"Earl Rogers' triumphs in court and his moral Geth-semanes outside, his life with women and with his enemy John Barleycorn . . . dames, booze, dynamite, bribery, murder, jealousy, fear, hatred, splashing vitriol, Chinese tongs, politics, poker, the payoff bundle, Clarence Darrow, Abe Ruef, Hiram Johnson, young Jerry Giesler, even Pearl Morton, the madam, and her girl Dolly."

"Far and away the most moving and powerful volume to come from Adela Rogers St. Johns, the kind of writing which deserves to be described in those felicitous words of O'Neill, 'written in tears and blood.' . . . An unforget-table narrative of human relationships . . . unashamedly sentimental, haunted by nostalgia . . . an enduring book."

THE POWERFUL HUMAN DOCUMENT OF A GREAT

"Moments of greatness and compassion . . . a tender love story that will touch the hearts of all who read it."

AUGUSTA CHRONICLE

"An amazing man whose passion in life was to aid the underdog in every legal fray."

RICHMOND NEWS LEADER

"Newspaper people will read it for Mrs. St. Johns' unerring skill at dramatic, pithy comment. Lawyers will read it to refresh their knowledge of Earl Rogers' technique of cross-examination which has become a model in all jury trials since. The general reader will be fascinated and shocked at the author's merciless reporting on the so-called great Clarence Darrow in the famous perjury trial when he was defended by Rogers."

BOSTON HERALD

"Intimate, soul-baring . . ."

DETROIT FREE PRESS

MAN'S DEGRADATION AND A DAUGHTER'S LOVE!

"One of the greatest defense lawyers in the history of the bar."

CHICAGO SUN-TIMES

"A fascinating, intensely personal study of law, its heroes and villains, victims and defenders."

DALLAS TIMES-HERALD

"A brilliant, colorful account of a trial lawyer who livened up his courtroom appearances with such antics as pulling a gun on a witness and putting a dead man's punctured derby on the head of the prosecutor."

MIAMI NEWS

"Almost frighteningly frank, revealing, deeply understanding and truly loving book. Some may be shocked that a daughter could write so frankly and fully of her father and his tragedy."

INDEPENDENT STAR-NEWS

ADELA ROGERS ST. JOHNS
FINAL VERDICT

BANTAM BOOKS · NEW YORK · YOUR ASSURANCE OF QUALITY

FINAL VERDICT

*A Bantam Book/published by arrangement with
Doubleday & Company, Inc.*

PRINTING HISTORY

Doubleday edition published August 1962
2nd printing .... *August 1962*
3rd printing .... *September 1962*
4th printing .... *September 1962*
5th printing .... *December 1962*
6th printing .... *December 1962*
7th printing .... *December 1962*
8th printing .... *February 1963*
9th printing .... *August 1963*
Literary Guild alternative selection October 1962
Bantam edition published January 1964

*Front-cover photo: James Viles
Back-cover photo: Engstead*

All rights reserved.
Copyright © 1962 by Adela Rogers St. Johns
*No part of this book may be reproduced in any form, by mimeo-
graph or any other means, without permission in writing.
For information address: Doubleday & Company, Inc.,
575 Madison Avenue, New York 22, N. Y.
Published simultaneously in the United States and Canada.*

ACKNOWLEDGMENTS

I would like to express my gratitude to the following people in connection with this book:

My daughter Elaine, who, with sympathy and a rare gift, edited and questioned these many pages. My son Richard St. Johns, who gave me advice, legal judgment, and a strong shoulder to lean on. My son Mac St. Johns, who has that blessed faculty of always *being there* when you need him, as I so often did. To all the rest of my family who gave me the faith and affection that inspired me when I needed it most.

My dear friend Ralph Wheelwright, who took time out from his own work for discussion, digging, and decision, and more than anyone else contributed balance, information, and unfailing practical encouragement. Ned Brown of MCA, without whose determination I do not believe I should ever have embarked on this long, sometimes heartbreaking and uncertain task of trying to relive and remember my life with my father so long ago. Ned, bless him, kept at me and *at* me, as the saying goes, because he said it was one book he was determined to read and how could he unless I wrote it?

Only other writers know the need for protection and uninterrupted time, and when your own home is filled with friends, family, and responsibility the best place for *me* to work is a good New York hotel, where somebody else looks after the laundry and where I can walk to the Metropolitan Museum and Carnegie Hall. Eugene Voit, Gail Benedict, Augusta Bornn, and the entire staff of the Savoy Hilton Hotel gave me all this for three years with patience, interest, and understanding you don't always find in those who are supposed to know more about writers and their problems. My minister, Dr. Ethel Barnhart, who prayed for me without ceasing. Kenneth McCormick and Margaret Cousins of Doubleday & Co., who *waited* and kept on believing that the book would be finished.

My son Bill, Mother Meyer, Hazel Holmes, and Elizabeth

Wood, who aren't here to read it now that it *is*, but without whose love and help at many times in my life I don't expect I'd have been around to write it at all.

To all of them deepest gratitude from my heart, and I can only hope what I've done is anywhere near worthy of their kindness and their faith.

Adela Rogers St. Johns
New York, N.Y.
March 31, 1962

FINAL VERDICT

ONE

We were sitting, my father and I, in my library, which at that period was also my office, workroom, and withdrawing chamber.

For a long time there had been silence between us.

When Papa broke it, the famous voice which had made juries believe that black was white and, sometimes, the guilty were innocent was almost the same as of old. "The truth cannot hurt anybody," he said. "In the end, the truth is light—always. Remember that, Nora."

No one else ever called me Nora, second of my baptismal titles. Papa always did. It was his own "small name" for me. Looking back, Nora—the girl Nora—seems part of another incarnation. Some of it I have forgotten, most of it is clearer to me than yesterday.

My heart was heavy just then with hope that had exploded, a red balloon blown too full, and he knew that.

A few weeks before he had come back from Loma Linda, looking just great. I'd taken that check for $50,000 in good faith. Or—I thought I had. We needed it *so bad*. You could have erased three zeros and we still needed it. So I might have been kidding myself. Then—he had disappeared for two days and though there he sat, back again safe and sound, under my rooftree, *my father*, he wasn't Earl Rogers, the greatest criminal lawyer of his day, to whom a man charged with murder would gladly pay that sum as a retainer. If he had it, and this one did—or his friends did.

Likewise we had just composed and sent to a distinguished law firm a letter thanking them but declining their offer of a sizable yearly fee for Earl Rogers to act as adviser and consultant for them on trial and courtroom work.

"Frankly," Papa said, "I'd rather be dead. Wouldn't you? To advise legal dullards, to be consulted by puddingheads who have no inventive cells of their own, then to sit back as

1

though you had a broken wing and watch a lot of blithering nincompoops make antic hay of your lovely design—"

"I thought you wanted to," I said.

"No no," my father said. "Good God! Certainly not!"

"You like to teach," I said, "to help young men who might—"

"That's another matter," my father said. "Then, they are teachable. How can you advise men who prefer *not* to go into court? Whose main objective is to stay *out*, in any compromise? How can you fire them to trial tempo? You might as well try to teach a peace-loving truck driver how to fight Jack Johnson in the ring."

"You can stay right here and write," I said, "write your own story. Write all the things you've always said you were going to if you had time. Write a plea to abolish capital punishment. Make a record of your own *firsts*—the first time something was *done* in a courtroom—"

His smile stopped me in my tracks. Our eyes met and held until I knew that he knew what he didn't need to go to any doctor to find out. He said, "I couldn't tell the truth, few men can about themselves. They don't know it. Also—we all must give ourselves the best of it. Only an egomaniac like Cellini, or the occasional objective historian, can write a truthful autobiography. You write it, Nora, when the time comes. I give you permission. On one condition."

"Ah," I said, and rolled a cigarette and handed it to him, "I know there's a catch in it."

"The truth," he said, and the words rang in the old way, "the whole truth, nothing but the truth. Little men are dissolved in it. If there is any gold, truth makes it shine the more brightly. I'll chance it. Promise me that, Nora."

I promised.

Then I said, "What about Mama?"

His face went white, it showed the fine bones, I saw the sign death had etched, *I'll be along presently, don't go way.*

"No," he said.

He still hates her, I thought. He must have really loved her, when they were young, through the chaos of their own long civil war.

I said, "Papa, why should she be the only one? If the truth is right for you, how can I ever tell that truth about you without telling her part of so much of it? How could it be the whole truth?"

He didn't answer me.

I had promised.

So I have never written the book.

All the years since his death, a few weeks later in a cheap rooming house where he'd gone so that I should not see the end of our tragedy, people have kept saying to me, you *must*. You must write a book about your wonderful father. Jerry Giesler kept saying to me, I've only got bits and pieces of it, you're the only one who knows the whole story. Judges, other lawyers, Max Steuer and Bill Fallon and Leibowitz, would corner me and say Rogers was the best of us all, there should be a record of his work. Teachers in law schools all over the country have written to ask the facts about some of his cases. The reporters, the bailiffs, old-timers around the courthouses in Los Angeles and San Francisco keep saying to me, Nobody like Rogers around now, never been anybody like him, best trial lawyer that ever lived, they say. Senator Hiram Johnson, the great Progressive, used to seek me out in Washington to say, "You ought to write a book about my favorite enemy and most-feared opponent." When he was getting ready to make a picture called *State's Attorney*, Jack Barrymore urged me on, he said, "I know you did it as fiction and my sweet-scented brother Lionel got to play the role. *I* watched Earl day after day in court, courtrooms were my favorite playground and class room, I saw all the lawyers who got star billing, Earl Rogers was the only genius among them. Write the *true* story and this time let me play him." People Earl Rogers had defended wrote me, traveled miles to find me, to say, "He saved my life. Why don't you write a book about him?" The innocent he had saved from the last injustice pleaded with me.

I have been too frightened.

It is not easy to write of anyone so close to you. I have been afraid that I could not make the truth do him justice. Because it was a tragedy, I have feared I might not be able to make anyone else understand him and what he was. Times change, you begin to see with different eyes, a little wiser perhaps, things startle you that at the time were splendidly part of your life. I am closer to him now because I have caught up with him in time.

Another reason entirely brought me in the end here to Carmel, where he and I and Jack London, his friend and my godfather-by-adoption, used to visit California's poet George Sterling.

Something else has driven me. Shoved me into the chair behind my typewriter to try once more. To tell the truth and nothing but the truth, though maybe not the whole truth. A few things are to me outside that promise still. What is here is the truth as I remember it, as I lived it, my eyewitness account, my I-was-there story. This may not always be exactly what happened, it is what I think happened. I am chronologically a bad witness and ask your indulgence as to dates. There are parts of my own life I have left out because they were not important to us—Papa and me. I have said so little about my three brothers, because in the early days our family somehow got divided into my mother and her son on one hand, Papa and me on the other. My father loved his son Bogart, but Mama somehow separated them right in the beginning. And of course the little boys, who made such a difference to me, were born too late, they never saw Papa to remember him, and he hardly knew them, which was sad. So—this is the story of my father and of me his daughter, Nora, nothing else.

Just lately, as I myself have come to the time when I begin to wonder what I am going to say to God about certain things and what I am going to ask Him about others, or as I examine my heart to find what the Recording Angel has probably set down in his great golden book, always and always I come upon one great unanswered question in my life.

A *moment of truth* haunts me now and I know it always has.

Whenever I try to find out what the score is, the question that takes hold of me and that I ask myself over and over is about that day in the courtroom when I was so young, so strong, so torn and baffled, the day when I made the decision which determined his fate.

On the witness stand, when he said, "Look at me, Nora," and began his cross-examination, I had his destiny in my hands. I, who loved him more than anything else in the world.

I know that. What I don't know is whether I was right or wrong in what I did.

So the story must begin there so that it is plain why at last I must tell it.

TWO

Every detail of that courtroom is vivid to me. I can walk right into it. Everybody in it still exists for me. *Then* is *now*.

Of all the courtrooms where Earl Rogers fought to save a man's life, I remember it best. I know it by heart.

This time his own life was at stake.

I, his daughter, was chief witness for the prosecution.

It felt like a nightmare, but I knew it wasn't. Too real and accustomed, the big, ugly, stately room, with the huge windows, dark woodwork, green walls, and shadowy corners. A shaft of light from the gilt head of the flag hit the court reporter's pencil that moved to keep a record of all that was done there that desperate day. Empty dark chairs in the jury box—no jury this time. Only the judge. What day, month, number of the Superior Court of Los Angeles County I can't recall, but I know Louis Myers was on the bench. Years later, as the circle moved, Earl Rogers' grandson was to be part of this judge's distinguished law firm, O'Melveny and Myers, and by then he was a revered elder statesman of the Bar. On the day that decided my father's fate and mine, he was very young to be a judge at all. I can see him there, on the bench, intent upon a long legal document, tense and grave and judicial, unhappy in foreknowledge of this case about to come before him in which he would have to rule upon the present sanity of the greatest lawyer of his time and space.

At the back of the room the reporters were gathered, restless and suspicious, their faces expressionless to cover the realization that they had bound and gagged themselves by the promise they'd made me. One I've never known them to make voluntarily before or since. To me, not for me—for Papa. Because he'd been their idol. Why, Earl Rogers' office was a *beat*, same as the police station, the city hall, the Federal Building, the D.A. "I hope you know you only got a job on a paper because you might be a leak out of your old man's office," they had said to me when I showed up, looking down their noses at my pigtails. Oh—he was their boy all right.

Today the room was almost empty. Usually when Papa tried a case, the court and corridors, often the lawns and sidewalks and streets, even the windows across the walls and the branches of the trees were jammed. For instance when we tried the case of McComas for shooting his mistress, or of Gabrielle D'Arley in her Red Kimono, they'd had to call out the riot squads. This time, the boys had kept their word, hardly anybody knew what was going on.

In the middle of the last row I saw Earl Rogers' sister, my Aunty Blanche. Her red hair was pinned back tight, she had on her fighting face, to buffet the tears no doubt. She'd been the tent-pole, the burden-bearer to help put her big brother through college, she'd toured as a pianist on the Orpheum circuit, played accompaniments for opera stars on concert tours across the land, while Earl got his start, his chance, she adored him. To give me moral support, there she was, though she hadn't been able to bring herself to sign the papers. For just being there, he never forgave her, never spoke to her again, he could not bear it that she had come to look upon his shame. I saw a deputy or two, a stray female confused in the wrong place, and hidden just inside the door, the district attorney himself. For a moment my heart sank. Then I remembered that he was a Southern gentleman, he was there to see that a fallen foe who had made his life hell for him over the years got a fair deal.

Hugh Baillie, all-time great newspaperman, reporter, war correspondent, editor, head of United Press, in the chapter "Rogers and Darrow" in his memoirs, *High Tension*, speaks of that courtroom on that day. "Only Earl Rogers saved the Great Defender [Darrow] from ending his career prematurely within what he called, in his closing address to the jury, 'the dim gray walls of San Quentin.' Now Rogers was nearing the end of the road. He had always been a heavy drinker and now his family was forced to attempt to commit him to a sanitarium for a cure, against his wishes. He conducted one of his last great trials in his own defense. The high point was his cross-examination when he had his daughter Adela on the stand."

That was the high point, all right.

I was "the family." I, his little girl, the only person on earth he had trusted. Against his wishes, I had done this to him.

I sat inside the railing by myself, I suppose partly because in courtrooms with Papa that is where I always sat. Too, I had to be by myself. I had thought a good deal about what I should wear, Papa had always been so particular about clothes for court. I really didn't know exactly, I ended up in a dark blue skirt and a white blouse starched stiff, with a high collar. By then, I had pinned my pigtails up around my head in two braids, and I wore a sailor hat. For the taste of those times I was much much too skinny, I must have had some looks or something I don't recall, because several young men had asked my hand in marriage. Papa had not liked any of them much. Nor had I.

Came the old familiar stir, the rushing sound a ship makes as it drives through the water. Or was it only an echo in my mind as I sat there trying to swallow the lump in my throat.

Papa came down the aisle just the way he always had and sat down at the counsel table. Of course he was the defendant, he was also acting as his own attorney. Who else? *If you can get Earl Rogers to defend you*—he could.

I tried hard not to look at him, but it didn't make any difference. I could see him just the same. His shoulders in a dark blue coat, exquisitely tailored by Eddie Schmidt, were held like a general's. I saw he'd had the suit pressed. People waited on Papa, they *wanted* to, it never seemed right or possible that he should do things for himself. I was glad to see he had on a clean collar. Clarence Darrow liked to be dirty, it was part of his conception of being The Common Man, though we knew lots of them and never met any as sweaty-dirty as Darrow, but for a man like Papa, who was a gentleman and a scholar, nothing was such a badge of degradation as a soiled collar. With him, sitting beside him, was a big man, sort of easygoing. Papa spoke to him as though he was somebody on *Rogers' staff*, instead of a male nurse-attendant and deputy from the county hospital who had him in custody.

My heart began to hammer as I looked at that man. For a minute I thought I was going to be sick, I'd have to go out.

I was remembering Papa once when he'd had a murder jury out for the second night. That particular time the D.A. hadn't asked for the rope—the rope which was Papa's deadly enemy. To have a man he defended hanged was a horror he'd never been able to contemplate. When it came, at long last in the Bundy case, it broke him. But that night as the long hours crawled over us, his client was facing life imprisonment, and Papa burst forth madly, striking a clenched fist into his palm, against his temple, the wall, the table, shouting, "Maybe the death penalty is more merciful. To spend your whole life locked up in a cage like a wild animal, never to taste freedom again, to be in the power of jailers some of whom may be fiends—right now as he waits for this verdict the man is locked up, he can pace only so many steps each way, man's inhumanity to man—I'd go mad, I'd go *mad*. Men who are locked up must go mad in some degree—as beasts do—"

As I thought of this, Jim Pope of the *Herald* knelt down beside me and said in a whisper, "The judge sent word he's going to accept what's in the complaint, unless Mr. Rogers insists on calling all the witnesses."

Of course I knew what was in the complaint. I had read it before I signed it.

The testimony of the cops who'd picked him up. He'd been *driving*, which he couldn't do well *sober*. One of the motorcycle officers—Papa had a bias against motorcycle cops—had a broken nose, which he said was the result of Papa resisting arrest with an *oar*, though where he got an oar unless he'd been rowing in West Lake Park I couldn't imagine and anyhow a cop should be smart enough to know Papa would resist arrest and been looking for it. There was also the record from the emergency hospital, where he had delivered a lecture on medical jurisprudence to the ambulance drivers, which they said was brilliant but made no sense, though whether that was their fault or Papa's who could say? Then followed the round of examinations and his behavior in the ward at the county hospital out near Alhambra, where they were obliged to take people who refused to come up with their names and addresses. Or couldn't remember who they were and send for somebody.

A lot of what happened had been left out, otherwise half the nurses and doctors would have been fired on the spot, that much I knew.

The trouble with people like Papa and Willard Mack, the top playwright, of the moment, was that they could always get around everybody no matter how hard-boiled. I picked up a lot from nurses I knew, and Marjorie could always get anything from any male—Marjorie Rambeau, theater and movie star and beauty, at that time married to Willard Mack, who had written for her such Broadway hits as *Cheating Cheaters* and *Eyes of Youth*.

Tell you the truth, a lot of it was legend. Years later when I was doing an exposé for the Los Angeles *Examiner*, of the County Hospital where six men had died from injections of a new wonder drug called neosalvarsan, or 606, they were still telling the tale of the high jinks that took place once when Earl Rogers and Willard Mack were in the ward at the same time.

Some of that was in the complaint too.

They hadn't, it seemed, arrived simultaneously.

Only on awakening in adjoining cots had they discovered each other.

"Ah," said Mr. Mack, trying to make sure he could see, "it is you. I was just going to call you."

"Do," Earl Rogers said. "Keep your mouth shut and call me."

"I intended to ask you to come to see me—" Bill Mack said.

"I can't do that," Rogers said. "I'm already here. One of the gravest miscarriages of justice since those ward heelers stabbed Julius Caesar, but these things will happen in a republic."

"—and get me out," Bill Mack said.

"As your legal adviser," Rogers said, "let me caution you. Think this over. Don't act hastily. Are you sure you want to get out?"

By this time they had managed to sit up and, being without their usual elaborate nightwear, had draped themselves in sheets. Mack was a six-foot-two Irishman with curly black hair and a smile as winsome as the first tulip. They wore their togas with an air of having been born on the Appian Way. Quite a pair. No wonder that soon the other patients, inmates, internes, nurses, and orderlies were gathered to make up the audience to which both were accustomed.

"There are advantages to being *in*," Earl Rogers said. "Peace. Quiet. No arguments. No domestic pressure."

"The great disadvantage," Mac said, "is that pathologically my system requires a certain amount of Old Grand-Dad, from time to time. I become dehydrated and this causes frothing at the mouth."

"We are not without resources," Rogers said. "Nurses have bowels of mercy. Let us try what can be done."

Oh—it could be done.

Always. Papa was a tough man to say no to. There was a tenderness about him, as though he was doing *you* a favor. Out of the kindness of their hearts; because Mr. Rogers was so wonderful or had done something so great for somebody they knew; or was always helping poor people who couldn't pay a big fee; or they loved him or they were too goddam stupid to see that sneaking him just one little one was a devastating catastrophe.

After they had imbibed a nondehydrating draught or two

they were so debonair everybody began to dance the cake-walk.

"I'd have paid to see it," one of the internes told Marj Rambeau when, a couple of days later, she located her missing spouse. "It was funnier than the Orpheum." "I thought so too," Marjorie said, "the first three years." But the interne was lost in his beautiful memories. "We played charades," he said, "even Dr. Duvalles. You should have seen Dr. Duvalles land on his behind trying to portray the fall of Lucifer." One of the nurses I'd met before said, "Honestly, we *died*. Of course gentlemen always think we nurses know everything anyhow—not that Mr. Rogers wasn't always a gentleman I assure you, it wasn't actually—anyhow, Mr. Mack was acting out *something* and pretending to be *somebody* and Mr. Rogers guessed Napoleon when he was too constipated to come out for the battle of Waterloo, and Mr. Mack was furious. He said Nobody with a soul could mistake his impersonation of Mona Lisa for Napoleon *anywhere* and then Mr. *Rogers* said, Come come, dear boy, haven't you ever suspected that constipation might be the causa belli behind that smile, hasn't it sometimes looked a trifle bowel-bound to you? Then Mr. *Mack* said, Oh *I* see, she was on the waterloo too, imagine! Well, as I said, we were in stitches—"

One of the doctors was having a discussion with them about reincarnation and Mr. Rogers said he'd been an acrobat at least *once* and Mr. Mack said modestly, "You know, I'm almost sure I was the mother of the Gracchi" and fell flat on his face. Then it crashed upon the doctor that somehow they were right back where they came in three days before and all was to do over.

At the same moment, Earl Rogers dropped the bright mask of comedy and madcap roistering that had had everybody in stitches and the doctor saw the gray despair and desperation in a death-sweat on his brow, and felt the palpitations of a driven heart that shook him in an ague and it turned him serious faster than ever before in his medical career.

When they sent for me, I didn't go to the ward, I went to the doctor in charge. A fine man, a sound mental as well as physical diagnostician. He'd known us—Papa and me—for years.

"What do you think I ought to do, Doctor?" I said. "I'm sort of—stumped."

For a few seconds he sat with his eyes closed. Then he

said, "I wish we could persuade him to go up to Loma Linda, the Seventh-Day Adventists do a remarkably successful job with this up there. Or I know several top men who have sanitariums of their own, where he could have the best treatment. Obviously, if he continues this way—"

"He won't go," I said. "I've tried and tried. His own doctors, his doctor friends, have told him. I even got Bishop Conaty to talk to him. Not that Papa believes in God but he does believe in the Bishop."

"We all do," the doctor said absently. "Then, my dear child, if he won't help himself, you and I must help him whether he likes it or not. A man as noble as Earl—oh yes, I know a great deal about him—must be saved from himself in spite of himself."

Or as Hugh Baillie puts it, "against his wishes."

As I drove back to town I thought I'd better consult Jerry Giesler. In our office he was still the "No" man, he always knew the worst. On the other hand, he'd come into our office as a boy, he'd read all his law under Papa, his exterior was colorless dry-as-dust, but he had a stupendous brain and a flaming admiration for and devotion to Earl Rogers. I always knew the only reason Jerry wanted to marry me was because I was Earl Rogers' daughter.

If Jerry saw the worst, the bad side, he also faced it. So as Papa had taught him to do with precision he made out the case against Papa, the way he always saw the case against our client. There was the day Papa had gone into a new judge's court and started to try the wrong case, the judge had been unimpressed by the Earl Rogers name and reputation and turned quite nasty. There was a client who'd paid a real big fee for which Papa forgot to prepare the case or show up to try it. Milton Cohen, so good with money, had a barn dance trying to square that one. The out-of-proportion number of continuances, the disapproval on the faces of the judges as they regarded the more and more dubious doctors' certificates. Complaints by clients to the Bar Association when blustering Frank Dominguez and Paul Schenck in his white ten-gallon Stetson appeared instead of the great Earl Rogers they had engaged to defend them.

With that, there peered at us the specter of which Jerry and I were terrified. Had long been terrified.

Disbarment.

I had also some *woman*—mother-daughter—fears of my own. When I was quite small Papa had bounced me out of the back seat of an open touring car going over the Casitas grade. He ought not to *drive*. And that rooming house where I'd found him—he didn't *eat*. Nobody to take care of him.

"We've got to do something," Jerry said. "Let me talk to him."

A lot of good that would do, I said. It jolted my hopes lower, though. I saw how panicky Jerry was, he was the last man alive to talk to Mr. Rogers about anything personally unpleasant unless he figured it was life or death.

I said, "Okay," and then I went up the hill to the Press Room in the courthouse. In the bare, dirty old room with its battered desks and antique typewriters and telephones, I asked the beat man if I signed a commitment so that my father would be held in a sanitarium and given a cure in spite of himself—would they keep it out of the papers?

Their first reaction was that I had lost my wits.

Earl Rogers was headline news, always had been, in their opinion always would be. A man couldn't fool around with *news*. That only was sacred to them.

Desperately I said, "No man ever played fairer with you on news than Rogers, did they? He made news for you when you didn't have any, didn't he? He was a newspaperman, you know that, before he was a lawyer. Two or three of you'd be on a weekly in Azusa if he hadn't saved your hides. Or in jail or still paying alimony to one of those babes you collected if he hadn't done your legal work for nothing. Did he ever refuse to take care of your family or your friends or some bum in some story of yours? If it's going to be on the front page I can't do it, it's tough enough—"

To my chagrin I began to cry.

Papa would never forgive me for bawling in front of reporters.

Anyhow, Johnny Grey of the *Examiner* said, "You've got something there," and Jack Lloyd of the *Times* thumped me on the back and said, "Never mind the tear-jerkers, we'll go along—we won't print it—"

So there they all were in Judge Myers' court. Watching. Not working.

As usual Papa crossed everybody up. He didn't cross-examine the doctors at all. So I knew he had another plan. Especially when with a little wave of the hand he dismissed them as negligible. Unimportant. His fame for making monkeys out of doctors on the witness stand was national.

Papa saw, I figured pretty quick, that this time there was no jury to impress or sway. Only the judge, concerned, trained, a little sad, cool and judicial. The judicial mind, which Papa knew and respected, meant above the appeal to sheer emotionalism.

"No no, no questions," Papa said to the last doctor, and waved him away.

The clerk of the court said, "Miss Rogers—Miss Adela Rogers—will you take the stand, please?"

I had never been on the witness stand before.

I'd always been looking *at* it—never from it.

Everything looked different, felt different.

As best I could, keeping my voice as steady as I could, I told it. At first I thought I couldn't. Then I went hot all over with a wave of anger. How dared he put me in this position? I was filled with the fury you have when a child has stayed out after dark and caused you terror and suspense and worry, you pray just let him be safe, let him come home safe, if I can get him in my arms safe and sound that's all I ask—when he *does* come, you yell at him in a rage and probably put him over your knee and use the rod.

My heart hurt, it was getting hard to breathe, but I was sore, too.

I said to the judge that from the same facts and statements he had read in the complaint, from the medical testimony, from my own daily observation I'd come to know that my father must have care. He was, I said, too tired, he had worked too hard for many years, always with a man's *life* at stake or what was then considered as important or even more dear, his reputation, and nobody knew as well as I did what this had taken out of him. Now I thought he was so worn out that he could no longer judge what was best for him. All we wanted, we who loved him, I said, was to give him time to rest, to provide care so that he would be himself again and go on with years of service to the poor—those who needed him—the people who had a right to the *best* defense—the underdogs who had always been his special care.

Judge Myers nodded. Very quietly, he said, "Mr. Rogers, have you any questions to ask this witness?"

Papa got up from his chair for the first time.

Then I had to look at him.

I'll never forget that. No, not as long as I live.

How many times with a man's life at stake had I heard, "Take the witness, Mr. Rogers?" Now I was the witness and he was walking slowly toward me, the way I'd seen him do a thousand times. For a moment he stood before me, as slim, as elegant, as dynamic, only his face—it didn't look the same. From his pocket he took the famous lorgnette, the golden eyeglasses with the golden handle on their black ribbon, the lorgnette that had become his trademark, photographed on front pages all over the world. Columns had been written about the various ways he could look at witnesses through it. As he held it there between his right thumb and forefinger, tapping the back of his other hand with it in a familiar gesture, it was as though it became a magic wand and in that flash of thought that can go round the world faster than a beam of light some of those witnesses paraded before me.

The Queen of Chinatown, who had caused a tong war, flirting her fan.

William J. Burns, head of the famous detective agency and onetime of the Secret Service of the United States. Three years, holding a bitter grudge, Earl Rogers had waited to get even with him—to get him on the stand.

The beautiful girl in the morals charge case against the chief of police saying, Oh *yes*, Mr. Rogers, coyly, when she was supposed to say, Oh *no*.

Papa spinning like a first baseman to fire the crucial question at a respectable rancher which broke a multimillion dollar will.

Mrs. Griffith J. Griffith of the Social Register, who should have been the corpse in the case lifting her veil at Mr. Rogers' request.

Above all, the final questions to Rudolph Spreckels, the millionaire reformer behind the Lincoln Steffens, Hiram Johnson, Francis J. Heney muckraking graft prosecution in San Francisco.

The greatest authority on trial work in the country, Francis P. Wellman, said, "Earl Rogers invented the art of cross-examination as it is now practiced."

Now I was on the stand waiting cross-examination by him.

For a moment he swung the lorgnette on its ribbon, then he looked at me and shook his head, with a rueful little smile he shot it back in his pocket.

I was glad of that!

With a courtly bow to the bench, he said, "Only a question or two, if it please Your Honor."

Only a question or two, I thought frantically, God help me.

"Nora," he said, then after a moment, "look at me, please."
So I did.

He said, "Nora—do you really think I'm crazy?"

"No, Papa," I said, "Oh no—oh no—"

"Then do you want to go on with this"—his hand indicated the long legal document on the judge's bench—"this farce and have me locked up?"

"No, Papa," I said, and burst into tears.

One of his great cross-examinations. Of course that was all there was to it. Later I dismissed the complaint, just then I stumbled off the witness stand, half falling because I couldn't *see*, and he put his arms around me tenderly and comforted me, we walked out past my aunt and the reporters, who looked relieved, and he kept saying, "Don't cry, Nora—please —I understand—"

I didn't.

How had we come to this pass, he and I?

Starting out so bravely, saving an innocent boy who would surely have gone to the gallows in an awful final injustice, how had we come into *this* courtroom? How had we come to the place where I had made my plea to the newspapermen and now had gone back on what had seemed to me *right* and *inescapable?* What had happened to us, the most successful, spectacular criminal lawyer the West ever saw and his daughter? The man of whom Jack London had said to me, "Never forget that this man your father is an authentic legal genius, going out far beyond what had been thought before him."

His record proved that.

In his hearing, someone called Clarence Darrow the Champion of Lost Causes and Papa said sweetly, "And of Lost Cases." For it was true that Darrow considered life imprisonment for Leopold and Loeb—a murder *guilty* plea for the McNamara brothers—the jury convictions in the Scopes and Massey cases to be *victories.*

To Earl Rogers, they seemed, would always have seemed, defeats.

No such blots, no such half-compromises, were part of his achievement.

"As long as there is such an inhuman and ungodlike law as capital punishment," Earl Rogers said in a plea to the Supreme Court, "I will defend with my last breath any man who might be its victim."

He had done that.

Yet there we were.

The guilt, the uncertainty, the doubt that kept clanging like cymbals, the qualms that did not stop.

Do you want to go on with this farce and have me locked up?

No, Papa.

I couldn't! Oh no—I couldn't.

To lock him up—*a man would go mad*. To rob him of his freedom—like a black panther in a cage. *Papa.*

Yet didn't I pronounce his death sentence?

"Only in his forties," the doctor at the county had said, "we'll put him in shape for many years to come. A little drastic now, maybe, but in the end it'll be worth it."

If I had said—if I'd had the guts to say—Yes, Papa, I do want to go on with it. I love you so much I must go on with it, don't you see that? I have to save you from yourself.

Would it have saved him?

He was only fifty when he died.

The decision was mine, there on the witness stand.

Or was it? Had it been his, all through the years?

I have never known whether I was right or wrong. I do not know now. That is the real reason I have decided to write this book. His story and mine. If I put it all down from the beginning, our lives together, all the big cases and trials, all the long fight the girl Nora put up, the best she knew—perhaps I can find out.

Find out why we destroy genius. Over and over again. Why?

Guilty, not guilty.

If I can find the true verdict, it will set me free.

THREE

When I was about eight, my father, coming home in the twilight, found me crouched behind a palm tree. In my hand was his big, black, loaded Colt .45, an extra gun he kept in the drawer of his chiffonnier under his handkerchiefs.

"What are you planning to do with that, Nora?" he said casually.

"I'm going to kill Don Brown," I said through teeth clenched the best I could with the front ones missing. Don was the boy next door, a lot older and bigger so that I saw no hope in my usual hand-to-hand attack.

"What has Don been up to?" Papa said.

"He killed Tom with his slingshot," I said, "for *nothing*, Papa. Tom was walking along his own back fence, and Don said *black cats* were bad luck and then he"—here I began to howl—"and I'm going to shoot *him* too."

"I see your point," Papa said. He took the gun and we sat down on the curb and he put one arm around me very kindly. My favorite character at the time was Bagheera in *The Jungle Book* and since it was obviously impractical to have a black panther in our neighborhood Papa had given me Tom as the next best thing. He understood my grief. Nevertheless he said, "Stop that noise at once. You cannot think when you are crying, that's why on the whole it wasn't necessary to give women anything to think with. Listen to me. It's better not to kill anybody. It accomplishes no practical end. All men and women, boys and girls, except saints like your grandfather, still feel the impulse to kill when they or someone they love have been sufficiently ill-treated, humiliated, or betrayed. They are tempted to believe whatever is wrong can be solved if they get rid of some one person. Usually it can't, the problem comes back wearing another face. What you must accept is that it is against the law under which humanity must live to survive. Your grandfather has taught you *Thou shalt not kill*, hasn't he?"

"I forgot," I said.

"Poor souls, we do," Papa said. "I now instruct you it is also against the law of man. In the State of California, where it is a major crime, if they catch you at it they will hang you by the neck until dead."

"That's killing somebody too," I said.

"It is," Papa said, "and I try to make them see the shame and horror of it, but they insist that the fear of such punishment keeps other men from doing it. It doesn't, but that's the theory. Neither will it be any answer for you to shoot that young savage, Don Brown, though I admit his killing your innocent cat was sufficient provocation and if you *had* done it I would have defended you."

"Oh Papa!" I said.

He gave me a quick, bright-blue look and grinned a little sheepishly. "Justifiable homicide is very rare, in the eyes of the law," he said, "yet by the very nature of the crime so often it's done by the underdog."

"Yes," I said, "but Tom was the undercat, wasn't he? Don was so much bigger and he had a *slingshot*. I wish Tom had been Bagheera."

"There are always two sides," Papa said soberly. "It's not always possible to replace the victim of a murder—but I'll get you a new cat."

"He won't be *Tom*," I said. "Some black cats do not like to sleep on the foot of your bed even when you put a red shawl there for them—"

"That's true," Papa said. "Well, we must do the best we can. Remember too that at least when they have arrested and charged a man and everything is against him, when the state has used all its forces and trained men and power to collect evidence that he committed the crime, he must then be presumed to be innocent so that—"

"If he's supposed to be innocent," I said, "why do they arrest him? It seems silly to me."

"No no no," Papa said, "the presumption of innocence is the best thing in the jury system. Having acted with full power to find the guilty man, we will now lean over backwards to be fair to him. We will act as though he was innocent, we will take upon ourselves the burden of proving he is *guilty* beyond any reasonable doubt in the minds of twelve others who are his equals. All twelve. Your grandfather will explain to you that no man over eternity can escape justice and retribution, *I will repay*, saith the Lord, *don't you have any vengeance, I am the only one wise enough for that, you'd make a mess of vengeance*—so better a hundred guilty men go free than that one innocent man be *unjustly* executed. That's a nightmare, you see that? Have you ever been punished for something you didn't do?"

"Yes," I said.

"Then you know how it feels," Papa said, "and the penalty for murder is so final. Once you've hanged a man, like Humpty Dumpty you can't put him together again.

"Also, remember the accused is entitled to defense, not just a defense, *the best defense*. That's only fair, baby."

"Yes," I said again.

"No man presumed innocent must hear the verdict Guilty until a jury of his peers in spite of the best possible defense is convinced beyond any reasonable doubt that he *is* guilty.

"There are many defenses, not just technical ones. Whether if he *did* it he did in self-defense, whether he knew the nature of the crime.

"Beyond that—sometimes in the final verdict of pure justice, clear as crystal—the man who drove another to do murder will be found guilty, not the man who wielded the knife.

"Sometimes Society is the guilty party—remember the O. Henry story? Those who grow up in slums, in poverty that feeds crime, in ignorance and hunger and fear, not taught the difference between right and wrong?

"You know your *Rubáiyát—Some there are who tell of one who threatens he will toss to Hell the luckless Pots he marred in making*—we have to defend the luckless Pots, too, we can see where they were marred in the making—

"So the jury in the box starts with This man before us is *Not Guilty* yet. The State can now throw everything it's got at him, they must make us believe he's guilty before we, the twelve good men and true, vote that he is. You and I, Nora, *we* are always on the side of the accused. He has a moral and a legal right to have us on his side, to show his side, his defense, whatever it may be, so the jury has that before them as it considers its verdict. That's our job. Our—life. Everything's against him except the presumption of innocence and the best defense. Only then does he get a square deal. You see that, Nora?"

I wonder again and again how it was possible that he could talk to me as though we were equals. Different—but equals. So that even when I didn't know some of the words, the meaning was clear to me, the rhythm of the meaning. He never talked down to me and he always listened. I knew that at any age I had a right to speak and to have what I said taken seriously. I know that evening when he took the Don Brown murder gun away from me it never occurred to me that we weren't the same age.

Looking back on it all, I know I create—I have to be creating some details, some words. It might be what I think happened or must have happened and not what did happen. I—don't think so. My father, our years together, left such a strong feeling; such a deep impact of all emotion on the clean, sensitive unused film of my young mind; such a vivid, dramatic sound track; such clean bright images impressed on my heart that I know it is there in my consciousness. It seems to me to unroll when I start up the magic of memory, like a motion-picture reel on a projection machine. What's been laid on top since slides off and there it is, that *first* clear record of my life. I may make mistakes in facts, or dates, or put them together wrong, but I don't think I will make any in truth itself.

The psychological fashion for young people today, I'm told, is to resent having a famous father or mother. At the beginning of the twentieth century many things were different and I think that is one of them. Myself I was always busting with pride at being Earl Rogers' daughter, determined to live up to it and take advantage of it, and when through force of circumstance or in desperate emergencies Papa ran the city or the state or defied Teddy Roosevelt, President of the United States back in Washington, I took it for granted and did my part in it the best I could.

A partnership had been formed that very evening when, sitting on the curb he first said, You and I, Nora, *we* are on his side. That the life and works of a criminal lawyer were not the best way to bring up a girl-child, nor a criminal-law office full of gamblers, murderers, and underworld characters of all kinds the best place, never entered my thought. I had no frame of reference. I never knew any other girls. From that day on, it seems, Papa and I lived and worked as one —*always with a man's life at stake.*

If that magnifying tempo *a man's life at stake* wasn't the best—or the usual—it was the only one I knew.

True, the women of Papa's family kicked up frightful rows about this. Papa seldom paid any attention to them. Once in a while they made such a ta-ra-ra, or Papa had a particularly guilty conscience, as I realize now he must have had about Dolly, and I was shipped off to Europe with one aunt to study music. To Arizona with another when I'd had scarlet fever. Or into a convent at San Jose, where Sister Mary Regis of Notre Dame knew how to handle Papa so well I stayed there in school several months.

Then Papa would come and get me. I always knew he would, so I managed to live through them.

He thought I was his good-luck piece, he sort of wore me on his watch chain as a charm.

"We have to defend everybody," he said as he sat beside me on the curb contemplating the big black .45.

We did. We defended everybody. Papa knew why they'd killed, or how they felt, he found excuses and loopholes for those poor, poor souls whom he conceived to be tormented

and driven to kill or steal or forge or betray a cause. Papa
loved Jesus Christ then as his father, a Methodist minister,
had loved his Savior. But if Judas Iscariot hadn't hung *himself*, if he'd been brought to trial as an accessory before the
fact, my father would have said he had a right to a defense
because as Jesus said probably Judas knew not what he did.

In the beginning when I was so small, I had no idea how
fatal a path this could be for a man to travel—*defending
everybody*. Especially *without God*, to guide him. A woman
named Pearl Morton, who was the madame of a high-class
sporting house, told me first—before long. It changed my
whole life.

Certainly I had no idea of those dangers on that hot clear
August evening when my father took me with him to the Los
Angeles County Jail to see a dark-haired boy named Boyd,
accused of the murder of the Louisville Sport in a poker game
at the world-famous Metropole Hotel on Santa Catalina
Island.

FOUR

Quite a while after that, months I think, our summons to
the Boyd case came from Oscar Lawler, later an Assistant
Attorney General of the United States, then a big corporation
lawyer.

It read:

Dear Earl; Alfred Boyd, youngest son of one of the first families of
Atlanta, has been charged with murder and is now in the County
Jail. His father, my lifelong friend, has telegraphed me that the
boy's mother is dangerously ill and he cannot leave her and asks
me to represent his son. I do not feel myself the proper man to
handle the trial work in a criminal case and ask your help. Will you
take charge as chief counsel for the defense? Please go to see young
Boyd as soon as possible. With my highest regards, Oscar.

Before the momentous telegram arrived, I had set up the
checkerboard. If Papa got home in time either we had a game
before dinner or he read to me. There was no radio or tele-

vision, there weren't even movies then. We had to entertain ourselves and each other, and I was lucky because I do not hear much on TV for that for me could compare to Papa reading Dickens and Kipling and Shakespeare out loud. Anyhow, he was late that evening and the minute he got inside the front door Mama started in on him. I was curled up in the big black leather chair behind his desk in the library, but as soon as I heard her complaining and telling him about some man who'd tried to flirt with her on the streetcar, I knew there'd be a row. No matter how hard he tried, she'd keep at it. So I went in the front room and began to bang on the piano as loud as I could. I never could bear to hear them quarrel. Sometimes it made me throw up, which children do easily.

Beneath my discords and theirs, deep down, I kept saying to myself I wish she'd drop dead.

I might as well face this.

I had wished it before and I would wish it again.

Not really, I guess. I had never seen death. I had no idea what it actually was. A manner of wishing her *gone*, sending her *away*, that was all. People were always saying where I could overhear it how much better *off* Earl would be without her. My grandmother, my aunts, even my Uncle Charlie, who was her own brother. When he'd come to visit us one time he'd told me that when she was young they called her Beelzebub and he said he couldn't see she'd changed any.

From my stool I could see them, he was smiling at first and trying to make friends, he said, "Belle, I've had a hard day, must you have a scene before I get my dinner?" and put his arm around her. She shoved him away and he went upstairs two at a time and she followed him. Anybody, it seemed to me in my fury, ought to know enough not to say mean things to him before he had anything to eat, even. She'll get him upset and then he'll shout at her and then she'll run out in the back yard screaming to make the neighbors think he hit her. He never does. *I* would, I thought.

In my ferocious child-mind I thought, I don't *like* her.

I couldn't possibly understand that she was madly in love with him, had sensed her own failure and the fear of losing him rode her like a witch. Much later I saw that, while her appetite for male admiration was greedy, the need to prove to him that she was attractive to other men tripled it. How could I, with my feet not yet able to reach the piano pedals, have even a hint of what it had meant to this spoiled, seventeen-year-old small-town belle, with the smoldering beauty of a Goya and such small brain power, to marry into the Rogers family? To move three thousand miles away from her home in Upstate New York to be a stranger in so strange a land as California?

Her father was a direct descendant of General Nathanael Greene, right-hand man and intimate friend of George Washington. Perhaps it was from his wife Kitty Greene that my mother inherited the dark beauty and warmth of temperament so welcome at Valley Forge that both her husband and General Washington insisted Kitty remain with them all winter. My grandfather Greene, as shrewd a horse trader as David Harum, had married into the Knickerbocker aristocracy, the Bogarts. My great-grandmother Bogart told me once that Belle was so much admired by the opposite sex as a girl she was soon quite uncontrollable.

Like his father before him, Earl Rogers had gone east to Syracuse University, where he played end on a football team which wasn't as famous as Syracuse teams became later. At a college dance he saw for the first time a dark, flaming young creature in scarlet gauze. They waltzed together and two months later she was his wife. He must have been off-his-head in love with her, therefore she expected him to put up with her stormy disposition and her vain coquetry for the rest of his life, and felt unjustly treated when he wouldn't.

At the same time she married him she also became the daughter- and sister-in-law of the Rogers women. Except for a good deal of Irish wit and gaiety these were bluestockings. A term which meant overeducated, highly intellectual *bookish* ladies. My grandmother, Adela Andrus Rogers, had been on the faculty of the early California college of which her husband was president. She read Greek and Latin as part of the ordinary run of things, spoke French, German, and Italian, as she assumed all educated women must, and in any of these languages could hold sparkling conversation. Her passion was baseball. When I first went to school, in the third grade, I was allowed to join my grandmother behind first base afterwards, to watch the Los Angeles Angels. Many times the official scorer sent down from the press box to ask the handsome erect old lady her opinion on a difficult play. I was crazy about her, but she was prickly as a hedgehog and I never ventured to be familiar, nor did her son. My father's sister Blanche was already chairman of the Los Angeles Symphony and their younger sister Madge was a concert cellist and music teacher.

Giving everybody the best of it, the situation was painful and destructive. The young wife found herself in a circle where her beauty and her arts and wiles were undervalued. She would make no effort to *learn*—as Grandmother Bogart said, she always resisted education—and try as they would the Rogers women and their friends were stunned by her unrestrained temper and her talent for making scenes. She didn't like women, *any* women, she felt them to be her natural enemies, out to do her in if possible.

As for me, I was a girl-baby when she had hotly desired a son. At two days old when I opened blue eyes to prove myself another Rogers woman, I must have seemed to her one more trick of a malignant fate. The fact that I was at once the apple of my father's eye added a bitter and bewildered enmity which increased as I grew. I was no Little Lord Fauntleroy for looks, and nothing so disconcerts a beautiful woman as a plain rival. She never could figure what Papa *saw* in me. She took it out on me all right.

The terrible danger, as his sister Blanche saw from the first, was that his wife was incapable of giving Earl Rogers any keeping-up-to-the-mark social life. Her attempts to make his home a place where he must maintain friendships with men who were his equals and his superiors were embarrassing.

I remember much better than I wish I did a garden party given on the magnificent Slauson estate for society's favorite charity, the Barlow Sanitarium. The dark, spectacular Mrs. Earl Rogers wore the costume of a Spanish dancer, selling cigarettes from a tray strapped over one bare shoulder. Romping, defiant, and coquettish, she was triumphantly trying to make more money for the cause than anyone else by giving a kiss for every five-dollar gold piece or over. I stopped riding the merry-go-round and went to stand beside her. My stomach was full of the hot lead of shame but I thought I ought to. I might have forgiven her if I hadn't heard a lady I admired say, "I don't think she means anything, she's just skittish, but it does make such a *fool* of Earl."

She *didn't* mean to make a fool of him. She just wanted to show him how popular she was with other men, that the women were cool to her because they were jealous. All men have too much vanity, it is the most devastating of all weaknesses of the human soul, only because men are so vain do they deny its omnipotence, and Papa was vainer than most.

For him to be married to a woman who humiliated him was in itself a catastrophe.

Years later when my father was dead, we forgave each other as best we could, my mother and I. In her last days of pain and regret and remorse and angry anguish, she clung to me. Daughters come in handy then. But *even* then, we didn't understand each other, we never spoke one word in the same human language, nor once saw the same thing when we were both looking at it.

As I peer back, most of the time I can't see her in our life at all. Some of the time she must have been there. I can't connect her with anything. My memory has rejected her, eliminated her, cannot apparently bear to remember her. She went home often to her own people in New York State, came back, went again, always taking my younger brother Bogart with her. She and my father were divorced and remarried, separated and reconciled, often my father and I were shooed out with a broomstick and went to live in hotels or apartments, finally they were divorced for good. And I can see my stepmother, the redheaded Irish-Canadian girl with the glorious voice who died too soon—*too soon*—much more clearly.

As a child I saw only my father's side *ever*, and I suppose I sensed all this without in any way being able to explain it.

Make a fool of him.

As I sat banging on the piano it was what she was doing *to him* that made me want her to drop dead. I wanted her to stop screaming like that, making Papa so angry and miserable that his face was white. He was a gentleman and couldn't knock her down and jump on her with his boots the way Bill Sykes did to Nancy in *Oliver Twist*, which I was reading at the moment. I wanted her to *stop it.*

I began to sing at the top of my lungs.

Come away with me, Lucille—in my merry Oldsmobile—

My Aunty Blanche didn't allow me to play popular music, but I'd sneaked it somehow, it was better for me just then than the Chopin nocturne that was my practice piece. Even so my father's voice, steel-cold, cut in through it. "Don't go on with that, Belle," he was saying. "It's not true, you work yourself up into these tantrums—"

Down the road we'll quickly fly—automobubbling you and I—

Oh God please make her shut up.

Wong put his head out of the kitchen door, his queue flapping above his white coat, and yelled that dinner would be spoiled and just then the doorbell rang a shrill warning, and a Western Union boy handed in a yellow envelope and all was still, in that divided house of chaos.

A telegram was a big event.

By that time, some people had telephones.

As a matter of fact, we had had one ourselves.

It had once rung three times during dinner and Papa, with his sweetest smile said, "Get me the ax, Nora." To my delight, the rest of his remarks were punctuated with ringing blows from same. "Privacy is the most civilized of all virtues. (*Crash-bang.*) In privacy a man has some chance of loving his neighbors which he cannot do if they are permitted to invade his home with no more notice than the jangle of a bell. (*Wham-slam-slam-wham.*) And from any distance. I have little privacy left, I refuse to tolerate this untimely and meddling intrusion. (*Bang-bango-bangitty-BANG.*)" As it came off the wall with a splintering rip-roar I cheered loudly and Papa grinned and said, "Get the unpleasant thing out of the house, please, Nora."

Per his instructions I had gleefully obeyed, depositing it in the gutter, and as a result the first news of the Boyd case, which was the turning point in all our destinies, I think, coinciding as it did with quarrel, came by wire.

With highest regards from Oscar Lawler.

This was the first time my father had been called upon by a firm of such prestige to do their trial work in a criminal case. My father had not started out to be a criminal lawyer. At that time there was no such clean-cut specialization in the legal profession as exists today when a tax lawyer would no more defend a libel suit than an obstetrician would remove your tonsils. In an early lecture at the University of Southern California Law School my father foresaw the end of the legal general practitioner, who had so long been vital in community affairs, but I doubt if even he realized that there would be tax, labor, industrial, international, political, civil, criminal, oil, marine, motion-picture, will, libel, title, banking, water-rights, and many other legal experts in less than fifty years. His complete dedication to criminal law had come as a result both of his own nature and of circumstances which played upon it. The pulse of triumph I saw in his face was for the recognition in his field that Oscar Lawler's request gave him. I knew that, though then I had not called his driving force by the name of ambition.

Within me it was just a throb of delight because Papa was happy. I had a desire and a determination to see that he was happy. Much has been written about the tigress and her cubs, but there is in the tigress cub the same violent potential, a tigress in the making.

My mother said, "This ought to mean at least a decent fee. The Lawlers always seem to have plenty of money, so he must get paid once in a while."

"Papa gets paid," I said recklessly. As a matter of fact all too often he didn't.

"You be quiet!" my mother said.

"Tell Frank to harness up," Papa said, and went upstairs. Even to go to the jail he had to put on a clean shirt and another tie. He didn't take a shower because we didn't have showers. My mother didn't move, she just stood there with her great, black eyes following him. When she was angry, there was a heavy purple cloud around her. I did not know the word "aura" but I suppose that is what it means. Strange —I had no mercy on her then, no sympathy for her, children can be very cruel. Now that I think how my father and I must have looked to her, united against her, two of a kind, my heart aches for her. At the time she was to me an enemy to my father, Kipling's rag and a bone and a hank of black hair.

I told Frank, the stable boy-gardener-handy man, and he went out to the stable, Wong came in dancing up and down, waving one of his big knives. "Mr. Rogers not eat dinner?" he shouted. "Very fine dinner, you tell Mr. Rogers very bad on empty stomach—" He followed me into the hall and I said, "He won't have time, Wong—"

"You're giving orders around here now, I suppose," Mama said.

When Papa came down I said, "Papa—take me with you?"

I wasn't crying. I always tried never to cry in my father's presence, he had no use for crybabies. It was to be one of his dumfounded surprises in life when he found his idol, Clarence Darrow, so constantly and publicly in tears. But I suppose my voice came out in a croak. I was scared. I never did like to be left alone with Mama when she was in what Papa called a purple rage. Also, I was a ruthless, self-seeking, self-serving brat, I wanted to go with Papa if possible and I was putting it on with all I had.

Papa said, "It's late, miss." He came over and looked down at me. Photographic proof positive that I was not a beautiful child abounds. I had a pug nose, my front teeth were missing, knocked out too soon in a neighborhood juvenile gang war,

and freckles. Fortunately I thought I was beautiful, because
people had begun to say I looked like my father. *Chip off the
old block, Mr. Rogers,* they would say admiringly. I knew my
eyes were the same Irish blue and had long black lashes. It
disturbed me that my hair was tow-colored but Papa consoled
me with the information that his had been, too, when he was
my age and mine would get as dark as his when I grew up.
"I'm going down to the jail," he said. "I can't very well—"
"Papa—" I said.

"Take her," my mother said, "take her. Get out, get out of
the house, both of you. Take her if you want to and for God-
sake don't bring her back."

He stood facing her, his face without expression. "All
right," he said.

When Papa and I walked out of the house together that
evening I think it was the first time he took away from my
mother a love he had once hoped he could feel for her. She
didn't want it, she couldn't meet it—and he gave it to me, his
daughter.

Men do this with daughters.

It has glories, but it has terrible troubles, too.

For always there must be another woman. In a case like
this she can be almost anybody. Dolly, one of the girls from
Pearl Morton's, who played the piano like Eddie Duchin. Or
the great blues singer Blossom Seeley. Or Mrs. S., who wanted
him to get her a divorce. Or the tall slim San Francisco
debutante who really lost her mind over him as well as her
heart and who was the first lady I ever saw take a drink of
whiskey. Sometimes—the other woman was Mama.

A daughter, especially when she is little, must do the best
she can.

Times when I couldn't see my way, when I was frightened,
when the pace and suspense and game in which men's lives
had to be fought for got too much for me, I ventured back to
my mother's side, my heart bursting to tell her, to ask her
help. She *was* my mother and his wife.

It never worked.

I see now, too, that there must always be something different about a child who has never lain down at night secure,
safe, wrapped against all evils in a mother's love. That's the
truth, you know. There is no real substitute.

I knew none of this, I promise you, on the night I walked
out of the house with my hand in my father's. I was the
happiest, most triumphant girl in the world. Papa kept saying,

"Hold still, Nora, you are not a whirling dervish, I hope. What is wrong here?"

We stopped just as he was helping me into the buggy, and with some exasperation retied a big red bow, which was flapping loose at the end of one pigtail. "Hold still!" he said. I did.

Life began in the county jail, where we went to see young Al Boyd.

Oh—I was sitting in the catbird's seat that night. I turned out to be right about my first murder trial, when everybody was against me, and Papa never forgot it.

FIVE

The new county jail was a stern building of gray granite blocks, its barred windows set deep in narrow recesses. Across the street, on a little round green hill, stood the rose-stone grandeur of the courthouse, its tiled roof copper-gold-red in the long last shaft of late summer sunset.

A jailer swung back heavy doors made of thick iron bars enameled white and said, "Good evening, Mr. Rogers," as we went through. He gave one of my pigtails a tweak. This was a familiarity with which I was not prepared to put up, so I kicked him in the shins and my father shrugged and laughed and said, "You fired first, Danny."

At the sound of his laughter a sense of adventure invaded me.

Never, so they say, is it given us to look upon the faces of our beloved dead in our dreams and as far as I know this is true. What I cannot understand is those—and they are many —who tell me they can't remember them, can't *see* their faces in the mind's eye, can't be sure any more just how they looked.

I can see Papa after we made our entrance into the jail that night to see young Al Boyd as though I were looking at him through a stereopticon lens. As *plain*.

A deceptive man to look at, he always was. The big, bulky

shoulders, with the punching, throwing muscles bulging down the back along the straight spine. At Syracuse he'd played second base on the ball club and boxed as a middleweight. They were only half concealed now by the elegantly tailored coat, and they must have tapered to a small waist for he gave the impression of being slim, almost slight. Actually, he was barrel-chested. Under thick overlong black lashes he kept his eyes half closed, above them the dramatic slash of black brows that almost met and went up at the temple ends. When he opened them full they had the blue gleam of a drawn sword or a gleaming lake or a piece of unexpected sky. His face was fine-featured, the nose and mouth a little too thin, the high cheekbones too plainly marked. We didn't *get* tans, in those days. We rode and drove, on horseback and in open buggies, we walked from place to place, we spent Sundays at barbecues out on the open ranches, so we just naturally *were* deeply tanned—the men, not the ladies. The ladies used veils and parasols and big hats to protect their lovely white skins and they didn't go outdoors much anyhow. I was ahead of my time and a scandal to my betters because I was as brown as Papa, and I know that it made his blue eyes a lot bluer so I suppose it did mine, too.

I tell you one thing. My father was as fine a horseman as there was in California, where there were the finest horsemen in the world.

Nobody, I always thought, could resist the sight of Papa on a horse.

A Beau Brummell, the papers called him, which was the word for best-dressed man then. When he was as young as he was at the time of the Boyd trial, in his early thirties, he already had an elegant wardrobe and silk shirts and jeweled cuff links and about a hundred ties and custom-made shoes and spats. No matter how fast Papa made money he could always spend it faster. He was a *dandy*, that made him doubly dangerous, he looked foppish, as they said, like his friend Jim Corbett, who had surprised everybody when he knocked out John L. Sullivan. Papa was *tough*. Tough-fibered. On purpose, I always thought, he didn't look it.

Very often he said to me, "True, clothes do not make the man nor the woman, but they are the first thing you see. Why handicap yourself?"

I see him standing there laughing in the glare of the jail gas jet, tall, young—so *young*—so elegant in a gray suit with a white silk shirt, a heavy blue-gray patterned scarf knotted under the high-style collar held by a pear-shaped pearl stick-pin with two diamonds set in it and cuff links to match tight at his wrists. He had swept off a soft, wide black hat with a dashing brim, not Western—as a matter of fact it was Italian, a ruinously expensive Borsalino—and was drawing off heavy buckskin driving gauntlets. Across the flat expanse of his waistcoat was the gleam of delicate gold links of a watch chain.

There, too, was me, though I can't remember much about me except that I wore enormous buckskin shoes and a Mexican sombrero. Of course Papa had picked me up just as I was, but I never did develop his flair for clothes.

He went into the sheriff's office, Uncle Billy Hamell was sheriff then I think, he'd gone home. Juan Murietta, an ancient deputy who became one of my best friends, turned over to Papa a lot of reports from the police and investigators' statements from the district attorney's office on the case. Papa sat down at the sheriff's roll-top desk to study them while Juan and I exchanged in Spanish those inquiries and formalities and courtesies customary to race, time, and place.

A bailiff brought in young Boyd.

I was by no means the first girl from eight to eighty to be swept off her feet by a rakish Southern gambler named Cameo Kirby or Ravenal or Rhett Butler. After the Civil War they'd started to come West to escape the scalawags and the carpetbaggers, we knew the accent and the exaggerated manners, the flashing smile, the dark scowl. Add to this young Boyd's black curly hair, which fell over a brow marble white, from a few days in jail and many nights in barrooms, 'tis true nonetheless romantic, and a limp like Lord Byron's and plainly any female heart must be touched by his plight.

I was.

The important thing however was my instant conviction of his innocence, which had nothing to do with these things and was as powerful as if a mule had kicked me in the stomach.

The boy—he was no more—came in looking defiant and dark and sullen and sat on the edge of a straight hard chair. He held his thin hands locked together so tightly that the knuckles stood out.

Some men, some men cannot pass a card game.

By nature and heredity, young Boyd was a compulsive gambler.

His grandpappy, with the long white mustaches, had lost plantations. His pappy, even if he was a friend of Oscar

Lawler's, had wagered fortunes on blooded horses, though he had clung to the heirloom gold watch that was to play so large a part in the youngest son's trial for murder. Now here was this too thin, feverish teen-ager who had issued bad checks all along Sherman's march to the sea and back so that finally his family had decided to ship him West with a small stake to go into business.

One of the gents he met out West was known as the Louisville Sport. The Louisville Sport was a pro.

All this I came to know later, but I felt it then.

My father looked up as he came in, nodded, went back to his reading.

Somewhere in the jail stillness a train whistled down by the crossing where the Santa Fe came into the old River Station. A church bell echoed across the plaza, calling the faithful for prayers to Nuestra Señora Reina de Los Angeles. The smell which is in every prison that was ever built, of disinfectant, old rags, human misery, dank air breathed over and over by captives and sweat allowed to dry on bodies and stale alcohol, filled my nostrils. For the first time I knew the restlessness that jails gave. Quiet as Papa sat, I knew being inside a prison made him squeamish and restless, I made myself sit still, Papa would not like it if I wiggled, he wouldn't take me next time. My imagination got to working on what it would be like to be locked in his place with this restlessness fevering you and not be able to get out. My mother had locked me in the hall closet for running away, I knew Papa would come home and let me out. I thought if I were locked up here now and nobody were coming to let me out I would fall on the floor sobbing and maybe die, so I tried to smile at the boy but it felt like making a face at him and he just stared, so probably it was.

What Papa was reading, the charge with which he had to be familiar before he talked to this boy accused of murder, went like this:

The poker game had started five days before, on the hot clear night of August 12. The scene was the cardroom of the swank Metropole Hotel on Catalina Island, a resort twenty-six miles off the coast of California.

In the beginning, it had been a five-handed game. By the time Jim Davin the bartender went in to serve a drink at 4 A.M., only three men were left at the table. The Sport himself, wearing his derby hat as usual. A nice-looking young man in a checked suit, very blond, Swedish, Davin thought.

He learned later this man's name was Johnson. And the dark boy with the Southern accent, who turned out to be Al Boyd of Atlanta. As he set that round of drinks on the table, Davin saw some five- and ten-dollar gold pieces. No, he didn't notice an old-fashioned gold watch.

Davin's answers to the D.A.'s questioning before us on paper could not produce the rich brogue heard later in the courtroom. "True," he had said to the D.A. "Not to speak ill of the dead, I knew the Sport to be a cardsharp . . . and 'tis also true the lad Boyd was ordering drinks freely which his chum whose name you tell me is Johnson passed up on several rounds but the lad stuck to Bourbon and them Southerners have heads like rocks for it, so I expected no trouble from him and I'd have got no thanks fer trying to stop the game if I'd seen trouble coming which frankly I did not."

Trouble came with the sound of two shots.

Before he could reach it, the door of the cardroom swung open, there stood the blond young man white as a ghost to be sure, holding a gun in his hand, which Davin said was steady. Behind him, framed by the doorway in the glare of the swinging green-shaded electric light, he could see heaps of gold like a pool on the green felt table. He could also see young Boyd, shoved back by both hands, staring like he couldn't believe his own eyes.

Johnson kept shoving the gun at Davin, who finally took it, and hollering, "He shot him, he shot him, he shot him, oh my God he shot him," but it wasn't until he went inside that the bartender could see the Louisville Sport. This time he didn't have on his derby hat. The bullets had knocked it off before they went through the Sport's head. He lay face downward on green felt and his blood—Davin swore to this under oath at the trial—was trickling over the face-up ace of spades. This death card was the last ace the Sport was ever going to deal off the bottom of any deck.

Boyd, dazed, admitted to Davin without argument that it was his gun.

More he wouldn't say at the time.

Almost an eyewitness, Davin, who'd heard the shots and was the first man on the scene of the crime, thought there was no question that Boyd was guilty.

At this time, historic Catalina Island was virtually the feudal domain of the Banning family. Cabrillo had landed there in 1542 and found an Indian tribe in peaceful possession. Sailing ships touched there for years after that and in

1846 the last of the Spanish governors, good old Pio Pico, gave it under Spanish grant to his friend Don Nicholas Cova- rubias. It changed hands several times before General Phineas Banning bought it in 1891 for $200,000 and was to sell thirty years later for many millions to the Wrigleys.

While the Bannings held it, its connection with California, the mainland, its laws, courts, and customs, was purely incidental and coincidental. Law enforcement was invested solely in the Bannings' own constable. At the time of the murder of the Louisville Sport, this was a man who spoke little English. If people misbehaved he simply deported them by putting them on the first boat for the mainland. He was known to be especially severe on those who talked during the band concerts in the plaza. Cockfights, gambling, duels, bull- fights, stage holdups, and piracy never bothered him, but he felt it rude for them to interrupt music provided by the general.

However, when he sent Boyd on his way to San Pedro he did tell the captain perhaps he ought to notify the sheriff, since the boy had shot somebody.

Before the coming of Judge Ben Lindsey, there were no juvenile courts. A man old enough to kill was old enough to be hung. So Boyd went through regular channels and was by due process of law charged and locked up. Nobody had any doubt up until that very night when Papa and I went to the jail that by the same due processes he would shortly go to the gallows.

Papa finished reading, stacked the papers neatly, and sat studying young Boyd. The case against the boy was black, common sense told Papa that he was unquestionably guilty as hell. However, he also thought it was amazing that the Louis- ville Sport had been allowed to live as long as he had, that he was no loss to the world, and perhaps he could make a jury forego the death penalty. Papa hated capital punishment with deep fury.

"All right, Son," he said, "you're talking to *your* lawyer now, so it's better to tell the truth. Start with how you knew Johnson, how you happened to go to Catalina, how you got into the game with Yeagar." The Louisville Sport's name was William Yeagar. "We've got to save your fool neck somehow."

Still defiant, unsure, angry, Boyd sat slumped in the chair, staring at the floor as he talked. He had an offhand you-be- damned way of speaking that was probably both inherited and imported and which we associate today with the vanishing aristocrat. Though he couldn't help telling his story well, in the right words and way, I could see he wasn't making a good impression on Papa, who was estimating the effect of this sulky, sometimes flip arrogance on twelve men in a jury box.

He met Harry Johnson, Boyd said, soon after he came to California. He didn't know anybody, they took a shine to each other, Johnson had come from the Northwest a couple of years earlier, he'd made a lot of friends. Well, no, they weren't the kind of folks Boyd was used to in Atlanta, he was sick of Atlanta, no chance for a young man there any more. Pretty soon he and Johnson took a room together and planned to buy a cigar store with Boyd's capital. Here Papa suggested this would also mean a crap game and for the first time Boyd looked up and grinned. "Johnson's right lucky with dice," he said gently.

A partnership, nonlegal, was formed. Boyd was to put up the money, Johnson his friends and good will. They'd had only one argument—Johnson thought he ought to be boss. He was older. "I like to be boss myself," Boyd said, "and it was my money."

A place on Spring Street had suited them, they made an offer and decided to take a trip while the owner made up his mind. Whose idea it was to go to Catalina, Boyd couldn't remember. The first night they'd picked up a couple of girls at the city, where tents were set on wooden platforms under palm trees facing Avalon Bay.

The next evening, they ran into Queenie.

At that point, Boyd choked up. He was thinking if they hadn't met Queenie—a man always thinks things like that, they are hardly ever true. If they don't meet Queenie they meet Lulu Belle or Carmencita. However, they did meet Queenie and Johnson knew her. She suggested they go back to the Metropole and buy a drink. Boyd realized now that she had been a come-along for the game of the Louisville Sport, who was waiting for them on the veranda. Unfortunately Queenie vanished when her boat got to the mainland so her story is lost, her role was simply to lead lambs to the slaughter, it was hardly her fault that the wolf got shot instead.

"You were looking for a game anyhow," Papa said.

"I—I reckon so, sir," Boyd said.

In the jail, the night black now through the barred windows, just talking about a game sent a restless wave through the boy. I didn't know its name, I didn't like it, I got down from my chair and walked over to stand by Papa and he put his arm around me. If I was an incongruous figure in that place, at that time, listening to that story, Papa and I didn't know it. To us it seemed perfectly natural.

When we got to the poker game, Boyd's memory was vivid, things came alive. With a smile that turned the corners of his mouth down instead of up he said, "You can't blame a man for risking money on a queen full, sir." My father gave him a straight stare and said, "What'd he beat you with, four deuces?" and at Boyd's ejaculation Papa said morosely, "They usually do."

I had to snicker at that. Papa did hate to be beaten at poker, or checkers, or driving our horses on an open road. In fact he was the worst loser I ever knew. *Boy*, how he hated to lose. A good loser, he said, was either a fool or a hypocrite. On the other hand he was a kind winner.

Look how tender he was when he beat Uncle Tom Hays playing chess. Papa loved underdogs, he was a benevolent monarch to all those below him in anything or any way, he could consort with ease and admiration with the really great. His trouble was opening himself up to his equals, he just plain never managed to be hail-fellow-well-met with them. Uncle Tom Hays was the real exception, I always thought he was the only man Papa ever really loved, which made it very terrible when he was arrested. I don't know just *why* Papa loved him so much except that Uncle Tom was plain *lovable* the way some women are beautiful or some trees green. Uncle Tom was a good chess player, he and Papa loved to sit out under the orange trees at Uncle Tom's big fine place in Riverside, with the board between them, Papa would be relaxed and merry. When he won, which was oftenest, Papa would say, "It took my down-to-the-bone best to beat you, you know that —plus a lot of luck." Uncle Tom, who was a good loser, would say with his smile that had wings on it, "Earl, you know there's no luck to chess," and Papa would look grouchy and say, "Yes there is—it was my luck you were off your game, my friend."

While we were talking to Boyd I thought it was odd, his remembering every single poker hand perfectly, every single card. Papa said, "No-no-no, a man's attention goes with his interest. You can count on his remembering that."

Papa got up and began pacing, back and forth, the length of the sheriff's office, swinging on the turns like a cat. He thought best on his feet. I can't imagine what he would do now when they insist a lawyer sit in his chair behind the counsel table like a clerk behind a counter. He would have done something. Babe Ruth and Joe DiMaggio and Roger Maris and Willie Mays would hit home runs in any league, with any kind of ball, in any park, any year.

Finally he stopped in front of the boy, who was sagging in his chair. "Did you kill the Sport?" he said.

The room filled with acute misery. After a pause, Boyd said, "No, sir."

Papa said insistently, "There are defenses, you know. Justifications. Did Yeagar carry a gun?"

"I—don't know," Boyd said. "I was sleepy and I'd had—a real lot to drink. I was leaning back in my chair feeling *low*, I'd lost the stake my family had given me that we were going to buy a cigar store with—" and that was as far as he could go. He was trying hard not to cry. For all his big talk he was just a *kid*. A grown man taking all his money, I thought angrily. He wouldn't let anybody see it but I could feel he wanted his mama.

"You should have thought of all that sooner," Papa said, and I realized he didn't believe *a word* Boyd had said. If there was one thing made him mad it was to have somebody lie to him and he thought Boyd was. He said, "Unless you tell me the truth, I may not be able to save your life." He stood staring down at Boyd, who wouldn't look at him, the boy had his head in his hands and it was almost down between his knees. You might have called him the picture of guilt. That wasn't all Papa was seeing, either. People in our part of the world knew a good deal about Southern hotheads who thought their war was still going on and took the law into their own hands. I'd heard the Rebel Yell myself when we were out riding with the Vaqueros on Sunday. Cheated in a card game and robbed of his stake, this boy wouldn't hesitate to shoot to kill. Again Papa said, hammering it home, "Did you shoot Yeagar?"

"No—no—" Boyd said, but it didn't carry any conviction.

I pulled at Papa's sleeve then and he looked at me.

"He didn't do it, Papa," I said.

"How do you know?" he said.

I used a gesture the Barrymores were to make famous later, only I put my hand on my stomach instead of my heart, "I know it *here*," I said.

"That," my father said, "is where the Chinese believe the soul resides."

"Never mind the *Chinese*," I said, "you have to get him off. If he didn't do it, it would be terrible if they hung him," I said, and I could see the boy's shoulders quiver.

"Even if he is guilty," Papa said, "they have no right to take his life. I don't see how we're going to save him. Somebody shot the Sport. They've got an eyewitness *and* a near-eyewitness. It's Boyd's gun. They can prove motive—and opportunity—cases do not get any blacker."

"That's where we start," I said. "You told me so. With the pre-something of innocence."

"The presumption of innocence," Papa said. "Yes. Hoist by my own petard. Now that every fact known to man proves him guilty, we presume him innocent. This is mad, it is also divine. It makes no sense so we propose to dedicate our lives to it. Better we should free a thousand murderers, leaving them to the final day of judgment, than that one innocent man—"

"Well," I said, "he didn't do it, Papa."

After a moment, my father said, "All right. Then we can't let them hang him."

I climbed into the buggy beside Papa and we started home. El Pueblo de Nuestra Señora Reina de Los Angeles was a much smaller place then, it is lost now beneath the sprawling, featureless city of millions which has flowed over it like lava. When I was a little girl it was in many ways part of the Old West. The Spanish influence was strong. We knew homes where it was not permitted to speak English, the hated language of the invading gringo conquerors. Our streets then were lined with hundred-year-old pepper trees, with magnolias and acacias. The adobe and red tile houses set far back in gardens belonged to the scenery and the climate.

The streets were quiet when we came out of the jail, the chill that came when the sun went down had cooled the air. Our black buggy with its red wheels skimmed along at a great pace and Papa let me hold the reins. An owl streetcar clanged its gong at us and I waved frantically. Papa was silent, intent, trying to see any way to acquit the boy back there locked in his cell. The horses' hooves drummed, above us the sky had the clear dry night blue of the desert. Long past my bedtime, but I'd never been so wide awake in my life. I couldn't contain myself. I was about to burst with love and felicity, I began to sing to let some of it out.

I liked a ballad out of the Spanish-American War, so I sang that.

> Good-bye, Dolly, I must leave you,
> Though it breaks my heart to go,
> Something tells me I am needed
> At the front to fight the foe.

Papa joined in. Neither of us had *voices*, we came of a musical family, we could carry a tune, we enjoyed singing, we sang with enthusiasm.

> Can't you hear the bugles blowing—
> Good-bye, Dolly Gray.

Wildly, I thought *I must never forget this.*

I must never forget the sky, the lighted windows, the smell of magnolias, our horses Steve and Ajax spanking ahead, Papa singing "Good-bye, Dolly Gray" and me sitting here beside him with the reins in my hand.

Whatever happens to you, or how old you get, I told myself, you must never forget it all just the way it is now this very minute.

I never have.

SIX

Two months later, surrounded by heat wave, Alfred Boyd went on trial in the superior court for the murder of William Yeagar.

Things looked blacker, if possible.

Only two people in the world believed Boyd could be acquitted. Me and Papa, in that order.

The district attorney himself, James Rives, led the prosecution. Assisting him was C. C. McComas, a borderline character of the Old West, a vast hulk of a man with a drooping mustache and hair worn long enough to curl over his collar. Tobacco-chewing, loudmouthed, braggadocio, bullying, and as able and impressive a lawyer as the D.A.'s office has ever had. McComas carried the prize asset of the prosecutor, a tough, paternal benevolence, this-hurts-me-more-than-it-does-you but it's my duty and I must do it.

Facing him, Earl Rogers, chief counsel for the defense, clean-shaven, foppish as a mere sprig, a stripling, and Mac soon made it plain that he considered this Johnny-come-lately an upstart not to be taken seriously. Patronizing and pleasant as big Mac was, the best young Rogers was going to get from him was a chance to prove his victories to date weren't flukes.

Some cases catch public interest at a high point, stir a wave of public imagination. Probably the Boyd case had all the elements in story and cast and might have made headlines anyhow. But it had also the concentrated and spectacular help of the man who was, I think, the best friend *to him*, the nearest to a partner, my father ever had.

Harry Carr was a reporter on the Los Angeles *Times*. A short, spare mouse-haired youth with a stammer, thick glasses, and a deprecating smile. Even at second glance, he resembled an owl strayed into daylight. In time there had to come into view the I-miss-nothing; the unmistakable all-doors-must-be-opened-to-me-I-am-the Press; the own-the-earth-walk of the representative of that most essential of the Four Freedoms; the strange, impersonal, stubborn, immovable won't-be-fooled challenge and tenacity of the great reporter from Charles Dickens to Allen Drury.

At that time the figure of General Harrison Gray Otis, publisher of the *Times*, was a colossus on the newspaper, political, and economic horizon of the United States and especially California. All his life Earl Rogers was to be on and off the General's black list, sometimes hailed as a legal genius, sometimes as an unscrupulous shyster. At the time of the Boyd trial these hot-with-ambition, loaded-with-ability young men were able to make a deal that got them both ahead faster. As attorney for the defense, Papa would always play ball with Harry Carr on timing, on exclusive stories, on any news breaks. Carr's stories and leads would increase and dramatize the new young criminal lawyer Earl Rogers.

Carr had already started this before we got into court. A hopeless case, a black outlook, the district attorney could hardly fail of a conviction and the death penalty. No one could blame young Rogers if the verdict was Guilty. If it was Not Guilty, all the credit would have to go to the chief counsel for the defense.

Opening day I heard for the first time as we made our ways

through crowds jamming the walks and lawns and hallways those words that were to become so big a part of my life. *There he is—that's Earl Rogers. There goes Rogers.* A thrill of pride I never got over—they love him too, I would think, beaming proudly back at them.

Crowds can jeer and hoot—laugh, too. I didn't know that then.

As we went up in the scary elevator—it operated in an iron framework attached to the outside of the courthouse—I could see across Temple Street to the gray stone county jail, and there flashed through my mind what a lot had happened since the night we first saw Boyd there.

The preliminary hearing, held over at Catalina in the Avalon court.

Nobody but Papa paid much attention to the mere legal formalities of coroner's inquests and preliminary hearings. Cases were won and lost by them, Earl Rogers always said. The trial was the showdown, the big battle, but it was sloppy work not to learn everything possible in preliminary skirmishes, lazy and dangerous not to gather all the ammunition, take advantage of the chance to estimate your opponents, familiarize yourself with the terrain. Every time a man opened his mouth, Papa said, he told you something. All men talked too much, especially liars, silence was beyond them, and given enough rope they would quite literally hang themselves.

On the stand in Avalon, Harry Johnson, that *rara avis*, an eyewitness to a murder, used the phrase "quick as a flash." Boyd, he said, drew his gun and shot *quick as a flash*. An ordinary, first-thought description. It was to cost him dear before Earl Rogers got through with him.

Also at Catalina, though he didn't fire it, Rogers wheeled a big gun into place for the defense, so carelessly that nobody noticed it at the time.

He was cross-examining Johnson, flubbing around, it seemed, and McComas pooh-poohed a question and objected that it was irrelevant and immaterial and Earl Rogers said, "All right—I withdraw it. Just the same I'd like to have Mr. Johnson instructed not to leave the jurisdiction of the court. I'd like to have him placed under bond as a material witness."

So they put Harry Johnson under bond.

On the way out McComas said to Rogers, "What in the

world did you do that for? We'll have him there, don't worry, he's our chief witness."

"A man has to make some kind of noises for his client, Mac," Rogers said mildly.

He had laid the foundation for the defense right under McComas' nose.

The worst problem I'd ever had in my life up to date got solved at Catalina.

A commotion and cat fit was going on about whether I should be allowed to attend the trial. A jaunt to the prelim in the open air of Catalina was one thing, a murder trial was another. Under the pressure of my grandmother and aunts repeating firmly and frequently that it would be *scandalous* at my age, Papa was looking at me doubtfully himself. After all I'd been through, all I'd seen and heard, with a feeling that Boyd was as much my client as Papa's, I was sure I'd die if I didn't get to go.

Besides the hearing, Papa and his own detective, a big guy named Bill Jory, did a lot of nosing around at Catalina. In the cardroom at the Metropole they reconstructed the crime in the manner of the new idol, Sherlock Holmes, not as yet any part of the legal tradition.

Papa had to have quite a few drinks at the bar with Davin the bartender before he'd let him take away the bloodstained ace of spades, which the cops apparently hadn't considered important. Davin said it had been good for business at the bar. Then we took the stagecoach across the island to the isthmus and back and Papa insisted on doing the driving. I was on the box with him and I want to tell you coming lickety-split hell-bent down a narrow, winding dirt road cut out of the side of a mountain with a rock wall on one hand and a thousand-foot drop on the other in a rickety old stage-coach and Papa full of *mucho tequila* cracking the long whip over four fresh horses was better than any automobile race ever run. The stage driver and I were waving our sombreros and whooping ki-yis the whole time and hollering *Viva el Papa* at the top of our lungs and when we got back we were all laughing so hard Papa nearly fell off the seat.

I could see he was all puffed up with himself so it seemed to me a good time to ask him about my coming to the trial. "I ought to be there," I said, "I am the only one who really knows all the time Boyd didn't do it. You're just *presuming* it. If I'm not there to remind you, you might forget," and Papa looked at me a minute and laughed harder than ever and said, "All right," and I said, "*Promise*, Papa, you know what those women are," and he laughed till he choked and said, "I promise."

As we went back to the mainland on the boat that time, McComas came up to Papa by the railing. He had begun to look a little puzzled. He said, "What in *hell* did you get Johnson bound over for? I'd like to know that."

Papa grinned at him. He said, "Well, Mac, *somebody* killed the Louisville Sport and I must assume the position that it wasn't my client."

For about a minute, McComas was thinking about that and he looked a little worried. He shrugged it off.

He was wrong. Earl Rogers was one-pointed as a Brahman. He kept at it and at it till he found the one point where he could break through and he never needed but one.

Going up in the elevator that was pulled by a rope and swung like a bucket, I was wishing we were back on Catalina Island.

My stomach was acting up again.

Whether it was seeing the jail one minute and palm trees and green lawn the next and then nothing but empty space, or because this was the moment my friend Boyd's life was at stake, I couldn't tell. Probably all of them.

Courtrooms, like baseball diamonds, are all different and all alike.

I was to spend a large portion of my life in them.

The old-fashioned room in Flemington, New Jersey, where they tried Hauptmann for the kidnaping of the Lindbergh baby and the press sent out a million words of copy a day.

The Chicago court where Clarence Darrow got life imprisonment for Leopold and Loeb, and he and I had our famous last words.

A tight little packed space where Alger Hiss perjured himself with a Harvard accent, and Whittaker Chambers, without one, fought to save his country.

All different, all as much alike as Yankee Stadium and the sand lot out behind the fire station.

The one we entered to defend Al Boyd for murder was my first. My own stake was so high that it's printed indelibly. My heart was in it for two big big reasons. That time, I was absolutely sure we were defending an innocent man. Moreover my credit with Papa had to be at stake. If I were wrong on this one he might never trust me and my stomach again.

A big square room painted buff, a very high ceiling, a row of long deep-set windows curtained in dark brown plush. Half of it was filled with seats, like a theater, where the public could sit. Inside a three-foot carved rail-fence, entered by a swinging gate, was the stage where the real, for keeps life-or-death drama would be played.

We faced the Bench, which was actually a huge desk of fumed oak, enclosing a kindly, plump little man of middle age who wore over his ordinary suit of clothes an air of quiet confidence and authority as impressive as a robe. Behind his head the American flag and the state flag of California, white satin with the golden bear painted on it, were crossed. We also faced, parallel to the Bench, an awkward, torturous oak armchair, in which the witnesses Boyd and Harry Johnson and Jim Davin and others would sit on a platform raised about three feet and surrounded by a protective rail of its own. On the floor in front and to one side of it was the court reporter at his table, where every word would be taken down, "nor all your prayers wash out a word of it." From his notes came those transcripts of the testimony which Earl Rogers insisted on having every day after court and with which we would sit up all night long the rest of our lives.

At right angles to us and the Bench, on our left was the long jury box with two rows of oak chairs fastened to the floor, backs and seats of black leather beginning to crack and to smell in the clear glazed desert heat pouring in like a furnace blast.

Facing the Bench across about four feet was the long counsel table, a shining expanse of polished golden oak broken by islands of white blotters, huge inkstands, at each end a tray with pitchers of water and three or four thick tumblers.

Bill Jory and I sat in the row of chairs inside the railing, a few feet behind Papa. I was staring at his shoulders and the back of his head. When they brought the defendant through a small door my heart began to jump up and down so I wondered if my ribs would hold out. Boyd looked small, limping between two big bailiffs with guns swinging at their hips but he had his chin up. He looked bad-tempered all right and Southern-aristocrat-arrogant. When he sat down in the chair beside Papa I was shocked by his color, starvation gray from jail food and that green tinge which was fear seeping through in spite of him. It made me giddy to feel how scared he was.

"What are the bugles blowin' for?" said Files-on-Parade.
"To turn you out, to turn you out," the Colour-Sergeant said.
They've taken of his buttons off an' cut his stripes away,
An' they're hangin' Danny Deever in the mornin'.

Those words spun around in my head and I knew they
were going to hang my friend Boyd unless Papa *stopped*
them.

Quick little silhouettes began to move on the edge of my
vision. The district attorney, spare, thin-lipped, cold of
eye. Blustering, truculent, paunchy McComas, dribbling tobacco
juice on a checkered vest, self-confident as a grizzly. After a
while a changing panorama of men young and old, big and
little in the jury box. Reporters buzzing around Earl Rogers
and the defendant and Harry Carr giving me a pat on the
back. On the other side of my father his assistant Luther
Brown, sleek, oily—I loathed Luther Brown, of which more
later.

My first murder trial. My feet still inches from the floor.

Without warning, I was visited by clammy panic. Between
my shoulder blades I felt icy sweat trickle. Then with a
motion of extraordinary violence my father swiveled around
his chair, got up, and stood in front of me. He put his hand
on top of my head so hard it hurt. His eyes were blazing.
"*For luck,*" he said, "for luck, we're going to need it. You still
think he didn't do it?" "Yes, Papa," I bleated. "Don't worry,"
he said, "we'll be all right as soon as the umpire says play
ball."

Twelve good men and true in the jury box, to give the boy
a fair trial as guaranteed by the Declaration of Independence,
the Constitution, the Bill of Rights and for all I knew the
Magna Charta.

The clerk's voice in a long singsong.

People of the State of California—

The people, baying, giving tongue, a wolf pack tying cans
to this puppy's tail, throwing rocks at him, that was the way
I saw the People of the Sovereign State of California, of
whom I was one.

Witnesses moved to identify the body, Jim Davin his
brogue increasing as he testified. Papa was quiet with him, he
gave an impression of regarding him as unimportant, the
questions about the moment when Johnson appeared in the
doorway, the gun in his hand, shouting, "*He shot him,*"
sounded like nothing-at-all.

One-pointed. One-pointed to the moment when the clerk said *Johnson*—Mr. Harry Johnson take the stand please.

Heads all turned in the jammed courtroom as he came down the aisle. Tall, square, dapper in a blue suit neatly pressed, a blue and white dotted tie neatly arranged in a bow under the clean stiff white collar, shoes shined.

The truth the whole truth nothing but the truth.

I got hold of Bill Jory's big paw and pinched it.

What I wanted to ask him was whether the jury would be able to tell for sure when to believe him and when not to. Would the truth carry a light? Would it go out if he started telling lies? How did the jury know when it was or wasn't the truth?

Having been told I must not *talk*, I didn't ask him, instead I studied Johnson's face. A square face, a square jaw with a slight dimple, broad forehead with fair hair growing low and neatly parted in the middle. His gaze at the jury was wide and frank from blue eyes—light light blue—set well apart.

A great apprehension filled me.

This was at the moment the American prototype of an honest young man. The All-American boy.

He did not look like a liar.

The D.A. let McComas take the examination of their star witness. Mac, with his long experience as a trial prosecutor, an old hand versed in all the tricks of his trade, always a favorite with juries in his gruff rough you-and-I-understand-each-other manner. The D.A. watched, directing strategy, making suggestions, manager in the dugout.

On direct, McComas led his witness confidently through the story he was telling again under oath.

Johnson spoke quietly in an ordinary flat young voice, pausing to think, to be sure, weighing his words carefully. Once or twice he looked at his former friend, now the prisoner at the bar, with a sort of concern, an apology, and Boyd gave him back a hot, black contemptuous stare, utterly without appeal.

Conciliatory, self-possessed, Johnson went through the poker game. From this Boyd emerged a reckless, hot-tempered, generous but wild young rascal, mad with gambling fever, regarding the world as his oyster and resenting bad luck as a personal insult. Here we were, staring, breathless, in the cold gray dawn as Boyd looked across the green table and saw his fortune in gold, his diamond studs, his jeweled cuff links in a heap in front of the faintly smiling Louisville Sport.

Offering, as a last resort, the precious old gold watch which had been his great-grandfather's, a sacred family heirloom, meeting the crude contempt of the professional cardsharp who'd wrung him dry. Haggard, desperate, Boyd pleaded for cash or credit on it. "You know how gamblers are," said the young man in the witness stand, glancing toward the jury box, and some of them looked as though they did. The last race, the last roll of the dice, the last hand of cards, the luck will change, it *has* to. "Boyd was sure he could pull out if he had one more chance," Johnson said. Yeagar wasn't having any. Loudly, he said he'd won the money in a square game, it was time to quit, and anyhow the old watch wasn't worth two bits.

With that apologetic duck of the head in Boyd's direction, Johnson said Boyd always got mad if anybody raised their voice to him. He drew his gun—and fired.

The transcript says here:

Q. (by McComas) Now when Boyd had shot Yeagar what did he do immediately thereafter?

A. (by Johnson) He stared at the gun and tossed it under my chair. He didn't seem to know what to do.

Q. Well, now, what did you do?

A. I picked up the pistol.

Q. Then what?

A. I started to the door.

Q. What was Mr. Yeagar doing when he was shot?

A. He was through talking to Al and he went on counting the gold pieces stacking them up.

One of those blind rages of which children are capable took hold of me. I could tell by Luther Brown's smug Iago face that *he* believed Johnson, he *would*. Johnson had made him see Boyd in a livid rage shooting the man who'd belittled his heirloom. The jury was looking at Johnson sitting there so sad and sure, and *they* believed him. Boyd was looking at Johnson with his lip curled back and I knew he would not say anything about Johnson, not if they hung him, and I thought, That's *crazy* but there you are.

A man may lie to clear his friend in trouble. The Brand of the Dog is on him who reveals a secret that will condemn his friend no matter what! From his great-grandfather's cradle Boyd had been taught that. The whole Civil War was full of it.

Desperately I looked at my father. Do something, I cried to him in silence. To my amazement he seemed totally undisturbed. Interested. He felt my stare or got my plea, he turned around and winked at me. I felt some better but not much and not for long, at this moment McComas threw the bomb that wrecked, as far as I could tell, all his defense plans.

Q. (by McComas) Now Mr. Johnson, you've told us of your arrangements with Mr. Boyd—share and share alike.
A. Yes sir.
Q. Did you have any other arrangements before you sat down to the table that night to play cards?
A. Yes.
Q. Tell us about that, Mr. Johnson.
A. Well, I had arranged with The Sport, Mr. Yeagar, that I'd get back a cut of whatever Boyd lost because I had steered Boyd into the game.

McComas turned to look at my father to see if this had hurt him and I couldn't see Papa's face so I don't know whether he showed it. It must have hurt all right. If this was true the motive Papa had been going to give *Johnson* for doing the killing was gone. By the time I could crane to see my father he was looking at Johnson as though he'd turned into a tarantula.

Q. (by McComas) Then you couldn't lose?
A. No. You see I do not like to gamble. I never do if I can help it—I was trying to—

Earl Rogers came to his feet, his voice rang out as though he just could not possibly help asking this tidy, careful young man who didn't like to gamble a question. *Couldn't help himself*, his voice sounded like that. "You're telling us you went into that game ready to double-cross your best friend? To get a sure thing you would play with the other man and betray your chum—"
Bellows from McComas to the judge finally drowned him out. Under the judge's stern reprimand my father sat down, his unbelieving eyes remained on the witness. This was worse than murder, his eyes said, and McComas moved shrewdly to get Johnson off the hook.

Q. You stood to win no matter who lost, was that it?
A. Sure. It seemed to me—

Q. You were partners with Yeagar against Boyd?

A. Yes.

Q. In what way were you partners?

A. I explained to him that I would help him in the betting, like when he gave me a signal and we had him between us.

Q. Boyd, you mean? When you had Boyd between you?

A. Yes I thought it was a very smart move. You see, Al was looking for a game. I knew he'd find one some place, he always did. I thought if I got *in* with Mr. Yeagar then whatever happened to Al if he lost, you know, we would have something left. To me it was a matter of percentages. I am a bookkeeper and I look at percentages. This way I thought the percentages were with me or like I say with us. If I had a piece of Mr. Yeagar's play, if Boyd had one of his bad nights I would get at least part of it back. Then I could split with Boyd afterwards. I thought that was good business.

Q. In other words, you planned to cut Boyd in on whatever Yeagar gave you?

A. Yes I did. So we could still buy the store.

Triumphantly McComas said, "Take the witness, Mr. Rogers."

Papa got up and went around to stand beside Johnson. His face was grave and unhappy. Puzzled, trying to be fair, he began gently to give this young man a chance to repudiate a double-cross that to a Westerner in the West at that time was next to horse stealing or shooting in the back. Boyd had been his pal, he'd been paying Johnson a small salary to investigate business opportunities, they'd lived together like brothers, he'd eaten Boyd's meat and drunk his whiskey, they were on this Catalina vacation at Boyd's expense. All this was true, wasn't it?

Johnson's naturally pasty color never changed. He said, "That's why I made a sharp deal with Yeagar."

Q. (by Mr. Rogers) When did you have a chance to sell your best friend down the river?

A. Well, when we met Queenie—

Q. You knew Queenie?

A. Sure. At the hotel, she and Al went to have a drink, so I explained to Mr. Yeagar that Boyd had a big roll on him. I said there were plenty of other games in town and unless he played along with me—

Q. So if you helped Yeagar win Boyd's roll and he cut back to you, you'd own the cigar store, that right? Boyd would be working for you, was that it, Mr. Johnson?

Johnson got a pinched look around his nose. He said, "I am a business man. I have to do the best for myself.

With a grunt that sounded like *Faugh,* Earl Rogers walked to the table and picked up the blue-covered transcript of the hearing at Catalina. I knew he knew what Johnson had said there by heart, the way an actor has memorized his lines. To impress the jury, sometimes, he would read it as he read Johnson's, or he studied it and spoke from it.

Q. You didn't mention anything about this smart bargain with The Sport at the preliminary. What caused you to change your story?
A. I remembered it later—
Q. You mean you'd *forgotten* a dicker to cheat your friend and only remembered it when I had you bound over as a material witness because you had the same opportunity and motive to kill Yeagar that Boyd had, until you thought this up?

The district attorney and McComas were both up at that, but Johnson didn't need any help—yet.

A. No sir I guess I just didn't want to tell it. If I could help it. I thought people might misunderstand, lots of people out here do not understand business deals very well—
Q. Not that kind, you're right there. They might misunderstand.

A sick feeling came over me that they didn't misunderstand at all. They didn't like Johnson so well, yet in a sheepish way they figured him for a smart hombre who'd put over a shrewd trade. If Boyd hadn't lost his fool head and started the gunplay, they'd have come out on top.

While Earl Rogers was going into all this, another character had come into the courtroom, he was there all the rest of the time, sometimes in the center of the stage.

The murdered man.

The corpus delicti, being dead, yet speaketh. Who, what, why, when, and how. The Louisville Sport stalks the courtroom in derby hat and yellow vest as clankingly as ever the ghost of Hamlet's father walked the battlements in armor. In every trial, it happens. So that in days to come we would almost shriek as Charlotte Noyes flung the vitriol and her lover's six gun barked, or watched the figure of Bill Broome come down the single dusty street of Antelope Valley at high noon.

The murdered do not seem to rest well.

We had the Sport with us. While Papa moved slowly behind Boyd, dropped his hand on the boy's thin shoulder to show confidence and reassurance, he'd left them a picture to look at—the Sport, face to face with Johnson, bargaining coldly, contemptuously.

When he spoke to Johnson again, Earl Rogers' tone had changed completely, steel-edged with scorn, bright with disbelief, the questions came faster and faster, piling one on top of another, leaving no margin for thought.

Q. Yeagar was counting his money when the argument started?

A. Yes.

Q. Putting the bills together, stacking the gold pieces?

A. Yes he had to give me my share, didn't he? As soon as Boyd had gone to bed he was going to give it to me. I'm a bookkeeper, he knew I'd insist the money be counted. You can understand that.

Q. Mr. Johnson, you can't be that naive.

A. What's that?

Q. Naive—artless, simple-minded, gullible. You are a young man who has been around. You describe yourself as a business man. You indicate you're a smart guy. You couldn't believe that Yeagar meant to fulfill this preposterous bargain you call a sharp deal?

A. You bet I thought he would.

Q. Mr. Johnson, please. A man like the Louisville Sport? Why should he? Did you have anything in writing? Were you likely to go around telling people you'd made a deal to double-cross your partner. You yourself have said they might misunderstand this—people might. Why should he give you any money even if he had agreed to do it?

A. I told him—

Q. With a gun to back it up? The truth is, isn't it, that he was sitting there giving you the horse laugh? He'd played you for a sucker, hadn't he?

A. I don't think anything of the kind—

Q. You signalled him you wanted to collect your cut, and he was laughing at you. He was putting the money in his own pockets and leaving you holding an empty bag, wasn't he?

Somehow Johnson recovered. He stopped, waited, his face a blank. While the jury stared at him, he made a careful and impressive answer.

A. No, I don't think he was. I certainly did not have any such idea at all. He gave me a wink, he counted and I was thinking how pleased poor Al would be when he woke up in the morning and I could tell him he wasn't dead broke, we had a stake left. Yeagar had a reputation as far as I knew of being a square gambler.

The shadow of the gallows fell across the white face of the boy sitting beside my father. I saw it. Father saw it too.

Up to the moment that the judge adjourned court until ten o'clock the next morning, the jury believed Harry Johnson.

SEVEN

As we came out of the courtroom a woman stopped my father in the corridor, and I had my first glimpse of Pearl Morton. A potent factor in my young life, she was to be.

After my grandfather died, my fierce, young, pigheaded unreasonable, unreasoning loyalty to my father left me nobody I would talk to about anything *wrong*. *I* could fight with him, *I* could criticize him, let anybody else so much as suggest a fault or flaw and, God help us all, I exploded like a string of firecrackers. (Still do.)

Knowing men as she did, Pearl Morton was able to show to me not a flaw, not a sin, not a weakness, but a man's battle against his besetting enemy, baffling, cunning, powerful. A temptation against which we must unite to protect him. Above all, as a danger—a *danger*, under which we must live, against which we must watch. Every time she had a chance,

Pearl Morton helped me, and I could accept her help on account of a love and loyalty she had for him that held no grain of condemnation. I have since known ladies who were pillars of society, models of conduct, strong in self-righteousness, who I am quite sure Pearl Morton preceded into the kingdom of heaven as we are told the harlots do go in ahead of scribes and pharisees. Her charity for all, her malice toward none, must have swept her through the pearly gates somehow.

As the crowd jostled us, I saw her first as a big woman, in the age when Lillian Russell was the most famous beauty in America. Pearl was laced into tight corsets, her figure in a suit of plum-colored silk was hourglass. Even on a hot August day Pearl dressed respectably, when she went out in public, a man would have had to pay well to see Pearl or any of her girls in the bikini thigh-length skirts, backless free-show fashions of today. A big picture hat with black ostrich plumes framed her hair, which was hennaed, though that was a word we didn't know, we just called it dyed. From her I got the first whiff I'd ever had of perfume. A tiny drop of Palmer's violet, a dash of rose water perhaps, but our ancestors had ruled that *perfume* was an aphrodisiac along the road to hell, only used by fast women or fancy ladies.

Pearl Morton was a fast woman, a madame. When in *Gone with the Wind* I read about Belle Watling, who ran the sporting house in Atlanta, the description of her brought Pearl plainly before me in all her buxom, colorful, worldly-wise might. As I read of how Belle Watling loved that great lady Melanie Wilkes, I had to wonder whether Pearl had managed with her great heart to endow me with a tiny bit of Melanie's strength and goodness. Not really, she *couldn't,* but she once said to Papa that I was the only child she'd ever had. We were united in our feeling about Papa.

In the shoving shouting mob outside the courtroom that day, Papa managed to get us to one side and say, "Nora, this is an old friend of mine, Mrs. Morton—Pearl, my daughter."

I dropped the curtsy my grandmother had taught me and Pearl Morton laughed. "A chip off the old block?" she said, and Papa said, "I'm afraid so," and he looked down at me and laughed too.

In a low voice Pearl said, "I know where Queenie is, if you want her."

While Papa thought, I could tell by the way she watched him how kindly she felt toward him, how much she loved him. Nobody had ever told me then about the corny bad-woman-with-a-heart-of-gold and it wouldn't have mattered, it never does when you are looking right at it, the kindliness of her face was as real as the glow of a fire in the grate.

Papa said, "Can Queenie help us?" Pearl Morton said, "She's a flighty critter," and Papa said, "Keep an eye on her, I'll let you know." The plumes on Mrs. Morton's hat danced as she nodded.

The next time I saw her was in the rear of the church all in black, at my grandfather's funeral. I was hurt because she didn't recognize me or return my wave.

Back at our offices, Papa summoned a council of war.

"Can I come, Papa?" I said, and he almost hollered back at me. "You're doggone right you can come," he said. "This is your case, you're the one who knew he didn't do it. You still think so?"

I said, "Yes I do."

Everybody else, I could see, thought things were beyond recall.

Our office was up one flight of dark, narrow wooden stairs, in a three-story brick building on the corner of First and Broadway. Half a block up First Street toward Hill, was the police station. The courthouse was two blocks up Broadway to the north and the city hall a block and a half south. The county jail, on Temple, faced the courthouse.

Earl Rogers' office was dead center of everything that was going on.

Sometimes I'd driven down with Frank when he came to get Papa and a few times I'd ridden down after school on my bike without anybody saying I could and got whopped for it. Now, in the Boyd case, I was allowed to be there all the time and already it felt like—it felt like the place I liked best in the whole world.

Until they tore it down a couple of years ago I used to go by, and walk up the steps and sit down. The steps were worn in the middle. By our feet, by the running feet of those in trouble trooping to see Mr. Rogers, the desperate, pursued, galloping feet of the underdogs coming to ask Mr. Rogers to defend them.

We defended everybody.

At the top of the stairs was a hall from which opened glass-paneled doors. On one, in gilt-and-black letters, EARL ROGERS. Nothing more, ever. Many men worked in our office, it was never a law firm. Earl Rogers never had a partner. It might have been better if he had. Not quite so godamighty cockahoop. Anyhow, it was then and always just Earl Rogers' office.

A big corner waiting room, dusty, dirty, untidy, noisy, crowded twenty-four hours a day. On the walls, pictures of Lincoln, who saved the Union, Papa's idol Grover Cleveland, James J. Corbett, young Ty Cobb, and two originals by Remington, the West's greatest painter. I forget what Papa had done for him. The furniture consisted of large brass spittoons, a couple of oak hatracks, two secondhand leather divans and half a dozen chairs around the walls, which were painted green. Two windows on one side looked across at the gray granite *Times* building, two on the other at Mr. Simpson's excellent saloon, where they had the best free lunch in town —hot, fresh homemade buns with baked ham in them, pumpernickel with Swiss cheese and little hot tamales. Sometimes *Wanted* men slipped into Simpson's back room and sent to ask if Mr. Rogers would come over there and see them. After dark, sometimes.

Adjoining was another office facing Broadway primarily inhabited by Luther Brown, beyond another for the rest of the staff, presided over by Bill Jory and later Rosy and Cowan and Hawley. Jory slept in the office, if he ever slept. Up those dark, narrow stairs came strange characters from many worlds. Second-story men, pickpockets, cops, cabdrivers (horses), detectives, official and private eyes, bartenders, messenger boys, prize fighters and their managers, jockeys, Pinkerton men, gunmen, politicians, mayors, senators, governors, fortunetellers, pawnbrokers, safecrackers, reporters, undertakers, newsboys, doctors, poets and painters, bookmakers, bankers, forgers, inventors, shoplifters. The underworld usually saw Bill Jory, who had come from there, first. When I worked for years alongside Damon Runyon I used to say, "I wish you'd seen my father's office, nobody else could really do it justice but you."

On the First Street side was Papa's private office. Lined floor to ceiling with law books in light calf bindings. Jerry Giesler swears that Earl Rogers knew everything in every book, but never which book or where. Jerry spent his young life in our office locating them—*there was a decision—there is a case in which*, Mr. Rogers would say. There *always* was.

Papa's family-heirloom walnut secretary desk was against the wall at the rear, he faced clients and staff from behind a big table down the middle.

Whether we lived at the Van Nuys Hotel or the Alexandria, in a small house on Bush Street or a big white one at Vermont Avenue and Los Feliz Boulevard, where the Standard station now stands, in an apartment on the ocean front between Santa Monica and Venice, or traveled back and forth to San Francisco and New York for months—years—on end, our lives centered in that office. Eat work sleep wait—I suppose to me when I was first allowed to *stay* during the Boyd case it was like moving to Coney Island. I could hardly believe my luck.

When we got back there on the afternoon Earl Rogers had begun his cross-examination of Johnson, we sat around the table, five or six of us. Luther Brown, Fred Spencer, Bill Jory, me—I'm not sure whether the others yet included big Paul Schenck with his white Stetson or not.

In other books, Luther Brown is described at this period as Earl Rogers' right-hand man, who made the contacts in the nationally important San Francisco graft trials. A former schoolteacher, deacon of his church, sound lawyer respected by all, looked on as a steadying influence for the brilliant temperamental young Rogers as he soared. Probably he was.

Children have prejudices of fantastic violence. I had seen Luther Brown at our house, sometimes he came in the evening or on Sundays to consult Papa, sometimes socially. He was my No. 1 choice of people I couldn't *bear*. Part of it was Papa-he-makes-my-flesh-creep, but I had another reason I didn't tell my father and have never told anybody and am not going to now.

When I read about a man who took arsenic to condition himself so he could share the poison cup with his victim and show no ill effects himself, I think of Luther. The sleek shining hair; the soft white skin; the moist luminous eyes. Probably Papa should have taken a razor strop to me, as he did from time to time, for my impudence to Mr. Brown, but he never did. Way down, I believe he didn't really *like* him either.

"A remarkable witness," Luther began as soon as we settled down, "and I fear, Mr. Rogers, a creditable one."

I said, "He's a big bandar-log liar."

Luther smiled benignly. "He didn't impress me as lying," he said.

"You wouldn't know a liar if you heard one," I said. "Oh, Papa don't you see, the one who did it would be the one to say he saw the other one do it, he would be the murderer himself and have to lie. If he didn't do it then he would not want to tattle on a friend, that would be the *Brand of the Dog* by whom a secret is revealed, you remember, Papa, you *asked* Boyd if he saw Johnson shoot the Sport and he said he was sleepy and wasn't looking, but Papa *if Boyd* had shot Yeagar he would have said Oh yes of course I saw Johnson shoot him with my own eyes because if he was a murderer he wouldn't mind lying and he would not have any secret to protect his friend—" I ran out of words, breath, and stuttered to a close.

His eyes closed, his lower lip folded over the upper one, Papa sat very still.

Nobody spoke.

The daylight had gone. Somebody came in and lit the big green oil student lamps. In the glass doors of the bookcases I could see reflected the distorted faces of the men around the table, as a background for Papa's dark head and shoulders. He looked a different *breed*.

After what seemed a long time, Papa said, "I am inclined to agree with you, Nora. Bill—" and Bill Jory said, "Yes, Mr. Rogers," and Papa said with a grin, "Are there any pawnshops open?" Jory said, "I can always get in anyhow." Bill Jory always had friends.

It turned out to be a good thing for us that one of those who came up our stairs to see him about then was Jim Davin, the bartender from the Metropole.

As soon as McComas walked into the humming, milling, shoving courtroom the next morning, he began to bark objections like a seal who'd missed his breakfast.

To be sure, things had been moved around some. In the space between the witness stand and the jury box stood the green felt bloodstained poker table, rakish and disturbing as rock 'n' roll in a church.

After a couple of minutes of McComas' uproar, the district attorney himself took the situation in hand. Dignified, self-contained, he made every man in the courtroom, even the presiding judge, feel the weight of his responsibility to the People, whose duly elected servant he was. In formal, well-chosen words he deplored this attempt, without precedent, to turn His Honor's court into a theater, nay worse, a circus. Tactics smacking of the charlatan, the trickster, the ringmaster were dangerous and prejudicial and must not be tolerated.

As he sat down Earl Rogers was on his feet. In morning attire of striped gray trousers, short black coat, pearl-gray

Ascot tie, he meant to look older than he was. There he failed, but he was before their eyes, neither the charlatan nor the clown the district attorney had attempted to describe.

As quietly as a man could speak and still be heard, he said, "If Your Honor please," and waited until Judge Smith said, "Mr. Rogers." Then he went on without emotion, every word clear and distinct. "I wish to offer this table as Defendant's Exhibit A. I also offer it as a permissible effort to take this jury to the scene of the crime, therefore a proper legal procedure."

After a pause, his voice began to escape from the rigid respectful control. He said, "In Your Honor's court, we are trying a boy not yet of age for the most terrible of all crimes and the district attorney has asked for the supreme penalty. Should this jury find him guilty, it would be their duty to condemn him to death. If we err in this court, Your Honor, surely we must err in favor of giving him more of a fair trial rather than less.

"My learned opponent speaks eloquently of his obligations to the People of the State of California, of which we are all aware. May I remind him that my mandate from the People is no less clear and powerful than his own? The *People* insist that this boy, whom they have instructed you to presume to be innocent, shall have the ablest, boldest, strongest defense it is possible to give him. They have decided in their might and majesty that the burden of proof is with the district attorney. I am *their* qualified, duly accredited counsel for the defense as truly as he is their counsel for the prosecution. In their hearts the People are passionately anxious that no injustice shall be done in their name. No innocent man convicted and hung unfairly to haunt their peaceful slumber.

"I am defending an innocent man.

"Your own law says so.

"I need not remind the district attorney and his chosen assistants that they, like myself, have one aim in common—to see justice done here. They are prosecutors, not persecutors.

"In my effort on behalf of my innocent client, Your Honor will not deny me the right to do something in my client's behalf for the reason that it has not been done before. Once men's heads were chopped off without any trial at all. In Star Chamber sessions, behind locked doors, without representation or defense for the accused, men were convicted and hung on gibbets in the public square. One of the greatest steps ever taken in the cause of humanity was the first fair, free, open trial by jury. Thank God no one stepped back from that grand concept because it was without precedent.

"If this is the first time a man's counsel has produced for the jury the exact scene of the crime, does that entitle his prosecutors to call it a trick? In God's name, I say NO.

"The witness Johnson says certain things happened which I do not believe happened nor could within space and time have happened. I have a right, a duty, to reconstruct the scene and ask him *there* to re-enact what he swears took place there. So that the jury may see for itself whether to credit the story Johnson tells or not. If this be theater it is the enlightened theater of the Greeks, or of the Shakespeare tragedies, of *Hamlet* and *Lear* and *Richard the Second*.

"I ask Your Honor's permission to question the prosecution's witness in the physical setting of the crime.

"One of two roles are possible to him.

"He was an eyewitness, as he claims he was.

"Or he was the murderer.

"I want to test his story by every means in our power, under all circumstances possible. The district attorney must wish to see it so tested. If he is telling the truth, he has nothing to fear from the stage which I have set. If he is lying to send another man to the gallows for a crime he may have committed himself, we all must want to find the truth.

"If this is the first time a courtroom has been arranged to turn into the very scene of the murder, others through the years who are innocent may have cause to bless Your Honor's name."

For a moment he stood so still it was impossible to look away from him.

Then we all became conscious of Judge Smith looking down from the Bench at the green garish table in his courtroom and then at Johnson, neat and veneered, waiting to return to the witness stand. At the defendant, sullen and feverish after a sleepless night.

"Mr. Rogers," the judge said, "upon me as well as upon you and the district attorney, rests grave responsibility. In the end, gravest of all will be that of the jury. They will set this defendant free or declare his life forfeit for this crime. In their dread task, I wish to give them every chance to arrive at the truth, to permit them every smallest piece of evidence that may assist them to arrive at a just verdict. I will allow you more latitude than I would if a man's life were not at stake. As you say, this reproduction of an actual scene may help this jury and others in the future."

There can be no question that this was one of those *firsts* in trial law which Earl Rogers introduced. Half a century later I was thrilled when in a case against an insurance company one of Earl Rogers' grandsons was allowed to build an entire plastic model of a road, a driveway, trees, fences, garages and not only bring this into the courtroom for the jury to see but use exact toy models of the cars involved to demonstrate what could or could not have happened on a faraway hillside. This was taken for granted by judge, jury, and opposing counsel, who made no objection of any kind, much less ones of the violence and length District Attorney Rives and McComas had used in the Boyd case.

"You may proceed, Mr. Rogers," said the judge.

The green table stayed where it was. Much better for them not to have fought against it. They had given Earl Rogers an opportunity to counterpunch and any real defense lawyer has to be a counterpuncher.

As Johnson finally took the stand once more, Rogers' easy, pleased, conversational tone, the way he stepped around the poker table without so much as glancing at it, caused first McComas, then Rives, then the witness to relax. This had just been a bit of Rogers' dramatic showmanship. They were mistaking this preliminary bout over the admissibility of the scenery for the main event.

After staring at it coldly for a moment, Johnson turned his honest frank blue gaze upon his cross-examiner. His mouth was thin-lipped, tight. I do not remember how old he was, older than Boyd, that morning he seemed in the same age bracket as my father, thirty-two—thirty-three. A little more wary, cagey, watchful, he wasn't the least bit afraid of Rogers up to this point.

In the transcript, the first questions seem easy, routine, simple.

Q. (by Mr. Rogers) Mr. Johnson, I trust you rested well and that your memory of the sequence of events about which I wish to ask you in more detail today will be clear, so that you will not have to change any part of your story again. I would like to review the events before the murder, the exact happenings at the time of the shooting and what took place immediately afterwards. Now in order that we may give the

jury a true picture—you sat *here*, is that correct? (indicating
a chair) No no no, Mr. Johnson, do not answer without
looking. There's nobody in any of the chairs now. No accusing ghosts here in His Honor's courtroom. You were *here?*
Good! Boyd here?

A.   That's right.

Like a stage magician, Papa now held a hat in his hand.

Not for nothing had Bill Jory encouraged his friend bartender Jim Davin to come up the stairs to our office. For this
was a derby hat, the very derby which when he took Queenie
to the Thalia on the Barbary Coast must have looked dashing
indeed upon the Louisville Sport. As Papa put it down on
the table in front of one of the chairs, it was dusty and battered and there were, unmistakably, bullet holes in the crown.
For further identification of whose seat that had been during
the fatal game, there appeared, by further Houdini, the death
card, the bloody ace of spades.

With a vengeance, Papa was reproducing the gambling
table, the game conditions, and because he himself was in
it, his eyes stared at *something* in the chair he had so firmly
marked as the dead man. His voice was almost a whisper as
he said, "And—Mr. Yeagar *here?*"

A.   That's right.
Q.   When the first shot was fired?
A.   Sure. That's where he was.
Q.   And the second shot?
A.   He didn't move after the first shot. Not at all.
Q.   No no, of course he didn't. He had this hat on his
head?
A.   I guess so, he had a hat on all the time, he pulled it
down over his eyes, the bulb didn't have any shade, it was
pretty bright so that was the way he wore his hat, down over
his eyes.
Q.   About like this?

Without any fuss, Mr. Rogers sat down on the chair that
had been Yeagar's. As he put the hat on his head, one finger
tilted it down on his forehead. Banquo's ghost had sat down
at the banquet. The scraping of the chair rattled as loudly as
old Marley's chains in Scrooge's ears and my spine rippled.
Every eye in the courtroom was fixed on the figure in the
derby hat, including Johnson's, who somehow kept that hard

little smile of contempt. He seemed to be the only man in the courtroom unmoved by this calling up of specters.

Q. (repeated) About like this?
A. Near enough.
Q. When you first saw the bullet hole in Yeagar's head, the blood streaming down, where was his hat?

For the first time, there was something too small for a pause—yet there was something. *For the first time,* Johnson was back in the murder room on the night somebody shot the Louisville Sport.

A. I don't know, I wasn't thinking about his hat.
Q. Were you thinking about the gold watch? Let's find out if you will please about the gold watch, the family heirloom.
A. Well of course all that was before—
Q. Before the shots?
A. It had to be before the shots didn't it?
Q. Yes yes. Now what I am asking you about is the time when your boy friend Boyd was asking Yeagar to give him some money on his watch, his grandfather's watch, wasn't it? You remember about that?
A. It was me told about it in the first place, wasn't it?
Q. Of course it was. I just want you to remember everything as it happened. Little things can be such a help to us here. Now. We have Yeagar here—

Again on his feet, he put down the dreadful, comic, tragic derby in front of the dead man's chair.

Q. Mr. Johnson, would you object to taking this seat, the one you occupied that night? I am not quite clear about a couple of minor points, I believe it will help the jury to reconstruct—

Johnson looked at McComas. McComas surged, the D.A. touched his arm and held him silent in his seat. A wily man was he, he saw where this would lead. To refuse was to give Rogers a point. If Johnson was telling the truth why shouldn't he return to the seat from which he swore he'd seen Boyd kill Yeagar?

As he came down from the stand and walked to the chair,

I saw Boyd stir. While the drama that concerned him more nearly than anyone else was going on, he'd sat slumped, weary, not wanting to look, forgotten. Now he sat up straight, following Johnson with eyes ablaze. He and Johnson weren't but a few feet apart now.

Courtrooms are so small.

Now Rogers was able to get closer to Johnson, he began a series of questions to which McComas shouted one objection after another with increasing vehemence. "I can't hear my own witness," he kept bellowing, "my own witness has his back to me," and finally Earl Rogers, friendly, concerned, persuaded him to take a seat at the table so he could see and hear Johnson better. By chance he took the seat of the corpus delicti and, absent-mindedly, Rogers put the derby hat on *him*. A roar of tense, nervous laughter swept the courtroom, the judge's gavel banged, Rogers apologized to everybody. I saw that his eyes were on the jury. The jury had laughed.

Q. (by Mr. Rogers) Now as I understand it, The Sport wanted to quit. It was getting very late, the game had gone on a long time, he said he'd given Boyd every chance to get even and now he was through. That's correct? Yes. You say Boyd was desperate. He wanted to keep on playing in an attempt to retrieve his fortunes. So he dragged a watch out of his pocket (Indicating his own watch pocket) and held it out to Yeagar. Is that the way it was?

A. Sure. That's about right.

Q. What did he *say* exactly, please?

Here began one of the things which lawyers, when they discuss Earl Rogers to this day as they do so often, say made him the great cross-examiner. Jerry Giesler called my attention to it once years ago when we were examining some of my father's most successful cross-examinations about which Jerry used to lecture from time to time. Note that though the record from here on shows the use of the word *say*—*said*— what did he *say* exactly—his exact *words*—it can't show the emphasis, the expression, pause, glance, always as though the importance lay with what was said when actually Mr. Rogers couldn't have cared less what anybody said. All that mattered was what they did. Rogers focused on speech instead of action, drawing the witness's attention from his danger area, getting him alert to defend against an off-tackle play so he would leave himself wide open for a pass.

Q.   What did he *say?*

A.   Oh he said he had not wanted to part with an heirloom but he had a strong feeling that his luck was about to change. He asked Yeagar to lend him a hundred smackeroos on the watch.

Q.   He asked for a hundred dollars? That's what he *asked* for? Wasn't that a large sum?

A.   More than Yeagar would give him, you bet.

Q.   Just exactly what did Yeagar say to him?

A.   He kind of snickered and said No. He said he wanted to quit and anyhow the watch wasn't worth anything.

Q.   What did Boyd say to that—now, all this time, while they were talking to each other, Boyd had the watch in his hand? Holding it out while he was *talking,* to show Yeagar when he *mentioned* a hundred dollars, trying to convince him, wasn't he, while he *asked* for—show us how he held it.

A.   Like this. (Taking the watch)

Q.   Did he—he was holding the watch in his right hand? Yes. Now, did he say anything?

A.   Yes.

About here, McComas gave a convulsive start and turned to the district attorney. He reminded me of a big whale they harpooned off Redondo Beach, the way he came up blowing and jumping. Too late McComas saw where the chief counsel for the defense was headed, just the same he started trying to help his witness with a lot of routine objections and was overruled, under *res gestae,* anything said at the time of the commission of a crime in the presence of the deceased and the accused was admissible as evidence and could never be hearsay.

Q.   You could see the watch? Now Mr. Johnson you're sure you could see it?

A.   Sure I could see it.

Q.   You didn't just figure from what he *said*—

A.   I could see it as plain as I see you.

Q.   In his hand while he was talking to Yeagar?

A.   Yes *sir.*

Q.   Well now—

With a swift motion Rogers went to the watch pocket of his dark trousers.

This time he took out a watch.

Now in his hand he held a gold case the size of a tomato.

As he went around the table, detaching it from his chain, I knew why he'd sent Bill Jory to a pawnshop. This was twice as big as his own watch. He was smiling politely at Johnson, asking a favor, it looked like.

Q. Just use my watch. Show the jury how Boyd was holding it and tell us what he said about it.

A. He held it out like this, I don't know any other way he could of held out a watch—

Q. No no, probably not. He just held it out as you are doing now and then he asked Yeagar to give him a hundred dollars?

A. I told you that.

Q. Yeagar was insulting? He said the watch wasn't worth two bits?

A. That's what he said.

Q. At that insult to his family heirloom Boyd reached for his gun and pulled it and shot Yeagar?

A. Yes well maybe not he was sore—

Q. Did he say anything?

A. He wanted a chance to get even—

Q. When Yeagar wouldn't agree quick as a flash, as you said, he pulled his gun quick as a flash—

Sure-footed as a cat, Papa kept moving backward, he was watching the witness now from the right elbow of the juror on the end seat of the first row. All of them stared at Johnson, behind the table, the neat square figure, the frank blue eyes.

From where he stood beside them Earl Rogers' thin, chill, icy whisper swept over the jury and hit Johnson.

Q. What did he do with the watch while he whipped out his gun quick as a flash?

A. I—didn't hear the question—

Q. Don't play for time, Mr. Johnson. It's too late. Your hearing has been acute up to now. Just tell us what Boyd did with the big gold watch in his right hand while he whipped out his gun quick as a flash and fired accurately at Yeagar's head.

McComas was on his feet, trying to give the witness time, protection, and Johnson still had the watch in his hand, staring at it.

Q. Answer the question, please.

A. I don't know I don't remember I wasn't paying any attention to a watch.

Q. Quick as a flash—you can't do it.

Johnson came off the ropes, still fighting.

A. It was just—that was just it, it was all so fast, done so quick, one minute I saw the watch then the next the gun was in his hand and I—I don't know how—

Q. You can't explain now how it was possible to do this?

A. I don't have to explain—

Q. Oh yes you do. *Try.*

The murder gun, picked up from the clerk's desk as Earl Rogers wandered restlessly by, slithered across the green cloth and came to rest two inches from Johnson's hand.

Q. You've got 'em both, the watch and the gun, and your hand, let's see by what sleight-of-hand Boyd managed the action you have described.

Johnson put down the watch.

Q. You have to put down the watch—and that isn't quick as a flash!

Johnson did not pick up the gun, he just stared at it and McComas, blowing and sputtering, got it and put it back on the desk. People's Exhibit B.

Q. You didn't seem to be able to do much with that, let's try something else. After he'd shot Yeagar, what did Boyd say?

A. Nothing.

Q. Nothing at all?

A. No nothing not a word.

Q. What did you say?

A. Nothing.

Q. You didn't cry out?

A. Oh well I may have cried out, sure, like what have you done or something, I don't remember about that.

Q. You had just seen a man shot to death?

A. I was speechless with horror that must have been it, Mr. Rogers.

Bill Jory jammed an elbow into my ribs so hard I thought he had broken a couple of them. I didn't get it, but Jory said to me in a hiss that it was the first time Johnson had called his cross-examiner *Mr. Rogers.* When they did that, he said, it meant Mr. Rogers had begun to get him.

Mr. Rogers went on re-creating the murder, the murder Johnson had told.

Q.   All right, Boyd held out the watch and asked for a hundred dollars, he pulled his gun quick as a flash when Yeagar said No, this hat here spun off his head and bounced on the floor and a hole appeared in Yeagar's forehead and the blood spurted and he slumped forward on the table *here* and this ace of spades was in the way and the blood flowed over it, the murderer stared at him and nobody said anything or made a sound, Boyd then shifted the gun with which he'd just shot The Sport from his right hand to his left—why?

A.   I—what do you mean?

Q.   Why didn't he just drop it naturally at his own right hand?

A.   How should I know?

Q.   You were sitting on his left?

A.   Yes on his left.

Q.   If you had shot the gun and dropped it at your right hand where you say you picked it up, that would have been natural—

A.   I didn't have the gun I never had the gun it was Al Boyd's gun.

Q.   So he either shifted it from his right hand to his left or he swung it all the way around and dropped it on his left side next to your chair where you could just lean down and pick it up? Which did he do?

A.   I guess I didn't notice one way or the other I guess so.

Q.   You didn't notice one way or the other?

A.   No I guess not.

Q.   You didn't yell out don't point that at me?

A.   No I didn't.

Q.   You didn't jump back and holler and shove back your chair?

A.   No I didn't.

Q.   Just sat there without moving saying nothing.

A.   I expect for a second or two I was sort of frozen in my chair. I was stunned like.

Q.   Boyd had been drinking heavily?

The whole courtroom heard Johnson's sigh of relief as the questions shifted to a new subject.

A. He'd drunk a lot, he did a good deal of the time.
Q. Drink made him argumentative? Belligerent?
A. Well, usually it did.
Q. Almost always wasn't it?
A. Well that's what he said himself he said drink made him quarrelsome.
Q. Looking for trouble most of the time, wasn't he?
A. Yes.
Q. Pick fights?
A. Yes.
Q. He wasn't too drunk to understand what was going on, I mean he could ask Yeagar to go on with the game, ask for a hundred dollars on his watch, a watch he said he'd never meant to part with, is that true? He wasn't too drunk to remember that?
A. No, he was sort of what you call maudlin about it.
Q. Not too far gone in drink to know when Yeagar had insulted him, to take offense because Yeagar wouldn't give him a chance to get even, he could draw his gun quick as a flash and shoot straight?
A. No, only when he was drunk he didn't know sometimes exactly what he was doing he got real mad at things —sore—
Q. Did it occur to you, Mr. Johnson, that he might have spotted your little deal with The Sport?
A. Oh no I'm sure he didn't.
Q. Still you said you and Yeagar had got him between you didn't you? In the betting. You were watching Yeagar count the money you say so he could later give you your share. Didn't enter your mind that as Boyd leaned back in his chair thinking he might have had just a suspicion of this before he pulled out the watch and said he wanted to go on playing—could he have spotted anything between you and Yeagar?
A. Oh no, I'm sure he didn't. We were careful.
Q. You knew him to be dangerous when he was drunk and sore and by the time he dropped his gun you knew he was capable of murder—you'd just seen him—

Papa was sitting there beside Johnson, questioning him in a way as natural as one man discussing something that had happened with another, something they both regretted. At that moment Rogers gave the impression that he had shot his bolt, tried to break this witness and failed. Until suddenly he had a gun in his hand, not the murder gun, his own .45. For a fraction of a second, it pointed straight at Johnson's stomach, Papa's lips moved, just as well we couldn't hear what he said.

We could hear Johnson, though.

His yell rocketed in the courtroom, his chair crashed, the derby bounced twice and settled against the jury box. Breathing in gasps, his face blanched white, Johnson backed against the counsel table where the district attorney sat, he tried to shove it over to get farther away from Rogers.

Bailiffs charged forward, McComas was shouting curses not usually heard in court, spectators were screaming, the judge's gavel beat a mad tattoo. A deputy grabbed Papa, took the gun, kept saying heartily, *Now Mr. Rogers, now Mr. Rogers—*

Mr. Rogers, however, stood in utter bewilderment. Staring at Johnson.

At last they got things quieted down. Silence fell. Into it, Mr. Rogers said, "This is the man who claimed—I can only ask Your Honor's pardon, no one has higher regard for the decorum of Your Honor's court—I merely wished to ask the witness a question concerning the manner in which he has testified the defendant handled the gun, which I question. And to test the witness's own behavior at that point. But now —Your Honor, we have here a witness under oath who has testified that he saw a man enflamed with drink and gambling fever, whom he knew well to be a dangerous, belligerent man who picked fights on the slightest provocation. He'd just seen him kill another man over an insult. Over what the other man considered an infringement of his gaming rights. Then, our witness Johnson testifies, the murderer in the process of dropping the gun pointed it directly at *him*, at *Johnson*. The witness knew that he had double-crossed this murderer, and that the murderer might have gotten wise to it. *That* gun was smoking, the hand that held it was red with blood, figuratively speaking, yet Johnson told us only a few minutes ago that he didn't jump, didn't try to get away, didn't yell, didn't crash over his chair or do one thing that Davin across in the bar must have heard. He sat still, he said to us, and did and said nothing. Your Honor, my gun hasn't been fired in some time. Mr. Johnson may suspect my private opinion of him, but he cannot think it includes murderous intentions. I am a member of the Bar in good standing. Could he believe that I would shoot him down without motive in open court in the presence of judge, jury, and district attorney? Surely a man with the cold nerve to face Boyd's gun, the man who says he *froze*, wouldn't have behaved as we—"

The judge interrupted there. He said, "Mr. Rogers, always with the best intentions, I'm sure, you seem to cause a good deal of commotion in this courtroom. You have made your point. Have you any further questions to ask this witness?"

"Thank you, Your Honor," Mr. Rogers said. "I have several more questions—vital ones."

Danger mounted with those quiet words. I began to bite my fingernails until they hurt. A murder had been re-enacted in front of our eyes, but we began to wonder now if it was the right murder. The tension was almost unbearable. In the box, the jury showed this plainly.

Johnson got back on the witness stand. Literally, he looked thinner, as though he'd lost weight the way a fighter does in the ring. In the atmosphere Rogers had created of the room where it happened, we began living over the words and actions after the shooting. The action moved along as the Q. and A. revealed them, we pictured Johnson leaning down and picking up the gun from the floor under his chair where Boyd had thrown it, he must by now be moving very fast, Davin in the bar had heard the shots and run to the door and met Johnson there with the gun in his hand crying *He shot him* and then Davin looked in and saw Boyd, his arms on the table staring at the dead man.

Q. (by Mr. Rogers) You gave the gun to Davin?
A. Yes.
Q. You told him Boyd had shot Yeagar?
A. Yes.
Q. And that Yeagar was dead?
A. I think so yes.
Q. Then the constable came?
A. Yes.
Q. You told him Boyd had killed Yeagar?

Quieter and quieter, each question, more and more softly like a man speaking so as not to disturb a wild animal.

Q. You told him Boyd had killed Yeagar?
A. Yes I said he shot him.

Q. What did you do then?
A. I went to the washroom.
Q. To the washroom?
A. Yes yes—
Q. Did you wash the powder burns off your hands?
A. Did I?—Did I?

Chill horror held the courtroom.
He's got him, I thought, with my heart bursting.
He's got him.
Papa broke the icy silence.
"Yes, Mr. Johnson," he said. "Yes. You did."
We all knew that for one of the only times in history the chief witness for the prosecution had just confessed to the murder on the stand in open court.
Papa gave him a bleak look of pity before he turned to grin at the innocent boy we'd saved from being hung.

EIGHT

That was all there was to it, really.
Boyd took the stand and Earl Rogers said, "I am going to ask you two questions. Did you kill William Yeagar?"
Boyd said, "No sir, I did not."
"Did you see your chum Harry Johnson shoot Yeagar?"
"No, Mr. Rogers, I didn't," Boyd said without hesitation, white-faced but perfectly steady. "I'd had quite a lot to drink and I was sleepy. I didn't see anything until after I heard the shots."
The code learned at Grandpappy's knee. *The Brand of the Dog on him by whom a friend is betrayed. If the blackest of lies is needed to clear*—The jury liked it better.
McComas cross-examined briefly and without conviction.
With those words of Johnson's—*Did I?—Did I?*—it was all over and McComas knew it well.
A great deal was made then, has been made ever since in print, in classrooms, by admirers and imitators, by lawyers

and detectives and professionals in trial work and crime, of Earl Rogers' use of the gun and the way he made Johnson react to it. The gun trick, they call it—and tell of Johnson's scream, the crashing chair, the white face and shaking hands. Among all the Rogers stories that are part of his legend, this is a favorite.

To Papa, it wasn't much. To him, that final moment with Johnson back on the stand was one of the things that satisfied him most. All the time he was trying to do one thing, one thing only. To hypnotize Johnson back into the cardroom of the Metropole on that August dawn. To bring back the truth of what took place there so powerfully that sooner or later it must conflict with the lie Johnson had commanded himself to tell. Somewhere, step by step, detail by detail, Johnson would forget which was which and make a fatal mistake. It only takes one, Earl Rogers always said.

By the business with the watch. The quick-as-a-flash testimony given at the Catalina preliminary. By the trick with the gun, of course, as part of it. By the hand-is-quicker-than-the-eye changes of pace and sound. The emphasis on what was said which didn't matter. Put together, Rogers was attempting to crack that cold, unscrupulous Swedish shell. To throw Johnson off balance so that he would throw himself, so that he would somewhere confuse the real story with the false one he had constructed.

Once out of the death room, away from the ghost of the man in a derby hat, the story of the murder as he must tell it, *stick to it*, must have seemed safely behind him, Papa said later. Now he was on his way to the washroom. The tense, exhausted, hard-pressed young murderer who'd been fighting Earl Rogers for hours could relax at last, this had to be harmless.

Nothing could happen to him in the washroom.

He was just going to wash his hands.

Everything led up to Johnson sitting there on the stand staring at his hands, from which he had washed the powder burns.

Q. Did you wash the powder burns off your hands?
A. Did I?—Did I?

That was what Papa was proud of. Not the trick with the gun.

The jury was only out about twenty minutes. So I didn't

have to learn in that case the hot-and-cold hell of waiting two
or three days and nights for a murder jury to come in. Twenty
minutes only got you nicely stretched on the rack, it didn't
have time to turn any of the screws.

Not Guilty was the first verdict I heard.

Nobody had believed Papa could win the Boyd case.

I didn't realize then that Harry Carr, in his front-page
stories, pinned down that victory to make my father the leading criminal lawyer of the West when he was only a little past
thirty.

Get Rogers to defend you.

The Boyd case built that into an axiom.

The night of the verdict we all went to the Hollenbeck
Hotel on Second Street where the headwaitress Delia and the
headwaiter her husband, whose name I can't remember, were
great friends of mine. Boyd looked sick and shaken still, but
his manners of being grateful impressed me a lot. He was
going back home the next day for good, he said.

"Will they try Johnson?" he asked Mr. Rogers.

Papa said no, probably not, the district attorney's office
wouldn't be anxious to call the public's attention to the mistake they'd made in the case. Better to just take a Not Guilty
and let it go at that. Probably by now Johnson had jumped
his bond, we wouldn't hear any more about it.

"Yeagar really isn't worth any more of the county's money,"
Papa said hilariously. "Johnson's too scared to ever do it again
—he was purely an opportunist murderer—those cold men
are."

That was exactly the way it worked out.

What was important to me, when we got back to the office
after dinner, I said to my father, "If you hadn't been there
would they have hung Boyd when he didn't do it?"

The smile that I loved best came over his face. He was very
pleased with himself, I must say. He said, "I think we may say
taking one thing with another the probability is that if you
and I hadn't been there they would have hung young Mr.
Boyd permanently."

"Oh Papa!" I said.

When I leaned against him I could feel him shaking like a
leaf. He said, "You stay here with Bill Jory for a little while.
Take a nap. Or read a book. I'll come back and pick you up
later."

In a real loud voice Bill Jory said, "I can take her home and meet you somewhere, Mr. Rogers."

"I don't want her to go home without me," my father said harshly.

I was surprised. His face was blue-black by now, the way it always was if he didn't shave a second time before dinner. Something funny was going on because he was very tired and white under the whiskers, yet he was all eager and excited and his forehead was glistening with little beads of sweat. A disarming gaiety about him melted me down, but it didn't disarm or melt Jory, I could tell that. Bill said doggedly, "I could take her to her grandfather's."

"What's the matter with you, Jory?" Papa said, laughing. I could tell under it he was angry. "Do as you're told."

Harry Carr came then, bouncing off the ground, he'd finished his story, he was gay and excited too. A feather in both their caps. Carr was blinking faster and faster like an owl, he and Papa pummeled each other and then Papa kissed me on the nose and said, "Get a nap, I tell you. I'll be right back." We could hear their feet *clattering* down the stairs and a burst of talk and shouts and roars of laughter floated back up. I ran to the window but they had disappeared down First toward Spring Street.

I wasn't sleepy. I'd tried once to teach Bill Jory to play checkers, but he couldn't keep his mind on it. I'd heard somebody say he was a top man with dice so I'd brought down my parchesi board. He said he thought he could learn, but that night he couldn't keep his mind on parchesi either. Pretty soon he put the cup down and said, "I'm going over to Simpson's for a beer and find out what's going on. I'll be right back."

I sat by the window and watched him walk across Broadway, a huge heavy-set man moving with unexpected lightness. The street lights were not very bright, my father was hollering about that only then nobody paid any attention to him. He said crime was a work of darkness and that one street lamp was worth two policemen. A clang broke the quiet and the police wagon came tearing out of the station alley, the white horses already galloping full speed, their manes and tails blowing. I hung way out to see them as long as I could. The *Times* building was lit up, in those days there were no night editions, the morning paper only came out tomorrow morning, so the night shift worked hard and late. People were coming up and down the broad stone steps. I knew which windows were the City Room, where my friend Harvey Elder worked as an assistant city editor. After the long hot day our offices hadn't really cooled off yet, they seemed cozy and safe and comfortable. It wasn't any use Luther Brown saying it was a shame, I ought not to be there, running to tattle to my Aunty Blanche, whom he knew because he sang baritone in the Ellis Club, a men's chorus of some kind. I felt more at home there than anywhere, I suppose because they belonged to Papa.

After a while I went over to the basin in the corner and washed my hands and face and retied my hair ribbons as best I could.

I had begun to feel restless, for no reason. My stomach had a knot in it.

I wished I could have gone with Papa.

Also the way Bill Jory was stewing worried me. Like he knew something was *wrong*, or he had a hunch that somebody or something bad was coming.

When he came back he brought me a lemonade with a maraschino cherry in it. Whether he'd got over whatever it was or not, I couldn't tell.

Footsteps coming up made Jory jump to his feet. A young Chinaman without a queue came in. He said, "Where is Mr. Rogers?" and Jory said, "Not here, what'd you want?" The young Chinaman shook his head and said, "I will come back tomorrow." As his footsteps went down again Bill Jory said, "Them Chinks!" A little later it was Harvey Elder. I loved Harvey, I'd known all his family out in Whittier for a long time, his grandmother was a friend of our family, and his sister Grace was about my age. He said, "Hello, sweetheart, where's your old man, out celebrating?" He held out a free lunch bun to me, which I usually loved, but for once I wasn't hungry. I had eaten an awful lot of dinner and besides there was that knot in my stomach. He said, "Well, don't forget I'm going to wait for you," and I said, "I don't think I'm going to marry anybody but if I do it would be all right if it was you," and later I wished to God I had a chance. I said, "Harve, where's Papa?" and he laughed and said, "He's sure got a right to howl tonight if ever a man did, don't worry, he'll be all right."

As soon as he had gone Bill Jory said to me in a hard, loud tone, "I gotta go—" and I said, "What's eating you?" He sat down on a chair and looked at me, finally he said, "Are we going to be pals or not?" I said, "Yes." He said, "Then you gotta start trusting me, nobody is pals unless they trust each other." I nodded, by then I was too scared to speak, he said, "I'm going to take you out to your grandfather's now."

This made me dig my heels in. I said, "Papa told me to wait here."

"I oughta be with him," Bill Jory said in a painful bellow, and I saw that though the California night had begun to chill, Bill's big red face was covered with sweat. He said, "There's going to have to be times when sometimes we have to know better about something than what he does."

In spite of himself. Against his will. Whether he likes it or not. A whisper into the future. My first.

The words then had no real meaning to me as Jory spoke them. Only I knew the knot in my stomach had begun to hum and buzz like a beehive. I chewed the end of my red hair ribbon to help me think. It didn't. I only felt I ought to do what Bill Jory said, he ought to be with Papa, so I said, "All right."

An old night-owl hack driven by a man named Spider who was a friend of Bill's stood in front of Simpson's. The horses names were John L and Wiggy. We got in and I must have gone to sleep right away and not waked up when Jory carried me into Grandpa's, I don't remember anything more that night.

Our whole lives were undoubtedly launched by the fact that in the Boyd case I had been right. As it had turned out, Boyd didn't do it.

A hundred squirms, turns, tours de force, self-defenses, justifiable homicides, evidence possible to manipulate to give a jury that smidgen of reasonable doubt lay ahead of us. In that first big, smashing, headline success, Earl Rogers was defending an innocent man, a boy who had actually not committed the murder for which he was on trial.

To defend the innocent, as Bill Fallon once said to me, is every criminal lawyer's ideal. It can't come to him too often. Leibowitz drove members of the New York press crazy for years wanting them to write a play about the only man, we all decided, he ever defended he was sure was innocent. Under our laws, our expert investigation, our highly trained personnel, our grand juries, not too many innocent men can be falsely arrested and charged. Even the magnificent work of the Court of Last Appeal, which tries to save those who have been, doesn't show a large percentage of injustices. More often the reverse is true. Corruption and graft and political influence allow the guilty to escape punishment.

Guilty-Not Guilty is legally, morally, spiritually a most delicate balance.

Naturally anybody could see that I couldn't know Boyd didn't do it by any process of reasoning, logic, or legal acumen. However, the Irish are always ready to believe in second sight, sixth sense, pixies, the little people, leprechauns, and psychic conclusions arrived at by convolutions of the soul and the stomach as well as the brain.

Thus Papa was easily convinced of, and accepted happily, an emotional superstition about his daughter Nora. The child's *fey*, he used to say, *very* pleased with the idea.

So a terrific pact was formed when we started our life and our work together, Earl Rogers and his daughter, by saving from the noose an *innocent* boy who would have been hung but for my intuition and his genius. The combination was great.

We defend everybody.

So—the guilty came too. A trial somewhere around this time in which Earl Rogers defended a man who was not innocent, a man named Mootry, most certainly guilty of murdering his wife Martha for the foulest of motives, and this is evidence of another kind of intuition, of spiritual insight.

This case was I think part of the greatest tragedy that ever struck Earl Rogers.

Or his daughter, for that matter.

His father died.

My grandfather.

A saint, said everyone who knew him, a saint if ever there was one.

PART TWO

NINE

My grandfather had some warning.
A month before he died, he wrote in the back of his Bible:

Today a signal comes that I
May any moment go.
What faithful joy 'twill be to me
If he doth will it so.

No one else had any idea. I wish he'd told Papa—faced it with him. Even I who saw him in the big old house on Hope Street on the mornings I had my lessons, or when he and I and our dog Samson strolled around the block discussing God's grace, always his favorite topic, saw no signs of anything amiss.

I have tried to see some way to highlight and dramatize Grandpa. Plain goodness is supposed to be dull. A putty nose such as Rostand put on Cyrano? A suit of armor such as good old Don Quixote wore? I've found it of no use. A good man he was, simple, unassuming, without guile, fearless and joyful. Goodness came from him as warmth from a pot-bellied iron stove, anybody could warm his poor, shivering soul at it. I can see the square, clean-shaven face with the short nose, the long Irish upper lip, the wise kindly blue eyes. A pattern in the Rogers family from earliest days and in my own time my brother Thornwell, my own son Richard, my daughter's son George. Not my father. My father was an Andrus like his mother, thin patrician face, lean punishing jaw, arched nose. Nor did his eyes always stay blue, the way my grandfather's did. Papa's changed from blue to gray to green, sometimes they looked black.

Grandpa was as utterly unself-conscious about his goodness as he was about everything else. The pure goodness that is always the main concern of Dostoievsky, which he gave at last and alone to Aloyosha, distilled love appearing in man as the goodness of man, love for anybody, without return.

I accepted as a child that my grandfather knew Jesus Christ.
How, it was not necessary for me to understand, any more
than I understand what the scientists say I must take for
granted about the galaxy of stars and the speed of light. I
could see a light when Grandpa spoke of His Friend, a radiance was there and I was quite sure about it.

On the front page of his Bible in scholarly script, fine and
now so faded, it says:

> Lowell L. Rogers
> Book Divine
> Thou art Mine
> Make me Thine.

A minister's edition, pages were inserted at the back for
notes, sermons, outlines. There, when he was pastor of the
Methodist Church of Globe, Arizona, in 1887, my grandfather
had set down a poem. As poetry, it couldn't be worse. I wish
I could be sure of ever writing anything as love-worthy or
sweet-scented to the Lord.

> I'm getting near His Dwelling,
> I long to see His face,
> There's room for me, I'm trusting,
> Though but an humble place.
>
> I have not on apparel,
> To let me near Him stand
> But, then, He knows I love Him
> And wait on His command.
>
> I bring so small a tribute,
> I have so little done,
> To notice me it may be
> He'll be the only one.
>
> But I remember sometimes
> When working in His fields,
> I found Him standing near me,
> To me this comfort yields.
>
> I did not fear His Presence,
> He spoke so sweet to me,
> Of course He knew I loved Him,
> He seemed my heart to see.
>
> And now I look! He cometh,
> He takes me by the hand,
> How happy, oh how happy,
> Close at His side to stand.

The man who wrote that poem would have to be profoundly disturbed when it was reported to him that his son had said to a client whose acquittal of murder he'd just achieved, "Get away from me, you slimy pimp, you're guilty as hell."

1

How long it was before he died that Lowell Rogers spoke to his son Earl of the Mootry case, of all it implied, of the profession Earl had chosen, I don't know. Not very long, I think.

I have told about the Boyd case first because it was the beginning for *me*.

Many things I learned later.

A man who had devoted his own life to going into the wilderness after lost sheep could hear and understand the cry of the sinner, the underdog, the downtrodden. Reverend Lowell Rogers had always pitied and forgiven the doubting disciple, the mistaken anguish of having been betrayed in Judas, the many who turned back and followed no more after Him when the way was hard and narrow. So beyond doubt my grandfather had led his son Earl into criminal law. His fears didn't stir for quite a while, then he kept silent about them.

They only came out into the open when he himself in the courtroom, unknown to his son, heard Earl Rogers say to a jury, *You cannot hang even such a man as Mootry on the word of a pimp, a prostitute and a policeman.*

But later—to his client, "You're guilty as hell."

Christianity has not been tried and found wanting, it hasn't been tried, somebody said that. Quite simple and literally, as two and two make four, my grandfather tried to live by it, in all things every day. So now with plain honesty he applied the teaching of the Master. Two parts were clear in the Way of Jesus Christ in these matters. Neither do I condemn thee— *Not Guilty.* The second part, the warning, the instruction that made it work, Go and sin no more. In the end after seventy times seven of forgiveness the verdict *Guilty* would be without repentance and reform. Repentance must be the key.

Feed my sheep was no less imperative than *Seek those that have gone astray.* If a man were only a young lawyer, brilliant, ambitious, not as yet truly redeemed himself, not a consecrated minister of the Gospel and even many of them failed, what spiritual food could he offer those he had saved from retribution? How bring them to repentance?

At that moment I think my grandfather must have sat down in prayer, to face this, and his own responsibility for persuading his son to become that defender of lost sheep, a criminal lawyer. For he saw that without active faith in God and what my grandfather believed in as the present help of the Christ, this had to be a lost and dangerous task. It was, he was sure, not the will of the Father that one of these little ones should perish, but how much *help* a man needed to carry them back and not get lost with them! Making the state of these men worse than the first. It must have been an awful moment for Grandpa as he looked back.

In the beginning, Earl Rogers did not intend to specialize in crime.

When I was working for the Los Angeles *Herald* before the First World War, the society editor was an unforgettable character whose by-line read "Juana Neal Levy." One day when Mrs. Levy heard me say, "This is Miss Rogers of the *Herald*"—a title of which I was passionately proud—she snorted, "*Rogers—Rogers,* it was on the door you know, *Rogers and Creighton.* If Earl Rogers had stayed in partnership with my brother Telfair Creighton with me and your Aunt Blanche, a *go-getter,* behind them, they would have represented the biggest people, the largest interests in the state. *Respectable.* No reason they shouldn't have had as much prestige and made as much money as the O'Melvenys or Hunsaker and Britt. No. Earl has to go off defending *criminals.*"

Ironically, a title fraud turned Earl Rogers to law in the first place.

In the eighties, my grandfather gave up the academic world for the church. Getting out his horse, he declared his Lord required him to go into all the world and again preach the good news of God's love to all the people. His circuit was from San Bernardino to Redlands, from Colton to Riverside, Pomona to Ontario. Each Sunday, with simple faith, he preached in a different wooden box to a handful gathered in His Name.

Those were the days when land-poor Spaniards couldn't pay the new taxes on their royal grants, the government was giving homesteads away, land was cheap. Somehow, Grandpa acquired vast acreage out beyond San Berdoo, sand, tumbleweed, unwatered cactus referred to as a ranch.

Today it is worth untold millions. All early real estate in California is. Present generations look disconsolately on prop-

erty their ancestors were not smart enough to hang onto.
In the Rogers family there was the block at Slauson and Main,
now heart of industry, which Earl Rogers once took as a fee
in the Lomax murder. Acres along Los Feliz Boulevard which
he refused to bother with as a gift in a murder fantasy in high
society known as the Griffith case. The victory of which Papa
boasted with many a snicker was when he had made O. T.
Johnson give him three thousand dollars cash instead of title
to the corner of Fourth and Broadway where the Broadway
Department Store now stands. "It takes real estate brains to
hold real estate," my father once said, "just as much as it
takes musical brains to play the violin. We do not have them."

What infuriated Papa about the ranch in San Bernardino
County was that his father had been bamboozled by bunko
artists.

As soon as men who understand such things saw that in
time California real estate would produce as much gold as its
mines, land frauds were worked successfully the length and
breadth of the state. Political manipulators got laws passed in
Sacramento. Among other things, these had to do with water
rights. To most early settlers, land and water rights were
simply the same thing. These crooks now proved otherwise.
Since the land was valueless without water, it turned out the
Reverend Rogers had to come up with a great deal of money
or let the men who now owned the water rights take over his
land. They might as well have held a cannon to his saintly,
ignorant head.

Coming upon this on his return from college, young Earl
Rogers was wild with indignation. "What you needed was a
good lawyer," he said.

"Good lawyers are too expensive for poor men like me,"
his father said. "Perhaps it was better for me not to have
riches. I might have become like the rich young man who
turned sorrowfully away from Our Lord."

"I think I'll study law while I'm working on the paper,"
Earl said, having intended till then to be a newspaperman.
So the first impulse to the law came because Earl Rogers'
father had been made an under-prairie-dog by a lot of land
sharks, to mix a few metaphors. "There must be a lot of others
like you," Earl said to his father.

In those days, a man did not have to go to law school.
Papa read in the offices of Stephen M. White, known as the
Little Giant, and he and Joseph Scott, leading Catholic lawyer
of the West for fifty years, stood together before a board of

judges and took an oral Bar exam. "Just the two of us," Joe Scott delighted to tell me down through the years, "just Earl and me. Youngsters. He kept saying to me, 'I've got to pass this one, Joe, I've just become the father of a baby girl.' " At this point Joe Scott would laugh with relish and add, "*You* were the baby girl."

Papa passed the Bar all right. After that he worked in Steve White's office for a while and then formed the one and only partnership of his career, with Mrs. Levy's brother. There was as yet no powerful labor movement with new laws to interpret, no oil rights, no taxes or tax returns to speak of. However, there were the all-important railroads, land and banking and corporations and wills, and Rogers and Creighton were to be business and corporation lawyers, with Papa inclined toward protecting the property rights of poor people like his father Reverend Rogers.

One thing was definite. The new firm would take no criminal cases. This was true of most corporation law firms.

However.

My grandmother knew a woman named Blackman. Grandpa knew her too.

My grandfather knew a freight conductor named Mellus.

My Aunty Blanche knew a plumber named Alford, so did Grandpa.

The whole Rogers family knew more lame ducks and underdogs and penniless people unjustly accused of murder and embezzlement than any other family from Shasta to San Diego.

2

George Blackman was an official of a Los Angeles public utility corporation. Indicted for embezzling company funds the case against him was so hopeless and so black that no reputable attorney would touch it. Mr. Blackman was a man, my grandmother admitted quietly, not to be trusted. As far as she was concerned nothing worse could be said of anyone. *Mrs.* Blackman was another matter. Grandma's long-time maid, Nannie Scott, had a sister who worked for Mrs. Blackman. One night Nannie's sister brought her mistress to my grandfather's house and Nannie persuaded my grandfather to talk with her. Grandpa sent for Papa and said he thought Papa ought to give Nannie's friends what help he could. Blackman was convicted just the same. Whenever the Blackman case was mentioned, Earl Rogers winced. He had

weaseled out with a reversal in the Appellate Court, to him
a most dubious victory. With this my grandmother agreed.
"Escaping a deserved penalty on a technicality is not justice,"
she said. "If he was guilty, he should have gone to jail."
"Then," said her son, "you shouldn't have asked me to defend
him in the first place. The people who ought to go to jail,"
he told her, "are the ones who trusted a puddin'head like
Blackman with a chance to steal all that money. Pay him
pennies and entrust him with millions."

"Let us hope his poor wife's sufferings and the loss of his
good name will teach him a much-needed lesson," my grandfather said. "But innocent or guilty he had a right to a fair
trial."

"He got it," their son said. "What will teach him is he's
scared. To succeed as a big-time financial thief, you have to
have cold nerve and no scruples. You have to do it *well*.
Blackman is a fool. If he tries it again, he will go to the
penitentiary and he knows it."

"Well," Grandpa said, "every man perhaps has a right to a
second chance."

3

While Grandpa was a circuit rider, a Santa Fe freight conductor named Mellus used to come to church in Colton to
hear him preach.

During a violent brawl in a caboose, this former parishioner
killed a man. So while ninety and nine of Grandpa's sheep
lay safely in the fold, this one was far out in the hills away,
in other words he was now in the calaboose charged with
murder. He had to be rescued and brought back if possible.
So Reverend Rogers took his lawyer son out to see what could
be done for poor Mr. Mellus.

The fight had resulted from a railroad strike.

The late nineteenth and early twentieth centuries saw
California dominated by the railroads.

Being the one vital means of transportation, they controlled
land values, price of crops, business trends, gold and silver
bonanzas, and were the real power politically, economically,
and even socially. And the shining rails across wide open
spaces, the sound of an engine's whistle blowing in the night,
a bell ringing as we pulled our horses up on their hind legs
to let the train go by, the smell of coal smoke as a train puffed
up the grade—these to us held as much adventure as space

ships and rockets to the moon hold for the young today.

At the time of the strike that got Grandpa's friend Mellus into trouble, there were no automobiles, no trucks, trucking, airplanes, or jets. If we wanted to go someplace we rode horseback, we drove in surreys, victorias, and carryalls, we went on the train or by river boat. Freight was sent by wagon, sometimes by water inland, mostly by train. A transportation strike is always a horrible nuisance and inconvenience at best. In the days when the horse couldn't begin to take up the slack it was a great deal worse. Feelings ran proportionately high and hot.

This one, centered in San Bernardino, displayed violence, property damage, costly delays, destruction of cargo, and soon threats had the non-railroad population terrified, and the railroad leaders on both sides, labor and management, steamed up to a sizzling pitch. The day of labor was only a dim light on the horizon then. Thinking men knew it was a real issue, knew the unions must and should be reckoned with. As yet, the public was neither vitally interested nor honestly concerned.

At last, settlement by arbitration was agreed to by both sides. A committee was formed to discuss terms offered by the railroads in answer to demands of the strikers. One man from the company; one elected by the workers; one respected citizen chosen by both to act as disinterested representative of in-the-public-good.

Mellus was chosen to represent his railroad union.

After discussion, he voted with the railroad company member. The Santa Fe's offer was thereby accepted.

A yellow-bellied turncoat, a Benedict Arnold, a worm, and a traitor were among the names his fellow unionists called him.

"Reverend Rogers knows I've tried to be a churchgoing, God-fearing man," he kept saying frantically when the young lawyer who was Reverend Rogers' son came to see him. "I don't say I've been a saint but I've tried to do what I thought was right. Your father taught us about not bearing false witness and what I done on that committee was not to bear false witness against the company, neither. Nobody could of expected no better offer than the one they was willing to agree to. I thought our side wanted what was right. Turned out they wanted to get the best of it and down the company. They never gave me another minute's peace. They wouldn't speak to my wife and they had their kids throw rocks at my kids. No man that has got any red blood can help getting sore about a thing like that even if he is trying to be a Christian."

On a day when a Santana, blowing off the Mojave Desert, turned the flat little town of Colton into a suburb of hell, the long slow freight of which Mellus was conductor pulled into the yard through blasts of blinding, stinging, burning sand and dust. While Mellus in the caboose checked his invoices, a crowd of union men gathered outside and began to jeer him. One of them, a hogger named Landon, jumped aboard. "He comes into my own caboose," Mellus said, "and calls me names no man wouldn't allow no other man to call him, he says I betrayed my brothers for blood money and starts telling what he is going to do to me like a big bully, until I couldn't take no more, so we got in a fight."

Both were big men, in those days all railroad men in the West had to know how to handle themselves in rough-and-tumble brawls. They were a rugged breed. For real, with no breakaway furniture and no pulled punches, those two put on that crunching, bruising, knockdown fight which has since become famous and omnipresent on television. Back and forth, the length and breadth of the caboose, one on top of the other, slamming from wall to wall, crashing against the windows, no holds barred. Blood began to flow freely. Sweating, with language which would singe the hair on a dead man's chest, grunting, gasping for breath, evenly matched, the spectators standing on boxes and baggage trunks looking through the windows began to make a noise like bedlam as the raw contest roared on.

Landon slugged Mellus and Mellus catapulted back and caught him, throwing him over a table that gave under his weight.

Landon went down and didn't get up.

The coroner's jury said he'd been killed by a blow on the head caused by striking the fender of the iron stove as a result of Mellus' attack. "I don' know how Landon come to get himself killed," Mellus said. "He didn't have no call to that I can see, any more than I did, it was just bad luck his banging his head on the stove."

My father then and always believed in labor unions.

Nevertheless, as he said, they always gave him a bad time.

Sitting there that day in the hot little jail in San Berdoo, he knew the workingmen of America must have higher wages, a bigger share, a better way of life, more honorable working conditions, and only in union would they find the strength to get these human rights for themselves. As early as the Mellus case, he saw that, like all pioneers, the labor union leaders would be ruthless, terrible in their struggle to achieve noble goals. A lot of innocent people were going to get hurt as usual. There had to be casualty lists in all wars. There would be blood shed in this one.

In the best American novel yet written about a strike, *The Valley of the Moon*, my godfather Jack London, a member of the Socialist party, a world-recognized voice for the cause of labor, showed what could happen to a man and a man's family if in fairness and honor he could not bring himself to strike against his long-time employers. I know that in some of their all-night sessions over a chessboard or a bottle of whiskey, in water-front saloons or in the peace of Glen Ellen, Earl Rogers told him of the Mellus case, it may have been a small part of what inspired the London masterpiece.

Earl Rogers' sympathy was with the union. His violent emotional drive was to prevent injustice anywhere. He leaned over backward on the theory that each man everywhere must be left with the right to obey his own conscience or he would find himself not free at all but simply the slave of yet another master. A union instead of a company might bind him in chains. When Eugene Debs came to visit us, my father warned him of this and years later after the Darrow trial he said it to Gompers.

So, of course, he took the Mellus case. His own brothers had made Mellus the underdog for not obeying the union, against his conscience. Also he was one of Grandpa's lost sheep.

There didn't seem to have been anything to winning it. As Mellus kept saying, it was his own caboose, Landon had broken in as it were, and his language had been abusive. The fight had been fair if bloody, the death entirely accidental.

No question, however, that in this matter Earl Rogers had appeared before the court as a criminal lawyer defending a murder charge.

Could he have allowed a man who'd been the target of mob threat and persecution of his family and who moreover had listened to the Reverend Rogers preach of a Sunday go without a rip-snorting defense?

The Blackman embezzlement, into which actually he'd been persuaded by Nannie Scott, a family retainer, had been small potatoes, besides being dull and of no interest to the papers.

Tried in an outlying county seat, the Mellus case hadn't

attracted much attention from a public still ignorant about labor and lukewarm concerning labor problems. Nor were the all-powerful railroad lobbies anxious that a killing resulting from a railroad strike be on any front pages.

The Case of the Man about Town and the Plumber, however, turned out to be a very different affair.

Though she never took the stand and her name was not mentioned, Earl Rogers' sister, my Aunty Blanche, was really the chief witness and practically forced Earl into the defense.

4

Versions of this in great detail came down to me through the years. Traveling with my aunt long afterward, I went to Bayreuth to hear *The Ring* and one night after *Götterdämmerung*, sleep being naturally impossible, she told me the whole story. For a number of reasons it had to be a famous trial, and reporters who covered it all went back to it, fascinated by its innovations and daring.

The continuity which ended with Earl Rogers appearing as chief counsel for the defense of a man named Alford against Stephen M. White, his own teacher and then the greatest lawyer in the state, began one night at dinner.

"Jay Hunter indeed!" Blanche Rogers said sharply and unexpectedly.

My father was devotedly attached to his sister Blanche, as he should have been. She was a woman of character as well as a lady of quality. The tone in which she spoke of Jay Hunter, who was at least a social acquaintance of theirs, surprised her brother Earl. For Mr. Jay Hunter had just been brutally murdered in broad daylight in the open hall of one of the city's newest office buildings.

"What about Jay?" Earl said.

"They've arrested that poor man for shooting him," said his sister, "the poor man says Jay Hunter was striking him with his cane and that he shot or he'd have been beaten to a *pulp*. Quite right, too. Why should a man just lie there and allow Jay Hunter of all people to beat him to a pulp? I could tell you things about *Jay Hunter*. They've actually put this poor man Alford in jail."

"They had to do that," Earl said. "He did shoot Jay, y'know."

"I'm sure he had a very good reason," Blanche said. "Jay Hunter was a man who deserved to be shot."

"De mortuis nil nisi bonum," their father put in mildly with a twinkle.

"Nonsense," said his daughter Blanche, shoving back her red hair. "Day before yesterday Jay Hunter was a vain, loud-mouthed, peacocking popinjay. Why because a poor, hard-working *plumber* whose bill Hunter hadn't paid shot him must we pretend he was *nil nisi bonum?* I'm sorry, Father, I can't see it," and before either gentleman could put further questions, Miss Blanche Rogers had taken herself to a rehearsal of her Chamber Music Quartette.

This bit of feminine special pleading turned Earl Rogers' attention to the murder of his fellow-attorney. Hunter had died on the table while surgeons were trying to remove the slug from his intestines. Public indignation had mounted to an alarming pitch. On all sides, young Rogers heard wails of wrath from the ladies. Who, they wanted to know, would lead the cotillions with that dash and style to which Jay Hunter had accustomed them? Respectable men asked soberly and seriously what we were coming to if a man wasn't safe within ten feet of his own office. The best and most influential people in town, many of them Hunter's friends, demanded immediate action from the chief of police, the sheriff, and the mayor. A plumber to attack and slaughter a gentleman like Hunter! Lynching parties by hot young bloods of a community were recent and formidable enough so that the sheriff was keeping Alford the plumber hidden in a solitary cell at the rear of the county jail under special guard. Here Alford was not helping his case any by declaring to what newspapermen were allowed to see him that he was glad the no-good cheating bastard was dead, he would do it over again if he had to, who did Jay Hunter, who owed him four dollars, think he was—hitting a man like that with his cane?

As Earl Rogers told his sister the next day, Alford's story was completely discredited. The medical report showed that the bullet from Alford's gun had traveled *down*. Thus it could not possibly have been fired while Alford was on the floor as he claimed.

Nevertheless, young Rogers wasn't happy about Alford the plumber.

Everybody was against the man who had shot Jay Hunter. Alford didn't seem to have any friends. If he did, they were afraid to come to his side. With the storm of public opinion beating on the doors of officials and newspapers, nobody was going out on a limb to start a special investigation to see whether there was anything to be said in Alford's defense.

The man had been out of work. That was the reason he had made such an uproar about the money he claimed Hunter owed him. Plainly, he wouldn't have a dime to put up for investigation or defense.

Possibly had a wife and family somewhere. No one had taken the trouble to find out.

One day while Earl Rogers sat smoking his usual *paisano* roll-your-own cigarette and mulling over this matter, Miss Blanche Rogers walked up the dark narrow stairs to her brother's office and startled whatever hangers-on and criminal characters or respectable clients might be loitering about by marching unannounced into the inner sanctum. There she lifted her polka-dot green nose veil, held her skirts well off the floor, and said clearly, "Earl, you must do something about this poor young man Jay Hunter was trying to kill with his cane."

Nobody ever made Earl Rogers laugh as much as his sister Blanche, not even Kolb and Dill. He said, "The poor young man took good care of Mr. Hunter, my dear sister. They buried him yesterday. There's not much more we can do to Mr. Hunter, is there?"

Blanche shoved back her hat and said, "Not Hunter, Earl. As Father said last night, we must think of this poor, friend-less little plumber. Did you know his wife is going to have a baby?"

"You can't blame that on Jay Hunter," Earl said.

"Don't be vulgar," Blanche said, and added darkly, "If he'd ever had a chance you probably could."

"Blanche," her brother said, "what have you got against Jay Hunter? What did he ever do to you?"

"He pinched me!" Blanche said.

At this point when he told it Papa always became hysteri-cal, flapped his arms, and cackled like a demented rooster. Something about this aroused the impish, unpredictable irides-cent mirth that lay close beneath the surface. He always said that his sister Blanche, with her foxy-red hair and white skin and green eyes, looked the way he imagined Elizabeth of England—and was just about as bossy.

Of course he got the story out of her then.

In an evening gown which showed her beautiful arms and shoulders, Miss Rogers was at her best. At a formal ball, she had waltzed with Jay Hunter to something pleasant by

Strauss. They had then strolled into the conservatory without which no third-floor private-home ballroom was socially acceptable. In its soft light they had paced up and down amid potted palms and hothouse begonias and Mr. Hunter had attempted to encircle her waist with his arm. This gesture she had repulsed without rancor, since it was regarded by young ladies as a legitimate conservatory maneuver. However, when Mr. Hunter so far forgot himself as to pinch her where a gentleman would be most likely to pinch if he dared such a dastardly deed, it was another matter.

"In her eyes," Papa would explain, "he took advantage. At a ball, a lady could not protest without making a scene which would prove she was no lady. Now, she knew Jay Hunter to be a whited sepulcher, capable of anything. Knowing this, she had decided we must come to the aid of the man who had given this pincher what he so richly deserved."

One other thing had aroused both his interest and his sympathy.

Alford had gone looking for the rich and social Mr. Hunter armed not only with a gun but with a hand-painted banner which said:

JAY HUNTER DOES NOT PAY HIS BILLS

This seemed to Earl Rogers courageous and imaginative and he felt that hitting a plumber who had come to collect his bill put a man outside the pale. Papa didn't always pay his own bills, but he was consistently sympathetic and courteous to anyone who came to collect them. He talked them out of *that* idea in a hurry and sent them away feeling somehow that having Earl Rogers owe you money gave you membership in a glamorous secret society. So, although this time he hadn't been sent for, Earl Rogers decided he must yield to his sister's conviction, his father's compassion for a friendless and forlorn fellow, and his own instincts and offer his services to defend the city's pariah, the plumber Alford. Also, it was a challenge —and an opportunity.

5

Soon after Alford had accepted this offer, Rogers ran into Stephen M. White, former United States senator, who said, "I hear you've agreed to defend Alford. You must be crazy." The statue of the senator on the grounds of the Los Angeles courthouse shows him with traditional drooping mustache, pointed goatee, impressive political uniform of frock coat, frilled shirt and oratorical gesture. Comment of the day on his appearances on the floor of the Senate refer to his piercing eye, his overpowering personality, his spellbinding oratory.

As an opponent, Earl Rogers always rated him as highly as he later did another senator, Hiram Johnson, who missed the Presidency when he refused to run on the ticket with Warren G. Harding. He said Steve White had a flair for trial law and that he had learned a great deal from him.

Whatever he had learned he now proceeded to turn on his mentor.

In the Alford case, White had been called by the indignant citizenry as special prosecutor to be sure the slayer of Jay Hunter got what was coming to him, a practice more common then than now, though of course Thomas E. Dewey's first step to national prominence was as the specially appointed Racket Buster.

"Stay out of criminal practice, you young fool," Senator White said. "I wouldn't be mixed up in this except Jay had powerful connections. You can't possibly win it, especially against me, it'll only make you unpopular. You'll get beat. What are you up to?"

"They seem to have stacked all the decks against him," young Rogers said. "He's got a right to a defense. Every man has."

The Senator shook his head glumly. "Never take a case you haven't got a Chinaman's chance to win," he said. "This feller went up there with a gun shouting threats at the top of his lungs."

"Does it occur to you if he'd intended to shoot he wouldn't have been so open and talkative?" Earl said. "The noise might have been an attempt to get Hunter to pay his bill. Alford was out of work, he needed the four bucks."

The Little Giant blinked suspiciously at his former pupil. "Nonsense," he said, "don't start splitting hairs. A jury hates a man to split hairs. Makes them think, no jury wants to think if it can help it. Simple case. This feller's a guttersnipe. Worked himself into a murderous rage and shot poor old Hunter down like a dog. Dr. Kurtz did the autopsy. Nobody better and he says Alford shot while Hunter was trying to stave him off with his stick. Open-and-shut case, son. You shouldn't have taken it."

Reporters say that always in every case in every court

there is the Big Moment. The appearance of Mrs. Hall's brother Willie Stephens in the Hall-Mills case. Of Lindbergh on the stand to identify the voice of the man to whom he'd paid the ransom money for his little son already dead. Of Evelyn Nesbit Thaw when they tried her husband for the murder of Stanford White.

As near as I can reconstruct it, the Big Moment in the Alford-Hunter case has to have been when Earl Rogers introduced a glass laboratory jar in which the intestines of Jay Hunter had been preserved in alcohol.

The Little Giant was right about one thing. An open-and-shut case. Which way did it open or shut?

Had the shot been fired by Alford standing upright while Hunter used his cane only, like D'Artagnan, to fend off a murderous attack? Or had Alford shot from the floor after Hunter had knocked him down and was beating him ferociously over the head?

Going into the ring, all the odds were in favor of Senator White. Even the defendant. The jury had Alford in front of their eyes and a more obnoxious, unpleasant little man never sat in the defendant's seat. Underdogs, having been ill-fed, uneducated, and sometimes embittered, so often are. Undersized, pallid by nature, as he sat beside his boyish, inexperienced, and unknown counsel, Alford lifted his lip in a perpetual snarl of antagonism against the world, the judge, the jury, Senator White, and the assistant D.A., whose name was General Johnstone. Seeing him there, the jury would believe this man could kill like a cornered rat. Arrayed against him, the courtly shade of that fine citizen whose death was a loss to country, state, and future cotillions took on an even greater impressiveness.

Earl Rogers thought the story Alford told him at their first interview in the county jail might be true. They sat together in Alford's cell, the bailiffs, saying he was dangerous, had refused to bring him to the waiting room.

"He was twice as big as me," Alford said resentfully, "when I says to him I wasn't going to leave without my money he owed me he turned purple like he'd bust a blood vessel and come at me like a crazy man. Why would I wanta shoot him for? That didn't get me my four dollars, did it?"

Hunter, so Alford told it, had started trouble the second he walked out of his office and saw the plumber in the corridor with his banner. He had then, Alford said, rushed forward waving his stick in the air, threatened to have him arrested, knocked him down, and beat him.

There had to be evidence to support this, Rogers knew. The man's word alone against all the jury would be told of Hunter's reputation wouldn't be enough to acquit him. More than that this client would be a catastrophic witness. From the very first moment, Rogers was in conflict with himself as to whether he would dare subject the ugly, ill-spoken, rancorous man to the dread cross-examination of Senator White. As early as that in his career, Earl Rogers established for himself the principle that the accused must take the stand in his own defense.

He never varied from that once, until many years later in the fatal Bundy case.

The jury had a right to hear the defendant's own story, to have it tested for them by the People. As a matter of trial tactics, Rogers thought it inescapable. Though the judge would instruct them that the defendant's failure to take the stand in his own defense should not prejudice them against him, Earl Rogers thought it would in spite of themselves.

A jury must suspect that the man who didn't want to take the stand with his life at stake feared he might crack and crumble under attack. The fatal weakness in Rogers' defense as he saw it was Alford—either as a *not witness* or as a witness under cross-examination by the blistering White.

In the weeks before the case came to trial this kept him pacing the floor most nights.

The way he solved it is one of the blackest blots on Papa's record. No matter how he excused or justified it, as he did to me, he was ashamed of it the rest of his life. And in time, it came home to roost.

The evidence of the intestines, Dr. Edward Palette as the impresario, came first.

The coroner had testified positively both at the inquest and again under careful questioning by the Little Giant at the trial itself that the bullet which ended Hunter's life had traveled *down*. Therefore Alford must have fired it while he stood upright on his feet. Every man on the jury was shown clearly how that had to be.

When Mr. Rogers took over the cross-examination of Dr. Carl J. Kurtz, chief autopsy surgeon, the transcript shows that to the surprise of the courtroom and the special prosecutor he did not begin with questions about this at all, neither the death wound nor the course of the fatal shot. He began by inquiring about the wounds on the head and body of the defendant now sitting at the counsel table before them. Nobody had given these any thought or attention hitherto, it seemed pointless and awkward. Always it is difficult to disassociate a man in his extreme youth from his later achievements, but at the moment Earl Rogers began his cross-examination of Dr. Kurtz he had no achievements, he was a kid lawyer, hopelessly outclassed and overmatched, probably trying to get a little experience in combat. White himself, the press, and probably the jury, who'd never heard of him, thought this merely a bit of inept even embarrassing fumbling by a novice.

ROGERS: With respect to the wounds upon the person of Mr. George Alford, Dr. Kurtz, you made an examination of them. Did you request a written description illustrated by a diagram as well?

DR. KURTZ: Yes sir.

ROGERS: From that which I now show you, are you able to give a good description of the wounds which you found upon the person of this defendant?

DR. KURTZ: Oh yes, certainly I can do that.

Using all the right technical terms, in utmost detail, the young defense attorney led the gray-haired, gray-bearded physician through a medical explanation of the cuts and lacerations on Alford's head at the time he had been arrested and taken to jail. Where—how—Earl Rogers got his medical knowledge I never quite knew—except that he read omnivorously, all the time, and seemed to remember everything. Always, medical witnesses thought they were talking to another doctor.

ROGERS: Within a few hours after Hunter was shot, you made this examination?

DR. KURTZ: Yes. That same evening. In the jail.

ROGERS: Doctor, could those wounds have been inflicted by this end of this cane? Just a minute, doctor, if you please, let me get the cane. (Mr. Rogers got People's Exhibit D and showed it to the witness.) Now, doctor, what I am asking you, could those wounds have been made with this small end —you see here—the *tip* of the cane?

DR. KURTZ: Oh no, I shouldn't think so at all.

ROGERS: Well, doctor, let's go a step or two further, let's

do better than that. Take the cane, please. Now look at the
size of the end—or *tip* of the cane.

DR. KURTZ: (examining cane) Most of the wounds were
too long to have been inflicted by that—by the tip of the cane
as you call it.

ROGERS: Thank you. Your Honor, may I have your permission to ask the jury to examine this cane, which Senator White
has had here identified as that which Mr. Hunter had in his
hand at the time of his death?

The elegant cane, a heavy polished brown shaft, a massive
gold knob, was passed from one juror to another. Most of
them had never before had a stick in their hands and they
grinned at each other as they balanced it. When Earl Rogers
had it back he held it so both the doctor and the jury could
see it plainly.

ROGERS: Now, Dr. Kurtz. By what part of this cane were
those scalp wounds you examined shortly after they were
made on this defendant probably or certainly inflicted?

DR. KURTZ: Oh certainly by this part. (Tracing the length)
Lengthwise of the cane.

ROGERS: I wonder—if—would someone please—

As yet he had no Bill Jory, no Jerry Giesler, no Buron Fitts
ready to spring forward as magician's assistant. He beckoned
to a young deputy sheriff. Rogers' first use of props, for which
he was to become famous—it must have been an effective
exhibition. With his usual meticulous care as an integral part
of trial work, young Rogers had gone to a fencing instructor
for information and instruction. With the deputy as his stooge,
he illustrated the differences. First a man parrying an attacker,
keeping at arm's length with the point of his cane-sword a
man bent on murdering him.

"This," young Rogers said, "is what the prosecution has
told you took place." He went on jabbing, lunging, the cane
extended at full length. Only the point would come in contact with the other man.

Then he shifted and began laying on with it. Like a broad-
sword, he belabored and lashed with the flat length of the
weapon. So it struck in a way, as the doctor had said, to make
long welts and lacerations. Not holes, as the tip must have
done.

Impossible for the jury not to see that only by a man

beating another with his cane could those wounds on Alford's head have been made.

To all the others, this was a small point in Alford's favor. The first and only.

"The senator didn't like it though," Earl Rogers used to say later.

Still, the medical evidence was that the bullet had traveled *down*. So what real difference could this make?

Enter the Intestines.

Chief witness for the defense.

According to the dictionary, the intestines consist of the tubular part of the alimentary canal, the bowels. In the human adult, the small intestine is composed of the duodenum, better known since the race began to develop ulcers of it, the jejunum, and the ileum; the large intestine of the caecum and vermiform appendix, the colon, and the rectum.

In court that day my Aunty Blanche was inclined to be grimly pleased that Jay Hunter must have had to appear in hell minus his guts. (Now listed in Webster as a permissible synonym for stamina, grit, and fortitude.)

A ripple of sheer horror shook the courtroom at the appearance of the actual portions of Mr. Hunter's human anatomy. Crowded as it was with the fashionable, the VIP top brass, Defendant's Exhibit as described above drew gasps, shrieks, and whistles which reached their crescendo as Senator White leaped to his feet, waving an accusing and denunciatory hand at his young opponent, and shouting, "Ghoul, ghoul, grave robber," in a fine fit of frenzy.

His former student gave him a look which combined hurt feelings and you-can't-be-that-silly. To the judge, he said quietly and with dignity that the jury had before them the clean, preserved-in-alcohol sections of the body, such as doctors and medical students worked with at all times, in the interests of humanity. If any of those in the courtroom without business there, he said, found them obscene or shocking it was their privilege to leave now. Those who had business there would not be so childish and unrealistic since this clinical exhibit was likewise in the interests of humanity as represented by his innocent client. If, he said further, the jury or the special prosecutor or even His Honor would look down at their own abdomens, there, concealed under skin and muscle, these same useful and miraculous organs were at this very moment performing functions necessary to life. Only the squeamish, the precious, the too nice could find anything ghoulish about proper medical testimony supported by a medically arranged display of human anatomy. This was surely not only the best evidence of what had happened to them, but the most dignified.

"There is nothing in the direct testimony of any witness for the prosecution to permit this unholy degrading exhibition," White shouted.

For the first time, Earl Rogers let his voice ring. "Oh yes there is," he said. "Chief Autopsy Surgeon Kurtz said the bullet from Alford's gun ranged *down*. That it must have been fired from above to penetrate the intestines as he found them. I propose now by this medical exhibit to prove beyond a reasonable doubt that the bullet didn't go down at all. It ranged *up*."

"You've lost your mind," Senator White said loudly.

"The testimony of the prosecution is that the bullet could not have been fired when the defendant lay flat on the floor. The defense proposes to prove to the jury that it couldn't have been fired from anywhere else. My client's life depends on my ability to prove what I've just said. I'm offering the best possible evidence, the bullet's actual path through the actual intestines of the deceased which I got a court order to have delivered to me by the coroner and if you think some gabbly females who pretend to be shocked by—"

"Mr. Rogers—" the judge began, and swiftly young Rogers said, "I beg Your Honor's pardon. Call Dr. Edward Palette."

As Earl Rogers qualified his medical expert, Senator White, reporters have told me, watched him with a strange expression on his face. In the newspaper profession, we have a phrase, "His boy's in town." Which means the boy who will one day take his place has shown up on the horizon. Joe DiMaggio looking at Mickey Mantle might have said to himself, *My boy's in town.* The Little Giant, as Earl Rogers moved ahead with his defense, must have known that feeling.

Dr. Palette, whose family is still socially and medically prominent in California, took the stand with imperturbable poise. A tall, dark, professional youngster with a clipped mustache, at ease on the stand, as young and slight as the defense counsel standing before him, to begin his examination. They had been friends since early days, now between them they had that air of patient kindliness and tolerance which the young in any science accord to the old and experienced, being sure those must be already out-of-date members of their professions. It gives them a vital and impressive air of almost unbearable superiority, you see it today in very young scientists.

As the two sweetly sure and infallible young men turned the courtroom into a medical amphitheater and proceeded to conduct a classroom lecture on anatomy, reinforcements began to appear at the counsel table beside the senator in the form of the coroner himself, Dr. Kurtz, with several other autopsy experts, laboratory technicians, and stacks of medical books. Steve White was a most able and resourceful man and he rallied all the opposition he could, which had to convey that he was in trouble.

Meantime charts in many colors appeared and were set up on easels. Maps of the lengths of the intestines were hung on racks before the jury. Clinical opinions and tests on the resistant power of tissue were offered and supported by photographs handed to the jury with extreme courtesy. In the technical language used to explain and introduce these the young lawyer seemed quite as much at home as the young doctor, which was understandable if anyone knew they'd worked together on this night after night for weeks.

As a presentation of expert testimony it was beyond anything the California courts had seen to that moment. Expert testimony is convincing and interesting only when the examining counsel knows what questions to ask and how to ask them and has some sense of stage management.

All this led up to three questions.

MR. ROGERS: So it was only because of the stooping position upon the part of Mr. Hunter, in which position the bowels were folded over upon themselves, only because of such a bent-over and doubled-up posture that the bullet could have punctured the intestines as we have shown they were punctured in Defendant's Exhibit here in this laboratory jar?

DR. PALETTE: That's perfectly obvious to the naked eye. In no other possible way.

MR. ROGERS: In other words, Dr. Palette, Alford must have shot from the floor.

DR. PALETTE: No other position could possibly account for the place in which we have seen the bullet entered and went through the intestines.

MR. ROGERS: At the instant the shot was fired, Hunter's shoulders must have been lower than his hips, as he bent over and struck down at the man on the floor below him.

DR. PALETTE: No doubt about that. You can see it for yourselves.

They could. They did.

Another strong point in favor of the defendant who wasn't supposed to have any points at all.

But—it was so-called expert testimony.

Triumphant as it seemed at the moment, young Rogers was afraid of it.

A jury might be impressed, yet he felt sure it was always *tricky* to depend on. There might be jurors who on second thought had no use for *doctors*. Jurors who thought, *Doctors will say anything, one thing for one side, something else again for the other. These experts, trying to put something over, a man better use his own common sense.* On second thought they might see Palette as a young whippersnapper putting his opinion against that of the official coroner and weighty autopsy surgeons.

He knew he had shaken the twelve men in the box, given his client a fighting chance for life. To save it, the bitter little man must go on the stand.

Two men had been in that fatal fight.

One of them was dead and could tell them nothing.

The other was the little man in the shiny brown suit sitting next to young Earl Rogers.

Let him tell them about it. He was *there.*

Put him up there where Steve White could get a crack at him.

Immediately court resumed after a noon recess, the moment His Honor was back on the bench, at twenty seconds after two o'clock, without warning Earl Rogers called the defendant to the stand.

At a clipped, machine-gun pace, in clear clean simple questions, he put the snarling little man through a vivid, resentful description of the killing. Hunter's purple rage, big man knocking down little man, the assault with the cane. Whether you liked him or not as the man on trial for his life told of them, the picture appeared with a violence that explained why the shot could have been fired in self-defense. Explained also Alford's resentment.

All well so far.

After seventeen minutes, young Rogers said, "You may cross-examine," and sat down, the muscles of his jaw rippling as he fought to keep his face from showing the white tension of suspense.

Breathless, the courtroom waited, in silence. The judge said, "Your witness, Senator—" and saw that White was not at the counsel table. Only old General Johnstone of the district attorney's office, who'd given a routine nod to the judge's routine "You are ready, gentlemen?"

One of the all-time great crime reporters, Dan Green of the Los Angeles *Examiner*, who was there, has told it this way:

"Senator White and Rogers ate lunch at the same place every day.

"This day we're talking about, White didn't come back on time.

"All around the courthouse everybody knew booze was Steve White's weakness, without it he'd have been a great statesman, and whether Rogers planned this or was waiting for it and took the opportunity, I can't tell you. He sure caught Johnstone, who was only in there holding the towel for the Senator, with his pants down. The poor old guy, who hadn't opened his mouth since the trial started, *goofed* and the first thing anybody knew Rogers was saying That's all Mr. Alford you may come down.

"Some of the boys swore Rogers put knockout drops in White's whiskey. When the Senator came strolling in a while later and found Alford had been on and off the stand he swelled up and said to Rogers in a whisper like a calliope, 'That was a damn dirty trick, Earl,' but of course he couldn't say it into the record without admitting Rogers had made a fool of him.

"Soon as the judge adjourned that afternoon I asked Rogers about it and he hit the ceiling. Stephen M. White he said had been admitted to The Bar some time ago. Also he had served in the Senate of the United States. If he could be led to betray The People's interests in such fashion he wasn't what he'd been cracked up to be. He knew White had one too many at lunch, he always did. Well, he was old enough to know better.

"I always thought Rogers had a guilty conscience, it was one of the only things he always got sore about if you brought it up. He was just a kid then, I figured myself *ambition* got the best of him, this was the big one for him to win. He took a chance at that. Steve White might have come back. It must have been real ticklish those few minutes when Johnstone was doddering around.

"I covered most of Mr. Rogers' big cases, and all the big lawyers around before and since. He was in a class by himself. To understand his story you have to see two things.

"He couldn't bear to lose.

"When a man's life was at stake he figured anything went up to bribing a jury or subornation of perjury, those he wouldn't go for. I was always looking right at him, I'd have caught him sure, the same way we caught Clarence Darrow when he tried it in the McNamara case. No lawyer anywhere has ever had the spotlight on him every minute day and night the way Earl Rogers did. He was *news* all the time. He never did any of the crooked things mouthpieces did later when being a criminal lawyer meant *you* were a criminal. Rogers' pride wouldn't let him, his vanity would have suffered. He had to win fair or it wouldn't have been any fun. I never believed he did a crooked thing and neither did any other reporter who covered him. We figured he was a trial genius, the only one we ever saw. His cases prove it."

One thing drove my father wild. The district attorney had the final argument to the jury. Starting with the Alford trial, Papa spent all his ingenuity and inventive imagination trying to overcome what *he* thought should have belonged to the man whose life was at stake. The last word.

As he finished his final plea in the Alford case, he went out into the hall and came back with a small blackboard, the kind children draw pictures on. Setting it on its easel, he said, "Gentlemen, over this entire nation, Senator White is famed for his spellbinding oratory. He can move mountains. In a few minutes you will be those mountains. He has the last word. I can ask no question, give no explanation after he finishes. I want to leave with you one question. If Senator White doesn't answer it, you must bring in a verdict of Not Guilty."

On the blackboard he wrote:

The Special Prosecutor did not recall Autopsy Surgeon Kurtz to the stand on rebuttal. Was this because he knew Dr. Kurtz agreed that the evidence of the dead man's own intestines and the testimony of Dr. Palette proved before your own eyes that the bullet travelled UP from the floor, not DOWN?

He must have looked rather young and frantic standing there, knowing as he told them there was nothing more he could do for his poor little rat-in-a-trap client. He put the palm of his hand against his forehead, took it away in a quick gesture, and sat down.

Senator White got to his feet trying not to look at the blackboard. Later he said he couldn't make up his mind whether or not to have it removed. It lay there like an unexploded bomb ticking away and the Little Giant, his face red, yanking at the high stiff collar which seemed to choke him, paced back and forth around it. His exasperation at this young whippersnapper who had dared to challenge him was seething. He decided to ignore the whole thing and roared and soared into as fine a speech as man ever made. The trouble was the jury didn't hear half of it, they were hypnotized by the blackboard. Taking its question with them into the jury room, the twelve men found Alford Not Guilty.

A big new courthouse was built in Los Angeles not long ago, one wall of every courtroom was a blackboard for use of counsel. I wished my father might have seen how his schoolboy one, which caused such a commotion as the first of its kind, had grown and come of age. Secretly, I sort of looked on it as a memorial.

A fine professional biography of Earl Rogers called *Take the Witness* by two AP reporters who had covered many of his cases, says: "Senator Stephen M. White had been beaten in court for the first time and by an erstwhile pupil, an obscure beginner. Earl Rogers had blasted the theretofore impregnable Little Giant and upon his ruin Rogers rose to glory."

My father's mature judgment in the Alford case was that the man fired believing he had to save his own life. "Probably he was wrong about that," Papa said. "I expect all Jay Hunter meant to do was give him a beating. He felt his impudence deserved that and he, the great Jay Hunter, had a right to administer it. However, this was something Alford couldn't wait to be sure about. Your Aunty Blanche continues to believe that a gent who would pinch a lady would also beat a man to death."

Step by step his heritage, his family's way of life, his temperament led him into the practice of criminal law. Made him champion of the underdog, defender of lost sheep.

Get Rogers Get Rogers Get Earl Rogers to defend you became a tide. The dramatic excitement, the rhythm of skyrocket success launched him at a pace swifter than thought.

Mellus—his father's parishioner.

Alford—his sister got him into that one.

Boyd—his daughter persuaded him to all-out fight for the boy.

All three of them were innocent. No no—all three were Not Guilty.

Inevitably, fatefully, rain or shine came a man named Mootry.

As a criminal lawyer—*Get Rogers to defend you—We defend everybody—Every man has a right to the best defense*—my father found himself defending Mootry, who because he was stuck on another woman shot his wife in cold blood—as foul a mess as a lawyer ever tackled.

To add to his chagrin over the low nature of the case and his client, this was one of the few cases where Earl Rogers threw himself into an emotional appeal to the jury. At all times, he distrusted courtroom eloquence as a dangerous method not to be depended upon. One of the many sources of his quarrels with Clarence Darrow was that Darrow wanted to depend on his own powers of persuasion way beyond what Rogers thought was safe.

Reading Papa's corny eloquence in the Mootry trial, I am surprised it didn't gag him right there in the courtroom.

Here it is:

You will remember those unforgettable days when you courted your girl, the girl who is still your sweetheart and always will be. And the thrill of that moonlit Sunday night when you sat holding her hand, maybe on the church steps, maybe in a fair garden, will never be forgotten.

But Charlie Mootry had no such blissful background for his romance. No church steps were his to sit upon when he held his sweetheart's hand. No, when he met his fate, when he realized that he cared for Martha with a love surpassing understanding, she was a chorus girl in a tawdry, unholy Club Theater resort of only dissipated and immoral men, of whom Mootry was already one.

But he took her away from her sordid surroundings, gave her his name, brought into her loveless life the only happiness she had ever known.

Which of us, had we suddenly found ourselves loving a girl in such an environment, would have ignored her past, would have taken her to the altar, and there entered with her into the holy bonds of matrimony?

He had not our moral concept to guide him. The men with whom his lot had been cast sneered at him for his weakness in marrying such a girl. On his social plane where none of them marry such women but only live off the wages their sin can earn, this was a ridiculous move. So contrasting his perverted viewpoint with our own more fortunate one, he was really nobler in his act than we would have been had we acted as he did in his place.

What greater proof could we ask of his love for Martha, his wife?

If they quarreled as testimony shows, which of us has not done so in the daily demands and difficulties of marriage? Do married quarrels of necessity lead to murder? If they did there would be many more murders my friends and you know that as well as I do.

Mootry loved his wife. He did not kill her. Martha, sitting there with her Bible—could any man no matter how low he had fallen slay his wife, as she sat in their home with her Bible open in her hands? Can you believe any man would dare to do that? Wouldn't he expect a bolt from heaven to strike him down?

No. Martha was growing stone deaf. She was in ill health that made her days a misery. She saw long years of pain and illness ahead of her in a world where she could hear no sound. So she dared to take her own life rather than be a burden to her husband.

An all-time low, that plea.

He then dwelt briefly on the witnesses for the prosecution.

Another girl from the same so-called theater.

A man who lived off that girl's earnings.

A policeman who said he'd been called to make Mootry stop beating his wife Martha.

"My friends of this jury," said Earl Rogers simply, "you cannot hang even such a man as Mootry on the testimony of a pimp, a prostitute and a policeman."

Nor, as it turned out, could they.

It was my grandfather's habit to ride downtown on the streetcar, and to sit quietly in the back row at Earl Rogers' cases, and leave without his son knowing he'd been there. By what others called chance perhaps, by what Earl Rogers called bad luck, by what my grandfather the Reverend Rogers called Providence, he'd gone down to hear his son's final plea to the jury in the Mootry case.

So profoundly had it confounded and confused him that

he sat through the brief closing argument of the prosecution. Then waited motionless in a dim corner of the last row for the verdict.

The jury found Mootry *Not Guilty*.

This shook that old saint the Reverend Rogers loose from his moorings. With that righteous anger which had poured forth from Jeremiah and moved Jesus to drive the money-lenders out of the temple, he watched Mootry, free, horridly triumphant, simper up with outstretched hand to thank the man who has procured an acquittal.

"Get away from me, you slimy pimp," Earl Rogers said in disgust, "you're guilty as hell."

My grandfather walked out quietly.

That night he sent for his son.

PART THREE

TEN

My grandfather's library, where I had school on mornings when it was too cold for the porch, was a big, high-ceilinged room walled with oak bookcases. A fire often burned on the hearth and beside it was a huge chair, upholstered in black leather, which was to become my father's and then mine. Against its gleaming, fragrant leather my grandfather's unruly white hair made what I took to be a halo.

Telling me about it long afterwards, my father said that what took place there on the night after the Mootry verdict could not be called an argument. They were not on terms which permitted what is usually meant by argument.

My grandfather did not believe it good, proper, or possible for a man to be friends with his son. Side-stepping his duty, he called that. A father had been placed in a relationship of love so high, so deep, so sacred that he dared not take the latitude allowed by friendship. No responsibility, not even that of a priest to his flock, was so great as that of a father to his children, and in the end he would be held to answer for his full measure of obligation to help build their souls.

That was why his old blue eyes, so loving and kind and compassionate, managed to be stern as he faced his son that night.

There was a passion of love between those two.

Even when I was a child, who knew so little of life, to be with them was to feel, *They love each other*. I accepted that Papa and I would love each other like that, father and child, all our lives. More than anybody else, I felt sure, when I was very young.

Grandpa had fired himself up to what he had to do and say.

In him were no quivering quibbles, riddles, dialectics. He tormented neither himself nor others with intellectual exercises, employed no hairsplitting to avoid simple unequivocal statements of his faith. No doubletalk to evade the challenge of answered prayer. Pedantry, odium theologicum, metaphysical gambits, or the proposition He-didn't-mean-what-He-said-He-was-only-employing-oriental-imagery, all of which were at that time keeping Oxford and New England in turmoil, never disturbed the Reverend Lowell L. Rogers. What C. S. Lewis has since called Mere Christianity was enough for him, and it was this he meant to practice now upon his beloved son. For all his unworldliness and see-no-evil, my grandfather had been a minister in Tombstone and Globe and Yuma and Nogales when Arizona was still a rootin' tootin' shootin' Territory, he'd preached his Master's Gospel to the men who came to make the West with a rope in one hand and a six gun in the other, the men you see daily on TV today as your favorite sons. When he had to go into battle about his Father's business, he was as ready to fight as he had been when he picked up his musket to preserve the Union.

So he patted his son's shoulder with consuming affection, went to his big chair, and attacked direct. "That was a contemptible victory for evil you won today, my son," he said. "We must come to an understanding about this. I see now that the practice of criminal law is beset with dangers, isn't it? You are allowed to be a *criminal's* lawyer but—you cannot be a *criminal* lawyer, you see my point?"

Straddling a straight chair backward, his son said, "I see it—from anyone but you, I'd be inclined to call it a pettifogging play on word, sir."

"Then you would call it amiss," his father said. "There is a line as clear and broad to an honest man as the line between good and evil or right and wrong always is. You must draw that line, Earl. The proper defense which is the right of every American citizen high or low in our republic. Those words *a proper defense* constitute a line of sacred truth. An attempt to save a man you know to be guilty from justice by dishonest or deceptive means crosses that line. You see that?"

"The debate on this has been going on for centuries between the best minds in the legal profession," Earl said. "As I see it, it is my business to defend everybody."

"Very well, very well!" his father said, and got up and came over and patted his shoulder again, emphasizing his words. "Defend everybody. I agree to that. But with honor. If you use your talent, your power, to take one step over that line you are one with the criminal. Oh my dear child—you become in a sense that hurts us both, one with the criminal. You would have to first excuse, condone, accept—even justify his crime. You have a right to state his case honorably, fairly, but not to help him by your persuasions and inventions and abilities to escape his merited punishment if he is guilty."

"How do I know exactly how far I go in using my best talents to give him a proper defense?" his son said. "Sometimes, Papa, it's hard to see—"

"No no," his father said, "no. You yourself—you know, Earl. This case today—"

"Aren't we supposed to forgive seventy-times-seven?" his son said.

At that his father blazed in a bright anger. "So—the devil quotes Scripture," he said sternly, and this time Earl Rogers got a finger pointed at him. "Let me tell you, my son, each one of those seventy-times-seven ends with *Go and sin no more*. Each one of them. Somewhere in those seventy-times-seven is the *one* a poor sinner, an unhappy criminal, is willing to accept and then there is joy in heaven over one sinner who has repented, one lost sheep brought back to the fold. But the man who cannot accept the grace of forgiveness and gets away with his crime, repeats it. Our Lord wishes to touch the heart to contrition, but often men insist on the hard way or retribution—and justice has to take over for mercy. Forgiveness cannot mean permission to repeat the offense. The results must prove to him that if he says two times two is nine or even four and a half, he will get a wrong answer."

There was a little silence then and he got up to put another log on the fire and stood with his back to it, flapping his long coattails. He said, "I was in court today when you made your final plea for Mootry," he said. "I was there when the jury returned its verdict."

Startled, for they had both been walking around this, his son rose and shoved back his chair and faced Grandpa, his head down, his lips tight, hammering against his thighs with clenched fists the way he always did when he was unhappy with himself.

"What you did there today was immoral, Earl," his father said. "Oh my dear dear boy—to say that a man could not possibly shoot a woman who was reading her Bible, and then a few hours later to say to that same man, 'You're guilty as hell'—why, Earl, this is black blasphemy and untruth. My soul trembles for you. To tell lies to the jury, to use your gifts—the art of oratory bestowed upon you, to speak with the tongues of angels to acquit a man you believed to be guilty of a crime against God and man—did you not then cross the line?" Only the fire crackling and singing broke the silence. Then his father pleaded, pressing his hands together, "Answer me, my son."

After a long breath, Earl said, "Yes. In the terms you have chosen to use—I'm not prepared to admit they are fair terms. If a man hires me, isn't the proper defense for me to use everything I've got to get him off? Isn't a proper defense to do my best to get him acquitted?"

"You know as well as I do where the line is," his father said.

"When you're there to show it to me," his son said, "yes Papa—when you're there to remind me but I haven't your faith. I seek God—I've—never found him except as I believe you. You say you've been there so I say it must be there. But to balance my actions—to interfere in another man's moral guilt or innocence—am I my brother's keeper?"

"Yes—yes, by God!" his father said, the fire alight in him now. "That is Cain's question. Just after he had slain Abel. Yes, we are all our brother's keepers. Brethren, the Master called us. I have high hopes for you. To see that the poor are never without a proper defense. To be sure that no innocent man is ever convicted. To acquit always if you may the man about whose innocence or guilt there is question. Even by honorable means sometimes to free a guilty man rather than take the chance that an innocent man pay an unjust penalty.

"But never—never—to use your gifts dishonorably to acquit a man to whom you can say 'You're guilty as hell' afterwards with the verdict of Not Guilty still in your ears."

I guess my father inherited his gift of tongues from my grandfather—people have told me so.

"Earl," he said solemnly, "you can never lie in word, thought, or deed to save a man from justice. It would have been better for you if this man Mootry had been found guilty as you knew him to be."

As always, he reached for his worn New Testament, in which the words of the Master were in red letters. He always made them sound as though they were being spoken for the first time on the shores of Galilee. So *new*. When he closed the Book, he said, "Let us pray," and quite simply they went down on their knees together as they had always done. A man listens to God better on his knees, my grandfather always said with a twinkle. He asked God in the name of His Son, Jesus Christ, to keep *his* son safe in this work beset by so many temptations and when he stood up his face was wet with tears—he was never ashamed of tears, he was too manly to need to be. He came the few steps and put his arm around his son's shoulders, patting him with restored courage and encouragement.

"Together," he said, "we're a match for the devil, don't you worry about *that*. Together we'll always be a match for him."

I was awakened in a cold, uneasy dawn. Some light came from a gas jet burning in the hall, and a thin silver glare had begun to lighten the windows. In the strange shadows, I saw someone sitting on the edge of my bed.

I sat up and pushed back my hair so I could see and said, "Papa?"—I wasn't quite sure.

Wrapped in a heavy dark overcoat, he wasn't crying any more, but I could see by his eyes all red and swollen that he had been for a long time. His mouth looked different, bitten and thin. Pain had set its mark there, I had never seen pain like that before so I didn't recognize it then. What had made me not quite *sure* was that he looked—*older*, and lost. He looked *lost*. Something else was there too, I had no name for it then. I have now, I've seen it many times and the name of that thing which shook the room and him and from him to me was fear. He put his arms around me and I remember my face against the rough overcoat, I remember fighting and struggling to get my *breath*. Against my ear his heart was galloping like a horse's hoofbeats, running, thudding in panic. In *panic*. Not just pain. I was frightened and I did not know what to do. Before, when I'd been frightened I had always gone to Papa.

He said, "We've been struck down, Nora, by the hand of God. We've been betrayed. Betrayed, I tell you. You and I have been robbed of our hope and our faith and our—our—oh, our better selves. The light—what can I *do*—the only light I had, Nora." I didn't know what he meant and he said in a terrible, shaking voice, "Your grandfather is dead."

"No he isn't," I said instantly.

He laughed and I said, "Oh don't, Papa," and he said, "I couldn't believe it either—but I saw him. I saw him. I saw him die in agony—this man who worshiped God, who prayed to him, who never did anyone any harm in his whole life, never hurt anyone—struck down like a dog run over by a wagon—in his prime—he had so many years to do good in— so many people needed him. What kind of a God struck him down without warning in the dark in torment?"

A rush of need to console him swept through me. I put my arms around him as far as I could, and I said, "Grandpa's all right, Papa. The trumpets will sound for him on the other side and his friend Jesus, he will come down to meet Grandpa and take him to the throne of Grace. Grandpa told me so. We mustn't—it wouldn't be very nice of us to cry if— if Grandpa is happy, you know yourself, Papa, how much he wanted to see His Lord."

"I'm not going to let you go on believing those—lies," my father said. "If there is a God of Love—don't you see I can't —all the faith I had, all the—prayer I had—how can I go on without him? What kind of a God would take him away from me now—*now*—how can I—"

He broke down, and I held him the best way I could, trying to keep him safe and I said, "Don't be afraid, Papa, please don't be afraid—we have each other, haven't we? We've got each other—"

We heard a sound from the doorway.

My mother was standing there in her nightgown, sobbing wildly.

"You needed him too, didn't you?" Papa said, very low. "He forgave you seventy-times-seven and that's more than I'll ever be able to do without him."

"Why did you have to wake her up?" Mama said. "You could have told her in the morning." Poor soul, she probably thought Papa and I had each other and now she didn't have anybody but my brother Bogart and he was awfully little.

At the funeral there were so many people weeping and Papa just kept staring at them, his underlip thrust out, his face like it was made of stone. When they told me my grand-father was in the black box and when they put him in the ground, Papa didn't say one word, but it didn't hurt me too much for a while. I kept expecting him to come back and walk along the road with me any day, the way his friend Jesus had walked on the road to Emmaus. Then Grandpa would explain everything and tell me all about it.

When I finally gave up, Papa and I decided not to talk about it any more. Nor about my grandfather. Nor God. Nor to say our prayers.

What was the use?

We went right on defending everybody.

Giving them the best proper defense and I guess that line my grandfather had spoken of the night after the Mootry case grew dimmer and dimmer.

No *Earl Rogers client* must ever be found guilty.

No no—we not only went right on defending everybody, we went right on acquitting them.

ELEVEN

Up at Acton, a small town in the Antelope Valley where we went on a feud murder as violent as any in Scotland or Kentucky, I had my long-overdue row with Luther Brown.

By the time we rode down the dusty main street where Melrose and Broome had shot it out at high noon, I should have seen and known what was going on. Or maybe not. As Bill Jory used to say, if you do not know a rattlesnake is a rattlesnake you may wish to take it home for a pet. I didn't have any idea of our danger, nor did I know its name. Nobody wanted to tell me, I was such a kid and probably they didn't think it was safe to tell me, either. Look what happened when Luther Brown tried to tell me that day on the veranda of the hotel in Acton! Though I would have taken it better from a friend than an enemy, it is also possible that none of my friends—his friends—recognized it either.

If I listen carefully to the sound track of my memory, I can discover the first high clear warning, a distant thematic discord beginning with the first time Papa didn't show up at a trial, the first time Luther Brown produced one of those doctor's certificates saying he was "too ill" to appear, and leading up to the blare and drums as Luther and I yelled at each other so *all Acton* could hear.

The things I am about to tell happened before we went to Acton on that first high-noon-walk-down-the-main-street murder, chronologically some of them belong way back before my grandfather died, some I knew only by hearsay and osmosis, that constant repetition and assumption which later makes it difficult to be sure whether you were there or not.

But to me now they have a strange straight line of their own, one step following another as the hands of a clock set on another time still move steadily minute by minute, against the same background but with a life of their own, or like the woof thread woven separately from the warp into a tapestry.

I remember that at home my mother had been in a dark cloud a good deal of the time. Our social life was nonexistent in the ordinary sense. That's up to the wife, and Mama didn't know or do anything about it and Papa was too busy unless it had just happened naturally or been forced on him. He adored the theater. The Mason Opera House, up Broadway half a block from our office, had New York companies on road tours with *The Prince of Pilsen* and *Old Heidelberg*, David Warfield in *The Music Master*, Mrs. Fiske in *Salvation Nell*, Mansfield in Shakespearean repertoire and, for *me*, above all things Maude Adams as and in *Peter Pan*. My mother did not like the theater, she said it was silly, especially comedy or musicals, so I got to go with my father. Every Sunday and sometimes Saturdays we tried to go to Chutes Park to see the Los Angeles Angels play baseball. One day somebody started the yell that became a tradition in the Pacific Coast League for many many years. *Kill the umpire, we'll get Earl Rogers to defend you.* I have to admit Papa *loved* it. He'd wave his hat and shout back at the fans.

Things at our office accelerated all the time. My father said that every hour which elapsed after a man was arrested before he talked to his lawyer, *if* that lawyer was going to be Earl Rogers, he wove a strand in the rope with which they'd hang him. Thus there were no nine-to-five hours in our office. Any hour of the twenty-four, clients sent for Mr. Rogers or came to see him. Besides murders, other citizens got picked up for climbing second stories or blowing safes or signing bum checks or holding up wayfarers. One little man was the king of the pickpockets, he tried hard to teach me but he concluded I'd never be any good at it, he said I was clumsy with my hands.

Politics also made its entrance into our lives.

Luther Brown was more interested in this than he was in the practice of law. Our office at First and Broadway could become the balance of power not only in the city but the county, the state, in time have national recognition. Brown was a staunch higher-up in the Republican party. Papa, of

course, was a William Jennings Bryan they-shall-not-crucify-
the-underdog-upon-a-cross-of-gold Democat. This made it possible for Luther Brown to play both ends against the middle.
His plan was to have them become overlords through control
of the city's crucial Eighth Ward. Politics, I thought, never
really got any hold on my father, but he was always in favor
of being an overlord wherever possible.

This was the swift, moving, changing backdrop.

Against it, as examples, were the case of the stolen horse
and our first and only divorce case, in which the whistle of
danger must have sounded if my years had been older.

1

Stealing a horse, unless it is the favorite in the Kentucky
Derby, no longer ranks as a major crime. At the time Papa
defended Alaska Pete—and came up with the first of those
"doctor's certificates"—a man could get lynched for it.

Alaska insisted he had not stolen the horse. A large, rock-
ribbed gent, he had only one eye left, but with that he faced
Papa reproachfully and said, "Mr. Rogers, I never so much
as seen this here horse. Out there around Saugus they might
shoot you for such a thing and I am not figuring to get shot."
Papa said mildly, "The plaintiff says he saw you," and Pete
said, "This has got to be a case of mistaken identity, he has
got hold of either the wrong horse or the wrong man."

On his first appearance in our office, Alaska Pete was wearing overalls and a flannel shirt. Sitting beside Earl Rogers
in court, he had blossomed in an unfortunate store suit of
alfalfa green. Also he had either fallen in love with his new
Stetson hat or he'd been *out*side so long he had forgotten
he was supposed to remove it when he came *in*side. Every
single time, Mr. Rogers had to remind him to take it off.
Knowing Alaska, Bill Jory was surprised to see Mr. Rogers
consulting with him more than he usually did with much
brighter defendants.

On the second morning of the trial there were no Earl
Rogers and no Bill Jory.

Without anybody giving it a second thought, Luther Brown
got a postponement with a doctor's certificate. The next day
there Mr. Rogers was, some sticking plaster on his jaw, but
in high spirits. Bill Jory was still absent.

With such good fellowship that only beer and pretzels
were missing, Mr. Rogers took over the cross-examination of

the plaintiff, a German rancher named something like Kirchen-baum. They discussed the plaintiff's health, which was good; the fine effort of the Los Angeles Chamber of Commerce to tell the world about Southern California climate; happily Mr. Rogers noted that Mr. Kirchenbaum didn't have to wear glasses, and the witness said he could see a jack rabbit across a wash combing his whiskers and they both roared at this ancient desert wheeze.

After lunch, lounging beside the green suit and the new Stetson hat, Mr. Rogers courteously, apologetically, took up with Mr. Kirchenbaum the identification of the defendant. "—doubt the word of a man of your standing in the commu-nity—sharp eyes as any man in the state—matter of legal routine—if the man you saw steal your horse is in this court-room would you be so kind as to point him out to the jury—"

The plaintiff would and did. Mr. Rogers nodded. "Quite sure, of course?" Mr. Kirchenbaum was. "This gentleman sitting here beside me is the man who stole your horse, no possibility of mistake?" "Ya is him," the plaintiff said jovially. "I seen him plain then, I see him plain now."

Unfortunately for his case, the man he identified as the horse thief was Bill Jory. In his overalls and flannel shirt. Alaska Pete was sitting in the tenth row.

Pure clowning—and Papa's delight in his gag was conta-gious, a ripple grew into a roar which swept judge and jury.

The fact that Earl Rogers for the first time had produced a doctor's certificate to explain his inability to appear was lost in the rhythm of fun.

Papa did love fun.

The case of a beautiful lady I shall call Emmeline Steer-forth didn't have so many laughs but it was the first time Earl Rogers ever settled a case out of court—and almost the last.

2

The Steerforths' many-turreted mansion on Grand Avenue was just around the corner from my Aunt Blanche's house. Inside, we came upon different worlds.

According to the friends who spoke to Earl Rogers in her behalf, Mrs. Steerforth's husband didn't understand her. She had a poetical nature and a sensitive soul. Mr. Steerforth had a commercial nature and no soul at all. All he cared for was money and the fleshpots it could buy, one of whom was named Olivette. Mrs. Steerforth's name was Emmeline. This had given his romantic wife right to a divorce, and also a large bite of the silver Mr. Steerforth had been busily grubbing out of the hills of Nevada.

A society lady like Mrs. Steerforth, and delicate besides, could not be expected to make the trip down to our office, where she might meet characters not of her exclusive circle. We must go to her.

My mother was a great natural beauty, with no need to paint her face and no taste in dress to enhance her charms. My grandmother had been busy helping Phoebe Apperson Hearst found the P.-T.A., my Aunt Blanche even on the concert platform felt a Christian gentlewoman and a musician should be above fripperies. Entering Mrs. Steerforth's domain, I encountered femininity painted, powdered, perfumed, cared for by a French maid, dressed by Worth, surrounded by luxuries I had thought existed only in such books as *Henry Esmond* and *Père Goriot*. It is also quite possible that my young father had never before met anything like Emmeline and her boudoir. To my father and other men of that time and place, the line was as broad as the Grand Canyon. On one side, wives, daughters, sisters, and all good women. On the other, Pearl Morton and her girls. *Never the twain shall meet*. The professional had little if any amateur competition and that middle-of-the-road, now so densely populated, where it is impossible to tell the difference, did not exist. If a lady got involved in scandal, divorce, or was caught sleeping around, as we say so frankly today, she moved or was moved over onto the other side.

A lady who could maintain her amateur standing while playing about had to be very clever.

Our visits to Mrs. Steerforth as a client may therefore have been as unexpected an experience to my father as they were to me.

On the first of them, an English butler flung open the door and we saw a stately hall with statues and paintings in gold frames. A maid in frilled cap and apron showed us up carpeted stairs, with candles burning in gold-and-mirror sconces. A second maid at the top threw open a door into a large room exactly like the inside of a candy box a client had given me for Christmas. Pink-shaded lamps burned softly, drapes of shell-pink satin tied with golden tassels were held back over priceless lace curtains, white fur rugs flung on American

Beauty rose carpets, a small fountain tinkled scented water into a mother-of-pearl basin. On an Empress Josephine chaise longue, her golden curls resting upon tiny silken cushions, her body draped in chiffon and rose-point lace, reclined our new client.

I remember distinctly feeling as bedraggled as Br'er Rabbit in the brier patch. Also I could see that this was no place for a mining man. But Papa! His face changed to suit the luxurious scene. The pitch of his black eyebrows, the lock of his black hair, the gallantry of his walk, the boldness of his smile, his fawn suit so elegantly tailored, the white silk shirt and black cravat with an emerald stickpin became a costume as he bowed over Mrs. Steerforth's ringed hand. I was sure that was the way D'Artagnan had kissed the queen's after he brought back her diamond studs.

I choked with admiration and so, I guess, did Mrs. Steerforth. Her eyes were enormous, the lids delicately blue and her mouth a Cupid's bow of deep rose-pink, both brought from Paris, but I had never seen or even heard of lipstick or eye shadow so no suspicion occurred to me.

"You are too young!" she said to my father. "Ah—forgive me, for my lawyer I expected an elderly person with a beard —" and her laughter tinkled forth like the fountain.

Then she seemed to become aware of me for the first time. She had clearly not expected me. She drew me to her, she smelled like Wong's spiced peaches, she said, "What a lovely surprise," and then she called her French maid and said "Jeannette"—and I got words such as *"petits gâteaux—."* Then Jeannette was maneuvering me expertly into the hall, I was in a little dining room, *petits gâteaux* turned out to be little pink cakes with silver frosting. While I ate them, I saw Jeannette going back upstairs with a bottle in a silver bucket.

Bill Jory was sitting on a teakwood chair in the hall, so I asked him what it was, he said champagne. "Don't let anybody kid you," he said crossly, "you can get just as drunk as if it was good bourbon. The next day you feel like you had been bit by a Gila monster."

Evidently it hadn't bitten Papa yet, he came down in one of his carry-all-before-me moods. He needed it. When he informed Jory he was going to leave him there all night, Bill let out a squawk that shook the chandeliers. Papa explained Mrs. Steerforth's husband had written her threats when she told him not to darken her doors again. "Well," said Bill Jory, "they are his doors, too. Am I supposed to give him a roust?

Who am I supposed to be?" Papa said, "Did I get you a fine new shiny deputy sheriff badge a week ago or not? As her lawyer, the lady has asked me to get her police protection. You are it. If anybody wants to get in ask him to show you a search warrant." Bill said, "This is pretty highhanded, Mr. Rogers," and Papa laughed and said, "It is indeed." Of course Bill stayed, Papa always had authority to make other men do what he told them to.

After that we spent a good deal of time at Mrs. Steerforth's. They were having difficulty getting a property settlement big enough to suit her.

The food around there was sensational, Papa and Bill and I had our first real go-round on French cooking, which got us in training for the days to come in San Francisco.

Papa and Mrs. Steerforth had their dinner on little gilt tables in the music room, or the conservatory, because Emmeline ate almost nothing. A chicken wing, a little salad with French dressing, which was new to California in those days— we had lettuce sometimes and my grandmother put sugar on it. Emmeline would hold a bunch of grapes in one hand and pick them off one by one, if she'd thought of it she'd have asked Papa to peel one for her. There was a new phonograph in the music room. Often they played records. Other times we could hear them laughing, I decided she must have the wit and conversational power of Madame Récamier, which I had read about. I asked Bill Jory, who got mad every time Jeannette or the butler went by carrying a bucket, about this and whether he thought Papa liked her a great deal. And if he did, why. He said the whole thing was human nature and there had never yet been any explanation for that. Horses, except broncos, he said could be handicapped on past performances. A coyote or a bear or a wolf would act like you expected a coyote or a bear or a wolf to act most of the time. Weather, forest fires, floods, and Injuns were predictable after considerable study. The only way to deal with human nature was to ride along and keep your eyes wide open and your gun oiled and be ready for anything because human nature would never be the same once in a million times and that, he said, is too long odds for any man.

Then one night Emmeline said to Papa, "Let me have this remarkable child of yours for a visit. She needs a woman's touch. Doesn't she have anything to wear but Peter Thompsons?"

A Peter Thompson was a style made in Philadelphia, composed of a dark blue pleated skirt and a white middy blouse with a big collar and an enormous tie.

"I like them," I said.

Mrs. Steerforth laughed and kissed me, but of course I knew she did not want a visit from me any more than a bob-tailed wildcat. My mother had gone East again to her folks and probably Emmeline had heard the gossip that this time she wasn't coming back. So I thought maybe she was figuring on two divorces. Jory thought something like that too, because he said probably if it was anything else he and I wouldn't be around so much. A lot of *petits gâteaux* to which I admit I was partial, and kissing me, and Jeannette brushing my hair, and a new dress she was ordering me from Paris made me figure she knew what Franklin D. Roosevelt taught me many years later—the only important vote is the one you haven't got. Mrs. Steerforth had to know she didn't have mine and it was going to be tough without it.

A lot of silk sheets and satin puffs and lace pillows and scent and things went on the night I stayed there, so I couldn't sleep. I thought I'd go down and talk to Bill Jory. In the dark I got mixed up and went down the back stairs and ended up in the servants' dining hall.

Emmeline was sitting at the table and never in my whole life have I ever seen a woman as mad as she was when she saw me standing there, in one of her silk nightgowns which was too big for me anyhow.

I turned around and went back up those stairs like a cottontail.

Mostly I could talk things over with Bill Jory. Not this. My grandfather had always said people put themselves in your power when they invited you into their homes as a guest. Their privacy must be sacred to you. I'd stayed awake the rest of the night trying to figure out whether this meant Papa, too, and I had about decided it did. If she hadn't been so stupid the next morning probably I wouldn't have told him either. She said, "Now my dear you must be careful about telling your father any fibs. Your father may call it creative imagination but I call it telling fibs. I warn you if you tell him any fibs about me I shall be forced to tell him what a little liar you are."

I knew then I had to get rid of her. It wouldn't help any to exchange Mama for somebody just as stupid and not even as beautiful.

I brooded about it all day and the minute he came for me that evening and we got around the corner I burst out with it.

I said, "Papa."

He said, "Yes ma'am?"

I said, "Mrs. Steerforth is mad at me and I'm glad."

There was a kind of curbing like a low wall built along the edge of a lawn just there. The water running alongside it in a cement gully was fresh and made a lovely sound. Papa and I sat down on it. I took it for granted then that all days were hot and clear and all nights cool and clear, that all days smelled of sand and sage and sea and all nights of Cecil Breuner roses and lemon verbena. Papa took out his sack of Bull Durham and his little book of brown papers and rolled a cigarette with one hand, the way all horsemen had to learn to do. It rushed over me that in a way Papa lived in one world and I in another. His had so many things in it I didn't know about yet. Mine still had things in it I felt he'd forgotten about. Just the same they became one, we could always speak to each other.

After he got his cigarette rolled and lit he said, "Why is the fair Emmeline mad at you?"

I said, "You know the way she carries on about being too airy-fairy to eat anything but strawberries and cream and chicken wings, well, Papa, all that is a lot of horsefeathers. I bet she can eat more than you and me and my dog Samson put together. I bet she has an appetite like a boa constrictor."

"How did you arrive at this astonishing conclusion?" Papa said.

"Hells bells," I said, "I saw her. There she was, with a plate of grub, cold potatoes and that pot roast she had Pierre cook for Jory and me, and apple pie and I don't know why she can't eat when she sits down to the table like anybody else. Anyhow, she's a fraud, Papa, and she said she'd tell you I told fibs, but I didn't make this up, Papa."

"No no," Papa said, choking a little over the smoke, "no no. Remember always, people can only tell the lies they can think of. Lies within the realm of their knowledge and the range of their capacity. The story has to be one their imagination would reach for. Edison imagined the electric light, not the Ninth Symphony. I cannot see how you could ever have imagined anything like Emmeline eating cold potatoes in secret. Moreover I take it you are giving me your word?"

"Yes," I said.

We always had that understanding. I was free to make up stories, but on direct question I must tell the truth the whole truth and nothing but the truth.

"Of course," Papa said. "Now on the other hand, Emmeline acting a lie to increase her feminine fragility, her astral charm —a creature composed of fire and dew without the grosser elements—yes, this is plainly possible."

"She's silly," I said.

"I'm afraid so," Papa said with a sigh. "Nora, will you arrange to stay as you are or else grow up to be Queen Mab or—no no, don't grow up."

I said, "She did have pretty feet and ankles. You told me always to look and I did. So that was one thing anyway."

Papa had begun to cackle with laughter, it grew and grew, and he said, "To be made a fool of by a chicken wing is more than a man can put up with," and doubled up with mirth.

The next night Emmeline Steerforth tried to commit suicide.

The first of a number of women who didn't try quite hard enough. It wouldn't have done her any good if she had. Papa thought suicide was not only cowardly but ridiculous.

All Bill Jory ever said to me was, "Don't ever drink things that taste good, you never know when you're drunk, and that causes trouble."

There was a good deal of talk about all this, in a way it was a good thing for Mrs. Steerforth. She went back to her husband. Or rather she let him come back to her. All that about expecting Earl Rogers to be an elderly man with a beard!

It was years and years before our office ever took another divorce case. Earl Rogers said flatly they were more trouble than they were worth.

When he did the chief witness for her sister was the red-headed Irish-Canadian girl who became his second wife.

The first doctor's certificate . . . ?

The *buckets* of champagne and the way Bill Jory worried about them . . . ?

Very small discords stating high and thin the theme of our danger. No no, it isn't surprising that Luther Brown took me completely by surprise when he trumpeted it in Acton, to which desert town we'd been summoned in the high-noon murder of Broome by Melrose.

Acton was one of the most amazing and picturesque hamlets I ever saw, a combination of *Our Town* and a *Gunsmoke* locale, I don't remember any other quite like it. High up through the pass above San Fernando into the Antelope Valley, it had the traditional street, the saloons and gambling houses, the wooden buildings. All around it instead of cattle range and sagebrush were little ranches, exquisitely neat and green, and beyond in every direction the breath-taking desert backed by glorious blue and purple mountains.

I don't remember on which trip to Acton my fight with Luther Brown took place to the intense interest and horror of the bystanders. During preparation for the defense of Melrose we made a lot of trips up there. Papa always spent a lot of time on the scene of the crime, nosing around after the methods of Sherlock Holmes, who had just burst upon a startled and admiring world. This was especially necessary in the Broome-Melrose walk-and-wait killing, which might be entitled the Case of the Eyewitnesses. Only a few babies under six months and an old man who was bedridden had failed to see everything that took place that fatal day. All of the eyewitnesses had to be interviewed.

We went up to Acton on the train. I always felt lighthearted and buoyant on a train and moreover I would get to ride horseback, which I liked to do best of anything in the world except swimming in the ocean. While Papa was working with the records of all this feud's previous history, I went off by myself on a nice pinto pony belonging to one of the eyewitnesses who had seen it our way.

The valley floor was a sheet of pure gold in the sunshine and the snow on the mountain peaks was whiter than the clouds. I saw jack rabbits pushing themselves on their hind legs like miniature kangaroos and rattlesnakes stretched out peacefully on the purple and green rocks, bothering nobody if nobody bothered them. The prickly-pear blossoms were gold with rose hearts, and every now and then there was a little clump of cottonwoods, silver leaves always dancing though I couldn't feel any breeze. Even when I was very young the desert told me two great things. The wonder of silence and never to be afraid of being alone.

The sun told me it was time to go back, I tied my pony to the rack in front of the hotel, and standing there was Luther Brown.

In a way, I suppose, sitting on my pinto pony in the sunshine was the last moment of sheer, unadulterated clear bright childhood felicity I was ever to know. My grandfather's death had made my heart ache, but we do not *worry* about the dead. They cannot be defeated or humiliated. It is the living who keep us awake nights with our hearts beating faster and faster with anxiety, praying God not to let anything happen to them, not to let them pass the point of no return.

We stood together on the dirt walk. I can see the two figures quite plainly. The girl beginning to grow taller and skinnier, in a divided skirt of fringed buckskin and a big sombrero to keep off sunstroke. The handsome suave young politician, wavy brown hair, big brown eyes, patronizing yet ingratiating smile. I was as allergic to Luther Brown as some children are to goldenrod or cat fur. I knew he had already betrayed my father and would again someday. He was allergic to me, too, he knew that I knew what I knew. Too insensitive to realize that since it would have hurt my father I'd cut my tongue out before I'd tell him. As a schoolteacher he resented not having any authority over me, he was sure I ought to be in a classroom from nine to three instead of under his feet. Well, he was not the only one who thought that.

Anybody watching him as he followed me up onto the veranda, his hat in his hand, would have had to think he was polite and friendly, nobody but me could see how vindictive his big cow eyes were.

I can't remember exactly what he said. A version of an old plea. He wanted me to go to one of the saloons where my father was having a drink with a deputy sheriff and one of the eyewitnesses on our side. Luther said he was getting drunk and, he said, I should use all this influence I was supposed to have and get him out of there right away.

This had been there, as I've said, for some time—Bill Jory the night of the Boyd verdict, the doctor's certificate, the champagne at Mrs. Steerforth's. I'd had no idea what it meant, this was the first time it had come out in the open in actual words.

I said, "Oh you shut up. Don't you think you're smart enough to tell my father what to do."

"Somebody must tell him," Luther Brown said. "You are supposed to be the apple of his eye. You're the rabbit's foot he carries. Your mother says—"

"You shut up about my mother," I said.

He knew he'd made a mistake. He said persuasively, "Look, my dear child, if he isn't careful he's going to lose this case. He talks too much when he's had too much to drink. He makes a fool of himself in front of the whole town and they have to think less of him—"

I guess I just went after him like a wildcat, biting and scratching, kicking and spitting, sobbing and panting out crazy words. "You take that back," I said. "I know all about *you*. You take that back, I'll have my father put you in jail don't you dare say such things about my father you're a liar you ought to be put in jail—"

He had planted in me the nameless terrible seeds of apprehension, and I was taking it out on him.

It would never be a bright unclouded morning again.

It was worse because I felt him my enemy and my father's betrayer.

He couldn't do anything with me, I was too little, and a female, and I was quite uncontrollable by anything less than brute force.

So he walked away, leaving me—having eaten of the tree that is in the midst of the garden, the tree of the knowledge of good and evil, concerning which God said, "Ye shall not eat of the fruit thereof."

TWELVE

Part of the time during the Melrose cases I was in Arizona. I'd had scarlet fever, which scared my father into fits, and afterwards he sent me to Tempe to stay with his sister Madge. Her husband owned the hardware store and taught me to shoot quail with a .22 and break my own ponies, so I lived through the separation. Then my other aunt, Blanche, caught up with him about the probable effects of bringing up a girl between a criminal law office and a murder courtroom and I had to go to a regular school for a while.

Some of the trial I saw, a lot Rosy told me later when we were living on a ferryboat in San Francisco Bay. Rosy was the Melrose who shot Broome. It was interesting to listen to him because as he said the man on trial saw things from a different viewpoint than anybody else.

The thing neither he nor Papa ever got over was a witness named Miss Lillian Beecher Plato of Boston.

If Irene Adler was always The Woman to Sherlock Holmes, Miss Lillian B. Plato was the same to Earl Rogers.

Somebody was going to get killed sooner or later.

Everybody up in the jack-rabbit country had known that. Two men would walk down the main street of Acton, running parallel to the railroad tracks, with the steepled schoolhouse at one end and the hotel at the other. One of them would lie prone and motionless and the other would stand over him, gun in hand.

The feud began the day Melrose got to town.

Acton had been settled by Germans from Upstate New York. Whereas most of the valley was in cattle ranches, these farmers had dug up weeds, built neat productive acres with chickens to lay eggs and cows to give milk. They had truck gardens, grew some alfalfa for winter hay, some fruit trees, and what in early California were called muskmelons. Leading citizen of this frugal, hard-working, well-behaved community was William Broome, whose great-great-grandfather had been Colonel John B. Broome of Revolutionary fame and for whom Broome Street in New York City is named. Telegraph operator at the railroad station—not many trains went through—Bill Broome still had plenty of time for farming, and also to be on the school board, a deacon in his church, and unofficial mayor. An efficient, stolid, overbearing Prussian, he had everything going to suit him until Melrose, heading up a Go-West-Young-Man contingent, blew in from Kaintuck.

Hate at first sight bloomed between Melrose and Broome.

Melrose was a big, swaggering, fun-loving Southerner, addicted to practical jokes. Even his own eyewitnesses admitted he was a sight too ready both with his tongue and his gun.

Before long his wife got to be postmistress, and Melrose started easing into county politics, and finagled a job with the street department. The original settlers didn't care for these Newcomers, as they called them, nor their go-getting ways and big ideas and rambunctions. The future eyewitnesses began to line up for a tug-of-war, Broome heading one group, Melrose the other.

"It startles me sometimes to remember how young I was when I arrived there," Rosy used to say sheepishly. "It's a wonder I didn't break a laig. I *preferred* trouble. A man has to be considerably older than I was to prefer peace and of course some men never do."

No better way to trigger a smoldering blood feud than a dogfight.

Only good thing about that German so-and-so, Rosy said, was he loved his dog. However, the dog was a ferocious pit bull, dedicated to making life precarious for every other dog in town. Melrose's dog was for hunting purposes, a good-natured Llewellyn who had no idea how to take care of himself in a fight. "I jumped in to pull that bull off *my* dog," Rosy said, "and that bulldog turned on me and I killed him. I never denied it. I wasn't going to stand around and let Broome's dog chew on my pants *or* my dog."

For a couple of days the slow and stolid Broome mourned. Then he made an unexpected and law-abiding move. He had the sheriff arrest Melrose for shooting his dog, which was a felony.

Enter first eyewitness.

Miss Minnie Boucher, the schoolteacher, spent a lot of her time in her rocking chair on the porch of her little cottage. As with all the other eyewitnesses, as you listened you were sure there must be *two* Miss Minnies. Rosy said she was a real nice old gal, though she talked more than was reasonable even for a woman, but most of it was the truth. The Broome adherents said Miss Minnie was a snoop, a spy, and the truth was not in her.

Anyway, she backed Melrose's story one hundred per cent. He was acquitted.

This had to be unfinished business and for the next two years nobody in Acton ever had a relaxed or peaceful day. Accusations were profane, noisy, sometimes legal. Broome said Melrose deliberately tramped down the flowers on his brother's grave, Melrose said Broome poisoned his cattle.

Two major engagements took place simultaneously.

A suit was brought, this time by Melrose, charging Broome with libel for publicly calling Mrs. Melrose a railroad whore. "I should of shot him then," Rosy said, "it would have been simpler. But I'd agreed before a jedge to keep the peace. But I couldn't just let him say a thing like that. Hell, she wasn't but fifteen when I married her."

Systematically, the Broome forces set out to get Miss Minnie fired as schoolma'am. Naturally, Melrose and his Newcomers Clan rushed to her defense and the meetings of the school board took on all the aspects of the Roman Senate about the time Caesar was stabbed. When the board deadlocked, the county supervisors stepped in. Firing Miss Minnie was too drastic, so they transferred her. To take her place, Miss Lillian B. Plato was imported from New England, likewise her mother, Mrs. Daniel Webster Plato. If Miss Minnie had seen, heard, and talked too much, it was soon evident that Miss Plato had Sphinx blood in her veins. Her mother was stone deaf and couldn't see at six paces.

Here the judge issued an order that the ringleaders must not carry guns. To this naturally neither of them paid any attention and the sheriff, several hours' ride away in Lancaster, wasn't about to enforce it. "Man looking for me with blood in his eye," Rosy said, "and I'm supposed to go around with nothing to defend myself? Let the other man draw first, the sheriff says to me. That's what I done. Only like your pa said it's all right to let the other man *draw* first, just be sure you *shoot* first—I done that, too."

During this well-armed cold war Melrose always had his gun on his hip.

Came the inevitable hot high noon, when Broome came to town on his produce wagon with his shotgun handy across his knees.

Broome was dead with *five* bullets in him, which to the end of the Melrose trials were to trouble his counsel Earl Rogers exceedingly. "How could I tell?" Rosy said plaintively. "He was a hard man to stop, you know them Germans." And to be sure, Broome's shotgun, which had been fired, was still in his dead hand.

Politics, that strong factor in murder cases, entered this one immediately and, for our side, adversely.

A peculiar but familiar reason for swift, all-out prosecution existed in the office of the new district attorney. No man had campaigned harder for Captain John D. Fredericks than Melrose. He and his followers had held torchlight processions in Antelope Valley on election eve. Now the Broome mourners marched into Los Angeles and announced portentously that unless Fredericks prosecuted Melrose to the fullest extent of the law it would prove corruption, a D.A. allowing his supporters to get away with murder.

"Fredericks," Rosy said, "had to give his friends the worst of it to prove how goddam incorruptible he *was*."

Under the circumstances, Captain Fredericks didn't wish to appear himself, so he assigned McComas, a chief deputy who survived all administrative changes, to conduct investigation and prosecution. The Melrose Clan countered by getting Earl Rogers to defend their man and the fight was on. In no case Rogers ever tried was sentiment more violent and continuous. The armed camps of the Antelope Valley inundated the county. In defense of his honor, the D.A. had to win his first big case. On the other hand we couldn't allow a newly elected district attorney to set a precedent by beating Earl Rogers.

THIRTEEN

I'm sure Papa never really wanted people to know how much his victories depended on hard, careful work, infinite preparation, meticulous attention to details. He preferred to build the legend of brilliance, of inspiration, of the unexpected break-through.

The truth was plain on our trips to Acton partly because it was so difficult, in the continued feud and boiling emotional pitch, to find out anything reasonably accurate about anything.

For hours Earl Rogers pored over the history of the charges Broome and Melrose had brought against each other. He talked to every witness in the past and all the eyewitnesses of the present who would speak to him and most of those who wouldn't. He measured distances, paced off steps in the dust, peered up and down the one street, tested what could be seen and heard.

By the time the judge rapped for order and the People of the State of California, County of Los Angeles, went to trial against W. H. Melrose in Department 2 of our rose-rock courthouse, Earl Rogers' case was prepared, as all his cases were. He knew everything there was to know about it.

A magic carpet had transported the entire population of Acton and a good deal of the valley across the mountains and deposited it in the courtroom. The feud had come with it. Both sides were seething with determination to see justice done their way. The courtroom was so jam packed that Melrose, the man on trial, found himself in the adjoining seat to the teenage son of the man he'd shot. The widow of the slain man and the wife of the accused once had to be separated by bailiffs. Fist fights inside the courtroom as eyewitnesses gave each other the lie direct kept the judge hopping like a referee in the prize ring. Drawn guns in the streets called out riot squads.

Poor Miss Minnie, sadly demoted at the very time the Acton feud murder hit the front pages, nevertheless gave one bit of testimony that should be preserved. "I told Mr. Broome," Miss Minnie said on the witness stand, "that if he were to murder Mr. Melrose it would have a most unfortunate effect upon the community and might get him into serious difficulties."

On one point only the eyewitnesses agreed.

The time was noon.

Well-drilled as a British square, Deputy District Attorney McComas' eyewitnesses said the same thing in the same words:

Melrose came down the street. Broome was near the hotel and when Melrose heard his shotgun he let out one of the bellows of laughter and profanity. "Look at that yellow son-of-a-bitch shootin' them pore little tame doves with a shotgun," he shouted. To this Broome replied by telling Melrose to mind his own business or he'd make him.

They began moving toward each other.

At this point it seemed certain both wives ran out into the street, waving arms and aprons. Various citizens shouted, "Stop him." By the time the two men faced each other, the street was empty, spectators had taken refuge and viewed further action through keyholes and windows. As for what they saw, it was impossible to tell the Bad Guys from the Good Guys, there were two different versions and casts of the same show.

One after another the solid German-Americans took the stand. With slight but recognizable accents they told their stubborn immovable never-varying eyewitness stories:

Having insulted Broome at the top of his lungs, Melrose had then rushed at the other man giving tongue to a version of the Rebel Yell. Broome leaned his shotgun against a tree and came toward Melrose shouting, "Put up your hands and fight like a man," and swung. They exchanged a couple of blows and then, the eyewitness said, "Melrose his gun pulls and shoots down Broome same as he did Broome's dog, he falls and Melrose stands above him and fires four times more into

Broome as he is on the ground. From the tree he takes the shotgun and puts it in the road by Broome's hand and walks away off."

This made it murder in the first degree with the gallows mandatory.

As best he could, Earl Rogers attacked his collective story.

I have always thought one of Earl Rogers' overpowering advantages on cross-examination was his idea about the truth. Other cross-examiners assumed the attitude that the witness was deliberately lying and no one knew better than Rogers that sometimes he was. However, he believed also that often he was telling the truth as he saw it.

A man looking at a scene through rose-colored glasses would actually *see* something different from those who had green glasses locked over their eyes as they did before they were allowed to enter the Emerald City of Oz. Without those green glasses, Oz was not an Emerald City at all. Which side of the race track you sat on determined which horse you *saw* win the race. Railroad tracks were seen coming together and this would appear to be a fact until a man was taught that it was only an optical illusion. Back in the early days in New England, undoubtedly decent men and women saw some silly old woman as a witch who should be burned to death. Your eyes told you beyond question that the earth was flat, yet the truth was far otherwise and in time men would get up high enough to see the curve of its surface.

At the time, Rogers was convinced that the Broome witnesses were telling the truth as they believed it to be. His purpose was to make them see another picture by taking off their green glasses. To bring them to the truth as it was, or as Earl Rogers wished them to think it was.

It did not look as though he was ever going to get anywhere. With blank stares, flat pauses, nerves like clams, no German eyewitness varied his testimony by a syllable.

One August Schultz, who kept the livery stable, was the star witness for the Broome clan. "This bad man Melrose," he said, "he knocks down my poor friend, he keeps shooting him, he puts the gun right upon him and pulls the trigger over and over so bloodthirsty is he."

This, it turned out, was the first break.

Up to then, nobody had mentioned the gun pressed against the body. Quietly, Rogers began to investigate this. How close, he wanted to know. "Held the gun right up against him?" he asked, with what appeared to be merely curiosity. "Like this?" and he put his forefinger flatly against Mr. August Schultz's stomach.

"Ya soooo," said Mr. Schultz.

Rogers poked for each of the five bullets. "Must have bent over him?" he said, and when Schultz nodded Rogers said, "At such close range there must have been powder burns. Why haven't we been told whether there were powder burns?" and when McComas objected that the witness wouldn't know whether there were powder burns or not, Rogers swung on him, "No—but *you* should. Were there?" and August Schultz, not to be shouldered out of the act, said gravely, "It can be he uses the schmokeless powder, ya?"

"If this witness has told the truth," Earl Rogers said, "there must be powder burns."

That midnight, oil burned in the office of the district attorney of Los Angeles County. Nobody knew better than McComas that the autopsy had been a sketchy affair—why not? Seemed of no importance. By this time, old Mac had a wholesome respect for young Earl Rogers and he sent Captain Fredericks to a sleepless couch by saying, "Rogers is *up* to something."

Nor were they happier the next day when Rogers got on the stand the man who'd done the autopsy. By the time Earl Rogers stretched himself out on the floor and requested Dr. Anderson to show the jury the size, shape, color, depth, and position of every wound, it was plain that the State's medical witness didn't know what he was talking about.

Q. You didn't think to look for powder burns, did you, doctor?

A. Well now I can't say I did.

Q. So you really can't testify as to whether there were any powder burns or not, can you?

A. No.

Q. I didn't think you could. So you can't tell me at all whether the witness who says he saw Melrose put the gun right up against Broome's body is right or not?

A. No I can't.

Q. Thank you, doctor—that's all.

At the dread and witching hour of midnight, anyone passing the cemetery where William Broome was buried might have seen an eerie light dancing among the graves, shapes flitting among the tombstones, and heard mysterious, muffled moans.

From what should have been its last resting place, a casket came out of the earth and was placed upon some boards held by sawhorses. In utter silence, that lid, secured until the last trump, was slowly raised. The glow of lanterns fell upon the indifferent dead face.

Into that frozen moment of horror, other figures moved, as ghosts leaving the surrounding graves. Somebody screamed gruffly, somebody swore in harsh protest, voices began to babble.

"I thought I'd better see what was going on, Mac," Earl Rogers said softly, putting the rays of his lantern on the big face usually so red, now a graveyard gray.

"I might have known," McComas said bitterly.

"You knew I might ask for an exhumation order after your doctor fell apart, didn't you, Mac?" Rogers said, in a grim, unfriendly tone. "I thought after we brought up those powder burns nobody had thought to look for you'd try to make sure. You should think of these things earlier so you won't have to disturb a man's last rest. I brought my own doctors. I think your man August Schultz is a liar, I want to make sure to leave this in—"

What Rogers didn't mention was that he had brought along Harry Carr of the *Times* and a photographer.

DISTRICT ATTORNEY SECRETLY EXHUMES CORPSE OF MURDERED MAN

This headline over a story of Carr's in the best Edgar Allan Poe manner and a picture of McComas by old-fashioned flash powder looking like Dracula hovering over the coffin made dark reading for Captain Fredericks at his breakfast table. He had been against the exhumation.

Like everything else in the Melrose mystery there were two sides to the powder burns. Some said yes there were, others no there weren't. Charges of illegal tampering were hurled back and forth until the whole thing became meaningless except as my father succeeded in putting one of his trial principles into operation.

Try somebody else.

Keep the prosecution off balance.

He figured every man's attention followed his interest and impact and a man or a jury had only so much attention to give. Now whenever he wished to take the jury's attention off a weak spot in his case or a strong one in the prosecution's, he diverted it to the nefarious activities of the district attorney's office.

In the *Express*, top court reporter Johnny Gray said:

A spectator in Department Two of the Superior Court would have some difficulty making up his mind whether they are trying Melrose for murder or the district attorney for robbing a grave.

By question, action, innuendo, and aside he established McComas as a ghoul, a vulture, a banshee and possibly the Hound of the Baskervilles. It began to seem possible that they had buried Mr. Broome without knowing whether he was dead or not.

Upon a stage thus newly set, enter Eyewitnesses for the Defense.

They swore that they had seen Broome sighting pigeons along the barrel of his shotgun. When Melrose passed by with his dog Broome began a-cussin' of him fit to make your blood run cold. When *Melrose*, infuriated at such abuse, shouted, "Put down your gun and fight," Broome leaned his shotgun against a tree. In a minute, they were both rolling on the ground, back and forth in the street. Broome kicked Melrose when he had him down, jumped up and grabbed his gun and fired point-blank at Melrose, who leaped aside just in time. *Then* Melrose whipped out *his* gun and his shot hit, but Broome went down with his shotgun in his hand and he was still a-movin' when Melrose fired again.

The jury listened to this with interest and looked friendly—if skeptical.

With Melrose, a good-looking, easy-moving man with quick dark eyes, on the stand Papa brought the tree into the courtroom and leaned Broome's shotgun against it. Down from the stand came Melrose, undulating, graceful, masculine and Papa became Broome and they re-enacted the death scene according to the man who won. By some shadow boxing Papa had the shotgun at his shoulder, pulled the trigger, Melrose leaped aside and had his gun in his hand with what we could all see was a mighty fast draw.

Melrose said, "He pulled his gun first as you might say. He shot and missed, that was all. Iffen I wanted to stay alive I couldn't afford to miss."

In the office afterwards, white, tense, and absolutely furious, Papa said, "Something's wrong. What is it? We didn't get them."

Always in our office there were no-men. Everybody could disagree with Mr. Rogers. It was necessary to see the prosecution's case as well as we saw our own. They went back and forth, seesaw, and then Papa said to me, "Well, papoose, what about it?"

Looking back as I do now, I agree it seems strange that Papa *could* have asked my opinion seriously at a moment like that. Probably that's why Luther Brown disliked me so much. He'd given his august and worthy estimation, an educated man, a teacher, a powerful politician, a good lawyer. For Earl Rogers to set on an equal with *that* the prattlings of a brat who couldn't know anything about anything offended him sorely.

None of this occurred to me at the time. Figuring it out later, I came to think I know why he asked me, trusted me, considered what I said.

Child-sight.

This is not in Webster's. But it was a fact that my father thought, believed I had child-sight and set store by it. As life happens to people, it increases knowledge and judgment, but none knew better than he did that often it dulls instinct and vision. Those pure and undefiled intuitions which the records show do come to the young were very often blocked later by what the world said you couldn't do or must not attempt. His faith in second sight, sensitivity of impressions such as a souped-up photographic plate might have, was strong in any case. In our hours alone he read aloud to me from *The Jungle Book*, we lost ourselves in the worlds of Kim and Peter Pan, of Mowgli and Puck, or Treasure Island, in all of which child-sight was victorious.

So he wanted my child-impression to add to the others.

I said, "Well, Papa, with Melrose right there it's kind of hard to expect anybody to believe he didn't start any fight he was in. I don't believe it myself."

Circling around the desk, Papa let out what was practically a howl and began to bang with a lawbook. "August Schultz," he howled, "benighted idiot that I am, the jury has identified him as his poor friend Mr. Broome. They can see Melrose in the courtroom, wild as a mustang, they've substituted *Schultz* for *Broome* and, as Nora says, in a fight between Melrose and Schultz any sane man has to believe Melrose started it. *And* finished it."

We sat in silence while Papa tossed the lawbook into a corner and began walking around again. He said, "At this moment I am licked. Bill? The jury as of now will convict him?"

"Yes, Mr. Rogers," Jory said. "I think so."

"You remember a lady up in Acton named Miss Lillian B. Plato?"

"Yes, Mr. Rogers," Bill said.

"Go get her," Papa said.

"Now?" said Bill Jory.

"I want her in court by nine o'clock tomorrow morning," Papa said.

"We'll have to take a freight train out of there in the morning," Jory said.

"One thing I'll say for Miss Plato." Papa said, grinning broadly. "I don't think she'll mind riding in a caboose."

FOURTEEN

As a straight out-and-out gamble, the calling of Miss Plato as a defense witness in the Melrose case has seldom been equaled.

Papa did not know what Miss Plato was going to testify to. She might hang Melrose as high as Haman.

Her disposition had caused the D.A.'s investigators to skip lightly over Miss Plato. If there was anybody in Acton kept themselves *to* themselves, it was Lillian B. Looking down her high New England nose, she said the town feud was none of her affair. Others, taking into account how far away her house was from the scene of the shooting, said it was impossible for her to have seen anything anyway. Which it was.

Having talked extensively with the lady, Papa knew better. She had seen something all right. Moreover he knew how, far removed though she was, she had been yet one more eyewitness. *What* she had seen, or how much, he had no idea at all. For at that crucial point Miss Plato had said, "If I am called and sworn as a witness, I will testify as to what I saw. Otherwise it's mere gossip. I never gossip."

No charm, no persuasion on the part of Earl Rogers could

move her. Nor at the time of their interview did he press her in the interests of truth and justice, which just might be in Broome's favor.

Now things were different.

With a case he judged to be already lost he had to take chances. Under a pile-driving, acrimonious, and able cross-examination by old McComas, Melrose had grown aggressive and showed a quick violent temper and old Mac, a good judge of juries, sat down sweating but with a triumphant leer at the young defense counsel.

Early that night after Bill Jory left, Rogers had seen Melrose in the jail. "It's your neck I'm gambling with," he told the defendant. "You know what she may have seen better than I do. I'd like your permission to call her."

Rosy told me afterwards he felt so embarrassed over acting like a spoiled kid on the witness stand that he wasn't arguing about anything.

But Papa knew it was a ticklish business and he didn't pretend to go to sleep at all that night while Jory by horse and buggy and caboose brought *somebody's* star witness to the rescue.

A surprise witness.

Miss Plato was that all right.

In criminal cases it was customary to put the defendant on as the last witness in his own trial. Thus the surprise began when Mr. Rogers, having asked Melrose the last few questions of rebuttal, did not rest his case.

Instead he said, "Miss Lillian B. Plato, please."

The courtroom hummed and in the press row I could hear the reporters demanding of each other, "Who the hell is she? What's she going to testify to? Nobody can be named Lillian B. *Plato—*"

But she was.

She took the stand with self-possession, settled her skirts, and waited for school to begin. A small, spare spinster with an eagle eye, a firm chin, and that air of speaking only to God, which in New England is not the exclusive prerogative of the Cabots.

In spite of this, Earl Rogers went to work with a look of shining relief such as comes to a man lost in the desert when he spots an oasis. Nobody but Rogers knew how fantastic such of her story as he already knew was going to sound to a jury. The first thing before him was to make that plausible.

Q. (by Mr. Rogers) Miss Plato, when you and your mother came to California, you brought with you a family spyglass—a small telescope.

A. Yes.

Q. Often you looked through it at the heavens, the stars, the scenery—

A. No.

Q. You didn't look—

A. Not often. Teaching school leaves little time for sitting around looking at stars through a spyglass.

Mr. Rogers smiled at her affectionately. *My dream girl*, the smile said to one and all. This was a gamble too. Miss Plato might keep him after school.

Q. I quite see that. Now on this particular day to which we have reference, you had come home for lunch, you were on your front porch were you not—

All five feet of the lady had stiffened. "Young man," said Miss Plato as though addressing a backward member of the fourth grade, "don't you try to tell me what I did. Nor what I saw. I will tell you. I'm the witness."

To the sound of a gleeful snort from McComas, Mr. Rogers backed off. But he kept his friendliest air as he said, "What I meant, Miss Plato, what I was intending to question you about was this. You had always been in the habit of from time to time looking through this telescope, I merely wanted to indicate to you that what the jury wants to hear is what you saw on this day at a certain noontime—"

"If," said Miss Plato, "you will be quiet and allow me to do the talking we will progress faster. Kindly remember I was educated in Boston. I know a thing or two about lawyers. I am not to be led nor intimidated, I promise you."

"Miss Plato," said Earl Rogers, "you see that chair right there at the counsel table? I beg your pardon, and I am going over now and sit in it. You know as well as I do that *I* don't know what you saw through your spyglass, you have refused to tell me. I just want you to tell the jury about it in your own way. Will you do that, please, Miss Plato?"

Completely unmollified, Miss Plato said, "I was in the house when I heard a great lot of shouting and swearing down at the end of the street. I ran to the corner where I keep my spyglass and went out carrying it to see what was happening."

Militantly nonpartisan, she went off like a string of fire-crackers exploding. Minute by minute Rogers and Melrose began to relax.

The big gamble had paid off.

The testimony of Miss Lillian B. Plato, who through her spyglass had been the nearest eyewitness of them all, corroborated Melrose.

When McComas got up to cross-examine her, he moved with extreme caution. "Why," he ventured, "have you never told this extraordinary story before?"

She snapped his head off. "Minnie Boucher got transferred for seeing too much and telling the truth about it," she said. "Unless I was forced under oath I did not wish the same fate to befall me."

The defense chief counsel brought the little telescope into court and asked the jury to look through it. Then to verify the facts, he also produced Mrs. Daniel Webster Plato.

The old lady had an ear trumpet about the size of an army bugle, and Rogers pitched his voice to carry. "Now when your daughter came in to lunch on the day of the shooting," he said, "she ran to you and asked where Uncle Higgenson's spyglass was, didn't she?"

Trumpet to ear, she regarded him suspiciously for a long moment and then said, "My daughter's always been a good girl."

After considerable of this, Rogers let her go and McComas approached her fearfully. "You didn't see anything, did you?" he bellowed.

The old lady gave him a knowing smirk. "Oh yes I did," she said.

This rocked him, but Mac knew he was in for it. Nothing to do but ask her, "What did you see?"

"I saw the Grand Canyon," Mrs. Plato said, "and if I hadn't with my own eyes I'd never have believed it."

I still say waiting while the jury is out in a murder case is the concentrated essence of suspense. Tantamount to the torments of Tantalus.

In the Melrose case we had four dreadful days and three bottomless infernal nights. How right Papa had been that without Lillian B.'s testimony the case had been lost was borne out when our first leak out of the jury room showed the first ballot eight to four, which way the bailiff didn't know for sure.

Daytimes he spent in the courthouse. We must have walked

the distance from Los Angeles to San Francisco up and down
those dim gray corridors. Rogers' front was high-spirited and
confident while he talked to the crowd of reporters who followed him, only Jory and I knew the back of his coat was wet
as though he'd been in a Turkish bath. We left a sawdust trail
of Bull Durham, I kept sacks in my pocket and handed them
to him like an umpire with new balls.

"He has to *eat*," Harry Carr would say, then I'd yank his
sleeve and say, "Papa, I'm hungry," and with bursts of
apology he'd race us all to the Hollenbeck or Al Levy's, order
prodigious and epicurean meals, of which he could not swallow a bite.

Often he went to the jailhouse to reassure Melrose.

"I don't want him to worry about me," Rosy said. "I'm all
right," and then I remember he said with an admiring smile,
"He sure wouldn't like to lose, would he?"

At 10 P.M. the deputies took the jury to their hotel and
locked them up. Nothing could possibly happen until morning. If we hadn't dragged him home I swear he would have
spent the night under their windows, trying hypnosis, telepa-
thy, or the methods of Madame Blavatsky, whom he was studying at the time. With his imagination, he lived through all
the Infernos Dante invented, and added some of his own. His
closing argument, he said restlessly, had been puerile, without
rhyme, reason, authority, or persuasion. His cross-examinations
of August Schultz and Mrs. Broome had been *embarrassing*.
He ought to be disbarred for his failure to show how fast a man
could be getting a shotgun into action, for he should have
brought in Wells, Fargo guards. . . . He may have slept
some in those long, dark days and nights. I never saw him.

People were not as weight-conscious then, the only scales
in existence were too big for house use. As Bill Jory said, Papa
got thinner before our eyes. Flesh burned off him in a furnace
of anxiety and that sense of guilt with which all the Irish are
cursed. If Melrose paid the death penalty it would be Earl
Rogers' fault and failure.

By the time that telepathic stir beat the court bailiffs to
tell us the jury was ready to come in, at the moment the foreman stood up with the verdict in his hand, he had his head up,
his face grave and confident still, but he was haggard to the
bone.

This time it was neither Guilty nor Not Guilty.

It was a hung jury.

Nine to three. With, the foreman told the judge, no possibility of agreement. Soon we knew it had been nine for acquittal, three for conviction.

A great moral victory for Earl Rogers.

In his story Harry Carr said, "Rogers won again, with a hung jury in a case where the betting on Spring Street was 100 to 1 for conviction." Also Carr and most of the other reporters predicted that now the district attorney would doubtless dismiss the charge. Nine to three was not encouragement to spend the taxpayers' money on another costly trial.

Here we ran again into Captain Fredericks' adamantine political conscience.

He would, he said, continue to try W. H. Melrose for the slaying of William Broome until a jury either convicted or acquitted him. And Rosy, now out on bail, issued warnings to everybody never to support anybody for district attorney.

Everybody said Rogers would win the next one. Easy, they said. Oh sure. And Papa himself always said the greener the grave the less chance of hanging anybody for the murder.

All very well. *I* knew Papa took his hung jury as a catastrophic defeat.

He had begun to regard himself as invulnerable.

He picked up the challenge with a burning curiosity and the clinical enthusiasm of a chemist working in the laboratory to determine the elements in some stuff or substance. Literally, he was possessed to find out why he, Earl Rogers, having convinced nine men that Melrose was innocent, had failed to remove the reasonable doubt from the minds of three others.

All three of the jurors who had voted Guilty had soon told him their reasons. And one of them spent a good deal of time in our office, all I can recall about him is an ever-present cheerful grin and very large ears.

One objection they had all shared. From the day he got to town, they felt, Melrose had been looking for trouble. He was the one who started the whole thing. Until his arrival, Acton had been a nice peaceful place to live.

Some of the other reasons Papa mined out were strange, unexpected, and intensely personal.

The little man with the big ears, for instance, detested schoolteachers. "I had a teacher in the fourth grade just like that Miss Plato. I wouldn't believe one of them if I saw it with my own eyes. The lies they tell kids are something awful."

Another man felt that most Southerners had no conception of the truth. Melrose's accent had been, for him, the very voice of untruth. Besides, his father had been in the Civil War and

he had always said Southerners were fire-eaters. They liked
shooting, his father had said. They weren't ever content to
settle down and *work*.

The third man with a reasonable conviction that Melrose
was guilty owned a bicycle shop. For some reason this made
him in his own mind an authority on anything mechanical,
including firearms. Broome couldn't have done with a shotgun
what Melrose said he did in that length of time. On this, he
knew-it-all and was immovable.

The ghost of Broome's dog had arisen. One of the three was
a member of the Society for the Prevention of Cruelty to
Animals. To shoot a poor defenseless animal, he said, is worse
than murder. A pit bull, Earl Rogers said, a bull terrier trained
to fight other dogs in the pit, that was the kind of dog Mr.
Broome had. A dangerous animal. When Melrose tried to save
the dog he loved, this ferocious fighting dog clamped his
teeth into Melrose's leg. The juror kept on shaking his head.
A man who would shoot a poor innocent dog, he said, would
not hesitate to commit murder.

All of them were proud of their stamina. Lesser men would
have been worn down, wanted to go home, given in to the
majority, been brow-beaten by the opposition. When Earl
Rogers got in the leader of the Not Guilty forces it was plain
that his conviction that anybody who didn't agree with him
must be either a fool or a taker of bribes had caused the Guilty
minority to dig in their heels.

Out of these three Melrose jurors with whom he actually
spent many hours, transcripts of testimony open before them,
grew Earl Rogers' obsession with picking a jury. His build-up
of an investigative force. It took him three months to get
the jury in the Calhoun case in San Francisco. Years later he
told law classes at the University of Southern California that
often a criminal case was already won or lost when the twelve
jurors sat in the box. "If I had known a juror in the Melrose
trial was an active working member of the S.P.C.A.," he said,
"I would have refused to accept him, challenged him if necessary, and probably have avoided a hung jury. Always under
all circumstances learn all you can about a jury panel and find
out everything you can after the men are in the box. I've made
a closing argument to one juror on one point when I knew a
deep-seated prejudice had set him against me whether he himself knew it or not." This was true, often he'd say to me,
"*Nora, watch the third man from the right in the back row.*"

After a third failure to get a verdict, this last disagreement, eleven to one for acquittal, everybody including Melrose regarded the district attorney's dismissal of the murder charge against him as a victory. Everybody but Earl Rogers. To him, all three hung juries were searing personal defeats.

By the third trial I knew Rosy believed himself. This happens a lot, I saw it with Bruno Richard Hauptmann in the Lindbergh kidnaping case many years later. But—I wasn't quite sure whether I believed Rosy or not. I wasn't sure like I'd been about Boyd.

Once when Papa was in the depth of black despair I said, "Maybe you could not convince a jury he was innocent because he isn't."

"What's that got to do with it?" Papa blazed at me. "He's our *client*. I might have done so badly they'd have hung him. He had a right to a better defense."

Clearly, Papa *liked* Melrose. So did I, for that matter. If you knew him you could hardly help it, he was cheerful and courageous, he had what they call a love of life, he didn't believe that God had already predestined most of the human race to hell. In his own mind, Papa had fixed up some scales of justice on which *he* weighed that a man like Melrose should not be put to death for shooting a cumberer of the earth like the dour-faced Broome.

I tried the equivalent of "You can't win them all," to which he said, "Oh yes you can. You have to, if your mistake costs a man his life."

Finding himself vulnerable when he had just about decided he wasn't brought upon him an exaggerated fear that someday somehow a man would go to the gallows because Earl Rogers had not thought of some way to get him off. Used some gift to convince a jury that black was white.

> *If you can meet with Triumph and Disaster*
> *And treat those two impostors just the same—*

Between us, we had to try to learn that.

My hour was upon me.

Sometimes it is impossible to know that a certain thing at a certain time, a certain word spoken by some one person, changed the course of life. Sometimes you are aware of it. Remember it with complete clarity. There! *There* began a new cycle of existence. *Here* I came to the crossroads and somebody told me what lay ahead and which road I must take.

I am so sure of it now that I cannot really tell whether I

knew it that afternoon when Pearl Morton spoke to me or not.

I think I did.

FIFTEEN

Papa disappeared for a week.

We were in a *state*, the case of the three cops was coming up.

As a rule Papa didn't like cops. This time, Murphy, Cowan, and Hawley were the underdogs, victims of a ruthless exposé of the police department by a newspaper out to get circulation. If ever men's lives and livelihood were at stake, theirs were.

The Los Angeles *Examiner* reporters, our opponents in spades, seldom took their eyes off Earl Rogers about then. They must have blinked or he was too smart for them. He'd shaken them somehow. This was probably a good thing for us. In an exposé by a newspaper, everybody is fair game.

Unfortunately, Bill Jory, Bull Durham, our office staff, and the Bureau of Missing Persons, who was on our side this time on account of we were defending members of the force, had also lost him.

It was terrible. I thought he might at least have let me know so I wouldn't wake up in the night and imagine him shot dead, in a ditch or smashed up under a car.

To my amazement when they did find him, they all looked dark and discouraged. "He won't come," Jory said briefly.

"Why won't he?" I said. "Is something the matter with him? Is he sick?"

"He's all right in a way," Bill Jory said, "he just plain won't come. He says he is resting. He says all work and no play will not leave any footprints on the sands of time. He just sits there and laughs at me."

"He has to be in *court*," I said. "They'll have his blood if he isn't. This all sounds crazy to me." I had been alone a good deal at our hotel, I did not want my aunts to know we couldn't find Papa, they would say things and it wasn't any of their business any way that I could see, but pretty soon I think I was getting scared myself. I said, "Where *is* he, I want to see him."

Reluctantly, Jory said, "Well, he is visiting a friend of his. A—a woman named Mrs. Pearl Morton. He's been there all the time, only she gave us the big run-around. She says he needs rest. I don't know. I don't know what to do and that's the truth."

"I know her," I said, and Bill Jory said, "No you don't," and I said, "Yes I do too. She has red hair and she was at the Boyd case and my grandfather's funeral. Why couldn't you and Bull and maybe Hawley just pick Papa up and carry him home if he is sick or acting so foolish?"

"No!" Bill Jory said.

A funny thing. Nobody would ever put a *hand* on Papa. No matter *what*. I do not know exactly why, they just never would. When it would really have simplified things and protected him—anyway, they wouldn't.

"Well then," I said, "I will have to come and ask him," and like a flash Jory said, "You can't," and I said, "What is the matter with you, Jory? Of course I can and I am going to," and finally he said, "All right. Only I will have to call Pearl first and tell her."

We drove there in our automobile. I think it was a Duro. Many times thereafter I wished automobiles had never been invented or at least Papa had never learned to drive one or what he *called* driving one. He was absolutely the worst automobile driver who ever lived. However, that day I sat on the high front seat beside Bill Jory holding onto my hat and while I liked horses when people stopped to stare I felt proud. On the curb *I* yelled *Get a horse,* when I was in the car I surveyed them like a queen.

Bill said, "Mrs. Morton is—she's all right, and a good friend to Mr. Rogers. Just the same it'd be better if you do not tell anybody you ever went down to her house, Shorty. For once do like I say, will you? It might be misunderstood—you wouldn't know what her place is—"

"Yes I would," I said, "it's a whorehouse."

Jory drove the car up on a curb and just missed a tree. He was so horror-stricken he forgot how to reverse. After he stared at me, white and speechless for a minute, I guess he realized I had no more idea what the words meant than if they were in Chinese, so he said, "You mustn't say such a thing as that, where did you hear such a thing as that anyway?"

I said, "Mrs. Morton and some young ladies that work for her came in a victoria to see the Fiesta Parade and Mama said to Papa there is your friend Pearl who runs that whorehouse—"

Above the car's hellish noise and stench while Jory was getting it backed off the curb and started again, he started trying to explain to me something which meant a great deal to him, as I could see. Otherwise, even to get Papa into court on Monday, nothing would have persuaded him to take me to Pearl's house. What he had to get over to me was that I mustn't be shocked about Papa being at Pearl Morton's. Men, he said, sitting straight behind the wheel and staring ahead, the ear on my side of his head bright red, went to Mrs. Morton's for *other reasons*.

Nowadays when girls start going steady at twelve, with the pregnancy rate in high schools what it is, it may be difficult to believe that a little girl raised in a criminal lawyer's office could be as ignorant as I was about sex. We had but one rape case in our office and that was the son of a newspaperman we knew. Even in the lowest criminal classes I had never heard of a sex maniac or seen or heard of what I later knew to be a homosexual. Literature hadn't reached that point where sex became as common as turnips and often as unappetizing.

My only head-on encounter with it I didn't know by name or nature, it was my darkest secret, wild horses couldn't have dragged it out of me.

I did not know what a whorehouse was, now that they no longer exist to any extent it seems to me Mrs. Morton's had things in its favor beyond the present methods, which have infiltrated society at all levels, ages, and places. The disease is now epidemic and has rotted a good deal of our moral fiber.

At the time that Bill Jory and I rode down the street that afternoon, I had no idea at all what he was talking about when he spoke of *other reasons*. Men, Bill said, got lonesome. They needed companionship, especially if their wives were not companions to them. No man ever went to Mrs. Morton's, Bill said, if his wife was a good companion to him. Sometimes, too, a man wanted a couple of laughs and wives did not usually give a man any laughs at all. One time he said he knew a young lady at Pearl's who was the funniest white woman he ever met. She should have been on the stage, he said. Papa had been real depressed over the Melrose hung juries and working too hard and Papa's wife as we both knew could not even laugh *at* a comedian on the Orpheum.

"Do they have free lunch at Mrs. Morton's," I said.

"Call it that," Bill Jory said. After a while he said, "Your old man has a friend who is a young lady named Dolly." This was the first time I heard of Dolly. "Your father is not a man who has to be thinking all the time about *women*. He attracts them like flies and he brushes them off the same way. He likes Dolly because she plays the piano and also she is a natural born comic at all times. All I mean is she makes Mr. Rogers laugh and that is very relaxing right now."

Whether or not it could be true that Papa went to Pearl's without that reason which Bill only succeeded in veiling from me in mystery, I don't know. I doubt it. I am sure that Jory either thought so or was trying hard to think so. Otherwise he would have felt guiltier than he did, which was already killing him and shows how much he loved Papa.

The house was on a street only a block long. By then most of the buildings were red brick. Mrs. Morton's was adobe flush with the street, the iron railings and little balconies were like New Orleans, the windows were closed and heavily curtained behind full-length black shutters.

"If he sees me," Bill Jory said, parking around the corner toward the plaza, "it will make him mad." We walked up to the doorway and he pulled a brass bell handle and kept walking up and down. The last I saw of his face it had such misery on it as I'd never seen gathered in one countenance.

In an afternoon dress of purple voile with satin stripes, Pearl Morton opened the door herself. A bertha of lace fell around her shoulders. I suppose she was a coarse, overblown woman with dyed hair. To me, she *felt* safe and warm and strong.

She looked at me and wrinkled up her whole face, then she let me in and shut the door and I was in a ground-floor hall, with wide black polished stairs going up from it, and it smelled beautiful. I could hear a piano. My aunt being the best piano teacher in town, I knew a good deal about music and sometimes I practiced myself. Whoever was playing had a strong clear left hand, the tune was gay and brilliant. Everything else seemed very quiet. Mrs. Morton kept on looking at me, then she shook her head and said, "Are you hungry?"

I thought it was peculiar Papa's lady friends always wanted to feed me. I said, "Not right now. Is my Papa here, if you please?"

Mrs. Morton gave a kind of exasperated grunt. "He's here," she said.

I said, "The thing is, everybody is getting nervous because the case is coming up and nobody has any idea what Papa is going to do. The *Examiner* is exposing everybody connected with the cops and—" I felt a burst of desperate urgency, I said, "I better get him back to the office right away, Mrs. Morton."

Mrs. Morton gave a quick snort and said, "All right. Come along."

Probably the big room that took up the whole front of the house was lush and vulgar and ostentatious. Certainly there were cut-glass and gold chandeliers, swinging and tinkling. The French windows were draped in red plush and there were big overstuffed chairs such as I had never seen before, and what seemed to me hundreds of little tables with gilt legs and glass or marble tops. There were two concert grand Steinway pianos, and on the walls full-length mirrors in magnificent carved gilt frames. I liked the way my feet sank into the thick red carpets. On the walls were huge paintings of rather fat ladies, some with a great many clothes on and some without any, all done in oils.

I thought it was a very rich and comfortable place.

I could understand why Papa would come here after what he had been used to.

A girl who seemed very thin in that room, and beside Mrs. Morton, was at the piano. Now, of all things, she was playing a march by Sousa. Papa loved Sousa.

Then I saw him.

It was Papa.

It was a complete stranger.

Dealing with someone you love and know as well as you do yourself who is not himself, and you cannot get through to him any more than if he thought he was Napoleon in another century speaking another language—this is a terrible thing. To me, it is the most terrible thing that can happen to you. There he is. You cannot communicate with him. If your life or his depended on it, you could not make him understand.

This was my first meeting with John Barleycorn.

The Noseless One.

He is the king of liars. He is the august companion with whom one walks also with the gods. He is likewise in league with the Noseless One. His ways lead to naked truth and death. He gives clear vision and muddy dreams. He is the Enemy. The teacher of life beyond what man is permitted to see. He is the red-handed killer who slays the flowers of the forest, our golden youth.

Papa needed a shave. He was blue-black, as I'd never seen him, crumpled and sodden and—*ill-kempt.* I knew if he had been to sleep at all it had not been true sleep. His face was all peaked and white, black circles around his eyes made them stand out. He was like fireworks, going off in all directions in dazzling pinwheels and towering rockets, then going *out*—black—black and stinking—smoldering, fizzling, giving out pitiful feeble sparks and then going dead again.

The worst was his eyes.

They looked at me as though I was his enemy.

Or he was mine.

No, I remember, as though *I* was his *enemy.*

I had seen men drunk. Never a woman, of course. In Chinatown, and down on Main Street, I had seen staggering men, or men in the gutter.

They were not like this.

Inside of me I could feel something trickling down and I could not tell whether I was bleeding—if I could cry out some of it would flow in just common tears, but I knew that I must not.

The girl saw me and stopped playing. We stared at each other, the way it was arranged over her shoulder I could see in a tall mirror set between golden pillars what she was staring at. In my middy blouse and pleated skirt and with my pigtails I looked to myself like Alice in Wonderland when she had nibbled on the wafer and got bigger and bigger and more awkward and out of place. "Off with her head," I said out loud, not meaning to, and Papa moved his hand quickly. Right away there was a new expression on his face. I do not know where he had been, nor what muddy dreams he'd had there, but when he came back and saw Nora-cum-Alice chewing her red hair ribbon in Pearl Morton's parlor, he got a—a *foxy* look. He was wily, he wasn't going to admit anything. He couldn't. Where we were or that it was strange I should be there or that he was drunk or that he knew Dolly.

Peering at me craftily, he said, "I know you. I know who sent you. Don't think for a minute you can deceive me."

I said, "Holy *cow*, we had better get back to the office right away. Or they are going to hang three policemen."

"Oh no they're not," he said, shaking a finger at me, "they wouldn't dare. Innocent policemen. They pay them slave wages and expect them to risk their lives guarding treasures of gold, bags of gold, they reap nothing—"

"Now everybody says you're scared," I told him.

He said, "This is a—a senseless canard. I know *you*. You're a tool in their hands—"

"Papa," I said, "will you please come home now? Please."

He blinked at me with hatred and pain and panic and such *love*.

The Noseless One.

"Yes," he said. "Yes—"

But he couldn't stand up. I said, "Just sit down a minute, Papa, and I will get somebody and we can help you into the automobile."

Dolly began to play again. I missed the top step and felt Pearl's hand under my arm, she said, "Are you going to be sick?"

I said I didn't think so. I said, "It's just—I mean—he won't *stay* like that, will he?"

I was thinking of a game we used to play called statues, where they whirled you around and you made a face and had to *stay* just the way you were when you stopped. Once I had got scared I'd be that way for always and I had to move and stop making a face, I couldn't bear it.

Pearl said, "He's just drunk." I could feel her jolt to a decision, she said, "Sit down there a minute, he'll be all right," and I was glad to sit down, my legs were as bad as Papa's, like the Scarecrow's in the Wizard of Oz. Mrs. Morton put me on a stiff teak chair against the wall and sank down herself on the stairs. Her face was furrowed and a queer color and I thought she was about as near howling as I was. Her purple skirts filled the staircase, her red head was violent against the polished ivory walls.

"I don't know if I'm doing right or wrong," she said. "*Men!* If there was anybody else—lots of kids a heap younger than you are have had to do worse things. Your Papa says you're awful smart. Well—if I'm wrong God'll forgive me I'm doing the best I know how."

I said, "Oh—do you believe in God?"

Pearl Morton looked at me in astonishment. "Certainly I

believe in God," she said. "What do you take me for? Now listen. Your father is a great man."

"I know that," I said.

"I know a lot about men," said the madame of the most famous sporting house in the great Southwest, "more'n they think I do. And about their wives. I know about your father, I know *him*, but also I know what other men say about him. You get that? I've got friends—well—people come here from Sacramento and Washington and New York. Big men. Men that run the state and—the country. Railroad men. I knew Senator White real well and—anyhow, most of the men that made this state. Just the other day a man came here from Washington. An old friend. He said to me, *There isn't anything Earl Rogers can't do—or be*."

I couldn't say anything. Somehow the wind had been knocked out of me and I was sitting there with my insides shaking, scared to death, and I didn't know why or of what. Pearl got up and came over and put her arms around me. She said, "We got to remember that. He said those very words. *There isn't anything Earl Rogers can't do or be if the drink don't get him*. I know that—he can be anything if he can stay away from the drink."

I said, "Then—what does he drink for? Doesn't he—know?"

"Oh—he knows," Pearl Morton said, "he won't admit it. I haven't got anything against drink if a man can handle it. Some can. Others—they can't touch it. Especially the Irish. I can't myself. In life it looks to me like everybody has got an enemy. Some it's one thing, some it's another. It's in themselves. That's what life is, doing the best you can against your enemy."

The Enemy was after Papa.

"I wish my grandfather hadn't died," I said.

Pearl Morton's breast heaved with the breath she took. She said, "So do I, baby. He was a saint, the Reverend Rogers was. I always said that—he was a saint. Drink—that's your Papa's enemy. I know him. I love him—like he was my own son. Drink's his enemy. There isn't anybody but you between him—and it. Oh—you can call on me, or Jory, or anybody and we'll do our best. You know that. Come right down to it though, on the level, there's nothing amounts to anything between him and it but you."

She looked at me and gave that funny grunt-snort.

"You're awful goddam *little*," she said.

"I am not," I said back.

SIXTEEN

I am not, I had said to Pearl Morton.

I am not so damn little, I meant.

What else could I say? From eight to thirteen, you cannot stand around letting grownup people tell you how too little you are. You cannot retort *You're so goddam big and what of it?* This does not meet the case. You *want* grownup people to be wise, trustworthy, all-powerful. To have *authority* over the universe around you. Somebody has to have.

The moment of nameless, organic suffering I had felt when I saw my father, the dire confusion that came from what Pearl Morton said, left me wobbly at the knees and in my brain, but I was not going to say so.

Somehow I went out and found Bill Jory and we went upstairs together. The shock of seeing me had sobered Papa, by the time we got back he had organized himself as chief counsel in his own defense.

Jack Barrymore used to say, "And Earl Rogers writes his own dialogue as he goes along." On this occasion he also created his own scenery and cast of characters. By this creative genius he now conveyed that we had met out in West Lake Park at a picnic, Dolly was the organ grinder and Madame Pearl had become Mrs. Swiss Family Robinson feeding us *tea* and cakes from her hoard. If you knew how to play this game, you could now also see the rest of the Swiss Robinson Family frolicking on the outskirts with the dogs. Papa and I had a lot of experience, he always made me practice *seeing* what we read—*Kim,* about my own age, with his lama on the Grand Trunk Road, or David Copperfield's first meeting with Aunt Betsey Trotwood or Huck Finn in the cave with Jim or Juliet coming out on the balcony and we loved it.

I must say I remember Bill Jory looking quite mad-hatterish as Mrs. Morton poured tea, and he finally dropped a teacup. That seemed to make Papa feel more kindly toward him and everything was better. Papa pushed back that lock of hair which came down in the middle of his forehead, and asked Dolly if she knew a song by Gilbert and Sullivan, "A

Policeman's Lot"—she knew the music and played it loud and free. Papa and I knew the words so we sang:

"When the enterprising burgler's not a burgling,
    When the cut-throat isn't occupied in crime,
He loves to hear the little brook a-gurgling,
    And listen to the merry village chime.
When the coster's finished jumping on his mother,
    He loves to lie a-basking in the sun;
Ah, take one consideration with another,
    A policeman's lot is not a happy one."

Bill Jory came in with a big boom-boom every once in a while, and it made Papa laugh until the tears ran down his face.

Then he said, "I have three policemen whose lot is not a happy one at the moment. It is time I returned to see about them." He stood up and put his hand on Bill's arm and we went downstairs all right. Of course we had an argument on the curb as to whether Papa was going to drive or not. In those days there were no driver's licenses, no speed limits, no traffic, no motorcycle cops. Finally we persuaded him to let Jory drive and they dropped me off and Jory took him to the Turkish baths.

I didn't expect him back that night but he came in rather late. We were living in the hotel while Mama was away again. I could tell he was very worried about my being at Pearl Morton's and seeing him there. In the evening he always put on a dressing gown. He had a lot of them, some were magnificent Chinese robes with dragons in gold that had been given him by the heads of Chinese tongs who were his clients. One was plaid like Sherlock Holmes's, my Aunt Blanche had friends in London and she'd ordered that for him at Christmas. The one I liked best was wine red velvet with black corded lapels, it's become common since but Papa's was the first I ever saw. He always had one and he put it on as soon as he came in and sat down in his own chair and began to go over some of the inquest testimony.

I sat on a big ottoman reading *Rebecca of Sunnybrook Farm*, I remember, because it seemed an odd choice, and rolled cigarettes for him. Sometimes the darn things would split and spill the tobacco, he pretended not to notice but it chagrined me, I kept practicing. A Bull Durham, brown paper cigarette would not stay lit, like modern ones do, you had to keep puffing, which I always did cheerfully when he was too concentrated to take it. Of course no ladies smoked in those days, only prostitutes and dance hall girls. Women were supposed to be superior to men, they had not yet come down to be their equals, so probably I was the first lady who did.

Without looking up, Papa said, "What did Mrs. Morton say to you?"

Well—there we were. I'd expected it.

We had a very definite understanding about *the truth*.

We lived a good deal in a world of books peopled by characters from them. For entertainments we had the stage from time to time and the great stories and music we went to hear in a concert hall or opera house or made ourselves, though by then we had a phonograph and a few records available to us. Our own minds were active, our imaginations were kept keyed up, Papa was pleased when I began to show a small flair for storytelling. I had already sold my first short story for one dollar. The Los Angeles *Times* ran a page in their Sunday magazine for young people. At nine I had written a tale about my grandfather and some watermelons (that's all I remember) and Papa was proud as Punch. This had brought us to the need for clarifying the difference between truth, storytelling, and facts.

Truth and facts were not always the same thing, Papa said. The same truth was not always visible to everybody at the same time. Or, he said, sometimes your heart acknowledged a truth which your mind refused to accept or admit. For instance, Papa said, when your grandfather was a little boy it was a *truth* that man could fly, but it was not a fact until the other day when two men named Wright did fly at a place called Kitty Hawk. Shakespeare's plays were true wisdom and humanity far beyond what most people knew, Hamlet however was not a fact, he was only a prototype of man's own tragic indecisions. The telling of stories was truth, not only permissible but divine. On the other hand, if a fact was asked for or required, or anything stated as a fact, it was not permitted to distort, invent, increase, reassemble, equivocate, or deny in relating it or answering about it.

Truth—fact—storytelling—these must be labeled. This was the Law of the Jungle.

Therefore, a choice presented itself to me when Papa said, "What did Mrs. Morton say to you?"

I could refuse to answer as provided in the Fifth Amendment of the Constitution, in Papa's opinion a cowardly confession of something rotten in Denmark.

Or I could state the facts plainly.

Or I was allowed to say that I couldn't talk about it because it involved somebody else.

I chose the last. "I don't know if she meant me to tell you," I said.

"Then respect her wishes, of course," Papa said.

I sat there, trying to think. By now, I had complete confidence and belief in what Mrs. Morton had said. I knew she was a woman wise in the ways of men, and I couldn't bear to take the chance of causing any break in her friendship for Papa, or *hurting* her. I kept remembering her face when she told me he always sent her a Christmas present. *Books,* she said, *imagine!*

Nevertheless, I was in desperate need of advice. Even if my mother had been there she wouldn't have been any use. I realized now that this could be a reason she made terrible scenes and wept and howled and threatened and got them into such tangles of emotions, and I knew all of that was useless. My grandfather was dead. My aunts and my grandmother—I thought of them as too *cold* and righteous and intellectual to understand, though I think now I was wrong about that. Naturally I couldn't discuss Papa's weakness, his enemy, with any of the staff except Bill Jory and the thought that Luther Brown was right about this, that he knew about it, made me froth. Not until we got to San Francisco and Jack London came into my life did I find anyone with whom I could talk about Papa.

So I thought the best thing was to tell him what Pearl Morton had said and let him decide.

"She thinks you ought not to drink so much," I said.

His face is in front of me now, clear as a Van Dyke portrait. At the Turkish baths he'd been steamed, massaged, had hot towels and ice packs, a shave and a hair trim, the rebellious locks groomed into place. The skin under his eyes was faintly black, and his cheekbones stood out too much, which always made my heart ache, I don't know why. I must have dealt him a blow, I know that now, for the elegant mask behind which he always kept his own secret was off, the tremendous pride and emotional violence, the passionate dislike of personal intimacies or prying eyes of others into the deep things about himself throbbed unconcealed for a little time.

At last he got himself under control and his eyes began to twinkle. He said, "Does she indeed. She's a worrier, Madame Morton. It's her maternal instinct. By the way, better not mention to the ladies of your family that you have met her. Forgetting as they do that according to their own teachings the harlots go into the kingdom ahead of the whited sepulchers they tolerate without protest, they might have difficulty recognizing what a kind and motherly soul Mrs. Morton is. A worrier, though."

"Sometimes anybody has to worry," I said, "like when you drive the car."

"What is this conspiracy about my driving?" he said furiously. "I never heard such nonsense."

"You can't, Papa," I said, "you get to thinking about something else and an automobile is not like a horse that has sense enough itself not to run into things. So I do have to worry."

"Anxiety is as catching as measles," Papa said. "Avoid it if you can. To get back to Mrs. Morton's worry. Let us put it this way. I was not born with a calm nature. At times I find it impossible to turn off my mind, to shake loose a problem so that I can come back refreshed, with a new view of it, a proper perspective."

"Probably you're worrying about it," I said.

"Don't be impertinent, Nora," he barked at me.

Outraged, I yelled, "Holy cow, who is impertinent? If I do not see the difference between staying awake all night with your mind spinning like a top and *worrying* like Mrs. Morton and I do, is that impertinence?"

"Too close for comfort," Papa said.

"You started it," I said, "you asked me. It's not fair if you say what do I think or what did she say and then get mad and bark at me."

I puffed away at a brown cigarette I was keeping lighted for him until he said, "Come here, Nora." I went, and he put his arm around me. In that moment it came into me that there was something deep inside him that was miserable and I knew it was shame. Children always recognize shame. It is the first unhappiness they know, they know that shame is the worst thing there is. They would rather be beaten than humiliated. Papa said, "I beg your pardon, Nora. My nerves are not at the moment what they should be, far otherwise. My advice to you is, don't worry yet. A man doesn't become anything all at once. It takes time. True, when I cannot relax, when I cannot let go of my concerns about my clients, when I am too exhausted to rest, I sometimes fill the Cup that clears today of past regrets and future fears. It's an undignified process. Nothing to disturb us, I believe. If there is ever any danger I promise to tell you. Then you can start worrying."

Papa had always told me the truth. For the first time. I did not believe him. Later Jack London explained to me that John Barleycorn never lets the most honest man tell the truth. Or even know it. His spell on a man makes him believe his own lies, for if that man sees the danger he will recognize John Barleycorn as the Noseless One, instead of being mesmerized to think of him as the prince who makes dreams come true.

I do not believe you can ever make anyone who really loves you believe a lie that they ought not to believe. Truth is too strong for such a lie. Jack London said this was true, Charmian, his wife, he said, had never believed him when he told her there was no danger to him in alcohol.

"Everything all right now?" Papa said.

"I guess so," I said. Down in the pit of my stomach there was fear, like a tuning fork, like a violin string, it would always be there and it would always vibrate, no matter how far apart we were. From then on.

Some of the men from the office came in and Papa did one of those fantastic comebacks and swept all before him. Maybe he had some apprehension that they disapproved of his being gone so long at such a crucial time. He loathed being disapproved of. He needed approval a great deal. So he turned on the charm and his intense and minute command of this situation. Within a few minutes we all knew that he was fully aware of every small detail of the vital case of the three cops. Wherever he had been he hadn't forgotten any of it.

"Papa," I said, "these men are not charged with murder. It says here it is manslaughter. Just what is the difference?" I still thought then I was, of course, going to be a lawyer and so I asked questions as we went along.

My father said, "Murphy and Cowan and Hawley went to make an arrest in the regular line of duty. They had never seen the two men or so much as heard of them until they were ordered to bring them in. There could have been no malice aforethought, and while premeditation need take only seconds it wasn't present here. Without premeditation, it cannot be murder. Lack of judgment, perhaps, overzealousness in the execution of their duty possibly. This makes it manslaughter at the worst. As we said a short time ago, a policeman's lot is not a happy one." His eyes were very bright blue now, he was sparkling with good nature and enjoyment of life, it was

wonderful but at the same time the swing was so great from
the man I'd seen in the chair at Mrs. Morton's that I found
it painful to see and I thought if it was painful for me what
must it be for him? Like Doctor Jekyll and Mr. Hyde almost.
He was watching me and he said with glee, "Nora, there is
a theme song for this trial. Especially written as a theme for
us by Gilbert and Sullivan. Play it, Nora."

Of course I had had piano lessons from my Aunty Blanche
from the day I was born, so I went over to the big black
Steinway in the corner of our suite's drawing room and
began to play it. With great gusto, Papa led the singing and
Jory came in again with the boom-boom and somebody had
a nice tenor:

> "When the felon's not engaged in his employment,
>   Or maturing his felonious little plans,
> His capacity for innocent enjoyment,
>   Is just as great as any honest man's.
> Our feelings we with difficulty smother,
>   When constabulary duty's to be done,
> Ah, take one consideration with another,
>   A policeman's lot is not a happy one."

By this time we were all uproarious, following Papa like
a lot of kids with a pied piper and the words got funnier and
funnier and we all picked them up and hollered them so that
if it had been anybody else the house dicks would have had
something to say about it.

"All right," he said finally, "we have three policemen whose
lot is by no means a happy one. Innocent victims is what they
are. However, we'll see to that. Thank you, Nora."

"I didn't play it nearly as well as Dolly," I said.

Papa gave me an odd glance under lifted eyebrows. Afterwards I wondered if it was right then he got the idea that
it would be pleasant to have Dolly come and live with us as
my governess and piano coach, which was what she was
listed as on the hotel register. Dolly may have left much to
be desired, but as Pearl Morton said, she was better for Papa
than some other people. I knew of course that he did it partly
in some bitter retaliation against my mother.

In bed that night I thought a lot about my grandfather
and I found that my head was still full of all that he had
taught me and I wished very much that I could still pray.

Neither then nor at any time later did it occur to me to
criticize Papa. I do not exactly understand why this was true.

Just that it was. A battle was joined and I was on his side,
that was all there was to it.

Whether he liked it or not.

Ask, Grandpa used to tell me. *Never be afraid to cry loudly
for help. Your position will be defended.*

I could hear him say with a big smile, *Look unto me and
be ye saved*, and, he would add, *Legions of angels will be
about you, your guardian angel will never leave you.*

Of course I knew as Papa said that all that was old-
fashioned bric-a-brac and hogwash. A myth. Read it in the
Bible or read it in Bulfinch's mythology or *Grimm's Fairy
Tales*, Papa said, you'll find it more or less the same old
story. Man-made superstitions. Idols of one sort or another.
No intelligent man ever believed any of this, it had been
designed from time immemorial to keep humanity in some
sort of order. As the Ten Commandments had been a set of
regulations to control the health and conduct of the Jews so
that Moses could get them safely up out of Egypt. If he
wanted to surround it with burning bushes and tablets of
stone and voices, why not? That was good sound drama.

Only—it had been comforting.

While I had been fresh as paint with Mrs. Morton and
would go on being, alone in bed I felt small, to myself.

Then I remembered something else my grandfather had
quoted when he was telling me stories of his flock down in
Tombstone and Globe. *Life isn't in holding a good hand*, he
said with a twinkle, *but in playing a poor hand well.*

I went to sleep after a while thinking about that.

SEVENTEEN

The Case of the Three Cops was actually the greatest circulation war up to the St. Valentine's Day massacre in
Chicago.

In it, with the appearance of acrobats and a chambermaid
named Adell Milk, Earl Rogers reached the peak of what any
judge would allow in the way of courtroom farce. He also

introduced ballistics as a science for the first time in any court in the United States.

There had been cases in which sheriffs and officers and detectives were allowed to give opinions as to weapons and bullets. But as to photographs, scientific experts trained in the German schools and by the Army, I find nothing prior to the appearance of Jesse Hawley in Judge Chambers' court in 1904. J. Edgar Hoover, with whom I've often discussed these early *firsts* of my father's, says the FBI has no record of actual testimony prior to that date.

The case depended on who fired the bullets found in the doorjamb. My most exciting personal recollection of The Affair is taking my turn with Papa and Harry Carr of the *Times* shooting bullets into sofa pillows under the bespectacled eye of the young man just back from Germany.

Like many another, this case was blown out of all individual meaning, importance, or proportion by circumstances, time, and place and was used as An Incident to start a shooting war.

Regard, for example, these headlines.

Same day. Same year. Same edition. Same trial.

The Los Angeles *Examiner*
COPS KILL TWO IN COLD BLOOD

The Los Angeles *Times*
CRIMINALS OPENED FIRE ON OFFICERS

The *Examiner*
WITNESS TELLS HOW POLICE ASSASSINS WAITED IN AMBUSH

The *Times*
WITNESS ADMITS BEING IN PAY OF HEARST YELLOW JOURNALISM

This crime, which two giants of journalism, General Harrison Gray Otis and William Randolph Hearst, used in a death struggle for power, circulation, advertising, and future real estate and political values, opened with routine paragraphs on page 17. Three cops had shot and killed a couple of cheap crooks, wanted in Illinois, who resisted arrest. Mere gunfire wasn't enough in those days to make the front page.

Time, place, and circumstances were as follows:

The *Times* and General Harrison Gray Otis, its owner-publisher, had been running Los Angeles and Southern California without interference for some time and proposed to continue.

The General's military title was on the level, he was an authentic fire-eater. A delegate to nominate Abraham Lincoln for the presidency, at the first call for volunteers in the Civil War he had enlisted as a private in the 12th Ohio and was mustered out a colonel after being wounded at Antietam. Appointed brigadier by President McKinley, he commanded the First Brigade, First Division, VI Army Corps of the U.S. Expeditionary Force in the Spanish-American outbreak and "for heroism in battle" was made a major general. From all I've ever heard, he rated it.

An unforgettable character, the General. One day I was sitting on the curb in front of our office building with two of my pals, one of whom later became a great gambler and the other a famous fight referee. At that time they sold newspapers on our corner and across in front of the *Times*. General Otis came striding down the steps of the *Times* building, which I thought of myself as a gray granite horror, but the General loved it and when the McNamaras dynamited it, his heart was broken. (Papa saw that, too, but it is another story and comes later.) Today his descendants, the famous Chandlers, still own and publish the *Times* and have magnificent new buildings that take up whole city blocks.

As he swung down the steps that day with his pointed silver goatee, his slouch army hat, and a cane which he whipped around like a sword, to me General Otis was Sherman and Grant and Robert E. Lee rolled into one. He saw the three of us sitting there, he stopped and pointed his cane at me and said, "Why aren't you in school, young lady?" and I said, "My father doesn't believe in formal education, he says it rots more good brains than opium." At that, he grunted and said, "Harry Carr says your father's a genius. You tell him I said it's a fine line, a very fine line." I didn't know what he meant and when I told Papa he was furious. He said, "Why, that chin-whiskered old Yankee billy goat!"

The General and his newspaper ran the City of the Angels like it was his brigade until out of the north one day rode young William Randolph Hearst, whose newspaper career was soaring and who was said by some to have started the Spanish-American War by his new and sensational type of headline yellow journalism.

In those days San Franciscans, of whom Hearst was one,

regarded anything south of the Tehachapi as fit for nothing but rattlesnakes and cactus. The vast 300,000-acre Hearst ranch, now a state park at San Simeon visited by millions of tourists each year, was in the center of the state, which may have given Hearst a better perspective. Certainly he foresaw the incredible future and proposed to annex Southern California then and there to the newspaper empire he was building across the country. At his suggestion that he'd like to start a paper in Los Angeles everybody who dared speak to him above a whisper told him not to. Big interests warned him. Otis was a fighting man strongly entrenched, absolutely ruthless, owned a piece of everything in sight, had enormous political pull and would defend his position to the death.

William Randolph Hearst was a hard man to scare. He, too, had weapons. Gold mines left him by his father, Senator George Hearst. The love California women felt for his mother, the great philanthropist Phoebe Apperson Hearst. And what nobody had quite realized then, his journalistic genius, which was turning the whole newspaper world upside down and inside out for better or for worse, for higher pay forever. Hotly, he believed that competition and controversy were the very soul of that Freedom of the Press upon which, he always said, all other freedoms were based. Once when I was sitting beside him at dinner in the castle at San Simeon, he told me in dramatic detail how Napoleon silenced the Paris press so that the French people knew little of the dangers and defeats of his campaigns. Any time, he said to me, you find all the papers in one town agreeing about things, our country is in danger.

No such day could ever dawn in Los Angeles once he'd started the *Examiner*. It was about to have two papers that for many years never agreed about anything.

However, after the first two years the *Examiner* was in desperate straits for advertising. Merchants and manufacturers felt a grave reluctance to defy the General's flat dictum: *anyone who advertised in the* Examiner *would be refused space in the* Times.

Only a big, *solid* circulation figure on the other side could overcome this loss.

The *Examiner* had to have big exclusives, special features —above all they needed a rip-roaring Exposé.

Now a first-class exposé is one that the other papers must follow and cover. It must be NEWS. Naturally, the paper that started it is always on top of the story and one jump ahead of everybody else on coverage. Readers of all papers are vitally interested and begin to buy the *Examiner* (or whatever the Exposer is) because it has more, earlier, and better news.

Later I took part in a good many Hearst-planned Exposés. Once we got rid of a corrupt mayor, once we cleaned up a scandalous situation in a county hospital. While the aim was and is circulation, an exposé isn't much good unless it has the solid foundation of an evil that ought to be exposed and corrected.

About the cleanup of the Los Angeles Police Department, which got under way when the cops mowed down Joe and Louis Choisser, it's a little hard to tell. I can however write the script of how it all began.

A Midwest sheriff wanted two men named Choisser. These crumbums had persuaded some gullible farmers to let them drive all the cattle to market, where Joe and Louis collected the dough for same, and instead of returning home with it, took off for greener fields and pastures new. Rumor had reached the sheriff that they were now holed up in a fleabag in Los Angeles. Would the police round them up before they spent all the profits and return 'em to Illinois, please?

Three plain-clothes dicks, Bert Cowan, Johnny Murphy, and J. J. Hawley, went to the Bruxton Hotel. In order to be sure of proper identification, they waited until father and son got back from a neighborhood bar and let them enter their own room. Then they knocked and said *Open Up Boys It's the Law*. After some more rat-a-tat-tat and language, the door yielded. Whereupon the hotel was startled by a barrage of gunfire. Running footsteps, screams, oaths filled the narrow hall. When the racket subsided the father, Joe, lay dead on the bedroom floor. Louis, riddled with bullets, was gasping his last in the corridor.

The morning papers, both *Times* and *Examiner*, covered it in the same words, give or take a few. That's the kind of story it was.

At this point, some bright-eyed bushy-tailed reporter, long alerted-to and past-master-of circulation getting, noted this lowdown, second-class, colorless story on page 17 and felt its possibilities. Drifting over to the city desk, he would say to the city editor, "You see this?" The city editor would read about two-men-wanted-shot-by-police and the reporter would say, "Pretty high-handed, wasn't it?" At this the city editor would nod solemnly and they would agree that members of the Los Angeles Police Department were behaving like Cossacks. Give 'em guns and they got trigger-happy and went around murdering citizens. This was a terrible thing, wasn't it? For the good of our fair city the police department needed to be exposed and cleaned up and the *Examiner* was just the boy who could do it.

To the uninitiated, the first move showed no outward signs of the *Examiner's* fine yellow hand. This was a brilliant piece of Journalism, it created *news*. If those sterling reporters Danny Green and Johnny Gray had a hand as producer and author they remained hidden behind the fake-marble pillars of the Bruxton Hotel lobby.

Here, unrigged and unrehearsed as a TV quiz show, a Vigilance Committee of public-spirited, civic-minded idealists held a kangaroo court. Aroused by the dread events of the Choisser slayings, one offered to act as coroner, others as judge and jury, while everyone who had seen, heard, or heard about anything appeared as a witness. The stars were unquestionably Arthur Clough and his wife Minnie.

Minnie's testimony was intimate and unusual.

Responding, Mrs. Clough stated, to the call of Nature, she had gone down the hall to the only toilet on the second floor, to find it full of policemen. Returning to their own room, she had complained bitterly to her husband Arthur, who was about to go out and beard these invaders when they heard banging and bombardment next door accompanied by profane language. Arthur had then climbed up and peeked through the transom. So from this box seat he had been privy to the dastardly and bloodthirsty actions of the cops. Unarmed, taken by surprise, the Choissers had been blasted with ruthless cruelty. Them cops, Arthur Clough said, might as well have been savages with tomahawks. All shots had come from the weapons of these tigers disguised as detectives and if defenseless citizens could be treated like that what was our great free country coming to anyhow? Mr. Clough, unaware even of the existence of Adell Milk—chambermaids had not been invited to take part in this indignation meeting—said he had seen it all and hanging was too good for them.

With grave dignity, the jury considered its verdict. They decided that Cowan, Murphy, and Hawley were Guilty of Murder.

Under a succinct headline which said:

POLICE SLAY UNARMED CITIZENS

the *Examiner* the next day devoted the entire front page and most of pages 3, 4, and 5 to the story, featuring the demands of the citizens' court. A *Police Shake Up. An Exposé of the Force.*

This the *Examiner* backed by signed affidavits from witnesses and kangaroo officials; by solemn photographs of the full proceedings of this citizens' tribunal, which had been forced to take the law into its own hands in a city terrorized by its own police; by symposiums of well-known ministers, alienists, clubwomen, opera stars, and crackpots. At getting such testimonials Hearst reporters were adept.

Were such monsters as Cowan, Murphy, and Hawley to be allowed to prowl our city without restraint behind police shields? Were innocent men, women, and little children to be at the mercy of licensed killers?

Editorially, in its finest prose, the *Examiner* asked these questions.

The *Times* didn't have a word of all this.

Its front page was confined to a board-of-education meeting, some railroad legislation in Sacramento, and a divorce case of little merit.

Five minutes after the *Examiner* hit the street that morning, nothing that happened at San Juan Hill could be compared to what was going on in the *Times* city room. Attacked by the General's cane and vocabulary, the *Times* could only rush out an extra accusing the *Examiner* of yellow journalism, which actually meant it was covering the other paper's story. The *Times* pleaded with the residents of Los Angeles not to be stampeded into condemning our noble boys in blue.

Within a week, the mayor, Chief of Police Elston, and District Attorney Fleming could no longer take the heat generated by the *Examiner*. In spite of the admonitions of big business, advertisers, respectable majorities, and most political bosses to stand firm, the three policemen were charged with manslaughter. Public frenzy could not be denied. As Mr. Hearst once said to me under somewhat similar circumstances, Nobody ever agrees with us but the public.

Immediately after all this started popping, we heard Harry Carr's well-known footsteps climbing our wooden stairs.

"Earl," he said, "the General would like a word with you."

EIGHTEEN

"Papa," I said, real loud.

He lifted his eyebrows. Too busy on some papers he and Harry Carr had brought back with them to answer me, this was our signal that I was free to go on with whatever I had in mind.

"Are we going to be on the cops' side?" I said. He nodded and I said, "But how can we?"

To Carr, Papa said, "There has to be another gun. And bullets." He looked at me, finally saw me, and said ferociously, "They're our clients."

On the table was our lunch, tamales made especially by an old Mexican woman whose son Papa had kept from being hung, golden corn husks wrapped around yellow corn meal and beef and ripe olives and raisins and a sauce so hot with home-dried chiles it made the tears run down my cheeks. Gasping from the peppers, I said, "How can we have cops for clients? You said they are perjurers and Simon Legrees and dumb flatfeet, didn't you?"

For a minute under a real frown, Papa's eyes were angry, I stared right back. I'd been taught to express my opinions, just because they differed from his was no reason to choke up. Through his thick glasses Harry Carr's eyes glowed with that warm curiosity that has to be part of the equipment of any great columnist, and Harry Carr, with B.L.T. (Bertram L. Taylor) of Chicago, was the first of those.

"A bad thing," Harry Carr said, "if people came to look on our police force as unreliable and dangerous. Your father must see a grave injustice isn't done both to the cops and to the public."

"He always does," I said, "but they can't hang them this time, it's only manslaughter. What I want to know is, why didn't they just go and arrest them? I don't see myself why they had to shoot them, do you?"

"These thieves were bent on shooting *them*," Harry Carr said.

"You don't believe that," I said. "What with? They didn't

have any guns. Just because people are cops they can't go around shooting anybody they want to, can they? That's a reign of terror worse than anything."

"Out of the mouths of babes," Harry Carr said, reluctantly.

"The crux of the case," Papa said, walking up and down in hot gloom, "I know the Choissers had to have a gun. The bullets they fired have to be somewhere. Get those mastodons up here and let's find out a little more."

"Anyhow," I said, "I don't like cops and neither do you."

"It is true I have not always appreciated policemen," my father said. "Does this mean I must keep a closed mind about them the rest of my life?"

I felt upset and dogged. I just kept staring back at him. Then he began to put it over the way a good night-club singer does a song with a cold audience. "Nora, do you know what they pay a policeman? Cowan and Murphy and Hawley get one hundred and fifty dollars a month. For this, we cannot expect to buy brains. I have been thinking for the first time from their side."

"Lookit the way they chased Farmer out of the alley for shooting craps with the circulation truck drivers. What kind of nonsense is that?" I said.

"They were protecting the drivers," Papa said with a grin, and it was true that Farmer, who later ran the first big gambling house in Las Vegas, was rough with the dice. "Honey, lay aside paltry prejudice. These are very hard-working men. And brave men."

"What is so brave about shooting down unarmed clods in a hotel bedroom?" I said.

Papa ignored me, he forgot me.

Now he was selling *himself*, being obsessed, taken over, filled to the brim with *their* side. I could see it happening. He said, low, moved, as it all dawned on him, "A routine part of their day's work is to take a chance of getting killed by some hopped-up Chink with a hatchet. Look at those rich baboons on Adams Street—just last month the mother of your friend Hortense out in her Pierce-Arrow and a real good cop named McCarthy, God rest him, with a wife and four kids gets plugged protecting some bright shining rocks she wears in her ears."

"Hortense is not a friend of mine," I said. "I just went to school with her."

"That proves what I have said about schools," Papa said. "These men walk a beat in rain and snow and darkest night—"

"That's postmen," I said, "not cops," and that made us both laugh, but he was too excited by now to notice it much.

"Unsung heroes twenty-four hours a day, a man is expected to go up against temptation, corruption, bribery, tong wars, and drunken Indians and they have to buy their own guns and uniforms to do it in, did you know that?" Papa said.

"Buying your own gun still doesn't give you a right to shoot people with it," I said sullenly.

"Imagine what this beautiful, bombastic, half-baked growing community would be like if for twenty-four hours there wasn't a cop in it?" Papa said. "A street lamp is worth two cops but if there weren't any cops walking the beat it wouldn't take our friends down in Mexican town or on Central Avenue long to shoot out all the lights, would it?" I knew he was *seeing* that happen, he went and stared down at the lamp-posts, and he was right, when the anarchists bombed the *Times* across the street our lights went out. "I must see what I can do about getting their salaries raised," Papa said, and to tell the truth when, under Charlie Sebastian, Papa was really the mayor for a little while, he did get them something. "Let me warn you of one thing, my girl," he said, "once the people see their law-enforcement bodies as worthless for whatever reason, once the crook or the gunman or the shill is giving the horselaugh to the cop, the criminals will take over," and in a way that was a prediction of what happened when an underworld of four million took over during Prohibition. Looking me in the eye as though he had never seen me before, as though I was some stranger on the Other Side, he said, "Can we let the men prepared to die for us be butchered to make a circulation holiday for William Randolph Hearst?"

"No," I said. "Only they were the ones who butchered somebody—"

I felt dizzy.

Once when he was defending Madame Cleo, the most famous fortune-teller in the state, for breaking some ordinance or other, she had said to him that his heart ruled his head. Well, I suppose in the beginning that mixture of emotion, intuition, imagination, hot blood, was the driving force. Once he knew where he was and what he was going to do, his head took over, cold as an iceberg.

He could turn on a dime and if you didn't keep up with him he fixed you with a cold, sea-gull eye. Ever since I knew anything, he had taught me cops were our primeval enemies. In courtrooms I had watched him make monkeys of sheriffs, policemen, district attorneys, and Governor Gage. Now he was *their* lawyer and I was expected to change my whole approach in ten seconds and probably the twinges in my stomach were what are called qualms.

Being the charge was manslaughter, the cops were out on bail, and they came up to our office when Papa sent for them and, my gosh, they were big, they filled it like a herd of elephants.

Cowan did the talking as Earl Rogers began digging, digging, digging on sounds—times—distances—and what had happened immediately after the shooting. Who had searched for guns and bullets and how hard had they done it? Well, they weren't as dumb as I had expected. Not like Papa or Harry Carr, but common-sensible-smart like Bill Jory. By reaction or osmosis I saw the truth of my father's whole philosophy. Once you knew people and had heard their side from them you understood why they had done what they had done. Often people did not look like villains when you knew them. The *Examiner* was howling about desperadoes in uniform, cold-blooded assassins, bloodthirsty morons. When you were looking at J. J. Hawley sitting there uncomfortably on a black leather couch, showing you pictures of his three little girls, a big simple guy, *worried* to death—*This'll bust me*, he kept saying, *either way it'll bust me and I don't know what'll happen to my kids;* when you heard him with a vocabulary of about three hundred words trying to explain it all to Mr. Rogers, he didn't seem like a cossack.

You cannot send even such a man as Mootry to the gallows on the word of a policeman.

Then Papa had been on Mootry's side.

He had felt sorry for Mootry, much as he despised him, because he said he had been spawned in hell and grown under a rock and society had no right to let a man grow under a rock and then condemn him because he came out crippled, with a brain as flat as a snake's. Men driven beyond the breaking point, the man who cannot fight because he has no words and no character—the marred pot again.

Now he saw these big cops as the underdogs.

Justice was never enough for Papa.

"I do not have the judicial mind," he said once to Judge Benjamin Bledsoe, one of the greatest jurists this country ever produced. "I have the trial mind. The quality of mercy is not strained," he told Ben Bledsoe, and the judge said, "But without justice even mercy becomes a hollow mockery."

NINETEEN

Early in the case, which by that time was kicking up a hullabaloo second only to the coming of the gringos, Papa had his first head-on clash with General Harrison Gray Otis.

Harry Carr, who had been on tenterhooks as big as the Eiffel Tower all during the interview, told me about it many years later.

He and Earl Rogers went out one afternoon to the Otis mansion, a beautiful cream-colored house standing in splendor on a Wilshire Boulevard corner overlooking what was Mac-Arthur Park the last time I was there, but you never can tell in Los Angeles. The old Otis palace had become a Norman Rockwell Art School. By now there is probably a forty-story building there. Washington did not sleep in the Otis mansion but Presidents McKinley, Theodore Roosevelt, and Taft did. It was to be in that same magnificent library with four walls of bound books in their rich colors that Papa met William Howard Taft, on the desperate matter of the blowing up of the *Times*.

On the night when the question was the fate of the three cops, Harry said it was interesting to see young Earl Rogers, edgy as a bronco, boyish and clean-shaven at a time when few men were, facing the silvery-bearded old tyrant so used to command. Yet, Harry said, little by little the balance shifted into equality. Just as it did, Harry said, when *Cowan* had been telling Mr. Rogers his story as best he could.

In those days we had a preliminary hearing before a superior-court judge. The D.A. presented sufficient evidence to hold the accused for trial. More than any other lawyer of whom there is record, Earl Rogers, especially in murder trials, used this preliminary hearing to drag out and examine as much of the prosecution's case as he could. Most defense counsels, Rogers among them, reserved their own strong points entirely at this time.

Walking the floor as usual, and with gestures, young Earl Rogers presented to the publisher, seated in all his majesty, an entirely new plan. He proposed to make an all-out attempt to get the charges against the three cops dismissed at the preliminary. At this, the General blew up with a loud noise. A damn-fool notion, was the mildest thing he called this idea. First, last, and always a major general, he said that to give advance notice of your position, number of guns, amount of ammunition, and troop movements was craven treachery. His *No* rattled the windows, he expected it to be final, and rose to say good night with condescension. "We will wait and present our case to a jury of twelve good men and true."

He held out his hand and for maybe the only time in his life it stayed there unshaken and unwrung.

"You won't be able to find twelve good men and true," said young Rogers with a pixie grin.

"Now what in hell's fires do you mean by that, young man?" said the General.

"If we could get a fair and impartial jury," said Rogers, "I'd go along with you. We can't. The first thing I figure in any case is my jury. Let us therefore examine a few facts. Nobody loves a cop. NOBODY. You don't. I don't. The instinctive reaction of the human race against constituted authority, in the first place. Second, the average man on any jury does not, will not, believe anything a policeman says in court. No brighter, if as bright, as the man in the street, nevertheless the policeman is a trained observer. Ninety-nine times out of a hundred, he is more accurate at describing any fast-moving event, such as a murder, a shooting, an accident, than any layman. Automatically, he has been conditioned to know time, to watch people, to take in a whole scene and to remember details. Just the same, you cannot convict the lowest criminal on the sole word of a policeman. At once, the jury assumes the cop is prejudiced. Committed to get a conviction in any case where he has made an arrest. Ten out of twelve men in the box tend to bristle the moment a policeman puts his hand on the Book. Somewhere in every juror's life he has had a *brush* with the law—he or his brother-in-law or his boss or his kid riding a bike on the sidewalk or his uncle who is a drunk and there is a drunk in every family. He and his relatives were always right and it was all the fault of some bull-necked loud-mouthed cop throwing his weight around.

"Now we not only have cops as witnesses but as defendants. And a population aroused by the brilliant work of the *Examiner*—no no, sir, you didn't rise from private to major general without knowing that to underestimate the enemy is always fatal—so that when they see three large cops who have shot down two little pipsqueaks—rats, if you like—still, little men, prejudice will shoot up like a thermometer. It'll reach the guilty mark before we can control it, if we ever can. The very air the jury breathes will be full of this poison about cops who'd rather shoot people than bears.

"I never expect to try another case where public opinion is so solidly against me.

"Now, in our judicial system which is very good, we have this thing called a preliminary hearing.

"Here there is no jury.

"Here the judge, with his trained judicial mind and extensive legal experience and long study of evidence and witnesses, is the only one who makes a decision. He can hold these men for trial by jury. Or he can dismiss for lack of evidence on the conviction that there is no case against the defendants.

"I agree that often enough it's not wise to reveal your plans, your evidence, to subject witnesses to examination which can then be checked before the trial.

"This time I'm going to shoot the works. I do not propose to let any jury get their hands on my clients, who are so obviously policemen they would be recognizable stuffed in a museum."

The General lowered his white head like a buffalo with an arrow under his tail. "You don't propose!" he said. "I make the decisions as to whether these men—"

"No no, Your Majesty," Earl Rogers said sweetly, "concerning my clients I make all the decisions. I am the chief counsel for the defense. Nobody tells me how to try my cases."

"One man," General Otis said, "one man would be more easily swayed or browbeaten or influenced or—bribed than twelve."

"Not Judge Chambers," Earl Rogers said. "Not any judge, I think—but not Judge Chambers I *know*."

"You want to try for a dismissal by this judge at the preliminary?" General Otis said.

"Want to?" Earl Rogers said, still sweetly. "I'm going to," and then with an even broader grin, "General—I've *got* to."

This meeting didn't take very long and of course Papa was too steamed up to settle down so he came by in a cab and picked me up and we went to the theater. I read somewhere that Charles Dickens used to walk the streets of London all night long when he was writing the death of little Nell or of Sydney Carton's ride to the guillotine, weeping and talking to himself, too stimulated and wound up to think of rest or sleep. I must have been in some kind of trouble with my aunts or my mother or something because I remember I had gone to bed in my school dress, red and white striped cambric with a white duck bertha, which I detested, and Papa had come in a four-wheel carriage, of which there were still plenty and which I regarded as the height of luxury. All these things are relative, I have discovered, and no one alive today gets more thrill out of a Mercedes-Benz or a Continental than I did out of the leather cushions and the fine team spanking along ahead of us. Papa was full of fun and on top of the world, telling me about the General.

It seemed to me it was too bad he did not get more of that kind of intoxication. So I said, "Why don't you and Mama ever go to the Otises to dinner? Aunty Blanche does. She goes to everybody's. The Slausons and the Sartoris and Mrs. McNeil and Mrs. Vosburg and gets her name in the paper."

"I get my name in the paper," Papa said.

"Only on the front page," I said, "about things like murders. Aunty Blanche gets on the society part alongside Mrs. O. W. Childs. Or in the music section, Miss Blanche Rogers and her Chamber Music Quartette gave a program in the ballroom of the Doheny mansion in Chester Place."

"I haven't got a chamber music quartette," Papa said.

"Mama has a new evening dress," I said.

After a moment, Papa said, "I know, I know. She looks—never mind, Nora, I don't wish to go to ballrooms to hear chamber music."

"One thing I'll say for Mama," I said, "she looks beautiful, if you come right down to it, she could be a Daughter of the Revolution. Her family tree is okay."

"What is all this about?" Papa said gaily. He was too pleased with himself to get sore at me about anything. "What is on your mind?"

"I—don't know," I said. "Only you had such a big time with the General—I wish you were with people like that more often—"

"You don't think the intellectual attainments of Luther Brown and our fine old Spanish grandee Don Francisco Dominguez are enough?" he said.

"They work for you," I said. "It's not the same. Somebody who wouldn't take any guff off you."

"There's you," Papa said. I got mad and said, "Don't be silly," and he said, "All right, come Sunday we'll ride out and

see your Uncle Tom Hays. His position is at the very top of
the social ladder in Riverside. Will that satisfy you?"

I said, "Well, you always like to visit Uncle Tom, I think
you love him best of any friend. Why, Papa?"

Papa thought a minute. He said, "His charm is like sunshine. It warms you into utter self-forgetfulness. He actually
seems to care more about you than about himself and that's
the greatest of all social and humanitarian graces."

"That's great," I said. "Uncle Tom is wonderful. But it
doesn't seem like you and Mama ever go places like other
people or have them come to our house or anything—"

He was about to give me a box on the ear when we drew
up in front of the theater.

When we got home afterwards, Mama was sitting at the
top of the stairs.

One of the things about looking back, sometimes you can
understand things, you know about them now, you are stunned
at your own cruelty and wish you had a chance to do it over
again. The trouble with that is you would have to be *you-as-
you-are-now* and yet be where you were *then* and that isn't
possible. The only person who understood my mother at all
was my grandfather. My little brother Bogart loved her but
he was hardly more than a baby.

I was real sore at Mama that night because I thought it was
all her fault that Papa didn't have more—more whatever it
was that was bothering me at the time. More contact with and
friendship of and stimulation by his equals—his superiors—
this kept coming back into my head though I didn't really
know just why or what ought to be done about it.

I thought it was too bad because Mama looked beautiful in
a white gown with a sort of purple kimono over it.

If she'd just quit trying to make him what she calls jealous
all the time and make some sense, I thought.

TWENTY

With both the *Times* and *Examiner* giving it a million dollars' worth of space per day, the case of California against three suspended police officers went to trial. Anybody who read them both could well have questioned his own sanity.

On the first day an assistant D.A. was in charge until noon, when Fleming himself walked in. Any seat was more comfortable than the political barbed-wire fence he was straddling alone in his own office. Whether the verdict was Guilty or Not Guilty he had to know his future probably lay behind him, poor man. He was a nice guy and an able lawyer and he went ahead, knowing he couldn't please everybody, and therefore would please nobody, presenting the seemingly unbeatable case for the prosecution.

Never in all my long courtroom experience have I known the victims in a murder case to remain as anonymous, faceless, and voiceless as the Choissers. Their poor shoddy little ghosts were never able to get protoplasmed in the courtroom. Nobody seemed to regret their passing, nobody showed up from Illinois. Everybody had forgotten who these little men *were*, sprawled lifeless on hotel floors. All the fury of the Bruxton kangaroo court had been against the police. The *Examiner* headlined it as the POLICE MURDER, the *Times* as the YELLOW JOURNALISM CASE. Nobody ever called it the Choisser trial.

Even their corpses rested in horrid nakedness, for their clothes were always being brought into the courtroom to show the bullet holes and it was impossible to think of them as ever having been stuffed with anything but straw. Undertakers handled them impersonally and pointed to pockets in which they had discovered ammunition and the limp suits and dirty linen were left hanging in their hands like the rags and tatters displayed by old-clothes dealers.

Whoever they were and however petty and venal, it was sad that human beings could have lived and come to a violent end and left nothing, nothing at all, behind them. Except for that one fatal moment when they had been hysterically brave enough to oppose the Law with a feeble gun, or when irresponsible representatives of the Law had slain them without provocation, the Choisser father and son might just as well never have lived at all.

In the first act, the dramatic surprise was Earl Rogers.

During an investigation, Sherlock Holmes called the attention of Dr. Watson to the strange behavior of the dog. But, said the puzzled Watson, the dog did nothing at all. That, said Sherlock Holmes, is what I mean by the strange behavior of the dog.

The strange behavior of Earl Rogers was that as the prosecution brought on its parade of witnesses he did nothing and did it very well.

The General, Harry Carr notified my father, was bouncing with wrath. Mr. Rogers said that would be good for his liver. Following the second afternoon session, when the counsel for the defense had waved an indifferent hand at four key witnesses, refusing to cross-examine, the district attorney said loudly, "He's got something Up His Sleeve." And Rogers, who happened to be walking down the hill just behind him, said amiably, "I hope you're right, Paul, I hope you're right."

Not until Mr. Arthur Clough had finished his sensational story of Murder as Seen Through a Transom did Earl Rogers so much as rise from his seat.

On direct, Arthur Clough had been definite, detailed, and melodramatic.

"Did the young man Louis Choisser have a gun?" the district attorney asked him.

"No sir. No *sir*."

"You saw his hands?"

"Yes sir I did."

"Both of them?"

"Yes sir both of them."

"Where were his hands?"

"Raised above his head."

"Raised above his head? And there was nothing in them?"

"No sir there wasn't. Not a thing."

"You saw no guns and no shots fired except by the police officers?"

"I couldn't, there weren't any."

A pause. Still not quite happy, the district attorney. Too good to be true, the way his case was rolling. Then he said, "Take the witness, Mr. Rogers."

Except in the press box, the courtroom grew still, stiller. As Mr. Rogers got to his feet and sauntered around the end of the table, the reporters took a tighter grip on their pencils. *Here it comes,* the *Examiner* thought apprehensively. *Here it better come,* the *Times* said to itself.

With a friendly, almost admiring smile, Rogers looked anything but dangerous as he stood in front of the witness drawing out his now famous lorgnette, adjusting it, lifting it to regard Mr. Arthur Clough through it.

In a feature article about that time, Joseph Timmons, a name held highly all over the nation in the fourth estate, spoke at length of this lorgnette. *To Earl Rogers, this gold-rimmed eyeglass with its long gold handle was what a spyglass is to the Indian Scout; the telescope to the Mariner; the fan to the coquette; the foil to the fencer. With it, he mows down the opposition, makes them dance to his music, sometimes ragtime, sometimes a macabre dance of death, sometimes a march or minuette. With it, he sights after the rocks of judicial rulings and gazes into the innermost depths of the soul of every witness.*

Whatever he saw in the depths of Arthur Clough's soul, it seemed to delight him. He shot the lorgnette back in the pocket of his grosgrain silk vest and said gently, "I don't want to bore you, Mr. Clough, it's so seldom we have a keen observer like yourself as eyewitness to a murder. You'll allow me to go over a few minor points? I was wondering why you looked through the transom instead of opening the door?"

"Well I certainly didn't want to put myself in the line of fire, did I?" Mr. Clough said patronizingly. "After what my wife saw in the toilet—"

"Forgive me," said Mr. Rogers, "just what did she see?"

"Well, she saw these brutes lurking there so when they started shooting people next door to death—"

"Still," said Mr. Rogers, "you didn't know that then."

"No, but my wife had seen enough of them and when we heard *shots,* we could figure—" Mr. Clough said.

"Yes yes," said Mr. Rogers. "You heard a lot of shots? A great many? A fusillade in fact—so that you wouldn't open your door?"

"That's right," said Arthur.

"Very quick thinking—the transom," said Mr. Rogers. "Just how did you manage it, Mr. Clough?"

"Oh it was easy," Clough said. "I got on the bed and then put one foot on the doorknob."

"Could you indicate to me—" said Mr. Rogers with great interest, and Mr. Clough made gestures with his feet and hands. "I see," said the defense counsel, "I *see*. Remarkable. Now then, through the transom—you leaned out somewhat?" Clough nodded. "So you are able to be positive you saw no gun in the hand of the young man who was fleeing down the hall?"

"I'm positive about that all right," Arthur Clough said.

"You saw the young man in his doorway, he threw up his hands to show the officers he didn't have a gun, and then he began running for his life?"

"That was it, Mr. Rogers."

"They didn't shout and order him to put up his hands or drop that gun or anything of that nature?"

"No sir."

"They didn't say they were officers come to arrest him?"

"Well—only when they knocked and said something like Open in the Name of the Law, something like that."

"After that nobody said a word, the policemen just began to shoot?"

"Nobody said anything."

"They just shot in grim silence," Earl Rogers commented thoughtfully. "The policemen were the only ones who ever fired a shot?"

"That's all. Only the policemen."

"These three police officers here?"

"Yes—those—those three."

"That's all, Mr. Clough—and thank you very much."

Without a mark, Arthur Clough came down off the witness stand. Apparently, Earl Rogers hadn't laid a glove on him.

The prosecution closed its case feeling sure it had proved it beyond a reasonable doubt.

The defense opened without fanfare or gunfire.

Two large gentlemen, Bill Jory and Melrose, who had come to work for us after his third trial resulted in a dismissal of the murder charge against him, wheeled into the courtroom several easels of the type on which paintings are displayed in galleries. On these they placed enlarged photographs, rather like maps of Death Valley.

Nobody had any idea what they were and Judge Chambers put on his eyeglasses and regarded them without expression. While he had no objection to the type of evidence Rogers had introduced into trial procedure, he proposed to watch it with care. There was no jury present and surely Rogers must know the Bench was not to be unduly impressed by the use of dramatic reproductions.

After a moment or two he said very sharply, "What does this purport to be, Mr. Rogers?"

"If Your Honor please," Mr. Rogers said, with a very formal bow, "these photographs have been taken by established commercial photographers. Each photographer has developed and enlarged his own prints. I have here"—he pointed to large stacks of heavy volumes, which had now been arranged on the counsel table under the wide but puzzled eyes of the press and the district attorney—"I have here some technical treatises from German laboratories on the science of ballistics which I shall relate to the photographs as I ask Your Honor's permission to place them in evidence as exhibits for the defendants."

"Ballistics," Judge Chambers said, "the science of propulsion, weapons, and trajectile gunnery."

"And *bullets*," said Earl Rogers in a tone that dripped poison at last.

Somebody in the press box said *Jesus H. Christ* in a piercing whisper and the judge glared in his direction. Nobody else even muttered. The D.A. and his staff were staring at the photographs in bewilderment, as yet without real apprehension. Along with the audience and the press, most of them at that time had never even heard of ballistics. Earl Rogers' secret had been kept even from Harry Carr and the *Times*.

This time, he had the use of the entire police department, men and equipment, day and night. By careful examination Rogers and the department's best detectives had found bullet holes and bullets in the walls and doorjambs opposite the Choissers' room. The prosecution had either failed to see these or if they saw them had missed their significance. No one at all had ever seen any other gun, except the defendants themselves, and naturally nobody was going to believe them, as Rogers had foreseen. If there had been a gun it was missing, possibly some of the gentry who lived at the Bruxton had stolen or lost it. If there were bullet holes *and bullets* in the walls they must have been fly shots as the cops banged away at Louis Choisser running for his life down the hall. If an undertaker testified that he had found a handful of bullets in Louis's vest, what did that have to do with the case? A man could not fire bullets without a gun and there was no gun on the Choissers, none in evidence, nobody had ever seen one.

To his clients as he prepared the case for trial Earl Rogers had said, "Unless we can prove to the judge that they fired at you and fired first, you are going to spend a lot of time in jail." To this Cowan said hopelessly, "Whatever you find, Mr. Rogers, them witnesses'll swear we fired 'em," and Mr. Rogers sat sunk in profound thought without answering.

The volumes now on the counsel table had not yet been published in the United States. No one but Papa connected with The Affair read German. As a result of the kind of all-night study he did on everything connected with his profession he'd heard of all this and now he was able to clarify things still further for Judge Chambers. "While ballistics as a science is still little known in this country," he said, "it has been highly developed in Germany, as fingerprints were by Bertillon in France. In Germany they have made extensive and successful experiments in identification of bullets and weapons. The United States Army is well aware of this."

"What do you propose to prove by it?" said the judge.

"With Your Honor's permission," Earl Rogers said, "I propose to prove by these photographs; by the testimony of a witness trained in Germany, and employed by the Army; by experiments he has made in conjunction with men trained in the use of weapons, that the bullets found in the *other wall* could not have been fired from the guns of the police officers present. And that the bullets in the doorjambs do match and are the same as the bullets found in Louis Choisser's pockets at the time he was killed."

"Proceed, Mr. Rogers," said Judge Chambers.

And all hell broke loose in the press box.

Within seconds, the *Examiner* was setting up type in which to shriek:

EARL ROGERS IN GIGANTIC COURTROOM FRAUD

While the *Times* in letters big as billboards announced its first triumph:

ROGERS TO PROVE CROOKS FIRED AT POLICE FIRST

After that, came a day of careful, scientific, documented testimony to which Judge Chambers listened with thoughtful, impartial attentiveness.

Jerry Giesler once told me that Papa would repeat over and over to him, *Qualify your witnesses.* Whether they are experts or not, Mr. Rogers held, impress the judge and the jury that they know what they're talking about, have some right and reason to be taking up the time of the court, either by special training or because they were present and saw and heard certain things, or because they are characters of great truthfulness, or were holding a spyglass or listening at the crack in the door. *Qualify them.*

"Mr. Jesse Hawley," Earl Rogers said.

Recovering from the shock of this surprise science, the prosecution now began yelping like dogs with cans on their tails. WHO, they demanded of the judge, was *this* Mr. Hawley? Certainly not one of the defendants whose name was Hawley. Who *said* he was an expert and of what? As far as the district attorney of Los Angeles County, State of California, U.S.A., was concerned ballistics belonged in Lilliput or Brobdingnag and had no more right on the witness stand than a magician pulling rabbits out of a hat.

This gave Earl Rogers additional opportunity, carefully, without heat, in a tempo designed for a judge not a jury, to qualify his witness, drawing from the uncommunicative Hawley all his degrees, consultations with the Army, and standing in his new work. At the end of this, Mr. Rogers said, "The witness will take any bullets from any guns the prosecution wishes to offer and guarantee to match them correctly with each other. I don't suppose Your Honor carries a gun?"

His Honor didn't. He said to the district attorney, "Do you wish to take advantage of the offer of proof made by Mr. Rogers as to Mr. Hawley's qualifications?"

Muttering something about the Orpheum and vaudeville turns, Mr. Fleming said he wouldn't descend to such nonsense.

"Mr. Hawley," said Earl Rogers, "have you made a chemical analysis of the bullets used by the police and given by the department to Officers Cowan, Murphy, and Hawley?"

"Oh yes," Mr. Hawley said.

"Have you also made a chemical analysis of the bullets extracted from the wall of the hallway of the Bruxton Hotel opposite the Choissers' bedroom?"

"Oh yes," Mr. Hawley said.

"What is the result of this chemical laboratory analysis?"

"There is of course a marked difference between the two types of bullets," Mr. Hawley said.

"Have you examined and analyzed the bullets taken from the bodies of the deceased, Joe and Louis Choisser?"

"Oh yes," said Mr. Hawley.

"Do those conform to the bullets carried by the police officers?"

"Yes," said Mr. Hawley.

"Do they conform to the bullets extracted from the opposite walls?"

"No no, not at all, entirely different."

"Have you examined and analyzed the bullets taken from the clothes of Louis Choisser after his death?"

"Oh yes."

"Do they conform to the bullets with which he was shot?"

"No. No. Entirely different."

"Have you compared the bullets extracted from the walls and the doorjambs with those taken from Louis Choisser's vest pockets?"

"Yes."

"What did you find as to those two types of bullets?"

"Oh, they're identical, of course."

With impressive skill, Hawley explained how and why he could offer definite opinion. The police bullets were of solid lead, with a small amount of copper fused into the nose. Much, he said, like army bullets. Those from Choisser's pockets and those in the wall had an element of tin mixed with the lead and lacked entirely the copper ingredient of the police slug. Step by step, pointer and lens in hand, Earl Rogers led his witness into the science of ballistics as it applied to the identification of bullets in the case now before the court. Looking back, it is difficult to remember the thrill with which we listened on earphones to a radio program or used an electric refrigerator or washing machine for the first time. We take everything for granted as having always existed. We accept ballistics now, but on that day the audience goggled and gasped before something new, unheard of, and hardly to be believed. A jury might have found it over their heads, had difficulty in following it, or, as the D.A. indicated, felt it belonged on a vaudeville stage, not in a serious trial. Judge Chambers however foresaw that in its field this would revolutionize testimony in many cases. At one point he took over the examination of the defense expert.

"Mr. Hawley," he said from the Bench, and the young man turned and peered up through his big glasses, "how do you know this bullet you are dealing with was actually fired into that wall?"

"Oh I also made a chemical analysis of the hole left there," Hawley said patiently. "It contained a residue of the same oily substance as is used on the *rotating* band of this bullet. The band only rotates if the bullet has been discharged."

Pondering a moment, the judge said, "Wouldn't the police bullets have left the same residue?"

"Oh no," said the witness. "This has a wax base. The police bullets had none. It's quite impossible."

When Rogers completed the proof that this was the bullet taken from the wall, ballistics had done a great deal to demolish the agreement of the hotel witnesses that only the police had fired any guns.

After seeing lots of eyewitnesses we came to feel that a few minnows in the milk were better evidence than nine men, none of whom saw the same thing, some being color blind and others cross-eyed. My father never put all his eggs in any one basket. Though he himself put eyewitness testimony pretty far down on the list he never made the mistake of underrating its importance to any jury or its legal weight with any judge.

Now between us and those two words which we spent our lives trying to win—Not Guilty—stood good old Arthur Clough, the boy with his head in the transom.

As a result of some of his own prowling and snooping around the scene of the crime, Mr. Rogers now called Adell Milk. One of his favorite witnesses of all time, I may add, who for twelve years had been a chambermaid at the Bruxton Hotel. With good will, and without fear or favor, Adell Milk hoisted herself onto the witness stand and faced Earl Rogers. Everything about her announced that her conscience was clear.

"Mrs. Milk—" Mr. Rogers began, "it is *Mrs.* Milk?"

"The priest married the two of us," said Mrs. Milk, "and a good husband Mike's been to me barring a brannigan on a Saturday night, all forgiven and forgotten the next day."

"I only wish I'd had the luck to meet you before Mike did," Earl Rogers said, and he and Mrs. Milk both laughed heartily. The judge, looking at Adell's round rubicund face, forbore to rap with his gavel. "Now, you were in charge of the room where the Choissers resided?"

"I was to be sure," Mrs. Milk said, "God rest their souls poor fellows."

"Do you recall whether you also took care of the Cloughs' room next door?" said Mr. Rogers.

"I did," said Mrs. Milk noncommittally.

"Would you be able to tell me," Mr. Rogers said confidentially, "when you last dusted the transom of that room?" and as Mrs. Milk reared back, surprised by the question, since probably no one at the Bruxton had asked when she dusted anything in all her twelve years, he added, "The transom over the door into the hall, I mean."

"Well now—" said Mrs. Milk, a little uncertain as to whether her professional honor was at stake or not, "I'm not sure about that—"

Earl Rogers twinkled at her with eyes as Irish blue as her own. "They don't really have as much help at the Bruxton as they should, I checked the books for that, and as hard as it is to get up there to the transom to give it a good going over it's too much to ask of one woman. It'd be quite understandable—"

Mrs. Milk relaxed. "If the truth must be known upon me oath," she said, "I daresay 'twas a month or two—"

"Before the shooting took place?" said Mr. Rogers.

"I'd do it on me monthly cleaning," Mrs. Milk said. "I remember when I was cleaning up all the mess them policemen and reporters made in me hallway thinking praise all saints it wasn't but a week until my regular monthly cleaning—"

"Nobody else would dust it?" said Mr. Rogers.

"Who would?" said Adell Milk.

More photographs. The dust of ages lay undisturbed upon the transom identified as belonging to Arthur Clough's room.

"Do you have any further witnesses, Mr. Rogers?" Judge Chambers said.

"One more, Your Honor," said Mr. Rogers. "I will now call Mr. Joseph J. Florillo."

Everybody turned to look at a large gent who came down the aisle with surprising lightness and vaulted onto the stand. Between cauliflower ears he had a friendly face. He agreed that his name was Florillo.

"And your occupation, Mr. Florillo?" said Earl Rogers.

A. I keep a gymnasium.

Q. Anything else?

A. Well, I was in vaudeville as an acrobat, the Five Florillos we were then, and now sometimes I teach tumbling and do exhibitions.

Q. How tall are you, Mr. Florillo?

A. Well, being as broad as I am maybe I don't look it but I'm six foot one without my shoes.

Q. Mr. Clough—is Mr. Clough still in the courtroom—Mr. Clough, might I trouble you to come and stand beside—ah, thank you—I should say you're two inches shorter than Mr.

Florillo. Now—yesterday Mr. Florillo—you may sit down now, Mr. Clough, perhaps you'd better—in my company, Mr. Florillo and that of the defendants and several disinterested witnesses—we all went to the Bruxton Hotel. We went into the room occupied by Mr. Clough—the manager admitted us in his absence, you recall?—and what did you do there?

A. Well, Mr. Rogers, I done like you asked of me. I tried to see could I get my head and shoulders through the transom while keeping one of my feet on the bed and one on the door knob—

Q. Could you give us a rough idea?

At this point I think Judge Chambers wanted to interfere but he was unable to speak.

A. Well, I suppose I could in a way—

Q. Remember you have to get in that position and get your head through the transom so you can see everything taking place in the hall.

Mr. Florillo rose and put one foot on the chair preparatory to mounting it.

Q. No—no, I think this may be dangerous. I'm sure we can visualize what took place without a demonstration. Just tell just what happened.

A. You know what happened, I fell on my face and come near busting my neck as if I fell off the roof.

Q. I see. Now you don't think Mr. Clough who is two inches shorter and not an acrobat could have stood—

The objections were loud and furious and varied but above them all could be heard the voice of Mr. Florillo raised in agony.

"Not unless he's a centipede or something," shouted Mr. Florillo with feeling.

All the reporters and photographers, carrying Mr. Florillo with them, were appalled and incensed when upon arrival they found Mrs. Adell Milk just coming down a stepladder. "You'll find it all nice and clean now, lads," she said, waving a dust rag at the famous transom, "as I'd have had it long ago I'm sure if I'd known folks were going to be snooping about like them Cloughs."

The next day Judge Chambers dismissed the charges against the three policemen.

All of them were restored to the police department in good standing.

At least for the time being.

TWENTY-ONE

Hawley, one of the three cops, found him, after five or six endless days.

Our phone was back in by then. In the middle of the night it rang and Mama answered it in a second, so she hadn't been to sleep either, I'll say that for her.

A peculiar thing had happened to me while Papa was missing, and this time he wasn't at Joe Fast's Turkish Baths moaning his way through the cold gray dawn of the morning after, nor at Pearl Morton's being pampered back to sanity by Pearl's cooking and Dolly's music.

From the time my grandfather died, we had renounced God, faith, and prayer. On those nights I couldn't stand it any longer. I didn't know what else to *do*. Besides, I figured, it was Papa's own fault. He shouldn't disappear like that and scare us all. So I got out of bed and onto my knees, which as my grandfather had taught me was one way to remind yourself that you were talking to God. I prayed then in the good, old-fashioned, and somehow *comforting* terms that my grandfather had taught me from the time I would repeat them after him. Please, dear Lord, temper the wind to the shorn lamb. Take care of Papa. Ninety and nine are safely home in the shadow of the fold but one is out on the hills away far off from the gates of gold. Don't let his enemy get him, Lord. Don't let anything happen to him. Even if he doesn't believe in you any more you loved him the same way you did Peter when he denied you three times before the cock crowed. You came to save sinners. Papa is not a sinner, he has an Enemy. Let me put on the whole armor of God to fight against this enemy and let grace be unto us.

A shrill shriek from the telephone made me jump out of my skin. A call from the French Hospital. Would we come at once? Bill Jory had a cab waiting for us. At first Mama wasn't going to take me, but I guess she had to, poor soul. I know I butted like a goat and got in the cab and kept kicking. Driving through the dark, silent streets we didn't know whether Papa was dying or not.

This was my first meeting with Sister Marie Josephe, a tall nun with starry eyes who loved my father. The nuns always came to Papa when any of their boys were in trouble or if they needed advice about any difficulty, even though the Church had its own legal counsels. When the Poor Clares arrived in his office for donations, they knew nothing of any wild extravagance or foolish generosity and there was no red tape or checks. Mr. Rogers emptied his pockets of cash, however much it was, while he sent across to the Pig 'n' Whistle for tea and cakes. Her prayers for him were piled high in front of her name saint. As we came in, she was standing on one side of the narrow white hospital bed. On the other was the square form of our late defendant, J. J. Hawley. Hawley's face had no range of expression and Sister Marie Josephe's coif gave her the serene look of a guardian angel.

On the bed, Papa was a fearsome sight.

A battered and bloody mess, even though his head was now done up in a turban of white bandages only spotted with the dire red-brown. His eyes were purple-black-green and swollen almost shut. One arm was in a cast held up by a sling.

Of these outward signs there could be no possible question.

He made a small gesture with his good hand and said in a whisper, "I'm dying, Nora."

To this day I cannot tell whether he actually thought he was.

Later on Jack London said to me that a man with a monumental hangover complicated by a broken arm and a slight concussion would not only think he was dying, he might hope so as well. In days to come when I learned that deathbed and remorse could be synonymous, that shattering fatigue and nervous exhaustion and too much alcohol could call up perfectly sincere last words and heartbreaking farewells which were a hundred per cent sincere, I was never never *sure*. Like the boy who cried *wolf wolf* until nobody believed him—in the end, the wolf would come. And did. So that I never dared to take a chance.

At that first deathbed I was sure, and I went over and

took his hand and said, "Papa, please don't leave me. I couldn't bear it."

Perhaps if I hadn't said that, Mama would have acted differently.

With her coat over her nightgown she stood there, darkly beautiful, her eyes blazing, her hair loose about her shoulders, and said in a high clear voice, "He's drunk."

Well—she was right.

On the other hand I did not think it was a tactful thing for a wife to say. With any of what she called *Earl's acting* she never had any sympathy at all. If he wanted to mix his own salad dressing at the Poodle Dog or stand up at the ball game and wave his hat when they cheered him, her lips got narrow and her face dark and she said, "Oh Earl, for goodness' sake stop showing off." I do not think it was possible for her to follow or comprehend that he was not acting and he was not showing off, any more than Jack London was when he wrote *Martin Eden* or Mark Twain when he wrote *Huck Finn* or Dickens when he wrote *David Copperfield*. Detesting the theater, Mama felt that all forms of make-believe were arrant nonsense, she had no—no *way* to follow anybody through the gateway of imagination, and realize that often it is more powerful in suffering and joy than reality. I have wondered since if she might have found a road in painting, if in those days people had painted for fun and relaxation as they do now. The Dutch have produced great painters always and she had an eye for color and created real glory in her gardens. It seems to me now that the one cloud of glory she trailed was her ability to make flowers grow.

As it was then, all she did was turn Papa's poor beat-up face away from her impatient belittling contempt to my small countenance, on which was depicted the imploring terror and adoration proper to the occasion.

I looked at Sister and she smiled a little and whispered to me, words of reassurance, and I managed to get my breath.

His story, and he stuck to it, was that a gang of circulation toughs, forerunners of those who composed the Chicago gangs, had been laying for him when he came out of a saloon on Spring Street and had taken him for an early version of what we came to call a ride. They had dumped him in an alley out near Central Avenue and Twenty-third Street and the cop on the beat had found him and called the station and they had notified Hawley, who went after him in an ambulance.

Hawley said, "Them goons can be real rough. Mr. Rogers

got the *Examiner* sore when he would not let them railroad me and Murph and Cowan. They could have laid for him or they could have just seen him and done it on the spur of the moment. Anyhow, somebody did."

Sister Marie Josephe finally persuaded me that Papa was not going to die, and so I kissed him and so did Mama finally and we left. I thought we would take a cab but Mama made Hawley take us home in his car. That was another thing that always made her mad. "Throwing money away like that," she said furiously. "With all we *owe*. The way he throws money around in saloons anybody would think he was a millionaire."

After a while Hawley said to me, "I had better resign from the department. Mr. Rogers needs me. You got a bunch of amateurs up there. You need a good professional."

I thought if everybody we got acquitted of murder wanted to come to work for us, we'd soon have a large staff.

As it turned out it was a good thing Hawley came.

If I'd been older I might have realized that night that Bill Jory wasn't going to be with us long. Sister Marie Josephe, who of course was also a nurse, stopped him in the corridor where small flickering candles burned before the saints in their wall niches. By the time I noticed he wasn't with us, they were too far away for me to hear what she said. Her lifted hand made a gesture toward a dark red patch on his face I thought was a boil, it looked kind of angry and disagreeable but I was so fond of him I just—kind of looked around it. The Sister spoke to him for several minutes very earnestly and after a while Jory nodded.

In a way it turned out it was Bill Jory's deathbed we had attended at the French Hospital then. He was the first person we ever knew to die of cancer. Sister Marie Josephe was too late—we knew little about this scourge then.

He was a very brave man. But—I wished it hadn't taken so long.

As far as I was concerned, nobody ever took his place with me.

Nor, I sometimes thought, with Papa either.

PART FOUR

TWENTY-TWO

Any foreign female is prohibited from engaging in prostitution within three years after being admitted to the United States.

My father's defense of the Queen of Chinatown, also known as the Pearl of same, on a never-before-heard-of charge of violating this immigration law, was one of the many things that led to his being called in by the tongs to try to settle the tong wars which were terrorizing Californians. The only American who ever sat in secret sessions with the tong war lords.

A tong was the active, warring, ruling faction at the head of a large Chinese family, which was of course partly relationship and partly political. The central control was, of course, in China but the tong itself extended from there to San Francisco, New York—as in the historic war between the Hop Sings and the On Leongs—to Limehouse and around the globe. At its best, it involved high finance and commercial enterprise and labor relations, at its worst it was just a Chinese Mafia. Gang tactics were certainly in operation and when trouble arose, it was often from territory disputes, like those of the Capone era over territory for illegal sales. Gambling—always the No. 1 fever with the Chinese—opium—white slavery all came under the tongs, who had their own methods. When war broke out, the tong leaders summoned their hatchet men, equivalent to the gunmen of the gangs—who buried their hatchets in each other's skulls and the Chinatown of every city in California ran blood.

More murders are expected either in Oakland's Chinatown or in this city within 24 hours, for the Bing Kong Tong is now five men on the wrong side of the balance in the present bitter blood feud. This simple, straightforward sentence in the *Chronicle* surprised no one when it appeared as a result of a murder on San Francisco streets. It did, however, cause the same kind of consternation that later arose from the gang murder of Legs Diamond or the explosive kidnaping of Dutch Schultz.

Later when I heard Thomas E. Dewey, the Racket Buster, wail to us, the press, that his witnesses were being found in cement blocks at the bottom of the East River, I was reminded of Wong Fong, who on a certain day didn't answer the call of the bailiff to take the stand in Judge Canaiss's court because he was on a slab in San Francisco's morgue with two holes through his head.

A typical tong tale, that of Wong Fong, mayor of Los Angeles Chinatown and of high standing in the Bing Kongs.

A Hop Sing member named Chung You was on trial in Canaiss's court for perjury. Two months previously, Chung You had sworn on the book that as he came down Washington Street he had seen no less than *four* Bing Kong assassins slay *one* peaceful Hop Sing member named Yick Wah. He had made this statement in a murder trial and now was being questioned concerning it. A fear arose among Chung You's Hop Sing buddies that Wong Fong had come north to help send Chung to the penitentiary for bearing false witness against the four Bing Kongs. So, the Hop Sing war lords called in their highbinders—hatchetmen or hired assassins— employed by each tong, as has been said, for purposes of assassination, revenge, and sometimes for a spot of high-level blackmail or commercial terrorism. The order was simple—Wong Fong was not to be allowed to appear as a witness. Since no cement blocks were handy as yet, as the Chinese mayor of Los Angeles came out of Hiram Johnson's office he was sent to join his revered ancestors by a long-barreled army revolver, of the type that was replacing the historic hatchet, in the hands of a Hop Sing highbinder named Fong On. Questioned about this, the highbinder swore that the mayor of L.A. Chinatown had long owed him a gambling debt. Approached about this by Fong On in a peace-loving manner, Wong Fong had started shoving with his little hatchet and Fong On had been forced to reach for a weapon he carried only to protect himself against pirates who came ashore along the waterfront. He did not, he said, know what a highbinder was and when informed by the Chinatown squad that it was an assassin paid by a tong he said he did not belong to a tong or any other secret society.

Anybody who believed this would believe the St. Valentine's Day massacre was a gentlemen's disagreement over when to lead trumps. They had taken care of Wong Fong the same way Murder Incorporated disposed of such troublesome witnesses as Abe Reles or Jake Lingle. Only I must say the tongs were more picturesque and colorful, had better manners and other motives than money, such as honor and revenge and family pride. They were often as ruthless and tigerish as the Mafia but they had something of the ferocious family pride of the Scottish clan.

Since then, everything has changed between China and California and the special relation that existed between them when I was young. The days when Earl Rogers was their favorite lawyer have gone with the wind. The other day a leftover merchant prince named Sui One took me down into his private treasure vaults beneath the asphalt and cement surface of a Los Angeles street. The yards of patterned golden silk he displayed made me catch my breath. "When this silk was made," said Sui, whose sons by a redheaded Irish wife were flamboyantly handsome and had been graduated *magna cum laude* from the University of California, "a man worked for three yen a day. Now—he gets three thousand yen per hour. This makes it necessary to sell the silk for three hundred dollars a yard." His laugh had the sweet metallic tinkle of glass bells. "This, however, it is very old. Accept same please as slight rememerance." To this I said, "Sui—it's worth a fortune," and Sui said, "Most unworthy gift for No. 1 daughter of my greatly honored friend. No more silk, no more Mr. Rogers, soon now no more Sui One. Mr. Rogers did much for the Chinese people of California. He was their most good and best friend. Allow me to honor myself with small present to him through you."

People go into ecstasies over the lamp shade made of this silk, but I have never been able to see it quite clearly, frankly I have tears in my eyes.

Oh—they have been written of in song and story, California and the days when its Chinese population spread over the whole state, and its towns existed in every big city. I always wish everybody could have known it then. True, we had highbinders and hatchet men—we had also great scholars among them, many of whom called Earl Rogers friend. We had house servants who served with pride and delight, made our homes miracles of order and color and grace and regarded our families as their own; arts and beauties of all kinds and centuries, woven deeply into our eyes and thoughts and decorations and ways of eating and dressing; philosophies and sciences deeper and older than our own, and so much character from top to bottom that was fine and merry and loyal and beautiful. I have known no man's word since as utterly invulnerable and entirely trustworthy as that of a good Chinaman.

They trusted Earl Rogers above anybody else at that time. In all things.

THE BOW WONG WUI
requests your presence at a banquet
to be given in honor of

THE BIRTHDAY OF THE EMPEROR

and to
Dedicate the Bow Wong Wui Hall
Saturday the twenty-ninth day of July
nineteen hundred and five
7:30 o'clock P.M.
409 Apablaza Street in Los Angeles
California

An invitation like that when it came to Mr. Rogers meant an evening of brilliant conversation, gourmet food beyond anything the best Chinese restaurant could then, or can now, prepare, exquisite decoration, and, my father always said, real fellowship, stately and yet warm.

Our whole lives were colored by "small presents." On the Fourth of July and Patrick Henry's birthday, for which they had some special reverence, wagons and truckloads of fireworks appeared at our house and office. No one else in the state had anything quite as fine as the display pieces designed for the palaces and the emperor which came to Mr. Rogers. Their spangled illumination was *splendiferous*—I remember Papa and me shouting that word back and forth at each other—never anywhere not even at Versailles have I seen anything to approach them. So many came that we used to go up the little hill onto Alvarado Terrace or even out to West Lake Park and Papa superintended setting them off for the whole neighborhood or even the entire west side of town. He would invite whole orphanages to see—and assist.

Jade came too, apple green and white, bracelets that were never exported for sale, my daughter still has a pair of the famous medallions in unsurpassed jade and velvety red Chinese gold. House pajamas, mandarin coats, kimonos and robes for Papa and me, shell-pink and lotus-flower and April-green and faintest lilac sheets of silk that could be pulled through a ring, all smelling of incense wood, of cinnamon and mint and new-mown grass and carnations and tuberoses and apricots. To this day, though I never find anything with its full-scale enchantment, a suggestion of it can make my heart *crack*.

Sometimes I found a lottery ticket in my pocket. Wong, our cook, explained to me that these were reproductions of leaves from a textbook known to the Chinese as the *Thousand Character Primer*, this added a touch of Marco Polo and his adventures to our conversations. At that time, actually, the Chinese lottery was operated all over the state about like the numbers racket later and was just as illegal. Not that anybody paid any attention to *that*. My father always said Americans, Chinese, Spaniards, Mexicans, Hawaiians, Eskimos, English dukes and Russian serfs and Swedish sailors and everybody else must gamble. Twice he tried to get gambling made legal but of course the churches bucked that, and he could not make them understand that you couldn't stop it and real crime was financed—and always would be—mostly by profits from the gambling houses—or syndicates as they came to be known later. If the *majority* of the people did not intend to obey a law and saw no reason why they should, it was unenforceable. The law became a broomstick in the hands of Mother Goose, he said, and about as inane, impotent, and nugatory. Look, he would point out, how the churches get into bed with the underworld at election time. And how pleased the world of corruption is, for these unenforceable reform laws benefit the men who sell vice. People must be educated into virtue and morality; they can never be legislated into it. That only raises the Old Adam, who insisted on eating of the Thou-Shalt-Not tree in the garden. That, the Old Adam in us says, ought to have showed you! Don't try telling me what not to do. Americans used to be worse about that than anybody. Especially Westerners.

My lottery tickets usually won, when I asked Wong about it he looked so blank I could hardly believe he was breathing. Of course he belonged to the same family as Wong She, the Pearl of Chinatown, but then so did about a quarter of the Chinese population of the state. Mostly our Wong wasn't blank at all. He was a particularly small Chinaman who wore a queue and must have changed his blue linen suits two or three times a day, they never had a spot or wrinkle in them. I brought my books home from Grandpa's, and from school when I finally went, and took them out in the kitchen to teach Wong to read English. He already knew the

Thousand Character Primer in Chinese. In return he was teaching me to play fan-tan and sing Chinese songs. Our pigtails, black and taffy-colored, swung over his big wooden table in perfect friendship and amity, but he could explode like all the fireworks ever manufactured. One afternoon I opened the front door and a peddler, when I said we didn't want any, put his foot in to hold it open. At which point Wong leaped out of the kitchen brandishing a knife in one hand and a meat ax in the other and chased the man clear up to Sixteenth Street. A good Chinese cook always brought his own knives, dozens of them.

To our door then used to come another Wong—Wong *Li*, who drove a vegetable wagon drawn by a dappled horse too old for fire engines. Wong could take money out of my ears, which infuriated Mama, who said all Chinks were dirty. Of course she had been brought up in Red Creek, New York, where there weren't any, but I thought it was odd of her to act that way because Uncle Charlie Greene, her brother, said we had a Mohawk great-great-grandmother back aways. Wong Li brought me packages of little brown balls, when you put them in water they expanded into flowers; nests of red-gold boxes; ugly brown bulbs to be put in a glass dish with pebbles where they grew into tall fragrant white lilies. Li's vegetables were grown in Chinese gardens, the Japs never knew nor will know how to flavor their truck produce with love and humor and imagination, but the Chinese did.

One day, Li arrived late, waited powwowing in the kitchen until Mr. Rogers got home. The next day it was announced that Earl Rogers had been retained to defend Wong She, the Queen of Chinatown. At the time I did not understand what Wong She was charged with. As a matter of fact she was the first person in the United States to be brought before immigration authorities for deportation under the ruling that no foreign female may engage in prostitution within three years of being admitted to the country. After that apparently she was on her own.

Two missionaries had tried to convert Wong She from the ancient teaching of Lao-tse and Confucius to what my father said were the similar ones of Jesus Christ. He was a student of them all and he said Jesus Christ was the greatest Teacher of all time because he taught anybody and proved what he said as he went along, and the Buddha and Lao-tse and Plato had to teach the same thing because there could be only one truth.

Having failed to persuade Wong She of the need for change, the missionaries asked Immigration Inspector Charles Wexley to deport her as an undesirable alien on the grounds that she hadn't waited the required three years to begin the practice of the oldest profession. Although all men in positions of authority were scared of the churches, I doubt if anything would have come of this if it hadn't been a fact that a new war had broken out between rival tongs for the exclusive favors of the Pearl.

Having seen the lady, as Papa said it was easy to understand that she was another of those who burnt the topless towers of Ilium.

When I saw her I wished I could take her home to add to my fabulous collection of Chinese dolls.

The Pearl was tiny, her tiny feet bound tight were indeed like little mice going in and out under the heavy rolled hem of her kimono. Her golden skin glowed under a veil of white rice powder in a day when American ladies did not use any powder at all. If you have ever seen a black opal, you know how her eyes glowed under poetic, slanted eyebrows. She wore her black hair elaborately high, with little fans and combs; it had a rich color and a polished texture such as I had never seen. Chinese ladies never washed their hair. They brushed and brushed it with some preparation that looked like oatmeal and then cleansed it with scented lotion and oils. They were horrified to discover that American ladies used soap and water and they said that was why their hair looked like dry straw. Wong She seemed to me about my own age, which was very young, but Papa assured me she was older than she looked. Probably, he said, as old as Lilith, who was older than Eve. About, he said, as old as Helen of Troy, or Cleopatra.

Anyway it was certain that the Hop Sings and the On Leongs were battling to the death for her to belong exclusively to their own tong. The harassed immigration inspector and the members of the Chinatown Squad all had troubles enough without the Queen adding fuel to the feuds and they thought this might be a way to send her back to China.

As the hearing began, a number of gentlemen obviously more used to raiding opium dens or breaking up fan-tan games testified to all this and more besides. She did have many visitors, they said. All male. One large cop said he himself had visited her in the line of duty. Turning a fiery red, he said she had offered him a cup of tea. At which the Pearl, who was not supposed to understand English, tittered exquisitely behind her busy fan.

Things in the chamber of the immigration authorities trundled along until Mr. Rogers put on his first Chinese witness.

Both tongs were well represented. Too well, for the comfort of the inspector and the police. Up till this moment they had made two rows against the walls impassive, unreadable, motionless, handsome, and very very watchful. Now the inspector introduced for the first time his own interpreter, one Lou Hoy, and what sounded like a row in the United Nations began popping off in several languages and dialects. It was belligerent enough so that the members of the squad took a couple of steps forward, hands on their guns, and the inspector halted the trial. These guys played for keeps all the time, anywhere, as well he knew. Both sides, it turned out, were yelling bloody murder; they said they were getting a bad decision out of Lou Hoy, a no-good and notorious procurer and thus unfair to the Pearl, who was Queen of Chinatown in her own right. Grave injustice was being done them all, both sides, by the way Lou Hoy was covering what the witness said, and probably this was true, just as people who speak Russian insist that a diplomatic job far beyond the rules was done by the interpreters who told the United Nations and the world what Khrushchev was supposed to have said there.

Mr. Rogers recovered from a fit of near-hysterical laughter, shaking behind his monogrammed handkerchief. The scene had been panache, mad, a high comedy of manners played on an erupting volcano to the tune of temple bells and war drums, and had filled him with delight in spite of the danger.

A compromise was then effected. It looked rather like umpires at a World Series—two for each tong and two for the inspector. Each side was to check each other and where this was to end nobody knew.

The missionaries were to be the principal witnesses against Wong She and their words would be translated from English back into Chinese for the tongs.

In retrospect, my imagination insists on seeing the ecclesiological witness who appeared first as I visualize the Reverend Davidson in Somerset Maugham's classic of a missionary and a girl from Iwelei named Sadie Thompson.

He had, he said, put forth every effort to bring Wong She

to repentance, to persuade her to change her evil ways and to abandon her immoral occupation.

Mr. Rogers looked at him for a long moment. Then he said, "And what was the nature of her immoral occupation?"

"She was a prostitute," said the missionary.

Wong She flung up both little hands, the fan between the thumb and forefinger of one of them spread wide, and Wong She held it far away from her while she, too, stared at the man who had just spoken. Then she folded the fan tight and held it straight up on her knee, like a scepter, and her head drooped forward under its weight of sorrow and tower of shining black hair.

"You say this—child is a prostitute?" Mr. Rogers said.

"She most certainly is."

"Sir," Mr. Rogers said, spacing the words, "my father wore the cloth. He was a man too good for this world, but out of respect to his memory I wish to show you every possible courtesy. Be very careful what you say."

"I know exactly what to say," the man said. "I shall say the truth."

Q. You know for a fact that Wong She is a prostitute?
A. I do indeed.
Q. Of your own knowledge?
A. Yes indeed of my own knowledge.
Q. But doctor you are a married man. I thought your position—

In scarlet fury, the preacher protested, "Don't you try to make something of it. Of course no such thing ever happened—"

"Then how can you know of your own—" said Mr. Rogers, and then, shaking his finger, "You peeped!"

"I did no such thing," said the witness.

Q. You said you knew of your own personal knowledge—
A. Everybody in Chinatown knows all about this woman. Her reputation is notorious.
Q. But that, my dear sir, is hearsay.
A. It is not, it's the truth and everybody in Chinatown knows it.
Q. Well, now we are getting somewhere, sir. Everybody in the world once knew it was flat, you recall. You just tell me now under oath the names of any men you know who

can testify here for us that they consorted illegally with Wong
She thus making her a professional prostitute in defiance of
the laws under which she entered the United States—or one
man who will swear here that he has seen or been present—

Deadly—*literally* deadly—silence descended upon the chambers of the United States Department of Immigration.

The yellow faces along the walls grew blank as though
carved out of Calabasas rock. Only the glittering opaque
black eyes slid sideways, eying each other. In the icy breath
of death that filled the room, the missionary froze in dubiety
and vacillation. How could any man ever tell anything about
the *Chinese?* Men had had their heads chopped off right
here in Chinatown, and not so long ago either. Or had been
found cruelly mutilated—oh, their codes could be cruel.
Primitive justice was still rendered by the tong councils.

Wong She was their private war.

A. I don't recall.
Q. One name—
A. I—don't remember.

At this age-old admission of defeat, Inspector Charlie Wexley and the squad heaved a sigh of relief. Gang warfare has
always been gang warfare and everybody knew it might have
busted loose any moment in any courtroom. Everybody knew
only a few months before in Watsonville a sheriff had been
shot right on the witness stand. This, too, had been a brush
with death.

True to his trial principles, Earl Rogers now called the
Queen.

Escorted to the witness chair by two enormous policemen
(in those days the regulations demanded that all cops be
enormous), the Pearl perched like a butterfly, with one gesture
of her fan blew away the deathful menace and with another
transformed melodrama into comedy-drama and the chambers
into a drawing room in which to stage it.

At Mr. Rogers' first question she retired behind the fan,
and spoke from behind it in a bird whisper to one of the
interpreters. He nodded and she began the exquisite mes-
meric sing-sing—in Chinese. And the interpreter moved with
her like a Greek chorus.

As a child picture-bride, Wong She had come to California.
To Lu Bong, to whom though he was an old man she had

been a dutiful wife, casting her eyes down except when he wished her to serve tea to his friends. Alas and alas, too soon Lu Bong died and Wong She pined with loneliness until one came and requested her hand. She was wedded then to Lee Boo and they were happy until—here the lovely dark tower with the fans and jeweled combs dropped in a hurricane of sorrow, a fever beset Lee Boo and she as a dutiful wife was forced to come to his support.

But how?

All eyes and ears in the utterly entranced courtroom attended now with ardent anticipation. The fan was used beneath her chin to hold her head high, the painted mouth opened to say, "The friends of my husband have been very kind."

"No doubt," said Mr. Rogers gently, "but how, my child?"

It seemed that they had always come to the Pearl's home when they were lonesome. A sad thing in this world, how often men are lonesome. Their wives it is true are busy with the children and the cooking and the family and matters of business and religion. Even in America, this is true, is it not?

"Thus it has been that the friends of my husband and the friends of my husband's friends, being lonesome, have come to me. They have said that it is sometimes a refreshment to look at me, and I fear sadly that sometimes the wives care no more to be refreshing in the eyes of their husbands. So they come to hear me talk of China, of art, of music, and the saying of Confucius of whose teachings my husband is a great master. At leave-taking they place money as an offering for the time in which I might otherwise have earned our livelihood in different ways, and this seems to me and my husband proper."

"I am sure every gentleman in this room would agree that an offering for the time given him to look at you and hear your discourse of art was proper and well spent," said Mr. Rogers. "You offered these lonesome friends of your husband's nothing else?"

The Pearl of Chinatown flung up her fan to stop him. "But —of course I offered him other things in the name of hospitality."

"What?" said Mr. Rogers, jolted out of this fairy tale he was enjoying as much as anybody.

"Tea," said the murmurous singsong in English. "From China."

"And that's all?" asked Mr. Rogers hopefully.

"Oh no!" said the Pearl, and this time she bent over and gave her lawyer a slap with her fan, she laughed in his face with bubbling and foreign abandon, she said still in English, "Cakes—lice cakes—with lice straight from China. Of the very best. I hope someday Mr. Logers and the so-kind inspector will come and partake of my lice cakes. It would greatly please my husband."

Thumbing through all his books, the inspector knew he couldn't send Wong She back to China for selling rice cakes and tea under the chaperonage of a sick husband. He suggested that she might broaden her scope and open a teahouse to the public. At this, the fan fluttered in a high wind. Her husband's family in China, it appeared, would be disgraced. Hospitality, said the Pearl, was one thing, *trade* was another.

The Pearl had defeated the Government of the United States and was allowed to remain.

Papa called on her several times, openly and formally, I guess. Once he took me. He said there were things an American girl could learn from a Chinese lady. But going home, I told Papa I was too big to learn anything from the Queen of Chinatown. Look at my hands, Papa, I said, and held them up. True, I am vain of my hands, the Rogers women way back have always had beautiful hands and though I have not been besieged by painters I have posed frequently for sculptors—especially my hands. Just the same, they were big. I'd ridden horseback since I was four, and yanked on the reins of a burro, climbed trees, and hopped wagons—a *tomboy* was what they called me then. My hands were certainly too big for all that business with a fan. "Look at my feet," I said to Papa. In my buckskin shoes, they looked like ferryboats. Remembering the tiny, bound embroidered slippers of Wong She, I felt hopeless and Papa sympathetically patted my shoulders and said all he'd meant me to learn was Wong She's good manners and desire to please.

Almost immediately, a real battle broke out between the Hop Sings and the On Leongs. One man of prominence didn't get the hatchet out of his skull in time and that sparked the blaze. As was to happen when Frankie Yale started shooting up in the Bronx, innocent bystanders got hit—and hurt. The thing spread like a forest fire, throughout the state, endangering cities and work on the railroads and the fruit ranches.

A few days later while the cops were trying frantically to locate any of the highbinders, or ruling tong members, Papa decided he had better pay a visit to the Queen. If, as many people believed, she had been the initial cause of all this, perhaps she ought to be removed both as and from a danger.

Somebody else had apparently thought of this first. The door was locked. The landlord, a Mr. Rheinschultz, said she and her husband had gone back to China. Just as well, Mr. Rheinschultz said dourly, they always get everybody into trouble, that kind do. *Sooner or later*. Not, he said, that I ever had any trouble with her as a tenant.

That night I asked our Wong why they hadn't sent for Papa and then maybe the Pearl wouldn't have had to go away.

His face, usually expressive of all his emotions, turned as inscrutable as the jack of clubs. "More better she go," he said. "In China, is easier. China much bigger. Here all the time things happening. I glad she go. Now I mix you a cake."

Just before I went to sleep, I found myself wondering why he had been so glad the Pearl had gone and that convinced me that she had, indeed, been as instrumental in starting the state-wide tong war as Helen had been in the one in Troy.

Someone had certainly removed her from our midst.

The meeting of a United Nations of Chinese tongs was held soon afterwards. Its purpose was to end war—as whose isn't?

My father was summoned as the mediator and adviser, probably because he had for so long represented the ruling heads and possibly because he had defended the Queen of Chinatown and saved all their faces from the ignominy of her deportation. It was felt, I know, that Mr. Rogers understood them as much as it was possible for any man in America to understand the Chinese.

Perhaps he did. Hardly anybody really could figure what was going on in Chinatowns or in the Oriental minds of the Chinese. A few members of the police force who'd been on that detail for a quarter of a century. A couple of brilliant and studious federal men and some sailors and merchants who had been much in China. A reporter or two like Hugh Wiley. Even they knew only a little, but that, my father said, was as much as anybody ever would. He always said that the first thing to accept about the Chinese was that they acted at all times according to their own lights, *which were never ours.*

They saw everything a little differently through their eyes, which slanted where ours were round. I knew them to be so kind, yet I also knew they were capable of deliberate cruelty beyond what any of us could ever enact. They were to be trusted; in San Francisco I have known a street contractor to take the word of a Chinese merchant up to a million dollars without a scratch of a pen, a credit he would have extended to no American alive. All their mad insatiable love of gambling, their besetting sin, ran under the high principles and calm behavior and conduct standards they set for themselves.

Nobody knew where or when this meeting of the tongs was to take place.

All I know now is that it was in one of the secret palaces in San Francisco which actually were there, concealed behind some small shops or flashy tourist buildings. At one end of the table sat Mr. Rogers. At the other, a Chinese sage, priest, wise man, philosopher, whatever we can find to call him. He wore of course the robes of his class and position, Mr. Rogers for the occasion was formally dressed in white tie and tails, with a set of pearl studs gleaming soft.

Peace, the heads of the warring factions agreed, must be found.

The present quarrels and bloodshed were demeaning and deadly to the best interests of both peoples and of all tongs and families.

A plan, a charter, a treaty for peace must be drawn up and here agreed upon.

How important this was can only be understood by, for a moment, being part of the California of those days in the first part of the twentieth century. A rich, glorious California stretched along the Pacific Ocean with its vast commerce, a California still almost as much Spanish as it was Southern and Midwestern American, and everywhere infiltrated by the Chinese elements. After '49 a gold-mining state, to be sure, still chiefly then a farming and fruit-growing acreage, controlled entirely by the railroads as the only means of getting their wares to market. These railroads had been built and were still being built by Chinese coolie labor, imported and controlled by the heads of the tongs and, behind them in China, the families.

Those Chinatowns in San Francisco, Los Angeles, Oakland were being set apart as tourist attractions to some extent as California began dimly to see tourist trade and climate as another gold rush. But those in Fresno, Stockton, center of the San Joaquin and Sacramento rivers business of cotton and sugar, in Oxnard and Ventura and San Diego, above all in Watsonville, capital of this foreign empire within our state—these were hidden, secret, lived a life of their own. At that time of course the coolies were as vital to California, its farming and industry, as the wetbacks became when they were smuggled over the Mexican border later. *Cheap labor.*

For nine long hours, discussion went back and forth, with formality and dignity around the table at this U.N. meeting.

Not once was the opium trade mentioned.

Several times, my father had tried to do something about this deadly menace. To work with the customs officers and the shipping heads. For thousands of years, the wise men of China had tried to break this habit among their people. Nobody had succeeded. Now, aided and abetted by the British and Americans, who were making fortunes out of it, it was protected politically in high places. It was outside any usefulness Papa could have in the tong wars and Chinese problems of California. "As Confucius must have said," Papa remarked ruefully, "a man has to know when he is butting his head against a stone wall."

At last, with Earl Rogers as arbiter, an agreement for peace was drawn. No more civil wars. Clan uprisings. Tong killings. No more blood feuds.

This was ratified solemnly by the heads of the four big tongs—the Hop Sings, Bing Kongs, On Leongs and the Sui Sings. For some years there was peace in California as far as the Chinese were concerned.

"The only thing I wish," I said to my father when he came back from San Francisco, "is that they'd won it before the Pearl had to go back to China."

"Well," my father said with a twinkle, "for that matter, so do I. On the other hand, I doubt that peace would have been possible if she'd still been here."

"Papa," I said, "did you help send her back to China yourself?"

"No no," my father said, sounding horrified. "However I admit I couldn't advise against it. As Mr. Rheinschultz said they do get you into trouble—sooner or later."

TWENTY-THREE

After the verdict in the Hays case, Judge Olin Wellborn said from the Bench:

In the opinion of this Court, this has to be as serious and unprecedented a miscarriage of justice as has ever taken place in an American court. I wish to say that this Court believes that an inquiry should be made into those records of fraudulent entry in the bank's books which are missing. The failure to produce them at this trial amazes me. You are excused, gentlemen of the jury, and may your consciences be clear of the failure to serve honorably in the jury system on which our judiciary and our justice and our law is built.

This was our first real brush with disbarment. Though I did not then call it by name, it set an alarm in my consciousness that was to keep going off long later.

Papa's love for Tom Hays had grown through the years. I suppose that is why he did what the judge suspected he had done. If he used Uncle Tom's keys to enter the bank on that first dark night, that was the reason.

The Hays case, too, started in our Chinese cycle.

In the dark of the night, in the dark of the moon, wrapped in a long dark silk gown, Wong Lo San, chef of the most exclusive country club in California, sounded the tocsin that sent us rushing to Riverside. He had already hidden Uncle Tom Hays in the club's vast storehouse and wine cellar so that a warrant, charging him with the embezzlement of a million dollars, couldn't be served as planned.

History books give John S. Chapman credit for associating Earl Rogers with him in the Hays defense. Actually, on a double reverse, the ball went from Wong Lo San to Earl Rogers to John S. Chapman, who passed it back to Rogers—and very glad Chapman was to get rid of it.

Lo San, invisible as only a good Chinese servant could be, picked the ball up in the elegant, candlelit dining room of the Riverside Country Club. On that rash and perilous night, he was in person supervising a special dish for a table of Big Brass. Only railroad men were really Big Brass in those days. Until Hiram Johnson became governor in 1911, *The Octopus,* as Frank Norris called the Pacific and Southwestern Railroad political machine in his great truth-as-fiction novel, had its tentacles around most throats *somehow.* The Chinese always knew what was going on with the railroads. Thus the fact that these men had met together, bits of conversation, and finally one particular remark Lo San overheard catalyzed all the gossip, information, and speculation that had seeped into Lo San's kitchen for some time past. The dining room saw him no more. Shortly he appeared to his cousin Wong in our kitchen demanding to see Mr. Rogers at once.

His tale was brief, incomplete but terrifying.

Tom Hays's resignation from the bank months ago had stunned the town . . . rumors of a huge shortage had started and spiraled . . . there was, as the dinner tonight proved to Lo San, a weird alignment of power going on . . . above all he now knew of a warrant to be served only at midnight so Tom Hays couldn't get bail and would have to remain behind bars until after a run of the depositors on his former bank, timed for the following morning.

A pretty plot. Not new by any means and outside my ken but I could feel that the three men in our kitchen understood it well.

"They make the fall guy of your friend," Lo San said.

"The goat with the longest whiskers," his cousin Wong said. "How you call the scapegoat."

"The infamous scalawags," Earl Rogers said, "the ruthless rascals. Villains villains villains—smiling villains. Their bowels of mercy are packed with gold dust. Yes, they'd make a scapegoat of a sweet guy like Tom Hays—or—you—or me— they forgot to reckon on me—and you, Lo San. Where is Mr. Hays?"

Under black sleeves, Lo San folded his hands. "They will not arrest him at midnight," he said.

Well, we were always getting dressed in the middle of the night. Papa liked it. "I am incapable of rest," I heard him say once. "Life is too short to waste." He was already awake of course and he certainly never minded waking anybody else up. If I protested he would yell at me. "People sleep too much. It's madness. More than three hours a night is nothing but *sloth.* The mind slows down to crawl among and under the rocks. Get your clothes on or I'll *leave* you." This being my supreme terror, I always got some kind of clothes on somehow. He had a saying about sleep which his father had taught him when he was a little boy. It said Nature requires five, custom seven, laziness nine, and wickedness eleven—hours sleep a night, it meant.

That night he probably would have waited five minutes for me. Tom had a perfectly beautiful daughter named Wanda and I called Uncle Tom's wife Tia, which means "Aunt" in Spanish. "You might be of some help," my father said. "This will be very bad. Never mind those preposterous hair ribbons —here, let me do it if you must. A man's life is at stake."

"They can't hang Uncle Tom for stealing money, can they?" I said as he tied the red bows and gave them a *yank*. "I mean even if they found him guilty, could they? I know in *Oliver Twist* they could and Little Dorrit—they hung people even for debt and for robbery but they don't now, do they, Papa?"

"You know your Uncle Tom," Papa said. "His good name is the immediate jewel of his soul. He's one of those precious fools who'd cry with Othello *I have lost my reputation, I have lost the immortal part of myself.* If they convicted him of being a thief, he'd die of it as surely as if they sprung the trap under his feet."

How we got to Riverside that night, whether we rode like Paul Revere, or drove the wheels off a buggy, or went on the big red interurban cars, I cannot remember. I don't think it could have been by automobile because it was quite a while before they had lights. The change-over from boots-saddles-to-horse-and-away to honking horns is interwoven inextricably in my memory. I remember crying because Mama broke her arm trying to crank an early automobile called a Duro. It was on a big red suburban electric car I rode to Whittier with Ike St. Johns to meet his family, a day I shall not forget this side of the grave, since Earl Rogers' notorious disreputable daughter was not what they had in mind for their eldest son—I was seventeen then. Must have been the big red car because I remember Papa and Lo San talking as I dozed and I heard something clearly about somebody Lo San was to find and I could tell by his voice that Papa was in between his top fighting-no-holds-barred mettle and trying not to break down and cry. Two or three times he said in a furious protest, "Couldn't they leave him alone? The best—he's the best, isn't he, Lo San?—I love the man, everybody loves Tom."

Lo San said, "Sometimes lovable now very weak man."

So already I knew this case was going to be different from any other as long as we lived.

I went alone up the white steps of the wide veranda. The light was on, before I could ring, the door opened. Big red circles around her eyes, swollen trembling lips showed how long Tia had been crying. So I hugged her and said, "It's all right. Papa's here." Tia hugged me back and kept saying, "It's a mistake, it's some kind of terrible mistake," and Wanda woke up in her chair, *she* was mad, she said, "You can sue people for false arrest, I'm going to sue them if they arrest my father, I'll sue them for false arrest." They wanted to know where my father was but I didn't know. He said to tell Tia just to tell everybody Uncle Tom was out of town and nothing else and to be surprised.

When the knock came after midnight, I hid. If the marshal recognized me he would know Tom Hays had sent for Earl Rogers and whatever Papa was up to he didn't want anybody to know he was there. Lo San had been smart enough really to keep his mouth shut and send for Earl Rogers and that gave him a jump. When they did arrest Tom Hays it would be much better if nobody knew he'd already talked to Mr. Rogers.

In her nightgown and bathrobe Tia went to the door. I was amazed at the way she looked as though she'd just gotten out of bed and her eyes were that way because she'd been waked out of a sound sleep. I decided women could deceive anybody whenever they wanted to. They told lies much better than men. *Nothing showed.* No muscles twitching along their jaws; no eyebrows wiggling; no eyes too wide open or too direct—just perfectly natural. Tia said, "No, I'm sorry, Mr. Hays isn't here. He's out of town. I don't know where—on a business trip, that was all he told me." I almost believed her myself.

With variations, she kept on saying that for three strange long days.

Wanda and I played duets on the piano to pass the time, noisy pieces like the *Overture from William Tell* and *Columbia the Gem of the Ocean*, and we got the giggles listing the *expressions* Tia put into her twice-told tale—*tutta forza, allegro, pianissimo, appassionata, con agitazione, abbandono, staccato, capriccioso, crescendo.* The *theme* never changed. To an ever-increasing number of officials with and without guns, with and without warrants, who wanted to see Mr. Hays badly, Tia said, "But he's not at home. No—I really don't know where he is."

The first night the marshal, who knew the Hayses, had taken her word for it.

On the third day he couldn't afford to be polite any longer. Aided by two federal men and a county detective, he searched the lovely serene home; behind the glazed chintz curtains, larkspur blue with roses and green parrots in the pattern; under the four-poster beds; in the gleaming mahogany wardrobes; opening the big closets that sent out clouds of lavender fragrance; picking up the silver tea service on the maple dresser that had been Tia's great-grandmother's. I loved it better than any house I knew, I have reproduced it on Long Island and in Beekman Place. As the search went on, I stayed hunched over the piano making *fortissimo scherzo* noises myself, I didn't want any of the reporters by now traipsing along to spot me. Also, I could hardly bear to see them just invading Tia's *home*, shoving around her family possessions, tramping on her Aubusson carpets as though they were jail linoleum —I'd never seen a house *searched* before. I could have chewed them up with my bare teeth.

They didn't find anything. Not in the stables-garage nor the chicken house nor in the orange orchard.

The marshal left watchmen around in the gardens. As we walked around in the house we could see them and every once in a while a face would appear at a window and Wanda squealed every single time. We were getting pretty doggone jumpy, to tell the truth. Cooped up and not knowing where anybody was or what was happening.

Naturally, they had thought of the country club. Golf and tennis were Tom Hays's sports, he had cups in them, he spent a lot of his time at the club, he was its most popular member and had been president the year before.

So they took their warrants out there.

Wong Lo San always seemed to be between them and any of the doors to any of his domain which they had been planning to enter. Every inch of the place where a Chinaman worked was always referred to by him as *his* and meant just what it said. Moreover, nearly always Lo San was sharpening *one* of the thirty-two little or large knives or the seventeen different meat axes small and great which he kept at hand. Just as the marshal or the bank officials or the D.A.'s dicks appeared, Lo San would test the *edge* with the ball of his thumb, where it left a thin red line. Lo San said tranquilly but with authority that he did not like anybody snooping around *his* domain when he had lunch—or dinner—to get. No, they could not go into *his* storerooms or *his* cellars.

He said he did not know what a search warrant was.

Somehow, nobody got up nerve enough to show him one and prove it to him.

Don't ask *me*.

I suppose it was the age-old mind-over-matter, the authority of a good English nanny who made the British Empire what it was, the one-pointed advantage of the man who means what he says.

Anyhow, they didn't.

As far as I know, this was the first time my father kept a client, or a man wanted for a crime, or somebody for whom a warrant was in the hands of the police or a United States marshal, hidden from the Law. In order to make an investigation, to do certain things, hide things, or conceal evidence *before* an arrest was made.

It's a T-formation quarterback's play to conceal the ball while his guards take their men and the tackles open up the holes and Earl Rogers was a remarkable ball handler. In the Hays case and other of Earl Rogers' cases Erle Stanley Gardner uncovered this particular hidden-ball trick and it became the consistent strategy of Perry Mason in most of his books.

In the Case of the Vanishing Bank Books and the Missing Million, Mr. Rogers was sure that, as Lo San and Wong put it, ruthless powers intended to make a fall guy or a scapegoat out of Tom Hays, a friend of his.

Over my dead body, said Earl Rogers. Right or wrong. May my friend be right if possible, but right or wrong—my friend.

Whereupon he took on first the United States Marshal's office.

Then the whole machinery of the bank examiners of the state of California.

Finally, a multimillionaire United States senator.

He and Lo San between them.

Just what the Hays case was all about and what really happened has bewildered many people who are supposed to understand high finance, as careful conspiracies about money are designed by geniuses to do.

However, history, fiction, and television have shown us clearly a simple fact. In the early days of the West, property and prosperity in all areas depended on the Coming of the Railroad. Some mighty bloody and unscrupulous fights took place. Somebody either wanted to get the railroads into their

town, or the railroads wanted to get some land on which to
build that somebody *didn't* want them to have. If a man knew
where a railroad was planning to go, he might make a fortune
by robbing a beautiful blond girl of the ranch her papa had
left her. Or by bribery, or gunplay, a villain might get the
railroad to lay its tracks on a right of way he owned.

This may be oversimplification or generalization, but all
drama comes within some one of the frameworks and this
looks like the one arranged behind the Tom Hays matter—
some version of it.

Back in Montana and Washington, copper multimillionaire
Senator William A. Clark wanted to get his Salt Lake road into
California, especially into Los Angeles, whose bright future
his stereopticon eye seems to have spotted while it was just
a little Mexican hacienda to lots of people. To do this, he had
to beat the Southern Pacific, whose lines were already entrenched, big, tough, experienced, and ferocious. The S.P.
didn't just have a powerful lobby in Sacramento—the Southern
Pacific lobby *was* the state legislature or vice versa. The
Southern Pacific also had as much money as the Salt Lake and
I guess on scruples, or lack of, they were even. This was the
old rough game, the power plays, simpler, more brutal, much
less subtle and easier to see than the passing game of today.
However, then as now, somebody always got the multi-
millions.

Looking for a soft spot to hit, the Salt Lake decided on
Riverside, one of the most beautiful little cities in the world.

Hard as it is to believe today, Southern California's largest
industry then was growing oranges. Of this, Riverside was the
center and capital. Orange groves stretched in all directions
around the town, when the trees were in blossom it smelled
the way I hope heaven will, if I ever get there. Orange blossoms were always used for bridal bouquets, I carried them
when I married Ike St. Johns. Now, of course, it is against the
law. Oranges have become too commercially valuable to use
the flowers that produce them for mere Romance. Somehow
I feel that they were warmer and sweeter and more real and
somehow *safer* than orchids.

Riverside was Pasadena's leading rival for social dictator-
ship in Southern California. It also had Mount Rubidoux,
where the Franciscan Fathers planted a cross and where the
first Easter sunrise service was held, and the most elegant,
picturesque, and delightful hotel on the American continent
—the Mission Inn.

Scouts for and from the Salt Lake R.R. probably saw none of this.

They did see an entryway into the land they needed and a bright prospect in Tom Hays. Head man in Riverside County, city, bank, real estate, society, country club, and political boss. Republican. Few Democrats lived in Riverside.

Nobody is ever satisfied with the industry they have, with things as they are. This is called progress. Beautiful and fragrant and reasonably profitable as growing oranges was, Uncle Tom saw that Riverside could do better. The Salt Lake promised him that Riverside would grow and multiply and outstrip Los Angeles if it had a real, good, huffing, puffing, root-toot-tooting railroad to bring industry belching from the East. It would become a *city*. Everybody's property would be worth more. Much more. *One* orange grove could be cut up to build six or seven factories on.

To these busy bees of industry, apparently, Uncle Tom explained the situation frankly enough. He knew everybody and everything, all the right men, and he showed them what had to be done to beat the Old Champion, the Southern Pacific, who or which would be waiting for them with lead in the glove.

The Salt Lake said go ahead and do it.

We will back you to an unlimited extent.

Tom Hays did.

Just *how*, just *what*—here was the reason for all the trouble. Nor can anybody answer it in full. Big deals like this are not hatched to be simple and by the time they get to be omelets it's hard to tell which eggs were whose. Or who broke 'em.

To everybody's amazement, a lot of stories got around that *Tom Hays* had pulled some crooked deals in buying up rights of way for the Salt Lake. In fact, some of these might be called fraud. This while he was still an official of the United States National Bank, which of course had given him a lot of his contacts, entries, and knowledge. Maybe after all young Tom Hays—such a *nice guy*, such a *sweet* guy, everybody loved Tom Hays—maybe he wasn't quite up to being a financier in that kind of company. In an agony of indignation and embarrassment, and possibly fear, against Earl Rogers' advice, Tom Hays resigned from his position at the bank. Papa was always against resigning. In this case, he thought the Southern Pacific might have started the rumors to scare people away from making deals for their land with the newcomer. Or the

Salt Lake themselves might be moving Tom Hays out front to take the rap, if anything was wrong. Dog eat dog, Papa said.

Following the resignation there was an ominous lull of a couple of months. We had ridden out a couple of Sundays to sit in the garden under the wistaria and have supper. I thought Uncle Tom seemed worried. Always before I'd thought of him as having what my grandfather had called a sunny disposition. The word *gay* had belonged especially to him. I suppose I was making my first contact with what I came to know so often was covered by irresistible charm—inability to take pressure.

Then a young congressman for whose election Tom Hays had been largely responsible made whatever move was necessary to have the bank's books examined. They found the shortage, all right. And a complaint was issued against Tom Hays. He had, it said, falsified entries to cover a misappropriation of bank funds to the tune of over a million. The court then handed the marshal the warrant he was trying so hard to serve. The story going around was that Uncle Tom had been buying up land and rights of way for himself as well as for the Salt Lake. One-for-you, one-for-me sort of things and that the Salt Lake had somehow left him holding the bag.

This was where we came in.

Wanda and me chewing gum, which we were NEVER allowed to do, and playing the piano. Tia answering the marshals. Uncle Tom hiding in the storehouse with Lo San sharpening his knives before the door. And Earl Rogers completely vanished.

TWENTY-FOUR

To give direct evidence of what Papa was up to in those missing nights is manifestly impossible now.

As Judge Wellborn thundered from the Bench, demanding an inquiry as to why the books in which the bank examiner testified he'd found the fraudulent entries were not in court, saying they must be the best evidence of the crime, I began to have a vague idea. If the books had been available Tom Hays's guilt might have been too plain to do anything about.

That night I told my idea to Papa.

"You are being carried away by your fertile imagination," he said.

"I know one thing," I said. "Tia told me. Uncle Tom still had his keys to the bank when he resigned. Probably nobody had the guts to ask him for them. Everybody had forgotten about that."

"All women talk too much," my father said. "It would be wiser if both you and Tia forgot such idle speculations. You see, don't you, that a man would be disbarred for such actions as you describe?"

"Oh—" I said, and then I said yes I saw that.

"Then you will see that it would be fatal to mention any of it to anyone else?" my father said.

"I wouldn't," I said, "I—*see*."

I did, too.

For years I saw it. For years I always knew what disbarment meant and how *easy* it was for a criminal lawyer to jar the thread by which it was held suspended over his head.

What else could Papa have *done* in the Hays case, with Uncle Tom being the man friend he loved best of anybody, ever?

He had to get him acquitted. I saw that.

On the third morning, Tom Hays surrendered. A bondsman was waiting, he never went to jail. At once Tom sent for his own lawyer, John S. Chapman, attorney for corporations, railroads, and banks who'd never taken a criminal case. This was the one case in which Earl Rogers ever appeared under someone else as chief counsel for the defense. He had refused to go to New York to help defend Harry K. Thaw, Delphin M. Delmas having been retained as chief counsel. Not that Delmas wasn't a good trial lawyer, but as my father often said during the trial he himself wouldn't have used the Dementia Americana defense. With the most beautiful girl in the world as a witness, one Evelyn Nesbit Thaw, he'd have plumped all out for the Old Unwritten Law. He'd prove an old roué Stanford White had ruined Thaw's bride when she was little more than a baby, and nothing more. Father never saw any great difference between getting a client sent to the insane asylum and getting him sent to Sing Sing, and a man didn't have to be crazy to kill under such circumstances.

In the Hays case, he saw at once that this trustee of the Bar Association, Mr. Chapman, would and could never be suspected of any little fun and games which the B.A. didn't sanction. Thus it was wise to leave him out in front as chief counsel while young Earl Rogers, who was busy trying to get that Not Guilty verdict, had been called in only to help in the trial itself.

One other thing was outstanding to me about Papa in the Hays case, more so to me than anybody else, I *knew* his ignorance about banking was a zero with the rim rubbed off. *His* bankers could have told them sad stories of bouncing checks, minus deposits, and bonehead bungling. In a mind tough, tenacious, broad in scope beyond any I've seen since, there was a lobe that didn't work. An aversion, an allergy, to figures, especially those on greenbacks of the United States. Gold pieces he understood better, you could *throw* those away, to piano players or beggars, bartenders or friends-in-need, tailors or nuns or anybody who could pitch a tale about wanting to go to college or home to see his mother. His estimation of money as without importance crippled and hamstrung him all his life.

Papa's idea of *saving* was to earn more.

He believed that his *earnings* were his *capital*.

Nobody could convince him that it was dishonest to spend on mad extravagance money already owed to other people—and in this the people he owed indulged him moronically. They came to collect bills and remained to beg him to charge more of whatever it was. In Papa, they seemed to think it was elegant and becoming and made their own lives a little more exciting for him to fling their money to the winds, as well as his own.

About money matters, I actually felt sorry for my mother. Her Holland Dutch ancestors were thrifty, her father Avery Green had been a shrewd Yankee horse trader, she loathed bills and bill collectors, and some of her bitterest quarrels with my father came because of them. I expect part of the time it was *the bills* she ran away from.

Yet as he came off the stand in the Hays case the bank examiner said he had never met a man with such a profound knowledge of every detail of banking, banking laws, and bank bookkeeping. *Papa*, who couldn't help me with my long division, much less fractions. In all things having to do with transactions, moneys involved, conveyances, deeds, reversions, deliverances and options, Earl Rogers, he said, might have been born in a countinghouse. For this he had stayed up nights, studying, absorbing, reading endlessly, as he did later also on all details of jewels and their weight and purity until in the Lomax murder he might have been a jeweler himself. His memory was phenomenal.

A fabulous performance, Judge Wellborn agreed, his lips pinched, his eyes cold and wary on young Rogers. And he was right. It was a performance. Just as John Drew hobbled about the wings bent in agony with rheumatism yet as soon as the curtain went up walked onto the stage as straight and sprightly as a man of twenty, so off-stage—out of court—Earl Rogers walked the floor all night, suffering as I'd never seen him before. Up and down, in and out, long walks in the darkness, preparing for the next day in court.

For in spite of the effectiveness of the performance, Judge Wellborn had from the Bench ordered a new and more drastic search made for the missing books. From all sides there was some unusual sense of pressure, in the courtroom we felt squeezed by it without knowing exactly what it was.

Guilty.

The word tolled in Rogers' mind through sleepless nights.

This jury, he said to me, won't look at me.

They don't look at Tom.

That's a convicting jury every time.

They will send him to prison, he kept saying.

"He'll die behind bars," Tom Hays's friend Earl Rogers said frantically, "he won't be able to breathe the air that comes through bars. Take away his freedom, he'll be a soul in pain, *gazing wistfully at the day.* He'll *peak and pine in sick surmise—*" I recognized that he was taking words from Oscar Wilde's *Reading Gaol,* using them as part of his own speech, a habit he had with poetry. "Better *with nimble feet to dance upon the air,*" he said, "*The dead so soon grow cold.*"

Pacing up and down, caged in his desperation, he began to quote the last stanza of it. "*A prison wall was round us both, two outcast men we were, the world had thrust us from its heart, and God from out his care*—some men would rather be dead than locked up—" he cried, suddenly, on one of these white nights, and my stomach fell like an elevator out of control. I had never fainted in my life, though ladies did often, but I thought I was going to then.

He had been drinking.

How could I have failed to see it before? Why hadn't my inner danger signal worked? I suppose because he had never—as far as I knew—done this during a case. Never showed up in court when he'd had a drink. He kept saying, "What can I do?" and my heart said it right along with him though we meant different things. I didn't even know whether to tell him right out that I knew. The bottle had been kept hidden. If he didn't know I knew it now, he'd still try to cover it up and not drink so much.

What can I do?

As soon as Rosy came in, I went to see Pearl Morton. To ask her. Of all things, she began to cry. I think his drinking in court, in the middle of a case, especially one where he cared so much, was a *first time* that told her more than it did me. She set a higher value on him than any other man, I felt it was partly the love his seeking refuge in her, trusting her, had awakened and partly he was the only black sheep she had worth saving. This I mean on top of just *loving* him. Her concern for him was an active volcano all the time. She blew her nose and between sniffles she said, "The way to tell whether a man is a slave or a master to drink, honey, is the ones who drink at the wrong time, not by how drunk they get. They drink at the worst time. For days when it wouldn't matter they never touch a drop. Then the one time they shouldn't, off they go. Sometimes I think I'll join up with Carrie Nation. Honey, I think you better put up a fight now. A man I know took the Keeley Cure, it did him a lot of good. Maybe you can get your papa to try it."

I must have made a lot of noise, looking for the bottle. He thought of strange places in which to hide it. I was pouring the whiskey down the toilet—I didn't know then how many women had poured bottles down the drain and that it never did any good—when there he stood in the doorway. His head was down, his anger came out of him like a blast, guilty anger is always hotter or colder than any other kind, and he gave me a real ugly look which made me mad too. He said, very haughty, "That's pretty fresh, isn't it? Besides being silly."

I said, "It's no sillier than you pouring it down your throat and it'll do you less harm." I took a long gasp and said, "It smells so awful. It makes me sick—I don't see how you can swallow it—"

In two quick strides he crossed the bathroom and pulled the chain. He said furiously, "Did anybody ask you to swallow it? Who's been putting you up to this Carrie Nation imbecility? You'll be going around smashing saloons with an ax next thing."

"They arrest her and shoot at her," I said, "but she is not dismayed."

"She doesn't do any good, either," Papa said. "It can't be done that way." The ugly look was gone, it left him white and —forlorn. Way way down underneath, I knew that he was frightened. It came out in the white flicker of forlornness, came and was gone at once but I'd seen it. I knew then that what he said was true. It wasn't any use pouring it down the toilet. This was the battle with his enemy of which Pearl Morton had told me. The good and evil of him, fighting to get possession. The good of him was so shining and gifted. The evil would send a fallen archangel like Lucifer, *better to reign in hell than serve in heaven*, we had to have a higher power on our side, too, I didn't know any higher power any more, just the same I sent up rockets of distress and I didn't care which archangel it was, Gabriel or Michael or Azrafel.

I said, "A long time ago, you said you'd tell me when to start worrying."

"Yes," my father said. We were still in the bathroom, of all places, and I sat down on the edge of the tub, my legs had begun to wobble like spaghetti.

"Isn't it about time?" I said. "In *court*, Papa. You know, Judge Wellborn is watching you all the time every minute like a gimlet. He thinks you did something phony with the books. You have to keep your head clear. Papa, you mustn't take another drink. Why, you'd be the one who sent Uncle Tom to prison, wouldn't you?"

His head down, he didn't look at me. He picked up the bottle, there was a little left in it and it swished around and I could smell it again. He said, "You remember the drink Dr. Jekyll made and poured and drank to become his lower self, Mr. Hyde, the fiend who trampled on children? This is it, Nora—this is it and always has been."

He threw the bottle and it smashed and he went out and I followed him. I put my arms around him and said, "It's all right, Papa. Just don't take another drink. You just have to promise me not to take another drink, anyhow not till the trial is over. It can't get out of the bottle, can it, and climb down your throat? And maybe after this case is over you might go and take the Keeley Cure—"

Well, I want to tell you, that did it. I never saw a man so mad in all my life. He let out a regular yell. "You're out of your mind," he shouted. "It's a joke—the Keeley Cure is a vaudeville joke—all right, all right, Wellborn has got his knife out for me and he's a good judge, I'll say that, and a respected judge, so I won't drink until the case is over. He might get bitten by this tarradiddle of yours too. You want everybody in this entire holier-than-thou overgrown village to think I'm a drunkard? I allow you a lot of leeway, my girl, but if you're going to be like any fool woman with this trumped-up father-dear-father-come-home-with-me-now yodeling—I'll put you over my knee and take a razor strop to you—"

"You can if you want to," I said. "You're bigger than I am—"

He was shaking, he put his hands on the table and said hurriedly, "I'm sorry, Nora—that was unforgivable, but forgive me anyhow."

"All right," I said, "but don't kid yourself, a lot of people do think it already and what's more you've got Uncle Tom worried."

His voice was different when he said, "I mustn't do that. You and Uncle Tom are really building up a Frankenstein here but just so you won't worry—"

"You said yourself," I said, "that it was like Dr. Jekyll and Mr. Hyde."

I meant to say more but suddenly his eyes were cold and forbidding. So I didn't. Then he held out his hand and we shook hands and he smiled at me. From his hand to mine, I knew I couldn't believe him. I could feel a fever in him; right then he wanted to take a drink. It didn't make sense but I felt it was true.

I was right.

When he went on that extraordinary visit to Senator William A. Clark he was just at the *peak*—where everybody who drinks wants to be.

By that time he was so sure they were going to convict Tom Hays that he was willing to take any chance. He should have been cold sober. The senator was not a man to fool around with.

Hawley had been staked outside the magnificent Clark mansion for some time. The senator was in residence.

Luther Brown went to the door and rang the bell and when a butler answered, he said that Mr. Earl Rogers, counsel for the defense in the case of Tom Hays, wanted to see the senator at once.

In a few moments, the two men faced each other in a library that might have come straight out of the stately homes of Old

England. The slim, black-haired blue-eyed young lawyer, on fire with purpose. The distinguished old senator, one of the richest men in the world and certainly one of the most powerful. His eyes were cold and his manner was ducal, not only used to command but to be obeyed. His reputation for vision, for mental capacity, for philanthropy was as great as his fortune. The opening in his armor was a true love of music.

"Good evening, Mr. Rogers," the senator said.

"Good evening to you, Senator," Earl Rogers said, without returning either the slight smile or the courteous nod.

"What can I do for you, Mr. Rogers?" Senator Clark said.

"I don't know whether you can do anything for me or not," the younger man said, and took a couple of steps forward. "For your own sake, I hope you can." He waited and the moment of silence lay between them. The senator was too old a hand to be baited into a move by this opening gambit. After a moment of it, Earl Rogers threw back his head as though appealing to whatever gods might be handy. "Ice water in his veins," he said, "ice water. I knew this. Listen to me, Senator. Somewhere somebody is putting a lot of pressure on a lot of witnesses to send Tom Hays to San Quentin."

This time, Rogers smiling pleasantly, outwaited him.

"Pressure," the senator said. "What do you mean by pressure?"

"I came to tell you one thing," Earl Rogers said, and he moved forward on the balls of his feet, swaying a little. "If Tom Hays goes to San Quentin, Senator, he will not go alone." He tapped his forefinger upon the senator's white dress shirt and began to laugh. "If he goes, Senator, you will go with him."

"Mr. Rogers," Senator Clark said, "you're drunk."

"Don't count on that, Senator," Earl Rogers said.

He made a rather more elaborate bow than usual and the senator nodded stiffly. "Good night, Mr. Rogers," he said.

"Good night, Senator," Earl Rogers said. He went across the big room, not quite swaggering, not quite staggering, a little of both. He turned and said softly, "You and I are the only two men in the world who know whether I can make good on that statement, aren't we, Senator? Good night to you, sir."

With that he made his exit, without looking back. Which is the sign of a really great poker player. As undoubtedly Senator Clark knew.

Perhaps it was that.

In his book on great lawyers, W. W. Robinson speaks of the plea Earl Rogers made in the Hays case as a masterpiece of eloquence, of exceptional emotional force, and one of the most moving ever heard. I have never thought of my father as a great orator, probably he underplayed everything and the contrast was too surprising for most of us, he was years ahead of his time. I agree that his closing speech in the Hays case was unforgettable and touching, terribly touching. Also it gave me a yardstick which I have used all my life.

Your Honor and Gentlemen of the Jury. The evidence is before you. I feel that you must judge it for yourselves. As to the Law, His Honor will instruct you upon that far beyond what I could do even if it were my place or my privilege to do so.

There is only one thing I want to tell you. One thing I am going to tell you.

By profession, I am a criminal lawyer. By the law of our land, as you all know, every man accused of a crime has a right to a proper defense. To a good defense. To the presentation of his side of the case as it should be offered to you. That is why trial by jury is the very foundation of our judicial system. And without an impartial trial in which the defendant is also represented, the fame of our trial by jury would not survive.

In the years during which I have practiced at the criminal bar of this state, with some measure of success, I have come to know one thing. To believe it with my whole being.

There are crimes of which each one of us is capable. You know that as well as I do. It must make us more charitable to our fellowman so that we combine mercy with stern justice. We also know that there are crimes of which we are not capable. Certain things we could not do. Under any circumstances, temptations or desires.

I have come to know that certain men simply could not commit certain crimes. In all honesty, let me say to you it has become almost second-sight to me now. *This* man could not have committed *that* crime.

With calm faith, I would risk my life on the lead-pipe cinch that Tom Hays could not commit the crime for which he has been brought before you. Tom Hays is not capable of cold-blooded, unscrupulous scheming to defraud his fellow townsmen. It would not be possible for him to stand shoulder to shoulder with his fellow workers, to greet his neighbors day after day while he robbed them of their savings. In some turmoil of the senses, some sudden lethal temptation he might yield for an hour, a day. But he could not *live* through weeks, months, of playing the fox consciously with people he knew well.

Not that. Not that.

Everyone in this community has known Tom Hays for years.

What word comes first to their minds if you mention his name? Honesty. Here is a man you can trust. A man we all have trusted. I myself have trusted him through the years to take better care of my earnings than I would do myself. Could such love and trust as his friends and neighbors have given Tom Hays be given to a man capable of this dastardly conniving? This low cunning? Some crimes, yes. I have known but one man I did not think might commit murder under extreme provocation, that man was my own father, who was a saint. The rest of us—you and me—if our blood was up, if revenge or hate or fear or any of the devil's snares caught us—I don't know. But to wake up every morning, to try to go to sleep every night, to look at his face in the mirror when he shaved and see not Tom Hays but Uriah Heep, that slimiest of all villains—I say to you NO, this is impossible. He would have died of it before now.

As is my duty, I defend everybody. To the best of my ability. That is our law, our jury system. Better, we say, that a hundred guilty men escape than one innocent man be condemned. It may be that I have under that principle freed guilty men. Ever since this case began, gentlemen, I have been haunted—*haunted*—by the terror that here this time I might fail to free the one innocent man.

Tom Hays is the scapegoat, the *patsy* as we say, of men—money men—who have lost all conscience in the pursuit of vast wealth and power, who believe all is fair in the war for gold.

And I tell you if Tom Hays is convicted of this crime of which I know him to be innocent I will turn in my license to practice law, in shame, gentlemen, in *shame*.

Look at him, gentlemen, look at my friend Tom Hays. And you will see why I say that to you.

Well, he was worth looking at.

So young, so charming, so clean-cut, his head held high, his eyes so kind and frank.

They looked at him and they believed what his friend Earl Rogers had said to them. They weren't out long.

We heard those words for which we so longed.

Not Guilty.

Then while we all laughed and wept over him, we were frozen by the cold heavy voice of the judge speaking in thunderous rebuke. I had never heard anything like it before and it was terrible, there was a thing beyond the man, there was the might of his office, the authority we had given him. Upon the incorruptibility of our judiciary our own freedom rested. All this was present, the thing itself, it swept and harrowed and filled the courtroom as though clouds had parted and Jehovah or Jeremiah had thundered at us.

. . . . *as serious and unprecedented a miscarriage of justice as has ever taken place in an American court . . . verdict of not guilty is without foundation. . . . this Court insists that an inquiry should be made into the records of fraudulent entry which are missing . . . failure to produce . . . you are excused, gentlemen, and may your consciences be clear of your failure to serve honorably in the jury system on which our justice and law is built . . .*

They slunk out. Yes they did.

My father stood there, his face stricken as a boy's. His hands for once hung down beside him absolutely still. The stunned horror on the face of Mr. John S. Chapman, poor soul, was near comic relief. After what seemed a long time, Tom Hays, with the tears streaming down his face, put his arms around my father. Then we were all able to move again and when we looked up the Bench was empty. The judge had retired to his chambers.

All this haunted me from there on in. I know now how close my father was to disbarment, even then I must have sensed it. Judge Wellborn was a man of enormous courage and integrity, member of one of the state's fine families of influence. I don't know why the inquiry he demanded never got off the ground. Perhaps others, of greater power, didn't want any investigation of anything to do with the Hays case . . . *If he goes to San Quentin, he will not go alone.* . . .

The specter of disbarment entered my consciousness then but of course I soon buried it deep under waves and heaps of spectacular success.

Nobody would *dare*.

Of course I didn't blame Papa. What else could he do when it was Tom Hays? Whatever Uncle Tom had done, he'd been roped into it. Could Papa let the higher-ups use Uncle Tom in their greed and then toss him into the jailhouse like a worn-out tool?

Looking back through the years is a strange experience. Sometimes it is looking through the wrong end of binoculars, big things are tiny. Or turning a spyglass into a room that remains dark. But often things grow clear and the truth is plain at last.

Uncle Tom was a man who had risen to responsibility on sheer personality. Charm—that amazing quality which implies magic, black or white. He looks weak, as I see him now, lovable and charming and *weak*.

Until the judge spoke to us like that I didn't care whether he was guilty or not. I didn't know whether it was the eloquence of Papa's final plea and promise, or one turning off the heat which freed him. At first what the judge said only made me defiant but after Uncle Tom died it troubled me.

About that, Papa had been right. His good name gone, his reputation tarnished, what remained was too mortal to survive. Papa was there when he died, he didn't want anybody else, Papa held him quietly in his arms. He said to me afterwards, "Don't ever let anybody tell you a man doesn't die of a broken heart. We have seen it happen."

What troubled me so much was that after all if Uncle Tom was guilty he—he had thrown away his own good name, hadn't he? If he was guilty even though he'd been a tool and hardly noticed and gotten into the quicksand and didn't know how to get out, it was his own weakness that had tarnished his reputation. Jim Corbett, heavyweight champion of the world, whom I adored because when we had a table-d'hôte American-plan dinner he ordered *all* the "choice of" cakes, pies, puddings, pastries, and ice cream on the menu for us both, had told me you never knew anything about a man until you found out whether he could get up off the floor or not. Uncle Tom didn't.

Just as in my stomach I had known poor no-good young Boyd hadn't *shot* anybody, I felt a weak man could have committed the crime of those missing fraudulent entries and died of it, hagridden by guilt, it was a weak crime that he'd think he could *cover up*. Put the money *back*. I still thought of course we had to get him acquitted. What else could Papa have done, I kept asking myself.

It was one of those moments when a sunny day stops being bright without changing. A one-per-cent mist of gray you could hardly see, a chill you couldn't really feel says summer is over.

All those magnificent things Papa had said to the jury. Could he have said them unless he believed them? When you defended a man did you have to sort of hypnotize yourself so you believed your own lies? Were you *supposed* to do that to give your client the best defense?

The judge hadn't thought so.

A serious and unprecedented miscarriage of justice.

To accept your own version—to become one with—to justify —to lose your own sense of right and wrong—

A lot—most of this—must have been instinctive and without words. I am analyzing it now, the cold feeling in the stomach of the child Nora, through the binoculars of long experience, but I am sure the analysis is right.

I feel that it is right.

I am of one mind with Frank Sullivan about footnotes and garlands of *ibids*. So how I came to know that my father's interview with Senator Clark took place as he used to tell it will just be part of our story here.

Years later my Aunty Blanche asked the senator.

Blanche Rogers Lott was then a top musical organizer as well as a concert pianist. Many of the musical affairs which she directed for the Los Angeles Symphony and later the Hollywood Bowl were financed by Senator Clark and they often met and dined together when they were planning an opera season or choosing soloists or conductors for their programs. She loved and respected him and was grateful for all he did for music.

So one day, being afraid of nothing and nobody, Aunty Blanche asked him if the story of her brother's call on him during the Hays case was true.

She said the old senator stared at her for a moment without expression. Then a wintry but admiring smile came over his face. "Your brother was a remarkable fellow," he said. "Understand I do not say whatever version he gave you of our conversation that night is the true one. His ideas were entirely erroneous. That he did come to see me and make certain—suggestions—is true."

After a pause, he said quietly, "Too bad. A man of such brain power and *daring* must be cold and sober as any good

gambler must be. I always thought he would have been Attorney General when the Democrats got in—if he had stayed
cold—and sober."

Then of course he would have been like Senator William A.
Clark, and never have defended Uncle Tom Hays in the first
place.

TWENTY-FIVE

Earl Rogers forcing the mayor to resign after a skittish vice
probe; Mama going East again; the Los Angeles Angels losing
the pennant by one game; the San Francisco fire, to which Papa
went on the first relief train; our last hunting trip to Arizona;
my meeting with the man of God, Dr. Bob Burdette; and his
with my father and Dolly; the sheer horror and macabre jests
in the Case of the Wife Who Didn't Die; the autopsy Rogers
himself performed on a man named Buck, after the state had
hung him! The arrival of Buck's ghost to haunt him forever
after—all these could not have happened simultaneously.

On the principle of television and Einstein, neither of
which had ever been heard of then, they did. The camera can
concentrate on Mantle at the plate, or widen its scope to
take in the infield, outfield, bull pens and dugouts, and the
fence over which Mickey hits a home run.

Looking back, the screen of our life at that time widens for
me and all these things do seem to have been going on more
or less at the same time.

One clear picture is in the garden of a beautiful school to
which I'd been sent after my grandmother's blistering tongue
convinced Papa that I was growing up an ignoramus and
would be unable to cope with my equals. I think Papa admired
his mother but he didn't love her as he had my grandfather.
I know I never counted on her having the slightest influence
over him. Years later when I spent a good deal of time with
the recently abdicated Edward VIII of England, I thought it
was much the same with him. He spoke to me of his father
King George with deep affection, of his mother Queen Mary
only with admiration. I thought that was why she had not

been able to keep him from giving up the throne of England for a woman.

Nevertheless Grandmother's dire predictions as to my future led to The Hall, where the headmistress soon summoned my father to explain to him that I Told Lies. Of this there was no question nor, when he arrived, did I attempt to deny it.

"Papa," I said frantically, "they don't know how to believe *anything*. Talk about ignoramuses. They've never even read *Midsummer Night's Dream*. It's no fun unless you can make them believe the stories. Don't you believe in Mowgli, Papa?"

"Yes," Papa said a little ruefully, "I do. Nora, the original storytellers throughout history were minstrels. They went from town to town, from castle to castle, from inn to inn, they carried the news, sometimes they spread a doctrine or whispered a mystical secret, sometimes they entertained with poetry and music and tales. Usually, they carried a lute. You can't do that, I agree, but you must work out some method to explain that you are telling a story, a *tale*. Nor must you allow your imagination to distort facts."

"Well," I said, "the ones they believe the least are the ones that really happened. When I make them up, they believe much better."

At one time when the lady headmistress, whose sweeping dark gowns and omnipresent smile I think I remember but whose name escapes me, sent for me, I was to hear a tale both true and tragic. "Your father wants to have a little talk with you," she said. "Perhaps you'd like to go into the garden."

We walked through the high-ceilinged white-paneled halls under massive chandeliers like the ones at Pearl Morton's, along gravel paths between rows of magnolias, the great creamy blossoms spilling a thick fragrance I've never been able to smell since without a sense of nausea.

He hadn't been drinking, I knew that. Sometimes people didn't know or notice, he blazed with brilliance and he could be awfully funny.

This time he was sober as a blight, his face had that white-blue-black look of the unshaven Irishman, he walked stiff-legged. Nothing that can happen to you yourself, I found out that morning, is like the pain of watching the unhappiness and humiliation of someone you love. Your father. Your child. This is the worst thing that can happen.

We sat on a bench beside a little pool-fountain, quite by ourselves.

"Your mother is going back to Red Creek, to her family,"

he said. At what was in his voice I began to shake inside but I tried not to let it get out for fear it would hurt him more.

"Is she coming back?" I said.

"Not this time," my father said bitterly. "Do you want to go with her?"

"Me?" I said in a horrified bleat. "Do I have to?"

"No you do not," my father said, "but she has offered to take you."

"She doesn't want me," I said.

"No," my father said.

"I—I'd rather stay with you," I said, which was probably my understatement of all time.

"All right," he said.

"Is she going to take Bogart?" I said.

"Oh yes—she's going to take him," Papa said.

"Can't we stop her?" I said. "Can't we stop her taking Bogart? I don't want him to go, do you?"

"No no," my father said, "no no."

He began to weep.

I'd never seen a strong man cry like that, from way inside him, with pain and wounded pride. I knew he was crying over an end. He'd kept hoping until right then, now he had abandoned that hope. I was too young to have been allowed to see it, I suppose, but I am glad I did. I knew then that the most terrible thing that can happen to a human being is humiliation. That was why they crucified Jesus Christ, a mean, felon's death meant to humiliate him, if he hadn't risen from it the very humiliation of it might have destroyed his teachings.

Because it was humiliation that crushed Papa he could speak only to me. When we used to go up to Carmel, Jack London and George Sterling could talk of personal things, defeats, disasters, infidelities. The poet could pour out his agonies about his beautiful wife who eventually killed herself. Not even to Bob Burdette, that man of God who had a right to hear and help him, could my father show himself humiliated.

When he talked to me that day in the garden I believe he hardly noticed that he was speaking out loud. He was talking to himself.

A great deal of what he said I couldn't understand. In the fragrance of magnolias that was suffocating me, to the tune of the tinkling fountain, I saw that even my father's clothes looked limp and humiliated to the dust.

I never forgave her for that.

A day or so later we went down to see Mama and my little brother Bogart off on the California Limited, which would take six or seven days to reach Buffalo, where they got off. Maybe the most pitiful thing about that was separating my father from his son. Mama had done it on purpose, without understanding why. A string tied to her husband, retaliation, a defense against the alliance my father and I had formed.

On the platform down at the little old red Santa Fe Station, Mama was crying terribly. She kept saying, "Oh Earl—oh Earl—" and I knew whatever she had done she was sorry.

Though I cried too, about Bogart, I was glad to see her go. It seemed to me all she ever did was make trouble for us.

I don't think it was until after the Buck case that we went down to Arizona on a hunting trip, where in a desert dawn he spoke to me again about my mother, as though he must explain the things he had said in the garden.

My father's younger sister, Madge, lived down in Tempe. Now an exclusive suburb of Phoenix, then it was a small town with a normal school attended mostly by Indians. Uncle Harry ran the hardware store there and he had everything ready for us all to go on a camping trip. A covered wagon drawn by two horses, with an Indian I'd known on my former trips to drive and take care of them. I had my own pinto and Papa had one of Uncle Harry's best mounts, a cow pony by the name of Piebiter. We were to take Uncle Harry's two dogs and be gone a couple of weeks.

At the last minute Aunty Madge decided not to go, she didn't really care much about camping, which was pretty rough in those days, and she couldn't ride. And then some ranchers came in to consult with Uncle Harry about orders for wagons so he couldn't go and to my delight we set off just Papa and I, with Juan and Rosy Melrose.

In a way it was the last quiet time we ever had.

From there on things broke so hard and fast we never had time to go away like that, to ride and rest and hunt and read and talk and cook over a campfire. I suppose, too, it was my last trip as a kid—I wasn't grown up by any means yet but I wasn't just a child any more either.

That time of year along the Gila River was just right, Uncle Harry said Papa would get lots of ducks and he did and I shot some quail with my .22 and Papa killed a big rattlesnake in my bed.

One night Rosy and Juan were sitting by the fire playing cards, and Papa and I wandered down along the river and sat on a big rock and watched the starlight on the water. Maybe there is something that smells more wonderful than flowing water under trees on a clear desert night but I have never found it. The song as the stream chuckled along over the pebbles made a nice accompaniment to quiet talk. I rolled a cigarette for Papa and one for myself and that was another thing, a cigarette you rolled yourself was sweet and clean, as different from "bought cigarettes" as fresh-baked bread right out of the oven is from bakery bread a day old.

Right away I knew that Papa wanted to get something off his chest and his conscience, and it was what he had said to me about my mother.

"Don't marry young, Nora," he said. "I married too young. It has been as much of a tragedy for her as it has for me."

"Uncle Charlie wrote me the other day," I said, "that it was an awful thing for the Lord to make a woman as beautiful as she is without giving her brains enough to handle it."

"The beauties I've known with brains were worse," Papa said, and paused.

"Don't follow the first impulses of an undisciplined heart," my father said after a while. I recognized this as what David Copperfield had said of his marriage to darling Dora. "You say to yourself *how beautiful, I could love,* and your undisciplined heart rejoices and says I *do* love. If you can discipline your heart a very little, if you can say I must not yield to this impulse until I know a little more, until my mind and my soul have sought to find out what time and reality may do to it, then either it *is* love or you save yourself from disaster. Romeo and Juliet on the balcony yielded to the divine impulse and it brought tragedy and the tomb. That may have been a better end than their tenth wedding anniversary would have shown them. To die is sometimes easier than to live."

"I don't see why we can't wait," I said.

"You will," my father said.

The river was very low and sometimes we couldn't hear it at all. No wind was stirring so that the cottonwoods didn't even murmur, though their leaves will flow and whisper at the flutter of a baby bird's wing.

"*The first impulses of an undisciplined heart,*" Papa said again, "Hers as well as mine. She has been lonelier than I have. I have my work and I have you."

"She has Bogart," I said, "but he's awful little, isn't he?"

He nodded, he said, "We do not fill each other's loneliness —only physically can we ever keep each other company. I don't blame her. A beautiful woman—she was born for the admiration of men. For applause."

He did blame her. He tried not to but he did. So did I.

Since at the time I had no idea of getting married at all I said cheerfully, "All right, I won't get married until after I pass my Bar exams. I promise I won't get married young."

It was a promise I didn't keep.

By then he had found a woman he had the impulse to love and it had become true love, though I can't say either of their hearts was what I would call disciplined exactly. It was too late—and she died too soon, my blessed Teddy.

Somewhere during that trip of hers to New York my father and mother did something about a divorce or filing a suit to get one or a legal separation.

At the time I didn't see any reason why he shouldn't marry Dolly. She was living with us at the Alexandria as my governess. They certainly got along much better than he and Mama ever had. She made him laugh and she could play the piano.

Dolly knew they couldn't.

Besides, she said, *she'll* come back.

She's got a hold on him.

TWENTY-SIX

To no one else on earth was there ever a moment of doubt, debate, or significance in the Buck case.

For the one and only time in his career, Earl Rogers appeared for the prosecution in a murder trial. And they hung the man *he* had prosecuted by the neck until he was dead and my father saw them do it. According to all the other citizens of California hanging was too good for Buck. The rack or disemboweling would have come closer. To my father, it was a wound that never healed.

On sleepless nights, he would go over and over the cold, brutal, unprovoked, premeditated murder of Mrs. Canfield, a woman of whom even the poor said, *If some people have money and some don't, she's one who should.* I knew her, you know, Papa would say, there is never enough kindness in the world, how could anyone want to shoot down this bright angel of kindness?

Somebody had, however. A man named Buck.

On a morning after he had been dismissed for neglecting the carriage horses and even, Mrs. Canfield feared, not always being kind to them, the former coachman came to the door, to ask for his job back. Failing that, to borrow a thousand dollars. Mrs. Canfield shook her head, spoke a word, and Buck raised his gun and blasted the defenseless woman and she fell dead at his feet.

No more brutal crime with meaner motive ever took place.

Her husband, an early oil millionaire, was a friend of Earl Rogers and came to ask him to act as special prosecutor. I want to see to it, Mr. Canfield said, that this born murderer doesn't escape justice. Over and over Rogers told him there was no chance of this, over and over Canfield said, "I'd feel better about it, Earl." Then it came to my father that in the pain of losing the wife he had lived with in such daily happiness for so many years the man had gone temporarily a little crazy. He feared his friend Earl Rogers might be persuaded to defend her murderer and by his magic formula get Buck off. *I'd feel safer with you on my side,* Canfield kept telling him cagily. Of course it was an absurd and impossible notion, this was one man Earl Rogers would not defend, but it was also impossible to refuse this anguish and torment. So Earl Rogers walked into the courtroom beside the district attorney as special prosecutor.

The trial was starkly brief. The defense was naturally without hope of or even desire to acquit. In a sort of unconvinced routine, it brought up an alleged skull injury earlier in Buck's life, and rested on the plea Not Guilty by Reason of Insanity. The jury was out long enough to take one ballot but even in those few minutes it was strange to be waiting and hoping for the one word *Guilty.*

Rogers went to San Quentin to see the sentence carried out. Strong men often cannot bear to see the trap sprung, the feet dancing on air, the limp body after its last struggle hanging by the twisted broken neck. Earl Rogers, so white Rosy thought he was going to faint, which plenty of men do, watched without movement or expression. The guards cut Buck down, the doctor pronounced him dead, the small, gloomy official crowd began to shuffle out on stricken feet and stopped with a jerk at a cry from Special Prosecutor Earl Rogers. Plainly, he couldn't stop that cry. "I was wrong," he shouted, "we're all wrong wrong wrong. We haven't any right to hang this man or any other man. Who are we to take life— life life life given to this man by whatever power gives life? To rob him of—his *chance* to repent, to expiate—to throw him straight into hell the way we did, like a bundle of old rags and bones. 'Thou shalt not kill,' it says. Who made us exceptions to this? I can't forgive myself."

The next day San Francisco papers reported that Earl Rogers had spent the night at the prison morgue.

Earl Rogers performed the autopsy himself, with the aid of Dr. Stone, the prison surgeon.

From the day he started to study and practice law, Earl Rogers studied and within its field practiced and later taught medical jurisprudence. In hospitals, prisons, with Dr. Clare Murphy and Dr. Ed Palette, who were his close friends in this common interest, he read and experimented and used medical testimony as no lawyer had used it before.

So he and Dr. Stone opened the skull, looking for lesions, cracks, pressures of bone, any kind of physical brain distortion, growth or damage by birth or accident. They found absolutely nothing. It did not comfort Earl Rogers.

"What do we know about those other forces that damage and distort the human mind?" he kept saying. "How can we tell what passions and resentments and starvations have warped the human soul which uses the brain as an instrument? A man who did what Buck did cannot be sane. We used to draw and quarter men for disagreeing about religion. Or put their severed heads on poles for debt or speaking ill of a lord. We still have much work to do. Someday we will be as ashamed of hanging Buck as we are now of hanging or pressing Goody Brown in Salem as a witch."

The papers picked up this crusade on which he went up to Sacramento to see the governor and to advocate a bill in the legislature against capital punishment. It happened that at this time he was, quite against his desire or design, running Los Angeles, Southern California, and a good deal else politically.

TWENTY-SEVEN

One day my father came dashing out of his private office asking for trouble. His client was a big, nondescript gent whose name I don't even remember, with no indication that he'd stirred a storm that was to blow the mayor out of the city hall and make Earl Rogers political boss of Los Angeles, to his indignation and annoyance. Much aggravated, I may add, when he found himself tied up with that eminent reformer Edwin T. Earl and his *Evening Express*.

"Somebody is making it tough for this poor man to conduct his business," Mr. Rogers said, "because he hasn't handed the ward boss his rake-off this month. Which he says he hasn't got and can't afford. What's going on in this town?"

"Well now Mr. Rogers—" Luther Brown said placatingly.

"The city hall is a den of thieves," Mr. Rogers said, not placated in the least. "This is pillage, plunder and piracy; we might as well live under the Camorra. From all I can make out the mayor is a thimblerig, the council is lousy with swindlers, the boards of all kinds are mooching around at their own little badger and confidence games. I dislike petty crooks in office more than I can tell you. I am going to do something about it."

"If you do," Luther Brown said in his mellifluous voice, "you are apt to step on the toes of some of your clients."

"Then," said Mr. Rogers, "let's get their toes out of the way. On his salary a policeman can still owe the last installment on Tiny Tim's crutches, and they expect him to defy the mayor, the chief, and the commission. Let's start by getting that misbegotten coyote out of the city hall."

Within twenty-four hours, we knew that Mr. Rogers' impulse to spray the civic dump coincided with that of a man as opposite to him as any to be found in the English-speaking world. A prune of a man, of whose millions Mr. Rogers once said, "God shows his contempt for money by the people he gives it to." A sillier thing to say cannot be imagined, and probably it had a tinge of sour grapes. Nevertheless when you looked at E. T. Earl it also had its point.

Even his wife thought so.

Exquisite, slim, in a day when a boyish figure was regarded as the early stages of consumption, Emily Earl came to our office as a liaison, as soon as it became apparent that even though they were fighting in the same war Mr. Earl and Mr. Rogers never could see eye to eye.

"The two Earls," Emily said, sitting across from Papa at the big table, clad in English tweeds and pearls and polished brogues—all of which were new and awe-inspiring to me, "are the final proof that politics makes strange bedfellows."

Speaking of bedfellows, it wasn't long before she wanted Mr. Rogers to get her a divorce. "On what grounds, Mrs. Earl?" my father said, too quietly.

Mrs. Earl paused to light a cigarette. She was also the first lady I had ever seen smoke. She carried her cigarettes in a gold box, on which her initials E. E. were entwined in diamonds, attached to a wide gold bracelet. The tiny rings she blew had a faint oriental perfume.

"Every afternoon," she said, "he comes home, lies down on a sofa in the drawing room with his shoes on, goes to sleep and snores."

"No man with red blood in his veins could refuse to get a lady a divorce on such grounds," my father said.

"I was sure of that," Emily Earl said.

From where I sit, it looks impossible that Earl Rogers and Emily didn't have at least an impulse to love. Although I expect she was a few years older than he was, she was a great lady, a wife who'd build any man into whatever he had it in him to be; she was Earl Rogers' equal in wit, daring, *savoir-faire* and *joie de vivre*. Which might be why he resisted allowing the impulse to become a permanent part of our lives. Or it could be the *lady* was used to all-kneeling and didn't want a man who wore the pants. I don't know. I don't even remember whether he got her a divorce or not.

After all, he wasn't our *client*. He was putting up the money and his *Evening Express* in a campaign against corruption that had begun to stink. Their motives in this were as different as Tweedledum and Tweedledee.

Edwin T. Earl wanted to make Los Angeles the Chemically Pure.

Rogers wanted to see that citizens didn't pay blood money to A Machine.

The *Express* and its publisher were against sin, especially dancing, card-playing, prostitution, and whoop-de-do.

Earl Rogers was against grafters and crooked politicians

taking a bite out of every tax dollar that ought to be spent on clean government, better schools, more parks and playgrounds, adequate fire and police protection, city and county hospitals, roads, charity for the old and sick, and help for any criminals who could be saved.

No man could have been more embarrassed by a prominent position in the Crusade Against Vice than was Earl Rogers. The company of reformers was something he avoided at all times. Blue laws were, in his opinion, totally without power to control human problems. "The greatest of them," he said once to Dr. Burdette, "the Ten Commandments, haven't done it. You know, my father, like yourself a minister of the gospel, believed the messages to Moses were intended not as commands but as prophecies. Look up, step aside for the burning bush, and thou shalt not—cannot—will not—then find it in your heart to bear false witness against your neighbor. Make for yourself no graven images, and thou shalt not then either covet or steal or commit adultery. Love the Lord your God with all your heart and thou shalt not—canst not—kill, for love fulfills the law in your heart. Prophecy of reward for loving the One God. Never *command.*" Bob Burdette said, "It's a beautiful interpretation. I wish I'd known your father."

Possibly my father went too far with it. He could never believe any *thou shalt not* was efficacious to save a sinner or restore a soul.

Earl Rogers' power to throw Mayor Harper and his larcenous cohorts out of the city hall came from his defense of the three cops Cowan, Murphy, and Hawley. From that day forward even the *Examiner* played ball. Above all he had the Los Angeles Police Department in his pocket. No small advantage for a criminal lawyer, and one never held by any other to that extent.

If there was one thing cops hated it was to have their brother officers discredited. Nothing could so undermine their prestige and belittle their persons. A member of the force either shot or convicted of carelessness or cruelty in pursuit of his duty shook public confidence to its socks. Brains in the underworld took instant advantage of this and the cops got pushed around. Any popularity of the cop on the beat, much loved and trusted and looked up to in those days, was sabotaged completely. J. Edgar Hoover, as great, just, and disciplined a law enforcement officer as the world has ever known, has always reacted with grave concern and justifiable anger to anything that could cast a shadow on a member of the FBI. Years ago, Mr. Hoover said to me, "The day I find the boys in the street want to be the G Man instead of Machine Gun Kelly, I will know I have a chance to defeat the four million members of the underworld."

To repay the debt they owed Earl Rogers, the whole police department united, from the newest rookie to the chief. They'd do anything for him.

Rogers also controlled, by his position as the city's No. 1 criminal lawyer, the Eighth Ward, known as the Tenderloin. This took in the downtown area, Chinatown, Central Avenue where the Negro population centered, Sonora Town or the Mexican quarter, the saloon belt, the red-light district, and the slums. The places, as my father said, where in hunger, ugliness, poverty, and ignorance crime bred, and also where it came to full harvest.

Since Luther Brown was a powerful wheel horse in the Republican party and Papa was a Democrat this made our office at First and Broadway about as near a coalition Tammany Hall control as we had.

At this time, public interest in national politics, affairs, and activities was so small I have difficulty in believing it myself. Most of us knew most of the time who was President but I can't say we cared much. Days—weeks—could go by without a story from Washington on the front page of any California paper or any mention of the President's name. When William Howard Taft beat William Jennings Bryan, and Eugene Debs got 402,000 votes as the Socialist candidate, California had ten electoral votes, way out there beyond the Rockies, and nobody paid much attention to her. We probably knew who our congressman was because we wrote to him for seeds and sometimes got them, and our senators on account of their being orators on the Fourth of July. The federal government, as a great centralized power running all forty-six states, hadn't occurred to any of us. There had been no big wars, only *Remember the Maine* and *Dewey Has Captured Manila,* which were storybook affairs, fought by the regular Army and a few hotheaded volunteers with less than four thousand casualties. Nobody would have believed a *draft* or military service or millions on casualty lists. War really had nothing to do with *us.* As De Tocqueville said in his *Démocratie en Amérique,* a book my father knew by heart, this was the true place for the first real experiment in democracy because, protected by our vast oceans, we didn't need any other foreign policy than the Monroe Doctrine, which simply said the American states were never to suffer the Old World to interfere in the affairs of the New. The only thing De Tocqueville was wrong about was the vast-ocean theory—he did not foresee nor did anyone else that the oceans would soon become a few hours' wide. No wars, no draft, *no income tax*. Our main knowledge of Washington concerned high or low tariff, which was always the main item in a party platform.

Our daily lives were tied into and affected by state, county, and city politics; the distances had not been bridged with the rest of the country in either transportation or communication. If you got a telegram you asked a friend to stand by while you opened it. A long-distance telephone call was almost impossible. No radio or TV or even movies seen by all of us bound us together as, for instance, Mary Pickford did when she became *America's Sweetheart*. No air mail of course—a letter to Washington or New York took at least a week—to Europe a month. No chain stores. We had our own Emporium in San Francisco and Hamburger's in Los Angeles until Woolworth wove the country together with the five-and-ten. Though we flocked to see Ethel Barrymore in *Captain Jinks of the Horse Marines* and Sothern and Marlowe in *If I Were King*, our own stock theaters were more important to us, week after week, than these road companies. If New York had its Weber and Fields, we had our Kolb and Dill. Only vaudeville, to which Papa and I went every Monday, was national. Our own writers, Jack London, Frank Norris, Ambrose Bierce, George Sterling, Mary Austin, interested us most. Above all, Henry Ford, who changed the map, customs, habits, and character of the United States more than any other man who ever lived in it, had only just begun to manufacture the Model T and put America on wheels. In my teens, there wasn't a foot of paved road in California. On the whole, we stayed home a good deal.

Ninety per cent of the news in local papers was local news. Ninety-five per cent of the pictures were home-town figures. We had no syndicated columns of any kind. With no movie or TV stars, no glamour boys in Washington, no real tie with New York, we created local idols. Earl Rogers as political boss, courtroom star of sensational murder trials, was a bigger popular favorite than one man could be today in any city or state. Known by sight to more people than a Vice President or an Attorney General, whose names we had probably never heard and whose pictures we had certainly never seen. When, on the night of a big fight, he walked down the aisle of Uncle Tom McCarey's Vernon Arena, dressed to kill, they started to cheer him the moment they saw him and kept it up after he was in his ringside seat. Always he had a court wherever he went, an entourage of his own, and also groups of admirers, hangers-on, hero worshipers, and while autographs hadn't come in then they "just wanted to shake your hand, Mr. Rogers." He divided the pedestal as No. 1 Matinee Idol with Lewis S. Stone, who was leading man at the Belasco, and once with an unknown young actor, Miss Barrymore's little brother John. All this was heady stuff for any man.

At first, Papa had fun and excitement chasing the grafters out of the city hall. He got the police raises he was after. The Crusade Against Vice he felt was dangerous and silly. When it was over he said to Edwin T. Earl, "You've driven the prostitutes into rooming houses where there is no medical inspection, you've sent a few fan-tan games into the cellars and swept some dance halls under the rug. The only way to combat vice is to pay your policemen a living wage and burn down the slums. Then you'll only have the big thieves to worry about."

Soon afterwards Willard Huntington Wright, then a music critic, later to become S. S. Van Dine, creator of Philo Vance, wrote a smashing indictment in Mencken's *Smart Set* entitled "Los Angeles the Chemically Pure." This caused great commotion especially in our town. "I was responsible for it," Earl Rogers said morosely when Wright came to talk to him about it. "I didn't intend to but I created it for you."

He was never able to let go entirely of his political power, he was always getting mixed up in things and of course the San Francisco graft cases were just around the corner; just the same, his heart was never in politics.

He was much more at home defending outlandish, grotesque, eccentric, and unbelievable Colonel Griffith J. Griffith in the case of the society wife who wouldn't die. How the man who could produce the first alcoholic-insanity defense could ever take another drink himself is still impossible for me to figure.

TWENTY-EIGHT

No need, this once, to summon from the grave the sheeted victim of murder most foul.

On the witness stand sat a lady in black, her face hidden by a thick veil. In a whisper that trembled, she was to testify against her husband, who by a hairsbreadth had failed to destroy her. *Don't kill me, oh darling don't kill me, you know I've never been unfaithful to you.* A gunshot cut short that piteous plea and now the shrinking, bewildered figure in black was the personal appearance of the corpus delicti in the courtroom.

"Mrs. Griffith," the district attorney said, "will you be kind enough to lift your veil?"

It was no kindness, now, for anyone to look upon Teena Griffith's face, though once Los Angeles society had called her a beauty.

We defend everybody.

He ought to be hung, the city growled, and if Mrs. Griffith had died, the sheriff said, there might have been one of its last lynching parties.

How could Earl Rogers agree to defend the millionaire mystery man and mountebank who had shot down his kneeling wife? Wasn't this worse than Buck?

For sixty sleepless hours Earl Rogers asked himself and dozens of potential witnesses that question. I am the only person who ever knew why Earl Rogers took the Griffith case, something which puzzled his staff and the newspapermen for years.

There was also a second question.

Could even Earl Rogers free Colonel Griffith J. Griffith on the charge of assault with a deadly weapon with intent to commit murder?

Call me and don't talk.

The reason Earl Rogers was summoned very late in the Griffith case was consistent with everything else about this phantasmagoria.

Colonel Griffith was a real estate promoter and financial wizard, a philanthropist who donated to Los Angeles the enormous and beautiful park which today bears his name, a member of the best clubs, a vain little Napoleon who knew more about everything than most men ever know about anything. When the cops who arrested him suggested he'd better send for Rogers, the colonel said that he, Griffith J. Griffith, would act as his own lawyer. He was, he said, smarter than any pettifogging ambulance-chasing shyster. With a high cackle of laughter he reminded the officers that Shakespeare had once said, *The first thing we do, let's kill all the lawyers.* Also, he told them, a man with his money had political influence, probably the district attorney wouldn't prosecute. The cops had heard this before but by this time they had taken such a dislike to him and were so revolted by the nature of the crime that they decided Mr. Rogers would be better off without him no matter how big the fee.

However, when Griffith heard that through his wife's Blue Book (our early version of the Social Register) family, her highly respected brothers and possibly her church, there had been brought in as special prosecutors former Governor Henry T. Gage and the city's leading Catholic lawyer, Isadore B. Dockweiler, he changed his tune. He sent his head man, a Mr. John Jones, to get Rogers. This turned out not to be as easy as it sounded.

The shooting had been horrendous. It had taken place in the palatial presidential suite of the Arcadia Hotel, overlooking the Pacific Ocean from atop the Palisades in Santa Monica, then a small beach resort some hours from Los Angeles, where the colonel and his lady were spending a peaceful vacation. The idea of Mrs. Griffith, a devout Catholic churchwoman, being unfaithful to her husband was obviously pure demonic invention. Papa wasn't afraid of either Gage or Dockweiler but they were awful good and he saw no reason to take a sure loser in which they had all the chances to make a monkey out of him. Especially for a man he had disliked more every time he'd ever seen him, and to whom he referred as a midget egomaniac. On principle he was against men shooting women, their wives most of all, perhaps because at least twice he'd resisted the temptation. He knew he'd have the unpopular side and this was important because it was unpopular with him too, which was his only reason for not defending everybody. Silly, he said, to be stoned for a cause in which you didn't believe. To begin with, he certainly did not believe in

Colonel Griffith J. Griffith as a cause or an underdog in any way.

Without realizing what he was doing or that he had done it, while Mr. John Jones sat in our office, Rosy said the thing which got Rogers into the case. "The man don't draw a sober breath one year's end to another," Rosy said.

"Nonsense," Mr. Rogers said. "He doesn't drink at all. Last time I saw him at the California Club he took a cigar instead of a drink and was slightly obnoxious in declaring he never touched what he called booze."

"Secret drunks—" Rosy began, but Mr. Jones cut in. "He's so brilliant, such a financial wizard," he said hurriedly, "that it hardly seems possible, nevertheless sometimes I wonder if he isn't unbalanced. But one thing I'm sure of, he doesn't *drink*."

Earl Rogers said, "Where do you get this notion he drinks, Rosy?"

"People tell me things," Rosy said.

"Let them tell me," Mr. Rogers said.

The word went out. *Mr. Rogers wants to see you.*

Griffith's multimillionaire eccentricities had been the subject of backstairs, front-office, men's-room, and drawing-room gossip for many years. The tales were as weird and wonderful, as varied and shocking as the procession that brought them up our wooden stairs. Hour after hour, eating off trays, drinking black coffee, Mr. Rogers digged and delved, stirred and stimulated, refreshed memories, cajoled and threatened and kidded and ordered carefully, as though these people were on an actual witness stand instead of in his office.

The president of one of the most exclusive clubs in the state, in a day when clubs were exclusive, said, "He made such huge donations to our charity program, we had to let him speak at dinners. He's long-winded as a camel but he loves to hear himself speak. One night after dinner—a lot of fellows thought he was kidding of course—he said he'd just refused an offer to become mayor because he knew they would soon ask him to be President—not of the club, of the United States."

"Had he been drinking?" Mr. Rogers said.

"Odd you should ask that," the president said, "I thought he was a teetotaler but now there's a rumor around the clubs—"

Whether Griffith had meant it as a joke or not, it all ceased to be funny after he shot his wife.

Rogers pursued the rumors around the clubs.

Did Colonel Griffith drink at the club?

Well not at the club as you might say, Mr. Rogers, I never served him a drink over the bar, he always refused to drink with the other gentlemen at the bar.

He did drink secretly perhaps?

Well sir that's another matter, I'm a bartender, them White Ribbon boys that have taken the pledge don't fool me. I'd say the colonel was half-shot all the time, taking snorts out of a bottle he had hid some place, not drinking at the bar like a gentleman should.

Did Colonel Griffith insist on changing plates with his wife, making her eat from the one you'd served him, at the Arcadia Hotel in Santa Monica?

Oh yes, Mr. Rogers, and the coffeecups, too.

Did he say why he did this?

He *told* me and all the waitresses the Pope was trying to have him poisoned off, he said, so his wife could give his money to the Church.

Did you believe that?

Oh no sir, Colonel Griffith was always joking.

You thought it was a joke?

Well, you'd have to, Mr. Rogers, wouldn't you, unless he was crazy or drunk or something.

I've understood Colonel Griffith didn't drink.

That's right, he didn't, only sometimes we girls would say among ourselves if the colonel was a drinking man I'd said he had a skinful.

Did Colonel Griffith ask you if you were a Catholic?

Yes he did. He said he wouldn't employ me if I was because his wife was one and she was trying to poison him to get his money for the Pope.

Did it occur to you at the time that he was drunk?

Not at first, sir. After I was driving for him a while, I never saw him take a drink not once, but it come over me he was either drunk all the time or he was sober all the time if you can understand that, Mr. Rogers, I got to know he *drank* but he was always the same, so the line of what you'd call is-he-drunk-or-isn't-he had disappeared totally so to speak.

You mean to say you sold Colonel Griffith two hundred cases of whiskey over this period of time?

He asked me never to speak of it, Mr. Rogers, but you can see it on the books for yourself. He said he gave it as presents to his friends and employees because he wasn't a drinking man himself.

A manicurist from his barbershop cast what turned out to be the deciding vote. A middle-aged respectable woman she was. "We get all kinds," she said, "in my born days I never did see anybody bite his nails as bad as the colonel. Down to the *quick*. I tried to get him to use calomel or iodine but he wouldn't. I felt sorry for the poor man, though of course he shouldn't have shot that poor lady. I used to see her at Mass."

After the manicurist had gone, my father sat for a long time, rolling cigarettes and smoking them slowly, not saying a word, the way his face looked nobody said a word to him, either. Then, by himself, he went out to see Griffith, who was in a hospital somewhere. When he came back he was thin-lipped and expressionless, except he had that very *young* look, which meant he had to do something he didn't want to do. Rebellious. As he walked through the outer office he said, "I've taken the Griffith case," and when an involuntary murmur of protest went up he shouted at the top of his lungs, "No back talk. I know what I'm doing," and went into his own room and slammed the door.

That night I asked him why. I said, "When Jones came in you weren't going to touch it for love nor money and we sure need the money."

"Are you going to start nagging me about money?" he said.

I said, "I don't care anything about the money. If I was a lawyer, I wouldn't touch this one with a ten-foot pole, that's all."

"Maybe you better not be a lawyer then," my father said thinly. "We defend everybody."

"I better not unless you're going to teach me why you went out to talk to this gentleman," I said.

"I didn't go out to talk to him," my father said. "I went out to see his fingernails."

"Papa—" I said.

"You heard the manicurist," he yelled at me. His eyes were so blue under the black lashes and brows—the set-in-with-a-sooty-finger Irish eyes—that they startled me. "Didn't anything inside you tell you that a man Griffith J. Griffith's age, with millions in the bank, a business he's supposed to be a genius at, a handsome wife—if he bites his nails down to the quick there has to be a reason? Something has to be very wrong with him?"

"No it didn't," I said.

I didn't know it, but already he was beginning to work on the hypothetical question that had everybody in such an uproar in court. He was trying it out on me, on himself, following it in his head.

Here we have a man, he said to me, who for years—year after year—has been two human beings. Sneaking his drinks, hiding bottles, covering up, slipping in and out, concealing this second self as carefully as Dr. Jekyll ever concealed Mr. Hyde. The outer man, an eccentric but reputable citizen, making after-dinner speeches, making more and more millions, a braggart and a clown but a success, received everywhere. All the time running away to feed this other self—this second self, guzzling the booze, as he called it, and deceiving himself that no one knew.

"When," he said, "did that other self take over completely? When did Colonel Griffith J. Griffith who had just completed a million-dollar deal, just sat on a board-of-directors meeting, become this creature with a brain that had in it more alcohol than blood? So that all the restraints and all the civilized practices and standards of behavior and all the truths of his life were submerged in fantasy and furor and he roamed in a jungle of his own making? In a human brain with more ounces of alcohol than the essential blood that feeds it, a man is not a sane human being, he is no longer capable of telling right from wrong or good from evil or reality from the chimeras of his fancy. Don't you see that as the alcohol accumulated over days, months, years, in this dank secrecy, breeding like mushrooms, the periods between growing less and less all the time, the tissues of his brain, the fibers of his character, the filaments of his soul, memory, emotions, desires are changed? The evil self has become the stronger, the more-often-present, taking up more and more time and space.

"Let me read you, recall to you, what happened with Dr. Jekyll. You remember, he had in his laboratory compounded a drink which changed him from a respected London physician to the fiend Mr. Hyde, who savagely struck down a beloved leader. Here it is—"

My father was turning the pages of the red-leather-and-gold volume of Stevenson, glancing at the pages, his pencil touching the words, his eyes intent. He went on putting it into shape for himself.

"When he had the first drink of this transforming potion Dr. Jekyll says *I was sold a slave to my original evil, at the moment this braced me and delighted me like wine.* . . . You see R.L.S. compares it to wine, he makes the indication plain . . . *this brief condescension to evil finally destroyed the balance of my soul* . . . yes, yes, now comes the day after, as Mr. Hyde, he has committed his murder. Without his consent or any action or volition, Mr. Hyde, his other self, his evil self, takes over, Mr. Hyde has become now the *dominant*, he has saturated the brain tissue, the fibers of the unbalanced soul, now there is more of him in this man than there is of the good self Dr. Jekyll and *now* Jekyll is helpless. He doesn't know it yet, he still thinks he can choose when he will allow Hyde to come back, when he will drink the glass that transforms a man into a beast. Dr. Jekyll is sitting in the sun on a bench in Regent's Park"—Papa turned a page or two and read again—"here it is—*I looked down, my clothes hung formless on my shrunken limbs, the hand that lay on my knee was corded and hairy. I was once more Edward Hyde,* not Dr. Jekyll but Mr. Hyde without his own volition, *A moment before I had been safe of all men's respect, wealthy, a cloth laid for me, now I was the common quarry of mankind, hunted* . . . I, Griffith J. Griffith accused of an attempt to murder my poor wife, of having shot her, stood over her and watched the blood run from her eyes and mouth—I Mr. Hyde or the drunken self of Griffith J. Griffith, a known murderer, *thrall to the prison bars now* . . ."

The shift was so swift it jolted a scared grunt out of me, the way he built up Jekyll and Hyde and then turned them into Colonel Griffith *as* Mr. Hyde Griffith. *Real.*

Papa kept flipping the pages in a growing excitement.

"Now . . . here . . . Hyde has taken cover at an inn . . . *thenceforth he sat all day over the fire in the private room, gnawing his nails* . . . you see? I must have remembered that sentence . . . the manicurist said *down to the quick,* gnawing his fingernails down to the quick . . . I went to see for myself.

"This fantastic, posturing, braggadocio monkey of a man, this is his Hyde self, now beyond his control. Taken him over, so that he could believe his wife was trying to poison him. A

man in his right mind would know her true as honor itself,
his wrong mind would create an hallucination of her unfaith-
fulness. The alcoholic delusion takes on reality as a man
smoking opium believes his pipe dreams. So many selves in
all of us to be dealt with. Why shouldn't this man's brain,
wet with alcohol, accept a religious persecution as other men's
brains see pink elephants? His delirium tremens sees his wife
of spotless virtue in adulterous embrace as another man will
climb up a wall to escape a boa constrictor that isn't there.

"Nora, when your grandfather was a circuit rider in
Arizona, he tried to send to jail all the men who sold whiskey
to the Indians. He said the moral guilt for any crime committed was *theirs*, they knew, your grandfather said, that
firewater made an Indian *crazy* drunk.

"*Crazy* drunk, they called it.

"Not only Indians. White men—some white men—get *crazy*
drunk too."

We sat there a minute. He wasn't looking at me now. I
had a terrible time choking down whatever it was in my
throat. I thought of bottles I'd found hidden. I wanted to go
over and put my arms around him but I thought that might
be making too much of it, it might *humiliate* him to feel that
I had made any connection.

In a voice so quiet it was really amazing I could hear it,
he said, "You see, that *I* must defend Colonel Griffith?"

I said yes I did.

A second reason, too. In a funny voice he said, "No woman
ought to have to live with the knowledge that her husband
has murdered her. Even the Roman warrior Caesar beholding
Brutus among his assassins, cried out. If their daggers had
missed the mark, this alone would have stabbed Caesar's
heart to death. *Et tu, Brute? Then fall, Caesar.* If you, my
beloved friend, my Brutus, came here to kill me, Caesar does
not care to live beyond the hour that revealed to him this
betrayal, this hate for love. Nobody can conceive how a
woman could love this vainglorious toad, Griffith, but love
him she did. Every man on the jury must see that the heart
and soul of this woman have been done to death. Do you
know what I think, Nora? She forced her broken body to
survive, when the doctors said it could not, to save him from
the gallows. *Don't kill me darling* wasn't a plea for her. *For
him.* Don't become a murderer. A *wife*—one flesh—I would
like to console her. It would have been easier for her if he

hadn't missed, the dead so soon grow cold. I think it will comfort her now to know that he didn't do this in his sane and reasonable mind, that he was—*crazy drunk*. Don't you think it will comfort her?"

I said I did and burst into tears. So I got to cry anyhow without humiliating Papa.

TWENTY-NINE

Crazy drunk. Drunk as a wild Indian. In the courtroom he called it by a new name, Alcoholic Insanity. That was to be Earl Rogers' surprise defense of Griffith, though neither the former governor of California, Henry T. Gage, nor Isadore Dockweiler, the impressive special prosecutors, had any idea of it until Mr. Rogers began to cross-examine the living murdered woman.

This defense opened up by the fact that a man bit his fingernails.

Governor Gage said, "Mrs. Griffith, will you be kind enough to take the stand?"

A nurse in uniform on one side, the governor on the other, Mrs. Griffith limped painfully down the aisle. Strange it was to see her pass within a few feet of the bellicose, fidgety, twitching defendant who was still, and always would be, her husband. She did not look at him as she made her way to the raised platform on which stood the witness chair. He peered at her sideways through his fingers. The first time they had been in the same room since he shot her. He was sober now, but it had left him with his dry brain still fluttering in his skull.

Once she had been tenderly settled in the chair, they were face to face.

I have never known such a moment of deathly stillness in any courtroom.

We could not fathom all it really meant to them, the thralldom was so great we couldn't move, we could hardly breathe.

My heart was thumping words to a death march. *We made no sign, we said no word, we had no word to say.* They had loved each other, married, it seemed stranger to me than anything I had ever known in my short life.

Her face was veiled, the soft dark netting like a widow's weeds hung to her waist. All we could see was a ghostly shadow. From behind the veil, her voice was a whisper we had to strain to hear, and the pauses were long and empty, like falling down a well. As she faltered out her story, behind the dark curtain, she put a delicate handkerchief to her eyes. Governor Gage stood close beside her, in courtly protection. A handsome man, he had a reputation as a fine lawyer, now he seemed only concerned to help this trembling lady, he repeated her whispered answers sometimes in a resonant, unhappy baritone.

She and her husband, Teena Griffith told us, had been going to the Arcadia Hotel in Santa Monica for years, they loved the sight and sound and smell of the sea, the quiet days and peaceful nights.

"We had a—lovely time," she said. "We were—going back to the city the next day. I thought my—husband was rested, he had been—tired and—nervous. I had begun to pack when—he came in—he suggested a walk along the beach. I thought how nice—that would be—to say good-by to the ocean—we were—both of us—we had always been—fond of the ocean. I went into our sun parlor and—put on my hat—I put my arm in his and—we went for a walk. I stopped at the little curio shop and—bought some post cards to send to friends—in the East. From then on we went to the plunge and watched some children diving—and then we went to watch the ocean—we only stayed a few minutes—my husband seemed to grow—restless—"

On it was that stamp of absolute truth nothing can dim or distort. This veiled woman, who'd never been inside a courtroom before, sitting there racked by bodily pain, telling in her well-bred, educated, ladylike voice of that last hour in her whole life that would ever be simple and normal and unafraid again. She seemed to linger over it, remembering how pleasant it had been. Like all those other hours before it when, she kept saying, her husband had always *tried* to be kind to her. Through it came her own pitiful *astonishment*.

"When we returned to the hotel he said I had better finish packing, we would leave, he had decided, early the next morning. So—I addressed the post cards and then—I opened the lid of the trunk and began to pack. I'd almost finished when—when Mr. Griffith came into the room again."

She could not go on.

She saw him come in, the familiar little feisty figure, her husband.

It was plain to us all that she could hardly believe what she had to tell. A nightmare—and perhaps she would wake up.

Then she went on, "He said to me, 'Now take this book, get down on your knees.'" She took a long breath. We heard it, and then she said, "I—I was alarmed. I said, 'Why, Griffith, what do you mean?' and he said, 'I want you to get down on your knees and swear to some questions I am going to ask you.' So I took the book—it was my own prayer book—I did not know what else to do—so I got down on my knees and then—then I saw the—the revolver in his hand. I said to him, 'Griffith, put that away—you might hurt yourself, it might go off.' I pleaded with him, I thought he might—injure himself. He only said, 'Close your eyes and do as I command you.' When I saw he was determined I knew—something dreadful had happened to us and I asked him if he would let me pray —so I prayed and I felt I was in the hands of a man—I could feel he was desperate though I did not understand—after I was through praying he took out a little tiny piece of paper and—read me questions from it."

We saw it happening, the judge and jury, the spectators, the reporters, their pencils still, the lawyers at the counsel table. The big, old-fashioned room, the huge windows draped in lace, the heavy furniture, we caught the scent of sand and sea and ice plant and eucalyptus. The lady in her neat wash dress, her long hair in a bun, kneeling with her prayer book, her eyes raised to the desperate little man waving a gun. We heard him shout wildly, *Remember I am a dead shot.*

Then he asked the questions.

"Have you ever tried to poison me?"

"Why, Papa darling, I have never tried to harm a hair of your head."

"Have you ever been untrue to me?"

"You know I have not. Don't kill me, darling, don't kill me —please—"

A moment of stillness in that room, in this courtroom.

"Then I was shot," Teena Griffith said in amazement.

Perhaps that plea *Don't kill me, darling* had made the hand of the dead shot shake a little. For she could run, run for her life, blood flowing from her head, shaking with astonishment and terror. She found herself beside an open window and flung herself out, landing on the piazza roof. She climbed along on her hands and knees, she couldn't see very well, she found another window and crawled through it, she tried to staunch the blood with the table cover, she could hear her breath coming in shrieks and sobs.

"Then Mr. Wright, the manager, came in and behind him I saw—my husband. I said to Mr. Wright do not let him come in, he has taken something against me, I think I am wounded to death."

Governor Gage took a fine handkerchief from his sleeve and pressed it to his eyes. When he could speak, he said quietly to his witness, "Mrs. Griffith, will you lift your veil?"

She did not stir. She was going to refuse. Or it might be she could not move. Governor Gage leaned down and with a hand that was not steady lifted it for her and held it there. When the jury had seen the bullet's red track, the fearful burns, the black patch that covered the empty socket of one eye, he let it fall again.

How such a shot had failed of its murderous intent the doctors could not explain. That the intent had been murderous no one who looked upon Teena Griffith's face could ever doubt. The shocked silence held. Into it came the most unexpected sound in the world. A laugh. Somebody had *laughed*. A squeak and a gibber of hysterical jeering derision. We all turned, we did not believe our eyes when we saw the defendant on his feet, waving his hands and grimacing. Yes— it was he who had laughed. His chief counsel piled on the next surprise. With a leap he was on his feet, he had picked up the capering little figure and flung it back in the chair, the whole courtroom heard Rogers shout, "If you don't behave yourself I'll save the hangman the trouble." And no one including the special prosecutors doubted his intent. The little man quailed, he sat hunched, twiddling his thumbs with their bitten bleeding nails.

I thought frantically that we were on the wrong side as we had never been in all our lives.

I thought probably they would lynch our client in the courtroom.

Governor Gage made a subdued gesture toward the black-clad lady on the stand and said, "You may cross-examine, Mr. Rogers."

I was glad when my father said to the judge, "If Your

Honor please—I suggest to you that Mrs. Griffith should not be subjected to any further questioning today."

"You propose to take some time in cross-examination, Mr. Rogers?" the judge said, and he sounded as surprised as Gage and Dockweiler looked, they hadn't expected he'd ask any questions at all. Any lawyer in his right mind knew that the sooner he got Teena Griffith out of the jury's sight the more chance he had, if any, to save his client.

"Yes, Your Honor—quite some time," Earl Rogers said.

"Then I agree, Mrs. Griffith should have some rest—we will adjourn until tomorrow morning at ten o'clock. The jury is admonished—"

If the jury refrained from discussing the case at His Honor's instructions they were the only twelve people in the city of Los Angeles who did.

"Papa," I said, "if she feels about him the way you said, why did she tell the story that way, couldn't she have said it was an accident or something?"

"Ah—" my father said, "if she'd had time to think, I expect that's what she would have done. Remember she was between life and death when she told it the first time. Then it was too late. I think she'll help me now. I'm going to give her a chance."

With deference as great as Governor Gage's had been, with the utmost consideration and sympathy, waiting quietly each time for her to regain her composure, Earl Rogers began to cross-examine the woman who had lived to tell the tale of her own murder.

Very difficult it had been to find somebody else to try in this strange case. Earl Rogers had succeeded. He was going to try John Barleycorn. Alcohol, baffling, cunning, powerful, his own bitter enemy.

Nobody else had seen him but within ten questions Rogers put him on the stand right beside the veiled lady in black.

Q. Before this, your relations with Mr. Griffith had been pleasant?

A. Yes.

Q. Had he been unkind to you?

A. No.

Q. He had been solicitous of you? Your health? Your comfort?

A. Always.

Q. Then he began having such delusions as his questions indicated. You didn't—forgive me for asking, you did not ever try to poison him, did you, Mrs. Griffith?

A. Never.

Q. Of course that is the truth.

A. The God's truth.

Q. You never even remotely thought of such a thing, did you?

A. Never.

Q. This wasn't the first time he had made these accusations?

There was a long pause, this time, and Mr. Rogers waited, he made a sign with his hand and Harry Dehm brought a glass of water, and he offered it to the veiled lady, but she shook her head.

Q. This wasn't the first time?

A. No.

Q. What was his condition when he did this?

A. I don't know what you mean.

Earl Rogers spoke directly to her, they might have been alone in the courtroom. He said, "Mrs. Griffith, it is too late to try to cover this up any longer. You are a loyal wife, you have been a loyal wife, like all loving and loyal women you have tried to conceal what you considered your husband's disgrace, his terrible fault. It isn't a disgrace, it isn't a fault—it is an illness, a disease, if you are to give him a chance to be cured you must speak the truth now for the first time in all these years. Mrs. Griffith, what was your husband's condition during all the times that he made these accusations?

A. He had been—drinking.

Q. He was drunk, wasn't he?

A. Mostly he was—drunk.

That was where Earl Rogers began the first alcoholic insanity defense. Perhaps the first—certainly one of the first— times that alcohol was called to account in an American courtroom as a disease, a mental illness, not just a sin or a crime or an indulgence.

Q. After your husband had been drinking, and sometimes when he had not entirely recovered from the effects of drink?

A. Yes. It was—principally from drinking—that he would ask those questions.

Q. Foolish questions. Questions like a drunk asks. You had never given him any cause to believe such things were true?

A. Oh no, sir. Never Mr. Rogers, never.

Q. He never had any sober sane reason to doubt you, did he?

A. I was always a pure woman and a faithful wife to him.

Q. But he made this accusation?

A. Yes.

Q. Many times.

A. Lately—

Q. When he was drinking? Wait a moment, Mrs. Griffith. Had you ever in your life seen a drunken man before you saw your husband drunk?

A. No—not close to—never.

Q. At first you did not know your husband did not drink in public?

A. No sir.

Q. So you never saw him take a drink?

A. Not for a long time.

Q. So you didn't have any idea what was the matter with him?

A. No—no. Not at first.

Q. And when you did find out as a wife must, you didn't tell a soul?

A. Only the priest.

Q. You were ashamed to have anyone know?

A. I—I didn't know what to do.

Q. You'd had no experience of any kind with drink, had you?

A. No—no I hadn't.

Q. You were bewildered and unhappy and didn't know what to do?

A. I told him—my husband—he got angry and said it wasn't true.

Q. He denied there was anything to worry about?

A. He said he did not ever take a drink, I was mistaken.

Q. Now at this moment though, Mrs. Griffith, you do realize that it was when he was drunk or when he was still under the influence to some extent that he did these things?

A. Yes.

Q. After the shooting when you spoke to Mr. Wright and told him you were wounded to death—what else did you say?

A. I said my husband shot me.
Q. Anything else?
A. I said he must be crazy.

That was what Earl Rogers had been waiting for. *Crazy.*
"You said he must have been crazy?" he asked her again.
On a long-drawn breath, the witness said, "Yes—I thought
he must have been crazy."
"You knew, didn't you, Mrs. Griffith, you know now," Earl
Rogers said in a comforting voice, "that your husband couldn't
have shot you or tried to kill you if he hadn't been crazy—
crazy *drunk*—insane from alcohol?"
"Yes—yes—" she said.
"Thank you, Mrs. Griffith," he said, and helped her down
from the stand. "I apologize for keeping you so long—you
understand that I had to."
This time Mrs. Griffith walked down the aisle, back to
where her nurse waited for her, on the arm of Earl Rogers.
She seemed to lean upon it heavily and with confidence. As
he handed her to the nurse, gently, Mr. Rogers said in a low
voice, "Don't worry." Nobody could have seen a smile through
the black widow's veil but everybody in the courtroom felt it.

Actually, a hypothetical question is one which can be
summed up in the word IF.
This is all unexplored territory, Mr. Rogers, had said Dr.
C. G. Brainerd, then the country's leading brain specialist, in
answer to Earl Rogers' hypothetical question in the Griffith
case.
We called them brain specialists or alienists then, being as
free of psychoanalysis and its uses and terrible misuses as we
were of other horrors the twentieth century was to produce,
world wars, income tax, traffic, and juvenile delinquency.
Nobody in the United States outside the medical profession
had heard the dread name of Freud, nor the words libido,
extra- and intro-vert, id, schizophrenic. A doctor could specialize in brain and nervous disorders but he consulted frequently
with the family doctor, who knew all there was to know
about his patients, mentally and morally. So Earl Rogers put
his IFs to eighteen sound reputable medical men with no
psychiatrists present.
So that later, sitting at ease on the witness stand himself,
it took Mr. Rogers over an hour to propound his hypothetical
question, followed by so much furor and controversy. The

unexplored territory referred to by Dr. Brainerd was the
matter of alcoholism as insanity, as a disease of the brain and
mind. Up to then it must be remembered drunks were *drunks*.
At best, figures of low comedy in vaudeville. True, almost
every family had one. A disgrace, a blot on the family es-
cutcheon, as evidenced by the fact that years later the best
spiritual means of saving them had to be Alcoholics *Anonymous*. Everybody wanted to keep theirs as anonymous as
possible if the poor souls died of it. Drunks ended in the
gutter, in jail, or if they had money in private sanatoriums
with male nurses. The churches did their best to get those to
whom drink was disaster to sign The Pledge. Just the same,
drunkenness was then a sin and a shame and had no other
connotation.

Alcoholism itself was a word not then in the American
vocabulary. Later the whole nation had to face this question.
By that time we were aware of a serious alcoholic percentage.
It verged on the disaster area when we blithely substituted
the cocktail lounge, where past, present, and future wives
and mothers could get drunk, for the bar, which had been
open only to men. The fate of all nations being determined
always by the moral strength of its women, this had to become a dangerous situation. The moral strength of drunken
women is low.

The first part of Earl Rogers' question covered the testimony already heard at the trial concerning the drinking habits
of the defendant.

IF a man secretly drank two quarts of whiskey a day would
this in time *become*—and then on into involved and technical
questions of brain tissue and nerve reaction in the body of
any human being.

This broad display of fireworks ended in simple enough
questions.

Q. (by Mr. Rogers) Doctor, is there such a thing as
alcoholic insanity as I have defined it here?

A. I had not before considered it—yes, oh yes, I believe
that is so.

Q. You have had an opportunity to examine the defendant
in this case and to check the records of the facts I have included in my question?

A. Yes.

Q. Was Griffith J. Griffith alcoholically insane when he
attempted to kill his wife?

A. Under the terms in which you have defined alcoholic insanity, I should say so beyond any doubt.

Q. Then at the time he was not able to tell the difference between right and wrong, he could actually have been possessed by a delusion that she intended to poison him?

A. Oh yes.

Q. Then he should be given medical care and treatment as an insane man?

A. Yes, I'm sure of that, quite sure. As I say it's unexplored territory but I'm sure help can be given in time.

> *Miss Adela Rogers, you feel that*
> *your father must have medical care*
> *and treatment in spite of himself?*
>
> *Yes Your Honor that's what I believe.*
>
> *Nora, you don't believe I'm insane, do you?*
>
> *No no, Papa, no no—of course not.*

When you can see both ways as the river of time flows beneath you, echoes come back from the future, too. I was in a cold sweat all the time about this question.

The trial went on, a dingdong battle.

My father and Governor Gage came to swords-drawn personal combat and a fine exciting spectacular pair they were, unafraid of dramatics. Their clashes were more equal, more deadly, than Papa had been getting lately, though soon now he was to face Hiram Johnson and Frances J. Heney, whom legal history records as among the greatest. Once he really caught Governor Gage off base and produced a moment of light and brilliance.

"Answer the question Yes or No," Governor Gage trumpeted at a defense witness, a bartender from the Jonathan Club.

"Come come, Governor," Earl Rogers said good-humoredly, rising from his seat, "you know better than that."

"Sir!" said the governor, haughtily.

"If you don't," Earl Rogers said, grinning at him, "His Honor will be glad to instruct you."

Governor Gage swung all the way around on his booted heel—he still wore the elegant patent leather boots—and stared at the slim young man. "May I ask what this is about?"

"If," Earl Rogers said amiably, "you can find anywhere in

any lawbook a ruling that a witness can be made to answer any question Yes or No, my client will plead guilty."

"I want him to answer Yes or No," Gage thundered, "No shilly-shallying or beating around the bush. I want a simple straightforward honest Yes or No—"

"Then as my father used to say, your want must be your master, sir," Earl Rogers said. "You can insist on a witness answering the question without excursions into irrelevant fields, but you cannot make him answer Yes or No, because there are questions to which Yes or No is perjury. You cannot force a witness to commit perjury for you."

"Mr. Rogers," said the judge.

Instantly, Rogers swung to face him with a quick apology. Very seldom did Earl Rogers permit himself to quarrel with a judge. In a speech before a class at the U. S. C. Law School, he said that he believed that the office of judgeship ennobled men. As long, he said to them, as the judiciary is incorruptible, the United States cannot be safely attacked from within. As long as the republic is united within it can never be successfully attacked from without.

"Am I to take it you wish to make an objection to the question Mr. Gage has just asked the witness?" said the judge in the Griffith case.

"If Your Honor please," Earl Rogers said, "I take exception to his instructions to my witness that he must answer a question Yes or No. That answer to many questions such as the best known *Have you stopped beating your wife?* is injurious and often false. It's a favorite trick of Cicero's and many others who moved in devious ways to entrap witnesses."

The judge said quietly, "Mr. Rogers, I will now instruct the witness that he does not have to answer any question by the words Yes or No. It is his right to answer fully enough to convey the truth as he sees it."

"Thank you, Your Honor," Earl Rogers said, and winked at Governor Gage.

On the other hand when in Gage's final argument he stressed the point of Griffith J. Griffith's many millions and cried, "A rich man has committed this brutal attempt at murder. No rich man has ever been punished for such a crime in these United States. A rich man thinks he cannot be punished," Mr. Rogers blew his stack in objections. The rest of Gage's argument was well-organized ridicule of the alcoholic-insanity theory and plea. "Are we to say," Governor Gage demanded, "that because this man has been a drunken hog in secret most of his life, he may in this beautiful state of ours slaughter the innocent with impunity? These so-called hypothetical questions are so much hogwash, put before you to confuse your manly judgment of a creature like this defendant who in his drunken indulgence and stupidity becomes a criminal of the lowest order and attempts to slay his true and loyal wife. I beg you to stand for pure womanhood and decent manhood against this man who adds the crime of murder—for such he intended—to the sin of his indulgence in drink."

So that the governor had clearly defined the old stand on alcoholism as Earl Rogers was attempting in unexplored territory to define a new one.

And, one of the jurors later told Mr. Rogers in detail, the twelve men fought it out in the jury room on these grounds for two days. To put it frankly, he said, it had been a real brawl. All of them had been impressed by the alcoholic-insanity defense. Most of them at one time or another had known a drunk. They were convinced that Griffith was as crazy as a drunken Indian when he pulled the trigger. On the other hand, as Gage had said, a man couldn't condone crimes because the criminal allowed himself to get blind *and* insane by pouring alcohol down his gullet.

Besides, what could they do with him?

How could they ensure that he'd stay sober for a while? Or maybe for good and all? They finally decided that until he got over drinking two quarts of booze a day and having murderous delirium tremens he had better be locked up where he couldn't shoot any other innocent party.

Commit him to an institution against his will.
In spite of himself.

Charmian London, Jack's wife, wringing her hands and saying to me, *What can I do for him in spite of him, what can I do to save him?*—the greatest novelist in America from the Enemy he called John Barleycorn.

The jury found what they thought was a start.

They sentenced Griffith J. Griffith to two years in the penitentiary with instructions that he there be given "medical aid for his condition of alcoholic insanity." The juror said, "We figured you'd think it was a sensible verdict yourself, Mr. Rogers. After the prosecution got through we were all for hanging him if possible. We thought you put up a good case for him and something ought to be done for the poor galoot. On the other hand, we weren't just going to turn him loose, either."

As too often happens, this sane compromise, punitive, remedial, and protective as it was, pleased nobody except, oddly, Griffith.

Governor Gage and ninety per cent of the public thought it was weak and ridiculous.

As for Earl Rogers, he took it—the word *Guilty*—as black defeat. Somewhere, sometime, a man must learn to live with his defeats. Nobody, as I learned to say when I became a sports writer, can win 'em all. Papa never accepted this. He wasn't just a bad loser. He was determined not to be a loser. Such a man will win more than his share, but when defeat comes it is disaster.

When a jury says, "We find Bundy GUILTY of murder in the first degree and recommend that he be hung," it may break him.

They *cured* Griffith J. Griffith.

> *You don't want to go on with this*
> *nonsense, do you, Nora?*
>
> *No no, Papa, no no, of course not—*
>
> *Lock him up? Take away his freedom?*
> *No no, Papa—*

With time off for good behavior, Griffith J. Griffith came out of the penitentiary after a year a new man, another man, if ever there was one. An objectionable personality still, but chastened, quiet, pathetic in a strange clown fashion, apparently sane, and still very very rich.

Some months after his release I stood with him on a hilltop, the ocean side of that enormous park named after him which he donated to the people of California. The hills were covered with pine and oak, eucalyptus, sycamore, mountain laurel, and the yucca, which the Spaniards called the candles of God, stood tall and ivory against their brown-green. Colonel Griffith was trying to give me ten or fifteen acres of what is today the exclusive residential district on the north side of Los Feliz Boulevard.

Hopping about like the dwarf that got his beard caught in a crack of the earth, he said, "Man like Mr. Rogers needs a hideaway, where people can't get at him and he can breathe some fresh air. I've paid his fee, this is a present I'd like to make him. I'll build a house and stable for a couple of horses —your father's the biggest man in this state. I know men. You can't make money unless you know men. I had brains—and always a wrong personality. Rogers has brains and a great personality. Few men have both, I know that. I'd like to help him."

I still couldn't like the man. Nevertheless he stood before me sane and sober. He was devoting most of his time and most of his money to prison reform and to helping convicts who came out of the pen with no place to go and no money and no job. His wife was still an invalid and she lived with her family; they were never reconciled but many of the works he did and the millions he threw into that work were in her name—he told me so. As long as he lived he gave his organizational ability to reform where it was needed most.

"Prison helped me," he said, "it don't help most. It ruins them, a lot of them."

Of course Papa wouldn't take the ten acres.

"I don't want to be saddled with a lot of real estate to pay taxes on," he said gaily.

"All right," I said, "you did a real good job on that Griffith, anyhow. No wonder he wanted to give you a present."

He only turned a dark face on me. "I'd rather be dead myself," he said furiously.

THIRTY

I remember once when Dolly and I were waiting for him and I'd begun to pace-the-floor.

At that time, Papa's drinking was still reasonably anonymous. Or at least confined to our own circle. For weeks, months Earl Rogers wouldn't touch so much as a Pisco Punch, even when he went into Simpson's or Joe Fast's or the Waldorf. Then he'd bust loose in what started out as a rowdy but elegant raz-a-muh-taz and come home with an orchestra or a pickpocket or, once, a camel. He said he had never had anything but hearsay evidence about a camel and he proposed to find out. It wasn't like Colonel Griffith, either. The hidden-bottle trick happened only when he was just deciding to go on one or was just coming off one.

For a while his binges were irresistible. Motley and madcap extravaganzas and the bright dancing waves of wit and the scintillating froth of drollery and danger hid the rocks.

With Papa, they always ended in a wreck. In trouble.

"You'd think," I said to Dolly, "after what he said to that jury about alcohol, he wouldn't ever want to take another drink. Wouldn't you?"

"Not any more," Dolly said. "I mean I wouldn't think that any more."

"Like what it said in the *Times*," I said.

Reviewing the unprecedented parade of medical witnesses, male nurses, bartenders, rubbers from Turkish baths, hack drivers, waiters, and saloon-keepers who had appeared in the Griffith case, the *Times* had commented wryly, *How anybody could ever summon up enough courage to take another drink after listening to all the testimony in the Griffith case, we cannot imagine. Earl Rogers put up a fantastic and great defense for Colonel Griffith. But it will be a long time before the brass rails on Spring Street will recover.*

Dolly and I decided to play duets. This is a pastime which has disappeared from our national scene and I have as yet seen little on television to replace its delights. Dolly made very satisfying arrangements of anything we liked, whether it was published in duet form or not. She spent a lot of time at the piano and she was giving me music lessons and since she wouldn't play duets with me unless I *practiced*, I *practiced*. This I had to conceal from my Aunt Blanche, who would have regarded it as the Last Straw—and did, when she found out.

"Men like him," Dolly said, bringing up the left hand so it rolled like drums. We were trying out a new for-two-hands instrumentation of Liszt's *Hungarian Rhapsody* Dolly had made. She was crazy about Liszt. "Men like your father cannot disconnect their minds from what they are thinking about like you and I can. In the first place our minds are not much and we are not thinking about much of *anything*. Musicians are the only great men who never drink, that is because they are entirely wrapped up in themselves and their music and never know anything about other people or the world so they do not get *involved*. They don't have to. Also men like your father are very lonely. They have to be. They *exist* at another dimension. He thinks beyond what is here and now, you know that, honey. If I were married to a man like that I would think of that first of all. To keep his idle time full up with people as near—as near as can be in his own—wherever it is he is. Like Guy Barham and Harry Carr and men from universities—"

I stopped playing and Dolly didn't notice, she went on with the *Rhapsody* by herself, and it was like a phosphorescent fountain of sound instead of color.

Right then I had an idea.

Papa and Mama were at the time legally separated or getting a divorce or something. I missed my brother badly and sometimes I would ask Papa if they were ever coming back. Ever since that day in the garden he always said, "No, never."

So I waited until Dolly crashed into the grand finale. Naturally the quiet after that was very pronounced. So I said in just an ordinary voice, "Why couldn't you and Papa get married?"

Her hands, which had begun to play Chaminade's *Scarf Dance*, stopped and were perfectly still. She had pretty ivory-colored hands, with long strong fingers, and she buffed her nails a lot so they were glowing and rosy. We did not have any polish for our nails then, we used a little powder and rubbed them with a chamois buffer until they were bright and shiny. She always sat very straight at the piano. That, at least, I thought would please my grandmother. *Lounging* was one road to hell; if Grandmama caught me in such a position I had to sit, and walk, with a book on my head. Dolly had a straight back, her head was held up properly, and only seemed to droop a little because her black hair was so heavy in big rolls and puffs. That would help too, I thought, because both my grandmother and my Aunty Blanche thought only blondes were bad girls.

Dolly went back to the *Scarf Dance*, very softly, and over it she said with a hearty laugh, "Don't ever say such a thing again, honey. It wouldn't be suitable. He is going to be a great man. The way Harry Carr and that big judge that were here the other day talked I guess it could even be the Supreme Court and the robes and all."

"Papa hasn't a judicial mind," I said. "He says it's different from the legal mind and the legal mind is different from the trial mind. I suppose he might be President or Governor, only he hates politics so much."

"Besides," Dolly said, "he's a Democrat. Democrats hardly

ever get to be anything like that. Well—any kind of a great man—he can't be married to me."

I thought about my grandmother and my aunts and even my Uncle Harry down in Tempe, Arizona, and I agreed probably there would be objections.

Dolly laughed again and she said, "I want to tell you something now that it may be good for you to know someday. The only reason girls who have been what I—was have a man marry them isn't for the reason most women think. I would like you to remember that, honey, because you are certainly no beauty and though I think you are going to turn out all right in time, you will need some understanding. Beautiful women never bother to get much, they don't have to, that's why on the whole they make such a mess of everything. Anyway, men marry girls like me because we usually have a sense of humor. From what I hear wives hardly ever do."

I thought about that for a while and decided from what I knew that most of them did not. My Aunty Madge didn't. I remembered once my mother saying with great *torment*, "I wouldn't mind not thinking a thing was funny if I just knew *what* you are laughing at, but I never do."

Dolly, I know now, had a rough and ready wit which sparked off whatever was going on. Not the kind that travels well over fifty years or so, just the kind that illumined our big luxurious suite at the Alexandria Hotel with its huge black Steinway concert grand, its big drawing room hung with dark green plush curtains, the teakwood tables and overstuffed furniture and the piles of books everywhere on everything. Also she never took it as *personal* when Papa was too tired to go anywhere or wanted to read instead of talk to her or came home in a violent mood about something at the office.

Of course I see now that this state of affairs couldn't go on. The roof caved in and I was miserable because I had been responsible.

I had never escaped entirely from those prayers my grandfather and I had said together before school. Nothing I have seen or done since, and that takes in a good deal of ground in all directions, has ever really altered the fact that Grandpa talked to the Risen Christ and *I knew it*. A man who has seen the light may go blind, and be bitter at having been robbed of the light, but it is impossible to tell him there is no such thing as light.

I was too young to have had the violent estrangement from

God that filled my father with passionate darkness and doubt. God had taken his father from him so ruthlessly, so mercilessly as he felt it, that he cried out in hatred, resentment, a defiance as flaming as Lucifer's. Better to be a man in hell than grovel to a God who didn't care what happened to his children, who struck down his most devoted servants without warning. This was an age of rebellion in religion, Papa and Jack London and Ambrose Bierce and George Sterling and all of them read Robert G. Ingersoll, the great iconoclast, and were in intellectual revolt against God all the time.

It didn't help any that right about then my Aunty Blanche got healed of a cancer in Christian Science.

My father was crazy about his sister, she made him laugh too, and he admired her very much. He'd been in a state about her. All his medical friends were summoned, big consultations of doctors were held, and yet there she was in the Good Samaritan Hospital waiting to die. Cancer was a new scourge, terrible to behold.

There seemed to me no question about her healing. She didn't die, she lived another fifty years, playing the organ in the Christian Science Church and becoming one of the outstanding women of her time and place. I was able to accept the healing then and always have been, since I saw it myself.

My father *flipped*. He said the doctors had been wrong; Aunty Blanche had built nervous dyspepsia and indigestion into something the medical profession knew nothing about anyhow. He read Mark Twain's brilliant humor about Mary Baker Eddy with gusto. But at the time the effect was to drive him further away from church, he said all churches were humbugs, hypocrites, and hysterics. While a good deal of this rebellious agnosticism had seeped into me—not all of it took. I was still a secret prayer.

Dolly had been brought up to go to church so sometimes we slipped out on Sunday morning and walked up to hear Dr. Burdette. One day as we came out he greeted us. I felt a little shy for once, but not enough of course to keep me still. I said, "You speak like my grandfather." He asked who my grandfather was and I told him and he held my hand and said, "Then you must be Earl Rogers' daughter," and I saw that he gave a quick glance at Dolly who looked very nice in a gray tailored suit with a Merry Widow sailor hat. He spoke with admiration of my father and said he would like to call on us someday. I knew how my father felt about most preachers, but he loved some, Bishop Conaty for example, and I knew Dr.

Burdette was a scholar and I figured he'd have tact and sense enough not to talk about *religion*, but would know other subjects. They might have some fine conversation, an art my father loved, so I said I knew Papa would be glad to see him.

One evening he walked in right after dinner.

We were having a very happy evening. The big lamps filled the room with a warm and comfortable light and made it quite homelike. Dolly was playing a piece she'd been practicing all day and Papa was complimenting her, he liked the new French composers; he said they had true gaiety. He and I were playing chess, he was patient with me, it had been obvious for some time that I was never going to be a chess player. He looked surprised as he got up to welcome Dr. Burdette. Neither Dr. Burdette nor I said anything about my invitation, he just said he'd been in the hotel visiting a friend and he wanted to pay his respects, he'd known my grandfather.

Papa said, "Do you play chess, Doctor?" When Dr. Burdette said he did my father said, with great friendliness and hospitality, "Perhaps you would enjoy finishing this game? Nora's a beginner, we might let her see how it is done." I didn't care about the chess, but I watched and listened, I thought it was wonderful to see them together, those two men, laughing and talking while they contemplated their moves. They seemed to have taken a great liking to each other. I was so happy and occupied I didn't notice the music had stopped and Dolly had gone away without saying good night.

I remember exactly the conversation with which that evening ended. Sometimes my sound tape is blank and I have to write what I feel was said, or invent it from what I knew so well of the people. Sometimes words are etched in, as fresh as the moment they were spoken. Perhaps because I kept saying them over to myself afterwards.

Papa had won. He said with that smile that would enchant anybody, it had such singular sweetness and good will, that Dr. Burdette was out of practice and must come again and have another chance.

For a moment Dr. Burdette stood there looking at him. He put his arm around me and when he spoke my stomach turned over. This was something and somebody—entirely different from that man I'd watched at the chess table. He said, "Of course you know you can't continue this. You are doing it, I am sure, mostly out of a desire for revenge. Unfortunately, as so often happens with that evil passion, you are not hitting the person you wish to hurt but—an innocent bystander. This is not worthy of you."

"It doesn't harm her," my father said in a clear voice. "There are better principles and morals *here* than in the homes of many reputable ladies protected by their marriage lines and their husband's names. As I have reason to know."

Dr. Burdette didn't back up, the way most people did with Papa. He stood his ground, whatever it was. "Two wrongs have yet to make a right, my son," he said though Papa wasn't that much younger. "You are going to put too heavy a handicap on—the innocent bystander."

"I will not pay homage to scribes and pharisees and whited sepulchers," my father said, and what surprised me was that he was explaining himself, which he usually didn't do, "or to worn-out superstitions. I want—I want her to be a free soul. To see good because it is good, not because it is protected by conventions and wealth and social position."

"As you know," Dr. Burdette said, "there is freedom only inside the law."

"I don't know that," my father said, "and I thought the founder of your church came to save sinners, not the righteous."

"There were terms to the continued forgivingness," Dr. Burdette said, "*Neither do I condemn thee—go and sin no more.*" Just as my grandfather used to say it.

"I assure you, Dr. Burdette," my father said in a voice that made me go over and stand on *his* side, "no sin is going on here."

"Thank you, my son," Dr. Burdette said. "The difficulty there is, I am the only man in California who would believe it."

My father laughed, really laughed. Then he said, "You are a brave man, Bob Burdette. I am inclined to think—a just one."

"Like your father," Dr. Burdette said, "I try my poor best to follow My Master." He looked at me and said, "Your grandfather was my friend. He was very fond of you."

"I know," I said, "I wish he was here."

He smiled and started to say something but had too much sense. He shook hands with my father and went out.

"Go to bed, Nora," Papa said, with absolute finality.

The next day, Dolly was gone.
I never saw her again.

Let me tell you I was in a fury with Dr. Bob Burdette. I thought he had double-crossed me and betrayed me and I hoped there was a hell so he could go to it and I was convinced Papa was right; it was better not to have anything to do with *God*. All you got was trouble.

My father didn't say a word about it at the time.

And not very long after I was carried off kicking and screaming on a trip to Europe with my Aunty Blanche.

There was no way to escape an awful fate, though I tried. A remarkable gal named Elizabeth *Bunny* Ryan, who holds more tennis championships than any other woman ever has, told me not long ago her impression of the time I did succeed in getting expelled from Marlborough, then the most exclusive Young Ladies' Finishing School in the West. Bunny Ryan was senior head girl, captain of the basketball team, already a tennis champion. "I'll never forget it," Bunny told me. "We were all absolutely mad about your father, we cut his pictures out of the paper, whenever he came to see you I suppose it was like Clark Gable or Marlon Brando coming to call as far as we were concerned. That night Mrs. Caswell had sent for him; you hadn't come back to school for hours after a basketball game out of town the day before—you were small, but you were a scrapper, I used you as a substitute guard— and we were all hanging over the banisters and hiding behind the portieres and peeking through the windows. Mrs. Caswell took you into the parlor where your father was waiting and she said, 'Mr. Rogers, you must understand I can't keep Adela here; her marks are excellent but she has no idea of community life, she tells most outrageous untruths, and she will not accept discipline. She is a source of continual unrest in my school.' Well, your father began buttering her up and just then she looked at you and you looked like the cat that swallowed the canary. Mrs. C. was a bright lady; she'd run that school for years, she could see it was a plot you'd cooked up to get out of there, so she said, 'If you will co-operate with me, Mr. Rogers, I'll give her another chance—' of course she'd fallen for him too. Well, no siren ever equaled the yell you let out. One of the girls fell over the balustrade. You kept shrieking, Oh no Papa please I can't stay here it's like Colonel Griffith in San Quentin you said I didn't have to stay if I didn't like it—and of course he said, All right, don't holler like that, and took you away and we all envied you more than anyone we knew and we got caught and were confined to barracks for a week or something."

I tried it again when Aunty Blanche said my music was good enough now for us to find out about it. I should study at the Gewandhaus in Leipzig; it was best for piano. Aunty Blanche always said a woman could live *with* a man only if she couldn't live *without* him, and she'd been advanced enough to remain an old maid until she was thirty in spite of many suitors. Then she married a fine singer named Harry Clifford Lott. They were going to London and Berlin and Munich and Bayreuth and Leipzig to study; I should come along.

This time I didn't get away with my pleas and protests. My father said music was one of the greatest graces in life; if I could play the piano it would be better than becoming a criminal lawyer and he said, too, that while he didn't believe in schools my Aunty Blanche was right, travel would give languages and polish.

So there we were in London. Fortunately for me my Uncle Harry Lott just had a magnificent baritone voice; he wasn't a dedicated musician like my aunt. He had some other interests, so we went in the pit to see Lily Elsie and Joe Coyne in *The Merry Widow,* and Mrs. Patrick Campbell and Ellen Terry, and Sir Beerbohm Tree and rode on the top of buses on the Tottenham Court Road and walked up Baker Street, where Sherlock Holmes had lived. Then we stayed at a *pension* in Leipzig and I worked at the Gewandhaus and a man told me in German that I would never be better than a second-rate pianist, than which we both agreed there was nothing worse. In Berlin I heard Geraldine Farrar sing *Madame Butterfly* and everyone knew the crown prince was madly in love with this American prima donna. John McCormack sang Lieutenant B. F. Pinkerton and I cried so hard I couldn't see to come down the stairs. We had paid a mark to go in the top gallery with the students—sometimes Papa forgot to send the check and sometimes as I knew he was probably broke himself. We went to Russia. In St. Petersburg, as it was called then, I saw the little czarevitch with his beautiful mama in floating white and jewels, and the four beautiful grand duchesses, with long flowing curls, going into the great church of St. Isaac. They were the most beautiful *people* I had ever seen; they took my breath away. Nothing could have made me believe that in a few years they would all be butchered in a cellar at Ekaterinburg.

I have always been glad my father made me go. Just the same I was very homesick and lonesome for him all the time.

I knew Mama was back. Dolly had said she would be. She's got that *hold* on him, Dolly had said. So I figured my chances weren't very good but I kept writing asking him to let me come home just the same. I was getting so sad that if it hadn't been for Uncle Harry I might have contemplated jumping in the Volga or the Rhine.

Then Papa went to San Francisco on the graft cases and sent for me.

It turned out that it was Patrick Calhoun, president of the United Railroads, Papa's client, who made the move. Years later at the Santa Anita race track when Mr. Calhoun was well over eighty he told me about it. People around Mr. Rogers said they told him if he really wanted to get things going right he had better send for Mr. Rogers' little girl Adela. I know now that they had all begun to worry. I didn't know then and I wouldn't have cared anyway. The cable opened the gates of heaven to me in spite of the fact that nobody thought to send me any money to buy my ticket.

PART FIVE

THIRTY-ONE

I can't remember anything about the trip home on the *Baltic,* except that I was met in New York by Uncle Billy Pinkerton, head of the Pinkertons, a great friend of my father's. He put me on a train which made its way across a continent so slowly I was wild with suspense. Just the same I was happy and filled with excitement and glory. Papa needed me; my exile was over, I'd see him in a day—an hour—a few minutes.

Only Rosy was at the train to meet me.

This was, I knew, the kind of a trick the Noseless One always played if he could. The one time—so I didn't say anything. Neither did Rosy.

We went to the St. Francis Hotel, where Earl Rogers had a big suite facing Union Square. He used it for an office, for meetings, as a hideout and part of the time lived there. He and Mama had a big house out on Washington Street, near the entrance to the Presidio.

When Rosy and I got to the big suite at the St. Francis, Papa wasn't there.

A new man met us. His name was Bull Durham, a big man with a pugnacious face, I liked him right away. I was introduced to half a dozen men I'd never seen before and they all wanted to know if I'd had a good time in Europe. I said yes.

Rosy and I watched the clock. We always did, I guess. The hands were straight up, on the witching hour, when we heard the footsteps we'd been waiting for, praying for, in the corridor outside. The door opened and he stood there, swaying. A heavy frown on his face.

I stood up.

In simple sincere surprise he said, "*What* is that you've got on, Nora?"

Well, they used mirrors then as much as they do now, only instead of being whole walls they were in gilt frames, like pictures. The one at the end of this hotel drawing room showed me a very thin young girl, the awkward age, all right, wearing a gray wool suit ornamented with heavy black braid and large black frogs across the front. On my grandmother it might have been suitable. My braids were half looped up and on my feet were large black Oxfords and black lisle stockings. I had to admit it was no improvement over what I'd seen some time back in Pearl Morton's mirrors.

"You look like an orphan," Papa said.

"I feel like one, too, if you want to know," I said.

I wanted to die. I said, "Oh Papa—" and he came across the room and put his arms around me like I was the straw to a drowning man and we both laughed until we cried. Then he held me off and studied me, and hugged me again and said remorsefully, "I'm sorry, Nora, I was taken by surprise; let us thank God you are in San Francisco where live the best-dressed women in the world. Tomorrow we will see what we can do to make you as charming as possible. We can burn these atrocities you have on."

"Or we can give them to some old lady," I said.

"No old lady deserves such a horrible fate," Papa said.

He pulled one of my pigtails and I realized that an extraordinary phenomenon had taken place. I was to see him do it often in the future, but right then was the first time I remembered. He had been weaving drunk when he opened the doors. Now he was cold sober and sparkling. He said accusingly, "You're not growing up, are you?"

"You cannot thwart nature," I said. "A man named Mayer whose father is a big impresario told Uncle Harry he wanted me to stay in London. To educate me so I'd be a proper wife for him. This is the custom in Europe, he said."

"I'd have had to shoot him," Papa said, "and who would I get to defend *me?* Still, if he could see any charm in you in those clothes—" and he began to laugh again, I could tell it was because he was *happy.*

"I didn't have these until we got to Vienna and I got too tall for my old ones," I said. I didn't tell him how pleased I'd been when Aunty Blanche let me have this suit with a long skirt, and a black felt hat with a plume, for fear he would think I had no more taste than she did—or Mama for that matter— and actually I didn't have much more. I said, "Where is Mama?"

He didn't stop laughing, he said, "I'm the last man in San Francisco to know that." I said, "Where's Bogart?" and he said, "At school down the Peninsula; we'll go see him Sunday." He came and untied my pigtails and let them hang down again, he said, "Never mind that. I want you to go with me to see a man named Abe Ruef. Is your *stomach* still working?"

I said, "It was beyond my control on the boat, but it was all right this morning—when I got off the train."

He gave me a funny look and said, quietly, "I'm sorry, Nora." A thought seemed to dawn on him, he said, "Who sent you the money to come home?"

I said, "I borrowed it from Mischa Elman. He is a very nice boy about my age and he can play the violin better than anyone in the world."

He said, "I guess you are growing up. Remember I'll beat you if you don't behave yourself. Now listen. Since you can't play the piano you may have to be a criminal lawyer at that."

My father was regarding me with a speculative eye. I knew already that his entire mind, heart, and imagination and even memory were now absorbed by the two cases he'd come to San Francisco to defend. The charges of bribery against the president of the United Railroads and its chief counsel, Patrick Calhoun and Tirey Ford.

"You've got a fresh view and a clear eye on all this," he said. "Listen and I will now give you the key to the entire case against Ford. No matter what else goes on or is told you, keep this one thing before you as we go into it. Will Abe Ruef testify against Ford? Whether you know yet what it means, hang onto it. In his opening statement to the jury, Special Prosecutor Heney, my esteemed opponent, promised to put the Little Boss, Abe Ruef, on the stand. No one else alive can connect Tirey Ford with guilty knowledge of any intention to bribe the supervisors except *Ruef*. Will he do it?"

He stopped and looked at me, his head down. I couldn't believe I'd been away. Piccadilly and Unter den Linden and the Rue de la Paix were unreal as a forgotten dream. "How much do you know about this graft prosecution which is shaking San Francisco worse than the earthquake?" my father said.

"Not much," I said.

"Well," Papa said, "give me your attention. I will try to reduce its intricate and astounding ramifications and absurdities, which will intrigue and confuse historians for years to come, down to some bare facts for you."

Somehow he made the bare outline, the skeleton, come out reasonably simple.

Theodore Roosevelt in the White House was a president the country *did* know, intimately. They loved him, they liked to read about him, he was close to their hearts because he was the colonel of the Rough Riders who'd been the hero of San Juan Hill. As the youngest President ever, Teddy had bared his teeth in his famous grin and taken off on another rough ride. To bust the trusts. To clean up political corruption, manifest in pork-barrel dishonesty of officeholders, all spoils systems, all pillagings and cheating, which had indeed risen to be a mighty scandal in our land. Somebody gave this reform movement of T.R.'s the name of "muckraking." As such it was soon the major headline interest of newspapers and magazines and swept from coast to coast and border to border in every state, county, and city government.

For some years prior thereto, San Francisco had been controlled politically by a picturesque young Jewish lawyer named Abe Ruef, better known as the Little Boss. He had elected a mayor, a board of supervisors, a district attorney, a city council, and whatever other offices were necessary to run the town. On the whole, such procedure was accepted by one and all as a necessary evil. Politics were corrupt and politicians were crooked. The Pay-off was a Fixed Expense of Business. After the fire, however, the corruption of Abe's reign had begun to show plainly and the President's Operation Muckrake encouraged some prominent citizens to activate a Reform Vigilante Committee. They then asked the President to help them. One peek into the horrors going on had aroused the city and soon indictments flew and prison sentences for the grafters were possible.

This time, I saw as soon as Papa talked, he was going against the heaviest guns he'd ever face. For he was defending two of the Big Business financiers accused of bribing public officials. On the opposition's graft prosecution team when I got home were Rudolph Spreckels, multimillionaire business genius and financier, heading this Clean Government movement out of, he said, civic pride. With him were many respected San Franciscans, including former Major James J. Phelan. Fremont Older, of the San Francisco *Bulletin,* was recognized as the greatest crusading newspaper editor in the country and was, Papa said, an honest, inspired, and dedicated man. Also into this particular battle zone had come riding Lincoln Steffens, who admitted to being the greatest of all the famous reporters following the red-hot trail of Roosevelt's campaign. Steffens actually made this claim stick; his series called *The Shame of the Cities* rocked the nation.

Also, to come right down to it, on the team was President Roosevelt himself, and to head the actual graft cases in San Francisco he had sent his top legal lieutenant, Assistant Attorney General Francis J. Heney, whom he named special prosecutor. Under Heney was the pugnacious, incorruptible fighter-for-right Hiram Johnson, the man who founded the Progressive party, in California, busy trying to bust the Southern Pacific machine, and after being governor and senator missed the presidency himself by one bad decision.

If there was any citizen in San Francisco not actively engaged in the graft prosecution on one side or the other, deeply involved in it some way already or soon to be, Papa said he had not as yet discovered him.

Up to the very moment when Papa was explaining all this to me, Heney had won 'em all. (Of course Earl Rogers hadn't been in any of those!) Heney had convicted the head of the Telephone Company of giving bribes. Sent Mayor Eugene Schmidt and others to the penitentiary for taking them. And gotten verdicts against Boss Abe Ruef for both, as well as for selling political influence and offices, fight and liquor licenses, protection of prostitution and all the old, old changeless patterns of Civic Corruption.

Now, Heney and the graft prosecution were trying for former State's Attorney General Tirey L. Ford, chief counsel for the city's streetcar system, the United Railroads. Pending was also a bribery charge against its president, Patrick Calhoun. Earl Rogers was in San Francisco as chief counsel of defense for these two.

"Just what are they supposed to have done, Papa?" I said.

Papa said, "The prosecution charges that Ford, as chief counsel for the United Railroads, gave Abe Ruef two hundred thousand dollars in gold fresh from the Mint. This they can prove. A number of supervisors have sworn they accepted bribes from Ruef to grant the United Railroads a new franchise after the fire, though a storm of public opinion was against it.

"Mr. Ford says he paid money to Lawyer Ruef on a regular yearly fee basis, for his expert legal advice on all political matters. That he never knew or even suspected that any of that fee was to be used for any corrupt practices or purposes.

"Now—only one man operated on both levels. Abe Ruef

received the money from Ford. He paid the head of the board of supervisors, his own liaison man, Big Jim Gallagher, to pass on to the board money to ensure their votes for the franchise. Only Abe Ruef can testify that Ford had knowledge or gave his advice or consent to a pay-off. You see that?"

"Sure," I said, "only I don't see how Ford could help—"

"Never mind what you don't see," Papa said. "When he went into court with this charge Francis J. Heney knew somebody had to forge the link between Ford and the bribes and bribed. Make the connection. Show Ford *knew*. So, as I've told you, in his opening address Heney promised the jury in these words, *I will put Ruef on the stand to testify to the fact that Ford not only knew of but ordered the bribery.*"

"What's his trouble?" I said.

"They are now playing ring-a-round-a-rosy," Papa said gleefully. "While he was promising, Heney promised Ruef FULL IMMUNITY if and when he gave this testimony against Ford and Calhoun. Heney said to Ruef, Take the stand dear Mr. Ruef and swear Ford agreed to your plan and the price of five thousand dollars per vote to each supervisor. Then, dear Mr. Ruef, you won't have to go to San Quentin where your pal Mayor Schmidt is already incarcerated. To which the Little Boss, Abe Ruef, with his customary caution, says, Splendid. Give me that guarantee of immunity in writing signed by you and I will so testify. It isn't that I don't trust you, my dear Mr. Heney, says the Little Boss, but I promised my mother always to get everything in writing. They are now dancing an Alphonse and Gaston reel. After *you*, my dear Ruef. No no, after *you*, my dear Heney. A pig-headed, cock-of-the-walk Irishman, against a tough, shrewd, imaginative Jew. So far it's a Mexican standoff.

"Now I've heard that Ruef is weakening a little."

"Where *is* Ruef?" I said.

Since the Little Boss had appointed or elected practically everybody in office in San Francisco at the time, including some judges, the graft prosecution hadn't considered any jail or jailers safe. With the immunity deal still to be closed they had to play ball with the key witness until they had his testimony before the jury. Under circumstances of this kind, the law provided that the court appoint an elisor, and Abe now had his own elisor and his own private jail, formerly a private mansion in an exclusive residential neighborhood, same referred to by the newspapers as the Little St. Francis, after the best hotel in town.

"They've got possession of him," my father said, "and they're putting on all the pressure from Washington down. Heney doesn't dare sign the immunity deal in full. I'll ruin him if he does. He has to persuade Ruef to take his word. My chance to acquit Ford is to be sure he doesn't. I must see him, that's all."

"How can you," I said, "even if it is his own private jail?"

Just then Bull Durham shepherded in a waiter bearing scrambled eggs and onions, a favorite dish of my father's, with loaves of hot French bread and sweet butter and pots of coffee and I realized I was starving. Other men had kept coming and going, some I knew, some I didn't. I saw Luther Brown in a caramel suit with a bow tie, I figured the measure of how glad I was to be home was that I was glad to see him. Papa introduced to me a man named Moore, a big lawyer on the Calhoun board of defense.

We were all eating around a big table in our dining room when Rosy came in. He was hurrying. He said, "My man's on alone tonight from three to six."

Everybody was very quiet.

Papa said, "Tonight. Good. How about it, Luther?"

I could see he still trusted Luther Brown's manipulations. However, Luther wasn't having any part of this one. He said, "I'm against it at any time. Say you get into the so-called Little St. Francis; if you are caught talking to Abe Ruef or even trying to talk to him this is tampering with a prosecution witness in the fullest legal meaning of that term. You know that, Mr. Rogers. You could not deny you knew it. Plenty of people would go a long way to get you disbarred right now. Or sent to jail till these cases are over. We are in the midst of a nest of snakes. Heney has his Burns operatives everywhere, following your every step. Fremont Older's best reporters never let you out of their sight. Four of them are in a dice game down the hall with the door open, right now. I say it's too risky."

Moore was strongly against it too. So, to my surprise, was the new man, Bull Durham, who looked like a scrappy fullback. He said all reformers were unpredictable and slightly cracked, they didn't know what they were doing themselves so how could you tell? Before this prosecution is over, Bull said, somebody will start shooting bullets. It might be tonight.

"Rosy?" Mr. Rogers said.

Rosy was sore. He said, "It's my man out at the Little St. Francis. He says the coast will be clear at that hour. We can park around the block and come in through the cellar. I got to go along with my man."

"Nora?" Papa said.

I couldn't answer for a minute.

I'm not sure a moment of happiness like that comes to everybody in their whole life.

Even if I had grown, Papa had hung me back on his watch chain.

Here he was in the most important case of his whole career and up against practically the President of the United States, and until that second I hadn't admitted to myself how scared I was that I'd been away too long. Now we were back in partnership again, Earl Rogers and his daughter, and a wave of joy swept over me that practically drowned me so I could only sputter.

Finally I said, "I don't see you have any choice," I said. "If he testifies you lose whether he's telling the truth or not. If you think you can *do* anything with him, you have to try."

Papa grinned at me. He took a thin gold watch out of his vest pocket (wrist watches didn't come in until the First World War). He said to Rosy, "You will have to arrange it so we can go through the next suite and down in the freight elevator," he said. "Suppose we leave here at three. That will get us to the Little St. Francis about three-fifteen to three-thirty—how is that?"

"I'll be back," Rosy said. He winked at me and went out, with the same old horseman's walk.

"I'll fill Nora in on a lot of the background while we wait," Papa said, and that made me even happier; it was just like old times and I could tell he was really so glad I was back he didn't want to let me out of his sight and I didn't either.

Also, he was keyed up like a starting pitcher the night before the first game of the World Series and it passed the time.

THIRTY-TWO

As he talked I discovered that for the first time Earl Rogers held a bitter, personal hatred and contempt for an opponent.

From the jump, he was out to get Rudolph Spreckels.

His utter, emotional conviction that millionaire Spreckels was a self-serving villain, fishing in San Francisco's troubled waters to gain more millions and new power for himself, turned out to be what, in the end, broke the graft prosecution. The day somebody called it that they opened a hole through which Earl Rogers could crash—and did.

Papa painted for me that first night a big canvas.

"Always remember," he said, "Teddy Roosevelt is a man of shining integrity, an aristocrat with money, the first idealist in the White House since Lincoln. These are great and dangerous men. He's done an idealistic and practical job of cleaning up the Shame of the Cities—the nationwide stinking corruption of our civic governments. But I'm afraid he doesn't see or understand yet that San Francisco is different."

This, of course, was legendary.

As long as I'd been alive, the feud between San Francisco and Los Angeles had been potent, though San Francisco didn't take her southern neighbor too seriously as a rival. I remember on the day of the earthquake I had been standing on my roller skates in the middle of the morning and all of a sudden I fell down flat on my behind. That was our echo of the quake five hundred miles north, and when I got home my aunts and grandmother and lots of people they knew were saying openly that a patient Jehovah had grown tired of this wicked city. At last he had wiped it out in twenty-seven seconds, as he had wiped out Sodom and Gomorrah long ago. The trouble was San Francisco didn't know when she was licked. Symbolized to herself by the phoenix, she rose from her ashes, glittering, triumphant, and irresistible. If she'd been the wickedest city in America, she rose bloody but unbowed. Muckraking her untamed seven hills, Papa said, would be more complicated than any other of the cities had been.

San Francisco: A Labor Government. So Lincoln Steffens

titled his chapters covering these years of civic civil war. Therein, Papa explained to me, lay so much of the ferocity and heartbreak and trouble. For it was not only A Labor Government. It was the First Union Labor Party Government ever elected anywhere in the world.

This makes what happened around it, as I am about to tell it, a focal point in history today.

"Wait a minute," I said once. "What you call the reformers only want to give the city an honest government. Get rid of the grafters. And we've always believed in unions, haven't we?"

His face darkened with anger. "Unfortunately," he said. "in this, it happens that the union men are the rascals. Nothing will be accomplished if we simply support the exchange of one set of rascals for another less bright."

Of course, Papa had known Ruef for years. Nobody could have done legal business in San Francisco otherwise. In the best and most readable book of the many written on this sensational and violent period, by Walton Bean, University of California's distinguished historian, he titled it *Boss Ruef's San Francisco* and so it was. The Abe Ruef now in his private prison. The Abe Ruef we were going to see in some dark and dangerous pilgrimage before this night was over. To understand all that was happening, Papa said, you had to understand Abe Ruef, the man and his part in it, so he told me about him.

A graduate of the University of California. Cultured, subtle, charming, of French parentage. "An hypnotic orator," my father said, which none of the other bosses of the cities were. "I saw him hold a hostile audience once for four hours and send them away cheering. A native San Franciscan. Didn't drink, smoke, gamble, nor consort with women. But these are not the sins by which the angels fell. From his cradle, one of his sisters told me, he was consumed by one ambition. Politics. A man whose end and aim is political power will stop at nothing. Nor did Ruef."

At, it seemed, a crucial moment when the Hearst newspapers were shrieking prophetically UNIONS ARE HERE TO STAY, the Republicans and Democrats of the Bay Area ran into the nightmare of every political party. No attractive candidates. Ruef saw the level of the balance of power was possible in a new Union Labor party, which had been started by an honest dedicated labor leader named Patrick Henry

McCarthy. Ruef took over from the fumbling, inexperienced, unknown laborites. In no time at all he had become the Little Boss and both parties bowed to his rule.

His formula was simple.

Be their lawyer. Get the pay-off in legal fees.

"Is that ethical, Papa?" I asked.

"In the highest sense, certainly not," Papa said. "However the way Ruef arranged it, it was legal. There are experts in the law, as there are elsewhere. There will be more. The structure of our government will grow so complex that no one man can know all the law. Each will select his own field. Ruef had already done that. He was an expert on political law, franchises, government contracts, labor rights. A formula legal, if morally questionable. Unless and until they can link such a man's fees as pay-off for political favors, unless he controls officials he has elected for personal interest, he can get away with it. Then, everybody goes to jail. On the books of all the big corporations in the United States, and all the public utility companies they were listed as *Fixed Expense*. Had been for years."

Ruef had political genius. No one else, my father said, would ever have thought of Eugene Schmidt as candidate for mayor of San Francisco.

Schmidt was the leader of the orchestra at the fashionable Columbia Theater. "Ladies at matinees swooned over him," my father said. No political experience, except as president of a dinky little outfit called the Musicians' Union. (Not even Petrillo ever ran a violinist for mayor.) Abe Ruef took one, tall, dark and handsome, with a silken curly beard, an actor-ish manner, and a ringing baritone and made him mayor. "He did not fiddle while San Francisco burned, either," my father said. "Give him his due. I was there after the earthquake, during the fire, when Mayor Schmidt said, 'I have ordered my men to KILL anyone caught looting or taking advantage of any other man or woman in this time.' He meant it. He was in danger spots all the time, directing, reassuring. A very brave man.'"

His election, of course, had given Abe Ruef immediate control of the police, crime and punishment, gambling, prize-fighting, Chinatown, prostitution and, through the Union Labor party, of all the unions. "Schmidt was over six feet, a fine figure of a man," Papa said, "and Ruef always looked as though he'd come into the Winner's Circle after riding a hard race. It should have been the other way around, but Schmidt sat on Ruef's knee while Ruef pulled the strings and spoke through him as a ventriloquist's dummy. An amazing pair.

"In Schmidt's first run for the roses, they had no hopes of the board of supervisors. The next time Ruef ran a full Union Labor party ticket. But he had so little hope he hadn't told one of the candidates he was putting his name on the ballot. Nor had he even met his candidate for district attorney and this was a fatal mistake. It had never occurred to Ruef in his most optimistic moments that any of them would be elected."

Nor was any politician in the world, unless perhaps Napoleon the day the Chamber of Deputies elected him First Consul, ever so dumfounded as Abe Ruef when he discovered the entire ticket had won by an impressive majority.

"Nora," Papa said, "do you know what a board of supervisors is and does?"

"No," I said.

"Neither do the voters," Papa said. "The board of supervisors has unlimited financial powers in the city and county. What concerns us is that it grants the franchises under which the city railways and all public utilities function. Its power over them is absolute and final.

"Look at this," he said, his finger on a sheet of paper he'd taken up, "and you will understand that at the very moment Abe Ruef became aware that the gods had poured all the riches of San Francisco into his lap, he must also have had some chill premonitions." His finger touched one name after the other. "This," he said, "is the board of supervisors Ruef put up and to his amazement elected. What is now known as the Boodle Board."

I read it following his finger.

Daniel G. Coleman ...member of the Retail Clerks' Union
James F. Kelly ....president, Piano Polishers' Union
Patrick McGushin ....saloonkeeper
Jenning S. Phillips ....official, Printing Pressmen's Union
George F. Duffy .....proprietor plumbing company
Cornelius Harrigan ...grocer, South of Market Street store
Max Mamlock ....vice-president, Electrical Workers
Thomas F. Lornegan ..president, Bakery Wagon Drivers' Union
John J. Furey ....blacksmith, president, Iron Trade Council
Sam Davis ....drummer, Tivoli Opera House,
                    representative, Musicians' Union
Michael W. Coffey ...hack-driver, president, Hack-drivers' Union

Edward L. Walsh ..... machine operator, official, Shoeworkers'
                                Union
Ferdinand P. Nichols ... carpenter, president, District Council
                                of Carpenters
Andrew Wilson .... furniture dealer

I was amazed at the pain and fury in my father's voice as he
read them aloud. "Yes, I believe in unions," he said, "I always have. But don't you see—I tried to explain this to London
—don't you see this is stark unmitigated tragedy? I'm not
looking down on these laboring men. I am saying there is no
darkness like ignorance, and this is bad luck for them, and
for their cause as they now represent it before the world.
Ruef had a team of illiterate greenhorns, unfit to hold public
office of this kind. Men with no executive experience or business judgment, on the whole. Bound to make mistakes. To
be used by the unscrupulous. More than that, here were
honest enough citizens when they started. Ordinary records
of average men. But remember. They have been taught that
the laboring man is downtrodden. That he has a right to all
that other men have. These were men just climbing out of
poverty. Poor men, who'd been hungry. Men who all their
lives have been without the glittering baubles of luxury and
vice around them. Men who couldn't afford things for their
families that they saw other men take for granted. Were these
men prepared to meet the temptations of bribery? Of more
money than they'd ever dreamed of offered for small favors
that didn't seem very important or very wrong? No no.

"Thomas Lornegan, who drove a bakery wagon for a salary
too small to give him and his family everyday comforts. Can
they elevate him with no training or education to refuse more
money for a small license than he's ever made in a year? So
you know what happened to him? The paper money he 'took'
was under his mattress the night of the earthquake and fire.
Now the poor ignorant, superstitious creature thinks God
engineered this catastrophe just to destroy and rob him of his
dirty ill-gotten gains.

"Where but in San Francisco with her prankish humor, her
weird and wonderful extremes, could such raggle-taggle
rabble as their bartenders and piano polishers have been
elected to power over vast corporations? Many of these have
taken generations to build. They need training and talent to
operate successfully. Now they must buy from men who
have no understanding of their problems.

"It's a joke on San Francisco, in San Francisco today. But it's a bad joke on labor, can't you see that? They weren't ready for power.

"Ruef's antennae warned him," Papa said more quietly. "The pay-off is an art. Done with mirrors. Now you see it, now you don't. Ruef was a magician. Schmidt himself never collected a penny. Now, one second after election, here were these petty pilferers making enough noise for a herd of elephants. Their greed threatened Ruef's domain. He took up his whip, but when he got into the cage he found no lions. Only jackasses in lion's skins and he knew that in politics nothing is so dangerous as a fool.

"At that moment Abe Ruef had been dreaming he might go—all the way. Napoleon. These poor little men! The spark lighted in San Francisco was to unite the Common Man everywhere, in a new Union Labor party. Schmidt, growing in stature, a front man for all the forces of labor beginning to move at last. With Ruef as his campaign manager, to influence the public, build the party, why shouldn't Schmidt become governor? Then the dream of the American politician, the house on Pennsylvania Avenue. Power not only corrupts. It distorts, creates mirages. Ruef cared nothing for labor, nor about the Common Man. But his prescience told him their day was coming; he felt the stirring around the world.

"He did his best to control his Boodle Board. Issued orders immediately. Money they must have, pay-off was customary. But nobody must TAKE anything on their own. Never let the left hand etc. etc. etc. If he'd had any idea how left-handed his lieutenant and go-between, Big Jim Gallagher, was going to be," Papa said, "I think Abe would have shot him."

Sometime before the fire, just about when the board was elected, a strong opposition to the renewal of the United Railroads' existing franchise had developed. A body of citizens felt San Francisco should have a new system with conduits and wires underground, to eliminate the ugly poles. Among these civic leaders was Rudolph Spreckels.

According to recognized practice and formula, Tirey L. Ford, having retained Mr. Abraham Ruef on a yearly basis to act as special legal adviser and expert to the United Railroads in political matters, saw this as part of Ruef's work. So he certainly passed the matter to him for action.

Before the date of the hearing arrived, April 18 intervened. When the matter of renewal did come before Ruef's board,

San Francisco had been laid waste, there was no transportation of any kind in a city where the ashes were still hot.

I kept a transcript of Earl Rogers' closing argument in the
Ford case. At one place, his description to the jury of that
time and place is almost in the exact words he spoke to me
that night.

Let us go back to the days right after the fire. Let us trans-
port ourselves, disagreeable as it may be, to those old days
when every man who had a cigar cut it in two, every man
who had a sandwich handed half of it to his neighbor without
being asked. To those days after the holocaust we remember
as though they were yesterday, when we took each other by
the hand, when we took strangers into our homes—what was
it like then? The dead were unburied. The wounded lay on
sidewalks. Children were lost in the ruins. You didn't ask
then is he a friend—a cousin—all you asked was is he another
human being? I am not going to harrow you with moments
or hours of pain and glory and horror and heroism—we lived
through those days together not long ago. Let's remember
now what the situation was when I got here on the first
relief train that pulled into the stricken city, bringing with
me what I could of help from your sister city down south—
all rivalry forgotten in that hour. Every man *walked* wherever
he was going. Every woman walked to get where she had
to go. No cars ran. Fifty dollars for a hack to take you two
blocks if you could find one. Who was here on the ground
ahead of us all? Tirey Ford, who had been the state's Attorney
General, blackened, grim, grimy, working with his hands in
the worst spots, above all using his authority to restore and
to maintain order.

The people of this city wanted street cars.

Nobody knew then whether San Francisco would ever raise
her head from the ashes. How long it would take. When
another disaster might come in a peaceful dawn. Nobody
knew whether San Francisco would ever get a *dollar* invested
in her again. Remember how people talked? Might be another earthquake tomorrow. Investors were bound to think
that. Who would put *money* into a city built on an earthquake fault? Many people said the city would have to be
put across the Bay. Why did everyone insist—why do we still
insist on calling it The Fire? Never say *earthquake*. Don't
remind people. We thought maybe San Francisco with all its

glorious history had become a ghost city, its fame ended, ships coming through the Golden Gate would turn away to other places to dock.

Who were the first people to announce *We Stand by San Francisco?* We will put our lives, our blood and our MONEY into this city right now as she lies in ruins. Who said that? Patrick Calhoun and Tirey Ford. While other millionaires sat back and said Let's wait and see, who took millions and said *Here*, give us a franchise and we'll get your street cars running as fast as we can, Calhoun and Ford of the United Railroads which didn't seem at that moment just a soulless corporation.

That was what Earl Rogers said to the Ford jury and I suppose in a manner of speaking he tried it out on me that night.

Looking back it was an extraordinary *feeling*, living in the midst of history, having my father unfold it, make it come alive, and I thought to myself that he was rather like a minstrel—the ones he used to tell me about who carried the news from castle to castle and town to town in the old days.

Like all good newspapermen, he said, Fremont Older had a feel for the times, for what was happening in the world around us.

A house could get too dirty to live in and suddenly there would be a great flourishing of mops and brooms and buckets. In the White House, T.R. was not only launching drives against graft, corruption, and moral turpitude in any government, as well as against trusts. The hero of San Juan Hill was also booming a book called *The Simple Life*, by a Lutheran minister, which advocated the elimination of all luxuries and any extraneous aids to happiness. Also Colonel Teddy had inspired the first epic to make the cowboy our national hero. *The Virginian*, the classic Western of all time by Owen Wister, was dedicated to the President. Upton Sinclair had just rocked the nation with his indictment of Chicago's stockyards, *The Jungle*. In newspaper, book, and magazine Lincoln Steffens was exposing the Shame of the Cities—graft. A new editor of S. S. McClure's muckraking magazine, Willa Cather, was devoting the genius that made her later *the* greatest American woman novelist to exposing the long-entrenched and accepted corruption of government. Writers, editors, reformers, smart politicians were on this band wagon. If sometimes Roosevelt's choice of instruments seemed governed by zeal and enthusiasm rather than sound judgment, Papa said that all too often only visionary and faulty and inexperienced men were available to die for a cause. Also, he said, there were other pigs who wanted to get to the trough and they shoved in wearing do-gooder masks.

"Fremont Older of the *Bulletin* was the leader with a torch," my father said. "He had known what was going on all the time. Ruef was skillful and sure-footed, Schmidt was popular as Jimmy Walker was later in New York, and so Fremont Older was a voice crying in the wilderness until the turn of the tide by the Man in the White House *and* the Boodle Board gave him his chance.

"Older went to Washington," my father said. "When he got back Spreckels was waiting on his doorstep with an offer to finance and supervise a graft investigation, exposé, and prosecution."

Oh, Papa was stalking Spreckels all right, though nobody else seemed to be. The moment he spoke the name, Papa was on his feet, walking back and forth like Bagheera. As soon as I saw Spreckels in court I could understand why. I was just back from Germany. In Berlin, Leipzig, Munich, I'd seen this same square, red-faced, thick-necked, heavy-footed German. I had lost the illusion that all Germans were kindly and good-humored. I wasn't to be as much surprised as most Americans when they marched into Belgium a few years later. One look showed Mr. Spreckels as the typical, bull-necked, round-headed, pugnacious Prussian who ordered everybody around.

"The Spreckels Method," my father said, "is slick, it's unvarying, it's always been successful. Rudolph's father, old Claus invented it."

Claus, it seemed, was an immigrant to California from Hanover, in northern Prussia. Feuds and fights were his specialty. With German thriftiness, he spotted the waste the easygoing Spaniards had allowed in refining sugar, sailed back to Prussia to find out how they did it cheaper and also how to refine sugar out of beets, cheaper still. That way he made his stake. Shipping his product, he got into a hassle with the Southern Pacific Railroad. So he started a railroad of his own in the San Joaquin Valley. There was a lot of flag-waving and speechmaking about small subscriptions to small businessmen, the farmers themselves to be the chief shareholders; Claus went around saying we must shake off the tyranny of the Big Railroads. Not long after the first train ran, however, Claus Spreckels sold his controlling interest for a huge profit to the Santa Fe Railroad, the S.P.'s big rival. Farmers and small businessmen were dropped on their heads and Claus was a millionaire with a rate deal for shipping his sugar via Santa Fe.

This was what my father called the Spreckels Method.

There were other instances with light and power companies.

Up to a day in March of 1907, all they had on Ruef and Schmidt was vice. The liquor licenses of the famous French restaurants such as the Poodle Dog in which no lady had ever ventured above the first floor. And a slight variation of Ruef's known as the municipal cribs.

Eleven months after the fire, however, Spreckels, Older, Heney, and William J. Burns lowered the boom on Abe Ruef.

All the guilty supervisors, fourteen in number, went before the grand jury and confessed to bribery and corruption so blatant and unmoral that all America from the White House to the newsboys who screamed the headlines was shocked to the core. Of all the Shame of the Cities this was the blackest.

"Wouldn't you rather be a musician?" my father said as I rolled him a cigarette.

"I can't," I said. "Anyway I want to be a lawyer."

"I will give you a law lesson right now, one most people seem to have forgotten around here. Let me remind you first," my father said, "that *criminal* law above all others is the collected, tested wisdom of the ages. What people have come to agree upon through all the centuries gives humanity its best chance.

"Here is one of its basic laws," my father said. "*A man ought not to be convicted of a crime on the testimony of an accomplice*. Why and when was it made?"

"I don't know," I said.

"After the Inquisition," my father said. "Under torture, witnesses confessed to things they hadn't done. On the rack, they implicated the innocent as well as the guilty. Good men and bad lied to get the screws loosened. For immunity from pain and danger, witnesses *talked*.

"Let me tell you that the method used by Spreckels and Heney and their man William J. Burns to get the confessions and testimony in this case is against the law. It is not only

the testimony of accomplices, but it was gotten on the rack.
With screws.

"Traps were laid. That is against the law.

"These guilty slobs were hooked once more, with witnesses.
Callously, with malice aforethought, they were tempted by
men representing the law. Supervisor Lornegan was tempted
by them to commit another crime. This time he took a bribe
to give an ice-skating rink a license. When they had the
evidence, they showed him he had been bribed by a *federal*
detective acting for an *assistant attorney general of the United
States*. Now they could send him to jail for this crime *they
had decoyed* him into committing. So they said to him, Now
go before the Grand Jury and testify to the guilt of Abe
Ruef and Tirey Ford and Patrick Calhoun. When you have
done this, we promise you immunity for all your crimes.
Whether it is true or not, testify under oath so we can convict the men *we* want to convict. You will then be free as
air. *Refuse* to do this and we will use the evidence we have
obtained, we'll put you in jail for taking a bribe *from* a man
employed *by* a government that asks us to be *incorruptible*.
The prosecution against *graft* will not prosecute you if you
help to convict the men IT has decided should go to jail. So
we have now government not by graft but by threat, blackmail, entrapment, and lies.

"When their toenails were about to come out, the shadow
of jail was on them, their children were faced with disgrace—
oh yes, then they confessed, then they named names. Probably Lornegan is a guilty man, poor boob. Who has determined his guilt? Not a jury—*the prosecution*. Of what? Of
acts committed under the sly conspiracy of sworn officers of
the Law. I tell you this is a method that is *against the Law*.
It is a cynical abuse of all the safeguards the centuries have
given man. In brazen insolence, it says to me, also a sworn
officer of the Law, we will present a case gathered on the
rack. Under torture. We are above the Law, we set it aside
for our own purpose which we declare to be good for all. We
have now become the Law because we are on the side of
reform.

"Spreckels—that arrogant man—he will find in me a man
he can't browbeat in the name of reform.

"Mockery of the Law is worse than any crime it attempts
to prevent or punish. Put your filthy hands on the judge's
ermine and you have corrupted something more sacred than
a mayor or a board of supervisors. Bring before him an en-

trapped witness and I tell you the cure is worse than the disease."

When Papa talked like that, a fire burned in him.

THIRTY-THREE

For a brief moment, I would like to move ahead in time.

On the cover of Lincoln Steffens' autobiography, it calls him America's greatest reporter. I can't go all the way with that, because there are Bill Shirer and Damon Runyon and William Allen White and Ernie Pyle—but he was among the greatest.

Years after the graft prosecutions were history, I was in Carmel when Steffens was living there. He was old and not well but I asked if I might call and pay my respects. In the course of our conversation I asked him why in his story he hadn't mentioned Earl Rogers. Pulling at the gray goatee which had been his trademark when he was a press power in our land, Steffens said, "He beat us. What could I say about him?"

"In your book," I said, "you wrote that to get the bribe-*givers* it is necessary to have the testimony of the bribe*takers*. To get this, you must agree to let the bribe*takers* go. You were for letting everybody go, weren't you? Now that the house was clean you were for forgetting the past and starting all over again. All had been guilty. If any were let go, all must be. Part of a corrupt system that had been exposed. Even though you were on their side, you called Spreckels, Older, Heney, and Burns *four willful obstinate men*. You might have found Earl Rogers more in agreement with you than any of them."

"Your father wouldn't have let Spreckels go," Lincoln Steffens said. "He was bound and determined to get him on the witness stand."

"Well—" I said, "but *after that,* he might have."

THIRTY-FOUR

That night at the St. Francis, while we waited for Rosy to come back, I kept looking at my father. I had never seen him look better. Yet I knew he had changed. Not because he had been drunk a few hours before and pulled himself back to sobriety with that effort of will which was as racking and harrowing as Hyde changing back to Jekyll. I could see that he was what Lionel Barrymore used to call *en flammes* with his role, with the time and place. But I thought, too, that he looked more exhausted—more as though he hadn't *slept*—didn't sleep, and I remembered how he'd refused to come north on these cases.

"Come to think of it, you refused the graft cases—Schmidt and Ruef—" I said. "How do you happen to be here?"

Well, it seemed that when Schmidt had been convicted, Garret McEnerny, for national prestige and reputation the leader of the California Bar and the titular head of the Calhoun-Ford legal array, said to his client Patrick Calhoun, "I think we must send for Earl Rogers."

"We have," Mr. Calhoun said, "he won't come. He won't work under you or the Moores or Alexander King. He has to be chief counsel."

"Then," said Mr. McEnerny, "we will make him chief counsel. I'm not sure Rogers can beat Heney but I know no other man can."

"What is Heney like, Papa?" I asked then.

He had begun to look at his watch now. It was one of those times when on one hand the minutes flew by in listening to him. On the other they crawled waiting for the moment of action to come. Papa put the watch back and said, "A smart lawyer. *I* don't think he's sincere in all this cause business, but *he* does. The Irish are the only people on earth who can successfully kid themselves to that extent. Right now he's riding a white horse and he has as much self-control as a boiling pot. None of that matters. Only one thing about Heney matters right now."

"What?" I said.

Papa took a long puff of a cigarette and the smoke surrounded him with that blue haze of a roll-your-own that no other cigarette ever has. "Ruef doesn't like him," Papa said, and gave a bellow of laughter that shook the room.

"Neither do you," I said.

"Bless you, I don't mind Heney," my father said. "That temper of his lets me lead him around like a bear by the nose. No no—what is vital is that Ruef doesn't like him and he doesn't *trust him.* You see how vital this is?"

"Not—exactly," I said.

"Your lawbooks will tell you," my father said, "where a man attempts to get you to find a fellow citizen guilty upon evidence of less value than that which he has in his possession, you must assume the better evidence is against him. The best evidence that Ford gave Ruef a sum of money knowing it was to pay off the board for the franchise is *Ruef's testimony.* They have *Ruef.* If they don't put Ruef on the stand, we have a right to ask the jury to assume that his testimony would be that Ford *did not know* any money was for that purpose. That he thought it was merely the routine Fixed Expense of Ruef's legal fee.

"Now Heney is up against this matter of trading immunity with Ruef.

"*Somebody has got to trust somebody.*"

Things had been going on. People coming and going. Luther Brown said a loud good night and went out slamming the door. The lights in the hall of our suite were out now and as the door opened and closed I could see that the corridor was dim.

"I only want to ask Gallagher a couple of questions," my father said, "and Spreckels six or seven. They'll never put him on the stand!"

A tall young man named Barrington came in. He nodded to Bull Durham and Spencer, a new man on our staff. Everything changed. Bull said, "Okey, Mr. Rogers."

I was on my feet. Papa said, "You can't come, Nora, you wait here."

I thought I was going to perish on the spot.

"There's been considerable unpleasantness," my father said, "Burns has patrols all over town. Way down in his gumshoe soul, he knows I'm going to beat him. He's playing rough."

I didn't say anything because I couldn't. I should never have let them send me to Europe, I thought. Something between us had broken and he was probably ashamed of me in these *clothes.* My voice came back and I said, "Where you're going this time of night it doesn't make any difference whether I am the glass of fashion and the mold of form, does it? They will think I am Abe Ruef's grandmother."

He stared at me, he said, "It's not your *clothes*. I don't want to get you shot." If I cry I'm done for, I thought, so I didn't. He doubled up his fist and pushed it against my jaw and said, "I'll never get used to you with all your teeth in," he said, and we went out all together.

One by one, in different directions. Barrington had left right away. Papa, Bull, and I walked through some more rooms, down some backstairs, took a service elevator, and went out through Solari's or someplace into Geary Street. A night-owl taxi was cruising and it hesitated, then stopped. We got in. A few blocks out it made a couple of turns and there was a big dark car with Barrington at the wheel.

You have to remember this, I told myself. This is one of the ones you have to remember. I never saw anything like that night. So beautiful. I didn't know San Francisco, now I had one or two long looks as we climbed up and down and around hills and there went my heart. For good and all. Kipling once said it was a difficult city to leave and I guess nobody ever does. You love where you are if you can, *and* your home town—and San Francisco. There we were and I was sitting beside Papa in a corner of the back seat and it was as though I'd never been away. Bull was up in front and Barrington was the best driver I'd ever ridden with. We went by one spot several times, there was a man out in front, the next time he wasn't there and Papa got out and we went on, very fast. I didn't like that. Then I realized it was Rosy, in the shadow of a telephone pole. The night felt chill all of a sudden. About two blocks away we picked up Luther Brown and swung back. We hadn't been gone more than three or four minutes, but Papa was coming down the steps as fast as he could. He had the trick that fighters have of moving very fast but not looking as though he was. Barrington opened the door behind him and Papa got in. We were very quiet until we'd gone several blocks, and I could feel Brown was upset.

"You didn't get to see him, I assume," he said.

For the first time I realized Papa was laughing. He'd been keeping it down, now it broke out like a hen that had just laid an egg and didn't stop even when Barrington swerved and we took a hill and swung over, up, and down without changing speed at all.

In the record of the Ford case there is this in Mr. Rogers' closing argument:

MR. ROGERS: Now I have not had Ruef in a private house instead of a jail under my custody for six months, seeing him every day. I have not had that. Heney has. I have not had it, so when I went down there and said I would like to ask you a few questions, Mr. Ruef, Mr. Ruef said to me You cannot do that Mr. Rogers here comes the guard—

MR. HENEY: I submit that Mr. Rogers has no right to make any such statement as he has just made upon the ground that there is no evidence in the record to support it.

MR. ROGERS: I am telling *you* why *you* did not call Ruef—

MR. HENEY: I ask the Court to instruct the jury at this time to disregard this statement upon the part of Mr. Rogers as to what occurred between him and Ruef.

MR. ROGERS: You were the one who said you were going to call Ruef—

MR. HENEY: I have no objection to your argument as long as you proceed on legal lines, but when you undertake to state what has not been shown here in evidence I will call the attention of the Court and ask the Court—

MR. ROGERS: You are correct. I'd forgotten it's not in evidence.

THE COURT: The jury will disregard the statement of Counsel, it was not proper to be made.

No, it wasn't in evidence as of course Earl Rogers knew but he also knew, human nature being what it is, you can tell a jury to disregard something until the sands of the desert grow cold without much success.

The evidence wouldn't have taken long.

As we lost the car that had followed us after we left the Little St. Francis, Luther Brown said, "What happened, Mr. Rogers?" and his voice was angry. He was supposed to be the fixer but *Rosy* had fixed this. I never thought much of Brown's fixing myself, like that stunt of kidnaping Fremont Older later which backfired and was silly anyhow, that was *all* Luther Brown.

"Rosy's guard was all right," Papa said, "but they must keep a double check because he heard somebody else coming along and said he'd have to take me out the other way."

"So you didn't get to talk to Ruef at all," Luther Brown said.

"Oh yes, I talked to him," Papa said still chuckling, "long enough. Abe and I have done business together before. He knows me."

Luther Brown said, "I should think he would hold it against you that you refused to defend him when he sent Asch down to get you."

"Oh no," my father said, "he's too smart for that. He respected me for it. He knew the dam had busted and nobody could save him."

I said, "Well, Papa, what I want to know is what did you say to him?"

"*Don't trust Heney,*" Papa said. "I said to him, '*Abe, don't trust Heney. You know he shot a man in the back down in Arizona.*' Abe nodded and I kept right on going. *Don't trust Heney*—if he doesn't that's all there is to this case."

"Not quite all," Luther Brown said.

"Oh, all that really matters," Papa said airily.

But when we got back to the St. Francis he looked exhausted and I said, "I hope you're going to get some sleep even if it is daylight." I don't think he did, though. He was still awake when I went to sleep and up shaved and dressed to the nines when I woke up.

THIRTY-FIVE

While I was growing up over the era of the graft trials . . . with their shooting-Heney-in-the-courtroom, shooting-at-Papa-and-me-in-the-park, kidnaping, living-on-ferryboats, and my-first-love-affair-and-last-spanking . . . with all these I kept a childhood habit.

This is something you must remember. This! This! This! Fix it now in your memory so you can never forget it.

One of these was when I felt in a wave of sheer felicity that San Francisco had fallen in love with Earl Rogers and he with her.

On a glorious morning not long after I got back, my father and I were coming down the steps of the St. Francis. I can see Union Square in the background, a cable car going by on

Powell Street, a corner stand of massed violets under an umbrella, and Jack Johnson in a pearl-gray cutaway and top hat stopping to bow and speak to us. It wasn't at the ebony black-panther heavyweight champion of the world, for whom every sports writer in America was then trying to find a White Hope opponent, that the crowd had gathered, the people passing in cars and on the cable car were looking. It was at the slim, elegant still-so-*young* figure of Earl Rogers. With gratitude. Why *gratitude?* I said to myself, they love him and they are grateful to him.

Years later our visionary, sensitive, high-principled enemy Fremont Older and I met as guests at William Randolph Hearst's San Simeon ranch. "I often wonder," he said rather wistfully, "what would have happened if your father hadn't come to San Francisco. That changed everything." I wonder too. Looking back, I have also wondered if a love affair with San Francisco, as she came madly alive after the earthquake and fire had razed her to the ground, wasn't worth it whatever the net result. "This *San Francisco*," said Rudyard Kipling, "is a mad city inhabited for the most part by perfectly insane people whose women are of a remarkable beauty. It has only one drawback. 'Tis almost impossible to leave."

The tide had been running high for the prosecution. In the beginning, San Francisco had been thrilled by the melodrama of the Great Muckraking. The *Bulletin's* brilliant crusade to save mankind. The orchestra leader who became mayor sent to prison. The Little Boss led in chains. Both sides cheered. The Classes, delighted by the debacle of the Union Labor party's Boodle Board, said, What did you expect of such low fellows? The Masses shouted with glee as the heads of capitalists fell into the basket.

Long live Heney and the graft prosecution.

Earl Rogers turned the tide for the defense for the first time. The reason seems overwhelmingly clear.

He was their boy.

None of the prosecution's leaders had ever really won their hearts or fired their imaginations or tickled their ribs. The cold-blooded thickset German, Spreckels. Big Jim Gallagher turned state's evidence in his iron derby. Wistful, starry-eyed, idealistic Fremont Older. Cigar-smoking, loud-but-not-funny detective Burns. Even that militant professional reformer Francis J. Heney, who pretended he came from South of the Slot in San Francisco but had been born in Lima, New York.

"If I'd invented you," Jack London said once to Earl

Rogers in a waterfront saloon they had sought together, "you couldn't have suited them better."

Of course there is a mystery about San Francisco. The fluffy, powder-puffy fogs that hide the Decalogue, their own Will Irwin called it.

The Golden Gate, opening to ivory, apes, and peacocks. Chinatown, more wicked and wonderful than in any other city, immortalized as it was then by Hugh Wiley's short stories. A girl named Iodoform Kate once put a red light in her window to guide her patrons through the fog. The other girls, seeing the results, followed suit and the Red Light District became part of the American vocabulary. Rebuilt after the fire and wittily renamed Maiden Lane, 'twas said that Kate's ghost still walked there, smiling sardonically. Beyond that, you came to the Barbary Coast, about which so many books have been written, where at the Midway and the Thalia they played jazz before anybody else north of New Orleans, and first danced the Bunny Hug and the Turkey Trot and the Grizzly Bear which were soon to sweep the nation. I know this because my next-to-last spanking was for going there to dance them with a Stanford halfback from Honolulu. Glittering, glamorous, the French restaurants and the Cliff House, out at Seal Rocks, had the best food on the continent. A theater town, a sports town, at nearby Colma, Joe Gans or Jimmy Britt or Stanley Ketchel or somebody was always training for a championship fight. The world's greatest-ever coloratura Tetrazzini used to stop on corners and sing in the streets and Blossom Seeley, still unequaled as a coon-shouter, was out at the beach—oh, music filled the air, as did the fragrance of its violets.

Her enemies had invented a little couplet about San Francisco—

> The pioneers came in '49, the whores in '51,
> Between the two they then begat the Native Son.

That was because they didn't understand *San Francisco*. High society was very high in those days, too. Jeweled, gowned, elegant, and *exclusive*. New York's "400" couldn't match it—only Charleston, Atlanta, Virginia herself had such an aristocracy. I remember a night at the opera when Nellie Melba was singing *La Bohème*. I've seen nothing since to compare for sheer *class* and color, even when royalty was present at Covent Garden. Papa and Mama were in a box. In that city of women remarkable for their beauty, the papers always called her the beautiful Mrs. Rogers. In a dress of white lace, her head shining and dark and glistening as a seal's, she was so beautiful that night I sort of understood why Papa was always taking her back. They'd been invited by some society dowager on Our Side—not all of them were, let me tell you—so Rosy and I sat in the gallery.

San Francisco, too, was producing more and better poets, painters, composers, editors, and writers to become famous than any other city, as everyone knows.

And its churches were fragrant and warm and crowded; there were always some old Irish saints from Kathleen Norris's neighborhood who hadn't missed Mass in their whole lives except when they were having babies, lighting candles, or saying their rosaries.

When Papa and I began to ride as often as we could, sometimes at dawn, sometimes on Sunday, along the bridle trails of the most beautiful park in the world, I told him he would never have to send me traveling again. Here it all was. An international canvas, a mural by Rubens or Da Vinci, or Michelangelo. There were Chinese in full costume, none of them had as yet put on American clothes. Italians from North Beach, from which was soon to emerge the Giannini family to control California banking. Japs, meticulous and mincing as Wallace Irwin's best-selling Japanese Schoolboy Hashimura Togo. Sailors from ships come into the greatest harbor in the world under flags of every country. Big blond Scandinavians. Dark Greeks. Slim Hawaiians showing their beautiful teeth and possibly bowing to the daughters of Liliuokalani, last queen of the islands, who had come to the mainland to school and rode by in their limousines. French families entertaining French sailors in their entrancing caps. The accents flowed around you from the Tower of Babel. The Southern drawl, the raw Irish brogue, the spiced French, the melodious Italian, and under it the ukulele beat of oriental voice and language, low and strange.

If I'd invented you, Jack London, born and bred by the Golden Gate, had said to Earl Rogers.

A slim young aristocrat, with arrogant but gracious manners. Not *in* fashion, he set fashions. The chevalier hat, the handkerchief up the sleeve, the spectacular collection and array of stickpins, the burberrys and chesterfields from Bond Street, the heavy scarves from Chinatown tied as a four-in-hand. His presence in a restaurant was an event which he did nothing to minimize. Earl Rogers making his own salads. Going to the kitchen for a conference with the cook. One night he was tasting a gourmet's veal of some kind when he let out a yell which startled the other diners into thinking another earthquake had rumbled. To the headwaiter, maître d', chef, and sub chef who came running he said affectionately, "Too much salt, my dear fellows." Accompanied by his personal retinue, half courtiers, half guards—with the lovely comedy touch of the Burns operatives following him and them in droves. Papa would stop, touch one of the big tails on the shoulder with his slim gold-headed cane, and say, "My good man, it's sloppy out tonight, come and have a bite of supper with me, I shan't be long." Or, "Now listen carefully, and I will tell you exactly where I'm going or you might get lost in this fog." Passers-by—he took care that there were always passers-by—would howl and repeat the story and the legend grew. It *suited* San Francisco. At Colma, at the ball park, at the opera, in the courtroom.

Nobody seemed to mind that he got uproariously fighting drunk. Once he and Jack London and heavyweight Jack Sharkey got arrested twice the same night for brawling on the Embarcadero, which wasn't considered safe or healthy. Over in Oakland, he and London and George Sterling went to jail and I had to go get them because, when the police apologized and released them, they refused to leave. Papa was going to bring suit for false arrest, he said. All this was printed in all the papers. Not so long ago the miners had been flinging their pokes of gold dust on bars and tables and dance floors and it was still traditional to throw gold pieces, at which both Earl Rogers and Jack London were all too ready and expert. In a way I was glad London was away most of the time just then on a voyage with Charmian on the *Snark*. The combination was too explosive.

I had, too, the same troubles that came later when I was a close friend of Rudolf Valentino's and when Wallace Reid and his wife Dorothy were so dear to me. Girls and women everywhere. Hidden in the back seats of the car, in closets, under rugs and in beds, coming over from nearby tables. At the time, on the whole Papa was too busy to bother. Though he adored Blossom Seeley and we took a singer on the ferryboat with us, but I thought it was just for songs. Women, too, were in San Francisco's time-space continuum.

He was always interested in women's clothes.
Right away the next day after my return it was obviously

necessary that I get some new ones. When I mentioned this, my father said he would go with me, I wasn't to be trusted alone in this matter.

"You were in Paris?" he said, as he instructed a saleslady at the White House, the smartest shop in town. "Why didn't you buy your clothes there?"

"I don't think Aunty Blanche knew Paris was supposed to be the place to buy clothes," I said, "besides, Uncle Harry was giving a concert, he and I had a time sneaking out to the Comédie Française and the Louvre."

Papa shook his head at a green suit. "You have one possible claim to beauty, Nora," he said, "your eyes. They are the true Killarney blue and, as your grandfather used to say, set in with a sooty finger."

"Do you think about Grandpa often, Papa?" I said, as the saleslady bore away the offending green.

"Yes," my father said briefly, with that pinched look of anger he always got—not at grandfather, at my grandfather's God, who had, he thought, struck him down so shabbily. "Now listen to me. Dress to your eyes. Not to understand clothes is unintelligent. What did your Aunt wear at this concert in Paris, may I ask?"

"To tell you the truth," I said, "it was something pink— and fluffy."

"*Pink?*" my father said as if I'd told him she'd grown a tail. "With her red hair? Now—are you aware that my sister has the most beautiful arms and shoulders I've ever seen?"

I said, "I—never noticed—I know she has arms and shoulders—"

"There you are," my father said, "a pianist, an accompanist, with an unparalleled opportunity to display arms and shoulders *and* the Andrus hands—you have them too, Nora—and she fails to take advantage of it. Don't you understand that, properly dressed and using the gifts she's been given, she might have achieved in that one night the European prestige and reputation for her husband that she's been slaving for all this time at the keyboard? Now, no matter how fine his voice, they have doubtless been dismissed as provincial—as minor-league performers. You inherit your aunt's unfortunate indifference in this vital matter. An ancestress of yours persuaded her husband to buy her a sable coat so she could go to prayer meeting in her nightgown. I will beat some sense into your Irish skull if I have to use a hammer. *Pink!*"

He bought me straight, simple blue tailored and tweed suits

with white shirtwaists, more grown-up Peter Thompsons. A
dark blue coat severe as a uniform. One-piece dresses with
flat white collars and cuffs. A traditional white dance frock,
held at the waist by a wide blue belt with a tailored bow. At
the bootshop, I got Mary Janes still and laced high shoes,
though I begged for heels and colored tops and buttons.
"Never as long as you live," he said. So that once when I
heard Hattie Carnegie say, "Never *never* buttons or frills for
Mrs. St. Johns," I surprised her by bursting into tears. It made
me miss him. It looks like I always will.

So going back into the courtroom with Papa my hair was
down my back again in braids with ribbons at the ends. I
wasn't nearly as grown-up as I had hoped to be when I bought
that Abe-Ruef's-grandmother suit in Vienna. I hadn't been
trying to be feminine or fashionable—just grown-up.

Nothing could dim the radiance of being Earl Rogers'
daughter once more. Of walking down the aisle of my native
heath toward the Bench, the counsel table, the witness stand,
and the jury box.

THIRTY-SIX

Big Jim Gallagher was the first important witness I actually
heard and saw in the Ford case. Keep-the-Change Gallagher,
my father nicknamed him. If Ruef gave him five thousand
dollars for a pay-off, the man he was buying got but four
thousand of it.

Preparation for this vital cross-examination kept my father
up all night every night right after I got back. Earl Rogers
always wanted to move sure-footed, watertight, and bullet-
proof with any witness; he wanted to be as familiar with
everything he'd ever said or done as a man is in his own back
yard. Heney kept telling the tale that Ruef was going to take
the stand, but nobody knew. The Little Boss sat there in the
courtroom, giving nothing away, his face as expressionless as
an oriental mask. On direct, Heney was doing a solid job of
making what Gallagher knew, had seen, heard, and been told
by Ruef as to Ford's knowledge of the intended bribery stand

up, if Ruef didn't. So Gallagher might be the determining factor with the jury, either way, and naturally Papa was more concentrated than ever on his previous testimony and actions.

He had to blast and destroy Big Jim.

While he studied the omnipresent long blue transcripts of each day's direct testimony, or talked with men who'd known Gallagher well at the time he became the middleman, from Ruef to the board and back, I went back and tried to get myself up on the record of the whole trial.

The reporters who hung around all the time and our own staff talked a lot about Papa's cross-examination of Thomas Lornegan, the first of the supervisors who'd Told All. So I got Jerry Giesler to dig up the transcript on that. Papa worked in a bedroom that had been sort of converted into an office for him; he'd prowl all over the place around from one end of the suite to the other, asking an opinion here, sending somebody on an errand, holding conversations about everyone on earth with the newspapermen. I had my backlog on the big table in the dining room, so I was there if he wanted me.

"What did Lornegan look like?" I said to Rosy as I read the stark Q. and A. Rosy said, "Before or after your Pa took him over the jumps?" I said, "Both," and Rosy said, "Well—*before* he looked like a kind of dumb guy who ought to be driving a bakery wagon which he had, and *after* he looked like a guy who wished he still was."

"What's all this about a magazine interview?" I said to Papa as he went by, but he only looked very sheepish and shook his head.

"Well," Rosy said, "there was Lornegan on the stand, the poor bastard and your Pa walked up to him, not looking at him, reading from a big typewritten document he had in his hand. You know how he does."

I did. I could see it as I picked up the Q. and A. . . .

Q. (by Mr. Rogers) Ever see this manuscript before, Mr. Lornegan?
A. Yes sir.
Q. That's your signature on the last page.
A. Yes—yes yes sir.
Q. You signed this after reading it.
A. Well I—yes, I did.

At that, Rosy said with happy reminiscence, Heney had gone nuts, hollering and yelling and making grabs at the manu-

script, which Mr. Rogers kept holding just out of his reach.
At this point, between the objections of Heney, the explanations of Earl Rogers, the stammerings of the witness, and the
rulings of the judge, it got through to the jury that this was an
interview given only the day before by Lornegan to one
Dorland, a writer for a national publication. Since Mr. Heney
now insisted on knowing what was in it, Mr. Rogers said he'd
be real glad to read it.

MR. ROGERS: (reading) This is a quote, from Thomas
Lornegan. We have always been proud of our civic duties as
Supervisors of San Francisco, to uphold its ideals and honesty
in highest regards, to discharge our functions as civil servants
to the benefit of our beloved community—

MR. HENEY: What the *hell*—

MR. ROGERS: I know, Mr. Heney, I know. (Reading) In
the matter of the building of a new pest house, there arose a
public need, and the Board of Supervisors has most gener-
ously—

MR. HENEY: Your Honor, Your Honor, what has this drivel
about pest houses got to do with the case before Your Honor?

MR. ROGERS: I thought you wanted the whole article, it
makes good reading—

MR. HENEY: So does the Bible, what's that got to do with
the case?

MR. ROGERS: To us, the Bible always has a great deal to
do with a man's moral guilt or innocence, all Law is based on
moral principles—

MR. HENEY: I don't need you to teach me the Law.

MR. ROGERS: You need somebody. I don't insist it be me.

At this point, reading over my shoulder, Rosy said with a
chuckle, "Here you gotta picture Heney like a coyote in a
fight with a tarantula. Heney don't ever seem to learn. Spreckels was trying to calm him down, he usually is. That Spreckels.
He's made out of ice. I don't know what will happen if Mr.
Rogers ever gets him on the stand, that'll be a battle of giants
as the saying goes."

We went back to the transcript, I could feel how pleased
Rosy was.

THE COURT: If there is any more of this exchange between
counsel, I will find everybody in contempt. If you have objections, Mr. Heney, address the Bench. Mr. Rogers, connect

this document with the matter before the Court or I shall rule it inadmissible.

MR. ROGERS: Yes, Your Honor. (Reading) The Board of Supervisors recognized the urgent need of a new transportation system at once, following our great disaster. We acted promptly, for the best interests of our city, with no monetary consideration either offered or accepted by me or by any other member of the Board as far as I know.

Rosy yelped, "That connected it all right. It contradicted every word he'd told the grand jury about how he and the others were bribed."

Papa came by then, and hearing Rosy making such a cackling, stopped and bent to look at the transcript. "No no," he said, and I could feel he was chagrined as he would be to this day if he knew the Lornegan cross-examination took up a lot of time and space in the history books. "He was not much better than a moron. It's too much like Ketchel beating up on some village bully. You know, this business of an expert, trained for years, experienced in courtrooms, knowing all the tricks, at home and at ease in a courtroom, cross-examining the average witness, can be a very unfair contest."

(Many years later, I used that comment as the basis of a magazine serial called *Take the Stand, Mrs. Langtry*.)

Most people regarded the whole Lornegan thing as a comedy. Papa didn't. With further distaste he said the man whimpered. "Heney tried to give a false impression of the weight of Lornegan's testimony," he said, "so I had to demolish it. And the poor boob with it. Nobody noticed the only important thing, which came after Heney took Lornegan back for redirect. Except"—he paused a moment, stood there very thoughtful—"except," he said, "Mr. Rudolph Spreckels. I fancy he noticed it." He found the place for me.

Q. (by Mr. Heney) This Dorland, who pretended he was a magazine writer for a non-existent magazine in order to furnish this material for Mr. Rogers, you say you saw him often? He wined and dined you, took you for spins in his auto and for picnics in the Park?

A. (by Lornegan) Yes sir. Often.

Q. He attempted to introduce you to young ladies.

A. Yes sir.

Q. Who were no doubt pretty young ladies.

A. Well—yes sir—they were.

Q. It seems that faking magazine articles comes high, doesn't it? Your witness, Mr. Rogers.

Q. (by Mr. Rogers) Mr. Lornegan. You don't think however that Mr. Dorland spent anything like $450,000 on your entertainment, do you?

MR. HENEY: Now what is all this? How is this recross-examination? Has anybody on direct said anything about it costing anybody $450,000?

MR. ROGERS: You spoke, Mr. Heney, of magazine articles coming high—which meant spending money, didn't it? I understand that the $450,000 put up by the Municipal Street Railway Company for expenses, such as the staff of Mr. Heney, the operatives of Mr. William J. Burns is now sadly depleted. Mr. Rudolph Spreckels of the so-called Graft Prosecution owns the Municipal Street Railway Company, doesn't he?

My father said, "Keep your eye on that." He put his finger on the words *Mr. Rudolph Spreckels owns the Municipal Street Railway, doesn't he?* Papa's face was grim. "I think Mr. Spreckels noticed that," he said. "That's my main line of attack."

Late on Friday, Heney closed his direct examination of Gallagher. Big Jim had done well for him. He had testified with impressive ponderosity to the whole corrupt grafting setup; to the money Ruef had given him to pay for supervisorial votes for the United Railroad franchise; to the fact that Ruef had told him Ford knew what the money was for. Now Heney wanted to give him all the time he could before he had to face Earl Rogers on Monday.

The whole town was seething with excitement. All around us, it was as wild and woolly as Tombstone on a Saturday night or the eve of a Big Game. Everything was overrun with reporters. Headlines announced the coming conflict as though it was a world's heavyweight championship.

BIG JIM GALLAGHER TO FACE ROGERS
ON MONDAY

Big Jim was no Lornegan. A lawyer himself, and a good one, with many years of courtroom and trial practice. Until the explosion of the national muckraking came to San Francisco, he had, as liaison man for the Little Boss, been regarded as an incisive and efficient lieutenant and executive, helping Ruef and Mayor Schmidt to run the city. He simply got careless with success and fumbled. Criminals always do. As a state's-evidence witness, he had accepted the immunity-promise deal, refused so far by Abe Ruef. Therefore if his testimony didn't suit Heney, Gallagher might still go to San Quentin. So he would be in there fighting for his life.

My father decided we'd go out to the house on Washington Street, where Mama and the servants were. He'd take all the Gallagher material and spend a quiet weekend going over them.

So with the usual trail of our own men *and* Burns men *and* reporters, out we went.

It turned out to be about as quiet as another earthquake around there.

THIRTY-SEVEN

After dinner, my father said, "Want to take a little walk?"

Our house on Washington Street wasn't far from the gates of the Presidio, San Francisco's army post. The gates were tall and stately and wide open. This was at a time when we all knew war was outlawed, no civilized people would ever go to war again. The flag was flying and it looked beautiful and safe in the clear crisp evening air. A few soldiers, in the uniforms and leggings and army hats they were to wear to France not too many years later, went by on their way to catch a streetcar downtown. Otherwise it all seemed quiet and deserted as we strolled in. I thought we would go for a walk, maybe through the Presidio grounds to the water, but Papa found a little grove of trees right inside the gates and began to prowl around there. There was still some light, and he seemed to be looking it over, his lips tight and his eyes very bright. No man ever looked more pleased with himself and whatever he had found there.

We went right on talking about Maude Adams, which we had been doing all the way from our house.

Papa had the worst crush of his whole life on Maude Adams, then the shining star of stars of the American theater. Maybe her delicacy, her gleaming comedy, her faith were what he really wanted in a woman. One Sunday morning we had actually gone to church because Papa knew she was going to be there. We sat in a pew right behind her. When we stood up to sing "Rock of Ages," Miss Adams saw a thread on her sleeve and started to pull it off. She *kept* pulling and it kept unwinding, pretty soon she realized it was attached to her, probably to a little woolen undervest most ladies wore, I had one on myself. From where we were we could see the immortal Peter Pan profile that millions of people loved getting pinker and pinker. She felt Papa's eyes, she turned, and then she really got red. Papa smiled and then he took a little gold knife he carried on his watch chain, and cut the thread. Probably it wasn't as romantic as if it had been a tress of her hair, but he rolled it around his finger and put it in his vest pocket as though it was something he would treasure forever. On the way out, the crowds on the sidewalk recognized them both, and so Papa made her a bow and said, "Miss Adams, my name is Rogers and this is my daughter Nora, one of your devout admirers. Might I offer our services to take you home?" So she got in our car with Barrington at the wheel and we took her home and that was the only time he ever saw her in person, but we went to see her five times on the stage. In the same play. I think it was *What Every Woman Knows*.

I said, "Do you think it is a *magic* people like Maude Adams have?"

Papa said, "Oh yes, no question about that. Wouldn't you rather try to be an actress than a lawyer?" and I said, "No, of course not."

For those few moments it seemed a different lovely world, the late twilight, the scent of trees, the stillness.

I enjoyed it, I thought it was good for Papa. By that time I knew the whole mad tapestry and whirligig of events that sometimes made it more like a Mardi Gras than a dignified court of law. Luther Brown and William J. Burns on opposite sides putting on their side shows outside the main tent—like that idiot Luther Brown *kidnaping* Fremont Older. The main tent was the Jewish Temple. I felt very sorry for the rabbis who had to come in and tried to have their rites and cere-monies, the trial had to be held there, there wasn't any other place built since the fire. And of course there was Luther Brown on our side stealing what his operatives had filched off the Burns operatives and vice versa and vis-à-vis as it were, skirmishing around. We had men inside their lines and they had men inside ours. The Banjo-Eyed Kid and several others guarded Mr. Rogers even in the courtroom and Heney had his body guard too, though in the end they let him get his head nearly blown off.

But it was peaceful and quiet, we thought, in the Presidio.

"Papa," I said, "I wish we had seen Miss Adams as Babbie in the *Little Minister,* I have just finished the book by James M. Barrie and—"

That was as far as I got about *that.*

I heard a strange sound, rather loud, and a bullet came zinging over my head and missed Papa's left ear. Papa hit me right on the chin, it knocked me ten feet away on my face, I heard more shots and over them Papa yelling, *Keep still, Nora, keep still.* I was stunned, but I peeked and I saw Papa behind a tree shooting back, then feet running and the sound of an automobile going away. I rolled over. My mouth was full of dirt and grass and my jaw hurt, and I said, "Are you all right, Papa?" He was kneeling by me and examining my face and wiping it with his handkerchief. He never swore but he was calling them jackals and hyenas, condemning them to hell to have their eyes burned out and hoping their gun hands would rot off with leprosy. He was green-white with rage.

Just then some men came running up. The streetcar had got to the end of the line, which was right in front of the gates, the conductor-motorman had heard the shooting and two other men were with him, and they recognized Papa, who was saying to me, "You're going to have a black eye and maybe a broken jaw but that's better than a bullet hole in your head, the mangy, misbegotten curs." I said, "They weren't shooting at me, Papa, they were shooting at you." My heart was simply overwhelmed because he had hit me before he thought of getting behind a tree himself.

Then he noticed the men and the streetcar standing there. He said to the motorman, "Let's get out of here," and picked me up and carried me. I suppose he figured this was a good deal safer than walking the blocks to our house on Washington Street; there might be more men hidden in driveways or behind trees. He sat on the floor and made me lie down and held my head in his lap. No streetcar ever went so fast. People were in the street waving their arms and yelling, but our motorman just clanged his bell, *ding-ding-ding* like mad, and dashed on by. With the San Francisco hills it was worse than any roller-coaster ride I ever took and I was sick at my stomach though I tried my best not to get it on Papa. He was grinning like a spitting cat; he said, "This is not particularly courageous, but until I get you safe we'll put up with it. I will make that yellow-bellied herring-gutted German brute eat his Municipal Railway and vomit it up in public inch by inch like a tapeworm, the greedy ape."

We got back to our suite at the St. Francis. I do not mind telling you all hell broke loose. Rosy said he had a man there but he got pulled off by somebody in the bushes, the reporters thought Papa was safely in for the night and had gone for a drink, everybody had let down with no court the next day. A doctor came, he said my jaw wasn't broken and Papa said, "I must be losing my punch." Whatever it was he washed my face with it stung and I yelled, Papa said, "Don't start belly-aching now that it's all over."

The doctor said, "Mr. Rogers, you look—may I suggest that you'd be better for a night's sleep and some rest and quiet?"

"Rest and quiet?" my father bellowed so loud they must have heard him down at the Ferry Building. "With them shooting at my daughter? With their ignominious, greedy brains they think they can scare me that way, or if they'd killed her or me I wouldn't be in court Monday morning to dissect Mr. Gallagher, they'll do anything to stop me, even fight children, I'll show 'em. I'll be there. I know one place I'll be safe."

THIRTY-EIGHT

The ferry slid out of its slip without a splash.

No gleam showed except the red and green riding lights, fore and aft. The waters of the bay were thick and flat as satin, dark rich brown-bronze, the swells gleamed coppery and then rust-yellow, then back to seal-brown again. The night was clear and dark and very still.

Nobody was aboard except the crew and us.

"The only safe place for my daughter until court opens on Monday morning," my father said, "seems to be in the middle of San Francisco Bay." I expect, until they laughed, Papa was just blowing off, but the laugh did it. He gave them as nasty a look as Caesar Borgia ever managed and went to a phone. I don't know what happened, I figured Mr. William Herrin, chief counsel and head man of the Southern Pacific, was bound to be on our side, probably a big anti-graft-prosecution man, and the S.P. owned all the ferryboats.

Silently, mysteriously, we moved on the river Styx, I thought, with Charon at the helm. I stayed by the rail, the side of my face burned and the air was cooling and was making me kind of sleepy.

With *us* on board were Rosy and Bull Durham and his wife, Cap, and a couple of Luther Brown's boys. We had stopped at the Black Cat to pick up a lady my father liked to listen to sing, and Stanley Ketchel was there, so he came along. He was middleweight champion of the world and a real idol. My father always liked prize fighters and baseball players and jockeys. For one thing, he said they had the only universal picturesque patois left.

Steve Ketchel—his name was Stanley, but everyone called him Steve, don't ask me why—stayed out on deck with me. We weren't talking, just watching the water and the stars, and it occurred to me he would know about my jaw, he'd been hit on his often enough even if he was the champ. I said, "How long before my jaw quits hurting?"

Steve looked at me, then he held my chin with one hand and ran the fingers of the other along the bone. His fingers were strong and careful. He said, "Your old man packs quite a wallop."

"I'd be dead if he hadn't," I said.

"It'll be as good as new in a couple of days," Steve Ketchel said, "Just don't run into a door or anything like that."

We didn't say anything more. I was kind of glad he was along. He would be a good man in case of trouble, you could feel that. From inside came a burst of laughter and then the player piano began a roll of "Way Down upon the Swanee River." Across the bay somewhere a boat hooted. All of a sudden I had a pain in my stomach.

I moved and Steve Ketchel put his hand on my arm and said, "Where are you going?"

I said, "I have a pain in my stomach. I better go in."

Steve said, "The bay's like a pond, you can't be seasick on this—"

I said, "It's not that kind of a pain—"

By that time we were lifting our feet over the brass sill and going in the door. The lights were on enough so we could see, they had pulled the shutters and the green baize curtains. Rosy and Bull Durham and a couple of other men were standing there watching Papa and the singer. I think her name was Lou but probably not. She was a real nice girl and had no idea what was going on, she was laughing merrily and why not? She and Papa each had a drink in their hand and were about to toss them off, when I came in.

Everything stopped. The singer saw something in Papa's face, I guess, she swung around and saw me and Ketchel, right behind me.

I hadn't had such an easy evening myself, my stomach was still going up and down from being shot at and knocked out and I was fit to be tied or I probably wouldn't have behaved the way I did at all. I never had before.

I just walked over and knocked the glass out of his hand and then I turned around and knocked the glass out of hers. Like Carrie Nation. Then I smacked Papa alongside the ear the way a mother smacks a kid who has done something naughty.

I said, "You are yellow. Don't talk about Spreckels being yellow-bellied. You are worse. I don't see why they bother shooting you, somebody might get hung. If they just let you alone you will do it for them. You aren't going to make Mr. Spreckels swallow his railway, you will probably be drunk somewhere and when you cross-examine Mr. Gallagher you will not even know who he is probably. You are supposed to be chief counsel, and you love General Ford and admire Mr. Calhoun and you are going to betray them worse than anybody because if you start on that you will be too shaky Monday to be one of Luther Brown's errand boys. Only I am not going to let you if I have to tie you up. I've had enough of *this.*"

I heard the singer say, Well-I'm-a-son-of-a-bitch, under her breath, and I saw Ketchel looking at me with a very peculiar expression. Then Papa's voice came out of what seemed to be a fog creeping in through the night that had been so clear. It said something like no man can satisfactorily contradict the truth and the deck spun under me dizzily and Papa said, "It's all right, child, it's all right—" and the fog got me.

The next thing I knew I opened my eyes and the room was full of bright morning sunshine. Papa was sitting at the table with a big plate of fried potatoes and bacon and eggs and Spanish beans in front of him. He was shaved and groomed and he had a lot of papers and pencils and things around him. I stood up and he turned and said, "Good morning, Nora." He stared at me and afterwards I knew it was because overnight my eye was blacker and my jaw had swelled up some. He said, "I have never given a lady a black eye before—I do apologize."

"As you said before," I told him, "it's better than a bullet hole in my head."

"You will be pleased to know," my father said, "that I only brought one bottle aboard and it is now being drunk by a hammerheaded shark at the bottom of the bay." I didn't know what to say. I was embarrassed. He got up and came over and grinned at me. He said, "A little fresh air might do you good. Go comb your hair and wash your face and come out on deck."

Well, when I looked at myself in the cockeyed mirror in the ladies' room I was really shocked. *Violence,* I thought. Why, we are in the midst of a *war.* Kidnaping and shooting at people and that trolley ride that was as dangerous as could be. Crime always led to *violence.*

On deck I said good morning to everybody and then I said, "Papa, what became of the motorman on the streetcar? Do you think he was shattered?"

"I think it was the big adventure of his life and nobody among his family and friends will ever hear the last of it," Papa said. "However we must see if we can't get him promoted or something, after all we do work for the United Railroads."

The contrast between the peace and beauty there on the ferryboat and all that I knew was going on in San Francisco made me feel odd and sort of disconnected. Swinging between two worlds. Papa said, quite low, "You know sometimes in my heart I think I'd like to stay here. In this peace and beauty."

I said something then from my stomach that my mind has almost caught up with. I said, I suppose, what was in my heart. It came over me that men like my father who think the world ought to be *different* are the ones who get in the most awful trouble if they do not have God. If they *blame* God. Men like that, if they do not have God, take to drink. Or something.

So I said, "You couldn't stay here in peace, though, Papa," trying to say what I meant and not quite knowing how. "I mean even you and I couldn't stay here in peace unless we believed in God, could we?"

He gave me a tormented look.

The singer and Steve Ketchel came over then and I saw she thought a lot of my father. When she turned and saw I'd been looking at her she said in a funny throaty voice, "Hell, I've been in love with him for years and a lot of good it's done me."

I felt sorry for her.

So I said to Steve that maybe we ought to do twenty or thirty laps around the deck. I still think he was the handsomest—no—that's a pale word—for a man he was the best-looking creature I've ever seen. He moved a lot like Nijinsky, whom I'd seen dance in Europe. Another strange thing I noticed too that morning. In size and color and type he did *look* a lot like Papa. They had the same middleweight build, the same black hair and blue eyes and fine punishing jaw line. I suppose naturally I would admire my father's type of good looks the most.

That night we tied up in a little slip way up the bay. There are more than four hundred miles of shore line in the San Francisco Bay. When the evening came we all sat on deck and Lou sang for us. She had one of those warm deep voices, and she knew German lieder—Schumann and Schubert—and Papa loved that and it was soothing.

Then he said, "Come on, Nora, let's show them what we can do."

We only knew two songs and neither of us was much shakes but we did love to sing. One was a San Francisco song called "Towsey Mongalay" that they used to sing down on the Coast. The words are pretty silly, I suppose, and the tune wasn't much, but—how can you tell why a song moves you?

It went:

> Towsey Mongalay, my dear,
> You'll leave me, some day I fear.
> Sailing far across the sea,
> To blue-eyed girl, in Melicee.
> If you stay, me love you true,
> If you leave me, how can do?
> Me no cly, me only say—
> Towsey Mongalay.

Which meant Good-by good luck God go with you, in Chinese. I told Steve that when he asked me.

Then we sang the other one and we'd been doing that ever since I could remember anything at all, whenever he was sad he liked to sing it. It was a terribly sentimental song, and it showed I always thought how *Irish* he was down deep. We Irish who laugh when we should cry and cry when we should laugh and get drunk at all the wrong times—we're sentimental no matter how brilliant.

> Wait till the sun shines, Nellie,
> Till the clouds go drifting by
> We will be happy, Nellie,
> Don't you cry.
> Down lovers' lane we'll wander,
> Sweetheart, you and I.
> Wait till the sun shines Nellie—
> Bye—and—bye.

In the end, we were both crying. We always did.

The starlight was very soft and bright.

For a little while, sitting there, it seemed as though the whole world was made of starlight and beauty and sentimental music. My jaw didn't hurt any more and Papa wasn't mad at me.

I think he knew there are times when a daughter feels more like she is her father's *mother*—I often did, I know that. It seems to be some kind of a circle of love.

After we got back to the St. Francis that night, Papa gave me a piece of paper. It had eight questions written on it.

"That's all I want to ask Gallagher," he said. "It'll probably take me a couple of days to get up to them."

He watched me as I read them. I must have looked amazed and confused because his face lit up like a sign. "Surprised you!" he said.

"Yes," I said. "I don't understand them."

"You will," he said, "just watch for them. When they come you'll see what they mean."

THIRTY-NINE

"Will you return to the stand, Mr. Gallagher," Heney said on Monday morning. "Your witness, Mr. Rogers."

The familiar excitement swept me, as I sat in the row back of my father at the counsel table. I had a black patch over one eye and in my hand the paper with the eight questions. Abe Ruef sat where I had a good view of him, each time it astonished me how little he was. A wisp. With his face indoor-white around his large, sad black eyes, very watchful. He wore the biggest blackest mustache for his size I'd ever seen. He kept on his heavy overcoat as though he was always cold. Probably he was. If he and my father exchanged looks I never saw it.

A few seats away was Rudolph Spreckels. His creator had made him square and Spreckels had continued the design. Square brown mustache. Square brown suit, worn like a uniform. I kept staring at him because I had begun to wonder if my father's detestation of him might warp his work—I had never known father to feel like that about anyone.

As we waited for Judge Lawlor to take the Bench, Heney kept moving around. A good-looking Irishman, only I always felt he ought to be carrying a hod. Everything about him testified to his being a fighter, with his hot conviction, his dynamic mind, his swinging fists—and gun for that matter.

On the prosecution side, only Fremont Older looked what in those days we called a gentleman.

Of all the defendants I remember, Tirey L. Ford was the most forgotten. Nobody paid *any* attention to him. A slim man, with a fine-cut face, now careworn, with considerable dignity. If they'd had their way, I felt sure, neither he nor any of the other big shot, high-priced defense battery would have tried this case the way Rogers was trying it. All of them were such a lot older than he was, Ford had been attorney general when young Rogers took his Bar exams. Most of the time these dignified corporation lawyers didn't know what Rogers was after, like many people they were deceived by the side shows and the fireworks. Trial work is so *different*.

A pause hung after Heney called.

Big Jim Gallagher, and he finally lumbered to the witness stand.

Haunch paunch and jowl. For the first time I realized, What a dangerous man. The old Irish con, the old Irish hocus-pocus now-you-see-it-and-now-you-don't, was laid on over greed and recklessness and violence. He had been the perfect tool in Ruef's hands, that was plain.

How close people who wanted never to see each other again had to be in a courtroom. As in the Griffith case, here it was again. People with violence between them, hatreds, grudges, betrayals, revenge. Gallagher had to pass close enough to Abe Ruef to reach out and touch him, but he didn't turn his head to greet his former boss.

When Gallagher was settled on the witness stand, he found it uncomfortable, the chair seemed too small for his bulk, Earl Rogers got up and went to stand in front of him. He took the lorgnette from his pocket, flipped it open, took a fine linen handkerchief from his sleeve and polished the glass, and lifted it to his eyes. I was nervous as a witch and I counted seventeen seconds by my watch before Heney spoke. "You want to sit in his lap?" he said with a snort.

Mr. Rogers, startled from his profound study, stared at Heney, returned to examine the witness, and then with a shiver of distaste stepped back. In a horrified voice he said, "No—no—certainly not."

The jury looked at Gallagher and wondered if they did either.

Gallagher only lowered his head a little and stared back with contempt. Somebody had obviously told him not to be afraid of Rogers. All that show with those gold eyeglasses—*Don't pay any attention to that.* Just don't let him get your goat.

From the table Earl Rogers picked up a newspaper and held it out.

"In this newspaper," Earl Rogers said very very quietly, "published right after the fire, a man named Gallagher, president of the board of supervisors, gave a fine and manly interview telling of the urgent need of his city for a new transportation system to be built at once to replace the one destroyed by the earthquake. He said San Francisco could not survive unless it had transportation at once. Were you that James J. Gallagher?"

"Yes," Gallagher said.

"When you made that proud and forceful statement as a leader of your city were you influenced by possible financial considerations?"

For one little minute, Gallagher drew about him some tatters of pride, he said, "No, I was not."

"You were a public servant?"

"Completely—I was."

"At that time, your city was without transportation of any kind?"

"That's right. At a standstill."

Mr. Rogers repeated the three words. "At a standstill," he said.

That is what I mean by *trial* work. Three words. My job was always to watch the jury reactions. I saw them narrow their eyes, remembering *a city at a standstill*, without a car running to get them to work, to church, to market, to the Ferry Building. I saw them nod one to another.

Over the three or four days of the Gallagher cross-examination, the witness felt he had done well. His self-satisfaction remained bright. On the whole, it had been an extremely dignified affair. Fewer uproars than usual. Every single possible thing had been asked and answered, he hadn't been tripped or caught, the jury would think him reliable.

Having set him up, Earl Rogers began on the eight questions.

He went after the one man he had always meant to get. The vulnerable man, the liability, the Achilles' heel of the graft prosecution, which nobody else had seen or evaluated.

"You know Rudolph Spreckels?" he said to Gallagher, and swung slowly, his arm at full length, the index finger leveled at where Spreckels sat, solid and square as usual.

Gallagher said, "Yes."

"When Mr. Burns was after the supervisors to get their statements as to these alleged bribes, did you meet with Mr. Rudolph Spreckels, that man over there?" Mr. Rogers said.

"Why—yes—we met—we did meet—" Gallagher said, wary now, unable to see where this was leading.

"*Where* did you meet, Mr. Gallagher?" Earl Rogers said, and I crossed off No. 1 of my eight questions.

"We met several times—we had discussions," Gallagher said.

"I know about the discussions," Earl Rogers said, "*where?*"

"Well—once or twice," Gallagher said, "we met in his office—"

"His office?" said Rogers swiftly. "Which office? Did you meet in the offices of the Municipal Street Railway Company, of which Mr. Spreckels was and is president?"

"No—I never—no, we didn't," Gallagher said.

"By the way," Mr. Rogers said in a friendly, confidential tone, "why is it called the *Municipal* Railway? It isn't owned by the city or the municipality, is it? It's a private corporation for profit, just like the United Railroads, isn't it? Founded by Mr. Rudolph Spreckels?" To Heney's scream of objection he said, "All right—all right—I withdraw it—I was just curious—*you met in the Presidio, didn't you?*"

There was the second question, like a rattlesnake sticking its horrid head out of a bouquet.

Gallagher hesitated, for the first time he looked at Spreckels. Rogers caught it, and slowly—as though fascinated—he walked around the counsel table and stood in front of Rudolph Spreckels. Every eye in the courtroom followed him. Then began the incredible performance of cross-examining a witness who wasn't on the stand. Rudolph Spreckels was under fire on every question just as much as Gallagher, who under this late and unexpected line of questioning, coming when he had relaxed, began to go to pieces.

Earl Rogers walked back and forth from one to the other.

He asked questions of the big man on the stand with his back turned to him.

He gazed quietly down at Spreckels while Gallagher hesitated for answers, with the hynotic effect that even the jury thought it was *Spreckels* they were waiting to hear from.

Heney did the best he could, which wasn't much. To draw too much attention to this double-cross would add to its weight and unless the judge wanted to create a special ruling there wasn't anything to do.

"In the Presidio," Mr. Rogers said again, then, "answer me!"

"Yes—yes—we met in the Presidio," Gallagher said.

"Where in the Presidio?" Rogers said.

"I didn't hear—" Gallagher said, and Rogers swung to him and said, "If you can't recall perhaps Mr. Spreckels can refresh your memory, he was there too."

On his feet, Heney objected that Mr. Spreckels wasn't on the stand.

"Put him there," Rogers said, "put him on the stand now."

"You can't tell me what witness to put on the stand," Heney said.

"I'd tell you to put Abe Ruef on as you promised," Rogers said, and went back quickly to Gallagher. "Have you remembered where?"

"I guess you'd call it just inside the gates," Gallagher said.

"In a clump of trees," Rogers said softly, "where you and Rudolph Spreckels could hide. *Why?*"

Why? The Kipling jingle about the honest serving men began to run through my head. Who and what and when and where and how and *why*—My father's third question had come—Why?

Gallagher—he was sweating now—said, "It was private—we could talk there without being overheard—"

Without an instant of time elapsing, like a bullfighter driving, Earl Rogers shouted at him, "As a lawyer yourself you knew you were on federal territory there, didn't you? You knew and could tell Spreckels that anything you said there and did there was outside the jurisdiction of the city or county of San Francisco or the state of California, couldn't you?"

It is no exaggeration to say that Gallagher began to wilt. A strange thing about all criminals. The word *federal* wilts them. I once saw a famous jewel thief confess to a big robbery because somewhere in it lurked something about a *post office*. Heney gave his witness a moment's respite, hammering with his clenched fist, shouting to the judge for help, saying this called for a conclusion of the witness and was irrelevant and immaterial. To which Rogers said, "You say it's not material and relevant that these two conspirators met in the dark under the trees, like animals in the jungle, on federal territory?"

It simmered down. The judge made a ruling. Rogers went to stand just beside Spreckels, close enough to touch him, looking across the counsel table at the weary Gallagher, who, though he didn't know it, still had five rounds to go—five more questions on my list.

Q. (by Mr. Rogers) Mr. Spreckels told you that they had the goods on you, didn't he? A threat, wasn't it?
A. We talked over—
Q. He told you all the other Supervisors were ready to squeal?
A. That was mentioned—
Q. He wanted you to confess, too.
A. To make a statement—
Q. Which must implicate Patrick Calhoun and Tirey Ford.
A. He wanted—he said he only wanted the facts.

Q. *Mr. Spreckels* wanted the *facts?*
A. Yes.

Again that swift dramatic hypnotic swing, creating a change
of scene as definitely as the shift of a movie camera. Now he
was cross-examining Spreckels again. The fourth question had
been the one about federal ground, now came the fifth.
"Spreckels told you if your testimony in this court in the case
against Ford suited him, he, Spreckels, would see that you
got immunity for your crime, didn't he?"

Gallagher floundered. "We—discussed immunity—if I testified—he said he wanted the facts—"

"The facts to convict the men who owned and operated
the street railroad built for the people when the city was at a
standstill? Mr. Spreckels, the president of the new Municipal
Street Railway wanted testimony to convict the president and
chief counsel of United Railroads? Mr. Gallagher"—he slipped
the sixth question in here without a ripple—"what did you
understand the position of Mr. Spreckels to be in this matter?
Why were you to talk to him instead of to the district attorney? San Francisco has a district attorney. Why didn't you
talk to him or to Special Prosecutor Heney?"

"Well—I did—" Gallagher said, "and Mr. Heney said, talk
to Spreckels."

"Mr. Heney said talk to Mr. Spreckels, did he?" Rogers
said. "Of course of course—Spreckels hired Heney—Spreckels
was the boss—so you talked to Spreckels a number of times
before you made the deal for immunity? Always at the
Presidio? Just inside the gates?"

"Yes—Mr. Spreckels was always waiting there," Gallagher
said, almost spitefully, as though he, too, now felt that
Spreckels should bear his share of all this.

Q. (by Mr. Rogers) Now when you used the grounds of
the United States Army, under the flag of the Republic, to
transact in the dark this deal—did Mr. Spreckels ever mention
to you that if you testified to the guilty knowledge of Mr.
Ford, which you have done as far as you could pretend to
know anything about it, did he mention that this would put
the United Railroads out of business?"

To that seventh question, Gallagher said no. But when the
camera of Earl Rogers' attention swung to Spreckels, the stolid
German control had broken, the square face was puce-purple,

he was glaring. Earl Rogers watched him until every juror and reporter had seen it.

Q. What did he say was his reason for getting involved in all this?

A. That his object was to see that the corporations responsible for the bribery and corruption of public officials be punished.

Q. But the public officials who were bribed were to go free. I see. Did Mr. Spreckels tell you he'd collected half a million dollars for this street railway of *his*? And that so far the only business of his Municipal Railway on which he has spent one penny is to finance a Graft Prosecution to *punish* the head of the *other* street railway corporation in San Francisco?

A. No—we didn't—that wasn't discussed.

I knew what was coming, it was on my list, so I was watching Abe Ruef.

"But," said Mr. Rogers, "you did discuss immunity for Abe Ruef, didn't you?"

"Well—in a way," Gallagher said, "he was to be included, if he testified."

Ruef's face showed absolutely nothing. He had played in very big poker games before. He did lean forward half an inch in his chair.

"So now, Mr. Gallagher," Earl Rogers said, "and please consider your answer to this question very carefully—now, *you* —Big Jim—you were making the deal for the Boss?"

The eighth question had the same effect on Gallagher as Ketchel's right, which Jim Langford said smelled like a hot brake. I thought he was going to topple off the stand, he almost did. He tried not to look at Ruef. The Little Boss drew him as a snake draws a bird. His terror shook him like unripe gelatin.

"By what right," Earl Rogers said, "did you propose to sell out the Boss to Mr. Spreckels who had no right to buy, either?"

"I guess—I didn't—it wasn't—" Gallagher said.

"That's all," Earl Rogers said quietly.

Heney did his best. He asked Gallagher if he'd ever heard such vile insinuations as those made by Mr. Rogers and Gallagher agreed he never had. It was no use. He wasn't able to get down from the witness stand by himself, a bailiff had to help him.

Heney knew he had no chance to get Abe Ruef on the stand after that, if he'd had a glimmer before. But he had to try.

He looked at Ruef. Nobody breathed. Their eyes held for what seemed an eternity.

Heney turned back to the judge.

"The People Rest, Your Honor," he said, and the press box broke down a door getting out. Their headline read:

HENEY FAILS TO CALL RUEF

or

ABE RUEF NOT TO TESTIFY FOR PROSECUTION

or

PROSECUTION RESTS WITHOUT PUTTING RUEF ON STAND

We had a recess until two o'clock. I went back to the hotel in Steve Ketchel's roadster. Papa had left quickly with the other defense lawyers.

A big conference had been called in Mr. McEnerny's office, with all the brass present. Alexander King and the Moores and Ford and Mr. Calhoun as well as Garret McEnerny himself.

What Earl Rogers wanted to do now was so unorthodox, so utterly without precedent, that it kicked up a gigantic ruckus.

In the end, young Rogers faced the weight of Garret McEnerny across his desk. And there was weight in every sense. Whenever I read about Nero Wolfe, I always picture him exactly as Mr. McEnerny looked to me when I saw him in those days.

"I came here," Earl Rogers said, "under an understanding with you, sir, that I am chief counsel for the defense."

"You did indeed," said Mr. McEnerny. "I abide by it. However, we wished you to know our opinions in the matter. We thought the fact that they are unanimously against you might have some influence upon your decision. But the decision is yours and yours alone."

"Thank you, sir," Earl Rogers said. "I'm sorry to be in disagreement with such lights of our profession. Only one man here, however, has what I consider a right to ask me to change my mind. General Ford?"

Tirey Ford looked at him a moment. "Oh no," he said. "You are my chief counsel, it is your case."

Earl Rogers grinned at them. He said, "Well—gentlemen, see you in court."

"Not me you won't thank God," said Garret McEnerny, who hadn't been in a courtroom in thirty years.

Judge Lawlor, in all his dignity, mounted the Bench again at two minutes after two.

Heney was already there and the press came straggling and staggering in, they'd had to file their stories and now *The Defense Opens* was upon them. The jury filed into the box. The stipulation that they were present went on record. The judge said, "You may proceed with your opening statement, Mr. Rogers."

Earl Rogers stood up. He looked at Heney with what appeared to be affection. Afterwards he told me he could read Heney's mind, all Heney wanted in the world now was his chance to cross-examine that briber and corrupter of public officials, the former Attorney General Tirey L. Ford.

"The Defense Rests," Earl Rogers said in a clear, carrying voice.

Nobody believed him.

Everybody went right on looking at him, in one of the biggest double-takes in history.

Without a single word of testimony, without calling one witness, Earl Rogers had said the defense rested. Hadn't he?

The judge looked at him inquiringly. Mr. Rogers said, "Your Honor, I do not consider that the prosecution has presented any evidence which in any way involves my client. I have listened, day by day, and examined night by night the testimony of the prosecution witnesses. If they have proved a case of political corruption and bribery I find no single piece of evidence to connect my client with it. Mr. Heney plays with a stacked deck, as well I have discovered. I do not believe in playing with the life and freedom of a man on trial, especially such a man as General Ford. When the special prosecutor failed to fulfill his promise to put Mr. Ruef on the stand to link Mr. Ford with this charge, I felt that there was no evidence to answer."

If Francis J. Heney had gone into apoplexy at this point,

it would have surprised no one. He etched a memorable picture of a man caught flat-footed, thirty seconds passed while the press hung flat-footed too, watching him. Then Earl Rogers, rolling a cigarette, strolled down the aisle, and out into the corridor and the scene dissolved.

Papa made a fine closing argument.

Nowadays of course that simple directness—that "My friends" radio technique of Franklin Delano Roosevelt's—is *a* —even *the*—favorite form of eloquence. Earl Rogers was way ahead of his time with it. The difference in the Darrow case was to show it up plainly—Darrow was as old-fashioned as William Jennings Bryan. The first man I ever heard use the simple clear form on the whole was Woodrow Wilson and he did not always reach the people. In retrospect, if I had to rate Earl Rogers I would put his over-all strategy and ability to find the weak spot—sometimes the only weak spot— in the prosecution, first. His cross-examination second, his oratory or speechmaking third.

He tied it all up carefully. He reminded them clearly and with incisive repetition of the failure to put Ruef on the stand and of Spreckels' self-serving interest in a street railway. "It appears in evidence," Mr. Rogers said, "that Spreckels has a rival streetcar company and it is his money he is using to *get* Calhoun and Ford involved in his graft prosecution. They would then be out of his way." He spoke movingly of Ford.

I thought Francis J. Heney's final plea was spectacularly good.

There he was, out on a limb this time, and within him all the fervor and frustration of The Defense Rests, all the anguish and disappointment of Ruef's refusal to testify— Ruef's final word, which we knew now had been, "I don't trust you, Mr. Heney. I'll go to San Quentin on my own with my skirts clean."

Into that final speech, Heney poured it all, painting so black a picture of corruption, political chicanery, a system of graft and greed that it horrified the country. A much more powerful and impassioned speech than Earl Rogers'; President Theodore Roosevelt had a right to be proud of his boy Heney that day. He generated sincerity. While I listened, moved myself, I kept asking myself how so strong and shrewd and intelligent a man could allow Rogers to make him lose his temper every single time—*every* time—so that he looked a fool. For instance the record showed:

HENEY: I wish Your Honor would ask Mr. Rogers to stop repeating that question. Besides how can the witness remember details that far back? I can't remember what I had for breakfast.

ROGERS: Then you ought to see a doctor, Mr. Heney.

HENEY: Don't you tell me what to do! You don't remember getting thrown out of a saloon Saturday night, either.

ROGERS: Yes I do. And so do the three fellows it took to do it.

Commotion as Mr. Heney attacked Mr. Rogers.

A lot of that kind of thing.

Nobody at the end of the Ford trial questioned the bribery of the Boodle Board. "We figured the $200,000 in gold was provided by Ford for Ruef and that he gave it to Gallagher to pay off with," a juror told us later. "But we thought it was just the usual for political favors, the way The System worked an outfit had to come up with it to stay in business. We never did see Ford had been tied up to that money as a direct bribe of that franchise which they'd have given anyhow with the city at a standstill the way it was. We knew Spreckels had an ax of his own to grind."

That jury disagreed. Eight for acquittal. Four for conviction.

The graft prosecution went on, limping a little. Heney made us try the Ford case again. The jury acquitted the general in twenty-six minutes.

Then San Francisco, exhausted, took a long breath, relaxed, began to think of other things, let the graft prosecution, in routine indictments against Ruef and others, drift into the background.

Until Big Jim Gallagher's house was dynamited, with the family present.

Until a man shot Francis J. Heney in the open courtroom.

The President himself went into Colonel-Teddy-Roosevelt-at-San-Juan-Hill action, rough-riding in demands for retribution against Heney's assassin, and begging all to have courage to carry on the fight. The nation's press and people screamed against this kind of violence in her courts. San Francisco zoomed to new heights of blood-boiling, fever-heat, fantastic madness without waiting to find out who had dynamited Gallagher's house or why Heney had been shot.

All that Earl Rogers had done to reverse the tide had been undone. The trial of Patrick Calhoun, direct descendant of the patriot of that name, the biggest prize the muckrake had gone after, loomed more deadly and dangerous than ever. Odds on that trial, in which at last by devious and terrible methods Earl Rogers came face to face with his arch-enemy Rudolph Spreckels on the witness stand, went high for conviction.

During all this, my father and I had the worst fight of our lives.

I think it ought to be told here because it had an effect upon Earl Rogers to find that his daughter Nora wasn't the little girl of the Boyd case any more. That she had begun to be what was then called a young lady, would have been almost a sub-debutante if they had stayed in their social orbit, a teen-ager of today, or at least a sub-teen-ager.

FORTY

Always look at a lady's feet and ankles first, my father said. The sight of my feet struck him with horror. I wore a four-and-a-half, triple-A to be sure, but in a day when the model size was three and many girls wore two or two-and-a-half, this did not help much. You will grow to them, Papa said hopefully. This presented another difficulty. I was already five feet four, taller than other girls and skinny in a day when it was not fashionable to be a bean pole.

Probably this was partly what kept Papa from realizing that my Gentlemen Callers, though they often stayed to talk to him, came to see me. I had invitations to the theater, to dances, to concerts. I even wore fraternity pins. So ignorant was I of their social significance that I took two, and when I got annoyed and gave one young gentleman back the wrong pin, I was ostracized. Somehow, with all that was going on, Papa didn't seem to notice any of this. I always had a guard or Rosy or somebody following me and to tell the truth I didn't pay much attention to any of it either.

Up to the moment out at the beach when Stanley Ketchel kissed me.

There may have been a girl or woman born into this world who wouldn't have paid much attention to being kissed by Steve Ketchel but, as anyone who ever saw him will tell you, this seems very doubtful.

At the time the search for a White Hope to take the heavyweight crown away from Jack Johnson was occupying about the same space we now give the Congo. I never could see what difference it made what color Johnson was, but they kept whooping it up and Stanley Ketchel, a dramatist and a ham in his own field, suddenly got the big idea that he ought to fight Johnson himself. This went to show, as Bill Mizner said to me once, that if Steve had a fault it was to overmatch himself. Ketchel was the greatest middleweight who ever fought but his best weight was 168. And Jack Johnson, who could lick all the heavyweights of this century except Dempsey on the same evening and maybe in the same ring, would come in at 203 or 4.

The match was made. A wave of excitement hit the country and San Francisco, where it was to take place. Like Damon Runyon, Paul Gallico, and Ring Lardner, my father thought no other sports event came near a great heavyweight fight, so we spent a lot of time at the training camps. I can remember sitting on a bucket watching Johnson stand at the end of a runway while three or four sparring partners threw tennis balls at him. Nobody ever hit anything except his forearms. A kindly man, outside the ring, with beautiful manners. My father, who was his lawyer, had told me a story which made me admire him very much. The woman he married looked white. Johnson took a terrible beating in the press for this, mixed marriages were then frowned upon and condemned by both sides. Sometimes when they appeared together, he was hissed. His wife was, my father told me, an octoroon, so light she had always "passed" for white and Johnson would never save his own popularity if it hurt her.

After we had watched Jack for a while we would go over to Ketchel's camp.

"He always reminds me of Nijinsky," I said to Papa, "the way he moves. But he is giving away too much weight, even for Ketchel."

My father laughed. He said, "Yes. A good big man always has to beat a good little man. But Steve's a magnificent boxer.

Johnson won't hurt him. It's just a show—and they'll put on a good one."

I was worried. I found I didn't want to see Ketchel get hit as hard as I knew Jack Johnson could hit. However, as Papa said, Johnson wouldn't. Steve was so fast he'd be able to keep out of his way.

To this day, I can't believe Mama did it on purpose. Once at school near Philadelphia, where Miss Elizabeth Wood of Hollywood High School had persuaded Papa they might tutor me into passing my entrance exams to Bryn Mawr, Mama sent me a pink organdy dress. I couldn't go to the senior prom in it though I had a Princeton beau from Nashville. Her taste was wrong, and I suppose it's a terrible thing for a woman who was herself a lush beauty, and what was then called *feminine,* to have a plain daughter of the boyish type.

Anyhow one day out at the Washington Street house, she gave me a new dress, of white dimity with a rose pattern, kind of like wallpaper. It had puff sleeves and a sash down the back with a froth of narrow pink baby ribbon bows. "Isn't it pretty, Papa," I said, prancing in to show off in it, and he said in a strange tight voice, "Nora—look, sweetheart, it's all a matter of whether a thing is becoming—" then I guess he saw my face and he said, "You won't have any place to wear a thing like that just yet—we'll talk about it later."

Ketchel came by one night, he was in strict training but he said he was going stale and I could tell he was edgy. He didn't know Papa had gone to Los Angeles on a hurry-up call from a client, and Mama was out as usual with Jake Samuels, who owned a big department store, or Ryan of the A.P. or maybe just joy-riding with our handsome English chauffeur, who turned over the big Pierce-Arrow one night and got killed. Mama was lucky nobody but Bull Durham and me ever knew she was the woman who'd been in the car with him. We never did tell Papa about that.

Anyhow, Steve said, "Why don't you come for a ride out to the beach," and I said all right, and I suppose if I'd had any sense the very fact that I went up and put on that dress would have warned me. Academically, I knew by now all there was to know. What Pearl Morton did for a living and why Dolly had been a shock to Dr. Burdette, what the words of the songs on the Coast meant, why Othello had killed Desdemona and the definitions of pimp and prostitute my father had used in the Mootry case. As for experience, I was in abysmal darkness. Nice girls in those days carried their own protection. Men did not make passes at virgins, it was both dangerous and out of bounds. Necking was unheard of, the pregnancy rate in high schools nonexistent, a girl's virginity was important since without it she couldn't make a good marriage and so for every reason, moral and social, fathers and brothers were quicker with their guns. Boys and young men who drank too much and *got fresh* were dropped from invitation lists and girls who permitted it were dropped altogether and soon *déclassé*. Life was a great deal more fun for us in those happy days of forbidden fruit and long courtship than it is now, when too many hors d'oeuvres spoil all appetite for the main meal.

Under these conditions, of course, the first attractive man who knows how to make love and does so outside the Marquis of Queensberry rules has a big advantage and that was what was meant by a girl being swept off her feet.

The drive through the park by moonlight was as beautiful as anything there was anywhere in the world. Steve stopped the big open roadster by the Cliff House and we watched the seals and laughed when they barked. Then we drove out along the beach road, slowly, not talking much. It wasn't a night for talking. He stopped the car and we got out and walked across the sand toward the ocean. Although we could see the waves gleam green-silver, crest up into moonlight white, and break in dancing falls of spun light, I don't suppose Steve could really see my dress, probably in the glowing darkness it even looked soft and floating.

He put his arms around me and kissed me and at first I didn't know what to do. Mother Eve took care of that and I put my arms around his neck and kissed him, too. I heard him gasp, and then he held me tight as he could, I didn't really care whether I ever breathed again or not, I was swept off my feet and so was he. We stood there swaying as though we were in a great wind off the sea, clinging to each other.

Maybe even Ketchel, who I know now had the morals and scruples of a tiger, realized a little how awkward and in-experienced and virginal I was.

Or maybe he remembered that I was Earl Rogers' daughter.

He let me go.

He put one arm around me, we walked back toward the car, our feet seemed to find the sand heavier than when we were going out. In the dim headlights of the car he said, "Give me something to bring me luck." I didn't have anything,

I never wore jewelry, and he said, "How about the sash, does it come off?" He unhooked it and stuck it in his pocket and helped me into the car.

I decided to go back to the St. Francis, I thought my father might come back on the Lark and be there in the morning. I wanted to be alone for some reason. So Steve drove me to the smaller door up toward Post Street and I got out and waved to him and he waved back and the car shot away. Waiting for me in front of the elevators was Rosy and he looked like he'd been hanging by his thumbs ever since I left. He said, "I never thought you'd play me such a dirty trick, *sneaking* out like that, your old man called up by long distance and wanted to know where you were and he thinks Heney has had you kidnaped and he's calling out the cops." In the elevator we didn't say a word but when we got inside he told the operator to get Los Angeles, which was a big deal. I had never spoken on long distance before, and Rosy kept yattering, "What'd you want to do a thing like that for—I never thought you'd be such a sneak—" and I said, "Oh, dry up. I was safe, I just went for a drive out to the beach with Steve Ketchel—" Rosy jumped four feet and said, "Do me a favor. Do not tell your Pa I lost you and you were out with Ketchel—"

Of course I'd intended to tell my father, but Rosy was in such a state I promised I wouldn't and when we got our big call through and I could hear Papa just as though he was in the next room I said I'd gone for a walk and my father was furious but said all right he'd be home in the morning.

So we thought it was all right.

It never entered my head to tell Rosy about the sash.

I didn't get to go to the Jack Johnson-Stanley Ketchel fight. Ladies did not go to prize fights. With the civil war that had San Francisco split in half then and the newspapers worse than ever about headlines on everything Earl Rogers did, he decided it would make too much of an uproar. He said, "You're getting too big." I tried to get Rosy to slip me in up in the gallery with him but he wouldn't. I had an idea that Mr. Calhoun's two daughters, Martha and Margaret, who were about my age and very beautiful and being brought up as ladies, had certainly never been to a prize fight and maybe this had something to do with all this.

The only thing I could get out of Rosy for keeping my trap shut was he said he would call me as soon as it was over and tell me how it came out.

Ketchel got knocked out in the twelfth round.

What happened, I found out later, was that Ketchel took a chance. No question he had a knockout wallop in his right hand. If he landed it full on Johnson's chin it could lay even the heavyweight champ on the canvas. For a fraction of a second, Johnson seemed to be coasting and Ketchel, a lover of the long shot, decided to take one. His Sunday punch was lightning, but the tennis-ball technique blocked it and in a reproachful voice Jack Johnson said, "You ought not to have done that, Mr. Ketchel," and knocked the middleweight champion of the world into the middle of last Tuesday.

Cap Durham and I were playing cooncan when the door opened. Papa was alone, which was unusual. Cap was a favorite of his, but he looked through her as though he'd never seen her before, and she went out. Papa kept walking toward me and when he got in the middle of the room I saw my pink ribbon sash in his hand.

Well, there is no use going into how hard he spanked me. It was the last time. He always used a razor strop. He kept saying, "You're too big to spank. Your grandfather always said spare the rod and spoil the child only he did not live up to it. I've spoiled you. I know you're too big to spank but if you behave like a guttersnipe I have to deal with it. I thought I could trust you."

To pretend I took this in courageous silence would be a lie. I howled like a northeaster coming in off the bay. I kept howling, I said, "Papa you can, you *can*, I haven't done anything, I haven't done anything bad—"

He got up and it dumped me on all fours. He picked the sash off the floor and held it up in front of me. "My daughter's favors hanging on the ropes in a fight arena—in a prize fighter's corner—everybody making bawdy remarks about Steve Ketchel's girl—" He dropped it in the wastebasket with a shiver of distaste.

"What was so awful about it," I said, with a gulp. "He asked me for something to bring him luck and I didn't have a rabbit's foot handy—"

"Get up," he said. I did and we looked at each other and I saw that under his fury he was very sad. He said, "Why didn't you tell me you'd been running around with this bum?"

"Well he's not a bum, Papa," I said, "he is a champion, you said yourself, and I was not running around with him. I didn't tell you—" I hesitated but it was too late now to save Rosy, so I said, "I sneaked past Rosy and he asked me not to tell you, that's *all*. I did it because I was wearing that dress with the roses you said not to. All I did was ride out to the beach."

He got the sash out of the basket and sat down and kept wrapping it around his fingers and staring at it, I knew he was going back to the moment he'd *seen* it there tied to the ropes in Ketchel's corner and recognized it, there couldn't be but *one* of it. He said, "Come here, Nora."

My knees buckled, but I managed to go and sit beside him. He said, "He is a prize fighter, honey. Stanley Ketchel is a *prize fighter*."

"I guess I know that," I said. "You took me to see him train often enough. What is the difference between that and Nijinsky?"

"If you could have seen him tonight when Johnson hit him," Papa said.

"I am sorry about that," I said, "but it is spilt milk—"

At this my father gave me the funniest look and began to laugh. He said, "All right. Listen to me, my child, my dear little girl, he's a prize fighter. There is a difference. Don't you feel it? You can go to see him train or fight—you can't accept him—this cannot be a man to whom you can give your—personal favors—"

For the first time, Papa was at a loss for words. "You never told me that, did you?" I said.

"Told you?" Papa yelled, and got up with such a leap his chair banged over. "Told you! Do I have to tell you a thing like that? Don't you feel it? Where is your sensibility?"

"It seems to me you are making an awful lot of this," I said.

"I'll make more of it if you don't behave yourself," my father said.

I had been going to tell him about Steve kissing me, I thought I had better not, the way he was acting he might shoot Ketchel.

"Can you imagine him at your grandmother's table?" Papa said.

I was getting a little sore myself. I said, "No, but we are not at her table either, are we? Not often anyhow."

A wry grin came over him. He said, "I took it for granted—there were certain things—your aunts are probably right—I've brought you up all wrong."

"No you have not either," I said. "I don't know what's got into you. You have always been able to trust me and you still can."

"You were a child," my father said, not looking at me, "now you'll be a woman. The way I've brought you up, can I trust you?"

"Yes," I said.

"I have to," Papa said. "You're all I have in the world."

He sat down in his big chair under the lamp. In the sweetest, kindest voice I ever heard, he said, "When you marry, marry a man like your grandfather. All the rest is dross. Nothing, Nora, is so deadly as the disparity of tastes, in marriage. The unsuitability of mind and character. The divergence of aim and purpose, this kills the soul. I don't want it to happen to you."

"I probably won't get married at all," I said.

"Nonsense," my father said sharply. "Of course you must marry. And have children."

I felt he had intended to say more, the effort was too much for him. A pang of fear shot through me. From Papa, sitting there so terribly *quiet*, not moving, his eyes closed, the agony of his fatigue went from him through me. Fatigue as though he was bleeding to death. Wildly I thought, He has used up all his nerve force, he has been operating on his viscera, he has sparked and hypnotized and driven and dominated out of his own heartbeats until he is tired to death. In his book *Sailor on Horseback*, Irving Stone speaks of the disease of which Jack London almost died in Honolulu. Where all of a sudden the strong virile sailor London looked entirely *white*. No doctor ever put a name to it. When we saw London at Glen Ellen soon after this I felt that with him it was as it was with my father—the giving of the life force itself beyond what the body can endure or sustain to their work, to what they want to do and must do, to dominating everything in sight. The sleeplessness. The white nights. The tremendous outpouring that could *literally* hold men and women spellbound. Take over the minds of witnesses like Gallagher, the will of juries, groups of men like McEnerny and Calhoun, cities like San Francisco. It drained them *white*.

Who replenished *them?* I felt guilty and shaking with disloyalty. He had been wondering if I was going to be like my mother. There was no use his telling me not to blame her. Something had happened only a few nights before and they'd had one of those terrible quarrels the whole floor at the hotel knew about. That drained him too. No, I hadn't any patience with her or charity for her that night. *Hurting* him, disturbing him, frightening him—seeing that silly *pink* sash on the ropes without warning. *She's not going to be like her mother, is she?*

I tried to get him to go to bed. He seemed more at peace, he was giving me that rueful grin, yet it was like collapse, as though he couldn't move. I sat down on the floor and put my head against his knee and he patted my hair.

"Everybody loves you, Papa," I said.

"For all the wrong reasons," he said.

He picked up a book from the table and began to read. I don't remember what it was. Could have been Carlyle's *French Revolution* or *The Iliad,* or Alfred Henry Lewis's *Wolfville.* His voice sounded cheerful again and I took a long breath of relief.

Just the same, two days later I landed in the Notre Dame Convent at San Jose.

"Whatever I do," he said to Sister Mary Regis, "or whatever I say, don't let me take her out of here. I want her to stay here where she's safe." He looked at my furious reproach and said coldly, "It hurts me worse than it does you."

"No it doesn't," I said.

Sister Mary Regis said, "I will keep her here, Mr. Rogers. And I will pray for you."

All the nuns were still always praying for Papa. So were the rabbis, the ones who kept trying to arrange the immunity deal for Ruef with Heney. Aunty Blanche was certainly giving him treatments in Christian Science. Of late, too, I had begun to ask Grandpa if he was anywhere to say some Protestant prayers. I didn't believe any of it any more but I didn't see what I had to lose. So I thought we had all fronts covered. Just the same I was crazy with *worry. Nobody but you,* Pearl Morton had said, *and you're too little.* I was bigger, but here I was in *school* and the Calhoun case coming up. He could lose it.

Sister Cecile Marie, head of the music department, saw what I was suffering. "I know well," she said, "nothing is so difficult as when the child has the true mother-love for the parent. You are not only his daughter to your father, in your heart you are to him as a mother. Sit down and I will play for you." She was a great artist, this tall stately French nun. She said, "You are too young for Mozart but, as we have said, these things mix up time and age so I will play him.

Save our Blessed Lord himself, Mozart is for me the great comfort."

Of course Papa came for me himself quite soon. Sister Mary Regis did her best but it wasn't any use and she soon saw it.

Just when my father told me that somebody had shot and killed Stanley Ketchel I don't remember exactly. An irate husband had picked up a shotgun. I was very glad it hadn't been Papa. If a woman was at last to be Steve's downfall I was glad it hadn't been me.

You always remember the first man who kissed you, if it was *right* the way it was that night at the beach. Whether he was a prize fighter or not. So I treasure the epitaph spoken of him by Wilson Mizner, who'd been his manager.

They told Mizner that Ketchel was dead.

Start counting, said the fabulous Mizner, *he'll get up before you get to ten.*

FORTY-ONE

A small, nondescript man, graying hair, untidy from the winds that blew up and down San Francisco's hills, walked through roped-off crowds, past the guards, and into the courtroom, where Abe Ruef was on trial for yet another of the sixty-five indictments against him. The judge had declared an afternoon recess and retired to chambers. The jury box was empty. At the counsel table, Francis J. Heney was talking to a staff member. People milled around, reporters scurried in and out, all was as usual. The small man, wearing a sweater under his heavy overcoat, was so commonplace, seemed so absent-minded, no one noticed him.

Until the shot exploded and they saw the gun in his hand.

Heney fell. Blood gushed from his head and spread over the carpet. It looked as though the whole side of his head had been blown off.

Instantly the place was a madhouse. A woman calliope

screamed steadily. Oaths of unbelief ripped out. The moaning of shock filled the room, the very sound of fear. Fist fights, hair-pulling, threats—sheer hysteria—produced chaos.

In that dreadful first moment, everyone believed Heney had been killed.

After a time shorter than it seemed, the bailiffs got things under control. A deputy sheriff had taken the man's gun, another put handcuffs on him. Nobody knew who he was and he refused to speak.

A stretcher appeared, they got the limp body and the terrible bloody head onto it; through a lane of frozen horror, men carried it away.

Francis J. Heney, Assistant Attorney General of the United States, prosecutor of the graft trials by special appointment of President Theodore Roosevelt, had been assassinated in the Superior Court of the County of San Francisco, State of California.

There had been the kidnaping of Fremont Older, an attempt by Luther Brown to put the beloved and influential editor out of circulation, which had been done without my father's consent and turned into a fiasco when Older was rescued by a train conductor.

There had been the dynamiting of Big Jim Gallagher's house. About that, people weren't sure. Could have been a plant. Very funny, one man would say, the family all being at home and every single one of them out in the garden as though they knew what was coming, so no one got hurt. Another would answer, Well, they could have had a hunch. On the whole, the man in the street shrugged that one off and withheld judgment. It made no real impression in the end, though it had startled everybody in the beginning.

Now, Heney, a national hero, a reform leader, a friend of the President, had been shot down. About this one, there had to be the devil to pay.

As Heney fell, Sam Shortridge, who was acting as Abe Ruef's lawyer in this case, looked at his client. The Little Boss made a hopeless gesture. This shooting of the special prosecutor in the courtroom where he was on trial had to cook his goose. His ticket to San Quentin would be along any minute, Abe thought, and he was right. It was.

Within an hour after the bullet hit, news came to our headquarters at the St. Francis that Heney was still alive.

The next bulletin said he couldn't live, but he was hanging on.

By midnight, we knew he had a fighting chance for life.

The newspapers sent reporters for what would today be called a press conference with Earl Rogers. This was the biggest story of the long long graft prosecution. A story with blood all over it always has more news value than one without blood.

"There's a rumor the defense is behind this somewhere," the U.P. said.

Usually, Mr. Rogers was good with the press. He and Harry Carr had been a team for years, he understood completely the press viewpoint, its need for news, its *right* to news. This time, he met them in an ungovernable rage and nothing I or anybody else could do about it.

"Let's assume I'm a murderer," he said, "and a cowardly one, who hires a thug to do the dirty work for me. *Why should I pick Heney?* He couldn't—he didn't—convict Ford. Calhoun is even more remote, one step further away from any possibility of knowledge of this bribery. This, I tell you now, this is the only thing that could beat me. The *only* thing. He'll come bleeding into the courtroom with arrows still sticking in him. He's got the cut and jib of a martyr, they'd rather be martyred than live to tell the tale."

"Heney is probably going to die," the *Examiner* said.

"He's too mean to die," Earl Rogers said darkly, "I'm too mean too, we're a couple of mean Irishmen. We'll finish this fight in this world, but I want you to know I think he's done an unfair, unexcusable bit of sharp practice getting himself martyred. The Irish will do it."

While they went on with their questions, Papa seemed to be waiting, watching for something. This was a time where there was no letup, no hands on the clock, no beginning or end to anything. No workday or bedtime. I knew he'd sent men out looking for something. He also had one of our boys with Chief of Police Biggy up at the jail where they were holding the nondescript little man. And pretty soon Bull Durham came in and handed Mr. Rogers a lot of notes, clippings, reports, and he began glancing through them.

"*Haas Haas Haas,*" he said, giving it out like a college yell, "I knew I remembered the name—"

"Morris Haas," the *Chronicle* said, "that's the man who shot Heney—"

"He is," Earl Rogers said, "he shot your knight in shining armor, did you ask yourselves WHY? No no—you just jump to the conclusion that it has something to do with Earl

Rogers and the defense—well, I was a reporter once myself and I've done some of your work for you. Your offices have probably got it by now of course but this'll get you off my back."

"What about Haas?" the *Bulletin* said.

"You don't remember?" Earl Rogers said. "Way way back in the first Ruef trial?" He took a long breath and began to tell the story. "Morris Haas was a prospective juror. A plain ordinary little man. He was living a quiet life. He had a wife, two children, a job to support them. His employer didn't know he had a prison record. His wife didn't know her husband was an ex-convict, nor his children that their father had done time. *They know now.* That righteous reformer, Mr. Heney, told them. Haas had paid his debt to society, was making good, but when Heney got through examining him as a prospective juror he had exposed Haas's past disgrace as ruthlessly as Heney himself once shot a man in the back. Haas loved his wife and children. When they knew of his shame, he began to brood. Of course he lost his job. For an ex-con, it proved impossible to get another. He determined to end Heney's life as Heney had ended his.

"No—Heney won't die. I say he got what was coming to him, but I am not a righteous man. I defend underdogs, instead of tying tin cans to their tails. Mr. Heney will live and come to court cast as a hero who shed his blood in A Cause. Don't, I beg you, let anyone think Earl Rogers had anything to do with this. The only life I value more than Heney's is that of Rudolph Spreckels. I want them both in court for the Calhoun case."

Big talk, and he talked it big. We knew it was a desperate crisis. While the words were still echoing, Morris Haas killed himself in his cell at the city jail. Reports were circulated that we'd sent him the gun with which to do it, how else could he have gotten it? Anybody who knew the ease and speed with which guns, heroin, and whiskey circulated in the jails knew it wasn't hard to do. Purported confessions by Haas telling nine or ten stories involving first one side and then the other kept turning up. Chief of Police Biggy said they were all fakes. He said Haas had told him before he killed himself that he had decided to *get Heney* that very day in the jury box.

What gave size, impact, and widespread conviction to the idea that the shooting of Heney was a plot against Operation

Muckrake in general and the graft prosecution in particular were the telegrams from President Theodore Roosevelt.

Sent from the White House as soon as he heard of the catastrophe in the courtroom, at a time when everybody except Earl Rogers was sure Heney would die, they were white-hot with sympathy, indignation, and accusation. The fact that the President could not possibly know what had actually happened, nor who the "infamous assassin" was, didn't lessen the appeal, prestige, and public relations powers.

This was the worst blow that had befallen us.

The tide had not only turned. It had become a torrent and seemed about to sweep the defense and its chief counsel into discredit, disgrace, and defeat.

FORTY-TWO

After months of delays, postponements, and continuances, Patrick Calhoun went on trial for the bribery of Supervisor Nichols.

The special prosecutor was Francis J. Heney.

His entrance upon the scene was spectacular. The great red scar across his right temple and cheek, the black patch over his eye, the snow-white hair, the emaciated figure made a frenzied and flaming impression. Often his hand trembled. His voice was edgy, irritable, without resonance. A formidable opponent against whom Earl Rogers would never again be able to use his old weapons.

When Heney explained to a prospective juror that he had to sit down while he questioned him because his strength had not come back since a bullet mowed him down while he was on service to his country, at the command of its President, Earl Rogers walked out of the courtroom white to the lips.

Hostility to the defense was simmering inside and out.

At the time Heney was shot, all the newspapers in San Francisco except Fremont Older's *Bulletin* had begun to play the graft trials with unbiased fairness. They did print the truth about Morris Haas and Heney's part in driving that underdog to take a gun to him.

Just as often, oftener, came up that first telegram from President Roosevelt to Mrs. Heney:

Inexpressibly shocked at news of the attempted assassination of Mr. Heney. Like all good citizens I hold your husband in peculiar regard for the absolutely fearless way in which he has attacked and exposed corruption without regard to political or social prominence of the offenders or the dangerous character of his work. Your husband has taken his life in his hands in doing this great task for our people and is entitled to the credit and esteem and above all the heartiest support of all good citizens. The infamous character of the man who has assassinated him should add not only to the horror and detestation felt for the deed, but also to the determination of all decent citizens to stamp out the power of all men of his kind.

THEODORE ROOSEVELT

Strong language. When Teddy Roosevelt was for you, he was *for* you. When he was after you, he was after you.

Just what the colonel meant by the "power of all men of his kind" it was difficult to figure out, unless he cared to lump all ex-convicts in this infamous character bracket. There was nothing else against Morris Haas. He was never at any time identified as an associate of any kind of corruption, nor of the rich and powerful who corrupted. The truth was that the public was nuts about the hero of San Juan Hill for his hot, partisan, exciting, and excitable personality and his tendency to come out fighting. It had its other side as well. Teddy Roosevelt didn't know Morris Haas from a hole in the ground. The same things that had made him wildly popular as Governor of New York, Vice President, now President caused him to holler that the man who shot Heney *had* to be of infamous character and a part of the battle against his boy Heney and the graft prosecution.

Thus he hung it around the neck of Patrick Calhoun and his defense like an albatross.

The telegram was printed in handbills and circulated widely. Printed in full pages. Read aloud by orators at the mass meetings which the graft prosecution soon began to hold as often as possible.

Another telegram had followed it immediately.

This one was to Rudolph Spreckels. In it, the President in unmistakable words put the seal of approval on Mr. Spreckels as presiding genius of the muckrake in San Francisco.

The wire said:

Dear Mr. Spreckels:

The infamous character of the would-be assassin no less than the infamous character of the deed call attention in a striking way to the true character of the forces against which Heney and you and your associations have been struggling. Every decent American who has the honor and interest of the country at heart should join not only in putting a stop to the cause of violent crime of which this man's act is but one of the symptoms, but also in stamping out the hideous corruption in which men like this would-be assassin are bred and flourish and that can only be done by warring as Heney has warred relentlessly against every man guilty of corrupt practices without regard to his social standing and his prominence in the world of politics or the world of business. I earnestly hope that Heney will recover and I give utterance to what I know would be Heney's wish when I say that I earnestly hope that whether he recovers or not there be no faltering in the work in which Heney has been so gallant and efficient a leader.

THEODORE ROOSEVELT

9:10 A.M. From the White House.

There could be no question of the weight of such words from such a man in such a position at such a time.

To read them carefully is to find they sound like they had gushed a hundred barrels a minute out of the well of his emotions rather than a thought at a time, with information, from his able mind.

The prosecution waved those telegrams like banners all around the town and crowds came tumbling after.

Too, there had been the suspense, the enormous appeal of the Fight-for-Life in the emergency right after the bullet hit and for a long time afterwards. All Americans love A Fighting Chance. The drama of this one swept the country. While Heney's life was in the balance every newspaper in the nation headlined hourly bulletins. Boxes of minute-by-minute reports on his condition by his physicians appeared on every front page. Crowds gathered outside the hospital to watch his window, and broke into sobs when his wife went in and out. Heney, they were told, had escaped death by a hairsbreadth and the mercy of God.

So to the special prosecutor's martyrdom was added a miracle.

As a result of all this, the mass meetings all over the state were heavily attended and hysterical in their support of Heney

and his sacred mission. The Citizens' League of Justice called
a mass meeting in these terms:

Francis J. Heney has fallen by the hand of a hired assassin,
shot from Behind while fighting at his Post in the Cause of
Justice for the people of this city. He would be the first
man to appeal to the calm reason of the citizens to preserve
order and proceed only by the processes of law; to look not
for Vengeance, but to demand swift justice through the
courts.

They had got some of their facts a little mixed. It was
Heney who had shot a man in the back down in Phoenix,
Arizona, and left the state shortly thereafter. Haas had shot
Heney from in front, directly in the right eye. Also, Morris
Haas had taken swift and final justice upon himself, which is
a strange—an almost unheard-of—thing for a "hired assassin"
to do.

However that mass meeting jammed the auditorium, the
present mayor, Taylor, and a former mayor, James J. Phelan
presided, and a large number of preachers and professors
spoke to a wildly cheering audience which gave the biggest
ovation of the night to Rudolph Spreckels.

It was only proper of course that most of the churches in
San Francisco should offer prayers for Heney at their Sunday
services while he fought for his life.

We also continued to exist in an increasing welter of delirium, brain fever, hallucinosis, charges and countercharges,
espionage and counterespionage and anti-anti-counterespio-
nage such as never existed before or since in any courtroom
in history. Our side had operatives in the Burns office, Burns
had them in ours. They snitched our stolen lists of prospective
jurors and we got theirs. Burns claimed we had dynamited his
safe and stolen priceless papers, we claimed vice-versa. Papa
and I were followed by what looked like the National Guard
and nobody was sure any longer which was which or who was
tailing whom. Around us a seriocomic reign of terror had
settled and we spent weekends on our ferryboat retreat and
went to Los Angeles a couple of times to try murder cases.

Also I have one very clear recollection of my father's
decision that playing golf would be a good idea.

"You've never played golf," I said. "Doesn't it take a while
to learn?" Papa was never very good at learning things, he
wanted to start at the top.

"I shouldn't think so," he said cheerfully. "How can it? It's a child's game really. All you have to do is hit a little ball with a stick."

We went down to Burlingame with a friend of his, Buck Travis, who owned all the taxicabs in San Francisco. On top of everything else it turned out that he played golf *left-handed*, which he did a number of things, so the *right-handed* clubs added to the general frustration and impedimenta. "All a man has to do is hit a little white ball with a stick," he kept saying. "The Scotch! No wonder they run the empire."

As we walked through the glories of the day and the beauties of the golf course, from time to time he talked about the Calhoun case and Heney. "The whole thing's a perfidious fraud," he said, and Buck Travis said, "It's been put over on the public, the President's telegrams did that." My father said, as he always did, "Those telegrams were *hasty*." He didn't say he had himself sent a telegram to the White House, giving the facts about Morris Haas, Heney's word-for-word examination of him in the Ruef case, Hass's final word to the chief of police. He bitterly resented receiving no reply. "Even if I am a Democrat," he said. "A man must not be afraid to look at both sides."

"The tide has turned against us," he said. "We have to turn it back."

"Can you?" Buck Travis said.

"Not until I get Spreckels on the stand," Earl Rogers said.

"You can't get Spreckels on the stand!" Buck Travis said.

"I can try," Earl Rogers said, and he had on that pixilated, furious, *profound mischief* face that only the Irish can produce and that meant big trouble for somebody. It was hard to tell whether it was genius or leprechaun demagoguery.

Anyhow, I knew we'd heard the whole plan of the Calhoun defense.

Keep Ruef *off* the stand.

Get Rudolph Spreckels *on*.

He continued to go everywhere, be seen at the theater, the opera, the ball games and fights, the restaurants and they loved him still. It was just that sentiment had been swept away by the tragic melodrama of Heney's assassination, as it was always called. So that when on the instant he had cried, *The only thing that could beat me*, it began to look as though he had been right. When the opening day finally came he faced not only the battle-scarred Heney, with the

black patch and the hair-gone-white-in-a-night; Hiram Johnson, who now took over much of the active trial work; Matt
Sullivan, later chief justice of the California Supreme Court;
and in the background the giant figure of the Man in the
White House, *but* also a weight of public opinion, which,
by the odds, had shifted heavily to and for conviction.

Earl Rogers believed in the telepathic weight of public
opinion on any jury, lock 'em up and keep the papers from
them though the bailiffs did.

Three months and 2371 prospective jurors later, the trial
itself began.

Those figures prove that there were no neutrals in San
Francisco. For a time it looked as though the judge couldn't
find twelve men who'd formed no opinion and might have to
change the venue.

My memory-diary of the Calhoun case has some pages
that time hasn't erased and that no other courtroom has ever
given me.

The first was the incredible contrast of all kinds of *witnesses*
upon whom justice calls. We had two further apart than any
others I ever saw, even in the trial of Bruno Richard Hauptmann for kidnaping the Lindbergh baby.

The first was named Sorenson, he was supposed to be part
of the backstage intrigue of the defense and Earl Rogers,
and he had ignored a subpoena. It turned out Sorenson was
the real name of the Banjo-Eyed Kid and Mr. Heney shouted,
"I demand that Mr. Rogers produce this witness."

"I can't produce him, Mr. Heney," Earl Rogers said plead-
ingly. "I don't have him. I don't know anything about a
Banjo-Eyed Kid."

"He's been sent from Your Honor's jurisdiction—" Heney
said.

At which point a harassed bailiff arrived to say, "Your
Honor, the witness is in jail. They got him at the door of
the courtroom because he had a loaded .45 on him. They
don't let in anybody with a gun any more." At which, of
course, there was a stir and everyone looked at Heney.

At last the Kid, entirely bald and certainly banjo-eyed,
was on the stand and Heney said to him, "What is your
occupation?"

"I," said the Kid gently, "am a clerk."

"A *clerk?*" Heney seemed overcome, so the judge said, "Where are you a clerk, Mr. Sorenson?"

"In the office of Luther Brown, Your Honor," said the Kid.

Heney had recovered. "As a clerk what are your duties?" he said. And added sarcastically, irritably, "If you know, that is."

"Oh, I know," said the Kid, smiling, "I sound out public opinion."

Heney had trouble believing his ears. "What public opinion?"

"Prospective jurors," the Kid said serenely.

"You carry a gun, I understand," said Heney.

Blander, more innocent if possible, the Kid said, "Every man carries a gun—sometimes, Mr. Heney."

"For what purpose do you carry a concealed weapon on your clerkly duties?" Heney said.

"I have other duties," the Kid said, and flipped his coat to show a large and tinny badge. Which Heney eyed with disfavor before he said, "You are an officer? Of WHAT?"

The Kid crossed his legs comfortably. "I am," he said primly, "an investigator for the Society of Prevention of Cruelty to Animals—the S.P.C.A."

It was no use. The judge himself was unable for a moment to bang the gavel, his head was bowed, and by then it was too late, the courtroom couldn't help it, it was hysterical.

When it subsided, Heney said, "In addition to these other duties, do you run a saloon for Earl Rogers?"

Mr. Rogers got up with absolute astonishment on his face. He said, "Mr. Heney, behave yourself, sir! I wish I'd thought to buy me one of my own in the beginning, I'd be way ahead of the game, but I didn't and you know that, sir."

A recess had to be called.

Earl Rogers had abandoned his old weapons. He was kindly, *careful* of Mr. Heney's health, but—he had them laughing at him. It helped some.

In contrast to the Kid, there was Patrick Calhoun.

To him, the President had been undoubtedly referring when he said Heney must not be deterred by the "social standing" of the men he prosecuted. He was a tall man, silvery hair, aristocratic face deeply marked now, and it surprised me that he had become a great financier. He ought to have been master of a plantation.

He asked the judge, with grave formality, a courtly bow, in a strong Southern accent, for permission to speak and when it was granted he said, "I am here, Your Honor, before a jury of my peers under the law of the country which my family has served for many years, on trial before you for my liberty and for my honor—" He had to stop and take a long breath. "This is the most important moment of my life. May I respectfully ask the protection of this court, as I have asked it of my chief counsel, as I ask it of the prosecutor, that I be tried only upon the allegations contained in the indictment brought against me." His jaw set, he drew himself to his full height, his voice trumpeted, "And not upon some cabalistic nonsense and extraneous proceedings the district attorney, who is not present in person at any time, has been imagining as a crusade having nothing to do with me nor my case."

My father looked at me, his eyebrows questioning. I had been, as usual, watching the jury. I nodded. I didn't think there was a man on it, or in the courtroom, who didn't believe the word *honor* meant much to Patrick Calhoun. They had been reminded with dignity that his was an honored name.

Maybe it was this attention to the jury I was doing for Papa that brought about Mr. Heney's next surprise move. He asked Judge Lawlor to throw Earl Rogers' daughter and the two daughters of Patrick Calhoun out of court for the duration. We were, he said, trying to influence the jury. Martha and Margaret Calhoun and I stared at him in violent indignation. The judge, it seemed to me a trifle dismayed, summoned us to the Bench. The jury, probably unaware until then of our existence, saw two of the prettiest Southern belles of all time in elegant appropriate tailored suits stand before His Honor. As for Miss Rogers in a neat Peter Thompson, she was at least, as they were, a lady. The judge admonished us. Mr. Heney objected to our flirting with the jury. Eyes cast down, we said we hadn't and wouldn't. It hadn't, actually, occurred to us before. Surely the Recording Angel can't blame me if, on my way back, I winked at the fat man in the first row. Whether the ripple of laughter was for that, or for the astounded gaze which my father turned on me at the idea of my *flirting* with anybody much less a *jury,* I cannot say.

FORTY-THREE

There had been another big conference on Earl Rogers' simple plan for the Calhoun defense. Again McEnerny had roared. *He's chief counsel, what he says goes.*

From the beginning, his tactics were different from what they had been in the Ford case. To the press he said openly he would call witnesses. Mr. Calhoun's brief moment had showed what kind of witness he would make, hadn't it? (I have always believed that my father knew Mr. Calhoun knew nothing personally of this bribery, though he might long have condoned The System. Whereas Ford *might* know enough to make him have to commit perjury, which he would do badly, if at all.)

The President was now in close, frequent communication with Heney and Hiram Johnson, leader of the new Progressive party. From Washington came rumors, dispatches, information. Earl Rogers was seeking federal court action, to find out whether, while acting as special prosecutor in trials with no federal aspect Heney had remained on the government payroll as an Assistant Attorney General. Or had he been paid entirely by the graft prosecution fund in California?

This fund was Spreckels' own.

Thus this was the first faint rumble.

Get Spreckels on the stand.

Link by link, it was forged. Rudolph Spreckels had to watch it. Hear it. I thought Spreckels began to come into court in the morning looking as though he hadn't slept as well as he used to. Heaven knows, Papa never let up on him.

In cross-examining the poor dolt who was the chief witness in this case, Supervisor Ferdinand P. Nichols, with whose bribery Calhoun was specifically charged, Mr. Heney accused Mr. Rogers of deliberately confusing the witness.

Q. (by Mr. Rogers) Mr. Nichols, do you agree with Mr. Heney's statement that you are a man easily confused?

MR. HENEY: I'm willing to stipulate he's no match for the trained mind of Earl Rogers. It takes a great deal to cope with a lawyer as tricky and misleading as Mr. Rogers.

MR. ROGERS: Perhaps the trained mind of Rudolph Spreckels will be able to cope—who can tell?

The press pricked up its ears and turned to look upon Mr. Spreckels, who had set his jaw and was staring straight ahead pretending he hadn't heard.

Several times as cross-examination of other supervisors and officials went on, Mr. Rogers would say cheerfully, "Oh we can skip that, we all know it by heart, as well as we know our Mother Goose rhymes. We know by now that Mr. Burns was quite as adept at bribery as ever they say Abe Ruef had been. Perhaps we shall have something *fresh*, a new light on all this, when Mr. Spreckels gets on the stand."

When once more he saw Big Jim Gallagher before him, Earl Rogers shook his head and heaved a sigh. Twice, three times, he said, "Never mind that, Mr. Gallagher. *This* time we shall have Mr. Spreckels' own version of the Treaty of the Presidio," or, "Mr. Spreckels' testimony as to what he said there will be the best evidence, I won't ask you about it," or, "Mr. Spreckels was there too, he can explain that to us."

Charlie Boxton, who had been mayor for a few minutes after Schmidt was convicted of malfeasance in office, sprang the trap himself. As a supervisor, he said he'd gotten five hundred dollars of the ice-rink bribe and while he had it in his hand, out popped William J. Burns with gun and camera.

"Did you know the money used in this entrapment, to force you to testify against Patrick Calhoun, came from Spreckels?" Mr. Rogers said.

"Not at the time, I didn't," Boxton said.

"But you found out later?" said Mr. Rogers, and as the witness nodded and Heney leaped up to object he went on very seriously to the judge, "Your Honor, we have in this case a special prosecutor. The district attorney of San Francisco has not chosen to appear in it. Surely we have a right to show that this prosecution was financed, paid for, by a private citizen *who owns a municipal railroad of his own*. When we have him here under oath, Mr. Spreckels will not be able to deny this."

Then as time passed came the "leak." A public relations technique of which he was past master long before the words *public relations* became part of our vocabulary and the profession a vital part of our lives. Somehow it began to leak out that *if* the prosecution did *not* call Rudolph Spreckels, Earl Rogers would. He would be Rogers' first witness for the defense no matter how hostile. The reporters came in droves to question Mr. Rogers. Was this a possibility? Mr. Rogers said it was indeed. It was more than that. It was a lead-pipe cinch.

Front pages had a big time with this one all over the country.

Years later in Washington when Hiram Johnson was the senator from California, and I was covering Huey Long for INS, I got the prosecution's side of this. I met the Johnsons at a dinner party at Cissy Patterson's, the great hostess who also owned the Washington *Times-Herald,* and Hiram filled in that piece of it. He always liked to talk of "my favorite opponent your father Earl Rogers. I consider him the best trial lawyer this country has ever had," he said, each time we met.

Before the trial began, he said, he and Heney promised Spreckels he would not have to testify. The fund he had raised could not be an issue. When they became aware that Rogers was trying to force their hand, rumors that he would call Spreckels if they didn't began to circulate, they assured Spreckels he could not be made to reveal details of prosecution finances. They would not call him. Rogers wouldn't dare.

Came the day, the headline:

ROGERS WILL CALL SPRECKELS AS FIRST DEFENSE WITNESS

"We had to face that," Senator Johnson told me, "Rogers might be bluffing. Heney thought he was. If he called Spreckels for the defense, he would be a hostile witness and Rogers, according to law, would be bound by his testimony. Heney took more hope from this than I did. We knew what your father would make of the idea that we'd been afraid to call him, or that Spreckels was as reluctant to testify as Abe Ruef had been. In the end we decided we had to put him on ourselves. Can you tell me, *would* your father have called Spreckels as a defense witness?"

"Senator," I said, "the Marines couldn't have stopped my father. His whole defense was to examine Spreckels. Besides, he wanted to get in the same ring with him."

The Big Moment that rocks the courtroom in every trial came.

Heney said, "Will you take the stand please, Mr. Spreckels?"

I never remember seeing my father happier than he was when he knew he'd won the first round. But as Spreckels walked heavily down the aisle and climbed onto the stand, nobody else was. *I* wasn't. I was glad Papa couldn't ask for a reading on my stomach at that moment, it was bleak as Greenland's icy mountains.

This was the most formidable man I'd ever seen. As he *settled*, filling the chair as completely as Gallagher but with muscle instead of fat, I had a sense he was a type my father had never dealt with. Spreckels was motivated by ambitions whose irresistible force my father never recognized or acknowledged. For the first time, I believed my father had committed the fatal error of underestimating an opponent, and this man's arbitrary power and authority.

David and Goliath. I wasn't sure a slingshot would do it.

I tried to comfort myself with the hope that the jury wouldn't *like* him. Still, at the Citizens' League of Justice meeting, Spreckels had been cheered for half an hour. He was a leading citizen, locally as big as Mr. Calhoun, a native son, a pal of Fremont Older and Jim Phelan, and I soon saw him as an impressive witness. Not eloquent, and the stronger for that. Square shoulders, head, face, an air of success shot out of him. He spoke as a successful man, used to giving orders, telling people what to do, and seeing that they did it. A jury of average citizens *weren't* his peers, they looked up to a successful millionaire. Any man in that jury box meeting Spreckels in a business deal would have been overawed by him, his position, his money.

Soon, *he* was leading Heney.

"You participated in this matter as a citizen of San Francisco?" Mr. Heney said with all the dignity and sacrifice turned on full blast.

"Yes, Mr. Heney, as a loyal citizen," said Spreckels.

"Deeply concerned for the welfare of the city in which you were born?"

"Yes."

"The disclosures of graft shocked you into action?"

"I think you may very well say so."

"Your one and only object at all times was to help right civic wrongs?"

"That is so."

"And the President of the United States is asking all good citizens at this time to do everything everywhere in this cause and has asked you, personally, to continue to do so?"

"Yes, that is a fact."

So there he was. The President of the United States. Heney had him in court now, on their side. As though he stood at Spreckels' shoulder.

For all I could *do* and though I got a big we're-all-right
expression on my face, I was a-cold. Yet as Heney said triumphantly, "Your witness, Mr. Rogers," I felt the first trickle
of hope like a prickle in your foot that's been asleep. Maybe
that big build-up about Spreckels and the President had been
a mistake. Spreckels huffed up like a bullfrog. As Earl Rogers
rose and came toward him, Spreckels looked down at him
with disdain, with contempt. Yes he did. And I knew *nobody*
had any right to look at Earl Rogers-about-to-start-a-cross-
examination with contempt. Not if it had been Teddy Roosevelt in person. So I thought, Ha! Maybe Old Ironsides is doing
a little underestimating on his own. Maybe the odds aren't as
long against us as we thought.

Rogers started quietly. No lorgnette. Nothing up his sleeve,
not even a handkerchief. He seemed anxious to get to know
Mr. Spreckels better. It was what we call a *soft* sell. Too soft.
As though he came out of his corner a little scared, sparring
to see what the other man had.

I didn't like it. I got so nervous that the sweat filled the
palms of my hands. My heart was thudding so hard I could
count it. I knew, I had to know, Papa had put the works on this
one thing. This long shot. If he could not break Spreckels, he
would lose the case. If he lost the Calhoun case, the graft
prosecution would be triumphant. The Ford case would be
regarded as one of those exceptions, Heney would be declared
the winner, Mr. Calhoun would go to jail, Earl Rogers' reputation would shrink. The defense lawyers would put all the
blame on Rogers, where of course it belonged.

All of a sudden Papa looked so *young* to me. He often did.
He and Spreckels were the same age, but Spreckels looked
middle-aged and Earl Rogers looked boyish. Like Ketchel
giving away so much weight to Johnson.

With much formality of manner, putting this on a plane
worthy of the President, Mr. Rogers took Mr. Spreckels for
a dignified walk back down the path Heney had just followed.

He elaborated it.

Emphasized it.

It made me sick.

With something verging on admiring interest, he led Mr.
Spreckels to make several speeches about Civic Virtue. The
duties of A Citizen. How these should be fulfilled, as exempli-
fied in the actions of the great Rudolph Spreckels. At length,
Mr. Rogers was concerned with, touched by, Mr. Spreckels'
love for the city of his birth, the plans for reform to be fully

inaugurated when Mr. Spreckels and his group came to power. They would rid the city of graft, which had prevailed in the reign of Abe Ruef, and—oh yes, of course, of vice also. With cold fervor, with guttural sound, all this began to echo into the future as *orders*.

Little by little a slight, a very slight, miasma entered the courtroom.

At the end of the day, the jury shifted in their seats, as though both their posteriors and their minds were getting tired.

Hours of reform could get a trifle dull.

Certainly Heney couldn't *object* to the detailed extension of his own direct questions. Nor could a judge, without objections being offered, halt a witness in such moral oratory. How could he?

But—under the manipulation of the soft-cross-examination, the image of Mr. Spreckels changed. When, on the second day, the chief counsel for the defense essayed a mild pleasantry, Mr. Spreckels wasn't having any. Life was real, life was earnest, humor was not its goal. By the end of the third day, his white plume was drooping. It almost seemed that the better one *knew* Mr. Spreckels—

Mr. Spreckels, let's face it, was *smug*.

"Now," said Mr. Rogers on the fourth day, "in this wide circle of your distinguished acquaintances, you included a Mr. Schmidt and a Mr. Ruef?"

"Slightly," the witness said, "only slightly."

"Prior to the fire, you did know a Mr. Ruef—a Mr. Abe Ruef?"

The witness unfolded his hands, which had been clasped over his stomach. "Slightly," he said again, "I may say very slightly."

"At that time," Mr. Rogers said, still friendly, "you had a discussion with Mr. Ruef, Mr. Abe Ruef, about calling a strike on United Railroads?"

For the first time, the witness hesitated. Up to then his manner had been so overbearing and authoritative that the hedging showed. "There may have been some mention of it," he said.

"*May* have been?" Mr. Rogers sounded surprised. "Mr. Spreckels, you have led us to believe in you as a businessman almost infallible in all your ways. Surely you must know whether there was a *mention* of a thing so unusual as calling a transportation strike on the city you love so well?"

"There was much chaos in the transportation operation at the time," Mr. Spreckels said.

"But it is your forte to bring order out of chaos," Mr. Rogers said. "Mr. Spreckels, please just tell us what was said."

"Well—among other things, it's difficult to recall, some conversation about the need for a municipal railway system," the witness said. "Ruef asked if I would be able to get assurance of capital—"

"You were discussing starting a street railway system with the Little Boss?" Mr. Rogers said. "Did you suspect then that Mr. Ruef was corrupt?"

"Everybody suspected it," Mr. Spreckels said.

"I see. Nevertheless, you discussed starting *your* street railway system with him. Now—Mr. Spreckels please—about the strike, remember I am asking you now about the strike that was to be called against another street railway company. What was said about that in any of these conversations you had with Abe Ruef?" Mr. Rogers said.

Everybody saw it, had to see it, my heart nearly jumped out of my mouth. Spreckels looked at Heney. The old old appeal. Unmistakable as a fighter looking at his corner when he's hurt, asking his seconds to tell him how much longer the round has to go. Heney was too smart for that, he didn't move, he knew they couldn't afford such an admission of weakness.

"Well—" said Mr. Spreckels slowly, "I—yes, something was said—he said something about it and I—I said it was impossible—or something—"

"Your memory has been so amazingly accurate," Earl Rogers said, "on all matters of civic corruption, of planned reform, of what great men have said in praise of your efforts, surely you haven't forgotten so unusual a conversation as that with the Boss about a street railway and a strike? You own a street railway yourself, don't you, Mr. Spreckels?"

"In a way—I am—" Again Spreckels was slow. He was a slow man, a deliberate man, he thought things through before he spoke at all times. Right here, however, it had to sound reluctant as a witness can get.

"Let's go into that later." Having lit that fuse under the man on the stand, Mr. Rogers left it. "Now can we conclude this about what Ruef said to you and what you said to Ruef. There *was* something said, wasn't there?"

"Yes—certainly—"

Then the gun barked for the first time. "What was said?

What did you say to the Boss? What did the Boss say to you? Answer me."

Slow, dark German anger turned Spreckels' neck dark. "He suggested a strike—I was horrified—"

"Doubtless," Earl Rogers said, moving in. "Yet a thing that could so horrify you was so easily forgotten that you had difficulty in recalling it. Go on, please. What did your slight acquaintance Mr. Ruef have to say, how did he dare to say it to a pillar of society like yourself?"

Watchful now, careful, a man walking through a field in the Black Forest he knows to be mined, Spreckels said, "He said of course I knew his connections with union labor, that he could tie up the whole town, when he did this he'd like to see somebody else bid for a streetcar franchise."

Smiling, shaking his head, Mr. Rogers said, "This slight acquaintance knew you might get the capital and then bid for a street railway franchise and he was offering to throw the town into chaos, bring it to a standstill before the fire did so, and then hand it over to you?"

"I didn't take him seriously," Mr. Spreckels said.

"You didn't take *Abe Ruef* seriously in a matter involving a franchise?" Earl Rogers said. "Did you report this extraordinary conversation to anyone?"

"Who was there to report it to?" Mr. Spreckels said.

"You had no faith in your grand jury then—such as you acquired when it was a matter of Calhoun's franchises later? Nor in Fremont Older's newspaper? You hadn't then become a crusader?"

"I didn't take him seriously," Mr. Spreckels said again.

"But you did organize a street railway company?"
"Yes."

"And call it the Municipal Railway Corporation?"
"Yes."

"You own the controlling stock?"
"Yes."

"Only the fire and the earthquake halted Mr. Ruef's strike?"

In open fury, Mr. Spreckels glared. He said loudly, "I don't know what Mr. Ruef might have done and neither do you."

"However," Mr. Rogers said, "you did take part in an activity later to get immunity for Abe Ruef, didn't you? In the plans to give your slight acquaintance immunity after he had testified to your satisfaction against Ford and Calhoun and the *United* Railroads?"

"I knew some form of immunity was being discussed, yes.

It was always my understanding that Ruef was to take some punishment."

"You're in favor of punishment, aren't you, Mr. Spreckels?"

My mind kept asking all the time *why* Spreckels was answering these questions. Why he didn't refuse to give any details? All in a flash, I knew the answer. Hiram Johnson, grim, tenacious, realistic, wasn't sure that in a pinch Mr. Rogers might not call *Abe Ruef*. He could, of course.

"You heard Mr. Gallagher's testimony," Rogers said, "seven or eight times, you've heard it."

"Yes."

Q. (by Mr. Rogers) You heard this man whom you knew to be venal and corrupt testify that you met with him on many occasions to plan immunity for the bribe-takers?

A. Yes, I heard him.

Q. You never heard Gallagher mention punishment without any hope of immunity for anyone except Calhoun and Ford, did you?

A. They were the ones—

Q. The ones you were out to get, weren't they?

A. They were the ones accused of serious corruption. Bribery—

Q. You heard Gallagher testify that you met with him inside the Presidio to arrange immunity for the officials who took the bribes?

A. Yes.

Rogers was crowding him now, hammering, punching like a piston, the Dempsey *one two one two one two one two one two*.

Q. He mentioned Ruef?

A. Yes.

Q. Was anything said about *punishment* for your friend Ruef?

A. I don't remember—

I swallowed a wild shout. When a witness said, *I don't remember,* he was on the floor. Not for the count maybe, but you could score it a knockdown. It went on and on. If the testimony of Gallagher was incorrect—Why on federal territory? Who suggested the meetings in the Presidio?—never pausing in his question, never taking his eyes off the man on the stand. Earl Rogers backed up to the counsel table. A member of the defense battery, A. A. Moore, put in his hands a sheaf of three or four sheets of paper. As he watched, Heney's face was a mask, the scar livid across it. If this man Spreckels gets angrier, I thought, he will be as dangerous as a wounded rhinoceros.

"You were the real head of the graft prosecution here, weren't you?" Rogers said.

"I was not, I am not," said Spreckels, "I am merely a public-minded citizen trying to do my duty."

Rogers spoke to Moore, at the counsel table, Moore dug into boxes, came up with another paper. Rogers took out his lorgnette, examined it, gave a big *that's-the-one* nod. He was saying absently, "The final decisions are always with you, aren't they?"

"They are not," Spreckels said, "they are with the special prosecutor."

"But Mr. Spreckels," Earl Rogers said plaintively, "*you* hired Mr. Heney, didn't you?"

"I did not," Spreckels said with terrible violence. "He volunteered to give his aid to the city and county of San Francisco."

"You wish to use the word volunteered?" Rogers said.

"I do, yes I do," Spreckels said.

A pause grew and grew and grew. Rogers studied the papers. The judge looked at him questioningly. When Rogers raised his head he said in a clear cold carrying voice, "How much money have you paid Mr. Heney?"

Once long afterwards, I saw that same movement made by another witness. Bruno Richard Hauptmann on trial for the kidnaping of the Lindbergh baby, moved back, shoved against the back of the witness chair, trying to get away from one question asked by Attorney General Wilentz. Heney knew what that back-pedaling meant, he came up now trying to divert the attack, he didn't throw in the sponge of course, but he did what he could in loud ringing tones. He was sure Spreckels would recover, he would give him a little time to get his breath. After a good deal of this, the judge held that Rogers could ask this question. "If Mr. Spreckels knows," the court said.

"Mr. Spreckels is a businessman and financier of note," Earl Rogers said. "I should find it surprising if he didn't know what he has paid one of his employees. How much have you paid Mr. Heney, Mr. Spreckels, *if you know?*"

"I can't say exactly."

"You paid all his office expenses?"

"Yes."

"You paid all the expenses of William J. Burns, a detective for Mr. Heney, and of his operatives who collected the evidence in this case?"

"Yes, I paid Mr. Burns."

"*If you know*, will you tell this jury how much you have spent on this prosecution to date?"

Into the valley of death rode Heney and Johnson, they volleyed and thundered, another battle of monumental noise took place. Finally the judge said yes, if Mr. Spreckels knew, he must answer.

Waving the papers, this time Rogers went right up under Spreckels' nose. "If he doesn't know," he said, "I am prepared to refresh his memory."

Only one word for it. The newspapers used it the next day. *Cringed.* They said Rudolph Spreckels cringed. I couldn't believe it. I had expected him to show fight. I thought when it got real tough he would be a menace, a threat, he had been looking at Earl Rogers for days threatening to have his entrails scattered in Union Square. Now here he was *cringing*.

"Do you KNOW?" Rogers asked.

Spreckels said, "I'd have to check my records—"

"Will you do that?" Rogers said, beaming, waving the papers, which not only the jury but everybody else could see were records of some kind. "If you don't care to leave the courtroom," Mr. Rogers said, "we will stipulate that these are correct." Well, they could have been a C.P.A.'s figures of what Spreckels had paid Heney or a new chess opening of Capablanca's. If it was a bluff, nobody called it.

After the noon recess, Spreckels took the stand in dark and sullen fury, and read the disbursements of his Municipal Railway.

William J. Burns	$123,250

Looking at his own papers through the lorgnette, Rogers nodded.

Francis J. Heney	$ 13,828

"No no," Rogers said quickly, shaking his head. They had some bits of wrangling over Miscellany and Associates and finally Rogers said, "It all comes to $215,374 to date—is that correct?"

"I believe so," Spreckels said.

"All this came out of the funds of the Municipal Railway, out of the half million dollars you put up to start yourself a street railway line in this city—is that right?"

"Yes," Spreckels said.

"Come right down to it," Rogers said, "this was your money actually spent by your Municipal Railway and by you, its president, to convict Patrick Calhoun, president of the United Railroads, wasn't it?"

There was no answer.

Suddenly into the guilty confession of silence, Earl Rogers said, "There is an item I don't understand. Perhaps, you can explain this $3785 dollars—isn't it?—and this word here—can you explain that?"

Rudolph Spreckels looked down at the paper Rogers held out to him. From the top of his stiff collar he went a fiery painful red.

"Turkeys," the witness said, mopping his brow.

Earl Rogers threw the papers into the air like confetti. He threw the lorgnette the length of its black ribbon. He threw back his head with a howl of uncontrollable, irresistible laughter.

"Oh Mr. Spreckels," he cried, "not Tammany Hall turkeys from the Reformers?"

The courtroom began to laugh, the jury began to laugh, to the lilting accompaniment of that laughter, Rudolph Spreckels obeyed the limp gesture of dismissal Rogers made and came down off the stand.

That was the end of the Calhoun trial, in all truth.

There was one more moment I like to remember.

During the last recess while Heney was making his last bid for martyrdom and his final attempt to save the graft prosecution, enter Miss Ethel Barrymore, San Francisco's favorite actress.

Sweeping into the courtroom, she embraced Earl Rogers, and sat down beside him, holding his hand and listening for a time to Heney's argument. At that time Ethel Barrymore was about as beautiful, queenly, and eye-catching as a woman could be. So that as she sat through the speech, courteously quiet and motionless as she was, the jury's eyes did drift toward her. As he finished she waited a polite time and then got up, went over and kissed Patrick Calhoun, and said, "Dear Mr. Calhoun, I'm sure you'll be acquitted. We all know you're innocent. And I'm so glad you had Earl, you know he defended my brother Jack—" She bestowed a sisterly kiss upon Earl Rogers and swept out again. Even Heney watched her go.

I think that and a good many other things about Earl Rogers always bewildered Heney. Nothing could ever make him believe that *boredom* was a factor in high political questions. Nor humor, for that matter.

The jury was ten to two for acquittal.

That turned out to be good enough. Francis J. Heney when he ran for district attorney at the next election was defeated, and Fickert, the big Stanford fullback who got in, never tried any more graft cases.

As I said in the beginning, it was difficult to know which side was right and I ended up thinking they were both right and both wrong.

In a magazine of national circulation, the famous graft prosecution never received the support it expected in the Ford and Calhoun trials. Papa was pleased when the highly respected *Harper's Weekly* ran a series of articles accepting, in the main, the contentions he'd made, practically admitting that the prosecution had been a failure and possibly done more harm than good. I don't believe that was true. For they were followed by Hiram Johnson and his Progressive party, which destroyed the hold of the Southern Pacific Octopus and broke The System. When Johnson ran for governor and later for senator, Earl Rogers supported him.

Nation in an editorial said, "Even a reformer cannot turn despot and run the machinery of government himself without provoking an immediate reaction. The best kind of reform is that which comes from the people themselves, by regular democratic means and not that which emanates from a handful of men financed by the well-filled purse of a business rival of some of the men accused of wrong doing."

That summed up Rogers' defense of Patrick Calhoun. To me, that was his real genius—always to *see* that one fatal point.

Again, Lincoln Steffens, who had been part of the muckraking, spoke with helpful honesty when he wrote, "President Roosevelt had given the Prosecution his full personal support, without being aware of some of the facts."

Such as the Municipal Railway and the reason for the Morris Haas disaster. This didn't make them any easier to defend against at the time.

Spreckels made public a long letter which he received from the President, exhorting him not to be discouraged because men of wealth and power had banded against him. "I want you to feel," Roosevelt wrote, "that your experience is simply that of all engaged in this fight." Soon after that, however, Roosevelt made the move to interfere in the matter of the Japanese school children and his support became a detriment in a city which feared then and until the day it happened the probability of a war with Japan.

As for men of wealth, Heney got what Spreckels gave him and $45,000 salary from the United States Government while he was acting as special prosecutor on Spreckels' payroll in California.

Earl Rogers ended up far far from being a man of wealth. From Patrick Calhoun he had received the largest single fee ever paid to a court trial lawyer up to that day.

He could always spend it faster than even Calhoun could pay it, especially in San Francisco.

So we ended up broke as usual. But *happy*. Fortunately, Papa had the temperament to do a lot of the things he did. You have to have the temperament to go with them, I found that out.

FORTY-FOUR

The McComas case was a fine, gory sex murder if ever there was one.

My father, who knew a lot about the subject, seeing how many murderers he defended, said murder always had, did, and would exercise irresistible fascination for people because it was the maximum passion.

"Above all things," Papa said, when the McComas case was our *cause célèbre*, "man yearns to feel. To care. To want or not want at the peak. He can never escape deep curiosity, response, even envy of the man who has cared enough about something to break the fundamental law, *Thou shalt not kill.* He is looking at the utmost height or depth of love . . . hate . . . greed . . . fear . . . revenge . . . which has driven a man to take human life. This heyday of the blood, hot or cold, of the murderer who kills the thing he hates or loves or fears or lusts after, casts a spell over the man whose emotional life is tepid, lukewarm, sluggish. Great writers, great stories, how many of them deal with murder? From *Huckleberry Finn* to *Hamlet*, from the *Iliad* to *Oliver Twist*, from *The Brothers Karamazov* to *The Virginian*, the stories of our own West, of our Civil War—of all war—these are games of life and death. They let the reader live vicariously at the utmost horror and delight of feeling—his lust for life, too feeble in him to act, is satisfied by seeing it in others. When it's *real*—as the Mc-Comas murder is *real*—they can't escape it."

For over a year, McComas, a famed gambler from Arizona, had been keeping his mistress, Charlotte Noyes, in a fashion-able apartment-hotel facing West Lake Park. When the cops got there, Charlotte Noyes, in silk nightgown and black satin kimono, lay in a pool of her blood. McComas' face was raw with vitriol, by that time he was raving in agony. The empty bottle lay near Mrs. Noyes's dead hand, half-hidden by her long, loose black hair. She'd thrown the hellbrew, the man told them. He was insane with pain and shock, and his blind instinct had been to shoot his assailant. He was, everybody knew, one of the fastest guns in the West. The police had many questions, and some other theories. *All* the bullets had hit Mrs. Noyes in the heart. Granted McComas' reputation with a gun, this was too good shooting in the dark, blinded by acid. Neighbors in the hotel had heard quarrels, Mrs. Noyes crying out that he was tired of her, wanted to get rid of her, but she'd never give him up. There had been too long a delay between the shots and the time Mac called the police station. Furthermore in those days it was just plain held against a man if he shot a woman even if she was no lady.

Passions of many kinds, flaming whole-hog, wild and woolly had been loose in McComas' love nest on that hot sum-mer night.

Look how soon The First Murderer appears, Papa said. It is Cain, hands dripping with the blood of Abel, who cries, Am I my brother's keeper? The cry of the murderer. For man must be his brother's keeper, Papa said.

"Man has two great fears," he told me, "more haunting and terrible than the unknown, which he will always explore. He is more afraid of missing *life while he is alive* than he is of death. He is afraid to be alone, from the moment he's born until the moment he dies. In these, these fears, not in mere lust lies the dominant appeal to sex. Sex is not only a physical desire, a bodily heat. It originates in the heart of man, who desires not to be alone. In the mind of man, which greatly desires not to *miss* anything, not to go out into the nameless void from which he came never having known *life*. Sometimes he can believe that sex fulfills both these desires." He stopped there and looked at me with a great air of bravado. He said, "I have never talked to you about sex, I daresay I should, shouldn't I?"

Impossible today to imagine how taboo, how forbidden, what Bad Taste and embarrassment surrounded the *mention* of sex. A ban existed equivalent to a smallpox flag on the door. My mother never talked to me about anything, but if she had sex wouldn't have been included. My grandmother, advanced and broad-minded enough to take me to see the Angels play the Seals and teach me to keep a score card, would have smacked me if I'd asked her any questions about marriage relations. Books had it *in* them, but without any descriptions such as are now given wholesale, ad nauseam, ad boredom.

My father was not exactly embarrassed but he looked severe and stern and a little defiant in breaking this barrier. "Sex," he said, "is part of love, but it is not all of love. It's like money—if you have it, you don't have to think about it; it's when you don't have it trouble can come. Love begins in the heart not in the body. You must never let love become the slave of sex. Then the universe is without meaning, the potter is tool of the pot. Love begins in the heart, expresses itself in the mind—the body is the instrument for its fulfillment. If you let love become enchained by the body's needs or subject to the body's pitiless tyranny—sex is your master, degrading, cruel, without hope."

He wasn't talking to me. He had forgotten me. I could see him in some arid land of his own, carrying his chains across a hot desert. I could hear Dolly saying, *Oh, she'll be back. She's got a hold on him, she'll always be back.* I was shocked and scared to have such thoughts of my own father and mother but they had come without my volition. I knew now that the quarrels I'd heard and Papa crying that day in the garden at school under the magnolia tree could come only from sex. As the acid had been flung that night in Mrs. Noyes' voluptuous rooms by a hand gone berserk with jealousy. I thought *we* had been lucky not to have had a gun go off sometimes. Maybe everybody is.

Yet the things Papa said to me about sex were oddly gentle and simple.

Always the same theme. A man's reach was exceeding his grasp—I felt that. A thing that was *rare* brought joy and beauty, not a thing that was common. He told me never to forget that sex *without* love could never compare to the fulfillment of sex *with* love. He said that as to the act of love, there were three parts and if any one of them was missing, we were cheated. Anticipation, expectation, first. Then fulfillment. And then the shared immediate memory, which he said was closer sometimes than the act itself.

Somehow for once I didn't feel that Papa *knew* altogether what he was talking about the way he usually did. Maybe he was being poetical on my account—a father talking to his daughter. But I felt it was on his own account, too. He had missed this. He didn't want me to miss it too.

A strange way to learn about sex, the McComas-Noyes murder. Looking back, in some ways I can't imagine a better one.

It showed me, and everybody else in town who was talking about little else, what not to do.

And as the newspapermen said, this was one of those stories that *had everything*—including Indians.

McComas was a part Clark Gable played often. Or Jim Garner as Maverick. Mac was a big man with wide shoulders and a small waist and no hips; the way he moved it was impossible not to feel he usually wore a belt and a six-gun. His hair was powdered with silver, his eyes were blue, a little too light in color, and he had that mocking expression not quite a smile that turned up one corner of his mouth and lifted one eyebrow. Most of the time his voice had a faint rasp of banter in it. In Arizona, he had been considered a *when-you-call-me-that-smile* customer, on the wrong side of the law part of the time, but then who wasn't?

Though there was some squawk about it, my father got him out on bail because he still had to go to the hospital every day to have the doctor treat his burns.

One night he told Papa and me about the Indians.

His father and mother had been killed in a raid. His little brother was carried off and never heard of again but the older boy was left for dead. When he came to, he remembered it all. His mother in the grip of a naked savage with feathers and war paint. His father being struck again and again with the tomahawk, flung in a crumpled heap, lying beside him now.

The smell of the slaughter was in his nostrils. The wordless, witless terror of two days and nights alone with the bodies before he was rescued bit deep, so that he never got away from any detail of it and never would.

"When you live with things like that," Mac said, without any expression at all, "you have to live fast and furious. An hour or a day at a time. Keep a-movin'. Play for more than you can afford. Ride faster, drink heavier, never be alone at night. Eat drink and be merry because you saw people die *yesterday*, your people, and you know life isn't worth living so you're quite willing to die and that gives you a reputation for cold nerve."

Often I thought of Mac when, in the Second World War, I knew in Washington some of the famed Polish Squadron of the RAF, who had the reputation for cold steel courage and deviltry against the enemy. One of them said to me, "We are dead men. We are men already dead. After what we saw done to our mothers and sisters we must die as soon as possible. So we move toward it faster, we dare more than men who wish to live. Desiring death, we cannot fear it."

So McComas grew up with the West along with Wyatt Earp and Bat Masterson and Wild Bill Hickok; he roamed Kansas and New Mexico and Arizona; he got an education by reading; he called me Little Nell and I was rather touched because I thought he meant out of *The Old Curiosity Shop* but it turned out it was Faro Nell, who was the lookout for Cherokee Hall in Wolfville. He taught me to play faro, a game I have always liked very much. In fact he taught me what it was to have a gambling streak in you—he had it and so did I.

After he told us about the Indians, I said to my father, "Do you believe that?"

Papa looked at me in surprise. He said, "Oh yes. In the first place he isn't that good—either as a dramatist or an actor. And anyhow, I checked it. It's well known." He gave me a grin and said, "Don't start playing Desdemona to his Othello—he was just there, he didn't do anything much."

I said, "Don't be so silly," and Papa said, "Well, he has to beat women off with clubs, they tell me." "Not me he won't," I said.

This wasn't entirely accurate.

No man can ever be as attractive any other time or place as a man who knows how he can be on horseback. McComas was as good as they come.

One Sunday morning we were all riding with the vaqueros,

and Papa was way up ahead with Dr. Shurtleff and some others and Mac kept dropping back with me all the time. I had a mare named Rainbow and I was having a little trouble with her. She took off and jumped a gate, by the time I got her back on the trail we couldn't see a soul. As we rode along slow, letting Rainbow cool off, Mac said, "I saw Pearl Morton the other day."

"I want to see her," I said, "but she won't let me come."

He said, "She says you're too big now."

"First she told me I was too little," I said, "now I'm too big."

He laughed, and said, "She thinks a lot of you."

The laugh, the way he looked on a horse, in spite of the bandages under his hat like a white cap. I felt excited and angry. I'd been dying to ask him some questions, but I hadn't been able to get up nerve enough, now I could. I said, "Aren't you sorry you killed her?" His horse whirled sideways, as though the spurs had dug in unexpectedly. My breath came short and funny but I didn't care. I said, "Don't you wake up nights in a cold sweat and miss her? And she's dead and *you did it?*"

We let the horses walk along. I felt simply awful, honestly. I knew I had been fresh and ill-mannered but I couldn't help it. How would I ever again get a chance to ask a man face to face how it felt to *kill*—to *have* killed—the thing he loved, or had loved? I'd been eaten up with curiosity. Papa was right, this showed me how violence of emotion—*murder*—could get you churning around and around it, fascinated. That hand right there on the silver bridle, it had shot a woman he loved. I kept thinking about her, about Charlotte Noyes. I'd never seen her, but she'd had lots of pictures, they were beautiful. Not the way women in murders are always called beautiful, which of course in a way they are. A woman must have been Venus to whoever killed her, to inspire such passion. I have gone since to cover a story when I knew the murderer had walked around a house for hours in darkness consumed by jealousy as mad as Marc Antony's, and, unable to bear it, had gone in and killed the other man; when I went in myself I found a slattern with no chin and with greasy skin. Charlotte Noyes had been soft and dark, with a lovely, big, generous mouth, unusual in those days when the tiny cupid's bow was the feminine ideal.

What I was trying to understand was the *arc* of change, the degrees from love to hate, from desire to destruction.

These same two—the graceful, cold-eyed man riding beside me, the sun showing the silver hair on the side free of bandage, the gay handkerchief at his throat. And the beautiful woman who'd died in a silk nightgown and a black satin kimono. Many many nights when she'd heard his step she'd run to the door wild with joy to welcome him. He'd laughed with pleasure, he had a big warm *teasing* laugh, and hugged her so tight she could hardly breathe. I knew they had gone to bed together, and held each other, and talked and whispered and gone to sleep side by side.

How could it *be* that these very same two people—one night when he entered she wanted to burn his face, make him repulsive, give him *pain*, maybe rob him of his sight forever? How could he even to save himself feel so differently that he could pour bullets into her heart?

What happened? What happened to people? How could it?

It must be terrible for them and everybody around them, the coinage debased, nobody speaking the same language any more.

Mac had shoved his hat back and was grinning at me derisively. I was glad he didn't have anything to do with *me*. The skin on his face, I saw, was faintly red and very thin, like peeling after sunburn—that was where the acid had hit. In a low sarcastic voice he said, "Kids always ask embarrassing questions."

"Well," I said, "you do not have to answer them if you do not want to. I just asked because I am curious about people."

"All right," he said. "No, I am not sorry. It was her or me."

"But you are always saying you don't care whether you live or die," I said, "on account of the Indians."

"You can't let suicide be thrust upon you," Mac said. "You have to play fair or you might as well go do it yourself. That's a coward's way."

I said, "My father doesn't think it's cowardly, he thinks a man has a right to—he and Jack London and Sterling and all of them."

"They're thinkers," Mac said, "your father's a poet. For me—it'd be yellow."

"Did you—were you tired of her?" I said.

"Yes," he said, and I never heard one syllable mean so much.

So that was what the dark soft Charlotte had seen. Probably, I thought, his eyes didn't light up any more. Probably a woman in love could *tell*. It must be awful. I said, "Had you found somebody else you liked better?"

"No," Mac said, and gave me another funny look.

Mrs. Noyes had known. Mac has to fight the women off with clubs, Papa had said. I didn't see why but I knew already that *why* is of all words the one hardest to find the answers for. After he'd gone to sleep at night and she couldn't, her imagination, even if she only had a small amount, would remember what it had been like when she and Mac first met. Their first kiss. She would know how it would be when he saw some other woman. Even the same words, the same kisses. She'd thrown the vitriol so nobody else would ever want him, if she couldn't have him no other woman should, she'd known what it was *like* to be unwanted.

Of course she ought to have known Mac and that fast gun of his.

Maybe she did. Maybe she wanted to die by his hand.

My heart was beating hard just trying to understand what a man and woman had felt that led to *murder*.

"She loved you," I said. He looked at me and shut his eyes. I said, "Did you—" I felt ashamed, but murder makes you so *curious*.

He shrugged, he said, "Oh yes—for a month—a week—twenty minutes. Don't let anybody kid you, sister. Love goes up and what goes up has to come down. It's easier if you face it. You hit a peak, climb a peak, you try to stay up there but you never can. That's why your Pa drinks—"

I got sore then, I hadn't given him an invitation to talk to me about whether my father drank or didn't drink. After all he was just a man we were defending for murder. I turned and the mocking smile was back, he said, "He keeps looking for something that won't come down. See? Anyhow, I've done one thing for him." He pulled the hat back down so it hid the bandages, and the patch was back over his eyes. He sat there swaggering on his horse, the way a first-class horseman can. He said, "He's a genius, he cares more about his work than anything, that's the real joy he has. He'd sacrifice anything to build a perfect case, the way a painter does to paint a picture. I set him up a big canvas. This is one that's going to take all the genius he's got. That's the breath of life to him, he don't need anything else then."

I was surprised. I said, "This is an easy case, isn't it?"

Mac yipped. "You got any idea how unpopular I am around

here? They're out to get me. That D.A. would rather hang me than be governor."

"You specially?" I said.

"He's a gentleman," he said, "shooting a lady is outside his code. He's after your Pa, too, all out. He's figuring on making real trouble for him. He thinks he's got a hand that will take the pot this time."

"Has he?" I said.

"I think your Pa needs to fill his hand on the draw," Mac said slowly, "and—Pearl's worried about him."

"Pearl is a worrier," I said. "He's been all right lately."

"Pearl said stay in there and she'll come a-runnin' if you holler," he said. "So will I if I'm at liberty which I don't expect to be. The doctor give me my discharge, and so I reckon I'll be back in jail shortly."

I said, "Sometime ask Pearl whatever became of Dolly, will you?"

He swung around to me so quickly both horses reared a little and began to gallop. "Don't you know?" he said, and— I did. Whenever I'd thought about Dolly I'd never been able to *find* her. She'd gone. Mac said, "She was a good kid. She couldn't go back, it turned out."

I said, "I was too little, at that. I didn't think about—going back. She loved us. Wasn't there anybody—couldn't she— couldn't somebody help her?"

"Not after that self-righteous holier-than-thou friend of yours got through with her," Mac said in an icy rasp of a voice.

"Don't say that!" I said. "He wasn't like that." But I didn't know how to explain. Now it did seem harsh and unkind and unnecessary to me, too. Every time you got mixed up with *God*, there it was. Yet somewhere my—my instinct told me there was a *reason* way way back. If you added two and two and got seven and a half it would come out wrong. Come unto me and I will give you rest, my grandfather used to read to me; we didn't come to him and we got hell. Dolly doing what she'd done and then we blamed God—I blamed him—for being a scourge and a lash to us. I kept trying to find out *why* about so many things. I knew Dr. Burdette had done it on my account, and Dolly and I had loved each other, now it all seemed harsh and unkind.

I said in a rush, "Mac—do you think with Papa it could ever be like Dr. Jekyll?" It was *out*, I'd said it. It had been inside me like I'd swallowed a cactus pear for a long time, and no-

body I could ask. Now I knew Mac understood Papa, and
Mac was a man who'd had lots of experience, so though I
hadn't forgiven him for shooting Mrs. Noyes I could ask him.
"Dr. Jekyll took the drink and became Mr. Hyde, and at first
he could get back just as easy. It got harder, and harder, to
get back to be *Dr. Jekyll* and sometimes he turned into Mr.
Hyde without taking it, and in the end he couldn't get back
—he had to stay Mr. Hyde. Could that—happen?"

"No it could not," Mac said bluntly, and I felt better.

It was a good thing I asked it then. The next day the judge
canceled his bail and the sheriff picked him up and put him
in jail.

Our office was part of Danny Green's beat. Danny was the
Examiner's star crime reporter, a lean, redheaded, parrot-
profile young man, with the true reporter's walk, as though he
owned the earth and all doors would open to him, which must
be, otherwise freedom of the press is gone and we are lost.

He brought us news of what the district attorney was cooking up for us.

"I hear," Danny said, sitting on the edge of my father's big
table and lighting a cigarette, "that McComas called you right
after he shot her, before he called the cops and you told him
to put the vitriol on his face. *He* said to you that she had a
bottle of vitriol and had threatened to throw it. *You* said to
him that it would be easier to acquit him if she *had* thrown
it. So Mr. McComas *then* threw the acid himself on himself
and called the cops."

Paul Schenck was in our office by that time, a big loud
fellow, a real nice guy, and a lousy lawyer, and he started to
bellow and rave. My father held up one finger and Paul shut
up.

"That would take a lot of nerve on McComas' part," my
father said.

"It would," Danny Green agreed. "If there is one thing for
which McComas is noted and of which he has an abundance
it is cold nerve."

"Yes," said Mr. Rogers, "yes. However, this is all an imaginative concept created by the D.A.'s office in a fevered sort of
way. A fantasy. How does he propose to prove any of it, do
you know, Danny?"

"McComas did telephone you first," Danny said, making it
a statement.

"Many of my clients do," Earl Rogers said. "I have always

told them—Call me and keep your mouth shut. Too many men weave a rope of words with which to hang themselves, as I've said to you before."

"Did Mac call you first?" Danny said.

"Let us wait and see what Captain Fredericks can make of it in court," my father said with a grin. "I fear I loom too large in the district attorney's approach to a case. They are bent on causing my discomfort—"

"And disbarment," Danny said, tossing his cigarette out the window.

"I'm afraid so, poor fellows," Mr. Rogers said softly, "and of course they are embarrassed by the finding of the second gun."

"They are not embarrassed," Danny said, "they are hydrophobic. They say you planted it."

"Fredericks' own men found it," Earl Rogers said, "and it hasn't much to do with anything. You remember it was in the blankets at the foot of her bed? It merely gives weight to my idea that my client had reason to enter Mrs. Noyes' room on the alert for danger. His hand on his gun perhaps? She kept that little pearl-handled weapon and had tried to use it on him twice before."

"Can *you* prove *that?*" Danny said.

Earl Rogers grinned at him, his chin out. He didn't say anything more.

Paul Schenck was carrying on so about the *insult* to Mr. Rogers that I began to think *he* had let out the news about that telephone call. Somebody had. Bluff, hail-fellow-well-met, carried his liquor well, Paul loved to hang around Joe Fast's and the Waldorf with newspapermen and detectives. He never meant harm or disloyalty, he just talked too much. Not like big fat Mexican Frank Dominguez—our nemesis who took the Bundy case. Frank talked all the time in three languages and might as well have been singing "Juanita," for all the good it did anybody. Schenck liked to hint that he was in the know, had deep dark secrets, and sometimes the hints went far enough so a smart reporter like Danny could pin them down. Schenck was a useful, hard-working member of Earl Rogers' staff but sometimes he got spotlight-hungry.

Q. (by Mr. Rogers) Did Mrs. Noyes fire a shot at you that night?

A. (McComas) No no—she did not.

Q. But she had fired at you on two previous occasions?
A. Yes—

Naturally after objections from the D.A. this was stricken from the record by the judge's orders. Papa was familiar, however, with the jury's subconscious long before that word became part of our thinking and vocabulary. Even *honest* jurors who tried to strike testimony from their minds, and thought they had, kept it buried somewhere out of sight and mind and in the end it might add a grain of sand to a wavering scale.

Anyhow, that was all Earl Rogers ever did with the second gun, which Woolwine insisted hysterically Rogers had *planted* in Mrs. Noyes's bed. I am not saying he hadn't. I do say the D.A.'s own men found it, though they'd searched before, and that the murder rooms had been kept under lock and key at all times. Fredericks never explained how or when the planting was done.

After Danny had gone, from then on I was aware that my father did not have in hand or mind a real defense in the McComas case. Kidding Danny, sending men to Arizona, spending hours in jail with Mac, reading over and over reports of his examinations by police and transcripts of the preliminaries, he was balked, it was driving him loco, which meant running in circles, batting your head against walls and howling like a coyote. I thought about what McComas had said of Earl Rogers' being an *artist*. The case was an occasion for his genius, set up like a vast canvas, Papa was walking around and around it in a frenzy, unable to *paint*, drawing and erasing, experimenting and wiping it off, mixing colors that never suited him, flinging palette and brushes out the window.

They would *hang* McComas. And disbar *him*.

We went loco with him, we were an asylum of walking-around nervous-prostration cases, when on the night after we started getting a jury—or rather at 4 A.M. the following morning—he came charging out of his office in a war dance. In tones of a four-alarm fire he began hollering for Giesler.

He had found two words.

Literally, two words. In the flat, routine medical statement of Dr. Campbell, the autopsy surgeon.

Return spray. Those were the two words—*return spray.*

FORTY-FIVE

We went into court co-defendants with McComas.

The dramatic story that McComas had called Earl Rogers, who had told him to put the vitriol on his own face, had now been told, retold, and lost nothing in the telling. A majority of people believed it. A lot of them considered it a brilliant idea, forgetting that if the district attorney's office could prove it the Bar Association would promptly remove the name of Earl Rogers from the list of those permitted to practice law in the State of California.

When the trial of the state's charge that McComas had murdered Charlotte Noyes began before a jury, Earl Rogers' well-known insistence that the defense counsel must always put the defendant on the stand in a murder case meant that the prosecution would have a chance to examine McComas under oath in this matter. Captain John D. Fredericks had chosen Paul Fleming to head his battle attack and Fleming was a remarkable, appealing courtroom lawyer, a brave and intelligent man of talent and integrity. Like all Westerners of that day Mr. Fleming had a lot of chivalry where women were concerned. Women hadn't as yet come down to be the equals of men and Mr. Fleming, who as I remember it had the hot blood of the South in his veins, believed that all women had a right to protection and even the best of it if possible. Of all the district attorneys we worked against my father liked Thomas Lee Woolwine (another Southerner) the most, thought Asa Keyes was the most brilliant, but gave Paul Fleming top marks for courtroom ability. He was also aware and reminded us of it frequently that Fleming had a real tug at a jury's feelings, something most district attorneys' men lacked.

So with Captain Fredericks as coach, as it were, Fleming at quarterback, and the entire district attorney's office ready to play, we had as dangerous opposition as we ever got.

The district attorney's examination—made by Fleming—of Dr. Campbell was routine and dull. Turning him over to Mr. Rogers for cross, he had so little idea of what was coming that he looked surprised when Rogers got to his feet to approach the witness.

Nobody but Harry Carr showed any special interest until Danny Green, who always kept an eye on Carr to see what he was up to, noted that Harry didn't go out for a smoke at this point. So neither did Danny.

As a trial lawyer, Earl Rogers created new technique in examining so-called expert witnesses. Until his work pioneered this road, each side put on its experts, they testified for their own side, nobody knew enough about it to value their decisions, and nobody could ask any questions to discompose their conclusions. Juries quit paying attention; expert testimony had become a dirty word. Also the dullest part of any trial.

As did his favorite character Sherlock Holmes, Earl Rogers always knew the expert's subject as well or better than he did himself. The great Holmes could identify the ashes of a trichinopoly cigar at a glance, tell the murderer's height by the length of his stride, name the newspaper in which a story had appeared anywhere in the empire from two printed words, inform you what county a man came from by the dust in his trouser cuff. In what was then an entirely new legal tradition, Earl Rogers was as much master of ballistics for the three cops, banking in the Hays case, medical intestines in the affair of the plumber and the cotillion leader, and now return spray in the McComas—and it might be the *Earl Rogers*—case.

Another dazzling advantage this ceaseless all-night study gave him. Nobody can find anything dramatic or convincing unless they understand it. Up to now most expert testimony might as well have been given in Tagalog, Osmanli, or Zulu-Kaffir. *Simplify,* Charles Dickens cried to his writers on Household Words, and simplify simplify simplify was Earl Rogers' rule and word and deed with specialists and their specialties. Then he could impress and dramatize.

Watching him in the matter of return spray, I saw him catch first the judge, the reporters, one by one the jurors.

Direct examination had been short, dull, routine, of no importance, it appeared. Charlotte Noyes had been shot through the heart. Three bullets had been found. Death had been instantaneous. That's all, Dr. Campbell. No mention of spray, return or otherwise, of vitriol, nor any other acid had been made.

"Dr. Campbell," said Earl Rogers quietly, "you used the term 'return spray.'"

Instant activity in the prosecution's bull pen. Paul Fleming was on his feet. "Dr. Campbell did not use any such expression during my examination," he said warmly. "I object on the grounds the question is not proper cross-examination, Your Honor."

He had no idea what return spray was, nor why Rogers was asking about it. He and his first assistant, a young man named Horton, and a battery of seven other assistant D.A.'s were there to *watch*. They were not going to give Earl Rogers an *inch*. If you let him take an *inch*—

"Dr. Campbell did use that term," Earl Rogers said as he lifted one finger. Quietly, Jerry Giesler put a blue document in his hand.

After an intense if hurried conference with Captain Fredericks, Fleming said again, "It is not on evidence in this trial, Your Honor."

With the blue document in hand, Rogers walked to the Bench. "Here it is, Your Honor," he said still quietly. "Page Forty-five—Dr. Campbell used this term—return spray—in his original examination at the coroner's inquest."

Fleming, with a mind as quick as Alexander Hamilton's, had seen that return spray must have something to do with the acid-throwing business of this case. His strategy—and always the strategy was Fleming's—had been mapped not to bring this up until he had laid his foundation. The long interval between the shot, heard by several people, and the call McComas made to the police. The call from a nearby phone in another hotel to Earl Rogers' home during that same time lapse. *Then* cross-examination of McComas himself.

This was too early. Nor did he wish Earl Rogers to be the one to bring it up at all, though what return spray had to do with it he hadn't yet figured out.

He was to know very soon.

Both Fleming and Fredericks made a long and sound attempt to exclude the question.

Unless, *Fredericks* said, throwing all his persuasion into the objection, the question had been asked on direct examination in this court during this trial, the defense counsel could not cross-examine on it.

If at any time any place in any official hearing, said *Earl Rogers*, the witness has used that term in connection with this case, he may use it now and I may inquire into it.

The court now said, after some time, to the witness, "If

you at any time have used that term as a description of what
you saw in connection with this case, you may explain to
the jury as to the conditions to which you applied it."

Mr. Rogers said, "Thank you, Your Honor."

Now that the court had so ruled, he began to use those two
words as fulcrum. His tone was entirely professional as he
began. One physician consulting another. A general practitioner, uninformed at a high level of this special matter, ready
and willing to learn from a consultant of note.

"Dr. Campbell," he said, "what did you mean exactly, when
you used the term return spray?"

Dr. Campbell said, "I applied it to the form and line the
drops of acid took on the face of the dead woman."

Q. (by Mr. Rogers) The face of the dead woman, Mrs.
Noyes?

A. Yes, on the face of Mrs. Noyes at the time I studied
the case.

Q. Yes, doctor, I see. You studied the case carefully, of
course. Now would you be kind enough to describe for us
the condition left on her face?

A. Well, I found that from above *downward*, on the right
side of the face was a line of acid drops. Or rather the marks,
let us say, left by their passage. The lighter ones being above,
these marks gradually became heavier as they passed downward. Showing me that the line of fluid, of acid, had formed
itself by gravity and struck the face in that perpendicular
manner along the right side of the face.

Q. Therefore you think she was standing up?

A. Yes.

The doctor's manner had succumbed to that of Earl Rogers.
They had forgotten they were in a courtroom, it appeared.
They were two medical men. Doctors just plain never would
discuss anything with you, or tell a layman anything about
all these fascinating details, even when it was your own family.
Now, by the simplicity of manner and style and language,
the jury felt they were being allowed to listen in on a real
consultation. They were eavesdropping.

Q. This meant that in other words the acid was running
down?

A. Remember, the burns became deeper downward, the
lower part of the face contained considerable eschar.

Q. By that, doctor, you mean dead tissue?

A. Yes yes, I mean dead tissue or the crust or scab occasioned on the skin by burns or caustics.

Q. Then Mrs. Noyes was alive when the acid struck her?

A. Oh yes otherwise no eschar could form.

I remember looking at McComas then, where he sat at the counsel table. His face was blank as I'd never seen a face before. Without *anything*, pain or thought or memory, mind or heart, fear or remorse or guilt or anger. The other face they were talking about—*the lower part contained considerable eschar—oh yes, she was alive when it struck her*—I wondered if he remembered it alive and unscarred. This was the face of the woman he'd loved—if only for twenty minutes. Was it before him now the way he saw it the first time, or the last time? Now it was a poor dead face and a doctor and a lawyer were talking about it as though it was anybody's property, a piece of steak, and had never been warm and responsive. It *hurt* me. All right, so love must have a stop. *Not like this*. Right then I hated McComas, let them hang him. I understood why she'd stood—*she was standing? Yes*—and in the dark had thrown that flaming stuff at the man she loved.

Beyond Mac, I saw that Paul Fleming was looking almost as blank. He had seen what was going on.

Q. (by Mr. Rogers) Now, doctor, if you will, may we go a little further into your reason for saying Mrs. Noyes was standing up?

A. The acid burns had been caused by a return spray. The heavy drops took the lower course, showing that the force of gravity had lined it. She must have been in an erect position to receive it that way.

Q. Receive it? Mrs. Noyes had thrown the vitriol, she had flung the acid. Now you are talking about her standing erect to receive it.

A. She received the return spray.

Q. Dr. Campbell, speaking of your use of the term return spray, will you please now tell us very explicitly what you mean by it?

A. Well, I mean a comeback, from the acid striking something else, anything, and spraying back.

Q. You mean by that, then, what we might also call a splash back?

A. Yes, Mr. Rogers, as the ocean would strike a rock and spray back.

Q. In your best medical judgment, is that the way those burns were inflicted on this woman Mrs. Noyes?

A. Oh yes, most definitely. I'm quite sure about that. No other possible explanation from the nature of the burns on her dead face.

Q. When she was alive and erect she was struck by the return spray of the acid she had thrown?

A. Oh yes yes, had to be so.

Q. Did you so testify at the autopsy and at the preliminary hearing?

A. I must have. That's the medical fact, I couldn't very well have testified otherwise, could I?

Q. I'm sure you couldn't, doctor. Thank you, we all thank you, you have been of great help to us all.

Then, for the first time, Earl Rogers turned and looked at the district attorney's bench. Quietly, he said, "I haven't any more questions, Dr. Campbell. Perhaps the district attorney has."

But it seemed that the district attorney hadn't.

Paul Fleming must have known then—Fredericks never knew when he was licked—he could never involve Earl Rogers. His own witness had taken care of that. If there was *return spray* on Mrs. Noyes's face alive, McComas couldn't have put the acid on himself.

At the recess, my father walked over and dropped a hand on Fleming's shoulder. He said, "Paul, think how you'd miss me. A fire-eater like you." The voice was pleasant, but triumph flickered in and out.

"You make it look so *goddam easy*," Fleming said.

That was it! That was why they all got so furious and threw things at him and made monkeys of themselves. He made it look as easy as Willie Mays in center field. Nobody except me and the men on our staff and maybe Harry Carr knew anything about the hours of training, of running around the track in a sweat suit, of long days and sleepless nights. He didn't want anybody to see that. The flamboyant figure, the genius at work by pure inspiration, no trace of perspiration showing anywhere. All of a sudden, too, I knew what had done Heney in. Why the record shows that Earl Rogers could get his goat every single time. Heney was a snob from the wrong side of the tracks, the worst kind. Heney was overcome with being able to name-drop the President of the United States and Rudolph Spreckels. It riled him to see that Rogers wasn't impressed, that he honestly thought Roosevelt was "hasty" and Spreckels a German upstart who ought to be digging sugar beets. Nothing is worse than when two men wear the same ties but the ties do not look the same on them. Heney, the champion of the common man, should not have cared about this; unfortunately he did.

Fleming gave Papa a dirty look. He said, "I am still going to hang your client. A man can't murder women in California. After they get the vote maybe, but we still have some chivalry left. I'm going to hang your client."

All the fun went out of Papa. The mere words—*hang your client*—went through him. I felt my own stomach tighten up. Here we were face to face with his bête noire, and worse, the ghost of Buck moving along the battlements. He said, "You ghouls ought not to hang any man. I suppose you'd like to revive burning at the stake if you could."

A number of people in our office, among them Jerry Giesler and Cowan, who'd come back from Arizona with some tales about Mac, thought Paul might do it, too. The probable impression Mac might make on a jury was what gave my father the jimjams. Mac could be *arrogant* and no jury would ever forgive a man for shooting a woman and being arrogant about it.

Our Bert Cowan had also brought back from Arizona a lady who on the witness stand swore that her name was Lulu McComas Gaspar, or Hanson, or something. She helped a good deal, though Cowan was hoping nobody would ask for her birth certificate, I found out later.

"You are the sister of the defendant in this case?" Earl Rogers said.

Lulu looked at the defendant and nodded. "Yes I am," she said, heartily.

Well, right there as far as I was concerned she had busted her oath to smithereens. Not that I believed my father would suborn perjury. On the other hand, my hunch was that the way Fredericks had tried to get *him*, it was permissible to fight fire with fire. I expect he thought this was just a way of dramatizing the truth and why not? When he got *into a case*, living it, breathing it, sometimes the sharp differences between reality and fantasy were no longer clear to him.

Nor me either, I suppose. He had splashed a Hogarth character on his canvas in Dr. Campbell, a stream of color in the *return spray*. Now he was filling in until the moment of painting in the main central figure of McComas. This big, rawboned gal named Lulu didn't look any more like Mac than a Salvation Army trombone and of course she couldn't be his sister or where the hell was *she* when the McComases were massacred by those Apaches and the boy left all alone in the world? Her name was McComas all right, Cowan told me, so I figured she might be his first wife. I have seen some very peculiar first wives turn up in my time—look at old Lucky Baldwin, for whom my father did legal work, it turned out he had actually married Clara Baldwin Stocker's mother, which upset the oil holdings in California for a long time.

Lulu's story, with Papa asking her the questions in a nice gentlemanly way, held everybody spellbound.

Her brother, she said, had engaged in a number of mining ventures. This time, she was talking about, some sixteen years ago when he was practically nothing but a kid, it seemed there were six holes he wanted to blast into one, which sounded all right. So he loaded all six of them with dynamite, lit the long fuses, and high-tailed it up the ladder.

As his head came about ground level, he found himself face to face with a rattlesnake.

A huge rattlesnake, Lulu said, which, if it was coiled as she said it was, I thought was gilding the lily. I met a coiled rattler once in an outhouse and I have to say my blood ran cold when I thought of being between him above and six lighted dynamite fuses below. However, it seemed to me the kind of a position in which McComas might find himself. Before he could make up his mind or get his gun, the dynamite went off. When he came to, Lulu said, her brother was buried under about a ton of earth and a rock had hit him and destroyed forever the sight of one eye.

"Which eye was it?" Earl Rogers said sympathetically.

"The right eye," Lulu said.

Well, I thought the prosecution would make more of who she was, her identity, than they did. Lulu had a disconcerting way of tilting back her head and looking at them as though she was trying to see across ten or fifteen miles of desert, and anyhow Fleming's chivalry never allowed him to be any good at cross-examining a female. (Later when they were trying to find out who shot William Desmond Taylor what with

Mabel Normand and Mary Miles Minter *and* her mother, a district attorney named Thomas Lee Woolwine was so disconcerted by these ladies he never did try anybody though every newspaperman in town was sure he knew who'd done it.)

At first I thought Lulu was just atmosphere. Then I began to wonder about this *which-eye, right-eye* business. Papa hadn't mentioned it but he'd been on a sort of white-heat merry-go-round ever since the case started. I glanced over at Fleming and saw by the way the muscles at the end of his jaw were going back and forth that he'd begun to wonder about it too.

We were both right.

McComas came close to being our most controversial witness. Opinions varied from ladies who swooned to gentlemen who, if he was acquitted, hoped to take him out into a clump of cottonwoods themselves. Nothing my father could do removed the impression that he didn't give a good God damn whether the jury believed him or not. His cold contempt for them and everybody else in the courtroom chilled the air and in the end Papa let it ride. The only thing that embarrassed the defendant sitting on the stand as easy as though it was his own horse was the fact that he'd shot a lady—he called Mrs. Noyes a lady.

"If I'd known it was a lady I wouldn't have shot," McComas said, disdainfully. "Meet a grizzly in a forest fire, you don't wait to ask if it's a mama bear or a papa bear. I was trying to *de*fend myself. Vitriol hurts, all you got left to act with is your instinct. My instinct's to shoot somebody that's after me. I didn't have but one good eye, I reckon I reacted faster trying to save it. I thought more might come, so I just bunged away."

"Mr. McComas," Earl Rogers said, "will you please face the jury?"

The lid of his left eye was crumpled like a poinsettia petal. His *right* eye, Lulu had said, he lost the sight of his right eye. Earl Rogers said, "Mr. McComas, did you throw vitriol on yourself after you shot Mrs. Noyes?"

"I don't know as I'd have the nerve to do that," McComas said. "No, I didn't."

"If you had, surely you'd have thrown it on the right side where you're almost blind already?"

"I figure my instinct would have been to throw it on my bad eye," Mac said, "I'd be thinking then, anyhow, and I should think I had brains enough to leave myself one eye to see out of, wouldn't I?"

The "just bunged away" was the chief point of attack when Fleming took him on a fine, emotionally moving cross-examination. Withering, detesting a man who'd shot a woman, Fleming scorched him. He had a lot of facts, too. No man alive could put three bullets into a target in the dark blinded by acid. Were we to believe all the bullets fired by instinct went into the small range of this poor woman's loving heart? No one could be expected to credit so fantastic a yarn.

"Mr. McComas," Fleming said, "you were planning to get rid of Mrs. Noyes, weren't you? People heard you tell her so, it has been so testified here. You were tired of her, you wanted to get rid of her, you had a new love?"

"We'd come to the parting of the ways," McComas said. "I didn't figure I'd have to shoot her, though."

"And you mean to tell me," Fleming said, "you just reached for your gun in the dark, blinded by vitriol, and hit a woman in the heart with all three shots?"

"That's what happened," McComas said. "You familiar with guns?"

"I'm asking the questions here," Fleming said. "Do you expect any man to believe such a fantastic story as that?"

"I don't expect anything," McComas said. "I'll just keep on telling what happened. A man shoots at a movement, a flash, a place that's darker. He don't have time to think when he's shooting in a tight place. There *ain't* time. His hand an' arm are trained, automatic, by instinct. On my best judgment I'd say I felt the acid and replied to it. I must of sort of sensed where my enemy was and my hand and arm shot without me tellin' 'em to."

After that, we had experts. Produced by the district attorney, the majority of them did not believe a man could do what McComas said he had done. In his cross-examinations, Rogers asked them if any of their fancy shooting had been done under the stress of a face streaming with vitriol. A rhetorical question, of course. Men had shown superhuman strength in danger, hadn't they? Would any of them say it was *impossible* that under such extraordinary and excruciating circumstances there might not be some superhuman shooting? No—none of them would say it was *impossible*—they just didn't believe it, that was all.

As to why McComas, in such dire straits, had called Earl Rogers before he called the police, McComas said coldly that

he had never had any reason to trust the cops. He wanted
somebody on his side before they started messing things up
for him.

So the central figure of Rogers' murder mural, insolent,
defiant, cold as ice, blazing away with his gun in the dark,
stood up pretty well, dazzling in color at least. Nobody liked
him much. Yet—we admired his refusal to grovel. His cold
nerve. For the first time I would not have minded too much
about the *man* himself. As the terrible waiting began, again
and again and again, another jury to wait for, this time it
was because it was our case, this was my father's masterpiece, they mustn't hang his client. We were all obsessed by
this.

I can't remember how long the McComas jury was out. A
long long time, days and nights, nights and days. My father
said he believed the longer a jury was out the less chance of
conviction. "Hang a man in hot blood," he said, "not cold.
When they start to think, they can't take the life of another
human being." And I think we all knew in the case of Mc-
Comas it would be the limit one way or the other. This was a
whole-hog guy; hang the bloody bastard or let him go.

We stayed around the courthouse all day—in the courtroom,
in the witness room—walking mile after mile in the marble
corridors. My father was gay, confident, chin up—but he had
to change his shirt and his coat as often as Whitey Ford in
Yankee Stadium on a ninety-six-degree afternoon. Somebody
set up a chessboard. There was a pitch game going on. Desperate attempts at conversation started and flagged. A
quartet was singing "In the Gloaming" and for a minute I
thought Papa was going to be sick. Footsteps clattered and
everything stopped. The jury had sent for the doctor's testimony—the bailiff told us that. My father let out a roar of
excitement and nearly swallowed a cigarette and we had to
hit him one on the back. Sandwiches came and everybody took
one bite and they lay there about like a picnic in a cemetery.
We went home when they locked the jury up at night—or
we went to the Oyster Loaf over on Main Street and sat or
leaned yawning, exhausted, aching, eyes staring in our heads
but unable to sleep. *To sleep: perchance to dream* of men
hanging hanging hanging—Papa sent Cowan to the jail and
he came back and said Mac was asleep and Papa laughed
so hard we had to laugh too, though we were so tired by then
it hurt.

Suspense is torture. Even a little suspense is some kind of

torture. Waiting for a murder jury, and I do not altogether know why but it is true, I tell you it is true, I have done it so often and I have waited out most of the other things, too, but waiting for a murder jury is the rack. Minutes are red ants crawling along your nerves. You *cannot* really get your mind off it. You stir and stir your coffeecup, round and round it goes, your brain is muddy with it but it always goes back to the vortex of *waiting*.

We get messages from bailiffs, correct or not—how many ballots have been taken—nine to three for acquittal—eight to four—ten to two—

At last that painful mysterious stir.

Nobody has ever as far as I know been able to explain it. Nothing has happened. No word, no sign, no sound. We are all exactly as we were in the courtroom, like a hum on a TV set—the stir comes. It never fails. Nobody ever knows why it happens.

They're coming.

My father looks fresh, haggard but smiling, supremely confident, which I know he is not.

He knows he cannot lose. He is sure.

Sometimes, he expects the verdict to be Guilty.

This is being dragged in two directions by two teams of horses.

At last they file into the box. It takes them forever, they are in *slow motion*, dragging their feet, those final moments are of unendurable suspense, we grow old, we live years waiting for murder juries, the accused man never waits but once, my father waited every time, he had crawled into the other man's skin, he'd associated his life with him when he defended him.

How many times can a man feel like that and live through it? The toll is too great. I ask myself and go and put my hand in his.

McComas is there now. His eyes lighter blue than ever, too light, frozen ice, killer's eyes?

NOT GUILTY.

Only once they say it, it echoes above the running feet of the press, above hisses and applause, both my father and McComas are calm.

NOT GUILTY   NOT GUILTY   NOT GUILTY

In a book I wrote later, *A Free Soul,* which after the manner of early novels is partly autobiographical, I wrote that the famous criminal lawyer, played by Lionel Barrymore, told the murderer to put the acid on his own face after he'd killed his mistress. This was fiction, I took dramatic license.

On the other hand, here is my evidence on the McComas case. I was there when McComas called my father. At first I didn't pay much attention. Then I heard the engine change pitch, the urgency in Papa's voice, and I began to listen. The conversation had been—was—rather long than short.

Quietly but clearly my father said, "It is a good thing she threw the acid on you, my friend, or they would hang you. No jury would accept the mere threat as self-defense for you—you could have jumped aside, or overpowered her or knocked the bottle from her hand. You see that." He listened, then he said, "Go back. Hurry. Then call the police. Keep your mouth shut and call me and I will come at once."

The times—the *timing*—were difficult to follow.

Why McComas went a block up Alvarado to call Mr. Rogers that first time was mysterious. On the stand he said he was in such pain and so confused that he had forgotten the location of the telephone in the hotel where Mrs. Noyes lived— he said also that he hoped to find someone in the drugstore to give him something to help with his agony, but only the phone booth was open.

He said he did not go back to Mrs. Noyes's apartment—and they could not produce a witness to say he did. He found he was too weak, in too much pain, to go another step, and so when he saw lights, heard voices, he went into another hotel. He appeared in the lobby where the guests were dancing—the vitriol still on his face—and, groping blindly, asked to be led to the phone, from which he called the police station.

It is true that telephones were not common as they now are. Mrs. Noyes had none in her apartment. There was only one in the reception rooms and it was out of sight. The interval in time between McComas' first call to Rogers and his call to the police was never exact. It *seemed* that it was long enough for him to have gone back to the room where Mrs. Noyes lay dead with three bullets through her heart and then go to the ballroom of the last hotel he visited.

The investigation there wasn't up to Sherlock Holmes or M. Poirot.

If it weren't for Dr. Campbell I would be inclined to think

that when my father said, "It is a good thing she threw the acid on you, my friend, or they would hang you," it was a suggestion—it could have been a command. Not something that *had* happened, something that *better* happen if Mac wanted to stay alive.

Oh—McComas had the nerve for it.

Perhaps the picture Earl Rogers painted of the McComas case should be called *The Return Spray*. That, and that alone, come right down to it, was what kept them from hanging McComas.

McComas kept on having trouble with women. Later another lady love of his was found dead in her luxurious apartment in San Francisco. Mac found her. Fortunately for him, her body was lying inside across the door in such a way that it would have been impossible for him to get out *if* he'd been inside when she was shot. Oh yes—she was shot too. Through the heart.

The jury believed him.

I—didn't—I don't—I do—I don't *know*.

McComas might have been able to come through the keyhole.

In spite of the *return spray*, I've never been sure. This was one time when we may have turned a man loose to do it again. That's part of the calculated risk of the criminal lawyer. He must *defend* on what his client tells him.

I knew—I always knew one thing. A man like McComas could get tired enough of a woman to kill her, if that was the only way to get rid of her.

A motive overlooked most of the time. If people get tired enough—or *bored* enough—

Yet, I knew McComas really felt very bad about *Dolly*. But then Dolly was never in love with him.

PART SIX

FORTY-SIX

Accelerating with murders, excitement, growing national fame, spectacular offers, time led us to my father's defense of Clarence Darrow for jury bribery, the climax and tragedy of his life.

My father refused offers from Mr. Calhoun and a partnership in Garret McEnerny's firm. As long as he lived the door said *EARL ROGERS*, nothing more. We went to New York to discuss a proposition which Papa turned down. To South Bend, at the call-for-help of a lay professor at Notre Dame who had been falsely accused. In Chicago to advise on trial strategy. To Reno to see the heavyweight championship fight.

Poor Jim Jeffries, as nice a guy as ever lived, had been persuaded to leave his retirement and become the White Hope against Jack Johnson, who was certainly black. Just the same, Jack was a friend of mine so I rooted for him. If you go to Reno today you will see ladies at the crap tables, but at the time of the Jeffries-Johnson battle it hadn't become the Divorce-and-Dice Capital; no lady had ever been inside a saloon except to get her husband or father out, that modern equivalent the cocktail lounge had not been invented and would not have been believed. So I took long rides and persuaded a dealer in a small gambling house to let me act as lookout, the way Faro Nell had done.

As I take out my memory tape, the thing I hear best is neither my Papa, *nor* Jack London, nor Charlie Van Loan, nor any of the big sports writers gathered from all over the world. It's Jack Johnson's own conversation in the ring. Jim Corbett, a handsome clean-cut white man, was in Jeffries' corner and Jim knew whereof he spoke, having knocked out John L. Sullivan once upon a time. I couldn't hear Jim, but he kept up a running commentary not to his own challenger but to black Jack. I judged the words must be pretty awful because once I heard Johnson say in his soft carrying voice,

"Your mammy teach you to talk like that, Mr. Corbett?"
Jeffries was doing his best, it seemed to me Johnson tried to
fight him equal, giving him a handicap as you would a man
at golf. He kept looking at Corbett, finally he began to
maneuver Jeffries around, left jabs, couple of straight rights,
and then he said so the first five rows could hear him, "Look
out, Mr. Corbett. Here comes your white hope," and knocked
Jeffries kicking into Corbett's lap.

The story Papa always told happened when he was making
the contracts. All Jack Johnson would say was, *No pop*.
Turned out he wanted a guarantee that no soda pop would
be sold inside the arena. "If I beat their white hope," Johnson
said, "them bottles would be too handy to throw."

We also went to Glen Ellen.

The reason Jack London adopted me as a goddaughter had
nothing to do with me, but with my father and Jack's own
daughter, Joan.

Nobody ever forgot a visit to the Valley of the Moon,
where London lived. This way of life that he and his wife
Charmian had established in the clear air of a redwood forest
in Northern California was the dream I'd never been able to
make come true. If I'd been older, had any help, known
anything about getting or keeping the money, I'd have arranged something like it for Papa and me. It might have
served him no better than it did Jack London in the long
run—all is to do *within* first, I know that now. Then, there
was an ecstasy in imagining that we might find such a home,
have days of good plain living, riding, gathering friends who'd
stimulate my father and require his best, far from the maddening throng and our throngs did get maddening. It seems
to me the first time we went there it was a sort of glorified
camp. I slept in a tent. Later, while London was building
Wolf House, which burned down before he ever lived in it,
they'd added wings to an old winery, thrown up small houses
around it. In them Jack housed a bevy of Men Who Came to
Dinner, his philosophers he called them. In royal hospitality
guests were bidden by letter—*Come to Glen Ellen any time*.
They came—Luther Burbank from Santa Rosa, Mary Austin
from Carmel, George and Carrie Sterling from San Francisco,
publishers and editors from New York, painters from Paris,
playwrights from London, sycophants, bums, cops and rob-
bers, anarchists and statesmen, phonies and geniuses,
gathered under the giant redwoods beside the lovely river.

Stimulated, sparked, demanded by the insatiable mind, the loving heart, the deep understanding and restless spirit of the man who at that moment was the greatest living American writer, conversation flowed as I have never heard it anywhere else.

To see my father and Jack London together; to watch any audience held spellbound; to follow the heads of the listeners turning from one man to the other like spectators at a tennis match; to hear Papa arguing, discussing, laughing, agreeing, defending, laying bare his own causes, challenging or cheering London or any of his guests and philosophers—the thrill for me was unequaled and my heart turns over as I remember it.

Another big experience at Glen Ellen was Charmian London.

In his magnificent life of London, *Sailor on Horseback*, Irving Stone feels that toward the end Charmian was to blame for events in Jack's life that led to the overdose of morphine. The same way, I suppose, I blame Mama for lots of things. Remembering how completely Charmian fascinated me on those visits, I wonder which came first—her collapse or London's. Perhaps, if she loved him, no woman could have survived as Jack London's wife, at the level of the greatest love story of all time, which they had consciously joined together to create. Mates—Mate Woman—Mate Man —they called each other and London was rough and rugged enough to get away with it though I must confess it embarrassed my father. Perhaps London wore her down; exhausted her powers, over the years when she was wife, sweetheart, first mate literally on the cruise of the *Snark*, where they nearly perished; helping him to break horses and build Glen Ellen; nursing him twenty-four hours a day through his white illnesses in Hawaii and Australia; joining in his socialistic causes; being his hostess, running the place for as many guests as a hotel; trying to keep him sober in New York when he went for a showdown battle with his publishers and magazine editors. Above all fighting his monumental extravagances and spendthrift madness which in the end more than anything else destroyed him. Dealing with creditors and harassing daily debts. Putting up with his infidelities and never letting on she even knew of them.

I don't know. Stone is against her and my father didn't like her.

I have a woman's feeling that to live with London at the

fabulous, preposterous pace of high drama which he *chose*, to see him disintegrating under the alcoholism as he was—by the time Stone writes of, there wasn't much left of her. Some of the things that Papa found embarrassing were, I think now, pure hysteria. "Don't imitate her," he would yell at me, and insisted she was the wrong wife for London, once he had decided to settle down. There was, Papa said, no settle down in Charmian, she might be great before the mast in a storm but not in a quiet country life. I said I didn't think there was really any settle down in London either.

I greatly admired her thin figure, the clouds of bronze hair, the narrow topaz-yellow eyes that gleamed from under long lashes. To an admiring early-teen-ager not much used to the society of women, her flowing velvets for evening, her picturesque Chinese costumes around the house, her elegant riding habits, her queenly air of ruling Glen Ellen were overpowering.

The minute we got out of the wagon that had brought us up the narrow dusty road, London always had things to show us. My father would look over the growing acres, the vast barns and silos, the farm equipment, the houses under construction, and say, "I approve, this is a fine experiment, but it is feudal. Are you still a member of the Socialist party and what do they say to all this?" Jack London said he was and they too approved, but of course he resigned from the party eventually. My father said the man behind the big stack of blue chips seldom remained a socialist. He said of course there came a day when he had so many blue chips he didn't mind dividing them up one way or another because he could still keep enough for himself to play in any game.

On the morning when I had started out for a ride very early and found Jack London galloping after me, I'd never seen or met his daughter Joan. I knew he had two daughters, the older one named Joan about my age. As we rode out through the redwoods, sort of to my surprise, London began to talk about his first wife. I have to say here that he was a man utterly without reticences and I think this is characteristic of most writers. Emotional reaction to life is their business, the people are all *characters*, even themselves, and they can discuss personal matters with a professional detachment which may not be apparent to their listeners.

I began to get a clear picture of Bessie. A good girl, a rarity to the waterfront sailor, lusting for life, that London had been before he met her. A strapping, rosy-cheeked Irish beauty, Bessie had married beneath her when she took the illegitimate young oyster pirate as her husband, even though he'd managed to get himself a college education.

Looking right at a marriage, it's still impossible to tell why it failed or fails. I believed then that for a woman to be married to a genius was a *calling*. A life's work. Her whole being must be committed to it in complete self-sacrifice. Genius was so rare, had such infinite possibilities for all the glory we really know, it needed such care and protection. I was beginning to see, however, that being wife to a genius had more difficulties than being daughter to one, and that wasn't smooth sailing. Bessie had tried one way, Charmian another.

Just a while before this, London had been swept by a desire for, a need of, a son as violent as Henry the Eighth's. All he meant to do with his estate, his farm inventions, his aid to the farmer must have a *son* to carry it on. While he and Charmian waited for the baby to be born he was in ecstasy—confident—uplifted.

The baby didn't live—and the drop was correspondingly as far down as the climb to the heights had been. It always was for Jack London.

The whole experience had reminded him poignantly of the time his first child was born. Of the months he and *Bessie* had waited. His joy when he first saw his first baby. Yes yes, he dramatized it as he told it to me—he was a *dramatist*. Read *The Sea Wolf* again!

So, he'd been remembering Joan, her birth, her babyhood, as a sturdy little girl who looked exactly like him. And now he had a plan. Turning off onto a narrow trail, we came to a little valley in a circle of oaks. Right here, he said, he was going to build a house for Bessie and the girls. At first he had me so swept away that this seemed a wonderful idea, then there entered a chill little doubt. Charmian might not be enthusiastic about this? I asked him how she felt about it and he said cheerfully, "Oh—they won't need to see much of each other."

That the man who had written *Martin Eden* could say such a thing when even a half-baked girl like me could feel its plain lunacy, held me in stunned silence until he turned and stared at me. He said, "It seems to me this would benefit everybody." All that *brightness*. It illumines the place where I am now, after all these years, with a glow of life. A stocky man, not tall, a strong jaw, thick black brows—above all I

remember his eyes. They never *stopped*. Bright, searching,
eager, alight—wide open always—as though he kept them
open, praying to whatever gods there might be to let his
unconquerable soul *see*. Let me see what is over the next
hill, beyond that dark rampart of clouds, inside the depths
of that man's heart, through every window of every house
and every soul—let me see. *Brightness* lingers around my
memory of him more than anyone I knew in those days and
it shone around him that morning as we sat looking at the
site he had picked.

"It won't work," I said. "They're all women. You know how
women behave."

Maybe that was the trouble, maybe he didn't. The women
in his books are all made of straw. He created them himself
without any help from a pattern God had made before him.

I said, "What does Joan say about it?"

"She won't answer my letters," he said in sudden wildness.
"She hasn't answered any of them. Why doesn't she let me
talk to her?" His voice held heavy heartbreak and confusion.
Disaster signals were on his brows and in the set of his lips.

Used as I was to airing my young opinions anywhere as
though they mattered and might even be the Delphic oracle,
I felt miserable, I didn't want to say anything. From Chinese
cooks to dairy hands to social leaders, everyone was at ease
with Jack London, he with them, but just then I felt a
barrier between us.

"I'm her father," Jack London said hotly.

"Well—" I said, squirming around in my saddle, "maybe
she doesn't know that. You aren't somebody's father just
because you *are*. You can love your father best of anybody
in the world but wouldn't he have to—be there? Joan
doesn't know you hardly at all, does she? You're mostly a
stranger to her."

"I ask her to give me a chance to make her know me. Is
that too much?" he cried.

"Not too much," I said, "but it could be too late. If my
father had gone off and *left* me—when a person has showed
you they can live without you for years and go all over the
world, it isn't so easy to believe all of a sudden they can't
live without you any more."

A long minute, he just stared at me. His *response* to you
was like the blast of a furnace. He was not like most of the
grown-up people I had known who were only interested in
their side. He reached out to understand even when, as it

did now, it had to hurt and anger him. He said, "How can a child presume to judge her father?"

"No it's not that," I said. "She was a little girl and she had to make up her mind inside herself about you leaving her. I am trying to imagine how I would have felt if Papa had left me. Even just for a short time when he went down to see Boyd that night, left me with other people. I don't think she is presuming to judge you, she just has to do the best she can to understand what you did to her, doesn't she?"

"How can a child know what a man feels?" he said. "What he needs, the measures of his temptations, the obligations to his work—he must venture into the unknown because he is afraid of it, he lives in another dimension, he fights wars and sails the seven seas, dares death—"

I was caught up in it, by a miracle that was what he was able to put on paper, the love of life. When men can convey that to you—it was the secret of the greatest movie star of all times, Clark Gable—they sweep all before them—love of life, *life* being a great adventure at its worst. Look how in *The Star Rover* he did venture into The Unknown—of course all good novelists must be prophets.

I tried to steady myself. I thought, All right, but you are not understanding Joan, I ought to try to express Joan to him. I said, "You are expecting a little girl to know a lot when you probably did not tell her any of these things. Joan hasn't had my advantages. Papa has always tried to tell me as we went along. Besides, Joan loved her mother which you say she should, and her mother—loved her. My mother didn't want me to stay with her even if Papa would have left me. Joan would be aghast—she would blame you for what you did to her mother, leaving her, marrying somebody else, she would want to defend her mother. You have to think about Joan as she is, the way she has grown up. She's made a choice, she had to. I don't think she can be expected, the way you treated her, to understand you the way I do Papa."

We were off our horses and walking around the site, he was silent, thinking, when my father and Charmian came cantering up.

Oh—I wish I could see Papa on horseback again just once.

London said to him, "Can a man adopt a godchild when she's half-grown?"

"That would seem to me the best time," Papa said. "Becoming godfather to a six-day-old child is a gamble, it may turn into a pickpocket or a saint—either of which can be difficult."

"I have decided to adopt Nora as my goddaughter," Jack London said.

Papa and I both knew he wanted to substitute me for Joan, because I loved my father the way he was now determined Joan should love him. Charmian looked at me quickly, her eyes narrowed to golden slits, she swung down and came and kissed me and said, "I shall be godmother."

For once in my fresh young life I didn't know what to say, I got red and grinned at them. I hadn't realized much about grown-up emotions until, in a way, the McComas-Noyes murder. Now I felt these emotions jumping all around me, between husband and wife, dynamically violent people. Charmian was filled with sorrow, I could feel the memory of her baby heavy within her. For all the glorified illusion of perfect romance, great love, it added to her fear that she might lose him. She couldn't know that he wanted to bring his first wife here now, Bessie with her good nature, her earthiness, her warm, easygoing ways. He needed a family. Daughters to bring grandsons to the land. Charmian didn't know this but she sensed it, her claws went in and out and her ears went flat back like a mountain lioness.

I didn't want to see it, I got back on my horse, and Papa and I went on riding. He explained some of this to me. He didn't care for Charmian, he detested affectations and she had many, but he felt sorry for her.

Also he was tensed up about London as a writer getting bogged down and in debt with all this farming project.

At dinner that night he talked about it, he said as much as anybody had dared or would dare.

"A man," my father said, "finds a rut that interests him, it can still be a rut. A rover, a seeker, an adventurer of the body or the spirit, for him it's the same as a grave, only the man is buried alive. Line it with plush, put gold handles on, for the rebel, the revolutionist, it's a coffin!"

London shouted at him, "I am leading a revolution right here!"

I was surprised my father didn't go on, I saw him give London a quick look, a broad grin, I got the flash—I can't quite explain this—I often tuned in on my father's thinking. He knew Jack London would go a-roving no more by the light of any moon. He was not only sunk in building Wolf House, in new methods of farming, water-right suits, and labor disputes on his property. The spirit was still in there pitching, but the flesh was *through*. The long illnesses, the wild life, the indulgence, again and again the *sleeplessness*.

One of those nights London talked violently about writing and that was the first time I ever had any idea—any response —any inkling—that this might be for me.

"Strength," London cried, with his great sweeping gestures, "be careful not to prune away all the strength. To polish and prettify all the blood and bones and flesh out of the work. The world will always buy *strength*. The writer who did most to influence his times—*Dickens,* he is not afraid of sentiment, of great slashing smashing strokes, of power, an exaggeration to prove a point. More than life-size, more than mountain high. He makes the reader weep and shriek with terror and laugh with glee. He was echo to no man and puppet for no critic. Nor am I. Strength I tell you—look at the strength of Jane Austen. Look at the suspense. Hers is a different style—a different canvas—but it's *strong*."

FORTY-SEVEN

One afternoon Papa and Jack London took off down the road to visit some of Jack's cronies scattered around the neighborhood.

I wanted to say don't go. My stomach was buzzing with danger signals. If I spoke, they'd just laugh, pat me on the head, and promise to be home early. They did that anyhow.

For five days, nobody heard a word. It was difficult to believe that the most famous writer and the leading criminal lawyer in the West, *with* a team of fine bay horses *and* a high-wheeled buggy, could vanish without a trace, but so it was. At least nobody would admit they'd seen any such phenomenon.

This was the first time I'd kept this vigil with another woman. Now I was astonished at the way Charmian London took it as a personal insult. *What he's doing to me.* Her laugh

fluttered higher and higher and broke like a light globe.
Neither of us slept except in catnaps, starting at the sound of
a sleepy bird, the wind in the redwoods, the footfall of
imagination, or the ripple of the river. We were up at a sound
lower than our ears were supposed to be able to hear. Peering
out hopefully into the dark. Charmian was sharp and bitter.
Nothing was ever said between us about drink. A man's
family did not discuss this, nor admit it. Now I knew she
hated Glen Ellen. Her longing was to be back on the *Snark*,
breathing the high seas again, seeing strange places, new
horizons. I saw that she was about as domestic as a mountain
lioness, of which she kept reminding me more and more. Of
course if her baby had lived—now as she moved restlessly,
never still, I began to avoid her. This was not the kind of talk
I could endure just then. She had *quit*. It scared me so I felt
my insides shake. By nature, Charmian London wasn't a
quitter. Even people who didn't like her admitted she had
more guts than any other female they'd ever known.

As a result of this I did the first thing I'd ever done behind
Papa's back—barring Steve Ketchel and I hadn't really done
that, I'd just kept it from him.

I began to say my prayers again.

I gave God a chance. Without faith, without courtesy, regarding it as I told him, as a lower-case, unintelligent, chow-
der-headed, down-grade act of fear. I double-dared him to do
something about Papa because I wasn't making out very well.
My grandfather had believed. So had I, once upon a time
when I was practically a baby. God was a last resort but something—*something*—I had seen in Jack London drove me to it.
On my knees.

Obviously they came back.

The two of them!

We all knew they would though I don't think any of us
expected them to be riding *burros*. This was hardly the home-
coming of Ulysses, the donkeys were so small their feet
dragged in the dust, it rose in a cloud around them. We saw
before us two gentlemen blandly satisfied with themselves and
even cheerful. In fact they were *singing*. Oh yes they were.
In an almost childlike confidence of their welcome and an
innocent goodwill toward all, their voices floated up to us as
we sat on the terrace. Papa was carrying what tune there was,
in a poignant Barbary Coast baritone, and London was coming in with the tenor. The tune was an old water-front favorite

called "Whiskey, Johnny, Whiskey" and that's all I remember of it, thank God.

When they got closer they stopped singing and we could hear their conversation. "I am a little confused," Rogers said. "Why am I riding this burro?"

"You are confused," said London, "because at this moment you are not sure whether you are a man dreaming you are a burro or a burro dreaming you are a man. We all have these moments."

"I think I should prefer to be a burro dreaming I am a man," Papa said.

Dismounting proved a problem. "There is something wrong here," Papa said. "Could it possibly be true that the earth is round?"

"You mustn't fall for that fairy tale, my friend," London said. "You can see with your own eyes, that except for a pimple here and there, it is *flat*."

"At least," Papa said with immense dignity, "you have never heard me mention it in mixed company."

They found this occasion for hilarious mirth, as they came up the dusty path, swaying like men just off the deck of a ship. They became aware at the same moment of George Sterling, California's favorite poet, whose legend has survived longer than his poetry, as he rose to his feet and said icily, "You might have waited for me."

"Georgie," London cried. "Earl, why didn't we wait for Georgie?"

"*Wait* for him!" Papa said resonantly. "Wait for him! You must recall how long we waited at the mouth of the Yukon Trail. We waited until we heard the call of the wolf pack and had to move on."

With some slight difficulty, they came aboard the terrace and after bowing to the company found chairs. Papa did not so much as glance in my direction but Jack London went over and kissed his wife and she gave him a flashing, narrow-eyed smile I'd rather not have had myself and became busy with coffee and China tea. All too plainly neither of the prodigals had slept *or* bathed *or* changed their shirts since they left. They had drunk themselves sober, which is a dreadful thing to behold, and yet—it is difficult to explain this probably on account of I do not understand it very well myself. Ordinary men at this stage of a debauch take showers, drink coffee, and if they have any sense send for doctors, nurses, go to bed, and collapse. Sometimes of course my father did all three. Some-

times, as on that day at Glen Ellen, these two seemed to me
to have stepped into another dimension. Into a space where it
was as yet by no means sure man could breathe and think and
have his being—halfway between purgatory and paradise. They
were fallen archangels geared to silver-bright madness. Talk
was released, their bodies were no longer drunk, they were in
a state of dangerous *exhaustion*, down to the bare bones of
their *nervous* energy. Their tongues were touched with magic
and their brains were full of the white light of alcohol. A
discomfort so profound I could hardly get my breath took me
over. Even while they bubbled with wit, took us into their
good fellowship, the conviviality of drinking together, I began
to shrivel and want to cry, *Stop please stop*. Their thoughts
and words had gained uncanny power, like the blue-white aura
of a dynamo, yet the *truth* was not in them and without *truth*
—I knew that without truth, though I did not know what truth
was, man—genius—cannot survive. Only in the soil of *a man's
own truth* can he grow the fruits of imagination, which does
not seem to make sense but I knew it then. The truth that
was the foundation of London's *People of the Abyss* and
The Iron Heel and above all *The Star Rover*. I could not
understand what I was seeing, but I knew that now as they
created bright images in this garden, as Papa had created the
picture of Rudolph Spreckels or McComas, the visions were
mastering *them*, not they the visions. They were wonderful,
we were all laughing as we'd never roared with laughter before
—we were laughing and laughing and wiping tears off our
cheeks and my heart grew heavier and heavier. I thought we
must learn somehow to take better *care* of them.

Charmian turned the dial, or tried to, onto another station,
but she ruined it when at the end she said in a hard-knife-
edged voice, "You have had a long visit this time with your
old friend John Barleycorn."

Every writer knows that somehow somewhere you *talk* your
stories first, or *they* talk *you*. You begin to feel something you
have to say something about and you *hear* yourself and it
stops you like a red light or a bugle blowing. A writer is never
more than twenty-six letters away from putting it *down* on
paper. Nor is he ever allowed scruples, any more than Dickens
was when he turned his father into Mr. Micawber, that forever symbol of England and mankind's upward struggle. As
we sat there that afternoon in the clear late-afternoon light
at Glen Ellen, I had no idea I'd ever try to be a writer, but I
tuned in on my new godfather and I knew for the first time

that he was *talking* a book he would someday have to write, it would be required of him in return for the genius that had been bestowed upon him. Later I was to hear Sinclair Lewis, and once Mary Roberts Rinehart, and often Damon Runyon and Paul Gallico and Ring Lardner and recognize when the *inner* self of the writer had *taken over* whether they knew it or not. When I read London's autobiographical masterpiece *John Barleycorn*, still the best book ever written on alcohol, I jumped nearly out of my skin for I had heard so much of it as he walked up and down the terrace at Glen Ellen with the sailor's gait and answered violently what his wife had said.

"I am friend to John Barleycorn," he said, "I am, I was, I never was. But he is no friend to me. I am never less his friend than when he is with me and I seem most his friend. How can I be his friend when he is my enemy? He is the king of liars. He is the great truth-sayer. He is the royal companion with whom one walks with whatever gods there be. He is also in league with the Noseless One. His way leads to truth naked and shameless, and to death clothed in fine raiment, and to life in rags and tatters. He gives clear vision and *God help me* muddy dreams. He is the enemy of achievement and the teacher of wisdom beyond man's vision. He is the red-handed killer and he slays our youth."

Something like that is now a page in *John Barleycorn*.

Jack London spoke as he pleased, he never hesitated to speak in a language of poetry, of power, of the written word. I cannot now remember exactly what the differences were between what he said to us and what he later wrote. It all meant the same thing. His voice got deeper as the light faded around us, he had the same sense of theater that Papa did, that they must have, they were *hams*, they were *great actors*, they created all drama as Burbage had done, even the scenery. They were ruthless yet they gave themselves as I have never seen anybody else except a few others like them—as Ernest Hemingway did also.

"No friend of John Barleycorn's but get his bill," Jack London cried with a lusty shout of laughter, "do not fool yourself. He tricks you into forgetting the price you must pay but you will get the bill. He sends in time. He loosens the tongue so that a man babbles secrets he would die to conceal, he makes a man wiser than all the gods on Olympus, but I tell you—*I tell you*—we have been telescoping days, weeks, even years into a few mad magnificent instants, we must pay for this in shortened life, that is The Law. We have used up our years—*years*—in an hour, years that should be lived patiently, honestly, trying to scale the heights. The Noseless One lures and he demands savage usury, he gives dreams, he gives service, oh oh oh—he is the slave of the bottle, the genie of the glass, he is in revolt against *nothing*, he does things majestically and it is all empty empty empty—empty adventures, mockery of romance, sterile ones, as we become sterile masks of forbidden promises and behind them—emptiness. He takes away the wise fears by which alone man is enabled to stay alive. He kindles the fire and then puts it out so that he may choke a man with its ashes. He bestows the most deadly of all poisons, facility—facility—beware *facility*. He soddens the gifts just as we have begun to take possession of them, to know them our own. He makes us impotent, posturing mimics of our own lives. He rallies us to lost causes and strikes us down in the first ditch with ribald laughter.

"The Noseless One—why, it may be John Barleycorn is the Noseless One himself."

I think we were all hypnotized as by a great performance of *Lear*. Or *Hamlet*. Tragedy was played before us without footlights. I never got away from the Noseless One again, he was with me when I took the stand at last that day in the courtroom. Jack London had just come off a five-day drunk. Without sleep. We wanted to stop, we had to stop, this cold-sober hangover, it was excruciating and unbearable. None of us had ever heard anything like it, he was laying bare his soul and we knew it and could not look away and could not bear to look *at*. Jack London did this often, he was without any ambush or concealment, at least he had a soul fit to lay bare in all its fighting anguish.

He said slowly, "The Noseless One makes man school himself forever to forget the one great truth that man cannot live without the God in whom I do not believe. If we do not have God we must have the company of the Noseless One who makes us forget that we do not have God."

Papa stood up then, green-white, unsteady, his face etched in revolt. His right arm came up, the index finger pointing, and Charmian, panic-stricken, stopped it. She put her hand on my father's arm and he turned to her, I saw that tears were running down his face, tears of weakness, and I thought, *I have to stop this, he might remember it*, and then Charmian said in a high brittle voice, "Jack—dinner has been ready a long time and your guests—your *guests* are starving—"

Guests did it. Guests were his fetish, he had inherited some

vital hospitality from the kings of Ireland who were probably
his ancestry, bastard as he was, this socialistic stevedore and
pirate was the most royal host I have ever seen except Mr.
Hearst. His kingdom was always open to his friends his family
his guests—*Jack London's* guests. He said grandly, "I ask
your forgiveness—" he bowed and turned to lead the way and
fell flat on his face. He got up in a tigerish leap. He put out
one hand to my father, one to George Sterling.

He said, "Let us make a compact."

Beside my father's etched whiteness, like a head of Caesar,
London looked too filled with blood, too pulsing with violence.

"*Let us agree not to sit up with the corpse,*" he said.

Nobody moved.

"When our work is done, our life force spent, *exit laughing,*"
he said, persuading them, almost coaxing them. "Is it a
promise? We hereby agree not to sit up with the corpse."

A final melodramatic gesture of his.

Yet somehow they must have ratified it in silence. In their
souls.

Jack London and George Sterling kept the pact they made
that day.

My father didn't. I don't think Grandpa would let him. Or
maybe McComas' point that suicide was the supreme coward-
ice. He did it the hard way in the end.

It was probably because of that I asked Papa for a promise
which I think now was a terrible mistake. The Noseless One
loves promises. He uses the broken bits of them for needling
his victims into hopelessness.

Going home across the bay, with a world so beautiful
spread around us, I said, "Papa. I have never asked you
before. I guess there are men who can drink. You can't. Don't
you see? We all know it, you have to know it now." I waited
but he didn't say anything, I could only see his profile moving
a little up and down as the ferry shoved the blue waters out
of her way. I said, "All those things Jack London said—they
are true, aren't they, Papa? You are already so *high* if you
pour alcohol on you it will burn you up—"

He said in a perfectly natural voice, "Jack is an inventor of
Arabian Nights tales."

"Yes," I said. "Most of them are *true.* Papa, if you—you
might—that *promise*—it was terrible—"

Don't sit up with the corpse.

"I didn't agree to that," my father said, and put his arm
around me. So I put mine around him and we had our other

elbows on the rail and we rode along without saying anything.

In a low voice, he said, "Of course I can stop drinking if I want to. Perhaps I should. Perhaps you are right."

"A long time ago you said you'd tell me when it was time to start worrying," I said, trying to make it light for fear if I didn't he'd shy way from me. "I just want to—I mean I haven't anyone else to depend on to tell me but you."

He laughed then. The effort was showing but he did it. He said, "We will start worrying together, sweetheart. You have my promise. I shall with great aplomb climb aboard the water wagon. It can do a man no harm."

I wish I hadn't asked for that promise.

Always it makes it worse. It isn't the way. You have to fight John Barleycorn with your eyes wide open, *a step at a time, a minute—an hour—at a time*.

One of the things I want to ask Papa when I see him again is whether that promise—asking for that promise—was a betrayal. A lack of burning daily *faith*. There is something about a promise that is forced from a man that can break him when he breaks it.

I wish it hadn't been there when the curtain went up on the last act and Clarence Darrow walked onto the scene.

PART SEVEN

FORTY-EIGHT

Through the years I have seen, as has all the world, busts, portraits, book jackets, photographs of Clarence Darrow, the Great Defender.

I shall always see him face to face with my father in our office the night before Darrow was to make his closing plea in his own trial for jury bribery, in which my father was his chief counsel.

The seamed, rugged Lincolnesque countenance; the ridges of dirt in the deep lines of the skin; the lower lip thrust out in defiance; the lank Great Unwashed lock of hair falling over the noble brow—I see these more plainly than the legendary figure that has grown since in story and drama. A smog of pain and protest surrounded for me the huge, stoop-shouldered body in the always threadbare and unpressed suit.

In a low voice Earl Rogers said, "You would do anything, have done everything for the cause of the workingman, as you see it."

"That is true," Darrow said, with a sob.

"This jury is going to acquit you," Rogers said, "you are not going to jail. We know that now. Where will you go? Tomorrow you must speak and prove your innocence before the world, so that you can walk out of that courtroom not only a free man but a man vindicated, so you can go back to your work. You will speak not to the jury to proclaim your innocence but to the world."

Then he began to lead and harass Darrow, bait and argue with him, shout at him, force him out of the strange lethargy that had held him through the months of the trial. That speech which has become so famous, gone down in the books, taken a high place among all-time great orations, was made before ever he entered the courtroom, made for the first time all night long in our office. I heard it and other things as well.

I don't know even now whether the conclusions I drew were

right or wrong. I was very young. Nevertheless, my short life had been spent weighing evidence. True also, I contrasted him with my father. So did most people at the time. Remember, most of the cases by which he was established as the Great Defender came *after* this acquittal. Then he was a famous criminal lawyer, a labor leader, sent out from Indianapolis, headquarters of the anarchist wing of the Labor party, and he had fallen into deep disgrace.

The bomb that dynamited the press, in the building of the Los Angeles *Times,* was heard around the world in the war between Capital and Labor just beginning. I have some testimony, a behind-the-scenes inside story of this moment-in-history not told hitherto. I knew more about the personal, emotional factors off-stage, which so vitally influenced events in the trial the world was watching, than anybody but Clarence Darrow's wife, Ruby.

In his great book, *High Tension,* one of the all-time all-American reporters, Hugh Baillie, later president of the United Press, has written: *Only Earl Rogers saved the great Darrow from ending his career prematurely within what Darrow called, in his closing address to the jury, the gray dim walls of San Quentin.* A majority of the famed correspondents from all over the nation who came to cover this unique and crucial trial agreed with this.

If the story of Clarence Darrow had ended the day he pleaded James B. McNamara guilty of murder in the *Times* dynamiting, he would have gone down to his grave a failure, a traitor to his cause, a bumbling poseur. If he had not been acquitted on the odious charge of jury bribery, Darrow would never have had a chance to win the moral victories of the Leopold-Loeb, Scopes, Scottsboro, and Massey trials, all of which, of course, he lost in court. Let's face it, he would have been disbarred, in the penitentiary, or in his grave. The Great Defender came after and sprang from the acquittal Rogers won for him on a charge of which we believed he was guilty.

The bones of the cases are simple—the only things that are.

On October 1, the *Times* was dynamited. Twenty-one men and women died. Many were injured. The grand jury of Los Angeles County, on evidence presented by Earl Rogers, returned an indictment of murder.

The following April, James B. McNamara was arrested for the crime and his brother, John J. McNamara, for the dynamiting of the Llewellyn Iron Works. Clarence Darrow, who had defended and acquitted Big Bill Haywood for the bomb slaying of ex-Governor Steunenberg in Idaho, came to California to act as their counsel.

While they were selecting a jury in the McNamara case, the district attorney's men arrested Bert Franklin, chief investigator for Clarence Darrow, for attempting to bribe a prospective juror, Lockwood by name, on a street corner in downtown Los Angeles. Clarence Darrow was on the scene of the crime at the time.

Seventy-two hours later, Darrow astounded the nation by changing the plea of the McNamaras from Not Guilty to Guilty, in one of the most unprecedented court actions on record.

After Bert Franklin's testimony had accused Darrow, he was also charged with jury bribery in the cases of Lockwood and a second man, named Bain, and was arrested, appeared with his attorney, Earl Rogers, and posted $20,000 bail.

The case went to trial four months later.

To put flesh and blood, mind, soul, and heart onto these bare bones has to begin as historic events so often do, with a small bit of human interest.

My father was against the methods of anarchy to win freedom for the underdog, he thought they were stupid. I once heard him say to that slim, sweet-smiling, starry-eyed young socialist leader, Eugene Debs, that every time he put the letter R in front of the word "evolution" he set true advancement back a century. Nevertheless, to be on the side of the prosecution was against his instinct, principles, emotions, and sense of drama. So in spite of the pleas of civic leaders and men-in-the-street I don't think he would have set out to find the men who put that dynamite in Ink Alley if Harvey Elder hadn't been behind the city desk the night it went off.

We had known Harvey all our lives.

His sister Grace was a girl who had been my friend for years. His grandmother, a great lady of the old school, was a friend of my grandmother's. Most of their early California fortune had dissolved under taxes and water rights, as so many did. The Elders lived in Whittier, a Quaker suburb of Los Angeles, the same town the young man I was to marry, Ike St. Johns, came from—and still later Richard Nixon. Somehow Grace and her grandmother were always lovely, gentle, kindly and Papa adored Harvey's grandma. The eldest grandson, Churchill Harvey Elder, came back from the University of Berlin when it became apparent the family exchequer wouldn't stand for the Diplomatic Corps, dropped the Churchill and got a job as a copy boy, a reporter, and finally assistant night city editor on the *Times*.

Any night city editor would have drifted across the street during the long hours to Earl Rogers' office, where the lights burned all of the twenty-four. It was a beat bigger than ever. Only the width of First Street away, the telephone could bring a city editor back in two minutes and it was interesting and often newsworthy to talk to Earl Rogers. As a young old friend, Harvey Elder made himself at home in our office.

He'd been there two or three nights before October 1. What Gene Fowler called a *sweet* guy. Hard-hitting, high-class, clean-living, an honest newspaperman. His night off was Monday, when the bill at the Orpheum changed, sometimes he went with Papa and me. I can hear him *laugh* now, at the man—oh, I can't remember his name, who broke up pianos before Jimmy Durante, or at Rooney and Bent, or Bert Williams, or any of the great vaudevillians.

You see, laughter was a thing we sought. We thought laughter was a—a sign of courage, of faith in life, of it being worth while to put up a fight. One thing that made it so difficult for Earl Rogers to communicate with Clarence Darrow or vice versa, or me either, was that nobody *ever* heard Clarence Darrow laugh. I never saw either him or his wife Ruby *smile*. Gloom surrounded them, spread from him so that you began to think John Donne was mistaken when he said, "The spirit of God is not a dampe." It was real damp around the Darrows.

On that last night he was in our office, young Harvey Elder was exuberant. He brought with him buns with baked ham from the free lunch at Simpsons, and a bottle of beer, and he said Grace and his grandmother were coming in some night soon to see "where I work." He hadn't had his promotion long. He said he'd call me and meantime did I want to go some night to see Marie Dressler in *Tillie's Punctured Romance?* I said I did and he went out waving a hand that still had a bun in it.

A *sweet* guy.

On that clear afternoon, as the sun went down and the sky deepened, darkened to a midnight blue, a thin ferret of a man, carrying a suitcase, slipped unseen into Ink Alley, a corridor inside the Times Building where reserves of printer's ink were kept. Acting on orders, when the man came out he was empty-handed. Sixteen sticks of eighty-per-cent dynamite had been planted, timed to go off around one o'clock that morning.

The whole building was still alight and active when one
o'clock came. The city room was working on the late edition.
Pressmen were set to roll. A staff of reporters, copy desk men,
telephone and telegraph operators was on duty for this lobster
trick. Going happily about their usual business.

Similar suitcases had been planted at the Llewellyn Iron
Works, and at the Merchants and Manufacturers headquarters,
this was to be a night of organized destruction of the enemies
of union labor. A surprise attack in the long war going on
between the steel manufacturers and the International Bridge
Workers and Structural Iron Workers Union, in which John J.
McNamara was an official.

With a roar and violence which shook the city, at 1:17 A.M.
the dynamite exploded. People tumbled out of bed, rushed to
their windows, sure this must be another San Francisco earthquake. Seconds later, the sky over the whole city turned a
terrifying, lurid red, as the severed gas mains shot flames high
—higher—up through the three floors of the building.

One hundred men and women were trapped in this inferno.

Earl Rogers, at his desk in his own office, was one of the
first men to get across to the burning valley of death. The
pavement was still rocking. The heat drove him back and he
stared, unbelieving, as the wall on the Broadway side fell in,
then in as many seconds four or five more explosions repeated
like the detonation of cannons and above it all he heard the
wild, inhuman screams of the human beings within.

This is *war*, Clarence Darrow was to say to his lawyer, Earl
Rogers.

As in so many wars, it was tough to see the innocent, the
noncombatant in the path of the bombs.

Immediately, the streets were clogged with people from
nearby hotels, some in their night clothes. From open-all-
night beaneries and saloons. Senseless with horror, tears running down their cheeks, their mouths open, they stood fool-
ishly, hypnotized, unable to go away.

In the *Times* of that day, assembled by a frantic-gotten-
out-of-bed staff and printed on *Herald* presses, it read: *In the
time it took to run at full speed from the Police Station to the
corner of First and Broadway, less than half a block, the entire
building was in flames on three floors.* In his confession, J. B.
McNamara said, "I never meant to hurt anybody, I'm sorry
about that." But—surely this trained handler of dynamite,
picked for this job, must have known sixteen sticks of eighty-
per-cent dynamite were dangerous to play with? And when he

said he supposed everybody would have gone home by one o'clock, it was a barefaced lie. James B. McNamara had himself worked as a pressman, he knew the morning paper didn't go to bed until two o'clock or later and pressmen and others would still be at work.

Men and women mangled, crippled, imprisoned by tottering walls and sheets of flame made the night unbearable with cries nobody who heard them ever got out of their ears as long as they lived. Papa said the worst was the faces appearing in the windows of the editorial and city rooms like distraught fugitives from a graveyard, which indeed they were. For a moment these faces would be there in a rift of the smoke and vanish as it swirled and darkened and engulfed them. Rescuers seeing them, fighting to get to them, to save them, were driven back by blistering-hot smoke, leaping, hungry flames licked out hungrily against them.

Fire engines arrived. Hose carriers came first, instead of hook-and-ladder wagons. The mistake was costly. A policeman rushed from the station with two ladders. Harry Chandler, who had been out for a bite and returned to find his paper in flaming hell and chaos, worked like a madman, trying to help others hold these against hot, crumbling walls. They were too short; nevertheless, they saved lives as men jumped and were caught. Others leaped, hurled themselves anywhere to escape the torture of fire, the bodies crashed broken and screaming or—broken and silent.

Now from mouth to mouth ran the terrified, pitiful whisper. Telegraphers, copy boys, mail clerks, cleaning women, phone operators, linotypers—no one had been given one second's warning. For the dynamiters such a warning would have defeated their purpose of terror for the owners of the *Times*. Needed reforms trample unwilling victims as well as dedicated martyrs. True, at that moment certain union labor leaders believed that millowners, mineowners, those who employed child labor would do nothing to better conditions for the workingmen—many of them were as guilty as the little rat of a man who had planted the dynamite. They may have been right. Looking back fifty years it is easier for me to see this now than it was for my father that night, as he listened to the calls for help of the dying, and saw the broken burned bodies like bundles of old rags in the streets.

When I got there about dawn in our new Pope Toledo car, most of the cops on the fire lines knew Earl Rogers' daughter and passed me through. My first look at Papa made me cry

aloud. Black with soot, his clothes in ribbons, his face raw and
swollen with burns, he was holding his right arm away from
his body and his hand looked like a piece of raw steak on the
end of it. The *stench* was unbelievable. The cold, sick reek of
smoke hung over the whole area, our offices were filled with
it like a slaughterhouse. Every window was shattered, glass
crunched under my feet. Desks, chairs, floors were covered
with ashes not yet cold, chunks of metal and granite and
charred wood were all over the place. We have seen the
wiping out of cities often since then, but each air-raid warden's
small area of rubble, buried bodies, destruction of human life
and human hopes was a microcosm of the city, country, world
at war. Bombs were new to us, what I saw, smelled, heard
that morning was as terrible to me, to all of us, as any global
holocaust to come.

Papa was talking to himself through clenched teeth. *The
murdering fiends,* he kept saying. *The paranoiac assassins.*
They defeat their own ends, which are righteous. This butch-
ery of workingmen and women—as brutal and useless as the
St. Bartholomew massacre, it will turn all decent people who
sympathize with their cause from them. What did the French
Revolution do but turn loose Napoleon? These men who must
turn loose the red-handed slayer—do they expect us to believe
they can govern? That they have a right to freedom? They
have to be chained like dogs that bite!

His underlip was bitten through, his chin was covered with
dried blood. I got a towel and went to wet it so I could wash
his face. The mains had been broken, there was as yet no
water, I had to do the best I could with dry linen.

"I played this in blackface, I see," he said, and tried a tired
smile.

Rosy came in with coffee. Behind him, Bert Cowan black
and tattered as something straight out of hell. My coffee
wouldn't go down. A pause fell. We all turned to look at Papa,
as we always did in moments of stress and suspense. He had
closed his eyes and his face was a death mask and I saw tears
coming out, squeezed from between his lashes. I said, "Papa
—" It came out past the lumps in my throat in two rasps. Nobody had mentioned Harvey Elder. Nobody needed to.

My father looked at Cowan. Bert walked over to the window
and came back and said, "He—jumped. He's at the Clara
Barton Hospital, he was alive the last I could find out."

I had been taught not to cry. A man did not cry. A brave
woman did not cry, at least where anyone could see her. But

there was nothing I could do about my stomach. Probably it was partly the smells. I got to the washbasin in the corner just in time. When I came back Papa said, "You are exactly the green of a leaf of lettuce," and I said, "And you are as red as a lobster, so we are lobster salad," and we thought we laughed but we didn't, not really.

I said, "Does Grace know?" and Papa said he did not see how she could, the Elders lived out in Whittier still, the telephone wires were down for blocks around the disaster area.

We walked to the hospital. Five blocks down Broadway. Two or three west up Fifth Street, close to where the Biltmore Hotel now stands. We did not talk, I don't think even Papa could find any words. This is another of those clear recollections where I do not have to make anything up that *must* have been there. This is complete in itself. The chill autumn dawn that did not seem real to me. I kept thinking about Dante's *Divine Comedy* in hell. *And to a part I come where no light shines.* All I saw then was as though my eyes were filmed with smoke, thick and black and sickening. *Hell.* What men had a right to condemn their fellow men to hell? *As one who from a dream awakened straight yet still retains impressions of the feeling of his dreams*—the desert dawn was shining clear and yet the impressions of that horrible crematory I had seen and smelled I still retained. I knew bodies were in the ruins of that building so familiar to me, that we looked at every day, that I ran in and out of.

Did things like this have to be part of the new war between Capital and Labor?

A scrubwoman who'd left home and whose grandchildren expected her back when they came from school. Children watching for their fathers—maybe Papa and I were wrong, maybe we could never quite see things in terms of Humanity, we always saw them in terms of human beings. We did not see a Cause—we saw men and women. I think now this was one of Earl Rogers' real weaknesses. To see things as individuals, never to be able to translate them into an impersonal Cause so that what happened to individuals in a war to free millions didn't—couldn't—matter.

At the hospital we found a wilderness, all confusion. Many of those for whom there was no room at Emergency had been brought here, it was closer than the County. We stood in a small waiting room, Papa was mumbling to himself again, it came to me that he might be a little delirious with the burns and exhaustion and smoke he'd breathed, and shock. "Senseless," he kept saying, as though he were addressing a jury. "I tell you, gentlemen, this is senseless. I am for the same cause but we must use our Brains."

Just then I saw a woman in white, her head done up in a turban. I recognized her as a friend of my Aunty Blanche's, the first woman to practice medicine in California, her name was Hammond. I ran and stopped her, she stared at me with tired eyes out of a grim white face, and I said, "My father"— I stopped to swallow—"he ought to have—" She came with me and nodded to my father. Papa said, "Our young friend Elder —" Dr. Hammond said, "He died an hour ago, you may thank God for it. You need some attention yourself, Earl," and took him away.

I said to Cowan, "Somebody has to tell Grace and his grandmother."

"It don't have to be you," Cowan said.

As it turned out, he was wrong. It did have to be me.

Perhaps this makes it possible to see why my father and I had trouble adjusting to Clarence Darrow's point of view about the McNamaras, which was to figure so vitally later on.

I always saw Harvey Elder on one side of the screen and J. B. McNamara on the other.

I do not say this was right or fair. Just that it was a fact.

Darrow was looking at it from the broad humanitarian standpoint. People who got into the way of humanity's progress must be dynamited out of it. Well, young as I was, I might have agreed if those who were responsible for holding back that progress could, in this way, be forced to do something about it.

But—*Harvey*. I kept seeing Grace Elder's face, the little grandmother's eyes shining through her tears. Their courtesy. Their concern, that so difficult a task had fallen to me. Their gratitude to me and to my father—they had time and room for these things in their hearts even then. The only other time I saw anything approaching it was when Anne Lindbergh was on the witness stand during the trial of Hauptmann for the kidnap-murder of her son. Courage—courage was the best thing they could offer. Grace and his grandmother offered it to the boy who had died, wherever he was. He had always known them as brave, he would expect them to be now. They made, as it were, a wreath of courage and faith and laid it on his grave. This was the gallantry that made you shed the tears for them.

In one of the eulogies of Clarence Darrow it says that he
was pleased to find his client, J. B. McNamara, charged with
seventeen counts of murder, a clean-cut intelligent young man
of quiet and gentle manner, at twenty-eight lean of face and
figure, having an amused, bright gleam in his eye and a
poetic, almost mystical strain. Undoubtedly, that was the
way Darrow saw the man who, with highest ideals, planted the
dynamite in Ink Alley. On the other hand that brilliant
reporter, Hugh Baillie, remembers J. B. McNamara as "a
ferret of a man, small and nasty." To me he was the first man
I'd ever seen who really looked like a rat, not poetical or
mystical at all. Yet at the time I felt a great and—*terrible* ache
in my heart for him which I hated and resented. This thin,
undernourished, undereducated little man, this pinched face,
it all shows in his pictures to this day—*why* did he loathe
society, fear and resent it to the actual placing of death for
the innocent? Society must have done some of this, I knew
that. So did my father, who said J.B. was a tool as much as a
blackjack or a monkey wrench.

That is why I say if he hadn't been the murderer of Harvey
Elder, he might have gotten away with it, he would not have
had Earl Rogers, implacable and eager as Sherlock Holmes
himself, on his trail.

FORTY-NINE

Still wearing bandages like boxing gloves, Earl Rogers met
with leading citizens to consider steps about this outrage,
which had caused wholesale death and injury, property damage and crippling of business and terrorized the common man
and woman who didn't like or understand it.

At once, labor branded as ridiculous this loose talk of *dynamiting*.

Gas inside the building had exploded and caused a fire.
Defective mains were responsible.
No bombs or dynamite had been used.

Respected, admired, and feared but certainly never loved, General Harrison Gray Otis was nominated The Heavy. An explosion, whether or not the result of gas leaks, would be a golden opportunity for him, with paranoiac hatred of labor, to try to blame them for this disaster. *Dynamiting.* No such thing, said union labor. Ninety-eight per cent of labor did not agree with the conquer-by-violence boys, the small but fervid group in Indianapolis, and they really believed the denials they put forth. Jim Lynch, an officer of the Typographical Union, said publicly, "We *know* the trouble was faulty gas lines." From St. Louis, the day after the explosion, Samuel Gompers, president of the American Federation of Labor, a great and honest leader, said, "We had nothing to do with it. I am reliably informed by men who have studied the matter that it was the result of gas mains exploding and the deaths were entirely due to the fire caused by this mechanical failure." Obviously, with the ashes still hot and the bodies still buried in them, no such study of the matter was possible.

Even the Los Angeles *Express*, anti-labor to some extent, said casually, *Very Likely It Was Gas.* From Sacramento, a weak-kneed governor said with feeling, "Could it be that there are fiends in human form who will perpetrate such dastardly deeds?"

Only one man made a direct, sensible, and prophetic statement. Chief of Police Galloway, who worked closely with our office, said to my father, "It was dynamite. Done by out-of-town men imported for the job."

As it turned out, both the city and the country were too uneasy to be lulled into letting it drop. If this was a deliberately planned bombing, it was evidence that anarchy, as a method, had crept into the ranks of organized labor, however much labor repudiated them. Which it did. This could be the beginning of terrorism, it must be checked before it got a foothold.

The Haymarket riots had been in the midst of a direct-action strike. Locked-out workers at the McCormick plant had lain in wait for the scabs who had taken their places on the job when they struck. A pitched battle started. Police rushed in, killed one man, and shot five or six others. Clubs were used. Bombs had been tossed at open-air meetings where laboring men gathered to plan action against deadly working conditions, too long hours, too low pay. The Homestead Massacre, as it was called, had taken place when strikers at a steel plant in Pennsylvania fired at and/or were fired on by bargeloads of detectives, seven men were killed, all this as part of the demand of workers in the coal-mine war, which was to last until the great John L. Lewis won it for the miners.

But at the time of the *Times* disaster *nothing* was going on. No demands. No warnings, no negotiations. Some time previous the International Bridge Workers and Structural Iron Workers Union had called a general strike, to which none of the other unions responded, so it fell through. Indianapolis blamed this partly on the Los Angeles *Times*.

If it was a dynamite job, the combination of wanton disregard for human life and the fact they'd struck without declaring war shook the nation.

True, at this time Papa was not respectable. In spite of Aunty Blanche as chairman of the board of the Los Angeles Symphony, his mother as a leader of the Friday Morning and Ebell clubs, and his late father as minister and college president, his name had been dropped from the Blue Book, forerunner of the Social Register. Nobody had yet seen him "under the influence" in the courtroom, but they had in too many other places. He was spectacular about it. Woolly rumors of our doings in San Francisco, still regarded by Los Angeles as wickeder than Port Said, were circulated. Our social life was maverick. We went to the ball games, to the fights, to the Burbank, where a young actress named Laurette Taylor glowed with pure genius. Once at supper after the show she said to Earl Rogers that his daughter was a true-life version of her most famous line in *Peg' o' My Heart—That's what me father says and that's how he says it*. Over at the Belasco the star and matinee idol, Lewis S. Stone, horrified everybody by saying he might go into The Movies. The management, wishing to replace him with Ethel Barrymore's little brother, finally located Jack at Catalina Island. However, Jack refused to leave his paradise. "Fish cannot fly," Jack Barrymore said, "yet here they do. I am studying this phenomenon." Papa had defended him on a charge of assault and battery. A barber in the Van Nuys Hotel had put a too hot towel on the to-be-famous profile and Barrymore had reacted with a left hook. The greatest Hamlet of all time and his lawyer, Earl Rogers, had a jury *in the aisles* when they re-enacted this scene in the courtroom.

Nevertheless, in conclave the city state and national fathers decided for three reasons that Rogers was the one man to take charge of an investigation to get the truth. 1. His proven Sherlock Holmes type of ability. 2. An already functioning force of investigators. 3. The only man in California trusted by the underworld.

"*They*—don't like this," Earl Rogers told the meeting.

The professional criminal liked dynamiting no more than later he would like child-kidnaping. Certain crimes unite an aroused public opinion and put it actively behind law enforcement. At that time, a Murder Incorporated had never been dreamed of. The professional gambler, pick-pocket, second-story man, highway or bank robber, safecracker, con man, jewel thief, counterfeiter, or forger regarded murder as a private and personal affair, accidental or passional. Murder was not a profession. Guns for Hire didn't come in until Prohibition. A high-class, intelligent pro never carried a gun. He might use it in an emergency, then he would get hung, which was to be avoided if possible. All these, as well as bartenders, messenger boys, cabdrivers, horse handlers, waiters and waitresses, who were part of their underworld, if they knew anything would tell it to Mr. Rogers and nobody else. They always knew things.

However the city fathers had trouble persuading Earl Rogers. At the meeting Oscar Lawler told me it turned into a brawl between him and General Otis, who came in waving a *Times* headline.

BOMBS EXPLODED BY ENEMIES OF INDUSTRIAL FREEDOM/FEARFUL LOSS OF LIFE; OTHER CRIMES THREATENED

"I won't fight under that banner, General," Earl Rogers said. "If you don't give industrial freedom to the workingman; if you let capital hog all the profits and refuse to share with them; if you don't do away with child labor, somebody else will clean your house for you, *with dynamite*. I want it understood that to me this is a *murder* case. I am after a murder indictment. Somebody dynamited innocent men and women, my friends. They murdered a boy I loved. A boy I thought someday I might have as a son-in-law. I want to find the man who killed him."

As far as I know this matchmaking bit about a son-in-law was a spur-of-the-moment figment off the top of his imagination. I must say it was effective.

Three weeks later, Earl Rogers went before a specially empaneled grand jury. To them he presented one hundred and seventy-four witnesses, some who had been there, some bomb and dynamite experts, doctors, plumbers, gas company maintenance officials, city inspectors, engineers, and builders. After considering this evidence, the grand jury returned its indictments.

The Los Angeles *Times* had been dynamited. This constituted murder by a person or persons unknown.

A great deal of time, energy, patience and incredible capacity was spent by Earl Rogers in bringing about the arrest of the McNamaras. He worked tirelessly day and night to find the man who put the dynamite in Ink Alley.

This was the tribute of the Los Angeles *Examiner*, Papa's ancient enemy. Truer words were never printed.

Starting to locate the person or persons unknown, Earl Rogers had as direct clues some twisted pieces of blown sticks of dynamite, some spattered nitroglycerin and nothing else.

The word went out.

Mr. Rogers wants to know anything anybody knows about those bastards that blew up those poor working people in the *Times*.

As the *Examiner* said and knew, for they had reporters in our office twenty-four hours a day, Earl Rogers watched and waited, patiently.

Piece by piece, like a cut puzzle, the shape of things to come began to be visible. Impossible to hurry anybody. Men who give information in fear of their lives—dynamiters were new, they might do anything, they could be dangerous—cannot ever be hurried. Rogers waited as they came quietly, by night, listened to a small problem of their own, gabbed about baseball, Joe Rivers and Abe Attell, the Keystone cops.

In the midst of this, vaguely, somebody had heard that somebody told a guy he knew that a man was seen leaving San Francisco on a certain day carrying a suitcase.

That night, Rogers, Sam Browne, head of the district attorney's county detective force, Luther Brown, Bert Cowan, and Bill Abbott went north.

In San Francisco, they still loved Earl Rogers. He was their boy.

Such and such an ironworks—over in Sausalito . . . ?

There they pinned it down. The dynamite had come from there and could be traced.

Then began the process of identification and elimination, made famous by Scotland Yard. A crime bears earmarks, espe-

cially one that needs the knowledge and experience of carrying and placing *time-fused* sticks of dynamite. Men capable of
this can be narrowed down. Such criminals, too, have tricks,
habits, as distinctive as fingerprints, whether they are cat
burglars or safe blowers, con men or dynamiters.

A general list was made of bomb handlers. Now Earl Rogers
found himself working *with* an ancient enemy. At the end of
the graft trials, William J. Burns had gone east to open his
famed detective agency. Among his clients was the Erectors
Association, composed of the big steel companies. From that
end, Burns worked on the Indianapolis headquarters, where
the Philosophy of Force planned its strategy and dispatched
orders and operatives. He also began with the help of those
labor leaders who deplored violence to get lists of bridges
blown, aqueducts dynamited, new buildings collapsed, train
roadbeds destroyed, accidents in steel works—all this tabulated
as to cities and dates. Earl Rogers concentrated in San Francisco on Olaf Tvietmoe, the Western brain of the anarchy
wing.

How many men, known to be connected with these, were
capable of the *Times* job? Where had they been on the night
of October 1—and thereafter?

At long last, a woman in South San Francisco told Mr.
Rogers that she might be able to identify pictures of the men
who bought the dynamite. In a reluctant whisper, she said
one of them had something wrong with one eye.

What man on the suspect possibility list had something
wrong with one eye?

Burns sent Earl Rogers a photograph.

In utmost secrecy, Rogers showed it among a dozen others
to the woman. Her finger came down instantly. "That's the
man," she said, "his name is James Bryce."

His name was James B. McNamara.

He and his pal and co-worker Ortie McManigal were
picked up by Burns's detectives in Detroit and brought secretly
to Los Angeles. A couple of weeks later, after McManigal
squealed, Assistant District Attorney Joseph Ford went to
Indianapolis with extradition papers and arrested his brother,
John J. McNamara, whom Earl Rogers wanted as the man
who had planned and directed the entire attack.

On the evidence he had collected and that supplied by
Burns, Earl Rogers again went before the grand jury.

John J. McNamara was indicted on the charge of dynamiting the Llewellyn Iron Works.

James B. McNamara on seventeen counts of murder, including that of Harvey Elder.

Within a few days the news broke that Clarence Darrow was coming West to defend the McNamaras.

FIFTY

The McNamaras Are Innocent.

Red, white, and blue buttons bearing this slogan blossomed and were worn around the nation.

Save the McNamaras.

Likewise in red, white, and blue, banners with this appeal swung from barber poles, cars, front porches, and were displayed in store windows. Torchlight processions were held in the big cities, a socialist named Job Harriman decided to run for mayor of Los Angeles and splashed his platform *Save the McNamaras from the Capitalistic Conspiracy* in red, white, and blue billboards all over town.

From where I sat, it was hard to realize that millions of people, a large part of the civilized world, hadn't waited on any *presumption* of innocence for a trial, but had begun to scream a burning faith at once. *Money talks.* Three hundred thousand dollars, worth ten times that today, contributed for the McNamaras' defense said the contributors were sure of this *innocence.* Much of the money came in dollar bills, silver fifty-cent pieces, quarters and dimes, copper pennies. For men and women paid at labor's rate per hour then, this meant going without dinner the rest of the week. When I saw women congregated under J. B. McNamara's county-jail window, I couldn't keep my mouth shut to a girl blowing kisses at it and got into a hair-pulling match which I won but Papa said I was too old for any more.

Like Sacco and Vanzetti fifteen years later, the McNamaras became a crusade. Intellectuals, artists, and writers, always on the side of drama and revolt, which often also is that of truth and the rights of man, flocked to the support of the Mc-Namaras. Nobody wrote anything as brilliant as Edna St. Vincent Millay's *Justice Denied in Massachusetts,* Zola's

J'Accuse in the affair Dreyfus, or William Ellery Leonard's *Tom Mooney*, but Max Eastman, Lincoln Steffens, and John Reed were heard abroad in the land.

This time the issue was drawn, the guns wheeled onto the firing line. For this was the first time a real accusation of pure terrorism as a weapon of the labor movement wasn't against some fringe crackpot, some socialistic wild man outside the organized ranks, who could easily and honestly be repudiated by the leaders.

These men were *inside*.

The International Bridgeworkers and Structural Ironworkers Union was a member of the American Federation of Labor, which therefore had to be responsible for its activities. John J. McNamara was its secretary-treasurer. James B. McNamara had been a member in good standing for years. Thus this was perhaps the major crisis of the fight the unions, then still in their infancy, were making for better working conditions, higher wages, more reasonable hours, to all of which workingmen were entitled.

Of all this Gompers and Eugene Debs were naturally well aware.

Asked the big question direct by their leader, Samuel Gompers, J. J. and J. B. McNamara swore with tears in their eyes that their hands were clean, their hearts were pure, the cause of labor, the future of their brother workingmen could rest safely upon their innocence.

The president of the A. F. of L. *believed* them.

Eugene Debs cried, "They are innocent men. I know whereof I speak."

It is not possible to build suspense when everybody already knows who won a war. Looking back down the years now it is possible to see the whole broad screen, all the action on the surface and above and below it. To show what the McNamaras and Clarence Darrow did to the life of Earl Rogers and his daughter it gives an honest, clear perspective to place J. B. McNamara's confession right here.

The Sacco-Vanzetti guilt or innocence is still a raging controversy. So is the Preparedness Day Parade bombing and Tom Mooney's part in it. Books are still being written and always will be concerning Bruno Richard Hauptmann and the kidnap-murder of the Lindbergh baby, those of us who covered the trial continue to argue about it. Alger Hiss has never confessed to the charges of which the jury found him guilty.

In the equally famous McNamara case, J. B. McNamara did confess to what *we knew* when my father indicted him for murder. To read it here is to have no further questions as to the basic facts with which we had to cope as the drama unfolded in our office.

This is the statement made immediately after he changed his original plea of Not Guilty to *Guilty*.

I, James B. McNamara, defendant in the case of The People against McNamara, having now in court on December 1 pleaded guilty to the crime of murder, make this statement of fact concerning same; And this is the truth. On the night of September 30, at 5:45 P.M. I concealed in Ink Alley, a portion of the Los Angeles Times Building, a suitcase containing 16 sticks of 80% dynamite set to explode at 1 o'clock in the morning and it was my intention to injure the building and scare the owners. I did not intend to take the life of anyone. I sincerely regret that these unfortunate men lost their lives. If the giving of my life would bring them back I would freely give it. In fact in pleading guilty to murder in the first degree I have placed my life in the hands of the state.

Signed
JAMES B. MCNAMARA

That came in December, six months after Clarence Darrow had arrived in town, in the midst of seething uproar, and pleaded the McNamaras Not Guilty with trumpets blowing.

Those six months held the incredible chain of events which led up to the most amazing *change of plea* ever made in a courtroom, the change which rocked labor leaders and the whole country and culminated in Darrow's arrest for jury bribery.

When we heard that Clarence Darrow was coming to take charge of the McNamara defense, I said to my father, "Is there any chance that they *are* innocent?"

My father said, "No."

"Do you suppose Mr. Darrow thinks they are?" I said.

My father sat behind his desk, rolling a cigarette, letting the first puff drift around his head, his face screwed up in disturbance, very thoughtful. I knew of course that Darrow was one of my father's heroes.

In fact if he had an idol, it was this man he was to save, who had already been a successful criminal lawyer when Rogers was admitted to the Bar. Opposites attract? Or maybe in his heart Papa wished he'd found A Cause, instead of -

having to do it one by one for the least of these. Since he had
seen Buck hung he'd gone to Sacramento several times and
once to Washington, but the fight against capital punishment
was so far ahead of its time—apparently fifty years later it
still is—that he couldn't get any help for this weird idea.
Himself a sentimental, emotional Irishman, he was deeply
moved by rebellion against injustice. He never seemed to be
quite able to let his heart rule his head, he always saw the
mistakes they were making in Lost Causes. When Darrow
defended Eugene Debs in a strike dispute, Papa had followed
every word of the trial. He'd spent long nights talking to
Debs on his last visit to California. The testimony in the
case of Big Bill Haywood he had read aloud to us there in
our office, he'd been tickled as a kid, chortling in a way he
had, when Darrow defeated Borah, a foe, my father said,
worthy of any man's steel.

Believing the McNamaras to be red-handed, maniacal
killers of the helpless, Earl Rogers now found himself on the
unpopular side of the case and he did not like it a little bit
when Clarence Darrow rode to the rescue singing the battle
cry of freedom. He wasn't used to it. On the other hand, he
was also torn with concern for the man he so much admired.
No one knew better than Earl Rogers *all* the difficulties of
defending guilty clients. Also he himself, having indicted
the McNamaras, was committed morally and legally to giving
the district attorney all the help he could to convict them.
He was always uncomfortable on the prosecution side, no
matter what.

After a while he said, "A man afire, alight, inspired for and
by a cause, can deceive himself as to the facts of a case. He
sees with his heart, his blood stream, his bowels of mercy,
he is able to see what he wants to see and not to see what
he doesn't want to see. Or—he may have accepted that the
end justifies the means and be able to *believe* the crime is
justified, and that justification is the same as innocence. To
Debs, to Jack London, as you've heard him say, all workers
are always right and all capitalists are always wrong. None
of them are *people* any more. They have become pieces in a
war, they may be defended for any action they take in battle.
A fighting crusader like Clarence Darrow, a true idealist of
courage and endurance, may believe the McNamaras are
innocent, justified.

"And," he was even more thoughtful, more concerned,
"either way and even if he didn't believe either of those

things, he must now give them, poor benighted hypnotized madmen that they are, the best defense of which he is capable. It will be very good indeed."

"But Papa," I said, "Darrow was sent out by Johannsen. Wasn't Big Bill Haywood one of the headquarters boys? It's not possible Darrow doesn't *know*."

"Oh—I wouldn't be sure of that," my father said, "it is their custom not to let the left hand know what the right hand is up to. They may keep a man of Darrow's high ideals in a comfortable fantasy. Again, they are now his *clients*. He must give them the best defense possible."

Clarence Darrow, as it turned out, did not give the McNamaras the best defense possible or any defense at all.

Why did he change the plea of James B. to *Guilty?* A change which at the time labor leaders said set their cause back fifty years. Did he betray that cause in a frantic attempt to wiggle out of a charge of jury bribery, to save himself from the penitentiary? Or was this simply another instance of the Darrow methods of making a "deal" to get his clients a lighter sentence which he used in the Leopold-Loeb and Massey-Fortescue cases and many others?

My father came to know the answer. I know a lot of it myself.

The worst of burying things you don't like to think about for years is that when they do come up it is as though the subconscious had kept them as fresh as a freezer. So I am glad to get this out in the open, to see it more plainly now.

I must put it in here, for though I will try very hard to be *fair*, it is harder when it is someone you love than when it is for yourself. It is only right to admit that I saw through the eyes of young, indignant hostility and horror.

As late as the Leopold-Loeb trial, when I walked into a Chicago court to cover it for my news service and came face to face with Clarence Darrow, my hostility still gave off sparks. I didn't say a word and neither did he. I didn't ask him for the $27,000 *expenses* of his defense still on our books when my father died in poverty. I went to the telephone and said to Mr. Hearst, "I can't be a reporter on anything Darrow has to do with yet," and Mr. Hearst said, "Well then, you had better come home."

Doubtless through the years Darrow redeemed himself. Earned the right to be called the Great Defender.

I don't hate him now. Thank God for that.

But I did then.

FIFTY-ONE

From the day Darrow arrived in Los Angeles to take charge of the McNamara defense, he employed a man named Bert Franklin, formerly in the office of the United States Marshal, to act as his head investigator and to find out about The Wheel, a revolving roster of names for prospective jury duty. In this, Franklin said he went beyond the limits permitted and tried to bribe six of them, succeeding, he believed, with two.

After weeks of getting a jury, Lockwood had been accepted as the fifth man in the box. He'd been a deputy sheriff with Franklin and Franklin offered him four thousand dollars to vote "Darrow's way." Lockwood agreed to think it over. Franklin said he would bring the Big Boy—meaning Darrow—out to confirm the deal and bring the money. However, before this meeting could be arranged, Lockwood had thought it over to the point where he'd decided he didn't want to be mixed up in it any further. Remembering the men who'd died in the *Times,* one of whom he'd known, and shocked, he said later, by a man like Darrow employing such tactics, Lockwood went to District Attorney Fredericks and told him the whole story.

Here the D.A. could have pulled Franklin in and made him talk.

Naturally, he was after bigger fish than a third-rate greedy scavenger like Bert Franklin. To Lockwood, Franklin had certainly put Darrow right in the middle. They wanted the suborner of bribery, the man who put up the money, the Biggest Boy in sight—Mr. Darrow.

A trap was laid. A smart mouse, a mouse who didn't panic, wouldn't have come within smell of the cheese. Guilty or *not* guilty.

In his autobiography Lincoln Steffens, a pro-Darrow man if one ever was, a Darrow lieutenant and witness, writes: *When people ask me what sort of a man Darrow is, I ask them an apparently irrelevant question. When? And my answer is that at 3 o'clock he is a hero for courage, nerve*

*and calm judgment. But at 3:15 he may be a coward for
fear, collapse, panicky, mentality.*

How well we came to know that!

Take the Witness, a fine factual record of Earl Rogers'
work as a lawyer, quoted the above and added, *And now it
was 3:15 for Darrow.*

Either that or—a guilty conscience doth make cowards of
us all.

The district attorney's office laid careful plans after Lockwood had told them his story. He was to ask Franklin to
meet him at nine o'clock in the morning at the corner of
Third and Los Angeles streets. This was on his route to the
courthouse. He was to tell Franklin he preferred to wind up
their deal in the open, where nobody could be listening or
peeping through a keyhole. Franklin was to bring the four
thousand dollars to pay Lockwood.

Engineered by Sam Browne, who'd helped my father catch
the McNamaras, the stake-out was strategic, intelligent, but
overeager. Years later as a reporter I saw Hickman bring
little Marion Parker, alive and well, to a kidnap-pay-off ren-
dezvous, the place was crawling with cops and he drove on
through, the next time they saw Marion she had been hacked
into a hundred pieces. Cops have difficulty concealing themselves somehow and this would have saved Darrow right
then and there if he'd had any sense. This time also, the place
was alive with cops, cops riding motorcycles, having coffee,
buying papers, strolling along looking in the other direction,
hidden behind telephone poles.

Franklin himself waited and watched diagonally across the
street. One of his men, White, met Lockwood and passed him
a $500 bill, showing him at the same time a roll with the
other $3500 in it. Franklin then came over and said, "All
right, if it's a deal, you can have the rest now." At this tense
moment, Lockwood dropped the pay-off bill. To Franklin it
looked as though his hands were shaking, actually it was
Lockwood's agreed-upon signal. As he stooped to pick it up, a
man on a motorcycle dawdled by and nodded to Bert Franklin. Evidently, here Franklin got a whiff of the cheese.
Another man from the sheriff's office, name of Campbell,
passed by and wished Mr. Franklin the top of the morning.
He also spotted Captain George Home of the police department, a good officer who couldn't be taking a walk along the
street at 9 A.M. for his health.

Then Franklin knew. He said to Lockwood, "Let's take a

little walk, huh?" and steered him toward Second Street at a smart pace.

A few minutes earlier, according to testimony given by Darrow, the phone on his office desk rang. A voice he did not know said, "Darrow? If you want to save your man Franklin, you'd better hurry. They're onto him. If he passes that money at Third and Los Angeles, you're all for it," and the phone went dead.

Now, innocent or guilty, it was 3:15 for Darrow.

Stumbling, gasping, the sweat breaking out, he ran down the stairs and high-tailed it toward the corner mentioned. Where, whether he knew it or not, the pay-off to Lockwood had been scheduled to take place.

Sure now of the cheese, Franklin was trying to steer Lockwood out of the trap area, when whom should he see lolloping along the sidewalk toward him, waving his *hat*, but Clarence Darrow. When Franklin did his best to *shoo* him away, Darrow paid no attention. At risk of life and limb, dodging horses, cars, and bicycles, causing drivers and pedestrians to gaze at him in horror and even to shout warnings, he charged across the street to arrive panting at Franklin's side in a photo finish with Sam Browne and two other county detectives.

What was said then was a matter of disagreement in court.

Sam Browne testified that Darrow said, "They're onto us, Bert."

One of the other dicks said Darrow said, "They're onto *you*, Bert."

The third didn't know what anybody said.

Looking at Lockwood, standing a few feet away and observing all this, the whole setup was as plain to Franklin as the road to San Quentin. Still doing his best for his boss, he tried to stop Darrow's babbling. To hide the Big Boy's panic, he accepted arrest and was marched away, leaving Darrow under the cold eye of Sam Browne to make his way back to his own offices in the nearby Higgens Building—followed by Browne's two best tails, of course.

Once there, Darrow ordered his associate in the McNamara defense, a fine lawyer named LeCompte Davis, to spring Franklin with ten thousand dollars bail.

Now there was—and is—only one undetermined factor in these short and simple annals of the poor mice.

How much and what did Clarence Darrow know?

What was his part in this?

Had Bert Franklin been acting on his own or with Darrow's complicity and authority? Had Darrow put up the money?

What in the *world* was Darrow doing at the corner of Third and Los Angeles streets on that particular morning?

Immediately *after* Franklin's arrest, before Franklin had involved him, Clarence Darrow changed the pleas in the McNamara case from Not Guilty to Guilty.

For the first weeks after his arrest, Bert Franklin asserted his own innocence and steadily denied Darrow knew anything about anything. Then he began to dicker. If he pleaded Guilty and turned state's evidence—what about that? They wanted him to implicate Darrow. This for some time he refused to do.

Then came the news that Bert would go before the grand jury, plead guilty and put Darrow right in the middle. This, Darrow knew, meant that he himself would soon be indicted along with Franklin.

You'd better get Rogers, everybody told him.

So Clarence Darrow and his wife made a secret trip to a small town called Hanford, up in the San Joaquin Valley, where Rogers was trying a big will case.

FIFTY-TWO

The bailiff made seats for them in the back row of the small, crowded courtroom. Clarence Darrow sat down heavily and his wife, Ruby, *perched* as she always did, a sparrow expecting war.

We were all sunk in a lethargy of boredom so profound we were no longer capable of making a move to escape. Jerry Giesler and I knew what was going on, this was the anesthesia technique of cross-examination, one of Rogers' most danger-ous inventions. It now engulfed the judge, who had his eyes closed, the jury, which openly yawned in the box, the witness relaxed to torpor.

Jerry pinched me and I followed his eyes to where the

Darrows now sat and then back to my father, walking up and down slowly behind the counsel table. He didn't glance around. But he must have been aware of the entrance of this great trial lawyer and—there could be only one reason why Darrow was in Hanford, where we were trying to break what looked like an unbreakable will case on a contingent basis because my father had felt sorry for two young lads just over from the Old Country.

Conscienceless.

I don't quarrel with what has been said about my father Earl Rogers. Sometimes the writer knows only half the story, sees it from his side only, he has a right to his conclusions. My own are partisan with love for my father that has not, it seems, dimmed through the years and I feel he has a right that *this* side of his story be told at last. Because he came to a bad end, often the truth and the record and the emotions behind it all have been obscured, as though St. Helena was all there had been to tell about Napoleon or thus all else discredited or diminished.

The word *conscienceless* applied to Earl Rogers by one biographer is neither just nor accurate. No man ever tried harder to decide within himself on the rightness or wrongness of his own actions and affections. As his own sense of right and wrong grew blunted, as he began to have a *bad* conscience, not Macbeth himself was more tortured by it. But we didn't go around howling in public.

His decisions as to the rightness of his feelings were too *much* swayed by charity and tolerance. I find this a fault easy to forgive. Milton Cohen, the brilliant young Jewish lawyer who came out from New York to try to put our office in some kind of financial order, used to throw up his hands in horror and despair. "If you'd only get *expenses*, Mr. Rogers," he would say. My father would laugh. "You can't get blood out of a turnip, this man has a right to a defense, poor devil, and he hasn't any money." "But Mr. Rogers," Milton would say, "there are public defenders for this work." "Yes, yes," Mr. Rogers would agree, "but this man needs a *good* lawyer. A good lawyer, Milton, is on call like a doctor, isn't he? I'm in the business of saving lives too. Our law say the *best possible defense.*" Every newspaperman in town brought him every "no dough but innocent" case. "Look, Mr. Rogers, the poor kid hasn't got a nickel, but she's a good kid and I think she's getting a raw deal." Or, "Listen, Mr. Rogers, as a favor to me—I was on this story from the start and I don't think the guy did it. He can't pay a *fee* but I thought may-be—" and he always thought right. Mr. Rogers would defend the man. Even the cops brought clients saying, "Y'know, Mr. Rogers, I got an idea this fellow ought to have a good lawyer —" Hundreds of these.

I doubt if, in the beginning, it occurred to Milton Cohen that, considering the big defense fund handed over to Dar-row by labor, we could come out of that one in the red, but we did.

The day Jimmy and Dick McHale came into the office, I told Milton he was wasting his breath trying to keep Papa from taking the case. "Uncle Pat Talent," they said, in the soft brogue of our own country, "was a man of his word, Mr. Rogers. I've no sons of me own, he wrote to us, but you're my sister's boys, you come along and when I die I'll leave you the ranch. We'd not like to see what he intended go wrong, God rest his soul." "Have you the letter?" Papa asked them, and Jimmy, grinning amiably, said, "No sir, it seemed foolish to bring it back all the way across the ocean again, but you've our word for it." So Papa took their word for it, on a contingent basis and no expenses paid. This against a will executed by Uncle Pat's own esteemed lawyer, witnessed by his best friend, a highly respected citizen, with his wife, a woman looked up to by the community, as the beneficiary. To break such a will is the most insurmountable task the law can offer. I'd have nudged him into it if need be. It meant a trip out of town, away from home, quiet days with nothing but work in the courtroom, talk over the table in a small country hotel, where Papa usually ate and slept well, no chance to drop in at Joe Fast's saloon, sometimes a horseback ride in the dawn. This was good for everybody. Also, I can't remember whether young McHale had given me an admiring glance or whether Jerry Giesler had just begun to woo the boss's daughter—*something* romantic-like was going on.

So now Clarence Darrow was watching Earl Rogers, whom he had not before seen at work, cross-examining Phillip Ray. Ray was the well-known citizen who had witnessed the will made by Pat Talent—Uncle Pat—on his deathbed. At a sleep-inducing drone, Rogers was leading the man over a touching account of a friendship.

Q. (by Mr. Rogers) You and Pat Talent had been chums since you were boys, is that right, Mr. Ray?
A. Yes, sir, we went to school together.

Q. You remained close friends right here in Hanford all your lives?

A. That's right—we did.

Q. Marriage didn't change this?

A. Oh no, Pat and I went right on seeing a lot of each other.

Q. A lot of interests in common? Your work, fishing, hunting?

A. I suppose you might say that, yes.

Once, this was all right. Earl Rogers took him over it until hives of bees seemed to be buzzing in our ears. The opposing counsel suggested politely, then furiously, that these questions had been *asked* and *answered* a dozen times, which was true. The judge said, "Mr. Rogers, do you intend to pursue this much further?" and Mr. Rogers said, "If Your Honor will allow me a little more latitude?" and the judge nodded reluctantly.

A fishing expedition. Give a man enough rope of questions and *if he is lying*, he will hang himself sooner or later. This was getting later.

"Look at Darrow," Jerry whispered.

For months to come I was to see that figure sunk in deep and deeper and ever-deepening gloom. At that moment he was new to me and far, far beyond my ken. Despair sat upon his shoulders in a sable mantle. It worried me, I had not yet learned that it was in life in general as well as in particular that Darrow found little to smile at.

"Darrow don't think much of him," Jerry said.

"Neither does his wife," I said. "I wish myself Papa'd get on with it."

"*She* thinks her old man's the only good lawyer in the world," Jerry said.

A bull's-eye. Antagonism began for Ruby Darrow in that courtroom, before she spoke to my father or I put my foot in it, and it never faltered. On the eve of the second Darrow trial, it had serious results. The lies she told afterwards for her husband are probably somewhat like the ones I probably tell here for my father. That's the way it looks to me. That was the way it looked to her. Possibly she didn't know the truth. As far as she was concerned, their excessive display of poverty may have been on the level.

Now, at last, Earl Rogers came out of the nostalgic long-ago which he was re-creating for a jury, where two men named

Pat Talent and Phil Ray had played, worked, fought, and cut crops together. We arrived at the day Pat Talent signed his will and the man now on the stand witnessed it. I looked to see how our visitor was taking the way Rogers set the new scene. I couldn't tell, his wife was tugging at the sleeve of his sloppy gray coat, whispering in his ear, a sight with which I was to become more and more familiar.

Q. (by Mr. Rogers) You got up that morning and bathed?
A. Yes sir.
Q. Got dressed as usual?
A. Yes.
Q. Then what did you do?
A. I went and ate my breakfast.
Q. What did you have for breakfast, Mr. Ray?
A. I can't remember exactly—

Dixon Phillips, the counsel for Mrs. Talent, who had drawn the will, was on his feet with weary objections. Mr. Rogers withdrew the question. "I was only testing his memory of the events of that day," he said, and to the witness, "Well, then, Mr. Ray, what did you do after breakfast?"

A. I went to my office.
Q. You were sad that morning because your best friend was ill?
A. Yes.
Q. Did you know he was dying?
A. Well I didn't know but I was afraid.
Q. Not much hope held out?
A. Not much hope, no.
Q. Had there been any change at all in your friendship, yours and Pat's, before he died?
A. No, none. None at all.
Q. You were just as close as ever.
A. Yes.
Q. His death would be a real blow to you, change your whole life?
A. In a way, I suppose you might put it like that, yes.
Q. At any time, in the past, had there been any misunderstanding between you, any parting of the ways?
A. No, never. We were always warm friends.

Now we were in the time and space of the deathbed scene. A big bedroom, hushed and darkened. A doctor spoke a word, went out. Nurses in uniform moved about. Propped against pillows, Patrick Talent smiled at them weakly. The middle-aged wife began to weep, her hand in his. Now, Dixon Phillips, the lawyer, approached, presented a document, Pat Talent glanced at it and nodded and—signed it. Then Phillip Ray came out of the shadows and wrote his name beneath that of his dear old friend.

Without the hundredth part of a note's change of volume or tempo, Earl Rogers went on.

"Then what did you do?"

"Nothing."

"I mean when you had signed as a witness to the will, what did you do then, Mr. Ray?"

"I—I didn't—nothing more, Mr. Rogers."

"What words did you speak at that moment to Pat?"

"I didn't—I just signed—and then—"

"No word of encouragement or love to your friend—?"

"Well, no, I didn't say anything."

"Did you bid goodbye to your friend before you went?"

"No—I left as soon as I'd signed the paper."

"*What? What?*"

The words shrilled like a police whistle.

The hum of the bees had turned into the cry of the Valkyries.

"You mean to tell this judge and jury that you, the dear chum, the lifelong friend of Pat Talent, did not *bid him goodbye*."

"I—I don't think so—"

"You don't *think* so." Earl Rogers waited now, let it sink in. Then he said, "You mean you can't remember whether or not you said goodbye to your best friend? Wouldn't that be a moment never to be forgotten?"

"I—I suppose so—"

"Mr. Ray, did you say goodbye to Pat?"

"No."

"Why?"

The men around the courthouses, bailiffs and deputies and other lawyers and reporters, talked about it by the hour for years after he was dead.

Jerry Giesler told me that wherever he spoke to law students all over the United States they asked about this *magic* of Earl Rogers on cross-examination.

We saw later, we see now, that there were a dozen good reasons Ray could have given, even after he'd been surprised into admitting he hadn't said a final farewell. He could have said he was too moved to speak, he was weeping, or he thought it would distress his friend too much.

He *couldn't*. Somehow Earl Rogers had conditioned him—us all—to a particular other world, though we hadn't noticed it was happening. He had created it around us, then absorbed us into what was going on in it. With each new question it had become more *real*, the room was lighted, the colors of the walls and lamp shades were before us, the action and characters were authenticated, we were mesmerized into the scene *as it had taken place* at the time it had taken place. We were seeing the river of time and action not from a boat but from a plane so that the past was as real as the present, and could not be displaced. Mrs. Darrow was wrong when she said later that Earl Rogers was "nothing but an actor." He was dramatist, scene painter, stage hand, and—magician.

So the question WHY? came to that hardheaded man of business, Phillip Ray, not in the courtroom but in the room of death, he was hypnotized by what had actually been, and powerless to put forth what he had meant to tell.

"Why?" Earl Rogers said again, no answer from Ray so he answered himself softly, sympathetically, "There could be only one reason. You knew he didn't know you. You knew he was no longer able to recognize you, you knew he was too far gone for that." While Rogers stood letting time pass in silence, I watched Darrow. My heart jumped. He had identified the master touch. On the stand, Ray's eyes met those of the men watching him with compassion, and after a moment he buried his face in his hands and sat perfectly still.

Earl Rogers' closing argument in that case was the most emotional I ever heard him make.

The transcript says:

Suppose Patrick Talent came within this rail right now. He would ask, *What is all this about here in this courtroom?*

They couldn't know Rogers had spent hours with the McHales to get exactly right the touch of brogue which Uncle Pat had never lost.

I will tell you now the other side gibbered in their seats, as they stared at *this other Irishman* with the blue eyes and heard from him *the voice* of a man they thought safely dead these many moons.

"They'd tell him it was a contest over his will, wouldn't

they? And then he would say, Why, I never made a will. You were my lawyer, Dixon Phillips, you know I didn't get it done though you were always arguin' with me about it." Rogers stood quietly behind the chair in which Pat Talent's lawyer was sitting. With great indignation, he said, "*Dixon Phillips, you know I never made a will.* If Pat Talent was here now in this courtroom, that is what he would say and Dixon Phillips would jump out the window."

After that Pat Talent was back in his grave, but he'd been there long enough to convince a jury that the will should be broken. The estate was settled out of court, the boys got their share on the grounds that Uncle Pat was a man of his word, God rest his soul, and for once we got our fee, the McHales also being men of their word.

That night Clarence Darrow, like many another desperate man before him, came to discuss the possibility of Earl Rogers for the defense.

Later Ruby Darrow said she never wanted Rogers from the start. This is correct, she didn't. "He was too theatrical for my taste," she told reporters. "He wasn't a lawyer, he was just an actor." We can check the singular ingratitude of this statement against the facts a little later. At Hanford, she certainly threw the monkey wrench that almost prevented my father from keeping Ruby's husband from going to San Quentin, where I believe he belonged.

My father treated Clarence Darrow as the great man he believed him to be and gave him the chance to become. I, on the other hand, behaved badly. The truth is the Darrows were as far outside my experience as I was outside theirs. To show you a small thing as to how I got off on the wrong foot with them, one night when Papa couldn't leave the office they said, "Adela can come to dinner with us." I could have hit Papa when he said *how nice.* Anyhow I had to go. They took me to a cafeteria, and it just happened cafeterias were in their infancy at the time and I'd never been in one. Papa did not care for them. So I sat down and waited for someone to take my order. I saw the Darrows carrying trays and Mrs. Darrow called crossly, "Do not try putting on airs with us, miss, you're not too high-and-mighty to carry your dinner." I got it, and when I saw a slip with forty-six cents I handed it to Mr. Darrow. They had invited me, and anyway, the man always paid the check, but Mrs. Darrow said, "No, you don't, miss, you pay your own, we go Dutch." So I paid mine and theirs too and she was sore and said I was a show-off just like my father.

At my meeting with Lincoln Steffens in Carmel I told him I'd never forgotten the desperate hangdog despair of Darrow's face that night in Hanford. He said, "Darrow was a great man. So it is surprising that he was a craven. Perhaps that made him even greater." I couldn't see that, my stomach revolted at the craven, not even a scared *kid* like Boyd had showed the yellow streak like that. It threw me off balance.

Papa saw the great man. Their discussion came down to one thing.

"Mr. Darrow," my father said, "if I were the defendant, I would make you my chief counsel and trust you completely. So you must trust me."

It was my first chance to see the two men together as the whole nation was to see them for many months to come. Darrow, the Honest Abe type, heavy of movement and bone, sunk in his old clothes, powerful and somber and impressive as a face on Mount Rushmore. A resonant deep voice to be played like an organ. Earl Rogers, "tall, dark and handsome," "a howling swell" as the New York papers called him in a slang phrase popular at the time, afraid of nothing and nobody. The difference between a fullback who plows his way doggedly through the line for an average of four yards a carry and a halfback who sweeps around the end with speed for spectacular gains. Yet there in the beginning I *felt* an alikeness between them. A response, intimacy even, a kinship. The deep in each called to the deep in the other. As they sat talking the surface differences were not so plain as that profound brotherhood. My father was almost shy with this man, and when they began to speak of the coming indictment he gave Darrow admiration and respect, more—an *affection* and concern I hadn't heard since Uncle Tom Hays died. It made me remember what Papa had said to me about all men being so afraid of loneliness. I felt sure Papa was lonely a lot of times.

"You must trust me," he said to Darrow, "with what I know you value most in life, your usefulness to the cause of the poor and downtrodden. In our profession, there is always the saying that a man who acts as his own lawyer has a fool for a client. I don't want that to happen in your case." He smiled engagingly at the big man sunk low in his chair. "I would confer with you, hear you at all times, use your gifts, but I must be chief counsel for the defense or—*we shall lose*."

Darrow lowered his head, deep in painful thought. Once years later in Leon Gordon's studio in the Beaux Arts I asked Jo Davidson, the sculptor who had done a magnificent bust of the Darrow-of-the-legend, if he had ever heard Darrow laugh. After thinking a moment Jo shook his head. "He was a great man," he said, "with the weight of the world on his shoulders." Probably that was it, and probably it was natural that Darrow wanted to be his own chief counsel and his wife supported him like a hive of wasps. In fact, before he could speak, Ruby Darrow broke in with her bird twitter, "It is an unthinkable suggestion," she said.

They sat talking for a while about the coming class struggle which Darrow saw ahead. Of his own work on the side of labor, the men he said who had with their hands built this country and who must now have their fair share of its prosperity and glory. It was eloquent, but—it was very strange. I do not think Clarence Darrow ever talked to a *person*. He never had a—a human moment, a trivial second, any small talk, a thought of ordinary matters, any other interests. Always he seemed immersed in causes. He spoke ex cathedra, to large audiences.

After a while Mrs. Darrow said they would give their decision after a night's sleep and got him to go upstairs, and I said, "Papa—" This *wasn't* a jail, a dark-hotheaded boy named Boyd wasn't our prospective client, it only seemed the same crisis to me. Perhaps because my stomach was in a congestive fever as though I'd eaten Little Black Sambo's 179 pancakes.

"Well, Nora?" Papa said sharply. I saw he'd let down now that Darrow was gone, he was white with exhaustion of bringing a man back from his grave to testify for himself in court.

I said, "You didn't take the case."

"If he allows me full charge, I have agreed to take it," he said.

"Don't," I said "don't take it, Papa. Please." My stomach, which he'd depended on as an indicator, which he'd given a seat in the cabinet, was howling warnings at me. Something *wrong*, something *wrong* somewhere. A stomach has a major fault as a factor in decisions. Your mind, intelligence, knowledge will supply you with reasons and the words in which to explain them. Visceral reactions, subliminal *feelings*, which sometimes are little better than hunches and at others as good as inspirations, are all too often without words. I didn't know how to tell him so he'd believe me that this man to whom he spoke with such friendliness was a *phony*. It seemed a monstrous thing to say, yet I was pitifully sure that he would betray us anywhere along the road without a qualm for any reason that seemed good to him. I said, "I wish you wouldn't."

Papa said, "Mind your own business, Nora," I was so furious at that I couldn't say a word, and he said, "You don't understand this man. Like so many great men, his mistakes, when he makes them, are colossal. He must be saved from them. Genius always needs protection if it is to be used for mankind. We—all have our faults. I'm very glad I have the chance to help him and he needs help more than he realizes."

"Well," I said, "I needn't worry. She won't let him."

However, when the chips were down, Clarence wore the pants. Next morning he came down to say he would agree Mr. Rogers should be chief counsel. I had to look him firmly in the eye and say Mr. Rogers had been called back to town at the crack of dawn or even earlier though where he was I actually knew no more than Darrow did. We were to meet at our office the next day. I sure hoped we would and actually we did. That was the first time Earl Rogers vanished on Darrow. Darrow was never to understand my father's faults any more than I understood his.

No decision therefore had been spoken between Rogers and Darrow when we went back to Los Angeles. And if Ruby raised a rumpus with her husband for hiring Earl Rogers, she should have heard the storm that broke on Rogers' head at the idea of his defending Darrow. It made hers sound like a tempest in a henhouse.

FIFTY-THREE

When we saw our old friend Harry Carr, our new offices were already rocking with opposition to Rogers' taking the Darrow case.

Not long ago I had to consult the head of the Los Angeles County Probation Department. Till I got into the room, I hadn't realized it was my father's office, on the fourth floor of the California Building. It seemed smaller than I remembered it, but when we took those suites facing Broadway and Second Street, they were the most elegant legal chambers in town. Big waiting room. Inner doors on whose glass panels gold letters spelled Harry Dehm, Frank Dominguez, Paul Schenck, Barry Sturgeon, H. L. Giesler, Milton Cohen, Harrison Castle, Buron Fitts. Clean, airy, walls shining, carpets bright, mahogany furniture and linen curtains. A janitor came to clean every night. The receptionist had a switchboard. And *elevators*. Was that a thrill.

The day we moved, I forgot and started up the old worn wooden stairs. When I remembered I sat down and put my head against the dirty wall. Perhaps I sensed then that the story of Earl Rogers and his daughter, still blazing up and up, was almost over. That the best part of it had been lived when those dark, crowded, old-fashioned offices were the one permanent fact in my young existence, with Bill Jory, who had died in such pain, as my baby-sitter. I wished Bill Jory was still with us. I never trusted anyone else the same way.

A stranger clattered by me on the stairs, he had a right to go up to our rooms, I didn't belong there any more. In a way, I suppose there is a corner to turn in our teens when without knowing it we say good-by to—*the child*. For some time I had known I was getting to be what was then called a young lady. I'd been in and out of high school. I'd told them I was a senior because I wanted to get through as soon as possible, but though I'd done the work and written the class play they wouldn't give me a diploma; I didn't have what they kept asking me for—*credits*. How could I? I'd never been in one school long enough. I didn't mind growing up as much as I'd thought I would, as long as I could stay with Papa. He said he would promise to be unselfish when I wanted to get married, but I didn't. I could not just leave him to *Mama*, and I knew he would always be the dominant factor in any house. Yet, if I were somebody's wife that factor ought to be my husband not my father. Pretty soon Edna Landers walked into those new offices—oh—if she'd only come *sooner* and hadn't died. That is what is called tragedy.

Papa felt a little the way I did about moving; he was superstitious, I think. One morning when we got down as usual way ahead of everybody, he said, "Of course we had to move—" I couldn't help putting my head on *his* shoulder and he patted *mine* and said, "There, there, Nora" the way he always did right up to the day I fell off the witness stand.

Our old friend Harry Carr didn't hesitate. He came through the door into Papa's private office on the double bounce. In excitement or anger, Harry stuttered, now he sounded like a Gatling gun. "T-t-t-this can't be t-tt-ttrue, Earl," he said.

Earl said, "If you mean Darrow, it's true. I shall go up with him this afternoon to post the twenty thousand dollars bail."

"You can't do it," Harry shouted, and came around and shook his fist right in Earl's face. "You c-cc-cccan't do it."

Chubbier, balder, wearing thick spectacles, Harry had a way of nodding *Yes* or *No* involuntarily, as though his heart telegraphed his reaction ahead of his brain. Those who knew him only through his column, a pioneer in that field, loved him for its warmth and courage. As a person, he was a right jolly little elf. But his integrity was steel and his anger formidable. I was giving him a silent secret cheer. My stomach hadn't gotten better, it had congealed, here was the *one* man who might persuade my father to change his course. This deep friendship, begun in the Alford case when they were both poor, unknown, ambitious young men, was just as strong now that they were, in these few years, at the top of their professions. Once Harry had actually persuaded Papa to try the Keeley Cure, very secretly, he'd stayed with him, too. *G–g– greater love hath no man,* he told me, blinking like a little owl, *than to take the Keeley Cure he doesn't need for a pal.* No other friendships are like those woven with the memories of shared hopes, fantastic gambles, small embarrassments and humiliations, big triumphs, little hurts and big joys. Nobody else ever really believes them, or understands them, or —come down to it—*cares* a whole lot.

Harry Carr kept on shaking his fist at his oldest friend, shaking his head, *No, No.* He said, "You obstinate, sentimental Irish bastard. This man Darrow is a discredited mountebank. I don't believe in his cause or his fight—Rich *against* Poor— Capital against Labor—*I* think he's building up unnecessary class hatreds everywhere. But by God I thought *he* believed in it. Now even his own labor unions know he sold them down the river."

"He had to fulfill his obligation to his clients first," Papa said.

"Why, you misbeguided dupe!" Harry said. He pulled out his big pipe and had trouble stuffing it with tobacco, then he began lighting kitchen matches and flinging them into the wastebasket, where some papers caught fire, until finally he was belching blue smoke. "The minute his hide was in danger, he threw his clients to the wolves to save himself. Don't you know he used part of a check these working people he claims to love so much collected to save the men he told them were innocent long after he knew they were guilty"—he stopped for breath—"he used one of *their checks* to try to *bribe* jurors?"

"I doubt anyone can prove that," Earl said, keeping very cool.

"Yes, they can," Harry Carr told him. "I've seen it. Such a shoddy, self-serving, craven record, Earl."

"You've been listening to your boss General Otis," Earl said, angry now too. "You can't judge Darrow fairly because it was your building the McNamaras dynamited."

"Do you think your great man Darrow is such a fool he didn't know the McNamaras were guilty?" Harry said. "I'm glad he let them confess. With all this public sentiment they've built up for a couple of cornered rats, it might have been difficult to convict them. Or they'd have gone to the gallows as innocent victims of Industry in a Holy War. If Darrow had given them as good a defense as he gave Big Bill Haywood. Why in Christ's name didn't he? Because they almost had *him*. Now you listen to me. There are a few things that happened around the time he changed the plea of the McNamaras I want to be sure you know, or remember, before you go out in public with him and appear as his counsel. You listen!"

His hands were shaking so he had trouble getting out of his pockets a lot of those thin pieces of paper called flimsies on which wire-service copy comes to the city room. On one of these, the Associated Press reported that their correspondent had gotten to Sam Gompers on the Congressional Limited between New York and Washington with the very first news of the *McNamara* confession. Gompers broke down, the story said, and his eyes filled with tears. Harry read us what Gompers had said. *My credulity has been imposed upon. I am astonished at such news. Only a short time ago I visited the McNamaras in the Los Angeles jail and they asked me to deliver to the Labor interests the message that they were innocent. I knew nothing at all of any plan for change of plea or any reason for a confession. I was not consulted about this step. I had raised $300,000 for their defense, believing them innocent.*

"He wasn't consulted," Harry Carr said, "after the D.A. arrested Bert Franklin, Darrow didn't have *time*. They were too close behind him."

"What has this to do with the charge against Darrow?" Earl said.

"Listen!" Harry said. The next flimsy said a UP reporter got to the president of the United Mine Workers of America, in Roanoke, Virginia. The quote read: *I have never been more astounded. I have believed confidently in the innocence of the McNamara brothers, I had always sincerely believed the Times blowing up was an accident, not a crime. Darrow was sent to defend them because we all believed their assurances of innocence.*

Stuffing the papers back into his pockets, Harry said, "I believe him. I don't think labor knew or believed in murder as the McNamaras did. You know the only labor voice that spoke up for J. B. McNamara after he'd confessed to killing twenty-one men? *Big Bill Haywood.* He said, 'I'm with the McNamaras and always will be. You can't view the Class Struggle through the eyes of capitalistic laws.' Earl, these are not capitalistic laws. They are the laws of the republic, founded on the rights of men. These men now want to take the laws into their own hands."

"As did the men who founded the republic when they tipped the tea into Boston Harbor," Earl said with a tight grin. "Darrow believes he has a right to help the workingman throw off the yoke in what he recognizes as a war between capital and labor. He is a man who has dedicated himself and his gifts to the rebellion and the rebels, but he has always been against violence. He has entered the fight to help the poor man free himself of hours beyond a man's strength, wages too unbelievably small for him to live decently upon, conditions in the mines of terror and death and destruction for him. You will remember I told your boss if capital didn't clean its own house there would be those who would use dynamite to clean it with—but Darrow has not been one of them, he is a very gentle and kindly man, he has spoken always against violence."

"Papa," I said, "you made that up. You don't know it at all."

"I suppose his gentleness was what got him to defend Big Bill Haywood," Harry Carr said quickly.

"I tell you Haywood had to be defended," my father said. "So does J. B. McNamara."

"Then why didn't Darrow defend him?" Harry Carr said.

"A criminal lawyer has a right to plead a man Guilty to save him from hanging," Earl Rogers said. "They've caught Darrow in a trap, a nasty, cold-blooded planned, baited *trap*. I am against traps. An informer is the chief witness against him. I am against informers. You and I know so well, Harry, the stab-in-the-back of that denizen-of-both-worlds—the stool pigeon. I must defend Darrow, he's an innocent man!"

Profoundly moved, Harry Carr said, "If this was true, Earl, do you believe I'd lift a finger to stop you? It's not like that. You are being deceived now by the old fallacy of the underdog, who must be innocent of killing sheep because he has been *trapped*. I think our system of democracy is better than socialism, I didn't want to see Job Harriman elected mayor. But I felt sorry for the miserable son-of-a-bitch when he got the news of Darrow's double-cross in public. Darrow didn't have the decency to warn him of the coming confession though Job was a member of McNamara's defense counsel. Like Eliza crossing the ice, by that time Darrow could hear the hounds baying on his heels."

Carr hadn't been at the Labor Temple when the news came, but he had talked with reporters who covered it all the way through. He re-created that scene for us vividly, and unrolled the days that followed. When the news of the Guilty plea and McNamara's confession came, they tore down the fine brave banners, *Save the McNamaras*, and trod them underfoot. The gutters ran red, white, and blue buttons with *The McNamaras Are Innocent* looking shockingly silly. Yards and yards of red, white, and blue bunting and placards, *The Capitalistic Conspiracy Against the McNamaras Must Be Defeated, Vote for Job Harriman for Mayor*, were dragged down and hurled away. The unions, who had been made fools of, milked of their hard-earned nickels, dimes, and quarters for men whose works they would have repudiated had they known, were ready to cry, *Lynch the McNamaras*. When somebody in the temple called out the name *Darrow*, the echo came back *Traitor*.

"Do you believe Darrow is innocent?" Harry said.

"Of jury bribery, I'm sure of it," my father said.

Of course I knew that Papa could always, especially with such inspired help as Darrow was giving him, believe his client was innocent.

"There's not much more I can say," Harry Carr said, and he wasn't an old friend pleading any more, he was a dignified member of the press, a citizen enlisted against dynamite. "As far as you are concerned, this *must* do you grave harm. But it is simple enough. Did Darrow allow his client to confess and plead Guilty to save him from the gallows? Simple. We asked Darrow at the time whether the arrest of Franklin had anything to do with the rush change of plea and Darrow said, '*Not a thing.*' Yet the change caught the press by complete surprise. You will remember that Lincoln Steffens at that time had a big story in the *Express* about how he had been working with both sides to get a compromise in the McNamara case and it had been agreed upon *before* Franklin was arrested?"

"I know Steffens," Earl said. "A good newspaperman, but he always has delusions of grandeur."

"Judge Bordwell," Harry said, "gave us a statement to correct some of the flat misstatements and misconceptions caused by what he called Steffens' irresponsible articles. The judge was very sore. Here's what he said.

"The District Attorney acted entirely without regard to Mr. Steffens and upon lines he had decided to follow before the latter appeared on the scene. As to the McNamaras defense, the public may rely on it that the developments of last week as to bribery and attempted bribery of jurors were the efficient causes of the change of pleas which so suddenly brought these cases to an end . . . Those interested in the defense continued to urge the District Attorney's acceptance of propositions for ten days or more until the bribery development revealed the desperation of the defense . . . *then* it was that the change of the pleas of these men was forthcoming."

(Later, in his history of the Los Angeles Bar Association, W. W. Robinson says, "Judge Walter Bordwell's blunt statement, apparently overlooked by writers and historians, directly linked the disclosure of attempted jury tampering with the change in pleas of the McNamaras. It contradicted the statement by Clarence Darrow, made the day his clients pleaded Guilty. Asked then whether the arrest for bribery of Franklin, an investigator *representing Darrow*—had anything to do with the confessions, Darrow said Not A Thing!" True, no Darrow historian including Darrow has ever remembered what Judge Bordwell had to say.)

When Harry Carr stopped reading, Earl Rogers began to walk up and down. I rolled him a cigarette and handed it to him as he went by, but I must have been in a state too, it didn't hold, the tobacco spilled down over his vest. Obviously,

Carr's plea had moved him much more than the one of Oscar Lawler, who had asked a young Earl Rogers to defend Boyd and was now begging him *not* to defend Darrow.

"You don't understand this man at all," my father said, stopping.

Remember, in this moment of truth *this* man was a discredited *man*. He had seen himself hanged in effigy by his own followers. Was now charged with a most odious crime.

We defend everybody. The rule of the old office was to hold good in the new. When Darrow in his autobiography dismissed my father's part in his defense with one line, "I hired a local lawyer named Earl Rogers to assist me," he overlooked, or had forgotten, or perhaps never faced the fact that he, Darrow, was the *under-est* underdog the West's leading trial lawyer, Earl Rogers, ever defended.

"Will it help this rebellion, this Industrial War, to try now to convict an innocent man just because you think he was on the wrong side?" Earl said. "You refuse labor the right to blow up the *Times*. So do I. So does Darrow. *We* refuse your right to trap a leader on the side against capital. You are as blinded against Darrow as Darrow was against the *Times*."

With a frantic bounce, blinking and tossing his head like a bronco in a temper, Carr was on his way out shouting, "If he's so goddam pure and lily white, what the bloody hell was he doing *at the scene* when the money was passed?"

"If you had any sense of proportion and judgment left," Earl said, "you'd see that's proof of his innocence. A smart man couldn't have been there if he'd *known*."

"All right," Harry said, "what was he doing at the corner of Third and Los Angeles that particular morning—attending a Salvation Army meeting? You can't be so far gone as to think it was just a coincidence, can you?"

"No, no," Earl said, and began to laugh weakly. "He went to try to prevent what happened."

"You don't think you can bamboozle a jury with that?" Harry said.

"What's more," Earl said, and anger broke through for the first time, "you and the General keep your hands off my cases. And tell that to the other rich and influential and powerful citizens. Don't try to tell me who I can defend and who I can't defend. Tell them they're not going to get Darrow. That was the purpose of the trap and I won't have it. You tell the boys when I get through with Bert Franklin he'll wish he hadn't changed his coat, the two-timing, flap-eared sneak. I found the men who blew up your building and killed my friends, and they're on their way to jail for life. You can't have an innocent man like Darrow, too, so get ready for a real fight this time."

Harry stared at him through his big glasses. Then he went out, the door shut very quietly behind him. I handed Papa a new cigarette. I'd rolled this one carefully, but he only took one puff and threw it away. He said, "Harry didn't say good-by to his best friend either, did he?" and it sounded forlorn, like a bell buoy we used to hear out in the bay.

I said, "He's mad now, but he'll be back." We both knew he wouldn't.

"I—have no choice," my father said.

"Could it be that you are wrong for once and everybody else is right?" I said. "Nobody but Giesler thinks you ought to defend Darrow."

"Jerry's smarter than all the other men in our office put together," Papa said. "These are big issues."

He was right. This was one of the great key first battles in the Industrial War. The Class Struggle that Darrow said would grow fiercer and bitterer day by day for years to come. Two great contending armies were meeting in a civil war, a mortal combat, there was real hate now on both sides, it would be years before the scales began to balance, the compromises be possible. At the moment of the Darrow trial The Interests and The People were drawn up. Darrow said the real enemies of society wanted him inside the penitentiary and my father believed him and had drawn his sword to see that they didn't put him there.

For the next fifty years this conflict was to rage.

Only the figures, *the men,* in it were important to Earl Rogers.

I have always thought the man who would have inspired my father most, earned his love and respect, was Albert Schweitzer. A man who gave up big issues, big success, big position, big influence in affairs of devastating importance to take care of a *very few people* with leprosy and potbellies and running sores in Lambaréné. This may sound strange, but it is true that with my father it was *people,* not issues. Patrick Calhoun's fine patriotic name. McComas, who had seen his father and mother scalped by Indians. Rosy and his dog. Twisted minds and bodies that made criminals. Poor dumb Chief of Police Charlie Sebastian. God help us, the boy arch-criminal Bundy. That was why he had wanted to see Buck's *brain* inside his skull. And now there was the once great and idolized Darrow, an underdog cast out by his own people, with his foot in a trap, yelping for help, squeaking in pain.

In *Lawyers in Los Angeles*, copyrighted in 1959 by the Bar Association, it says, *Earl Rogers—true to form—would now work, successfully, to save Darrow from the Penitentiary. This was his work.*

He couldn't very well go off somewhere to Africa and set up a *court*, could he? But he could try to help those who needed him, and ignore the sides, which of course gave him a spectacular inconsistency which puzzled people then and has ever since.

"We are between two fires," Papa said, and began to laugh.

"We always are," I said, "double double toil and trouble, our native heath."

He kept on laughing and followed the Macbeth line. "So foul and fair a day I have not seen," he said.

Until Jerry and I eavesdropped on the first big row between him and Darrow, I really didn't know what he meant by "between two fires." I understood then—Harry Carr represented one fire. Darrow, his own client, was the other.

FIFTY-FOUR

Around the big, new mahogany table. My father at one end, across from him Clarence Darrow, with the usual grease spots on his tie and vest, though what they were intended to prove I never knew. The union men I'd known in San Francisco ate with their forks without spilling things. Harry Dehm, solid and careful. Frank Dominguez, who was to take the fatal Bundy case and drag Earl Rogers into it. Milton Cohen, shrewd, witty, an inspired poker player. Jerry Giesler. *Well, Jerry? Well, Mr. Rogers—*

At that first conference, Rogers let Darrow lead off. "That trap laid for me at Third and Los Angeles," Darrow said, "was part of the wrath of the criminal elements and The Interests of this country and their determination to get their greatest foe,

Clarence Darrow, out of the way. He's the man they were after—get Darrow. I have been pursued day and night by as cruel a gang as ever tried to destroy a man in all history, because I have been a friend to the poor and oppressed." My father said simply, "We must find the best defense." Again and again and again, Earl Rogers looking for the best defense. Rudolph Spreckels' ownership of a street railway. The two words *return spray*. Bullets that *didn't* come from the cops' guns. Jay Hunter's intestines. *You cannot send even such a man as Mootry to the gallows on the word of a pimp, a prostitute and a policeman.*

"Well, Jerry?" he said.

"It's a strong case," Jerry said, in his high, light penetrating voice. "Bert Franklin's testimony that he attempted the bribes on Darrow's orders, with Darrow's money. The defendant on the scene at the moment the crime was committed. We will have to do a lot better to prove his innocence than the fact that he says so."

Earl Rogers began laying out the case like a chess problem. Darrow looked up in surprise. Perhaps his wife had persuaded him that Earl Rogers was only the actor they'd seen for a brief time in the Hanford courtroom. Once when Jerry Giesler and I were working on a book a publisher had asked us to do about Rogers' trial work alone, a famous federal judge told us that the forty books of Darrow transcripts are chiefly remarkable for the exposition of Rogers' legal work, his grasp of law, his trial strategy, his undermining of the prosecution's case. Darrow was the man who made the appeal for sympathy, the actor's emotional outbursts, as he and my father agreed, since it was Darrow's freedom and future that were at stake. Nobody ever filed any charges of jury bribery against Earl Rogers!

As he set the pieces on the board, Rogers followed Jerry's line.

Bert Franklin.

Darrow refused in righteous indignation to take the threat of Franklin seriously. A man who has turned state's evidence. A man who admits he is a criminal and a bribegiver. A man who has in his own words betrayed his employer. *I will discredit him on the stand completely*, Darrow cried.

A strange pause fell. Our eyes turned to Mr. Rogers. In our office, the suggestion that Darrow would decide that he was going to cross-examine anybody was practically blasphemy. As a matter of fact, Darrow did very little cross-examining.

He started on Lockwood and others, but he got so emotional and off-the-track that Rogers took over.

Mr. Rogers only smiled slightly. He said, "It's not as simple as that. You hired Franklin as your chief investigator, as they can prove; you trusted him with vital matters over a long period. His reputation here as a United States marshal was good. He'll be a competent, cagey, cold, careful, tough witness."

Of course it wasn't the custom in those days to arrive at first names overnight, but I don't remember my father and Darrow ever got there. In public it was *Mr.* Rogers—*Mr.* Darrow. In private, nothing—or occasionally *Darrow*—*Rogers*—an *uneasy* relationship.

Jerry said, "Lockwood swears Franklin said from the beginning you were in on it, Mr. Darrow."

Rogers said, "Only his loyalty to you made him reluctant to involve you."

"He was telling the truth then," Darrow said, "pressure from, fear of the men who control this state economically and politically got to Bert. They told him to keep his mouth shut about everyone else—just testify against Darrow, he's the man we want."

"After the McNamara debacle," Dominguez said, "there would be pressure from the labor side, too."

Jerry said, "Franklin cracked when they showed him your checks."

"*My word!*" Darrow cried out. "My word against his. My life and long years of service at the Bar. Do you mean to tell me that my word against that of an informer wouldn't be good enough for any jury?"

The pause was awkward. I kept hearing Harry Carr . . . *discredited*, he had said, *a discredited man.* Didn't Darrow know that? For once, I kept my trap shut, Papa was being so considerate of Darrow. He said, "Unjust as it seems to you, Mr. Darrow, we must face the fact that you accepted the defense fund put up by people who believed you when you said the McNamaras were innocent!"

They took up the ten-thousand-dollar defense-fund check, a field in which I was a moron, so I began to think of other things. The group of doctors who were my father's friends. *Darrow's guilty as hell*, they said. If Rogers won the case it would be a disgrace, if he lost it a disaster. A political disaster already, to be mixed up with Darrow. Hiram Johnson had spoken publicly of Earl Rogers as a potential attorney general.

(Johnson missed the presidency when he refused the second spot on the Harding ticket and it went to Cal Coolidge.) Johnson's Progressive party certainly wasn't liberal enough to admit Darrow, who was Eugene Debs's lawyer and supporter. Fifty years later the nation had progressed to accept many of the planks in Debs's platform, but at the time he was the Socialist candidate for President he got only 901,000 votes. I didn't want Papa in politics. Nor did I want him cut off forever on account of Darrow. I began to stew about how awful it would be if we lost the Darrow case. We *might*. I was having a very unhappy time. For so long everybody had relied on my stomach's oracle, now *they* had abandoned it, but I was stuck with it, I couldn't get away from it that easily and never in my whole life had it been as sure of anything as it was that Darrow was Guilty.

All around me this scouting expedition for a defense was going on, as ruthlessly impersonal, as extensive, inclusive, broad, and deep as Stonewall Jackson preparing for battle. Nobody cared what I thought any more and it was *hurting*. Just the same, I also began to see where Papa was heading.

"Well, Jerry?" he said. "Their strongest point?"

"Darrow on the scene," Jerry Giesler said.

His appearance, his conjunction with Franklin and Lockwood as the money changed hands.

"We must make it work *for* us," Earl Rogers said. His lips were thin, tight, grim. His eyes had begun to blaze, the full measure of excitement which he had to generate before he was at his best, had taken him over. His antennae were sensitized to a half-tone, an eyewinker out of line, a coffeecup off center. *Anything*. His senses were ahead of us, we were sitting there just *talking* about what was already *happening* for him in the courtroom. He put the palms of his hands flat on the table and leaned across it to the defendant. He said, "What were you doing there, Mr. Darrow?"

"I went there in response to an anonymous telephone call," Darrow said, and let the organ roll. "I thought probably they were trying to frame Bert."

"If you were the man they were after," Rogers said, "didn't it occur to you that your presence might put you in the frame-up?"

"Not at the time," Darrow said. "If I hurried, I might prevent it. I never think of myself in a crisis."

"We must think for you," Rogers said politely. "Your salvation is the important thing. Now—we can't deny you were there. Half the police department seems to have seen you. Any intelligent mouse would have sniffed the cheese but you are not a mouse, you are a man of great emotional heat, dedicated, idealistic, selfless. You conceive it to be your duty to rush to the rescue of your co-worker. To prevent injustice you run, panting, race perspiring, take your life in your hands crossing the street, wave your hat so you may warn Franklin of the trap in time. Yes, yes—a rash and reckless and foolish thing, but *innocent* and only believable under that interpretation. On the other hand, you have been a lawyer thirty-five years. If you planned this bribery you would take pains to be twenty miles away from the pay-off. It is beyond the bounds of reason, probability, possibility that *if you were guilty*, you would arrive on the scene at the moment the crime was committed." He began to howl with laughter. He said, "Sam Browne, their top detective, *testified* that you were *waving your hat.*"

He pranced into the corner and took his own elegant Borsalino off the rack and began to wave it frantically. We saw it. Plainly. This was to be the visual, pictorial, unbelievable thing a man could not do if he was guilty, re-enacted before the jury.

What is Darrow like? I always answer, When? At 9 o'clock that morning a great man. At 9:15 after the phone call a panic-stricken coward.

Twelve men in the jury box wouldn't *know* what Lincoln Steffens had learned from long, intense association with Darrow under fire. Men in great fear, cravens, do the worst thing possible, run into the tiger's mouth, tell idiotic lies, wave their hats and plead clients Guilty.

No—the twelve men wouldn't know that. Earl Rogers didn't know it then, and so here we were at the Darrow defense.

Sam Browne said Darrow was waving his hat.

Everybody was pleased but Darrow. He was too green-gloom and damp to bristle, but he began tugging the arrows from his bleeding breast.

"Mr. Rogers," he said, "you call my presence on the scene where I went to assist my man foolish. To hear you, anyone might think you were my prosecutor not the counsel for my defense."

"Unless I see both sides, I'll be little use to you," Rogers said.

Darrow sat in silence, his chin sunk on his chest.

Papa made a sign to us. Another man's humiliation was the

one thing he thought nobody should ever be allowed to look upon. I could have told him that Darrow's ego did not permit humiliation to be to him what we thought it was. But I was for the moment without portfolio.

So the meeting broke up leaving Rogers and Darrow alone together in Rogers' office, which along with our phones, secretaries, and staff, Darrow was using as his own.

The office next to Papa's was Harry Dehm's.

Whether or not Giesler told any of this in the book he just wrote, I don't know. We agreed it would be better for us not to read each other's, it might influence our memories and get me, at least, in a sweat where we differed in dates and all and make me self-conscious when we had opposing views about people and events as we quite often did and do, or what's a lifelong friendship for? Probably Jerry wouldn't remember a little thing like this, or he might think it unbecoming for a now senior and distinguished member of the Bar to admit eavesdropping on a client. As an ex-reporter I have done a good deal of eavesdropping in my time and think nothing of it.

I can see those two young things, who no longer exist except somewhere on the past's stream of time, but who have *become* me and Jerry Giesler, all of whose ambitions for fame and fortune came true. I know him *now* of course, but at this minute I can see him more clearly as he was that day Papa skedaddled us out of the office so Darrow could bare his breast without an audience. Jerry's sandy hair, always a little thin, his bulging dome of brow like the Scarecrow's in the Wizard of Oz—in fact Jerry wasn't at all unlike Ray Bolger's screen presentation of that wonderful character. I can see the homely unforgettable face, background for the farseeing, lighted-from-within-by-brain-dynamo eyes. In every way, he was the antithesis of the man he idolized, Earl Rogers. Just as he had the moral courage from first to last to oppose Mr. Rogers if necessary, so he had the courage to discard imitation at once; to create a different character, a lawyer of simple sincerity, whose stumbling efforts to find the truth won a jury's sympathy at once. He didn't seem to be a very *good* lawyer, but they felt he was *honest*. They wanted to help his clients. The Giesler power was all masked and muted.

And the girl kneeling on the floor beside him, ear to the crack, long tow-colored braids—we called them "tow" before Jean Harlow invented the much more glamorous word "platinum" for the same color—pinned around her head with big black steel pins. How painful they were. Too thin still. Wearing the first suit that fabulous tailor, Eddie Schmidt, ever made for a female, but Eddie would do anything for Mr. Rogers—and wearing it badly.

I look at all this through a stereopticon of double magic lanterns. It is like another incarnation. Sometimes as you long to grow in grace and pray for wisdom over the years, the several incarnations which you have lived *in this one here on earth* separate themselves distinctly. My incarnation as Earl Rogers' daughter, Nora, is clearer. I can see and hear the essential things better than I can some that happened yesterday. The things that exist only for yourself, in faith—in art—in glory—in love. No one else has ever lived these, because they could not have seen them with your eyes and heart. You have created and re-created them in the pain and happiness of your memory ever since. Probably you have softened some things you can hardly bear and heightened those that bring joy. Where else can I spend my time, now, with my father except in this world of memory?

I know *the* Jerry Giesler of that time long ago better than I know the one today. Then we were always together and he was my best friend anywhere near my own age. He was to be trusted about my father.

We clung together in our youth, and our need to protect Papa, and it was a great comfort and affection for us both.

We waited until we were sure Harry Dehm had gone. He was a most moral man and would have disapproved of listening at door cracks and peeping through keyholes and was quite capable of tattling to Papa if he caught us.

I said to Jerry, "The doors were thinner in our old office."

"Shut *up*," Jerry said. So we hardly breathed.

My father's voice came clear and warm and by it I could tell that he was trying to comfort the man in there with him.

My father was saying, "When you take the stand—"

"I will take the stand and say on oath that *I am innocent*," Darrow said. There was a silence. He said, "You know I am on trial because I have been a friend of the less fortunate, I have been a lover of the poor, I have tried to serve the men who toil, I have stood for the weak and the poor—"

At this I pushed myself up and went and sat on Dehm's desk and I said in what you might describe as a piercing whisper, "You and Papa! He is a friend of the weak and a lover of the poor but he doesn't say anything about the fifty-thousand-dollar fee he got out of their nickels and dimes or the two hundred thousand dollars Milton says he had for expenses—"

"He had a right to a fee," Jerry said.

"For what?" I said. "The McNamaras could have pleaded guilty by themselves, couldn't they?"

"And got hung," Jerry said.

"Who knows?" I said. "He is not such a man as Mr. Calhoun, I tell you."

"He is a much greater man," Jerry said. "Mr. Calhoun had a code, and principles, he'd been taught them for generations. Darrow is a first-generation reformer and he is scared to death but he does it anyway, he is a nervous wreck but he keeps on fighting in his own way."

"Maybe he is a nervous wreck because he has a guilty conscience," I said, and rolled myself a cigarette, which I did not often do.

Jerry said, "If he was guilty, he would not have a guilty conscience. He would believe what he did was right and justified, the way men do things in war."

From beginning to end Jerry Giesler *said* he thought Darrow was innocent. That was his platform. Of course Jerry was so *smart* he could probably see farther ahead in some ways than Papa. He was cooler. His *Mr. Hyde* kept popping in and out but not strongly, like the time he pulled the old lady's chair out from under her at Ciro's and the night he and I shot at Charlie Sebastian. I always thought he drank monkey-see-monkey-do. He quit when he needed to. Probably he knew at the time of the Darrow trial that in the end in the future the popular side would be Darrow's. Then, there were only two million members of labor unions—*If the McNamaras did this terrible deed they are only two men out of our two million members,* said Sam Gompers. Fifty years later there would be twenty-two million members. The tempo and trend of public thought would follow Darrow to Scottsboro and Tennessee. If Earl Rogers succeeded in getting him acquitted in Rogers' home town, where at that moment few thought anything of Darrow but ignominy, Darrow would make a comeback and go on to big things.

Naturally, knowing how smart Giesler was, it didn't enter my head that he really thought Darrow was innocent. I knew how Papa could turn himself over to that dramatic excitement and convince himself of *anything,* but Jerry didn't and didn't need to. When, years later in his own luxurious office building in Beverly Hills, I saw the two enlarged photographs of Rogers and Darrow, exactly the same size, same frames, same position side by side, I wondered. So I asked him and he said he had always believed a hundred per cent that Darrow was innocent. I still don't believe it. He did say then and always that wherever he went to lecture or teach, it was always Earl Rogers they wanted to hear about, asked questions about, and not Darrow. That always surprised him. I said maybe that was because Darrow never had any fun.

As I went back to my listening post, "He's crying," I said to Jerry.

Jerry said, "He's very emotional—and he's a nervous wreck."

In the corner of our office there was a big blackboard. I said to Jerry, "What is he doing—can you see?" and Jerry said he was making out a timetable.

They were in there several long hours, with the door locked. Jerry and I went across the street to the Pig 'n' Whistle and got some sandwiches and milk and chocolate éclairs. I was always hungry. When we came back Dehm had gone to court so we went in and could hear Darrow crying out loudly from time to time, but not exactly what either of them was saying. Then Papa's words came through clear and distinct. He said, "We have got to prove that only your complete *innocence* is compatible with your appearance at Third and Los Angeles at that time. We have got to emphasize your brilliance as a lawyer and then show the bungling stupidity of this even if you are innocent. Then we have to say, Can you believe that Clarence Darrow would rush in where angels fear to tread *waving his hat*—"

In the silence that followed, we could hear Darrow sobbing, as though his heart was broken and I guess it was.

"The poor guy," Jerry said.

I felt sorry for him too. But not very. Gallantry where they let *me* do the crying for them has always been what really got to me. People who kept their chins up—like Harvey Elder's sister, Grace, and his grandmother. That day I cried all the way home.

Before long I got so I had learned to plain pay no attention to Darrow crying.

The young can often be very hardhearted.

FIFTY-FIVE

What went on in the Superior Court at the trials of Darrow has been written, millions of words, many books, endless official records and documents.

The tragedy, which I might call Feet of Clay, enacted in our office, our house, corridors, and public streets as the future Great Defender and his chief counsel went back and forth, has never been told.

Their struggles and soul-searching differences didn't culminate until the night before Darrow's classic address to the jury, which READS like Antony's oration over Julius Caesar. To *hear* it was, I think, something else. But leading up to that moment, we had an almost daily row over Darrow's courtroom behavior and continual scraps about the three lines of defense and which came first so that a lot of the time my father was as restless as a .400 hitter benched in the World Series.

One act of this long unfolding trial came at the time when Lockwood on direct examination said plainly that Franklin had offered him four thousand dollars for a Not Guilty vote in the McNamara case. The money came, Franklin had told him, from the Big Boy, identified as Clarence Darrow. Tempted to take it to pay off his mortgage, Lockwood said he and his wife prayed about it and then instead he went to Captain Fredericks, the district attorney, and told him everything.

On the night after Lockwood's direct testimony, our office reminded me of the streetcar powerhouse on the corner of Sixteenth and Burlington, where we had lived when I was little. Filled with hot, blue-white light and a *hum* that never stopped. The drive it took for my father to control Darrow's desire and insistence that the defense rest entirely on the conspiracy-frame-up basis was mounting into hot or icy quarrels. Reporters were perched all over the place, a pitch game was dealt on the reception-room table, shouts and arguments and beer and a crap game were going on in Dominguez's room, the big, fat Mexican was a great mixer. In a corner, Joe Timmons, the *Examiner* ace, was reading a volume of Macaulay's essays Papa had lent him. Leaders and writers from all over the world had come to help "save Darrow," for their cause, and added a degree of fury and intensity. As a whole, the press could take Darrow personally or leave him alone, in spite of the news value of the great defense lawyer as himself defendant. A press-box vote would have convicted him, that's for sure. Through the open windows, sage, from the foothills we could see in the daytime, and the dry river bed mingled; a late taxi hooted shrilly, tires squealed as a car came around into Broadway going at a late-at-night speed; the elevators rattled up and down, their doors clanged, the telephones rang wildly.

I kept pushing back the pressure, the tension. I thought sort of frantically that people had to sleep and eat *sometime*. What kind of a pace was this we were trying to live? Other men lived through it once, my father lived through it again and again. Now our new offices were beginning to be like the old ones, we had overlaid them, only there in spite of physical dimness it had always been—*bright*.

From time to time the shadow shapes of Rogers and Darrow came and went on the long, ground-glass panel of the door into my father's private office. Papa's thin and swift, Darrow's heavy and lumbering.

Papa had put me out. I saw Ruby Darrow, too, erect on a straight chair in Paul Schenck's room, her eyes snapping under her straight straw hat. Papa's manner to her was still courtly, but put her out he had and did. She spent the rest of her life getting even by the things she said about him. *Thank you* was never one of them.

After midnight, Papa put his head out and said send over to the Hollenbeck and get some food and whatever the boys wanted. The door shut so fast the newspapermen couldn't even ask a question. When the sandwiches and tea came I took them in. I thought maybe I could persuade them to get some *sleep. What is that—sleep?* Papa would say and grin at me. Isn't it funny that in this day of pale pink, rubbery tasteless tomatoes I can remember at a time like that a bucket full of dark red, luscious, ripened-in-the-sun ones? I can almost taste the flavor which has so long disappeared from all our lives. Maybe the machine that is going to compose music like Mozart's will put that back.

Darrow was saying, "We must destroy Lockwood—"

"With what?" Rogers said.

"I will cry it to the world," Darrow said. "Lockwood is

part of the Erectors Association-Los Angeles *Times*-Franklin conspiracy, planned and carried out by William J. Burns."

"But he isn't," Rogers said, putting hot pickles on a roast beef sandwich and pouring the china tea whose divine fragrance floated into the air. "He didn't take the money. We haven't a shred of evidence to connect him with a conspiracy we can't prove anyhow."

"His lies—" Darrow cried out, "his lies, his lies, his lies. Why if he is not part of the conspiracy to *get Darrow* does he tell lies about me? Why does he say Darrow was the Big Boy?"

"He doesn't," Rogers said. "He says Franklin *told* him you were the Big Boy *behind* this. Any man has an advantage in his own town. Here in California, Mr. Darrow, this jury knows a man like Lockwood. They can believe their fellow townsman loved his few little acres and could be tempted to do wrong to save them. They will not believe their fellow townsman Lockwood entered into a capitalistic conspiracy to knock off a labor leader. That's part of your thinking, bred by your experience in this movement, it doesn't belong out here. I wouldn't be able to make them believe it. It's a mistake to try."

At dawn when I was asleep with my head on the table, Papa came out. He looked the way a man does when he has just broken the record for the indoor mile. Darrow had that dead-and-dug-up color very unpleasant to look upon. Papa didn't speak all the way home. The only way I knew who had won that time was Papa's cross-examination of Lockwood the next day in court. Its emphasis from beginning to end was on whether or not he had any proof that Darrow was the Big Boy. On the fact that Third and Los Angeles was a *trap* of which he, Lockwood, had been part.

He went quietly over the initial bribe offer. Trying apparently not to humiliate Lockwood with his initial acceptance.

You never saw Darrow at that time? No. You never spoke to Darrow? No. If he was the Big Boy of this bribery you had no knowledge of it of your own experience or observation? Just the word—the reference—just the hearsay evidence of Bert Franklin? As far as you know of your own knowledge the Big Boy might have been John L. Sullivan or one of the Katzenjammer Kids? You have to tell this jury you had nothing but the word of Bert Franklin for Darrow's part in the *offer* of a bribe?

To all of this Lockwood agreed gravely and convincingly. "The first time you ever *saw* Darrow was at the corner of

Third and Los Angeles Streets at nine o'clock on the morning of November 29?"

So there we were! At Third and Los Angeles.

"Now," Mr. Rogers said, "this meeting where you first saw Clarence Darrow, this performance, this fake, this trap arranged against the law to *get* a man—" He was driving it in fast and hard like an engraving chisel.

Naturally hell seethed and erupted. If there was a better man at breaking all hell loose in a courtroom than Joe Ford I never saw him. Of course Captain Fredericks himself, the district attorney, was there, he was trying the case himself, but the *trial* man was Joe Ford. He was tough, a rugged little Irishman, with graying curls, a jaw like an English bulldog, and that same bulldog's ability to hang on, never let go, so that he aroused Darrow's ire more than any other man ever did.

He and Fredericks were both on their feet. "Rogers ought to be judged in contempt—he must not be allowed to get away with such statements—"

Facing the judge, Mr. Rogers waited. Joe Ford and Fredericks waited.

Behind them Clarence Darrow began to weep. Ruby handed him a dry handkerchief. I often wondered who used his handkerchiefs when they were clean.

Judge Hutton was a handsome man. Black hair, streaked with silver, thin, ascetic features. This was as difficult a job as a judge ever had and he did it at all times with fairness, amazing competence, and understanding. I think except for the ones who were actually prosecuting him, the Bar on the whole hoped Darrow would be acquitted. It couldn't be good for the eminence and trustworthiness of their profession to have a big lawyer go to the pokey for jury bribery, such things had to undermine the confidence of people in the legal profession. Except the crooks who naturally didn't care how you got them off.

"Mr. Rogers," the judge said, "this is a statement of intention to prove?"

"It is, Your Honor," Mr. Rogers said.

"The court will accept it as such," Judge Hutton said.

To the witness Mr. Rogers said, "You went to that engagement prepared to pretend to take a bribe and drop a bill as a signal for the detectives from the district attorney's office to move in for the kill?"

"I went there prepared to help the district attorney show

that attempts to bribe the jury in a murder case were being made," Lockwood said quietly.

"Your motives were pure, no doubt," Mr. Rogers said gently. "But it *was* a planned performance?"

"You can call it that," the witness said.

"I do call it that," Mr. Rogers said. "Now tell us, please, after you dropped the bill White had handed you, as previously arranged, Franklin came across the street, he appeared to be very nervous all of a sudden and he said to you, 'Let's take a walk.' This is correct so far? Then he saw a man coming toward you across the street and he began trying to *head the man off*? Did you see who that man was that Franklin was trying to head off?"

"Yes."

"Do you see that man in this courtroom?"

"Yes."

"It was Clarence Darrow?"

"Yes."

"Ah. Now you expected to see Mr. Darrow that morning, didn't you?"

"No sir."

"Don't you know that part of this play-acting, as it was written, was that somebody was to telephone Mr. Darrow to come down to Third Street right away? That was part of it, so you all could make it seem he was part of this?"

"No, I don't know that."

"Wasn't the meeting arranged with Franklin to pay you off at this place so you could involve Darrow?"

After another hail- and thunderstorm of objections had died down, Lockwood said, "Franklin chose Third Street."

"You'd seen Mr. Darrow, you knew what he looked like?"

"Never saw him before."

"Then why were you looking at him?" Mr. Rogers said.

"The way he was running through traffic."

"He was *running*?"

"Yes."

Mr. Rogers let a pause fall. He moved closer to the stand. He said, "Mr. Lockwood, I want to ask you a very important question. Will you take time and be sure before you answer?"

"Yes. I'll be sure," Lockwood said.

"Was Darrow waving his hat as he came across the street?"

"Yes—he was."

"Waving it—like this?" Rogers said, and picked up a hat that lay conveniently on the table and waved it.

"Yes."

Earl Rogers went around behind the counsel table and as he went he dropped a hand on Darrow's shoulder and grinned down at him triumphantly. Of course Darrow didn't see him. How could he? His head was sunk forward, the lock of hair was in his left eye, and both eyes were full of tears.

"Well," my father said cheerfully when we were all on our way down the hill after court, "he admitted you were waving your hat."

"A fine fool you made me look," Darrow said bitterly.

The newspapermen remembered the beginning of the row that started then. Somehow that got Papa—it had been a long ticklish day, Lockwood was as good a witness, as likable a witness, as he'd ever faced.

So it began on the street and in the elevators and crossing the reception room and on into my father's private office and they were too excited to remember to shut the door just at first and even after they did this time they were both shouting so loud they could be heard down in Joe Fast's saloon.

"I have to ask you to stop looking so guilty," Rogers said.

"I cannot sit there day after day and hear you make a fool of me," Darrow said. He was quivering all over, when he did that his flesh seemed to come away from his bones and have a life of its own.

"Nuts," my father said through his teeth. "We must insist that if you, Clarence Darrow, had taken to crime you would have been as good as Caesar, Borgia, or Moriarity. You couldn't have left such a *trail*. Were you watching the jury when Lockwood said you waved your hat?"

"No," Darrow said, "no. I can't bear to look at them."

"That's what I mean," Rogers said a little wildly. "Only guilty men hang their heads and won't look the jury in the eye. When I put my hand on your shoulder, why didn't you look up and share our triumph? Make the point! Why did you look like a dewlapped hound caught in the sheep pen? Jurymen have eyes and ears. I work all day to prove you innocent. They look at you and *see* a Portrait of a Guilty Man. They remember this at night—they will remember it when they take the case into the jury room."

"You want me to be cheerful when my heart is broken," Darrow said. "I am crucified daily, tortured by false accusations, burned at the stake in the flames of injustice."

"The saints sang hymns at the stake, didn't they?" Rogers said.

"My own people have repudiated me," Darrow said.

"Everybody's own people repudiate them some of the time," Rogers said. "You're a great man, above praise or blame, which are the same thing."

"Many of my friends do not believe in my innocence," Darrow said.

"Right now," Rogers said, "I don't care what anybody believes except twelve men on the jury."

"They would think me callous," Darrow said, "a hardened criminal, if I smiled and looked cheerful."

"You are not of a cheerful countenance, any more than Don Quixote," Rogers said irritably. "Out here, an innocent man keeps his chin up, comes out fighting, looks his accuser in the eye, proposes to continue on this line if it takes all the rest of his life."

"Injustice is the hardest thing of all to bear," Darrow said.

"So Socrates found," Rogers said, "but he drank the hemlock cup without a tear, it says. We must present a brave man, an innocent man fighting his valiant best against injustice. Not wilting under it."

A great man, Steffens said, *Strange he was a craven.*

"I believe in your innocence of this charge," Rogers said. "We'll get you off if you will stop looking so guilty. The jury's beginning to keep its eyes *away* from you. You know how dangerous that is."

"I am through anyhow," Darrow said. "My career is over. It's all right. I have done my best to serve. Let the young men have a chance."

"Moonshine," Rogers said. "You're only ten years older than I am. Your real work has just begun. If we can keep you out of jail this time, you'll practice law another fifty years." He gave him a *let's go* smile to which the response was a rueful shake of the head as usual.

Some of the newspapermen and a couple in our office agreed with Darrow about this. They thought his terrible suffering and mortification wove sympathy between him and the jury. Gave the common man in the box a feeling of identification. Watching that jury as I did, I never could see that at all. It embarrassed them to see a man so *naked* in public, showing such depths of grief and so many tears. I am still sure of that myself.

FIFTY-SIX

One night, the chief counsel for the defense vanished from our ken.

A couple of times after trouble with Darrow, or more specifically I thought with Mrs. Darrow, he'd stayed out of a session and let assistant defense attorney Horace Appel or Jerry Giesler or Darrow himself carry on. Now I had a feeling that he had begun to look at Darrow from time to time like a pitcher watching a shortstop boot away four unearned runs behind him.

Well—this time, Papa wasn't where we could find him on our first go-round. In our office, our house, the hotel apartment we always kept, his usual haunts, or with any of his usual companions. In spite of spouting off frequently that it would have been better if he had conducted his own defense, the moment Rogers didn't show up Darrow panicked. He pinned me in a corner and said, "Where is your father?" Though I thought Darrow was a *mess* and Ruby his wife was at the bottom of my list of women, he was such an outcast, for a moment I felt sorry for him. He was the one in peril, and as Papa said, not the one to be clear and calm of mind or mien. Anyhow, we had to get him *off*. If we lost this case we'd all go down with it.

I said, "He's taking a rest. He hasn't had much sleep lately."

"Do you know where he is?" Darrow said.

"I always know where he is," I said, which was a flat lie. I didn't want him in our hair while we tried to find Papa. I was afraid he was developing a slight distaste for Darrow and if he saw him he might go back in, like the ground hog.

"Is he drunk?" Darrow asked.

I could have smacked him. My feeling sorry for *Darrow* went off like a pinwheel. Around our office nobody ever *said* that. We had certain cover-ups ready by this time, a sheaf of doctor's certificates on hand, outposts in bars, honky-tonks, turkish baths, hospitals, backstage, and on the police force, prepared to notify us. I can see now that Darrow had a right not to have his chief counsel, on whom his very life depended, missing on a binge just prior to a vital cross-examination of

Bert Franklin. As per the unvarying pattern, of all slaves of the Noseless One, Papa always did it at the *one* time he shouldn't. We all regarded Darrow's use of the word "drunk" as a *faux pas* and stared at him blankly as though we didn't know the meaning of it. When I remember that loyal, united front we turned upon the world all I can think is, *How we loved him.* The fascination with which he literally absorbed us all, so that we lived Darrow's life, never our own.

Looking into Darrow's countenance, my stomach knotted into a prickly pear. All he cared about then, or ever, was why Earl Rogers wasn't in court to defend *him.* Never once did he think or speak of giving Earl Rogers understanding or support, a man, it seemed to all at that moment, believe me, with a chance of as great a future as his own. Never once did he offer a helping hand against Rogers' enemy, as Rogers was giving him a hand, heart, and head against the People of the State of California, the Labor party, and Rogers' own friends. For free, too. *I smelled liquor on his breath,* Ruby Darrow said, pinching up her mouth, so she looked like Missionary Davidson's wife in *Rain* when she saw a native in his lava-lava instead of a Mother Hubbard.

Just then, too, things were at their worst at home.

A period of relative peace, so that my brother Bogart and I had lived under the same roof again to our common satisfaction. We also had a new baby brother, Thornwell, born as an attempt at the tie that binds. But the terrible sickening quarrels had begun again. I remember my brother looking at me across the dinner table, where I sat like a stick, and saying, "They're off!"

One of the things I'd like to be able to ask the Recording Angel someday is where nagging rates in his book. To me it seemed the deadliest of all sins against *Love thy neighbor.* Nag, nag, nag—far into the night when he was trying to work. About anything and everything.

Especially *money.* Right then, anyhow. We not only weren't getting any money to speak of from Darrow, we were putting out a good deal. Money was something I didn't know how to worry about very well. I wish I had. My idea, like Papa's, was to *earn* more. What was so awful, people hollered to me, or pestered my mother, who once more was suffering agonies over bill collectors. The big stately white house, out in the foothills of what became Hollywood, was expensive to run, with house servants and gardeners and cars and chauffeurs, all of which my father took for granted. Mama didn't, and didn't know how to handle them. In consequence I suppose it was unfair that she should have had the payroll to meet all the time. Papa's extravagances drove her off her head.

The trouble was if Earl Rogers showed up, they began to apologize all over the place for having *asked* him to pay his bills.

Just before the Darrow case, I had an acute rumpus with Eddie Schmidt. Eddie became the most famous tailor in the West because he made Earl Rogers' clothes and took great pride in having him wear another suit at every court session so that the newspapers had a box on his wardrobe every day. There might as well have been a *Tailor by Appointment to Earl Rogers* royal patent over his door. Anyway, Eddie, who later made Gable's clothes and to whom I took Gary Cooper for his first dinner jacket, had sent me a couple of real nasty letters saying he must have something *on account*. So I told Papa, he would have to dig up a little money for Eddie Schmidt and of course Papa said why? I said well in the first place we owe it to him and in the second he is getting to be a nuisance, so Papa said all right, quite cheerfully. One day he actually invited Clarence Darrow to go down to Eddie's with him. Charlie Van Loan, one of the first great sports writers, went along and he said Darrow not only wouldn't order a new suit, he ran out of the shop as though the devil was after him. I must say, he was right. On Darrow, such a suit would have looked strange.

Papa finally went down to see Eddie about the bill and when he came home he had ordered *and* eventually Eddie Schmidt made *and* delivered twenty new suits from striped trousers and cutaways and tails to English tweeds, which Papa had just discovered. When I asked Eddie how it was possible for this to happen, Eddie said indignantly, "He *needed* them. I could not let Mr. Rogers go around looking shabby, could I? After all he's done for me!" True Papa had made him, as far as that went, but I did say to Eddie kindly not to bother me any more about *bills*. The identical thing happened at Oviatt's, the elegant men's haberdashery, so I quit sending Papa to talk to the creditors and just ignored them. I paid them all after Papa was dead, out of pride, I guess, though I must say it was all their own *fault*.

Our home broke up for the last time shortly after a second little brother was born and named Bryson. What to do about *them* complicated my life a good deal. This time—too late—the divorce was final.

So that when Papa disappeared on the eve of cross-examining Bert Franklin, I can't say I was surprised. It was due. Though there is never any *why* about this drink horror. That is the thing I learned so painfully. Not to ask *why*. I am sure Lucifer was an alcoholic, the archangel who set the pattern of abandoning heaven for hell. Why? You mustn't ask why. It does no good. This is the Enemy attacking. When Papa had been drinking, sometimes I got very sore, who doesn't? Still I knew I must unite with him against the Enemy, fight the Enemy. When he was most helpless under the potion that turned Mr. Rogers into Mr. Hyde it was most necessary. I wish I had known how to pray instead of being an atheist or an agnostic half the time myself.

But when Darrow said, "Is he drunk?" I said, "If he is you're enough to drive anybody to it, I will say that for you, Mr. Darrow." And it was just then that *she* came along and said, "I knew it. He drinks secretly all the time, I smell it on him." I said, "I'm surprised he ever lets you get close enough," which wasn't good manners, but at least I didn't say anything further about *smelling* people. There were no deodorants in those days so you had to be very careful about *bathing* and talcum powder and clean clothes and all.

"He'd better be here tomorrow morning," Darrow said heavily.

I had just been talking to Milton Cohen so I said, "Yes, and you had better be here, too, Mr. Darrow, with some cash of the realm on you, hadn't you? The men who are digging up testimony, and keeping track of Franklin, and trying to find out who put up that four thousand dollars if you didn't, and *who* made that phone call you say you got, are getting sore. If I was your chief counsel, I would not show up until you paid up *some* dough, so far we have put all of it up out of our own funds but we are not John D. Rockefeller, nor Andrew Carnegie."

Joe Timmons and Danny Green and some other reporters heard me blow off. I was bitter about it. Papa was so lordly, as though he was Midas. Once he borrowed from Arthur Letts, who'd have gone nuts if he'd known it was for *Darrow*. Letts was a Dickens character, come to America to make his fortune. He and Papa had a riding friendship and a running feud about his stable clock, a neighborhood curse which struck the quarters all night. Papa filed a suit about this and drove Letts to buy farms farther out where his clock wouldn't bother the gophers or coyotes or rattlesnakes. Under Letts's shrewd touch, these farms became Brentwood, Westwood, and West Los Angeles so that Arthur Letts could give the state a site for the University of California at Los Angeles as part of his philanthropies. Through admiration, in spite of their feud, Mr. Letts wanted to invest some of Mr. Rogers' money in this early real estate development but Papa was investing it in the Darrow defense. Though Ruby said I made scenes every morning trying to get money out of them, she's mistaken. I pegged her for Mrs. Turnip quite soon and, moreover, anybody who knows me will testify in court that I never got money out of anybody, except by hard work or across a poker table.

As soon as I got rid of the Darrows, and Jerry Giesler settled down to study the Bert Franklin direct-transcripts for Mr. Rogers, Frank Dominguez and I started to search again. Ever since Frank had come back from the Philippines, where he'd been governor general, and come onto Mr. Rogers' staff, he'd been a big help. He came of a family loved and honored in the city of La Reina de Los Angeles. He was a man of the world, he had friends everywhere. Of course if I could have foreseen the Bundy case I would cheerfully have shot him, though I know now if Bundy hadn't been the first Earl Rogers client to hang another would. Dominguez wasn't a good lawyer or a great brain, but he was gay, considerate, a kind friend. My mind made me begin to value kindness earlier than most.

Frank and Rosy and I went to Pearl Morton's. Sometimes she wouldn't tell anybody the truth but me.

I waited by the car. She came out, we held each other a minute. If it is without jealousy, nothing brings people closer than love of the same one. Pearl said, "He isn't here, youngster." We walked up and down the strange little street. She said, "Get him away for a rest, when this damn case is over. Nora—it happens now though he hardly knows it, or how it happens. He's worse when he's been drinking, men always are as they get older, but the *way* it happens worries me."

As though Dr. Jekyll didn't mix the crystal powder and blood-red tincture any more . . . *my clothes hung formless on my shrunken limbs, the hand that lay on my knee was corded and hairy. I was once more Mr. Hyde* . . . once a man consented to be the slave of the Noseless One even for a few minutes, unless he fought little by little in time, it happened without his consent . . . *I have set before you this day blessing and cursing* . . . no, no, Papa did fight.

When we found him and I saw him sitting in the stately teakwood chair shrunk into the rich embroidered silk, he seemed *small* and his face was gray white and his *eyes* . . . I couldn't do anything but run and put my arms around him and hide his face for him against my breast and hold and hold him and feel his hands hold onto me . . . *it was the horror of being Hyde that racked me.*

None of this showed when he came into the courtroom the next morning to cross-examine Bert Franklin, head up, eyes bright, groomed and dangerous and ready for trouble, looking for trouble. You have to take that kind of courage out of the lining of your guts.

As Jack London said, you live up a year in a day.

FIFTY-SEVEN

The obsequies for Bert Franklin, the Associated Press called Earl Rogers' cross-examination of the prosecution's star witness.

In the *Examiner,* Joe Timmons commented dryly that it was possible to hear Rogers' deadly contempt for Franklin all over Los Angeles, and the result had been deadly for Franklin and the prosecution.

Hugh Baillie of the *Record* and the Scripps chain wrote that in those long days Rogers struck at Franklin's story from every direction in a masterly exposé of its weaknesses.

I thought Harry Jones of the Chicago *Tribune* might be closer to the truth when he said, *The Witness floundered badly only once.*

To me, this was the coldest, hardest fought, an eye-for-an-eye-and-a-tooth-for-a-tooth battle I ever saw any witness give my father in any court. Yes, he had Franklin floundering, he wore him down, exposed glaring errors of course. I am sure he succeeded in planting a reasonable doubt as to whether or not Franklin was telling the truth when he implicated Darrow. At the same time, Franklin never backed up on his information about Darrow and he made some telling points himself.

I thought then, I think now, that Bert Franklin could have done this against Rogers *only* if he was telling the truth. No preliminary fighter, no matter how tough and well trained and conditioned and even smart, can stay twenty rounds with the champion *unless* he is fighting for country, home, mother, or truth. Then sometimes they can and do.

Truth, even in the mouth of an informer, a spy, a briber, can become bigger than anybody who tries to destroy it. Truth survives.

I think Earl Rogers was trying to destroy the truth with Franklin, though at the time he didn't know it and believed Darrow innocent.

We want Darrow.

Get Darrow.

Though he had refused to make the frame-up his main line of defense, with Franklin on the stand, he used it dynamically to bring out the man's betrayal and double-cross. Otherwise I thought the frame-up was hard to sell.

In certain cases, whatever is said or goes on in the courtroom, whatever each side is trying to prove there, there are certain things that are *known*, to the leaders.

One of the things they *knew* was that the McNamara cases had NOT been settled when the trap was sprung on Franklin at nine that morning, in which they hoped to involve Darrow though they'd had no real hope or expectation of getting him on the scene. The one thing *Captain Fredericks* knew positively was that he had refused up to that very minute to free brother John J. McNamara and that actually the negotiations were further apart than ever. Every offer ever made, however tentatively, by anyone for the defense had been based upon dismissing all charges against John J., who was a ranking official in a big A. F. of L. union. All the plans offered to plead younger brother James B. to something only if older brother was turned loose. Captain Fredericks knew he'd stood firm. John J. could not go unpunished. He knew there had been no deal until within a few hours *after* Franklin's arrest Darrow rushed in and consented to plead James B. guilty to murder in the first and take a fifteen-year term for John J. In record-breaking time of seventy-two hours, all points had been ironed out, pleas changed in open court, the confession signed.

These facts made the other line of defense Darrow clung

to—that he had no reason to attempt bribery since a settlement had been made—look very unconvincing to the press
and everybody else.

I knew these things too. Always there are some things certain men can do, some they can't, as Papa had said to the
jury in the Hays case. I could believe Darrow would do
anything for his cause, and then lose his head in a pinch. I
couldn't and never did believe that John D. Fredericks was
part of a conspiracy to get Darrow. Steffens was the only
man who kept insisting the deal had been made. Again I find
it possible to believe that Steffens' only grave fault as a
reporter, his own desire to play God to the story, led him to
exaggerate his part as treaty-maker, which Judge Bordwell
denied ever happened. To anyone who ever knew General
Otis, the picture Steffens gives of meeting with him and
winning from him a promise to be kind and lenient to the
McNamaras is too hard to swallow.

As the trial progressed over long months, it took on a
peculiar quality as though it might have been conceived by
Dostoievsky. I don't mean to indicate anything communistic.
The Russian Revolution hadn't taken place, no one had even
heard of Lenin, nor communism as an active part of life. Hard
as it is for present generations to imagine, those things which
now occupy time, thought, and horizons to such an extent—
war, income tax, traffic, communism—did not exist in our
world. We truly believed we had evolved to a peaceful and
progressive civilization. As a bloodless revolution, a civil war
without guns if possible, many people like my father believed
in the cause of labor and in reforms all along the line—believed
that capital could, would, and must clean its own house of
child labor, unfair working conditions, and unjust wages and
hours.

It was a *Russian* atmosphere that somehow seeped into
and took over the courtroom, like a gray fog coming in pal-
pably through the windows. As the chief actor, the star,
Darrow somehow imparted to the whole cast and proceedings
a wildly emotional, breast-beating, bleeding gloom and
wretchedness. As days passed, he lost weight visibly. His
clothes hung looser and looser. None of us had ever seen
anything like it before. We entered daily into the Slough of
Despond and stayed there. Any fire Rogers tried to get into
it sometimes fizzled out under Darrow's tears. Inkwells flew,
insults were exchanged, Papa was supposed to go to jail for
contempt, was pardoned, all inside an aquarium, as it were.

So that Papa's examination of Bert Franklin had a strange rhythm, a distinct beat of violence that was *cold*. Like a fight between sharks instead of tigers.

I can see Earl Rogers walking in that morning. The old aids on the outside, the sweat room at the turkish baths, the pummeling and kneeding to get the blood flowing, the icy showers, the shave and haircut and hot towels, the elegant striped trousers and cutaway coat with black braid outlining its elegance, had restored the outer man. I didn't like the transparency about him. I didn't know just what I meant by the word then, I came to know later. The heart wearing out.

Bert Franklin was a middleweight, stocky, in control of his hands and feet, not bad-looking. He wore a mustache cut straight across into a thick brown brush, and he had a large dimple in his chin. I was pleased and hopeful with this, I had a theory that men with dimples in their chin couldn't take it. Franklin made me eat that the first day. He could take it and dish it out, too.

They knew each other well, he and his cross-examiner. Had for years. Bert had been present in many courtrooms where Earl Rogers was chief counsel for the defense. His eyes, which Baillie described as like marble, were icy and wary. Confessed criminal and stool pigeon though he was, he was a fighter and he had watched the champ in training camp and knew what might be coming.

The sequence on which he floundered badly was the Lockwood bribe, and I think there Rogers took a line for which, with all his cold caginess, Bert hadn't been prepared.

"You'd known Lockwood for years, hadn't you?" Rogers asked.

"Yes, sir," Franklin said. He could make his voice utterly without tone, time or color. It gave nothing away, for or against.

"Worked with him as deputy sheriff, didn't you?"

"Yes, sir."

"Knew him to be a good officer?"

"Yes—a good officer."

"Knew him to be an honest man?"

"Yes."

"He was a friend—he was your friend—you counted him as your friend?"

"Yes."

"A good man to have beside you in danger—in trouble?"

"Yes sir."

Pretty soon there they were—*Damon* Franklin and *Pythias* Lockwood.

Q. (by Mr. Rogers) You told Mr. Darrow you thought, you knew, Lockwood as an honest man?

A. Yes sir.

Q. Why, if you thought he was honest did you think you could bribe him?

A. No man's that honest.

Q. You thought you could tempt him to his own destruction?

A. Well—I thought he had his weak spot. I thought the offer of enough money might influence him, yes.

Q. You knew he had a mortgage on his little ranch?

A. Oh yes—

Q. You knew how much love and work he'd put into it, how he and his wife loved it and hoped to spend their declining years there?

A. I guess so.

Q. So you, his friend, his old comrade in arms, you dangled enough money, $4,000 in cash, enough to pay off the mortgage, in front of him to seduce him from his honesty, to betray his honor—you did that?

A. I did—yes.

Q. Then in the end when you saw you were in a trap, you thought you'd take your friend up to the policeman on the corner and say *he* had solicited *you* for a bribe—you did say that to the district attorney, didn't you?

A. Yes. I thought I might make it look as though he started it.

Q. So you were quite ready to charge an honest man, your lifelong friend, with a dastardly crime, an innocent man as he was, to save yourself?

A. I was only doing the best I could to get out of the straits I was in.

Q. And are still in, aren't you, Mr. Franklin?

When he got into the matter of Darrow, Darrow's part in the bribery attempt, I could see my father turning on the speed. Speeding it up. I am sure he figured right there that if there was one place he had it on Bert it was in speed—Franklin was being slow but sure, timing carefully, not allowing himself to be hurried, giving an impression of serious consideration. But with the increased dazzling speed of the questions Rogers began to make it appear that he was hesitating, that he had to *think* before he answered—that he might be lying.

Yes, Darrow had laid the plan, given him the money. Yes he had reported all his moves with Lockwood and Bain to the Big Boy, Clarence Darrow. But he had of course kept Darrow out of it at all times.

"I told him," Bert Franklin said, "I told him to keep out of sight." He shook his head sadly. "But he showed up."

"You told him to stay away from the corner of Third and Los Angeles?"

"Yes I did. I told him, I said to him then they wouldn't care anything about me, they'd be after him. *You* stay out of it, I told him."

"And so you were very much surprised when you saw Mr. Darrow there—after you say you had warned him?"

"Yes sir, I certainly was."

"You were already aware of the trap when you saw Mr. Darrow?"

"Yes sir—I'd said to Lockwood, let's take a walk. Then I saw Darrow."

"What was he doing?"

"He was coming across the street like a bat out of hell."

"Did he wave his hat at you—like this—to catch your attention?"

"Yes yes—he did."

"Waves his hat at you while you and Lockwood were walking along? Darrow waved his hat at you?"

"Yes."

"You'd told him not to come—you'd warned him they were after him—the district attorney, the opposition wouldn't want you, they'd want him, yet you saw him come charging across the street in plain sight of all the world waving his hat?"

"Yes—that's about it."

"This must have surprised you very much—"

Of course there Joe Ford's crackling objections halted that line. But it was obvious to one and all twelve of the jurors that it had surprised Bert Franklin out of his wits.

I remember one flashing moment when Rogers went into the matter of the money. Of LeCompte Davis's testimony about the bail. Franklin lost control for a moment, he bared his teeth and his voice came high and shrill, "You want to know about that? All right—ask your client. *Ask Clarence*

Darrow. He knows all about it." He stared at Darrow, his very mustache bristling, his hands on the arm of the witness chair as though he was going to leap out of it and drag Darrow to his feet and confront him. Several times in several courtrooms I have heard defendants leap to their feet and cry out against a witness. I can still hear Bruno Richard Hauptmann screaming at FBI man Tommy Sisk, calling him a liar. I did it once myself. I remembered how Patrick Calhoun had stood up and spoken with dignity. Darrow never moved. Except that maybe his chin sank lower and lower on his breast and the lock of hair hung farther and farther to hide his face, abject, haggard, lower lip hanging loose.

Ask Clarence Darrow! He knows all about it. A damaging moment!

And Franklin landed one more before the days ended.

"Now, Bert," Rogers said, and he had assumed the I-know-you-won't-try-to-kid-me manner of an old friend, no, an old acquaintance, who'd always known these things, "the district attorney began asking you to implicate Darrow almost at once, didn't he?"

"He asked me if Darrow had been in on it, yes."

"And you said he hadn't?"

"That's right."

Slowly now and carefully, Rogers took him through his many denials made after his arrest. His statements in the newspapers were held before his eyes. His statements to many of his friends, to Job Harriman, defeated candidate for mayor.

"You said to them that Darrow was never in on the bribery?"

"Yes."

"That Darrow had never given you a corrupt dollar?"

"Yes."

"That Darrow knew nothing of what was going on?"

"That's right."

"That Darrow was innocent as a baby and if he hadn't appeared at Third and Los Angeles Streets that day they'd never have thought of it."

"I said he was innocent, I don't remember the last part," Franklin said aggressively. "I said he was innocent as a baby."

"Why did you say all those things if they weren't true, Bert?" Rogers asked him.

Franklin was dramatic then. Whether it *was* real—whether he turned it on—heaven help me, it sounded real to me. His cold mean face had a terrible look. He said, "To protect that man there—" He half stood up, he extended his right arm and pointed at Darrow, slunk in his gloom. "To protect him. Because he'd sold me a bill of goods, Darrow had. He'd made me believe in him—even when I was shocked that he'd plan jury bribery—"

That terrible look. It comes to human faces when they are staring at *feet of clay*. If this had happened to Bert Franklin, it would have been particularly horrible because probably he hadn't believed in anything since they took away his nursing bottle. If he had believed in Darrow—

Rogers did his best to retrieve it. "No, no," he said. "Let me ask you this. Didn't the district attorney begin at once to assure you that *you* wouldn't be in any trouble if you *played ball?* Didn't he assure you of that?"

Bert Franklin's shrug was the height of all cynicism. "Sure," he said.

"Bert," Rogers said, "the district attorney told you he didn't want *you*. We want Darrow, isn't that what he said? We don't want you, we don't care anything about you. *We want Darrow.*"

Bert shifted a little in his chair. He said, "They said if Darrow had been in this they wanted me to tell them."

"And you said he hadn't?"

"At first I did."

"That was a lie?"

"Well—"

"Then you said he was in it?"

"Yes."

"Which one was a lie—one or the other was a lie—you lied sometime, Bert, didn't you?"

"I didn't tell the truth when I said Darrow didn't know about it."

"But how can we tell? How can we be sure which time you lied? They told you they wanted to get Darrow."

King Darius said to the lions:
"Bite Daniel. Bite Daniel. Bite him. Bite him. Bite him!"

Thus roared the lions:
"We want Daniel, Daniel, Daniel,
We wanted Daniel, Daniel, Daniel,
Grrrrrrrrrrrrrrrrrrrrrrrrrrrrrrrrrrrrrrrrrr
Grrrrrrrrrrrrrrrrrrrrrrrrrrrrrrrrrrrrr."

That's the way Earl Rogers made it sound—for a moment or two. Bite Darrow, bite him, bite him, bite him. *Grrrrrrrrrrrrrrrrrrrrrrr.* The courtroom vibrated to the growls. *We want Darrow Darrow Darrow.*

"Didn't they tell you if you could get Gompers, if Darrow would give them the evidence against Gompers, they'd let Darrow go?"

Bite *Gompers,* bite him!

But there was Captain John D. Fredericks, well and favorably known, elected by enormous popular vote, peering through his glasses in honest bewilderment. Joe Ford, giving off sparks of indignation and throwing inkwells. At Papa. They didn't *look* like they'd said, *Bite Darrow, bite him, bite him, bite him.*

Rogers had created a despicable creature out of this witness, without honor, a double-crossing double-dealing informer without honor, hardened in disbelief in any good in any man. Ready to sell his own soul, or his best friend's. Yet—he'd stood up to Rogers, he hadn't quailed under blistering cross-examination or been confused in his own version of the facts.

As we walked down the hill after it was over I asked myself what the twelve men would take into the jury room as their unforgettable impression, higher and deeper than their thoughts. What did *I* remember? Two things.

Darrow running across the street waving his hat like a madman, or a fool!

That terrible look on Bert Franklin's face, the look that comes when a man beholds his idol's feet of clay.

Which time had Bert Franklin lied?

I wished Papa had made me sure, but I knew he hadn't. It was very uncomfortable. I was glad to find I was the only one. Jerry Giesler, who preferred to warn rather than praise, agreed with the Associated Press that Earl Rogers had indeed conducted obsequies for Bert Franklin, the most dangerous witness against Darrow.

At the dinner table, in icy tones, Rogers said to Darrow, "I am not Houdini. I cannot do this without some co-operation. Time and again, juries bring in verdicts against all evidence, and the judge's instructions. They tell you, 'We knew *he* couldn't have done a thing like that,' or 'She was one we knew could be up to a thing like that.'" He waited. Darrow said nothing. "The impression the accused makes on the jury can be fifty per cent of the verdict?" Darrow nodded.

"Then, you lugubrious wretch," Rogers said, "you are going to jail," and got up and left the table.

The first time he had spoken impolitely to Darrow in public.

FIFTY-EIGHT

The only entirely *un-Russian-novelist* bright moment in the trial came through Sam Browne, head investigator for the D.A., and was engendered by my father's relish for a spot of revenge now and then. Sometimes he dismissed a grudge as not worth the trouble. When he held one, it didn't fester but it kept watch for a chance to get even.

The build-up of Browne was again part of the hat-waving defense, of which at no time, *no time*, for one second, did Rogers ever lose sight.

Sam Browne had been on the spot and Darrow had spoken to him there.

Earl Rogers said to the court, "We will show that to the certain knowledge of Mr. Darrow, Sam Browne of the district attorney's staff, is the man who officially ran down the perpetrators of the *Times* horror. Sam Browne was the man who produced the evidence which led to the fact that Mr. Darrow, as counsel for the McNamaras, was obliged to plead his clients Guilty. We will show that Mr. Darrow had read the grand-jury transcript and knew of Sam Browne's part in the testimony that brought the indictments. He knew Sam Browne by sight. We offer it that it would be unlikely, knowing what he did about Mr. Browne, that it is more than unlikely, it is entirely unbelievable, ridiculous and manifest falsification, that Mr. Darrow should make any admission to Browne or any careless remarks in front of him or offer to 'take care of him.' Unless he was entirely innocent of all complicity in this matter, any connection with guilty knowledge, a man like Darrow would not stand there asking *Mr. Browne* questions as to what was going on."

Rogers had spoken in that perfect-enunciation the-jury-must-hear-this ringing way so that while the judge could order it stricken from the record he couldn't expunge the jury's sound track.

My father told us afterwards that just at that moment he saw the portly, pompous figure of William J. Burns enter the courtroom and take a seat. An idea, Papa said with a Machiavellian Mephistophelean grin, sprang full-panoplied like Athena from the brain of Jove. "I'd waited a long time for Mr. Burns to walk into my parlor," he said gleefully.

The long wait had been since the graft prosecution in San Francisco when Burns was on the side of The Weak and The Poor and the unions, riding lickety-split with those knights of reform, Fremont Older and Francis J. Heney, and paid by Rudolph Spreckels. He had then called Earl Rogers a mountebank and a deceiver, accused him of kidnaping Fremont Older, and insisted that he had tried to lure Lornegan with light ladies. For a short and surprising span investigating the dynamiting, we'd been on the same side. Now Burns, still on the steel-trust payroll, was our foe once more and *Get Darrow get him get him get him* was his theme song.

Suddenly, Mr. Rogers, if he had been nominating Sam for the Hall of Fame or trying to get him elected governor, couldn't have orated more eulogistically. None of us could figure out what he was up to and neither could the district attorney. Browne was his man, nevertheless, he didn't like any part of it. They were wary of Mr. Rogers bearing gifts. Deciding it would be better to get it over, the district attorney himself rose and said resignedly, "We will stipulate that what Mr. Rogers says is a fact *is* a fact, if we can thereby get on with—"

Rogers beamed at him and a stipulation as to the activities and full credit to be given Mr. Sam Browne for the capture of the McNamaras was entered. The press decided this was another of Rogers' balloons to keep the jury's mind off Darrow's guilt, which he often did for days. Nobody saw it as a *first* move until Mr. Rogers made the second which was to walk up to Burns in the corridor and say, "Did you call me a son-of-a-bitch, Mr. Burns?" when Burns hadn't opened his mouth to so much as breathe. Blows were exchanged. Commotion and deputies and finally Judge Hutton, a peace-loving Christian, demanded complete disarmament. Everybody was summoned into chambers and put their guns on the judge's desk and the place had a more homelike *feel*. As they walked out Rogers shook and waggled a warning finger at Burns—to call his attention to the future.

After this fracas, Burns took the stand to testify concerning the confession of McManigal, and Rogers began a razzle-dazzle of questions. In answering them, Burns tried to be belittling and disdainful. The Rogers questions implied in a welter of double-talk that Bert Franklin had actually been working for Burns all the time. That the money for the bribe had come not from *Darrow* but from *Burns* in a triple cross. That as head of the detectives for the steel trust this plot had been conceived and executed by Burns. He was the man behind the trap to trap Darrow. Burns's denials were stentorian and bombastic. All of it was a lot of camouflage and aimed at any suggestibility among the jurors that there *were* other ways all this could have come about. While the echoes were bouncing off the walls and even the judge was trying to sort out these accusations, Rogers switched completely. Toying with the ribbons of his lorgnette, he moved behind the counsel table and took up a favorite stance.

He said, "There is a reward in the McNamara case?"

Burns said, still at ease, that there was.

"A considerable sum—fifty thousand dollars?" Mr. Rogers wanted to know.

"Yes, that is the figure, I believe," said Burns complacently.

"You intend to claim this?"

"Indeed I do. Nobody else is entitled to it."

Mr. Rogers smiled at him sweetly as he came leisurely around to the witness stand. "You say, Mr. Burns, that you and only you are entitled to the reward money. Are you aware, dear Mr. Burns, that here in this court the district attorney stipulated that Mr. Sam Browne was the man who discovered most of the clues against the McNamaras? That Mr. Browne gathered the evidence which brought about the grand-jury indictments? That he was responsible for the testimony which forced the McNamaras to plead Guilty and thus put them in the penitentiary where they now are?"

You could hear the jaws of *that* trap close, the crunch of bones as Burns screamed with pain and the district attorney turned Stanford red.

"No such thing," Burns was shouting, "no such thing," as Judge Hutton rapped and, trying not to smile, said, "I believe there is such a stipulation, Mr. District Attorney?"

Fredericks rose, balanced precariously on the horns of this dilemma. Sam Browne was his own man, head of his investigative branch. If he threw him to the wolves, Rogers would see to it that he lost prestige and popularity. On the other hand there sat Burns, nationally famous, powerful in Washington, high in industrial circles. Probably he had been led to expect the reward. He said at last, "Well, Mr. Rogers certainly did make a long and—and very—*eloquent* speech of appreciation of—of Mr. Sam Browne's work—as it happens of course at that time Mr. Rogers himself worked with Mr. Browne in—in discovering the—the *Times* dynamiters—I believe I did state, I did stipulate that all that Mr. Rogers said in praise of Mr. Browne was true, however there was no question—nothing was said about the reward—"

"Something is being said now," Rogers said, dripping honey. "Just to refresh your memory—would you care to look at the transcript, Captain? You stipulated quite clearly that what I said was the fact and what I said was that *all the credit* for the arrest of the McNamaras should go to Mr. Browne—it seems to me this means *the cash* as well, doesn't it?"

He turned back to Burns, who was having what was beginning to look like apoplexy. "You've engaged an attorney, have you not, Mr. Burns, to collect this reward money for you?"

A. I have.

Q. And that attorney, my good sir, is the Assistant District Attorney trying this case, prosecuting it?

A. Yes sir.

Joe Ford came out of his chair so high far and fast that the jury jumped, and he cried out, "He engaged me as a person, not as an assistant district attorney!"

"But dear Mr. Ford," Rogers said. "You were sitting here not in your private person as separated from your person as assistant district attorney if this can be done. You were sitting here as assistant to the district attorney when the district attorney stated officially to this court as follows: 'We will stipulate that all the things which Mr. Rogers has recited about Mr. Browne as facts are facts.' " He laid the transcript down. "You heard that, Mr. Ford. You made no objection to the stipulation. Mr. Burns, *you* heard it and if you can understand English you must have realized what it meant. Do you still think that you and you alone caught the McNamaras, with no help from Mr. Browne or my humble self?"

Burns said, "Well, all I know is that I was in the courtroom a little while here and I heard Mr. Rogers saying all that rot, none of it was true."

Q. (by Mr. Rogers) Then if it was not true how did it happen that in your very presence the District Attorney in person stipulated that it was true that Mr. Browne and Mr. Browne alone was responsible for the McNamaras being in the penitentiary?

A. I heard something—a lot of rot—

Q. You don't think the District Attorney was telling the truth?

A. Oh, you know, Rogers, you were just getting off a lot of bunk, it didn't mean a thing to anybody except this fellow Browne maybe.

Q. By 'this fellow Browne' are you referring to the Chief Investigator for the District Attorney of Los Angeles County?

A. Yes I am.

Q. That's how you feel about him—'this fellow'?

A. Well, he's made himself ridiculous wanting part of the reward.

Q. You want it all, Mr. Burns?

The district attorney interfered here and the court upheld him. But Rogers had an arrow left in his quiver. As Burns came down he said, "By the way, Mr. Burns, you also expect to collect all the reward on Mr. Darrow?"

Burns blinked. "There's not any reward in the Darrow case," he said.

Rogers smiled broadly and made a little gesture toward the jury. "Oh—isn't there, Mr. Burns? I'd heard that in Washington they were going to make you—"

Storms and protests and Burns and Ford howled and raged. I doubt, however, if Rogers wanted or expected an answer to that or even knew how he was going to end the sentence.

He knew what the jury thought of Burns.

In the end, Sam Browne got the reward.

I was glad he had that bit of fun and folklore.

Shortly afterwards, he had to put Clarence Darrow on the stand.

FIFTY-NINE

Time, as it passes, takes a hold on what seems to each of us essential, screens out what in our feeling and thought didn't really matter. My excursion into the past to relive this story for myself I find like any other trip. Some scenes, conversations, places, times are vivid and indelible. I can smell and see and hear them *now*. Others I can reconstruct out of bits and pieces and make it *feel* right, as Irving Stone has done in his life of Michelangelo. I am a professional writer and it has been my whole life's work to *know* what would, did, will, and has to happen and be said to and by certain kinds of people in certain circumstances. I once did an imaginary interview with the woman who was in jail in Olympia, Washington, in the Weyerhauser kidnaping, and it was so accurately and exactly what she *had* said to the arresting agents that the matron and I were called up by the FBI on the theory that somebody had violated orders and let me in. Other things upon which other books have laid stress have vanished from me altogether, and I still find them unimportant. To me. I once heard Babe Ruth *replay* the game in Chicago in which he hit the home run he called ahead of time, with every pitch of the nine innings. Other games he didn't remember had ever been played at all. On the very next day, ten men, even those who have had training, will give you ten different accounts of what they observed, as J. Edgar Hoover has proved in his initial screening tests for FBI agents.

Given Mrs. Darrow, Jerry Giesler, Jim Pope, who covered the Darrow trials for the *Herald* and later became a superior-court judge, the bailiff in charge of the locked-up jury, Harry Carr of the *Times*, Anton Johannsen, one of the triumvirate of the anarchy wing out from Indianapolis, William J. Burns, a Gompers observer, and Earl Rogers' daughter, we have that many divergent and nevertheless honest reports. Like photographs of the finish of a horse race, taken from far right, far left, and straight on the wire, all true camera shots of the same event, same time, all showing a different winner.

On a few things, a majority agree.

One of these seems to be that Darrow was not a great witness for himself. Few of the historic accounts of the trials so much as mention his long days on the stand. Rogers, with a shrug, said, "The gentleman doth protest too much, as is but natural." Rosy said he was too damn indignant and mortified to make sense. Jerry said he had to be *awkward*, being on the stand instead of in front of it. Darrow himself said over and over that he had thrown himself open to Ford. If he hesitated it was simply to understand Ford's questions, he said he had made no more errors than any honest man always makes.

As for me, I thought he began too high and never could go anywhere. As though a prima donna began an aria on high C. He had no *pace*. He was too *personal*. He had the old debater's trick of sliding off a question—ask him about the ten-thousand-dollar check to Tvietmoe or the thousand-dollar check to Bain, and he would be found discussing The Rich and the Social Conflict.

About this time Mrs. Darrow had a nervous collapse. I don't think she was in court part of the time while her husband was testifying. I can see now that she held herself strung so tight that finally it had to snap.

I wish I had understood her better then. No use saying I did. This was a not very attractive woman who had by the turn of events become the heroine of a great love story. The wife of a famous man. His devoted and adoring wife, his very rib. A center of drama, tragedy, melodrama, violence. Like most women who had in themselves no possibility of such a full life, she was more Clarence Darrow than Clarence Darrow. Her god, religion, principles, activities all channeled through him, as him, he was the object of her affections, her *raison d'être*. Nothing is as devastating to watch as one you love being tortured, yourself unable to *stop it*. Hatred of the torturers, resentment against those who aren't doing as much as they should be for the victim drive a woman crazy. Ruby Darrow, thin, angular, old-maidish yet obsessed by a *grande passion* she had probably feared in youth would pass her by, saw the man who had been her life being burned at the stake. Her desire to help him made her jump off into space every once in a while.

From the beginning, her antagonism to my father cast the apple of discord. Without her needling, her jealousy, her insistence that Earl Rogers was nothing but a shyster, a ham actor, a drunk, Rogers and Darrow might have achieved what I *know* my father longed and strove for—a friendship. Women can play havoc in such spots. I didn't want it any more than Ruby did. I still had to cope with my stomach as best I could. *You think he's guilty*, my father would say. I had to say, *Yes I do*. Only to him of course. I did. I still do. So did *eight men* on the second jury, remember, the case my father *didn't* try. The charge is still on the books in California, outlawed though it may be, and the agreement that Darrow was never to attempt to practice law in this state.

Darrow's examination by Rogers and cross by Ford seem to have left no impression. All interest, response, applause focused upon Darrow's address to the jury.

So does mine, now.

Especially on the first time he made it so gloriously, the dress rehearsal in our deserted office on a night I can never forget as long as I live. Though why I knew with such utter, irremediable moral conviction that this was the turning point in our lives I still cannot tell you.

To understand the truth about this famous speech, it is necessary to realize what we had found out before it was to be made. In his book, *High Tension*, Hugh Baillie brings to print for the first time as far as I have read that *he* knew days ahead of the Big Speech that the jury had already decided to bring in a Not Guilty verdict.

I'm certain that the jury had decided to acquit Darrow even before all the evidence was in, Hugh Baillie wrote. *I knew how they were going to vote a week before the trial ended*. His foreknowledge came from a juror named Golding. It came before Darrow's famous final plea had been made.

We knew this too, and so did several other reporters. Among them Don Nicholson of the *Examiner*, who was a beau of mine at the time and came and told me, as well as his city editor Ray Van Ettisch.

Our office got it from a bailiff here and a deputy there, who accompanied the twelve men back and forth to meals and guarded them by night, to Bert Cowan and Rosy and Bull Durham and Dominguez, to Mr. Rogers.

This is by no means unheard of in trial annals. Attorney General Wilentz stopped in front of me and said quietly, *It's the chair*, some three hours before the Hauptmann jury came in, and if Judge Trenchard hadn't taken the precaution to lock us all in the courtroom I might have scooped the world. Usually it is the prosecution side that has the best chance of an in to the jury, since the deputies and bailiffs are in its employ, but again *Mr. Rogers* was different.

As far as I was concerned, I didn't think they'd made much effort to conceal it. My training had been to *watch the jury*. To use my eyes and ears, intuitions and instincts, heart, stomach, and bowels to read any and all of them on every pitch. What their reactions were to everything, whether we needed to press harder on one line of testimony or drop it altogether. To be sure whether they had laughed—or cried— or been indignant—or amused—by a piece of evidence or a witness.

Nothing in life has ever been so exciting as trying to get inside a jury's skin. A game of life and death. By that time I knew a jury would and could believe anything it wanted to. Find reasons for its own determinations. Neither voters nor golf balls are as unpredictable and baffling as juries. Supposition is greater than truth, Bacon says, and my father often said this was a motto for many juries. But a great trial lawyer's work is as closely geared to *the jury* as a pitcher's to the batter. I really suffered during the Darrow trial. If they pulled out my toenails, I would still know we had to get Darrow *off*. He was our client. Right or wrong I was for Papa, but for the first time I wasn't clearhearted rip-roaring all the way out, every once in a while I'd find myself drifting to the other side unconsciously. I knew he was guilty, and I couldn't seem to justify it. I couldn't figure he was such a great guy we ought to be for him anyhow. Of course he didn't try to belittle Papa then, that would have been too silly, but I had a hunch he was going to do us dirt somehow. I knew he didn't like Papa. He resented having to depend on him, resented his triumphs. I thought this was very small.

Papa asked me and I'd told him I felt after Bert Franklin's cross-examination the jury had shifted to our side. While I didn't consider it one of my father's big ones, I knew it had been a winner, and as the trial progressed the prosecution didn't have enough else. Moreover, as I told him they had all *laughed* about the hat and like all great gags it got better with repetition. They were familiar enough with it now so that it was their own thinking.

I told Papa we were in. They were making no bones about relaxing. A plump little juror had begun to wink at me as he went by, to assure me all was well. In the front row a heavy-shouldered man beamed paternally upon Mr. Rogers. They no longer avoided looking at Darrow so much. Then we got the direct word that they had already decided on a Not Guilty verdict.

Though there was speculation as to whether Rogers or Darrow would make the final plea for the defense, there was never any doubt about it in our office. My father said to reporters at the time, "It is not often your client is a great trial lawyer and famous orator. It is his right to speak to the jury himself last, and our good fortune to have him do so."

So Rogers made a simple, clean-cut summation of evidence. He set up charts and in his usual unoratorical way went through the testimony of each prosecution witness and showed where it had fallen apart. He put down and highlighted the contradictions and the character of the witnesses who had contradicted each other—the reputable well-known lawyer like LeCompte Davis against a man like Harrington, who was one of the informers.

He carefully set up the three lines of defense.

1. The conspiracy to get Darrow.
2. That the agreement to plead the McNamaras Guilty had probably been made and therefore Darrow had no reason to bribe anybody.
3. Above all, he came back to the inanity, insanity, stupidity of Darrow's appearance on the scene if he was guilty and knew what was to take place there. "Not very intelligent," Rogers said with a smile, "even when he was innocent, but Darrow is a crusader, he will always follow a white plume."

SIXTY

Darrow didn't believe our straight-from-the-horse's-mouth information that the jury had made up its mind to acquit him. Thus we entered the night before his final plea to them in a state of jitters and jeopardy as far as he was concerned.

My father was tickled with this. It meant the adrenal gland was working overtime. "Different people take it different ways," he said. "Unless they do take it they'd better stay home. If a man isn't on edge, he'll be no good. This man is a champion, once the whistle blows he'll be great."

This I found to be true over the years. Damon Runyon sweating it out in the snow the night before the Hauptmann case began in Flemington; Lucille Ball in a state of coma half an hour before her smash hit show opened on Broadway; Franklin Delano Roosevelt waiting for *Ladies and Gentlemen, the President of the United States* to say, *My Friends,* on a vital broadcast; Babe Ruth on the eve of a World Series; the thoroughbreds in Louisville who knew as well as jockeys, trainers, and sports writers that the next day was the Kentucky Derby—that same up, up, up nervous excitement throbbing through the blood stream into the brain, unbearable in its intensity.

As my father said, it took everybody differently.

He was like Nijinsky, on his toes, soaring, ready to leap, all over the place.

It seemed to have paralyzed Darrow into an increase of that lethargy and despair which had been upon him all the months of the trial.

As everyone knew, he always expected to be convicted. San Quentin haunted his conversation. That night as he shambled to a chair in my father's office, he was surer than ever. The life of the office flowed around him. Rogers was all over the place, the *chug chug chug-chug-chug* grew faster, faster. Sending for transcripts, for Giesler, for Dominguez, in hopes of last-minute news from the sacrosanct precincts of the jury.

At the last the clamor died. Voices shouted good night. *Need me any more, Mr. Rogers?* All our lights were still on, the glare emphasized the emptiness, the blackness of the night seemed trying to get in through the open windows. That eerie feeling of an office building by night descended. Only Rosy, half-asleep at the switchboard, and Jerry Giesler in a far corner with a lawbook were left. Because the August heat was still in the walls, the door into the private office where Rogers and Darrow had begun their final work was open.

"I will ask no man for sympathy," Darrow said, out of his thoughts. "I have never asked for sympathy. I would rather go to San Quentin. Ford has warned them I will beg for sympathy, why should I stand before the world and plead for mercy when all I have ever asked is justice?"

"Before the world," Rogers said. "Yes, this is your great chance to state your case to the whole world, to declare your innocence to all people."

He began then to stir Darrow, to bait him, argue with him, remind him, call upon him, entice and stimulate him. Sometimes it was brutal, and sometimes it was beautiful, it was a pep talk by a football coach, it was a poetic conception such as Vic Fleming gave Gable before the scenes with the dead child for *Gone with the Wind*. At first it was like trying to get an elephant out of a wallow, where his own peril weighted him heavily. Little by little. Darrow responded, came to life, climbed toward the light and the fight, the excitement began to get him.

"I was warned that union labor would turn against me if I pleaded the McNamaras Guilty," he said. "Those for whom I spent my blood misunderstand me."

"Tomorrow," Rogers said, "you can speak not just to the jury. You can speak to those who had misunderstood you."

"I know the mob," Darrow said. "I can love it at the same time I despise it. The masses are incapable of thinking, I've lived and worked with them, I know. I've been their idol. Now they cast me down and trample on me. On the highest pinnacle, I have heard the mob cheer me to the echo. Now in the depths they hiss my name. The same mob. The same masses. Such devotion to humanity I have called out of my soul that I have gone on serving them, unmoved by either their praise or their blame. Some men look at a man and see only the devil in him. Others build him into an idol. Neither can be true. I have tried to follow my conscience and my duty faithfully, to be a friend to every man who lives. I have felt his heart beat with my own. I've tried to help the whole world and to love my neighbor as myself and I know that these people who want to make my name a byword do it only because I have been a friend of the poor, the weak."

My father's face shone in response.

For the third time, I saw my father put his hand on Darrow's shoulder.

In all the years since I have heard nothing more eloquent. I said to myself, Why, you ignominious little whippersnapper, you fresh, half-baked punk, how dare you criticize this great man? How dare you judge this man who thinks of the poor and weak before himself? I felt the impact of his greatness. No matter what its weaknesses, how far short it may fall, greatness makes itself heard, seen, felt in the heart. Here was a measure of greatness and I knew it, yet all the time and all the more because of that, I was bitter about his behaving the way he had in front of everybody. I found out I wasn't the only young person who had been scared and upset by the way great people could act without any standards, the kind my grandfather had always spoken of. I thought I was the first this had happened to. I knew I was different than other girls such as I had met briefly in schools, on account of the way I had been brought up, yet I felt anyone would be shaking in their shoes, the way I was, if they were in mine.

I sat there sweating and listening. You did not sweat much in the kind of heat we had then in California before the climate changed, and besides the sweet coolness that came always when the sun went down was filling the room. I was sweating just the same, I could feel it under my braids and I pulled the pins out and let them hang down for relief. I tried, I had been trying, I figured it was petty of me to hate Darrow for the way he treated my father. Why should a great man like Darrow be expected to treat another lawyer like ordinary clients did? Only—anybody could have *manners* and friendliness. Now it was something else. It is very very hard on a kid—and I still was only a kid, no matter how I had been brought up, to see feet of clay. Worse than anything. While I was sure in myself that this was a great man, or anyhow he could be a great man, like a demon something kept chattering in my inside ear, *You, Clarence Darrow, let people wear red white and blue buttons saying The McNamaras Are Innocent* and all the time you knew they were not anything of the kind. They killed Harvey and if you go to San Quentin, as you say all the time you will, it won't be any conspiracy of the enemies of the poor and weak. It will be because you are guilty and couldn't play by the rules. If you don't go it will be Papa saving your skin for you and you will not so much as say thank you. I thought that my father was great, too, and he had his *Mr. Hyde* but bad as it was it was a lot nicer and more natural. Anyhow Papa does not pretend about it if you face him with it.

In my confusion and going around and around about it, I tried to put into some kind of shape that the publicans and the harlots like Papa and Pearl Morton went into the kingdom before the whited sepulcher. Anyhow they are not so *damp* and depressing, though maybe that is what is dangerous. Besides what right have you got, I said to myself, to call this great man Clarence Darrow, who has been on a pedestal to oppressed people and their *idol*, a whited sepulcher? How do you know he is? There might be nine other explanations, and then it came over me that only *idols* have feet of clay, probably the rest of us are *all* clay.

Papa thought Darrow was innocent—or did he?

"You think I'm guilty," Darrow said to Rogers sometime during that endless night, and Rogers said, "Prove to *me* that you are not, that's what we're here for tonight. Prove to any skeptic, any undecided juror, your own lawyer that you aren't guilty. Prove it!"

Papa had always told me he thought Darrow was innocent. This time, he said, I was all off base and didn't know what I was talking about.

Jerry—but Jerry was so *cagey*. Sometimes I thought he was even smarter than Papa, but not nearly as great. He had an ax to grind. I had figured that out or maybe I hadn't. Maybe he was just hardly more than a kid too, and he thought of Darrow as an *idol* to look up to, but he had Papa for an idol so what did he need another one for?

I could hear Darrow all the time as though I had a rubber ear that stretched out and listened to him while I myself was going through such a *time*. Feeling younger and more—more inadequate than I had ever felt in all my whole life. It wasn't often I felt inadequate, that's for sure.

. . . Will it be the gray dim walls of San Quentin . . . my life has been all too human but I have been a friend to the helpless, I have cried their cause . . . if this jury sets me free there will be thanks pour in from thousands of the poor that they have given me my liberty and saved my name . . .

Anybody can say one thing and think another, I said to myself. I wish he'd get *off* that poor-and-weak-and-helpless *refrain*. Something dangerous was there. I was afraid now. For all my spoiled, youthful arrogance and temper and prejudices where Papa was concerned, I wasn't often afraid. I felt alone. I was glad all over when I heard Papa's crisp, clear voice, and evidently he too thought it was time to get him off that *refrain*. He said that it wasn't wise to take the Not Guilty verdict entirely for granted, there were things they had a right to hear from Darrow himself as his last word.

His appearance on the bribery scene, Rogers told him, needed to be explained. Darrow cried:

If you can believe that, don't send me to San Quentin, send me to a lunatic asylum.

Bert Franklin. To this, Darrow answered:

No other testimony connects me with this crime. I tell you I'd
rather be dead than to live in an America where the lowest man
in it can be convicted by an American jury on the word of a
creature, such a man, as Bert Franklin.

Again and again, Rogers kept bringing him back to the
case. Burns?

I am going to tell the truth about that. They can send me to the
penitentiary at San Quentin if they see fit. It was a hard bitter
fight. The district attorney's sleuths, an army. Burns with his
pack of hounds. The steel trust with its gold. All arrayed against
me. Did I have the grand jury? Or the police? Or the government
in Washington itself so that The Interests could get the President
himself to force the union in Indianapolis to open their safe to
provide evidence against us? I stood alone for the poor and weak.

The full diapason was ringing now.

The poor and weak? Well—there was J. B. McNamara with
his sixteen sticks of dynamite, poor and weak for all his
narrow head and ferret eyes. Harvey's grandmother? The old
have to be dynamited out of the way of progress, only had
she been in the way? Of what? Had Harvey been in the
way? My head got dizzy trying to reduce the war for little
people *to* little people.

"Barring you make a surprise confession," Rogers said,
grinning, and getting no response, I can tell you, "this jury
won't send you to San Quentin. Have you thought where you
will go instead? You're no more willing to end your career
than Adelina Patti. Your career lies ahead."

My father saw clearly the Darrow of the defense of the
Darwin theory against the Bible; of the very rich Massey-
Fortescue case in Honolulu; of Leopold and Loeb, who did
more to really open up juvenile delinquency than anybody
else; and the Negro rapists who were convicted in spite of
him possibly because they couldn't get a fair trial.

"Win them back," Rogers said. "Show them your side.
Make those who have misunderstood you salute your innocence."

An overpowering yawn nearly dislocated my jaw and I
couldn't keep my *eyes* open but I couldn't tune Darrow out
to save me.

*Men of power said to poor weak Harrington unless you bear wit-
ness against Darrow you go to the penitentiary. So Harrington
bore false witness against Darrow. They took Franklin by the
throat and shook lies against me out of him. The doors of San
Quentin look grim to me as I face them now, and Harrington
admitted he told me all would be forgiven and I'd never need to
face them if I told him where Caplan was, a man The Interests
were looking for. Do you suppose I would purchase my life at
the expense of the life of one of my fellow men no matter if he
was a criminal? If I furnished evidence for their wild crusade to
destroy trade unions, so that men might be made to toil longer
for less pay, do you suppose I so much as waited to draw my
breath? I would not purchase my liberty at the price of my honor.
So I am pilloried before the world as a CRIMINAL.*

If he could make me feel like this, all squirreled up the way
I was about him and his never taking a bath anyway—what
would the jury feel? They'd been going to acquit him anyway,
they'd have to give him a *halo* and I would appear as the
devil's advocate.

I wondered if the jury was awake, locked up on the top
floor of the Trenton Hotel. They ought to be, one and all were
staying awake on their account. As the trial moved from weeks
to months the judge had ordered the hotel to put in a ping-
pong table, he'd invited them to dinner and ordered the
deputies to take them for drives to the beach. They weren't
serving a sentence, he said, just doing jury duty. Perhaps the
night they would stay awake until their eyes burned in gritty
sockets and they were too nervous to go to sleep would be
before they had to go into the jury room and decide whether
Darrow was guilty or not—only they had decided—

All of a sudden, fear slugged me.

Suppose they hadn't? Our inside information might be
cockeyed, it had been once or twice. These things were tricky,
I knew that. Besides, all this Darrow was outlining now, giving
out with like a golden horn, it would take him two or three
days, wouldn't it? If he was guilty maybe they would smell it.
Would twelve honest men get it through their pores, their
stomachs, their antennae or the soles of their *feet*, the way I'd
gotten it, the way you got measles and began to *itch* without
knowing where it listeth?

*I would have walked from Chicago across the Rocky Mountains
and the hot desert to tell J. B. McNamara not to place dynamite
in the Times building. Why did Mr. Ford relate to you the horrors of the Times explosion? So the horrors of that awful accident*

*might attach to me, get me into the penitentiary at San Quentin.
I do not retreat by anything I have heard from my conviction
that it was an accident. All my life I have counseled gentleness,
kindness, forgiveness of every human being. And now as I speak
for my own liberty I stand on that. Has this anything to do with
this case in which I'm charged with jury bribery? They drag it
in to prejudice your minds against me, to argue I should not have
defended J. B. McNamara. Do you suppose I am going to judge
him? I know him. Do you know anything about criminals? I take
back nothing I've said . . . men who are called criminals are no
different than you or me, there isn't a case where someone didn't
plead for a criminal, ask mercy because while his enemies tell all
the wrongs he's done a mother or wife tells the right ones. I know
that the same feelings lurk in the mind and heart of each man. I
cannot be responsible for the brain of J. B. McNamara, nor his
heart's devotion to a cause though it might have carried him too
far . . . this was a social crime, I do not say it should have been
committed, I say it grew out of a condition of our society that
McNamara wasn't responsible for. A fierce conflict in this city,
minds inflamed with hate, something like this could take place
. . . I say, hang these men to the highest trees, everybody suspected, send me to San Quentin, convict the fifty-four men who
have now been indicted in Indianapolis, but until you go down
to fundamental causes, over and over again such things will
happen. As earthquakes come, hurricanes uproot trees, lightnings
destroy, we as a people are responsible for these conditions . . .
let us look what comes in the face . . . that young man was my
client, in justice to him I risked my life, my liberty, my reputation to save him . . .*

My father said, "That isn't the confession I asked you
about, is it?"

I don't think Darrow so much as heard him, the tide rolled
on and on.

*What has this young man to gain? Love of money didn't inspire his
act. Fame—why if he was successful he couldn't tell anyone in
his lifetime. His heart was in a cause, he risked his life for it.
One thing, when you come to know the man, come in touch with
him, meet such men and know them, you feel the kinship between them and you, any of them, all of them, men charged with
any crime in any walk of life, burglars, bankers, murderers, you
see how human they are, they love their mothers and wives and
children as you do. They love their fellow men. Why they did
this dark thing or that remains the dark mystery of the human
mind, so this act of the McNamaras is only brought up to rouse
the passions of this jury against me.*

We were all utterly silent, immobile. Darrow was on his
feet, he cried out more and more loudly.

There never was a man charged with a crime that I am not sorry for, for him and for his crime and that I cannot imagine the motives that moved his poor weak brain.

We had been held in a trance. A scene from Dante, from *The Tempest*, from *Lear*. The glare of one room, the shadows leaping in the darkness where I sat as my father passed back and forth between its light and the doorway. The man Darrow shifting from one foot to the other, powerful as an elephant, sweat pouring down his face so that it glistened.

I clawed my way up through a miasma that slipped off me like seaweed around the rocks at Catalina.

I felt sorry, too. But there was some glaring flaw and fallacy and I could not explain it even to myself. The younger Mc-Namara had risked his life but he was alive and Harvey Elder was dead. James B. McNamara, Darrow said, loved his mother just like Harvey loved his grandmother—I couldn't find my way. *Weren't these the same things my father believed?* Society had to be held responsible, what was Society? Who fixed that up so it wouldn't be responsible? Would it make a difference if women could vote and if men got better wages would there not be crime and killing any more? My father got inside the criminal and found the excuse, the motive. Also, a man had a right to the best defense. All men must be pre-sumed innocent. Darrow was to cry somewhere in those des-perate night hours, "Wouldn't it be better that every rogue and rascal in the world go unpunished than that you and I give up the privacy that alone makes life worth living?"—and I thought wildly that I didn't *know*. We defend everybody. But what happened to the man who thus defended all crimi-nals?

My grandfather used to say something—"He loved right-eousness and hated iniquity." He came to *save sinners*. But he hated iniquity.

I had to grit my teeth to keep them from beginning to sound like castanets. *We'd* done it all always in a Robin Hood tempo. Picturesque game of outwitting the Law. Now Darrow in his deep, sociological way—I felt like I was looking into one of those silly mirrors in a fun house that show someone you love in a distortion with his head squashed as though somebody had hit them with a pile driver or else pulled his skull into a hot dog. It wasn't funny any more.

Papa loved people.

Darrow loved the masses.

Too young, too shaken, I thought my mind wasn't big enough yet or maybe never would be to put it into any kind of words myself and it was years before I found the key words in the first verses of the seventeenth chapter of Luke.

All I knew was I didn't agree with Darrow altogether, though the way he put it it could make you look like a hard-boiled Simon Legree who didn't love your fellow man if you said so. Poor weak brain, he kept saying. People were born criminals with poor weak brains. I felt sorry, but then what? John J. McNamara hadn't had a weak brain, he was a lawyer, a leader, a brilliant organizer. Twisted? Or a marred pot like it said in the *Rubáiyát? Darrow*—if Darrow was guilty, why he was supposed to have a gigantic brain size, an outstanding intellect. What about it if *he* went around *bribing juries* to save guys with weak brains?

It came over me that the physician Dr. Jekyll working in his laboratory, safe, respectable, using his science and education and brain to create the drink that turned him into Mr. Hyde—why, *he* was much worse than Mr. Hyde.

I hated myself for *doubting*.

All this was too much for me, far far beyond what I could cope with, as usual my stomach betrayed me. I was very sick to it. I came back limp and covered with the cold sweat you get all over you when you vomit. I was met by such a trumpet of Darrow's voice I closed my eyes and hung onto the door-jamb and saw that both Jerry and Rosy were listening now.

In the light of J.B.'s motives, can I be his judge? I cannot con-demn him. None of the perpetrators of this deed were ever morally guilty of murder. Never. Dynamite was placed there to injure property, with no thought of harming human life. No, I cannot condemn him, I will not, he was not morally guilty of murder, so I tried to save him.

My father stopped then in front of him, protesting, I could feel his anger rising like a wave. He said, "It is not true that the McNamaras were not guilty of murder. This will not restore you. This country rejects murder as a method of human progress. Except for the men indicted in Indianapolis, your own people—union labor—Gompers—leaders everywhere—know that violence sets a cause back each time. They don't approve the destruction of property and when the destruction includes a ruthless chance of killing human beings, they will not tolerate it. If J.B. was not morally guilty of murder, why did you plead him Guilty? To your last breath, you—or I—

must defend a man morally innocent. Above all other men."

Darrow sat down, his head in his hands, and my father prowled around and around the big table, keyed up like a batter with the bases loaded and two out. Talking too carefully. This made me very nervous again. Something was going to happen. My father was saying, ". . . jury may find a man not guilty and the public will disagree with that verdict . . . though he's acquitted of bribing a jury a lawyer can move under that shadow the rest of his life . . . it's very dangerous, Darrow, for a man to accept the feeling that everyone is part of a conspiracy against him. It leads to hallucinations. It leads to refusal to face simple facts. It loses him in a fog of alibis and lies to himself and about himself. Unless you prove your innocence other than by that cry of frame-up, your usefulness may be gone in spite of freedom."

At first the glare blinded me when I tried to stare through the doorway, I blinked a couple of times, then I could see Darrow, his arms flung across the table, his head resting on them, he could have been a dummy thrown from a high mountain. Well, I thought, he may never get up, and I should have felt pity for him, but the young are mostly incapable of pity except for those they love.

I wished we had never seen him, in all our whole lives. Unfair as it was, it seemed to me he had brought darkness upon us. A man could have a touch of greatness and be a destroyer, too. I thought it was like someone with a beautiful voice who never learned to sing anything. A dark angel—a fallen archangel—it was all mixed up in my head and besides I was by now fighting sleep, in and out of sleep, not knowing whether the nightmares were part of the moments of slipping into sleep or of the moments of propping my eyes open and pinching myself.

Sentences went in and out. Papa's voice and then Darrow's. He had the big man on his feet again, they both sounded angrier, sometimes Darrow whispered, a whisper of pain, I heard the pain but the words were lost. Then they would sing out again.

I have committed a crime like that against the Holy Ghost for which there cannot be forgiveness, I have stood for the weak, the poor.

If I am convicted it must be only on the story Franklin tells.

I think I have lived a thousand years in the last one.

God, God, if my word and character and all the years I've prac-
ticed do not weigh more than all the trash they have presented
to the jury I do not want to live, I want to die.

Am I dreaming? Am I brought to the doors of San Quentin peni-
tentiary with charges of such a despicable crime and with no
proof but nine informers and nine detectives telling lies?

My dreams of today will be the facts of tomorrow.
Here in your city there was a direct cleavage in society, on one
hand those whose hatred grew fiercer day by day. This is a class
struggle, two contending armies joined in mortal combat. The
rich and the poor arrayed against each other and many must die.
I am always on the side of the poor, they must use what weapons
they can.

I have practiced law many years. I do not say to a client, Are you
guilty? Are you innocent? Every man on earth is both innocent
and also guilty.

I heard my father trying to lead him back to the *case,* to
proof of his own innocence, for again Darrow had been
whirled away by his own eloquence. I had heard this in
courtrooms too many times, sometimes it was the pure gold of
sincerity, sometimes the magic from behind the footlights.

Men who stand with the workers strike out in their blindness. In
darkness, sometimes wrongly. They are the ones who built all
civilization, the men who laid the tracks on the railroad bed,
who run the locomotives so you and I can ride across country in
comfortable Pullman cars. These men go ten or twenty stories
into the air to construct high buildings, taking their lives in their
hands, and their mangled remains are found on the earth be-
neath. Every step civilization has taken upward has been upon
the labor of the poor. Every step the world must take is for the
elevation of the poor. Without it, no civilization can survive. The
progress of the world means the raising through organization,
through treating them better, through every and all means of
helping the weak and oppressed . . . often these people may be
wrong, blind, rebellious, riotous, they are doing more more more
than their part in their way in the progress of the world, more
than anyone. I knew this with the McNamaras, I felt it in and
with them. In this great social conflict any means—any means . . .

What had awakened me in cold terror was utter silence.
Darrow's words rang in my head like a melody repeating itself
*—any means—any means—any means—*but the silence was
louder. Both men might have just as well jumped out the

window, the room was so without sound or movement. Rubbing my eyes, I woke up even more. I was so turned around, I staggered and bumped into a piece of furniture, trying to get to the rectangle of light that had to be the doorway.

The two men were facing each other like something out of Madame Tussaud's waxworks.

In a clear voice my father broke it. He said, "It's not the way. The only wise man who ever lived said no to that way. He said no to Barabbas, the leader of the rebels, of the underground revolution to kill all the Romans and their own rulers. The mob chose Barabbas and hung the man who wanted to do it the only lasting way. What did Barabbas gain? Is there peace today, or brotherhood, in Jerusalem? Did Greece gain by killing Socrates, or Rome by slaughtering Caesar? Think, Mr. Darrow, *think*."

Well, I said to myself, Papa is making the speech Darrow ought to make and he's going to make old baggy pants like it or lump it. He was mad as a she-grizzly, I saw the way he meant to challenge Darrow, superior and reasonable as Plato, then his tide got him, too. He shook his finger at Darrow and practically hollered at him, "*You have forgotten a boy named Harvey Elder, Mr. Darrow.*"

The only thing about Darrow that moved was his lower lip, it hung down so, as they say, I thought, he'll trip on it if he gets up, and the creases in his face were like they'd been carved with a saber.

"And the little old scrub lady and the copy boys and the men working in the pressrooms," my father said, and he was breathing out fire and smoke now. "You cast a spell, Darrow, a deep spell. I listen to you and I am lost. But let me tell you man's inhumanity to man isn't the way to get what you want and never has been. Discord won't heal discord. It sows more seeds for a later crop, by all the seven gods of thunder it does. If you use this evil means, my friend, to gain what you call a good end, the evil means will gobble up the good end, *in the end*.

"I listen to you, Darrow, when you give tongue, and I forget that night of *shame*, that massacre of the poor and weak and helpless whom I heard crying out in agony while the man you say was never morally guilty skulked and scrambled in back alleys. I care as much for my fellow man as you do, though I don't talk about it as much. I swear to you there was a way to freedom for the French that didn't lead through the guillotine to the Emperor Napoleon's death and destruction of all

Europe. Your true labor leaders are looking for that way, this country's looking for that way, and sometime it's going to find it.

"Yes—the poor, the weak, the marred pots, the poor weak brains—there in J. B. McNamara but for the grace of God goes Clarence Darrow or Earl Rogers—but you leave out the heart of the matter. The *grace*—some kind of grace that's given man. You want to substitute dynamite and say there by the grace of dynamite goes J. B. McNamara as good as Darrow and Rogers. I tell you *no*. You can't make men equal by putting this progress into the hands of the sons of *Cain*. The first man to *kill* his brother, as J. B. McNamara killed, said, Am I my brother's keeper? No no, *you* listen to me. Raising the poor and the weak, and the weak brains you say you didn't make, to sudden power won't create a strong brotherhood. It will bring chaos, or simply other tyrants and bread and circuses. You set aside the fundamental law *Thou shalt not kill* and go back to the jungle, set aside what every wise man has taught throughout history, you and the boys in Indianapolis don't seem to have had time to read history, and you will only multiply your rulers. The new ones will be as cold and ruthless as the old, once they come to power."

In the silence that throbbed to a stop, Papa took his handkerchief out of his sleeve and pressed it against his forehead, his lips. His hand was shaking and he held it out and looked at it and made it stop.

"Dynamite is easier," he said contemptuously, and laughed. "Without the guillotine perhaps Marie Antoinette would have gone on saying, Let them eat cake, who knows? I say there is a better way of progress if we use *our brains*. Especially for us—we have the ballot." He was walking up and down again and Darrow sat stiller than ever. "I don't ask my clients whether they are innocent or guilty either," Papa said, "but— I know. You knew about the McNamaras. I didn't ask you, but you told me you were innocent."

The stare Darrow turned on him then, seen in profile, had what looked to me like the glitter of sheer malevolent resentment. He said, "You never believed me, did you?"

The door slammed shut, I didn't have the faintest idea which one of them had slammed it but somebody had. It was a good strong door but it seemed to be shaking from that slam, that's how hard it was. It must have been Papa, at that, I decided, he was on his feet prowling around switching his tail by that time and Darrow was slumped down in the chair. It

was pitch dark around me for about a minute. My mind
wouldn't think so it dredged up words I kept in my memory
for when I didn't want to think, poems I'd memorized, and
such. . . . *a glorious victory and may no misconduct in anyone tarnish it* . . . It was misconduct to bribe a jury if he had.

Quietly, the door was opened and for the first time I realized
that dawn had come. Pearly white and terrible as an army
with banners. Looking no more torn up by the roots than
usual, Darrow came out and somebody joined him. I was too
shaken up to know who it was, in a few seconds I heard the
buzz for the elevator going over and over like a drum and my
surface mind thought, What a hell of a good thing it was we
always kept an elevator man on all night, and then I heard
the opening and closing of the noisy door.

The moment when my father came out is etched into my
brain partly by the importance and suspense of the day that
had just dawned. All I knew was that I'd never seen him look
quite like that before.

I don't ever want to see any man look like that again. This
was a thousand years in a few minutes.

My father had gone into that room with Darrow believing
in his innocence, his honesty. That was why he got so furious
when Darrow sat there looking like Guy Fawkes or Dr. Crip-
pen or somebody. He came out knowing Darrow was guilty,
though we agreed we would never tell anyone and I never
have. Not even when the Darrows said things about us and
hadn't the decency to give my father an iota of credit every
record shows belonged to him. Not even when eight men on
the second jury *voted* him Guilty. I have to tell it here, or it
is not just to the story about Earl Rogers. It made such a
difference to us.

Not just Darrow being guilty, though that was a big disappointment. Nor that feet-of-clay or head-of-the-Medusa look
that had been so terrible on Bert Franklin's hard face. Hell's
bells, my father would have defended Darrow anyhow. And
lots of clients lied.

What it was to me and I know afterwards to Papa. If a man
entering the skin of the criminal, feeling he was both innocent
and guilty, always understanding his motive, always being
sorry for him and his crime, justifying it in the name of
humanity, if this could lead Darrow to that final betrayal of
their profession, tampering with the *jury*, would the day ever
come when Earl Rogers might do the same for a client?
Would the reckless *fight* in the courtroom, the thrill and ex-

citement of the battle, the life-and-death game, lead someday to *Earl Rogers'* putting unscrupulous hands on the most sacred of all rights to guarantee justice to man—the jury system?

Where was the line? When—how—why—where did a man cross it? Would Mr. Hyde move in without being asked? How long could any man walk that tightrope of playing God by eliminating the consequences of a man's own acts? Of finding a way to call evil good and guilt innocence? Of finding a way to call evil good and guilt innocence? Of dealing out forgiveness *without repentance?*

The *line* of which my grandfather had spoken so long ago—

Darrow, guilty, that night in our office had the hysterio-passio of *Lear.*

The opening movement of our symphony had been a brilliant scherzo—Melodrama.

The finale had begun to sound the great fugue-like adagio—Tragedy.

SIXTY-ONE

For the first day, Clarence Darrow's speech to the jury was as moving, eloquent, and truth-declaring as it reads.

Packed triple into every inch of space, his friends and his enemies, those who'd hung him in effigy, those who wanted him back on his pedestal, listened, were compelled, convinced against their wills, for the moment anyhow or for all eternity, by one of the great all-time performances ever seen and heard in any courtroom since Cicero.

His was the peril. A great man—a man who at least had the quality of greatness around him—in those middle fifty years that should entitle a man to respect, dignity, pride, now in the arena pleaded for his very life, his freedom from prison, his work and usefulness to a cause before twelve strangers. This was Daniel in the den with the lions, and as the noble words rolled out, the simple and majestic words, emotion was a great wind sweeping them along. Even those who thought him guilty or had called him traitor were stilled and tranced.

I, who had heard the dress rehearsal, knew every word already, began to doubt my own senses, my own knowledge and long-held conviction. As I stared around me from the jury box to the Bench, from the press box to the bailiffs t the door, who'd heard so many pleas in their time, from the men at the counsel table, who also had big stakes riding n this play, to the avid, greedy, thrill-thirsty audience, all I saw was deep interest, poignant reaction. Not an eye ever left Darrow. No noisy breath nor scuffling shoes nor whisper nor squeaking seat disturbed the silence into which his oratory flowed.

The jury had come in relaxed, my plump friend gave me a pronounced wink, they had a bouncy air of relief, soon they would be going home to their wives, their kids, home cooking, the office, the store, the job. No convicting jury on earth ever looked like that. Front-row seats at this spellbinding display of eloquence and drama—for-real drama—with the big man in the old gray suit as the sorcerer—what man could ask more?

Exactly when it began to go sour, I'm not sure. Along about the sixth inning, I should say, when a pitcher with a no-hitter going walks a man. Then an outfielder saves him with a spectacular catch—and then his magic is gone and they start to hit him. Nobody knows how or why.

My first inkling came from Judge Hutton, though he didn't know it. Leaning back in his big chair with the towering back, his head was bent in most courteous attention. A loud sob of Darrow's reverberated through the courtroom and the judge's eyebrows lifted involuntarily, his expression didn't change, but he glanced around. Settling back once more his fine eyes were fixed on a spot high in the right corner. I never after that caught him looking at Darrow. Slight puzzlement had misted over the press box. Don Nicholson caught my eye and made a what-the-hell-is-this? face at me and I shrugged.

On the second day, this—blight?—this shadow began to operate and my father began to look like something out of the Ice Age of Pitz Palu.

Darrow's mild tears and gentle sobs had taken on hurricane proportions. His great bony frame, from which so much weight had fallen in the long, long weeks, shook like a scarecrow on a pole in the midst of his convulsive sobs. He wept each handkerchief into a sodden ball, cast it from him and Ruby Darrow supplied another, which soon suffered a like fate. At last he began to wipe away the floods on his sleeves, they clung as though he'd plunged them into a rain barrel.

By this time, I had the feel of juries as a man who drives every day in traffic gains an instinct for what that other crackpot driver is going to do before he does it. I could have sworn that the Darrow jury, coming in prepared to enjoy and applaud their great moment, now damn well didn't know which way to *look*.

. . . they would stop my voice, they have hired many vipers to help them do it, my voice which from the time I was a prattling baby my father and mother taught me to raise for justice and freedom and the cause of the weak and poor. They would stop my voice now in the penitentiary. I who have defended the poor and weak as has no other man in America . . .

A bailiff handed me a note. Scrawled on gray copy paper I read "This is his second prattling babyhood if he don't look out, how about dinner? Don."

. . . I don't want to live . . . I want to die . . .

My father got up from the counsel table and walked out of the room.

His head was down so people thought he was overcome. As quietly as I could I tried to be invisible as I followed him. I found him in an empty witness room and opened my mouth to say maybe he ought not to be out while Darrow was making the speech. But I got a look at the maddest man I had ever seen, his eyes were that hot blue of an acetylene torch, so I shut up.

"He will get himself convicted yet," Papa said in a thin tight fury. "Where does he think he is, in Indianapolis? I warned him. That jury was ready to acquit him. If he doesn't stop this wailing-wall weeping-willow blubber and snivel— That's not a speech, it's a lament. They might change their minds and lock the melancholy Dane up somewhere."

His concern was real. He was like a cat on hot bricks.

Perhaps it is more common now to see men cry.

In those days before the First World War, we weren't far out of the old West and its rules and codes of conduct. Wyatt Earp lived in our town. Jack London with his stories of Alaska and the sea was the most popular novelist in America. Mark Twain had been dead only a few years. *Neurotic* was a word not yet in our vocabulary, the wide open spaces had not yet been covered with housing developments and bomb shelters. Most of us had never seen, read, heard or knew that there was a man called a homosexual. We were a fairly simple, emerging pioneer people, the sight of a man *crying* about himself for hours in public was unfamiliar to us. In time it came to be a gag, that "out where men are men," but then we simply took it as a basic fact of life that if possible a man faced a firing squad with dry eyes and fought at Dodge City the same way. Probably the good guys and the bad guys was much too rigid in our minds, Freud was as inconceivable to us as splitting the atom. Whether either has done the world any real good I do not know. In those days a man might weep for the loss of a wife, a child, a friend, but he tried not to. My father had wept when he told me my grandfather was dead, and that other day in the garden at school, but I myself had never before seen a man cry in public.

Many times it has been said that this speech was one of the greatest, and perhaps it was. As I say, it reads better than it heard. Because of its excessive self-pity, many men that day did not admire it. I didn't know then that self-pity is the final mark of the true egotist and sweeps him far beyond his own control.

As we walked back and forth in the corridor, Papa puffing on a cigarette like an engine going up the San Marcos grade and muttering between his teeth, Darrow's voice rang plainly in our ears.

> Oh you wild insane members of the steel trust.
> Oh you bloodhounds of detectives who are willing to do your master's evil will.
> Oh you district attorneys, you know not what you do. But if I must drink this cup to the dregs . . .

I said, "Papa, that's blasphemous," and Papa said, "No no, it's just a figure of speech. He has a right to that."

We stood in the open doorway then. Anyone could see that Earl Rogers was listening with all of him and that he was strained and shaken.

> I can tell you that all this grew from a social conflict. I know that though terrible were the consequences of this blind act of the McNamaras, consequences which nobody foresaw, still it was one of those inevitable acts which are part of this industrial war. The loss of life was an accident. These were good men, the McNamaras, I heard them speak of their brothers, their mothers, of the dead . . .

That was what Darrow said.

In a low faraway voice in my ear, Rogers said, "I am of two minds. A man loses power when he is of two minds. I said to him you cannot build safely on sand. You cannot exchange one evil for another and one set of evildoers for another set of evildoers—"

Holding himself very stiff and straight, his face now its natural color, Earl Rogers walked back into the courtroom and took his seat at the counsel table.

Broken, a shaken wreck, his face covered with tears, his arms flung out as though upon a cross, Darrow came to his climax.

There are people who would destroy me, crush me down. I have enemies powerful and strong. Honest men misunderstand and doubt me . . . if you convict me there will be people who applaud this act. If in our humanity you can believe me innocent and return a verdict of not guilty, I know there are thousands of the weak and poor and helpless throughout this land who will arise up and call you blessed for saving my name and my liberty.

He sat down, still sobbing. Rogers dropped a hand on his shoulder, took a clean handkerchief from his sleeve, and pressed it into Darrow's hand.

We didn't see the Darrows after we left court. I can only remember that my father congratulated him on the magnificence of his speech and we went back to the hotel instead of to the office. He was filled with a lot of different emotions, a sort of white anger and then acrimonious contempt for the way Darrow had behaved and then a release of warm admiration for the quality of greatness and a depth of compassion— yet he had long periods of a strange grim-faced silence. I had never known him so strangely silent for so long, and often he seemed far away and I didn't have any idea where he was. Except I could see he was between two fires and of two minds, as he had said, and once he said very sharply, "You think it's an acquittal?" and I said I was sure of it. And I was.

Out of the midst of all this I found out what was really setting off this uproar inside him. He turned and stared at me as stern and grim and furious as though I'd done something and he said, "You know if they acquit him the district attorney will try him again immediately on the Bain indictment, don't you?"

So that was it.

The grand jury had returned two charges of bribery attempts made to two jurors. The Lockwood case was by far the stronger, so naturally the D.A. had tried that first. The other, however, was *there*, if the D.A. wanted to pick it up.

This second trial was what was riding Papa like the three witches, though at first I didn't understand why.

When I woke up in the morning and saw him still sitting there in the window sort of smoldering like white ashes, I did.

He didn't want to have to defend Darrow again.

Fredericks wasn't a good speaker. On the dull and pedestrian side, he did the best he could for two long days. It wasn't easy to pick up the pieces of his case that Rogers had blown up, nor to follow a man like Darrow who had been pleading for his own life. Toward the end he gathered what natural dignity he had and denied that there had been any settlement in the McNamara cases prior to the arrest of Bert Franklin. He had been surprised when suddenly Darrow had made all the concessions he had hitherto refused. He said conspiracy to bribe was a difficult thing to prove but that tampering with a jury must always be resisted by every decent man and every official. And he believed Darrow guilty.

He was not a man, John D. Fredericks, who could rise above the anticlimax which Rogers and Darrow had arranged for him. Nor did he.

The jury was out twenty-seven minutes.
Long enough to elect a foreman and take one ballot.
Not Guilty—12.
Guilty—0.

Well, such a scene as happened then I'd never witnessed before.

This was real mass hysteria. There were fights and bloody noses and a man got shoved through a window. The crowds whirled and milled and cheered and yelled, some in wild joy that the champion of the poor and weak and helpless had defeated his capitalistic accusers and some still convinced that he was the defender of the McNamaras who had killed twenty-one people in the dynamiting of the *Times*.

They carried Earl Rogers down the hall on their shoulders in a triumph like a football coach and many of them embraced Darrow and even kissed his hands as he wept.

A moment came highlighted as by a giant spotlight.

In the wild undirection of the crowd it swept Rogers and Darrow face to face and people pulled back so that they stood looking at each other, surrounded by the staring eyes and excited faces and howling voices.

I wonder what would have happened if at *that* moment Earl Rogers had said to Clarence Darrow, *Don't come near me, you slimy jury briber, you're guilty as hell.*

SIXTY-TWO

Well, if there was one thing my father didn't need to worry about it was the second Darrow trial, it really was.

As he figured it, his strong sense of obligation to a client put him on the spot. *Necessitas non habet legem,* the lawyers say, but now it turned out the necessity was no more, for Darrow thought now he could escape having to take any help from Earl Rogers. Darrow was now flying high. *And* mighty. Back on his pedestal, as far as he was concerned. Quite indignant that the D.A. *dared* to put him through another ordeal when a jury had so unanimously and in such record time pronounced him innocent.

However, the verdict hadn't been popular with many important citizens and a large part of the public still remembered the *Times* holocaust. So the district attorney announced a date for the trial of the Bain case.

Then it was made plain that Darrow did not *want* Rogers this time.

Though Papa hadn't *said* anything to him that day in the corridor, it's just possible that Darrow could read his mind. Come right down to it, Darrow had to know what Rogers knew, he'd *been* there, hadn't he, that night? I suppose now that he was wearing that Not Guilty verdict like a halo there was one man he could get along without. Earl Rogers. It often takes a really great man, not just one with the quality of greatness, to forgive another man for such a favor as saving him from prison and for knowing things about him which he now wishes to convince himself never happened—and that he had never told.

They had one big row, and I always had a pretty good idea that Ruby had been putting her oar in. Having been acquitted with Rogers as his chief counsel, Darrow thought that in the easier and simpler Bain matter it would be better if he directed his own defense. He could afford to be chief counsel this time.

To tell the truth Papa was very glad. The whole thing looked like being an anticlimax, a ball game after the pennant is already won. And it certainly wasn't any *fun* to be with the Darrows together or even separately.

By this time Darrow had also decided stentoriously and vociferously and frequently that his speech and his speech alone had been responsible for the victory. The foreman, a very remarkable man named Williams, told us this was not true. Our men and Don Nicholson's men and Hugh Baillie's man Golding had been right when they said the Not Guilty verdict had been decided on long before Darrow's closing argument. Naturally Darrow wasn't going to believe anything like that. While as time passed he forgot a lot about the jury bribery trial, even that it ever happened at all, if it ever did cross his mind his great oration was apparently all he remembered.

Rogers didn't withdraw. He felt that this would have prejudiced Darrow's case. So when it went to trial, with Darrow as his own chief counsel and Jerry Giesler, who could reproduce Rogers' defense in the Lockwood case quite well, as his assistant, my father went into court several times and sat quietly beside Darrow at the counsel table.

The antagonism between the two men was so thick by then you could have cut it with a knife.

Obviously, it was a good deal the same case, with Bain a very much weaker prosecution witness than Lockwood had been. Jerry did real well. In this first test he showed he was going to be what father said he would—a great courtroom lawyer. Darrow made an even more moving speech inflamed and impassioned in defense of the inevitable actions taken by the McNamaras, who were morally innocent in dynamiting the *Times* and killing all those people. He was under no restraint at all this time and many thought it a greater oration than the first one.

I don't think any man who ever lived was more surprised than Darrow when twenty-seven minutes, measurement of the first jury, had flown by and the second jury didn't come in.

Thousands of minutes dragged by, multiplied into hours. Into days.

Excitement returned all over town, all around the court-house.

Several times the jury notified the judge that they could not agree on a verdict. Each time the judge sent them back to try again. At last the foreman sent word that if they stayed out three years instead of three days they'd never reach an agreement.

They filed into the box. The foreman stood up to report.

"You feel you cannot reach a verdict?" the judge said.

"We cannot, Your Honor," the foreman said.

"How do you stand?" the judge said.

Not Guilty—4.

Guilty—8.

What was known as a *convicting hung jury*.

It did look a little as though Darrow should have gotten that "local lawyer named Rogers" to "assist" him in this one, too.

Of course Fredericks could have tried him again since the result had been a disagreement. He didn't want to. Nobody wanted to. Mostly everybody wanted to see the last of Darrow. So when he agreed never to try to practice law again in the State of California, the district attorney let him go on back to Chicago.

The Bain jury left undecided in the records the question of whether Darrow was or was not guilty of jury bribery, but I never had any doubts on the subject. In my opinion Darrow was guilty—on the evidence which included his presence across the street while Franklin was passing the money to Lockwood; on his attitude and appearances during the trial; and on the basis of my private conversations with him. Only Earl Rogers—and four jurors in the second case—saved the Great Defender from ending his career prematurely within what he called in his closing address to the jury the gray, dim walls of San Quentin.

That is the impersonal final summing up of a great reporter who covered the Darrow trials—Hugh Baillie of the United Press, a man honored and respected in his work by presidents and leaders in many countries.

I never had any doubts, not even before one of my father's private conversations with Darrow included an admission of his guilt to his lawyer.

For a number of years, I used to blame myself a good deal for being so harsh and rude and inflexible with Darrow. It was because I didn't like him, felt he was a phony, and not because I always knew he was guilty that I behaved as I did. I hated myself for it for a long time.

I did not know then that Clarence Darrow would, for the largest fee ever up to then paid a criminal lawyer, defend two very very very rich teen-age delinquents for the brutal blood-and-sex-thrill murder of a nice little boy who wore glasses. That he would hurrah over a big victory when he got them life imprisonment instead of the chair or the asylum, and thus began the theory of compulsion for juvenile delinquents to kill and torture and slay. For if you will check it you will find the juvenile delinquency murder and the school of literature which sold such boys psychiatric pardon in open court began with Darrow's defense of Leopold and Loeb in Chicago. There also began the fear of using the rod, of parental discipline, of standards of conduct and rules of decent behavior. So when I walked into the courtroom and there saw Darrow as chief counsel for Loeb and Leopold, I forgave a *little* the hard-hearted, crude, high-stomached, overloyal, overbearing teen-age girl I had been.

Legends grow.

Facts are forgotten. Darrow went down in history almost entirely for cases he tried after his escape from the jury bribery charges in Los Angeles and, to pin it down, *few* of them had much to do with the poor the weak and the helpless.

If the Darrow legend is really founded upon a rock, this eyewitness account I've given cannot harm it.

If it was built on sand, it should fall like all else that is phony in the history books.

Of course the Guy Eddie case came in between the two Darrow trials and probably could be one of the reasons Ruby again kicked up such a furor of opposition. It must have shocked her into fits.

I must say that I myself was barred from the courtroom for most of this rooming-house-contributing case against the public prosecutor, but my father always thought it was the funniest case he ever tried and so, I find, do all the newspapermen who were there. Somehow the door with the holes that made it look like a piece of Swiss cheese sends all males into convulsions.

PART EIGHT

SIXTY-THREE

About then, there was literally *no room* in chemically pure Los Angeles for sex dalliance. Under its rooming-house ordinance, today a hundred million dollars' worth of motels would go out of business.

One of the leading lights of organized reform was the city prosecutor, Guy Eddie, a tall young fellow with untidy hair and glasses, a reformer by nature, heredity, and environment. His ordinance made it a crime for a man and woman who weren't married to be alone together in any room that had a *bed* in it. Another law sponsored by Mr. Eddie and his cohorts made it a prison offense to trifle with the affections of a girl under twenty-one. Fifty years before America regarded *Lolita* as witty literature, this was entitled "contributing to the delinquency of a minor" and under it Lolita's boy friend could, should, and probably would have gone to *jail*.

Putting the heat on the police department, with help from the churches and the press, the young city prosecutor had wreaked so much havoc on vice that the Progressive party was grooming him for district attorney. Already Mr. Eddie had removed from the police a source of income known as Protection. If he were elected D.A. things would get worse. Again, strange bedfellows, the underworld and the police department, decided Guy Eddie must GO. And in such a way that he could never be elected to anything again.

On the private staff of the chief of police was a fly-cop named Johnson and to him was assigned the task of *doing something* about the sincere and resolute, if naïve, young city prosecutor.

The difficulty with reformers is that they are so often naïve. That, incidentally, was why Fiorello LaGuardia succeeded where others failed. Believe me, there was nothing naïve about the Little Flower, whoever his opponents were in vice or crime, he was tougher. Guy Eddie was credulous and gullible, artless and unsuspicious. Or he would never have fallen for a plant in his own office, which was on the second floor of the police department. In the same BUILDING.

One fine day fly-cop Johnson walked in with Alice, just out from Milwaukee. "Make a great female operative for your rooming-house squad," said Johnson, and did not then call attention to the fact that she was supposed to be Jail Bait. Only sixteen. Mr. Eddie made an appointment to see Alice and the cops went to work. When gents had grown wary enough always to hang their coats on the doorknobs, thus obstructing the keyholes, a bright boy on Eddie's staff had invented an auger that fitted into the palm of the hand. Now that the script called for catching Guy Eddie *flagrante delicto*, the cops borrowed one of these and augered ringside seats for their witnesses. At the same time they oiled the door hinges so they'd yield at a touch. Well, Alice screamed, the peepers rushed in, Guy Eddie's protests were drowned in squeals and shouts. The police handcuffed the city prosecutor and locked him up cozily right next door in the city jail on the charge of contributing. A felony, this could land *him* behind the gray dim walls of San Quentin all right.

Sensation. Reactions were mixed. People who were glad to find reformers as other men snickered. Those who had approved young Eddie's fight against vice and corruption were indignant and unbelieving. The Progressive party, which on a "throw the rascals out" platform had busted the old S.P. machine, rushed Senator John D. Works, with bail, to the rescue of their young hopeful. The senator, taking one look at the eyewitness testimony of the arresting officer, called Sacramento.

Governor Johnson said, *You had better get Earl Rogers.*

We heard about this first on the California Limited coming home from New York, where we'd gone to hear Caruso sing *Pagliacci*. The Darrow case had been the worst thing that ever happened to us, in spite of the upset victory my father had won for Darrow. Sunk as we were in disillusion and despair, somehow the gargantuan laughter of *Pagliacci*, the beauty of the music, the creative force of some good shows had restored to us some faith in *joie de vivre*.

We had both drawing rooms in our car and Rosy and Bull and Cap Durham had both in theirs. Thinking back, that is where Papa's money went. We always had both drawing rooms and a Pope Toledo and a Pierce-Arrow and a Locomobile at the same time. Also three accompanying retainers.

To offers of everything from champagne to classic bourbon, Papa waved a dismissing hand. "I know you don't approve, Nora," he would say with a grin.

This was—a *happiest* hour.

I can see myself sitting on the hot red plush seat, cinders and smoke blowing in the open windows, wearing ivory Chinese palace pajamas. Papa opposite in a magnificent robe of green and gold. At Kansas City they brought aboard special steaks, at Trinidad we got mountain trout and Colorado celery. The head steward waited on Papa in person.

He read aloud to me and the others and sometimes the whole car would congregate at the open door. Red Dog from *The Jungle Book*. Macaulay's essay on Clive in India. *As You Like It*, which for some reason Papa adored, though the title indicates Shakespeare didn't regard it as one of his real plays. Also he had along the best Western short stories ever written, Alfred Henry Lewis's Wolfville tales of the Old Cattleman, Faro Nell, Cherokee Hall, Doc Peets, and the Colonel. One afternoon, when you had to look three times to believe the colors of New Mexico out the car windows could be real, he was reading and chuckling along when he came upon the following sentences.

You think the trouble lies with the man, not with the Whiskey, I said. The Old Cattleman and I were discussing temperance.

He came to a stop after reading those words. But he was game.

He went on:

"Right you be. This yere whiskey drinking," continued the old gentleman as he toyed with his empty glass, "is a mighty curious play. I know gents as can tamper with their little ole 40 drops frequent and reg'lar. As far as hurtin' 'em is concerned it's no more effect than throwing water on a drown' rat. Then again I've cut across the trail of some other gents—to them whiskey-drinkin' is like playing a harp with a hammer. What's medicine to one, is pi'son to another. Being a regular reliable drunkard thataway comes mighty near being a disease. It ain't a question of nerve, either. Some dead-game gents I know who's that obstinate and brave they wouldn't move camp for a prairie fire, couldn't talk back a little bit to whiskey, and them's the ones always start out to drink all the whiskey in Wolfville."

Well, there was no question about it, after the first Darrow trial my father started to drink up all the whiskey in California.

A binge in those days was more spectacular and outstanding. A man started buying drinks for the house and when he got tired of one saloon he took the customers along to the next one. Earl Rogers' progress from Joe Fast's to the Vernon Country Club, the Sunset Inn at Santa Monica, the Ship Cafe on the Venice pier, Canary Cottage at Arcadia might lead on to Tia Juana, Catalina, and Seal Rocks, moving like a Roman emperor with chariots. If I had all the gold pieces I've seen him throw, like Jupiter, to piano players, newsboys, beggars, waiters, coon-shouters, cab-drivers, flower girls, hobos, and sundry, I would be something no Rogers has ever been.

Every time I caught up with him on this state-wide spree, he started on the same song. "Why didn't that reptile McNamara go to the gallows and die for his cause? If he'd got himself hung he'd have been a martyr, no one would have believed him guilty if he hadn't confessed. If the great man Darrow believed him morally innocent, why didn't he fight for him?"

So that was why we'd been to New York as well as to hear *Pagliacci.*

No sooner were we home than appeared in our office the erect form of United States Senator Works. And unfortunately by that time again, all I could do was pray that the senator, a family man, a church deacon, and scholar, wouldn't notice that Rogers, sitting behind his desk, was drunk as a Piute just off the reservation.

"I am honored, Senator," Mr. Rogers said, "my poor office is honored." I admired the elegant bow but my stomach turned over for fear he'd go one inch too far and fall flat on his face. "Can I be of service to you, sir?"

He listened while Works explained the infamous plot against their once and future candidate Guy Eddie. His eyebrows came down in a heavy frown as he said, "Senator, at the moment I have a bellyful of politicians and poltergeists, captains and supercargoes and defenders of the poor and weak and helpless who are so bloody stupid any four-bit cop can put on a false mustache and sell them the Brooklyn Bridge. I don't want your young Galahad who can't keep his armor buttoned." He roared at his own humor, he said, "*You* defend him, Senator."

The senator pulled his beard. "I never was a trial lawyer, Mr. Rogers," he said. "The governor hopes we can persuade you—"

"One moment," Mr. Rogers said, getting—safely—to his feet, "I must consult my associates—"

He knew I knew he wasn't going to consult anybody, he never did, much less his associates. I followed him out and said, "If you take another drink, you won't get away with it. The senator will tell the governor you were under the influence—"

"Now my girl," he said in the grand manner, "do you intend to make a scene about this?"

"I do indeed," I said.

"Oh well," he said, "easy come easy go I always say," and went back in. "Get him up here," he said, and until Eddie arrived he discussed with the senator a treatise on California water rights, illustrating it with the story about how his father was cheated out of forty thousand acres in San Berdoo. "A saint, my father," he said with tears in his voice. So I said, "You want to look like Clarence Darrow?" and he glared at me but he quit *that*.

When Eddie came in, he stared at the young man through his lorgnette trying to remember who he *was* and then he said in a sepulcher tone, "You must agree in the presence of this gentleman [by now he didn't know who the hell the senator was either] to take the stand in your own defense or I can't take the case," and I thought, Well that's safe whether he shot his uncle or stole a barrel of pigs' feet. Guy Eddie was as dumb as a man can be and pass his Bar exams but he had guts. Most men if you hold humiliation and ridicule to their heads, show the white feather. He didn't. He agreed.

The senator got to his feet. "Then I shall withdraw—" he began.

A Rebel Yell came out of my old man. "Now I know you," he said. "No you don't, Senator, no you don't, fellow-me-lad. This is your idiot child, not mine. I would like to do Hiram Johnson a favor, he's a tough man to shave, but if I do you will stay in there and be counted. I want to ask Mr. Eddie one question. Mr. Eddie, do you drink?"

Guy Eddie wiped the sweat off his glasses and said, "No sir."

"Then," said Mr. Rogers, "I can't ask you to have one with me. So I must wish you gentlemen a very star-spangled good afternoon. I may decide to get drunk myself."

We watched the two members of reform leave.

"Or drunker," I said.

"There is not that much whiskey in Wolfville," he said,

dropping the Pagliacci mask over his face. "Do you suppose I shall ever again have a client who can take his little ole forty drops with no more effect than pouring water on a drown' rat? Ah well—I have your promise not to sit up with the corpse, have I not?"

I said he had and he went out with a flourish that flung a nonexistent cape over his shoulder.

ALICE TELLS ALL

Pictures of Alice doing this took up front pages and double trucks in California papers the next day. There she was, sure 'nuff, sweet sixteen on a spring day. After the prosecution had summoned her, the men came back to our office in a sort of cataleptic trance and my father, who did not startle easily, wore a startled look. I said, "You look like a parade of zombies," but it was some time before I could put the bits and pieces together.

In the first twenty questions, the masculine courtroom, judge, jury, lawyers, spectators, and cops, beamed upon Alice, who wept with delight if you gave her a smile and trembled with fear at your frown. Then they became aware of what she was saying and did a mass double-take. Not one gory detail was omitted. Words which had never been spoken in a Main Street burleycue house and for which a gent would be ejected *cum laude* from Pearl Morton's floated through the air of the courtroom with ease. This unabashed recital of the dirtier facts of life in Alice's little-girl voice held the inhabitants paralyzed with shock. When they emerged they turned bright scarlet to a man. A nice girl like Alice using dirty words in front of a nice girl like Alice!

Headlines hit the streets, mobs rioted to grab the still-damp extras, the skimpy accounts the law allowed were gobbled by a public which had as yet no obscene books, salacious TV shows, no smut on stage and screen.

Something bothered me as I watched my father leave for the courthouse to cross-examine sweet Alice Ben Bolt. New dark blue suit by Eddie Schmidt, blue silk shirt with darker satin stripes by Oviatt's, cuffs fastened with sapphire links by a trainer from Ascot Park we'd defended for shooting a bookmaker. A race-track case always got us diamonds we could hock to our good friends the Zemansky Brothers. No place ever knew more about *what goes on* from a criminal lawyer's point of view than the best pawnshop in town. It wasn't just that burned-out transparency that bothered me, I'd have had my tongue snipped with Chinese scissors (or I thought I would) before I'd have said it even to Jerry. Somehow it hurt, I had to keep a real go-to-hell grin sometimes because I felt a small bit of embarrassment for him. Maybe it had been coming on longer than I knew or would admit—this *exaggeration*. This is another *line* that is almighty fine. Behind footlights, on the flat-dimensional film, exaggeration in clothes and manner is necessary to gain the impression of life-size. In everyday *life*—it has a hint of—well, anyhow, I thought Papa was going a little bit too far—elegant but more like an *actor* dressed up to play a gentleman.

However, Alice didn't get this. When Assistant District Attorney Keyes asked her afterwards if she thought she was *Mr. Rogers'* witness Alice said, "Oh Mr. Keyes Mr. Rogers was such a *gentleman*." So maybe that was what Papa was up to. At Alice's level, only exaggeration would get across.

He made her tell the story so many times that even a jury had to see she'd been rehearsed till she was letter perfect and couldn't change a syllable any more than your aunt's parrot. Then he began to move away from it to where she had to think up answers. "Now Alice," he said, "when you first came to Los Angeles, where did you go?" Alice had never looked more demure, she was ready for that one. "To the Young Women's Christian Association, Mr. Rogers," she said. "And how long did you stay there?" said Mr. Rogers. "Oh—" Alice said, "oh—about an hour." Mr. Rogers permitted himself to smile at the jury, they smiled back and so did Alice.

For some reason Alice and her pictures annoyed the hell out of me. My curiosity got to be an itch, so I walked up to get a look at her coming out with her chaperon and an honor guard of cops. I said to Papa, "You ought to have a tin cup," and he said, "What's all this?" and I said, "Whatever Mr. Eddie is supposed to have done he could not contribute to her juvenile anything. I would sure hate to be hanging by my thumbs since Goldilocks was sixteen." I said to Don Nicholson I do not get this and he said I hope not! And Aunty Blanche when I said I did not see what was so *funny* said, "Men. All of them have a gutter streak." I am glad I learned this then, though I must say in my experience the female of the species lets joy be more unrefined than the male. Women get so *coy* when they are vulgar.

I could not understand how it was possible for men who

knew as much as our staff and the press was supposed to know to have believed Alice was sixteen, nor how they could have such a big time with this ribald, legal, strip-tease.

Because the next thing the newspapers splashed around the front page was Alice's *drawers*—not in a bureau, the kind females wore. From Mr. Rogers' questions, as printed, these sounded like the chastity belts knights locked on their wives when they went off on a three-year crusade.

The papers commented dryly that Mr. Rogers did not seem familiar with this garment.

Q. (by Mr. Rogers) The closed type—that's what you say you wore that day?
A. Yes Mr. Rogers.
Q. Did you put them on especially for this occasion?
A. Oh no.
Q. You have worn this—this closed type of—of garment at other times?
A. Oh yes I always do.
Q. Right now?
A. Oh yes Mr. Rogers right now.

Well, Mr. Rogers gave her a Groucho Marx look with his eyebrows going up and down and the courtroom focused like gimlets. Ten to one he was going to ask her for People's Exhibit A. And a hundred to one if he did she would. But old spoilsport Keyes began to holler, "I don't like Mr. Rogers' manner with this witness and I don't think it's proper—" and Mr. Rogers said, "All right, Ace, I'll take her word if you will."

As court resumed in the morning, Mr. Rogers unwrapped a package and held up a pair of closed drawers of repellent aspect. "Like these?" he said.

Alice studied them. So did the jury. "Yes—somewhat the same—" said Alice.

Mr. Rogers examined them doubtfully. He was heard to mutter something about ". . . Eddie must have been an acrobat . . ." at which they told me the whole courtroom fell in the aisles, Ace Keyes had to leave, and the judge ducked under the bench. This, apparently, was the funniest thing since the banana peel.

After Alice came down, Mr. Rogers went to work in earnest. By eyehole witnesses the jury soon had a geographic survey of Eddie's office as seen through auger holes. Following this he produced a bevy of technical experts, architects, builders, cartographers, oculists to say that unless laws of nature had. been set aside, and cops could see through doors and around corners, they had not seen what they swore to have seen. Shortly thereafter he himself carried in a door, painted a drab ivory. With great care he set it up, stood back, and said, "This is the actual door to Mr. Eddie's office though it does look more like Swiss cheese, will you have it with mustard or without?" Without a sound, he then arranged a chair which he and one of the experts measured with a tape. Then he put Mr. Eddie in the chair with a young lady no one had seen before.

To the jury he said, "I am going to ask His Honor if he doesn't think you would feel better satisfied if you made this experiment for yourself." His Honor did and the jury, rather hilariously, went through the enactment. They couldn't see a thing, either.

As a clincher Mr. Rogers produced a surprise witness. As the stocky middle-aged man walked in Alice gave him a smile of welcome and Mr. Rogers said, "You know who this is, don't you, Alice?" and Alice said, "Oh yes, Mr. Rogers, that's my husband from Milwaukee."

The marriage certificate proved I was about right. Alice would never see twenty-one again, much less sixteen.

The defense rested, after the arguments the jury didn't leave the box.

Apparently like a two-year-old who's had bad racing luck and never develops three-year-old form, Guy Eddie did not become district attorney, nor anything else in spite of that swift Not Guilty that exonerated him.

Maybe he decided he wasn't cut out for politics. It's still difficult to get good men who are.

As far as Papa and all the rest of the men were concerned they might as well have been to a burlesque show at the Grand Opera House over on Main Street.

SIXTY-FOUR

After the Darrow trials, the rocket of Earl Rogers seemed to reach its zenith. To hang blazing against a darkening sky before it crashed to earth.

For me, I am already in the midst of catastrophe beyond anyone else's imagination, moving with terrifying speed toward my own moment of truth. Each day . . . each event . . . each trial, our story must always tread around and between and in the midst of trials . . . as I look back they are blackouts from here on, not acts . . . twenty-four sheets, not chapters.

The morals trial of Chief of Police Sebastian. Earl Rogers running the growing city with that handsome half-witted puppet as mayor, on his knee.

The only one of my father's murder trials I covered as a reporter, the Frankie-and-Johnnie Case of the Red Kimono, when poor little Gabrielle D'Arley shot her man because he done her wrong.

Above all, my father standing in the Supreme Court, white and terrible, making his last frantic appeal to save that red-handed boy-slayer Bundy from the hangman's noose.

By then, I knew we were playing the harp with a hammer. When Jack London killed himself, distant thunder rolled, in the lightning flashes I saw that John Barleycorn had won that one. Don't sit up with the corpse, we promised. Nothing was said about a beloved ghost come to haunt me.

Truth, my father said. As we sat in my library that day, I mean. *You write it, Nora*, he'd said, *I give you permission. On one condition. The truth, the whole truth, nothing but the truth. Little men are dissolved by it, but if there is any gold the truth makes it shine more brightly. I'll chance it, so promise me that, Nora.*

So I can't invent a way for him to end his life as Dickens did for his Sydney Carton. I must go ahead *in truth*, to what in truth was our last courtroom together.

You don't really think I'm crazy, do you, Nora?
No no, Papa.

When I get there this time I pray I may at last know the verdict on what I did there.

Teddy played so great a part, this must begin on another witness stand, where my father saw for the first time the one woman he was to love so much and lose so soon. It hurts me as much now as it did then that Teddy came into our story so late. This tall, lovely young thing with a spirit that always gave encouragement. I remember that she lighted up their drab old courtroom like a stained-glass window.

One thing our office never took was divorce cases. Not since la belle Steerforth when I was a kid. By their nature, my father said, they could be nothing but inevitable disaster. Ignited by ignoble motives, hopped up with malice, riddled by a desire to hurt, belittle, destroy, and justify self. At best, he said, divorce was a disillusion, a crashing of hopes, and a betrayal of sacred vows. People were bound to be in an advanced state of emotional instability, unable to know or tell the truth. Nothing, he said, shook a man's confidence in human nature and intelligence and integrity like listening to both sides of a cause-for-divorce story when told by its principals.

Destiny decreed that a man to whom he owed legal obligations in Winnipeg, Canada, wrote him, "As a favor to me will you represent Laura Chapman? Her family are my old friends, you will realize how serious this is when I tell you she is a Catholic." So Papa took the case. To the quiet, dark young woman who was Mrs. Chapman he said, "You must have a corroborating witness," and she said, "My sister Edna is here with my mother and me studying for the concert stage. Will you need to see her?" Mr. Rogers said, "No no, she simply has to agree with what you've said."

Papa and Teddy used to laugh about it. Teddy laughed a lot.

When he walked to the witness stand he was reading a letter he wanted her to identify. He looked up and Teddy used to say, "*Finally*, the judge said, 'You have some questions to ask the witness, Mr. Rogers?' How could the poor man know we'd fallen in love right under his judicial nose! No girl ever had an odder proposal. Mr. Rogers said, 'Miss Landers, do you confirm the testimony your sister has given?' and I said, 'Yes I do,' and there we were, engaged to be married."

It wasn't as simple as that. Rough going came first.

Since I'd gone back to praying, I'd always prayed Papa would find the right woman. Now Teddy walked right into the mold without a wrinkle. A robust Irish wit, an aura of joy in life, a wonderful rich warm voice—she sang Irish ballads and "The Road to Mandalay" as well as arias from *Bohème* and *Louise* and *Butterfly*—and red hair, the color henna always hopes it's going to be and never is. The surge of hope was so hot it hurt. Scars would heal. Life would have meaning. The pace when nobody had time to *think* or *breathe* would slow to a fine normal existence. Papa would have a home filled with light instead of dark clouds. An enchanting hostess people would like, whose plan for the kind of guests he ought to be associating with instead of claques of applauders and hordes of sycophants.

One night not long after he met Teddy, he came into the apartment and my heart nose-dived. Whatever had happened had burned him bone-white, with a sad and rebellious anger.

He said, "You will be disappointed too, Nora. That's a futile word! My heart feels broken into small pieces, I can feel them bumping around forlornly inside me. I've found the one woman I love, with whom I want to spend my life, with whom and for whom I could make myself and my work into what—they should be. Now I am told I cannot have her. In the name of a God who is said to be loving, I cannot have her."

Well, I wasn't taken altogether by surprise. I'd wondered. We'd been thrown off by the fact we met in the middle of her sister's divorce, but as long as Laura didn't remarry, this was allowed by her church. When I was in the convent I had thought of asking to become a Catholic. Such a beautiful, comforting religion. My grandfather wouldn't object as long as I loved his Risen Christ. Still, in case they went to different places in heaven if I ever got there I thought I'd better stay on Grandpa's side, I wanted most to be with him. But I had explored the Catholic doctrine enough to know that a good, devout Irish-Catholic girl who was goddaughter of a cardinal was in a *jam* if she fell in love with and wanted to marry Earl Rogers.

"*Seventy times seven*," my father said once again. "I made one mistake and I've paid for it with a lifelong purgatory, but I cannot be forgiven even once."

I was trying not to cry. *Why*, every time Papa came near *God*, did some mean thing come up? The thought of giving up Teddy filled me with hot rebellion. Of course, *now*, they could have had a love affair and lived together without too much social or religious ostracism. Such an idea in connection with a girl like Edna Landers never entered our heads *then*.

"If I was Teddy—" I said, and rage boiled up suddenly like a pan of milk. "Oh Papa, you can persuade her. She loves you so much."

He was at the window, looking across the broad walk and sand to the ocean. He said, "Her mother scares her with this mumbo-jumbo. If I persuade her she will believe she is taking a chance of eternal damnation to please me." He yanked the curtain tassel so hard the shade came loose and clattered over his head onto the floor without his noticing it. "I am a bogeyman. Fe-fi-fo-fum, I have been divorced three times. It doesn't count that it's been the same woman all three times." His laugh filled the room with gall and wormwood, I tell you.

Willy-nilly I'd begun to cry. "You say yourself laws have to be made for the majority," I said. "Don't they grant special dispensations? If Teddy's godfather the cardinal asked the Pope—"

Papa said, "I've been into that. I don't see much hope. The last divorce was so noisy, it would be difficult to overlook it."

My heart sank. My fault, I felt it was my fault that the last divorce had been so noisy and front-page.

All this, ending with the scandalous and final divorce which now cast its shadow on their love, is a flashback and took place before Papa ever saw Teddy. It was my fault because I got into a *state* about one of my baby brothers, Thornwell. This lead to the headlines *Earl Rogers Attempts to Kidnap Baby Son*.

My mother always said that my little brother Bogart belonged to her side of the family. Which he did not. She had always taken him with her when she went away and this created a division. This happens in many families but in ours it recurred and lasted longer and seemed more violent. Came this last do-or-die reconciliation, we bought and moved into the big white house at the corner of Vermont and Los Feliz, Bogart and I were both there. They had two babies, though the second boy Bryson didn't arrive until a few months before they split up again permanently. Bogart and I both had such high hopes that this made the failure worse and pitchforked me into the first divided love and loyalty I'd ever known.

Until the first baby, Thorny, arrived, wrong side up, months too soon and weighing two and a half pounds, I'd never seen a new baby. When he was a few months old my mother, who was always a wife first as some women are born to be, persuaded my father to take a boat trip someplace. He *hated* boats because you couldn't get *off*—but she insisted. While they were gone Thorny almost died. Turned out the little fellow had no appetite. The head of a big German maternity hospital, imported by Papa to take care of him, kept him on barley water till he was like a tiny wax figure with nothing alive but big brown eyes that smiled at you. We had a colored cook named Bea and she said, "She starvin' him to *death*," so I fired the German, Bea laid the baby on the wide, warm shelf of her bosom, gave him a hunk of salt pork to suck, and by the time Mama and Papa got back he was in great shape. This was more than they were. Papa didn't come back to the big house at all, we took the apartment on Ocean Front, though it was almost more than we could do to leave Thorny. We went to see him often whether Mama made a fuss about it or not.

One Sunday afternoon I'd gone to visit him and just got him down for his nap when who should walk in but Papa and Charlie Van Loan, the great sports writer. He and Papa liked each other. Papa, it seemed, had decided to come for me himself instead of sending the car and I saw that he was in that smiling, bewitching, superpolite stage of intoxication when he *looked* like a seraphim. I said, "Come on, it's late," but he said he must first pay his respects to the beautiful Mrs. Earl Rogers. Her greeting was sour-sweet with sarcasm and my nerves jangled an alarm. Sure enough, the devils of alcohol had lit a red-green-yellow flame under the old humiliations, you could see it as plain as a chafing dish. I thought, Oh dear God the worst thing that can ever happen to a man is marriage to the wrong woman.

His look turned her into a rag and a bone and a hank of hair, and she said, "I don't know what you want here any more, Earl," and Papa said, "There's just one thing I want, it belongs to me and I'm going to take it," and went upstairs three steps at a time, like a boy. *One thing I want*—Oh, I knew what he meant. *You miss the little fellow, don't you? So do I!* We found out Mama had told the nurse to keep the door locked and never let Papa in. He was kicking it in when I got there, throwing his weight against the lock, saying, "You saved his life, didn't you, Nora? He's my son. She's not *fit*— we'll take him home with us—" The door gave, splintering, shrieking, the nurse was screaming at the top of her lungs, he went through and came out with Thorny in his arms, half-asleep, clutching him with both little hands. The nurse tried to grab him and Papa elbowed her. Now from below Mama's whoops added threatening discord and Charlie Van Loan's heavy rumble was saying, *Now now calm down everybody, let's not get excited.* With Thorny on his shoulder Papa walked right through them, saying, *It's all right, little fellow, it's all right.* The baby was frightened now and his wail went up above the chaos of sound and I thought, *If Papa gets him into the car*—so I lost *my* mind, too.

"Give him to me!" I said to my father.

Papa gave me a shove to take me out of the play, and that made me mad. *Babies,* I thought, are different. I said, "Give me the baby, you hear me?" and I said to Mama, "Shut up. You're to blame for this whole thing. You are our evil genius, that's what you are. If you don't stop that noise I will strangle you." I had Thorny by then, though my father kept on struggling. I thought of Solomon and his judgment and that we would tear him apart between us. I was quicker than any of them, so I ran up the stairs and Papa sank down in a chair and put his head in his hands.

I stayed in the nursery holding Thorny and making up my mind. Papa was a grown man, a big lawyer, senators took his advice, men like Mr. Calhoun relied on his judgment. In his own affairs he behaved as he'd never allow a client to do. Thorny and Bogart and I, I thought vaguely, are shoemaker's children. Pretty soon the baby was smiling again, so I gave him to the nurse and went down. I was going to tell Papa that if he tried to take Thorny away Mama would have him arrested. Besides we had no place for him, it was *wrong.* The best thing would be for me to stay there with him.

Something inside me began to hum with anxiety. The fight Pearl Morton had handed me so long ago—it seemed very long ago now—how could I give up? Especially when Papa just looked at me haughtily, as though he didn't give a damn. The baby is so little, at least he's a *boy* even if he is a *Rogers.* Mama won't let him go hungry and it's too early for him to get hurt.

I thought he had a long life ahead of him. Nothing told me he would be killed with the Marines at Rabaul, that brilliant young lawyer Thornwell Rogers, whose name was on the door of Jerry Giesler's office—*In Memoriam*—until Jerry's recent death.

But time was short in which to save my father.

I said, "We must go, Papa."

I let him drive, to reassure him. I do not think I have ever been so scared any one other time in my life. He wasn't a good driver when he was sober and now half-tight and half-crazy with not getting his own way and with memories that don't bless, just *burn*, with real anguish at giving up his boy— he was homicidal.

Newspapers the next day carried banners. Anyone who read the stories must have concluded that Rogers had been on the rip-roaring father-and-mother of all benders. Mama filed suit for divorce with Charlie Van Loan as her witness to these events. It served him right, he must have told his paper. No divorce in our time was ever noisier. I considered it my fault, I shouldn't have let him see how I missed the little fellow. Being in love with a baby was new to me. Papa missed him too. Just as well we hadn't known the little one, Bryson, well enough to fall in love with him, too. Two of them would have been more than we could bear to part with.

This much-publicized divorce was what he meant when I asked Papa if maybe Teddy's godfather, the Cardinal Merry del Valle, couldn't get them a special dispensation to marry, and he turned away from the window and said, "I don't see much hope. It would be a hard divorce to overlook." Actually, that wouldn't make any difference.

I was in bed with a good book when my father and Teddy came in late one night. They'd been dining at the Ship, which was sort of picturesque, though there wasn't a really good restaurant in Los Angeles. I remember that Teddy wore something shimmering blue and her feet were dancing six inches off the ground. My father, in a dinner jacket, was *triumphant*, practically carrying the goal posts, and waving flags.

He said, "I have persuaded her," and shoved back the glorious red hair so he could look down into her face.

Teddy came to sit on the edge of my bed. She said, "I don't see what else I can do. He says he can't live without me."

I said, "I'm so glad I'm dizzy. We—neither of us could live without you now, Red."

Neither of us had any idea either what it meant to Teddy to give up the Sacraments. Especially Holy Communion. The privilege of the last rites, though how anyone could have thought of Teddy and *death* I don't know. Teddy herself was

lost in a cloud of radiance which had dissolved the desperate
months of opposition from her mother, her family, her church.
I thought if he could make twelve hardheaded men think
black was white and the guilty were innocent, what could
he do with a woman who loved him and whom he loved?
He must have made their love seem nearer and realer than
creeds and ritual and a distant deity. Across a candlelit table,
with the sound of the waves and soft music, Teddy told me
later he had said, "You must choose now, we can't go on this
way. Oh my dear love, my only love, don't believe in a God
who would send us to hell for doing what he made us capable
of doing—loving each other as we do. That's superstition,
dear heart. That's man-made law. Don't believe in such a
God, my darling. I can't live without you."

Just as I was going happily to sleep I thought that my
grandfather would have had no objection to this, he would
have been glad too. He didn't have any rigid rules and
superstitious nonsense and then I was *wide awake*. Of course
it had to be in my head, in my memory, but it was just as
plain as if he'd spoken to me. "The disciple must accept the
discipline," he said. "I have always told you that." I hadn't
known what he meant when he said it, and I didn't then. I
had to learn the hard way. I am one of the ones like Judas
who has to learn the *hard way*. But I think now if my grandfather had lived he might have taught us that what Papa
needed was inspired loving discipline to protect his genius.

Naturally nobody wants anything to do with discipline if
they can help it.

The wedding was lovely. Teddy's mother had been ferocious
and adamant against her daughter's marrying Earl Rogers. But
when it was decided Laura had prevailed upon Mrs. Landers
to let them be married in Teddy's own home. My Aunty
Blanche was there. She was an active Christian Scientist and
surprised that her brother was marrying a Catholic outside
her own church, but she was so delighted with Teddy's
beautiful voice that she condoned it. My grandmother, stiff
and stately in gray satin and white ruching, detested my
mother so much that to her it would have been an improvement if her son had wedded a head-hunter's daughter or an
Eskimo. So, though Teddy's mother looked like a death's-
head, joy and beauty were triumphant.

Teddy took the marriage vows as pronounced by Judge
James with smiling grace and we all forgot that in them she

also renounced the church of her childhood. She said, *Till death do us part*, and meant to keep it. I felt that all by herself she tried to make this a sacrament. A woman as much in love as she was can work miracles for herself.

And somewhere as the champagne flowed I said to Mr. Hyde, *Now, you stinker, let's see you get out of this one!*

PART NINE

SIXTY-FIVE

About here I started holding my breath. I was under a long time.

Now now now the Noseless One couldn't get a hold anywhere.

Strange as the circumstances of a Dr. Jekyll were, as he wrought and fought with his lower self, the debate itself began, for reasons forever hidden from us, in the Garden of Eden. Common to all men, as old as Adam, the longing for good, the inducements and alarms of evil. I think after his marriage to Teddy my father was on his knees, not to God, not in prayers, just in gratitude. A man rescued from an avalanche. Often I saw tears in his eyes. Life had given him Teddy. Now he wouldn't grow weary, now he wouldn't be tormented. He would never admit the drinking to me then, he said he had locked the door on the past. He meant to redeem it.

He and Teddy took a delightful house at the beach and I had a room there but I kept our old apartment, too. I didn't think I should live with them, though to tell the truth I was there most of the time.

I had to take the 4:32 A.M. big red car to *work*.

This was the result of uproar and upheaval and of what at the moment seemed almost like a revelation. A directive. Rescuing me from a boiling caldron.

There are several reasons why I put the Guy Eddie case in this book, where probably it doesn't seem to belong, for it was in truth a totally undistinguished, piddling inane fribble of *mauvais goût*. No. 1, living it over, I could hear my father laugh, and I always liked to hear him laugh. I had been obsessed by a still-childish fear that Darrow might infect all laughter with leprosy or lichen. And I was pleased and restored when the silly Eddie case showed that Papa's still came roaring out of his belly when he was tickled.

Also, right afterwards, came the final decision about my own career.

One clear morning fragrant with pepper and eucalyptus, Papa and I were riding out through old Colonel Griffith's now beautiful and famous park. The sky was that blue painters call Our Lady's Mantle, and we breathed sunshine-made-air.

Homesickness for the past has many bridges to get back to it.

Strange that mine should so often be a song. Especially one sentimental foolish ballad.

Walking by the ocean at night, riding early in the hills, and only when we were alone, Papa and I sang it over and over again. Sometimes when he woke up in the cold gray dawn of the morning after he'd say, "Sing, Nora," like a kid frightened of the dark and I knew he meant this same song though I still do not know *why*. It repeated itself, the common words and tinkly tune, like a theme of a symphony.

> Wait till the sun shines, Nellie,
>   And the clouds go drifting by.
> We will be happy Nellie,
>   You and I
> Down happy lane we'll wander,
>   Sweetheart, you and I.
> Wait till the sun shines, Nellie,
>   Bye—ummmm-bye—eye eye eye eye.

Hope. Maybe when we couldn't bear to go deeper, it expressed a hope as deep and true as St. Paul's. In commonplace words, avoiding, not daring, big and powerful words. Hope—that had to be spoken, hope that plays her song on a harp with only one string. I'm singing it now in my head, you know. On that last bye-ummm-ummm bye-eye eye eye eye, I can ride back to the trail with my father.

On the very last note, I hear a girl's voice chime in. It says, "I think I ought to try for the Bar exams next fall, don't you, Papa?"

Even the ground squirrels and the little cottontails, the rattlesnakes sunning themselves on the rocks and the doves mourning in the scrub oaks paused to listen at the explosion from the man on horseback which this simple sentence brought forth. Both horses stood up on their hind legs in protest. When we had this situation under control I was listening to my father's vehement and varied objections in stunned surprise. I literally had no idea he felt so strongly opposed to it. Darrow had increased his consciousness of the dangers around criminal law. I knew I couldn't go ahead against his real opposition. I felt forlorn. Since I was eight, being a lawyer was what I'd set my heart on.

As soon as I was sure my voice was steady I said, "You keep saying a woman must be trained to earn a living for herself and her children, or she is a slave. I've tried other things—"

I couldn't play the piano well enough. Acting was the profession my father admired most for women. To please him, I'd tried a few weeks of summer stock in Salt Lake City and a small part in a play in Chicago. I disliked doing the same thing every night so much I eloped with the son of a railroad president but after we got the marriage license I changed my mind. Later Cecil De Mille wanted to make a screen test of me. I explained that trying to pretend I was somebody else was beyond me.

Out of nowhere, my father said, "Before he wrote *Pickwick Papers*, Dickens was a reporter. How about a newspaper?"

I said, "Girls can't work on newspapers!"

Papa said, "A few do. Women are bound to make headway in the press—wait until they get the vote."

"You think women will get to vote, Papa?" I said.

"Oh yes," my father said, "and I wish I could believe it will make as much difference as they promise it will. Nora, now I come to think of it, from the time you were big enough to spank, you have had difficulty telling the difference between truth and your imagination. That's the mark of a writer. He must think what he imagined is truer than anything else in the world. Jack London moved back and forth between his life and his stories as a man moves between land and water—both utterly real to him. A newspaper might be just right—"

Before he finished, I knew. I said, "Oh Papa."

He grinned at me, delighted. "You like the idea?" he said.

He took me to Guy Barham, the publisher of Mr. Hearst's new afternoon paper, the *Herald*. Mr. Barham took me to the city editor, Jack Campbell, who agreed that Earl Rogers' daughter might be worth $7.50 a week as a cub. Hours unspecified turned out to be 5 A.M to 9 P.M., and I loved it. Our office was half a block away and Campbell expected me to know what was going on there at all times. So I was in and out as much as ever. I was still in my teens, skinny as a Hottentot, fresher than paint, and Campbell taught me my

job with so much Terrible Man technique that one day I
hit him with a telephone. Ike St. Johns, the handsome young
head of the copy desk, picked up a pair of long copy shears
and ran him into a phone booth. Fortunately, Campbell took
this as a sign our adrenal glands were working.

The thing I remember best about going to work was Papa
waking me at four, and while I combed my hair, which took
half an hour, bringing me in coffee, and sitting there talking
to me. After he and Teddy were married, when I did stay
with them, our best talks were as the dawn came, before I ran
to catch the big red car.

We never had any trouble, the three of us. Still, when she
began to go along with his idea that he could drink a couple
of highballs before dinner and a little wine with it, I moved
sort of carefully to warn her. She didn't have any idea at all!
Her father always drank like a gentleman! She thought the
best way was to be normal about it, not to be *afraid* of it.
She thought I had what I suppose now we'd call a phobia
against drink and I guess I did. "Let's not make too much
of it, dear," she said.

The first night he didn't come home she wasn't too worried.
I was. I thought I was going to die.

SIXTY-SIX

And the gun went root-a-toot-toot.

In broad daylight, on a public street, Gabrielle D'Arley
killed Leonard Troop, who was buying a wedding ring for
another girl with the money she'd earned for him in a crib-
house.

I shot my man, because he done me wrong.

Root-a-toot-toot was the cue for the criminal lawyer, his
entrance music was *root-a-toot-toot* from a big black .44 gun—

> Oh put me in that dungeon, oh put me in that cell.
> Put me where the northeast wind blows
> From the southwest corner of hell . . .

And get Earl Rogers to defend me.

Q. (By Mr. Rogers) How old were you, Gabrielle, when
you went to work in the cribs?
A. Fourteen.

> Frankie went up to the scaffold,
>   As calm as a girl can be,
> And turning her eyes to heaven
>   She said Oh Lord, I'm coming to thee . . .

Don't worry about the scaffold, Gabrielle, Earl Rogers has
never had a client hung yet, not yet, there's a boy named
Bundy waiting in the wings, but not yet.

In Louis Untermeyer's invaluable, incomparable *Treasury
of Great Poems,* which would be the second book I'd choose
if I were going to be cast away on a desert island, is a section
titled "Five American Folk Songs." First comes "Dixie," then
"My Old Kentucky Home," and right after that "Frankie
and Johnny."

We were back in a murder trial, an American Folk Murder
trial, with a theme song, a poem set to music, weaving in and
out like *Porgy and Bess* or *West Side Story.* In the press box,
somebody rumbled, *Frankie and Johnny were lovers.* A bailiff
proclaimed, *Frankie went down to the pawn shop, she didn't
go there for fun, she hocked all her jewelry, bought a pearl-
handled forty-four gun.* I caught a juror whistling between
his teeth, the words to that were *Frankie lived in a crib-
house, He was her man, but he done her wrong.*

Now I was in the press box, the other side of the railing.
I could reach out and touch Papa, he could turn and speak
to me. I thought, Everything's changed, nothing's different.
A girl reporter. A sob sister was a title they gave me then.
It meant that I was supposed to make people weep over their
fallen sisters; or homeless babies or underdogs in the pound;
or a mother who had killed herself because she spent her
kids' Christmas money on a new dress, and we must get a
tree and presents for them; and over what had been done
to a fourteen-year-old girl like Gabrielle D'Arley. We dramatized all this in the newspapers as it is now dramatized on
the stage and in best-selling novels. Ours was *real.*

I was scared all the time. Of deadlines. Of the stories I had
to write in such a hurry. I don't think anybody knew it, but
I was. Besides I was worried about Papa all the time, at the
same time I never had been so excited.

Gabrielle D'Arley took the stand in her own defense before a house my father, with some help from Aunty Blanche, had packed with respectable womanhood. Lady doctors, school-teachers, presidents of women's clubs, preachers' wives, society leaders, Salvation Army workers in uniform, philanthropists, and celebrities like Madame Ellen Beach Yaw, better known as Lark Ellen. This classic gathering had judge, jury, and press box in an uproar. Packing an audience for effect was new. A *first*.

Curiosity beat upon the thin, dark, forlorn girl on the stand in a hot breath. When in *Gone with the Wind* I came upon the scene where Dr. Meade had been arrested in Belle Watling's house it took me back to the D'Arley trial and the good ladies staring at Gabrielle with the terrible interest that killed the cat.

"Doctor," his wife hesitated, "what did it look like?"

"What are you saying, Mrs. Meade?"

"Her *house*. Are there cut-glass chandeliers? And red plush curtains and full length gilt mirrors? And were all the girls unclothed?"

"Good God!" cried the doctor, thunderstruck.

"How can you ask me such an immodest question? I will mix you a sedative."

"I don't want a sedative. I want to know what a bad house looks like and now you are mean enough not to tell me."

Well, the ladies in the courtroom knew as little and wanted to know as much in exactly the same way. I suffered from profound shock myself. Cribs were not well-regulated houses like Pearl Morton's or Tessie Wall's in San Francisco, which I knew well. They were small ugly bare rooms opening on an alley, the girls sat in the doorways, like Sadie Thompson in *Rain* at Iwelei, the old Red Light District of Honolulu. A girl in the cribs had a lover who helped to sell her wares, called a pimp, and none of us had ever heard the word spoken before.

This girl, with a whirl of long dark hair, was still pretty—and so young so young so *young*. This was one of the poor and weak.

Q. (by Mr. Rogers) How old were you—
A. Fourteen.

Six years ago. She didn't look much older. Only—so *sad*. Leonard, her lover, had been a thin, blond young fellow with a loud laugh and a line. Gabrielle gave all her money to Leonard and as she told it, it seemed, that hadn't bothered her. He was her man. She was crazy about him, he was all she had in her whole life, you could feel that, anything she could do for him wasn't enough. As long as he loved her.

> Frankie and Johnny went walking,
> Johnny in a brand new suit.
> Oh good Lord, cries Frankie,
> Don't my Johnny look cute?

So the folk song has it. It was hard for us to understand. I asked my father and his look was strange and angry. He said, "That pimp was the only thing in the world she had to love. Women, God help me, must love something." We both knew we were thinking of Dolly. We hadn't forgiven ourselves for sending her away.

Q. (by Mr. Rogers) You and Leonard began to quarrel?
A. Yes.
Q. What did you quarrel about?
A. I wanted us to get married.

The courtroom took a startled breath and let it out in a shriek.

Gabrielle began to tremble, she looked up at Mr. Rogers and the tears hung on her eyelashes. I thought savagely, Here we are again. This one got to be an underdog when she was only a *puppy*. A female, we don't keep females, throw her in the gutter. Leonard found her there and patted her.

She made a mistake, but—she had always wanted to be *married*, Gabrielle said she thought they ought to. "There wasn't anything to stop us," she said, "I—nagged him about it, I guess." She didn't mean to give up her job, or anything foolish like that, she'd go on *working*, at least until he could support them. If she was his *wife*—she wouldn't mind how hard she worked. "I'd been saving up," she said remorsefully, "to get a wedding ring. I—once I did something terrible. A drunk came in, a sailor, and I—I picked his pocket and gave the money to Len. For the ring."

> Ain't going to tell you no story,
> Ain't going to tell you no lie,
> I saw your man about an hour ago
> With a girl named Nellie Bly,
> If he's your man, he's doin' you wrong.

One of the girls in the crib-house finally told Gabrielle what everyone knew. Leonard was going to buy a wedding ring next day. But not for her. For a plain and pallid virgin whose father had left her a profitable hardware store.

Gabrielle hid the gun in a tiny moth-eaten fur muff. At the pawnshop, she found Len bending over a tray of rings, words passed, and he began to run. The gun went root-a-toot-toot right through that little muff and by the time the cop from the corner got there, Gabrielle was kneeling on the sidewalk holding Len in her arms and pleading with him to answer her.

> *Oh bring on your rubber-tired hearses,*
> *Bring on your rubber-tired hack,*
> *They're taking my Johnny to the cemetery,*
> *And they ain't goin' to bring him back,*
> *He was my man, but he done me wrong.*

My city editor sent me up to the jail. All the time I was talking to her, Gabrielle kept three fingers pressed white against her lips and couldn't speak. Her eyes were so wide with pain they were like a dead woman's and might never close again. After she'd been on the witness stand I told Papa I knew I wanted to try to write. Since I was eight I'd known people. Masks off, no holds barred, fighting for their next breath, men and women in the raw of comedy, tragedy, melodrama.

My father said, "You might have a first-class imagination, too."

"A second- or third-class one, I don't care," I said. "I want to tell *real* stories."

"Imagination is the only gateway to reality," Papa said. "You can't ever know everything about anybody or anything. You put together what is real and if you have the gift of true imagination, you find the rest."

I did write a story about Gabrielle, Mrs. Wallace Reid and I made it into a picture called *The Red Kimono*. Actually, I think it was the first of the documentary films.

I thought perhaps someday I would make people understand each other better.

In the famous D'Arley murder trial, it was my father who was not *real*.

He was giving a performance. This I'd never seen him do before.

No jury would have convicted Gabrielle. We still operated

under a Code of the Unwritten Law. Homicide was sometimes not only justifiable but obligatory. Earl Rogers gave the case style and size, but she didn't need him except to give her a chance for a decent life after he'd saved her. What he did do for her— Lark Ellen took the girl home as soon as the Not Guilty verdict was in. I'd watched the women watching her. I remembered what my father had said about murder. Gabrielle had been a prostitute in a low crib, but sometimes their faces were stark and stiff with envy. She had cared enough about a man to kill him. I hoped I would always remember that *hunger to feel,* to be alive, as a driving power in people. This girl hadn't missed emotion at the nth degree even though it was degraded. In time she married a man in Arizona and made him a good wife. No one there knew her story and I used to wonder whether after a while she could believe it herself. I have known several murderesses who didn't.

For Mr. Rogers there had been no challenge. No fight. No snatching *this* underdog from the jaws of death or the gray dim walls of San Quentin. There are routine moments in the life of a criminal lawyer, of course, but this time he was giving a bad performance. Flamboyant, overwhelming, you couldn't take your eyes off him but—it didn't have it *there,* in the heart as of old.

In the press box I heard a *Times* man say to Johnny Gray, "Rogers is boozing too much." And Gray said, "First time I ever saw him under the influence in court." Another voice said, "Look at him, I'm damned if he doesn't think this is his private club or something." Another, "All those ladies think he's their host." They snickered in admiration. They had forgotten I was there. Johnny saw me and put his arm around me and said, "Never mind, kid. He's okay. He just needs a rest."

I said, "He won't take it." I didn't say the doctors and I had been trying to get him to go to a sanitarium for a bit. His heart wasn't quite right.

I didn't know what was going to happen next.

Somehow I couldn't *imagine.* Couldn't see ahead at all.

The boys knew the pattern, though. They weren't surprised when we moved into another fast three-ring Earl Rogers greatest show on earth that quite literally over half the time backed the First World War off the front pages in California.

This one went by so fast I don't remember much about it.

This is the one where Jerry Giesler and Rosy and I went out and took a shot at the chief of police to convince the public that the underworld was trying to get him.

SIXTY-SEVEN

Three rings three rings three rings.

Our life was a three-ring circus, we lived in the middle of many rings, spinning around us faster and faster.

The biggest criminal law practice in the West, biggest offices.

Sebastian's trial for contributing to the delinquency of his lady friend's little sister. More uproarious and scandalous than Jimmy Walker.

My father's determination that since Sebastian was an Earl Rogers client as well as candidate for mayor he must be elected as well as acquitted. He established an Earl Rogers *first* by winning a big city mayoralty with a man who was *at the time* on trial in open court for a felony carrying a ten-year prison sentence. What he'd forgotten was that once Sebastian was in the city hall, where he had as much business as a glowworm, my father must again *ipso facto* be mayor of Los Angeles. Every time anybody asked Mayor Sebastian how to get to the ball park, His Honor said, *See Mr. Rogers.*

Above all, there was Teddy. After all these years, I cannot write of this without pain and tears.

Inside the Sebastian courtroom was young Edith Serkin, a sallow, dumpy sixteen, who testified that she had been in a room at the Arizona Rooming House when the chief and her sister, Mrs. Pratt, dallied sexually. On many occasions, she had a front-row seat for this performance.

Outside, campaign processions were greeted with cheers, Papa got the famous Chinese dragons to join the fun, and I tell you now with all our electronics nothing as good has yet been invented. The very best one out of Chinatown was about two blocks long, carried by hundreds of Chinamen. All you could see of them was their slippers, which looked like they might be the dragon's own feet. His head was the size of Grant's tomb, he wove back and forth taking up a whole street, a gorgeous purple-green-gold in color, great flashing eyes, tall silver horns, and *breathing fire*. Don't ask me how they did this, the Chinese knew all we know a long time before we did. As Papa often said, Lao-t'se and his pupil Chung T'se were as wise as Socrates and Plato, and some centuries earlier. The dragons were followed by thousands of Chinese children in exquisite robes, squealing in singsong voices, by rickshaws decorated in flowers like the New Year's Parade, by stately elderly Chinese in rich silks with fans. Behind all this in a black victoria drawn by eight white Arabian horses came the chief of police in full uniform. True, he had been suspended on a morals charge but there he was and the torchlights caught all his medals—he had a lot, he was a brave man or he would have been where he really belonged happily walking a beat. Chinese rockets and pinwheels went off and crowds packed every foot of the route and cheered like mad.

Hanging out of our office windows, I had to admit Sebastian looked regal, and as handsome as Marc Antony coming home with his loot. What all this had to do with being mayor I didn't know then and I don't know now. It's the same on TV, I suppose.

My father said, "Sure as shootin' they're going to elect that poor geezer mayor."

I said, "Well, you can't squawk, it will be all your fault."

He gave me that sidelong quizzical look which was becoming more and more frequent. His clowning was growing on him, what else could he do with fantasies like the Sebastian case? He was either too arrogant to believe my eyes or in a pathetic way he was trying to keep me quiet by teasing, being real merry and bright, by impressing me that he wasn't kidding himself.

As the city got more steamed up and wild-eyed and loud-mouthed about the Sebastian affair—remember, we had few movies, no television, no radio, only our own home-grown melodrama—the charge that Sebastian was the crooked tool of the underworld kept recurring. So Rogers, with monumental glee, got up a parade of clubwomen and members of the W.C.T.U. and the Y.W.C.A. They rode around in carriages, wearing ostrich plumes, and holding large photographs of Charlie and banners which demanded, DO WE LOOK LIKE MEMBERS OF THE UNDERWORLD?

This, too, was when Jerry and Rosy and I went out one night and Rosy took very careful aim from behind a palm tree to miss Sebastian in his front window. Next morning Papa stormed into court saying that the Lowest Forces in our fair community were determined to remove his client as a candidate if they had to shoot him. It kicked up a lot of dust.

Our real problem was Sebastian. A man whose looks get him further than he ought to be for any other reason is always a problem. Dumb as he was, I've heard people say Sebastian was the handsomest man they ever saw. However, he had a low-grade common sense and he had never wanted to be chief of police or mayor of Los Angeles, Downey, or Playa del Rey for that matter. He did sense that the fierce light that beats on even so small a throne as the city hall would expose his weaknesses, such as Lil Pratt, and his troubles, such as his wife, to whom he always referred as the Old Haybag. So every few days somebody changed his mind about running for mayor. Papa usually changed it back only because he was too far in now to get out without admitting defeat, the taste of which Papa still disliked mightily.

Whether they acquitted Sebastian because they thought he was innocent, or out of automatic habit because Earl Rogers was defending him, or because they really didn't care if he walked around the corner from his arduous duties at the police station to the Arizona Rooming House for a siesta-fiesta with Mrs. Pratt and that as far as Edith Serkin was concerned her delinquency was bound to be contributed to sooner or later, I have no idea.

Acquit him they did.

We acquit everybody.

There he was. Mayor of Los Angeles.

On this Last Hurrah, Earl Rogers was taking over a city growing at a rate staggering even to the chamber of commerce ballyhooing its climate to the four corners. A city into which had come, because of the climate, The Movies, soon to be the country's fourth largest industry. Pioneered by Charlie Chaplin, by D. W. Griffith making *The Birth of a Nation*, Mack Sennett with his bathing beauties and Mabel Normand, who became my best friend, they were built up in Edendale, Burbank, San Fernando Valley, Culver City, and Santa Monica Canyon united under the name of Hollywood. They fascinated Papa and gave him some mad and exciting company.

Fortunately for everybody concerned Sebastian didn't last long.

One time I asked Papa what he thought was a real love story and I was dumfounded when he said Charlie Sebastian and Lil Pratt. Only Balzac, he said, could have written it. Don't be deceived by outward glitter, he told me, great love knows no time or place. While he was in the city hall, the mayor went right on seeing Mrs. Pratt. Not at the Arizona, but in an apartment nearby. And of all things, Charlie, an inarticulate character, wrote her some letters.

In a fateful one, describing an official trip on which Her Worship the Mayoress had accompanied him, he indited a little wistfully, "I wish you could have been along, instead of the Old Haybag." Forgetful as the next man, he didn't mail it, and his wife found it. Her desire to ruin him was greater than her own pride, so she took this limping sonnet down to the *Record*, an anti-Sebastian paper which made a very pretty front page of it under the headline:

THE HAYBAG LETTERS

The roar of laughter that swept the town did the work of a hurricane.

"How could a woman make herself so ridiculous?" I said. "How could she admit her husband said such things about her?"

"Malice," my father said, "is stronger than self-respect or pride or self-interest. Revenge is sometimes stronger than self-preservation."

Frantic word came from the mayor. Earl Rogers shrugged and said, *Resign at once*. So he did.

Papa was right about the love affair. For years, I used to see Mrs. Pratt wheeling Sebastian up and down Ocean Front in a chair. He'd had a stroke and she cared for him with such tenderness that, immobile as he was, not able to recognize us when we stopped and spoke to him, he yet radiated content from some carefully nourished fire within.

No question that Earl Rogers' defense of Chief of Police Sebastian was brilliant. He somehow held Sebastian and Mrs. Pratt to dignified and convincing denials that there had been "anything wrong" in their meetings. Knowing this was a lie, the jury yet believed it. His cross-examination of Edith was even more shattering than that of Alice, her mistakes on dates of which she had said she was so sure were legendary and absurd.

Headlines, backing the distant war in Europe onto the back pages. Courtroom dazzled, the district attorney, Thomas Lee Woolwine in one Southern rage after another, Edith not sure whether she was his witness or Mr. Rogers', the jury molded to believe the guilty innocent once more.

All the materials were there.

The importance. My father was the biggest man politically in the state at the moment, he was in control of the decisive setup that Governor Johnson had to have. More and more, crowds waited to see him come out, followed him as he walked down the hill, shoved each other to get nearer to him. *Hello, Mr. Rogers. There's Earl Rogers.* As yet, no more star had as much attention.

How shall I say it. Why was it happening?

As though all had begun at times to be meaningless to him. Therefore, this one was tawdry. His magic, his vital excitement, had made them causes, could—would—have made the defense of poor misplaced-person Charlie Sebastian—a misguided underdog if ever there was one—into a big battle. Without that, in the thin light of his indifference, his weariness, what we had taken to be velvet showed as cheap plush. Even real pearls worn with the wrong clothes at the wrong hours look imitation to the eye. My heart refused, beat back strongly, the thought that the greatest trial lawyer of his day was changing *at moments* into a theatrical poseur. Without his heart centered on his work, the simplicity and naturalness were gone—*at moments*—I refused that. Yet in those moments from which I ran away, turned away, there was a glimpse—no more—of an old-school Shakespearean actor in a new play by Bernard Shaw or Eugene O'Neill.

Only a breath, any of this, swift and chill as an autumn wind on an Indian summer day.

No one else in our three-ring circus, spinning faster and faster, seemed to feel it or shiver against it.

Except my father.

I think he knew.

Don't sit up with the corpse, Nora.

Promise me that.

SIXTY-EIGHT

Teddy, so warm and kind and generous, see no evil, hear no evil, speak no evil, didn't know we had an Enemy, cunning, baffling, powerful. In their new home out near Pasadena this was a time of peace, of gaiety and, though we did not speak of it in any such terms, Papa at first made a real fight. The air, the house, the garden on the edge of the arroyo were filled with music and laughter and love. Teddy was working at her singing again, coaching with Uncle Harry Lott, and Aunty Blanche, stern and uncompromising as Old Morality, was red-headed herself and could be merry and mirthful if all and everybody were doing exactly as she thought they ought to be.

Then—*cunning,* oh, cunning indeed and always—entered the Enemy in the character of *After all, Earl can drink like a gentleman.*

Oh—Earl bought it himself and then sold it. To everybody but me. The—Oh, let's not be narrow-minded, let's not be puritanical and prudish, let's not hold old fears and grudges. *One drink never hurt anybody.* At the home front, at the office, I was the only one who was worried. I began to get edgy, sore, my temper was too quick off the blocks. Couldn't they see? No. He had created an illusion again, baffling, baffling *sleight-of-hand.* Look at the great Earl Rogers, happy at last, who said he couldn't take this li'l ole forty drops like a gentleman? No possibility that *forty drops* could contain the transforming chemical that would turn him into Mr. Hyde.

Step by step. In the book that will stand your hair on end about yourself if you reread it, no matter what the name of your devil may be, Robert Louis Stevenson warns. Shows. Not against the great temptations, when somehow a man cries aloud for help and his god, whatever god, god as he understands him, rushes to help defend his position. The steps downward are little steps, hardly to be noticed. Underestimating the Enemy. Yielding one small outpost here. Another there. Words that twist the mind into drugged acquiescence. How can these little things matter? Whoopee! I can be a little bit cruel to my friend provided I am witty enough . . . I can be just a tiny weeny bit greedy and dishonest as long as I'm smart enough to make a buck out of it . . . I can roll on an adulterous mattress and laugh it off if the dialogue is brilliant and it proves I'm not puritanical . . . I can take one drink, forty li'l ole drops—Oh, Danger the great one shows the exciting, gay, fashionable, witty successful faces, moving in the pattern of compromise with our little evils, our small *imps*, but now they have pitchforks in their hands and the setting is the Inferno, and the music is the thunder on the Mount. Only true genius like Michelangelo's can beat the devil and create an image finer than the Golden Calf or the great god Pan.

Watching him with a bemused smile, Aunty Blanche would say, "Isn't it splendid that at least Earl has learned to handle his liquor?" or Teddy mixing him a weak one, "My father used to say one highball before dinner was a good thing for a man, it relaxed him." At the office fat old Dominguez blustering, "Mr. Rogers is in great shape, got everything under control these days."

Me, me only. A bear with a sore head. Seeing Charmian London's thin, agonized face. Hearing Pearl Morton's voice down through the years. *His mortal enemy.* Cunning. Baffling. Powerful. I felt too little now, all right. And alone. Papa was angry with me. He hadn't fooled me—and I think he had fooled himself.

One night I was out on the piazza of their house, the wash of the arroyo was filled to the brim with moonlight, the sycamores were elegant black witches etched against it. Papa came out with a highball glass in his hand, cheerful, at ease, and Teddy's song swept around us.

Seeing the glass, I said a word of protest, pain, dragged out of me as wives and daughters and sisters get it dragged out of them. "Papa—"

Oh, he got it. His face tightened with annoyance. He said, "You are getting to be a nuisance about this, Nora, I am willing to agree that in the past I drank too much, not wisely, that fatigue and strained nerves and unhappiness took that path of escape. That's all in the past. Can't you leave it alone, in the name of sanity?"

And I was desolate and sick of an old passion—why did that come into my head, our old habit of thinking in quotations, I said, " 'Twas in another country and beside the wench is dead but it never is, Papa." His look then told me I was what later we called Public Enemy No. 1. The ONE between him and what Mr. Hyde, pretending to be asleep, licking his chops, wanted him to do, raging inside his prison, thinking up a thousand thousand ways to be brought back to life out of this smothering, smug, smooth death. *Let me out let me out let me out.*

I said desperately, "Like the Old Cattleman said, to some it's pi'son." I was trying to get a laugh. "I know I sound like a bad actress reciting *Ten Nights in a Barroom,* but—it's just you and me, Papa . . ."

The song mounted and stopped. In the moonlight his face had violence under the fine-drawn surface, the nose was more arched. A fragrance of lemon verbena came out ahead of Teddy, the hot perfumes hadn't been sent to us then, we used sachet bags in our bureau drawers and closets and a little toilet water in flower scents. As long as I live lemon verbena with its sweet cleanness will take me back. I will see Teddy coming through the door that night and saying with love, "What are you two up to?" and Papa, laughing, his arm around me answering, "Your young stepdaughter is a thorn in my side. She's so used to bossing me all these years . . . all the Rogers women are like that, listen to my sister Blanche sometime."

Waiting.
Seven years, my Lord, have now passed since I waited in your outward room. Dr. Johnson said that. It seemed like seven years. Those nights when women wait are the longest. Once you have waited out a night for a man to come home it can never quite dawn a beautiful bright morning again—not quite.

Teddy and I, as it just happened, sat out her first night of waiting together.
The weariness, the endless pain, of waiting for someone to come who nevermore will come again. Every time I looked at Teddy, trying to be perfectly natural, the smile growing a little stiff around the edges but so bravely worn, hopelessness strangled me. The minutes crept by. A sound—and the gallant conversation broke itself off to *listen.* Not daring to breathe. Picked itself up lamely. The car had gone by, the footsteps faded, the breath of hope left the lungs and the heart flat with disappointment. The swing back into heaven itself as the telephone rang, the rush to answer, the desperate effort of "Laura darling—how's Mama?" or "I'm sorry he isn't here just now, I'm expecting him any minute . . ." After a while

the silences grow longer, they are bewildered, they swing between fear of *accident* . . . the way he *drives* . . . or fear of something we never mention.

Strange how *love* grows in such suffering, but it does.

We went to the piano and started playing duets. My hands shook so I made more mistakes than usual. These were the same duets I had played with Charmian London, I never heard music so forlorn . . . *now as then*.

The sun we knew would never come up again and it never has. Not *that* sun. Other suns, not that one.

There had come the terrible moment when *Dr. Jekyll* had tipped the scales too far, played this delirious game of yielding to minor temptations too long, it wouldn't *work* any more, little by little baffling, cunning, powerful, these had reached out and taken over the shape and size of the mind and soul, until they became *Mr. Hyde* again. The frantic effort to find the way back, the change back . . . too late, too late, they didn't make that medicine any more and there *he* sat *Oh yes Mr. Rogers of course Mr. Rogers* breathing the reek of the turkish baths again, seeing the naked bodies with the soft white *corporations* we called fat stomachs, hearing the shrieks of laughter, the smack of wet hands beating on sweating thighs in applause, the hoarse cheers as Earl Rogers told them tales; in very genius, he acted out the Guy Eddie door; cross-examined Johnson in the Boyd case once more; triumphed over Rudolph Spreckels and fought with Darrow. As magnificent and dreadful and pitiful as Jack Barrymore in those last TV travesties that made those of us who remembered his *Hamlet* wish that we were dead . . . or he was.

That first night's betrayal of Teddy's trust shocked him into cries for help. Glowing with hope, she said to me, "He's *promised*." And the battle was on again. She persuaded him to a sanitarium for a rest. There were long intervals. Hope—God's dear daughter hope—was resurrected again.

I was back at the beach and he could never really stay away from the ocean long. He came down often. We talked nights away. I always called Teddy to say he was *there*. Sometimes I would find she had gone to stay with her mother and Laura. Try as she would Teddy's mother was never happy in the home where her daughter lived with Earl Rogers. In sin, she believed it to be. So Teddy went to her.

One evening I'd found her there and reassured her. Papa was with me. The next morning Laura called me. At first she

was just, I thought, absent, tight—and then she said, "Adela—
Teddy's sick. I—don't like it. We've had the doctor and got a
nurse. My mother doesn't want me to tell your father. He
wasn't *there* when Teddy felt so sick, that's why she came
home. She's got a high temperature—she keeps asking for him,
I think you ought to come now."

We knew little of influenza then—but I didn't like it either.
I put up the phone and stood quite still, my back to Papa.
He was at the kitchen table with a pot of coffee in front of
him.

As soon as I'd seen him that morning, I had realized he
must have had a bottle hidden somewhere. It took so little of
it now. Her mother wouldn't want him there. Only—Teddy
loved him. Love is like grace, perhaps sometimes it is the only
part of grace we will accept. We aren't *worthy* of it—love is
always by grace. This much I know. I went on into my bedroom to pin up my braids and put on some clothes, I'd been
for my early-morning swim. The timbre of Laura's voice began
to penetrate. *She's got a high temperature.* I didn't want to
upset Papa. Once it got hold of him, it used anything as an
alibi, anything. *Cunning!* So I said, "Laura called, she says
Teddy's there and she's got a cold or something—they think
maybe it's this new thing they call the flu—"

Papa stood up, swaying, palm out to ward off evil. He said,
"She was quite all right—"

The phone rang again. Laura said, "Come quick, come
quick, we think she's dying . . ."

Well, I didn't take it in. I couldn't believe it. Teddy? Glowing with health, so alive, so filled with the joy of life . . .
how in a few minutes could she be dying? She was *young*,
young and strong and beautiful. We hadn't learned that the
flu loved a shining mark. There was Papa in his pajamas and
bathrobe, my mind made circles around him. If I didn't let
him stop to change he would *know* and if I did and there was
any truth in this insane fear of Laura's and we got there too
late—too late for what? *Teddy?* God help me, I was thinking
of what it would do to my father, how to do the best to protect him, maybe if she were dying it would be better for him if
he *didn't* get there. A stern terrible voice spoke inside me,
Don't try to be so bossy don't try to run things, you or Teddy's
mother, these two—*these two*—they love each other. They are
a man and woman it is their love, they aren't your possessions
yours and Teddy's mother's. So I got his overcoat and put it
on him, and I backed my little car out into the Speedway,

which was a sort of alley just wide enough for two automobiles to pass.

Papa said, "I'll drive."

I said, "No—no, I'll drive, Papa." I saw that he was going to drive, he was a strange white, sober now, still drunk and yet cold ashy sober. I thought, All right, if you get killed, probably it will be for the best if Teddy is dying. I forgot I was there too, until we had taken off up the Speedway like a sea gull.

He'd had a message over lines older than telephone wires. Come quick come quick. He was coming quicker than I ever rode in my life.

Inside the grounds of the Old Soldiers' Home at Sawtelle, then a collection of ramshackle painted wooden houses with old men from the Civil War and who'd been with Roosevelt at San Juan Hill and with Dewey at Manila, the car gave a swerve, and went both ways in a circle, came to a shuddering stop against a curb. We had blown a tire. In those days they blew about a dozen to the four-day drive to San Francisco.

I couldn't change a tire and neither could Papa.

He got out and began to walk. In his slippers with the overcoat flapping back from his pajamas. I said, "Papa—you can't —" and he said, "I must—I will not see her alive if I don't—I must—" and he began to run. I didn't try to stop him. Some of the old soldiers gathered around but they didn't know how to change a tire either. I was going mad, so I stood out in the road and began to wave frantically, a big heavy touring car came along and it slowed down and I told him and he said, "Earl Rogers? Get in. Where is he?" We could see his figure ahead, half-running, half-walking, and we caught up with him and I got him in the back and climbed in with him.

He was cold sober now, as though he'd never been drunk in his life. I almost wished he wasn't. His imagination had gone on ahead of us now and he was going through it all and he was a coward because it was *Teddy* and so he died with her a thousand deaths. Suddenly he said in a great terrible voice, "I would go to hell in her place. Will your God accept me?" I said, "Oh Papa, Teddy's going to be all right." He knew better.

Laura and her mother were standing at the foot of the stairs. Her mother made a sound and my father said, "I will go to my wife—" Neither she nor Laura stirred as he went past them. A nursing sister came down after a minute and she said, "He wanted to be alone with her." And I looked at her because I couldn't believe it. *My Teddy.* She must have seen the pleading for hope in my eyes, she shook her head, and went on into another room to pray.

In a harsh thin voice, Mrs. Landers said, "I thank God that she has had the last rites."

I said, "But—"

She had made her confession then and on her deathbed she had promised to sin no more. She had been forgiven and she had renounced her sins. That meant she had promised never to live in marriage with the man she called her husband again. She had renounced *him*. I felt as if I had been struck by lightning. Then I saw her mother's face. I knew then that to lose a child is something that you must never feel you can understand unless you have been through it.

Papa called me then. "Nora—Nora—" and I went up as fast as I could. Teddy wasn't dead! He had his arms around her and her hair was like a flame of life against his shoulder, and she was smiling. Papa said, "She wanted to see you." My heart was glad she had wanted to see me and I knew she wanted to tell me something but she couldn't speak. I couldn't either. I took her hand and held it against my cheek and I knew she had asked me always to take care of him and that she loved him and I had promised that I would do my best without her. Without a word or look. Then she turned her head on his shoulder and the flame curtain hid her face from me forever.

I went back downstairs. I thought, *This will kill him*, and I was going to ask Mrs. Landers not to tell him of how she must have promised not to live with him any more or be his wife ever again. The nursing sister went upstairs quickly. In just a little while Papa came down.

A miracle had been wrought upon him. He was quiet and sane and like he used to be when he was quite young. When I first remembered him in the Boyd case. His dignity was the way it used to be. He didn't look at me or at Laura. He went over to Teddy's mother and he said, "I would give my life, any hope I have—if she had—"

Mrs. Landers chopped it off with an ax. She said, furiously, "She had the comforts of her church no thanks to you."

Papa said, "Thank God, oh thank *God*." And it was the first time I had ever heard him speak of God since Grandpa died.

He began to weep then. From deep inside, quietly, and he walked around saying, "Thank God thank God—" and after a while Teddy's mother went and put her arms around him and they held each other, trying to comfort each other.

SIXTY-NINE

Standing before the robed might and majesty of the Supreme Court, Earl Rogers made his final plea to save his client, the boy named Bundy, from the gallows.

Up through all the lower courts he had fought this lost cause. This was his last stand, and it was marked with all the burning-white intensity of vain expectation, of faint hope still pursuing.

He wore dignity that day himself, a depth of respectful formality. Yet he spoke savage words beyond what were usually used in that place, or to those final supreme justices.

"The extraordinary brutality of this murder," he said, "one boy beating another boy to death with a club, with rocks, with his hands, a boy he knew, had gone to school with. For a few dimes and quarters, a handful of silver, this must in itself show you that Bundy is not sane. All the evidence shows you he has been insane since he was eight years old. Our burden. Our responsibility. I say to you, who are the highest court in this land, you dare not send this boy of unsound mind, of smashed and shattered brain, to his death at our hands. You dare not *order* him to be killed in his turn. *Thou shalt not kill.* Who gives you or any other man the right to take no account of these words? They are plain enough. Small enough. Simple enough. If you, in cold premeditation, send Louis Bundy to die by your words, by your choice, you will have done a deed as terrible as his own. More terrible, for we are men of sound mind. Grown men. If he, a poor wrecked boy of seventeen, broke a law of man when in a frenzy of fear and blood lust he murdered another boy, what if we, so high, so fortunate, so wise send him to be killed, haven't we broken a law of God? If he were as sane as we hope we are, still I say to you there is nothing anywhere but in the old savagery of an eye for an eye, a tooth for a tooth, which gives us right to take a human life. In no word that has ever come through inspired sages to enlighten mankind is there anything that says we may rob others of the gift of life, the thing we cannot create, the thing that it is not within our province to give—nor within our com-

mandments to take away. This boy—possessed with devils,
who take him and throw him so that he foameth and gnasheth
with his teeth and falleth to the ground—is it our precedent
and example to murder him? To cure murder with murder?
Or is it to give him time for repentance and help in healing
the sick brain which an accident when he was a little boy gave
him, through no fault of his own. I beg you to look deep into
your hearts and into your conscience before you say, *Kill him.
Put him to death*."

In point of time the Bundy case came earlier in this story.
The horrible murder, the trial, the conviction that made Bundy
the first client of Earl Rogers ever sentenced to hang.

But it dragged its way through such a long long time.

And from its first day it was the final danger and its menace.

We were in the county jail again, my father and I.

Frank Dominguez, and I could have throttled him, had
taken the Bundy case.

The custom of our office was that the men on the staff took
their own clients and cases if they were not busy on work for
Mr. Rogers. Sometimes Mr. Rogers came in to help them,
usually not. Dominguez was a friend of long standing as well.
In the old days, Papa and I used to ride out to the Dominguez
rancho on Sunday. The señora, who could speak English but
never did, was no bigger than a sparrow but she ruled thousands of acres and peons with maternal despotism and barbe-
cued whole steers in a pit for our lunch. Frank, not nearly as
bright as his mother, had been swept off his feet by the unexpected storm that broke over the Bundy horror.

The whole city rose in rage against this young fiend. A
seventeen-year-old boy who with cold premeditation had
called a drugstore, given an order, and asked them to send
change for twenty dollars with it; who had lurked in the dark
with a club like a savage in the jungles. I don't think we'd
had a juvenile-delinquency murder up to then. They are so
common now that it is difficult to imagine the roar of public
indignation that broke out at the discovery of poor little
Harold Ziesche's broken head and mangled body and the
arrest of his schoolmate for the crime. Having taken the case
without looking around, Dominguez was panicked and came
moaning and weeping for Mr. Rogers to help him. Or, said
the wily Mexican, a client of the Earl Rogers' office was going
to get hung. Only Mr. Rogers could save him.

After some argument, my father went up to see Bundy.

I went along. I'd already seen him, my city desk had sent me up the day after he was picked up. As I went back up the hill to the jail with my father I kept thinking I must have been mistaken about Bundy. He couldn't be the way I remembered him. His face that strange raw red, like fresh-cut beefsteak. Probably it had been my overheated imagination, from what the boys at the police station had told me of the sheer unnecessary bestiality of the killing. I'd seen him through the pool of blood in which skinny little Harold lay, seen it pouring over Bundy the red mist of Cain.

Now it seemed we had come around in a circle. Same door of steel bars had opened and clanged behind us, same voice saying, "Evening, Mr. Rogers," the turnkey didn't pull my pigtail, it was pinned up now, but he winked at me. Same office, same straight chairs and old roll-top desk. Even same Martin Aguierre, older, dried-up like a mummy, his one eye bright as ever. The same smell of Lysol and cigar smoke, cold sweat and imprisoned human breath.

As soon as they brought in Bundy I knew I hadn't been mistaken. A heavy-shouldered boy without a neck, spiky brown hair, and if murder had a color somewhere in the spectrum between crimson and purple, that was the color of his face.

"Papa—" I said. My father turned from Bundy to stare at me, his eyes very wide open. They were green. Sometimes they changed from blue to gray and once in a while to green. It was a danger signal. I didn't like it. Dimly my outer ear heard Papa begin to talk to—*at*—Bundy, who grew darker, redder, more suspicious. In fury, Papa barked at him and the boy cowered and snarled back. He didn't seem to take much interest, gave no help, showed no gratitude, didn't seem to have any feeling about whether Earl Rogers defended him or not.

I was too tall now to lean against my father's knee, my feet touched the floor all right, but they wouldn't stay put. I got up and went and leaned against his shoulder. I said, "Papa— *please*—" The boy's little muddy eyes swung to me suspiciously, they went over my figure in a navy-blue tailored suit and lost interest at once.

Back in the office I had to wait for Papa and Dominguez. They had stopped at the Waldorf, the Mexican was a man who could take his little old forty drops of Chianti or Dago red and I hoped it choked him. They came back, talking, naming doctors, discussing the accident. A baseball bat had hit Bundy when he was a kid, he'd been knocked unconscious for two days. They reviewed the nervous instability of his father and mother at length. I waited until Dominguez went out to start digging up the facts and evidence Mr. Rogers wanted. Then I said, "Papa—*please* don't take this case."

My father narrowed his eyes. He said, "Why not?" through tight lips.

"He's guilty, Papa," I said. "He knew all the time. He'd been running around with a girl. Out at the school they say she was what they call a teaser. He'd promised to buy her a present. He hasn't any defense at all. I know you don't believe in capital punishment and neither do I, but as long as we have it—no matter what anybody does if ever they hang anybody they are going to hang Bundy and they ought to."

My father came off his chair the maddest at me I'd ever seen him. He said then all the things he said to the Supreme Court later. "We have no moral right to hang this boy," he said. "He isn't sane. He's too young—seventeen years old. Has it ever done any good—hanging men? Do two foul wrongs make a right?" He came over and yanked me out of my chair and held me, shaking me like a rag doll, he said, "No no—he isn't handsome or romantic like young Boyd, he doesn't look like Byron. He hasn't a Southern accent or a gold watch that was his grandfather's.

"By the Unknown God, that's why I'm going to defend him! He's repulsive, repellent, he's Cain. But if I defended Boyd it's a thousand times more my duty to defend this human being. Who taught him to come out of the cave and not to kill? How do you measure the temptation of that twenty dollars to buy the girl he wanted a present so she might speak kindly to him, touch his ugly red face with her hand? Many men have bought love, Nora. The price is always the same whatever it is—a gilt trinket or a crown or their honor, two dollars or a million. If I defended Boyd I must defend Bundy, can't you see that?"

"Boyd was innocent," I said.

"As it turned out," my father said grimly.

"I—knew he was, all the time," I said.

"What do you know about Bundy?" he said, and gave me a look edged with bright anger. "So is Bundy innocent. The law says a man is *not guilty by reason of insanity*. When he cannot tell right from wrong."

"Bundy knows right from wrong," I said. "He just doesn't

care. Jack Campbell says he ought to be shot like a mad dog, he's just as dangerous."

"He's not a dog," my father said, "he is a human being. You give him no sympathy. No charity. Oh—he's not as easy to sympathize with as a boy like Boyd. He's ugly. Repulsive. I agree. So, too, it may be he was the man who hid himself in the tombs, or the one who falleth oft times into the fire and oft times into the water. Bundy has dizzy spells, too. Did you know that? They have no right to put him to death."

"They will," I said, "I *know* that."

His eyes were green and baleful. He said, "Do you remember Buck? He didn't have a crack in his head, I tried to salve myself with that, but he wasn't sane. He has haunted me ever since, he has walked the battlements with me night after night, keeping me from my rest. I was younger then, I've tried to forgive myself for persecuting a madman. Or for helping to hang him by his neck until dead. Maybe you're right, maybe they'll hang Bundy, but I'm going to try to stop them. If you don't want to come along—"

"Don't be silly," I said.

To see my father again, I don't think I'd want to have to go through those hours while we waited for the Bundy jury.

Papa wouldn't leave the courthouse. At first, I had no hope at all. None of the reporters did. Guilty with the death penalty, they said. As we sat in the empty courtroom, my father and I, or in one of the witness chambers, or walked up and down the corridors, and the minutes plodded by with booted feet in wet sand, somehow my father made me believe they would find him Not Guilty by reason of insanity and order him to an asylum. Or Guilty, with a recommendation of life imprisonment and hospital care.

I don't know how people live through those hours. It began to come through to me then and it comforted me afterwards. Papa *didn't like* Bundy. He saw him as we all saw him. Because he did, I began to see what it meant to love your enemy. If you love them that are lovable, if you pray only for those that it is fun to pray for, what closeness to brotherly love do you generate? All sides of the tree must grow green.

Papa loathed Bundy, that vicious, crippled, snarling underdog. But even stronger was the duty to defend him as a brother man. A fellow human being.

I thought of all the other jurors, in all the other cases, how our minds and hearts were wrung with them, my father's a thousand times more than mine or theirs, and I wondered if his heart wasn't just tired.

In the wings I felt the presence of tragedy standing and knew by it sometimes we learn. As I was learning.

Over and over, again and again as we waited—*waited*—he went back as he always did, counting over each day of the trial. Depressing, morbid, sickening the days of the Bundy trial. The invalid mother. The weak-chinned, bleary-eyed father. The heartbroken hysterical sister. Then the family of the boy who had been bludgeoned to death in the darkness, young Harold, who came and went as the murdered always do. I hated it all. It was miserable to listen.

Had he made the jury *see* that moment when the baseball bat crushed Louis Bundy's skull when he was only a little boy? Had he made them realize the boy had lain in a coma for days, and this had to mean a fracture pressing on the brain? Earl Rogers had not put the witness on the stand.

Everyone noticed this, spoke of it. After the jury had retired and we began sweating it out, this was the rack that hurt him most. He'd say to a reporter who'd come to ask a question, "I couldn't put him on the stand. He antagonized everyone. Jack Campbell said he should be shot like a mad dog. He makes people feel that way, I couldn't put him on the stand." I'd roll him a cigarette, he'd puff once, throw it away, and instantly hold out his hand for another. He'd say, "I never before failed to let a man accused of murder tell his own story. But you can see can't you what the district attorney would have asked Bundy? Did you strike your friend over and over with a rock? Nora gets sick when Bundy tells about that." Then with violence, with a fury of ill temper he would condemn himself. "I was wrong. They would have known this showed madness. No sane boy could have done it. Not Guilty by reason of insanity would have been the verdict. I have always said you cannot acquit a man of murder unless he takes the stand."

It was frightful to watch him.

I know now that the deep, emotional identification with his client was what made Earl Rogers the trial lawyer we have not seen since. I know, too, that a man may be tried *once* for murder. A man may be tried *once* for bribing a jury. But to go through it with that complete involvement of sinew, soul, and imagination over and over again will drain away a man's life at last.

Sometime after dinner—I don't remember how many hours they were out—the jury came in.

A *first*, too.

Guilty of murder. The death penalty.

To go through it even in memory twists my insides. In the long long night that followed he played over every inning, every pitch, every out, every error, every hit with a tape-recorder recall. While Jerry and Dominguez and I tried to ease his bitter self-condemnation, he shuffled the *if* deck. *If* I had done this, *if* I had done that.

"Oh, Papa," I said, "don't don't. You did the best you could."

"It wasn't good enough," he shouted at me. "Why wasn't it good enough?"

I couldn't tell him. All the way through the Bundy trial, he had seemed to me—oh, I don't *know*. His timing was off, or something. He didn't make it *happen*. This time the magic didn't work, it was spent.

Not that anybody who ever lived could have got Bundy off. Only—we always *did*. The impossible took longer—but we did it.

Guilty—Guilty—Guilty—the Bundy verdict.

Appearing before the Supreme Court in that last appeal, he was keyed two twists beyond concert pitch.

. . . from the age of 13, he was addicted to the excessive use of cigarettes. You have the word of the physician of the Juvenile Court that the excessive and inordinate use of cigarettes, the smoking of three packs a day, by a boy whose brain is still growing had an effect of deterioration and traumatic disturbance . . . I am not attempting in any wise to dispute that most unfortunately, regrettably, to my lifelong and inexpressible sorrow, Bundy did this extraordinary and horrifying thing, that he, a boy less than 18 years old, took a human life, in utmost brutality and cruelty. Do you believe we shall accomplish any good purpose to follow his example? To do as did his disordered, distorted, immature, retarded crazy brain, and likewise take a human life this time in cold-blooded cruelty? I beg we shall move forward in humanitarianism, that in both justice and mercy you will confine this boy for treatment and care . . .

He looked from one to another of those majestic, robed figures high above us, peering into each face. Then he dropped his hands and walked away.

I tried to persuade him not to go, I remember. I waited in the warden's house, feeling that strange terrible unrest of protest that is in a prison the day of an execution, while my father was in the death cell with Bundy. No one else was. Papa stayed with him until the last moment. He went up that flight of wooden steps to the upper room that held the gallows. They were on the outside of the small brick house—death house. One reporter fainted and slid down but Papa and Bundy went on to the top all right. When he came back, I knew that the trap which fell and broke Bundy's ugly murderous neck had broken that mainspring of which my father spoke to me. *After it's broken,* he said, *you can run along all right on the level but you can never climb hills any more.*

Maybe it broke before that, when Teddy died.

For me—it was that day in court, I know, I remember, so small—so *nothing*—

He was examining the girl for whom Bundy had done murder. He put up his lorgnette and—she laughed.

I damn near strangled myself coughing and so did Jerry Giesler, so maybe Papa wouldn't even hear it himself. Nobody would hear it or notice.

I—all right, the high horrid laugh of that cheap little girl they called a teaser. At Papa. It went through whatever it is we call my heart like a sword. It's still there—that sword. Permanently. Of all other things.

Perhaps, with Papa, it was when he knew Darrow was guilty, or when the district attorney rousted Darrow out of town and told him never to try to practice law in California again and Darrow went without saying good-by—or thank you. That did something to him, it's silly, but I always knew it did. Bundy didn't say thank you for trying, for sticking by me, either. I asked Papa and he said he didn't say a word. Of course Bundy had no manners anyhow and also—*he* was inside the gray dim walls of San Quentin. He hadn't gone free.

No no. None of these. If it hadn't been for the drink the drink the drink, he'd have licked those, climbed over them on his way up and up.

Only God can defeat the Noseless One. And we had decided there wasn't any, until too late. We had to do it the hard way.

PART TEN

SEVENTY

Having been through so many others, this story must end in the same courtroom where it began.

That courtroom, with young Judge Myers on the Bench, of which every detail is as vivid to me as it was when I tried there to have my father committed for care. Against his wishes. For his own good. Everybody in it still exists for me. I can go back. *Then* once more is *now*. Of all the courtrooms where Earl Rogers fought to save a man's life and honor I remember best the one where, at last, he fought for his own. Against *me*.

Take the witness, Mr. Rogers. *Me?*

Judge Myers saying quietly, "Mr. Rogers, have you any questions to ask this witness?"

This witness? I am this witness. My father is walking toward me the way I had seen him a thousand times. Down the telescope of years, I see him as clearly as ever. Slim, elegant, dynamic, only his face does not look the same.

He didn't live to grow old, but it was possible that day to see what he would have been like if he had. From his pocket as he stood before me, he took the famous lorgnette which had had its day on front pages around the world. His trademark before which witnesses had quailed. After swinging it on the black ribbon, he looked at me and shook his head with a little smile and shot it back into his pocket. I was glad of that. I wouldn't remember that anybody had ever laughed at it, I would deny it forever. Nobody ever had! Instead I would always remember William J. Burns looking so silly—and Johnson in the Boyd case—and Gallagher sweating, toppling off the witness stand. Still—I was glad it was out of my sight.

With his courtly bow to the Bench, Mr. Rogers said, "I have only two questions, Your Honor."

Only two, God help us. I thought frantically of the eight he'd wanted to ask Rudolph Spreckels, of the long agony of that cross-examination. Now I was chief witness for the prosecution. Had I ever thought to see the day!

"Nora," he said, and after a moment, "look at me, please."
So I did. I *am*.

He said, "You don't really think I'm crazy, do you, Nora?"

"No, Papa," I said.

"Then you don't wish to go on with this"—his hand indicating the long blue legal document on the judge's desk—"this farce?"

"No, Papa," I said, and burst into tears.

One of his great trials, one of his last great cross-examinations, they always said. Of course that was all there was to it. Later, I dismissed the complaint. Just then, I stumbled off the stand, half falling because I couldn't *see*, and he put his arm around me and comforted me as we walked out past my poor Aunty Blanche, past the reporters who'd made a deal with me not to print it if I had him "put away" for treatment for his own good. He kept saying, "Don't cry, dear. Please, sweetheart, don't cry. I know, I understand."

I didn't. One of the reporters said, low and bitter, "I knew you'd never go through with it." Right then, that soon, the young, very young, Nora began to panic, to wonder if she'd done right, whether she'd failed him, whether she should have stood against him—for his own good.

I had let him make the decision when we'd decided he didn't know what was for his own good.

As I wrote in the beginning of this book, something drove me, shoved me into a chair behind a typewriter to tell my father's story. The truth which he had said always brought *light*. It is not the whole truth here, I know that. Some of it isn't even "nothing but the truth." I know that, too. I have told lies to protect us but not enough to matter. Of course I have made honest mistakes and those subconscious errors which our souls have moved around and readjusted through the years, like oysters making pearls out of a grain of sand. Yet I know now that in spite of all that it is *the truth*. I wasn't driven by all those who said, You *must* write the story about your wonderful father. Nor even by a great wish to record his *firsts* and that contribution to trial law which all authorities grant him. Nor to correct some of the tales which as tales so often give spectacular and melodramatic moments, entertainment if nothing else.

No no. Three years ago I knew I had to tell this story for I had begun to wonder what I was going to say to God about certain things, when I had to bear witness to my own life. Or, as I examined my heart and conscience as honestly as anybody ever *can*—we always give ourselves the best of it—to find out what is already on the Recording Angel's books about me, I found that one haunting unanswered question in my mind.

One moment of truth that has haunted me and, I know now, had to at last be examined and answered.

Over and over I would ask myself about that day in the courtroom when I was so young, so strong, so torn and baffled. When I made the decision which determined his fate. Oh yes —I did. The doctor had said, "My dear child, if he won't help himself, I think you and I must help him whether he likes it or not." Against his wishes, as Hugh Baillie put it.

You see, through these haunted years only I *knew* all that happened before I made that decision on the witness stand.

Only I knew what happened afterwards. I'm not going to tell it here. I *can't*. I just plain can't.

It's an old story anyhow. No details change much. The power of the Noseless One grows. Little by little, step by step, fierce and terrible.

A qualm came over me, a horrid nausea, a deadly shuddering . . . these passed and left me faint, as the faintness subsided I began to be aware of a change in the temper of my thoughts, a contempt for danger, a solution of bonds of obligation or responsibility, a gibing disdain for honor or law . . . I looked down, my clothes hung formless on my shrunken limbs . . . the hand that lay on my knee was thin, evil, a claw of bones . . . a moment before I had been Dr. Jekyll Earl Rogers, safe in all men's respect as long as I stayed sober, wealthy as long as I cared to earn money as a defender of the underdogs, beloved, oh yes, so beloved, by so many, now I was John Barleycorn or Mr. Hyde or Earl Rogers on another drunk, bat, spree, binge . . . the common quarry of all men in bars who snickered with satisfaction to see yet another dragged down to their level, of sycophants in Turkish Baths laughing like the fiends of hell at the caricatures I made of myself, the cartoons I drew of my best work, of the cops who with shame dragged me from the gutter, of bailiffs who turned away their eyes from Mr. Rogers under the influence in court and of the judge's sorrow as he looked down upon the limp false worn doctor's certificate to excuse Mr. Rogers breaking his oath as an official of His Honor's court as a lawyer actually is . . . and of the pity of nurses and the riotous humor of low brilliant comrades . . . homeless, yes, I was homeless, I could not bear that Nora should sit up with the corpse of what I once had been . . . houseless, except for cheap rooming houses where at last I would die alone, allowing myself to die in a more genteel way than my great friend Jack London, alone except for John Barleycorn chalking up another victim.

Look at me, please, Nora.

Then he began his two-question cross-examination as though we were alone on St. Helena. "A man as noble as Earl Rogers, oh yes, I know a great deal about him, must be saved from himself, when he drinks he no longer knows the difference between right and wrong for himself." The doctor in the county hospital had said that in the midst of all the comedy-melodrama-tragedy written produced and acted by Rogers-and-Willard Mack. He had defended Bundy, who didn't know the difference between right and wrong. When I asked the doctor what to do he had said we must help him against his wishes if necessary.

I expect I was always hoping, I wanted him there with me. I had a vision of building a library around him, when I got the money, where he could read and study and write this book himself. Other books. One on trial law, on cross-examination, maybe teach in the law schools, or take the offer of a big firm to sit in a back room as a trial lawyer emeritus.

"Like Sydney Carton with a towel around my head no doubt," my father said, and then, with utter simplicity and sincerity, "I'd rather be dead. Again, like your hero Sydney Carton."

He can have many more years of usefulness, the doctor had said, and that came back often to haunt me too.

It wasn't true.

Only God can ever defeat Mr. Hyde and John Barleycorn and we had turned our backs on him because we didn't want to accept the discipline of the disciples.

Oh—if I had said, Yes, I do want to go on, it's not a farce, it's deadly earnest, we shall save you whether you like it or not, this would have been the bitterest of all defeats to him. Force is never a remedy.

Now that I have written it all down here, the life of Earl Rogers and his daughter, I can see what the other decision would have meant. To be *locked up*. Beating his spirit to the final anguish against bars. Inside instead of out, making fun, making laughs, kidding with the inmates and the kind of nurses they had then in mental hospitals—being grand and merry as he and Bill Mack were in the psychopathic ward and then weeping alone at night into his coarse pillow. How could he be born again within such walls? He had a right to live out his own life, *pick his own hell* if such it had to be. Above all, if I'd said yes instead of no, he wouldn't have had *me* any longer. I would have done that terrible thing to him and the wound would have been too deep. I would have sided against him. Every soul that comes into this world must have one person who is always on his side, right or wrong, always cheering for him, everybody is with you when you're *right*. No no, Papa, I don't think you're crazy, all the rest of the world may, but I don't.

If I'd said yes . . . ?

Papa, I *couldn't*.

When the trumpets blow, all the walls fall down flat.

The trumpets hadn't blown.

"It won't be for long," he said to me soon afterwards, "not very long."

Steel has its point of stress and so has the human heart. I used to beg him to come and live with us, I used to go and bring him *home* with me. I was married by then to Ike St. Johns, who loved him, I had my first two babies, a daughter, a son. They went to him as soon as they could crawl. A few days, a few meals, my heart high. Then one morning I'd come down and he would be gone, like a ghost. And I would wonder if he'd really been there.

"Let me alone," he said, "it is easier for me alone. Sometimes alone I can forget what I have been, what I should be, above all what I am."

One night when we were sitting in my workroom with only my green-shaded student lamp burning and the night shutting us in together like strong walls, he said, "You mustn't grieve, Nora. The best of me—how can you lose it? It's been yours all your life, hasn't it? You know how I think. You know my mind. Anything I've done or been that's any good you know. It's been yours as much as mine, hasn't it? The blessed gift of memory will create it once more and let you live with it again always. With me as I was. When you read our books, or hear music we've loved or go to places where we've been or cross the bay on a ferry, we'll be together. No way to escape that or want to. Perhaps that's what immortality is. When something new comes your way, you'll say Papa would have said this or that, or thought so-and-so about it. Your love for me, which has survived so much worse things, will survive death. Of course it will. And to love—that's the important thing always, whether it's a man alive or a memory. If there's a hereafter, which sometimes I doubt and sometimes I believe, because it's too altogether senseless without—mine for you will survive of course. It will survive, even if it only comes up some day as a hyacinth. I will not ask you to turn down an empty glass, Nora, but I do ask you to make me one promise."

I couldn't speak, but I put my hand in his.

"Don't cut holes in bedquilts and go around calling them your clothes," he said with a grin. "You didn't turn out as plain as I thought you were going to but not even a beauty can survive that. Don't be sloppy. I can't abide sloppy women."

We said good-by to each other then.

So I didn't see him when a few weeks later they called to tell me he was dead. Why should I? Death is always a lie about the one who is gone.

I wore my best dress to his funeral, where the underdogs gathered, God bless them. And though nobody could see it, a red ribbon on the end of a pigtail under my brand new hat. Celebrating the trumpets, or defying the thunderbolt, I know as well as anybody how sentimental that red ribbon he used to tie on the end of my pigtails was, but it comforted me a little, so who should say me nay?

He said I would never lose him and I never have and that *is* a kind of immortality. He was right, too, in that it is possible to live with him again, really live with him again, as I have done every single day for three years in this book. I am sure now that the trumpets have blown for him and all the walls fell down flat.

I have forgiven Earl Rogers' daughter Nora at last.

For as I've written it all out, here, I've seen that we cannot go back from where we are, and think what we would have done then if we had known what we have learned since, or blame ourselves because we didn't.

The little girl he hung on his watch chain as a kind of charm, the girl who was too little, I know now did the best she could, the tall young girl with her pigtails pinned up who said that *No, Papa* on the witness stand, seems to me another incarnation.

I have forgiven her because every page and word I have written has shown me one thing about her.

Right or wrong, she loved much.

That is the greatest gift life can bestow on anybody.